Guidance
Principles and Services
Second Edition

Frank W. Miller

Northwestern University

CHARLES E. MERRILL PUBLISHING COMPANY
Columbus, Ohio

A Bell & Howell Company

Library of Congress Catalog Card Number:
68-21284

PRINTED IN THE UNITED STATES OF AMERICA

Preface

Since the publication of the first edition of *Guidance Principles and Services*, the guidance movement has continued to exhibit the dynamic growth and constant change that has been evident since its inception. The roles of the elementary and secondary school counselor have been better delineated and more adequately differentiated. Guidance is now recognized as holding a central position within a comprehensive and coordinated program of pupil personnel services. Behavioristic views of counseling are, once again, coming to the fore. Guidance has gained increased professional stature through the adoption of an official Code of Ethics, structural changes in its professional organizations, and more sophisticated research and publications. New issues have arisen even though traditional ones remain.

This new edition has been designed to reflect these changes through the addition of new chapters on the *Role of the Elementary School Counselor*, the *Role of the Secondary School Counselor*, and *Guidance Within Pupil Personnel Services*. In addition, many of the original chapters have been given extensive revision, particularly those on *The Counseling Service, Guidance as a Profession*, and *Current Issues in Guidance*.

It is the addition of an extensive readings section, however, that constitutes the most significant departure from the earlier edition. It has always been the author's firm belief that an introductory text should present the reader with a variety of viewpoints. The inclusion of pertinent articles, each carefully selected to supplement a particular chapter, makes it possible for the reader to acquire an organized body of knowledge in the area of guidance (involving terminology, history, principles, personnel, services, and issues), and gain the benefit of divergent points of view held by noted authorities in the field, as well.

The author feels a great personal obligation to those students from whom he has learned so much during eighteen years of teaching the introductory course in the graduate program of Counselor Education at Northwestern University. He is particularly indebted to his doctoral students who provided helpful criticism and mechanical assistance in developing the text. To his colleagues who graciously permitted the inclusion of their articles, he extends his deep appreciation. Finally, he is profoundly grateful to his wife for her encouragement, her patience, and her permissive counseling.

Frank W. Miller

Contents

PART 1   HISTORY AND PRINCIPLES

Chapter 1 — The Meaning of Guidance 3
Chapter 2 — The Development of Guidance Services 19

PART 2   PROGRAM AND PERSONNEL

Chapter 3 — Guidance Programs Within Schools 53
Chapter 4 — Teachers and the Guidance Program 75
Chapter 5 — Role of the Elementary School Counselor 97
Chapter 6 — Role of the Secondary School Counselor 112
Chapter 7 — Guidance Within Pupil Personnel Services 132

PART 3   SERVICES

Chapter 8 — Student Appraisal Services 151
Chapter 9 — The Counseling Service 201
Chapter 10 — Information Services 231
Chapter 11 — Research and Evaluation Services 262

PART 4   ISSUES

Chapter 12 — Guidance as a Profession 285
Chapter 13 — Current Issues in Guidance 321

PART 5   READINGS

Chapter 1 — Attaining the Promise of Guidance for All 344
            Kenneth B. Hoyt

Chapter 2   The Progressive Heritage of the Guidance
                Movement   354
                        Lawrence A. Cremin

Chapter 3   Interferences to Guidance Program
                Development   363
                        Herman J. Peters

                A Focus for Public School Guidance
                Programs: A Model and Proposal   371
                        Merville C. Shaw and *John K. Tuel*

Chapter 4   Values and our Youth   380
                        Gordon W. Allport

Chapter 5   Consultation in the Counselor's Role:
                Invitation to Dialogue   391
                        Louise O. Eckerson

                A Differential Approach to Elementary
                Guidance   396
                        Marion Heisey

Chapter 6   Can the Counselor Function as an Effective
                Agent of Change?   401
                        Donald Blocher

                The School Counselor and Religious Liberty   406
                        Claud C. Crawford

Chapter 7   Administrative Deterrents to Guidance
                Program Development   410
                        Bruce Shertzer and *Shelley C. Stone*

                The Pupil Behavioral System   418
                        Herman J. Peters

Chapter 8   Culture-Fair Testing   427
                        Anne Anastasi

Chapter 9   Change in Values: A Goal in Counseling   433
                        Joseph Samler

                Behavioral Goals for Counseling   444
                        John D. Krumboltz

Chapter 10 Some Proposed New Developments in
Vocational Aspects of Counselor Education 454
John W. Loughary

Chapter 11 Some Missing Links in Counseling Theory
and Research 467
Milton Schwebel

Research in Vocational Development: Impli-
cations for the Vocational Aspects of
Counselor Education 477
Henry Borow

X Research in Guidance: Horizons for the
Future 492
Buford Stefflre

Chapter 12 Ethical Standards: *American Personnel
and Guidance Association* 499

Confidence and Confidentiality 507
John L. Phillips, Jr. and *Adam Margoshes*

The Two-Year Graduate Program in
Counselor Education: A Re-examination 512
Frank C. Noble

Chapter 13 Counselors Need Teaching Experience 515
George R. Hudson

A Rationale Against Teaching Experience
for School Counselors 520
Frank A. Nugent

√ The NDEA and Counselor Education 524
C. H. Patterson

INDEX OF NAMES 529

SUBJECT INDEX 533

PART **1**

HISTORY AND PRINCIPLES

1

The Meaning of Guidance

Human beings have always had problems. They have constantly sought help with these problems. Whether people today have more serious problems than they had twenty, fifty, one hundred, or one thousand years ago is debatable. We speak nostalgically of the "good old days" and complain that "the current generation is going to the dogs." However, since historical literature is filled with references to wizards, soothsayers, medicine men, fortune tellers, and phrenologists who flourished in those "good old days," we must conclude that previous generations had problems too. Fortunately, our methods of problem-solving have advanced greatly in recent years. The giving of *professional* assistance has become an accepted and vital part of our society. Today, we seek medical advice from the physician and bolster our mental health by consulting a psychologist or psychiatrist. During the past half-century, a new movement designed to give professional

3

assistance to the young people in our schools has developed. It has been identified as the *guidance* movement, a dynamic, constantly changing field in our group of professions. (In Chapter 2, we will examine the history of this movement.)

The wise traveler, planning an extended visit to some foreign country, usually starts by studying the language of that country, the customs of the people, and the principles or beliefs on which their society has been built. When he has acquired these understandings, the traveler usually finds it possible to play an active role in his new environment. He is able to exchange information with the inhabitants and become sensitive to their likes and dislikes, their problems, and their plans and goals. Teachers or students who are planning a brief or extended visit into the field of guidance should find it profitable to follow a similar course of action. Since this book is intended to serve as an introduction to guidance, this first chapter deals primarily with terminology or language and the principles or beliefs on which the guidance movement rests.

The Semantic Problem

In the last thirty-five years much attention has been given to the term *guidance* and its meaning in an educational setting. Payne (43),[1] as early as 1925, found 103 definitions of *vocational guidance*. By the 1930's, the confusion over the concept of guidance had become the object of considerable comment. Kitson (27), in 1935, spoke out strongly on this matter:

> Some members [of the NVGA] assert that vocational and educational guidance, if properly carried on, cover all that needs to be called guidance. Others insist that this is only one form of guidance; and that there are many other forms of "guidance," e.g., "directing," "leading," "orienting." When we examine guidance practices in schools we see similar confusion. The term is applied to a weird assortment of unrelated activities: counseling of individuals on any matter, group instruction in any subject, home visiting, trips to factories, probation work, teaching pupils how to study, chaperoning dances, club leadership, the giving of tests; whatever cannot be easily classified is called guidance. Then, too, everybody and anybody performs these services: principals, assist-ant principals, school psychologists, visiting teachers, deans, class advisers, homeroom teachers, teachers of subject-matter courses; all may claim to be doing guidance.

---

[1]See list of references at end of chapter.

Two years later, in 1937, Dietz (16), joined the critics: "The Tower of Babel had nothing on the guidance and personnel field when it comes to a need for a common language. We must agree among ourselves on what we are talking about."

In 1941, George Myers (39), in his book *Principles and Techniques of Vocational Guidance,* advanced the proposition that *guidance* should be used as a noun, with qualifying adjectives to give it some meaning. He, accordingly, discussed vocational, educational, recreational, civic, community service, "social and moral," "health," and "leadership" guidance in clear and concise terms. Myers' forthright statements motivated others to formulate more clearly their own concept of guidance. In a series of national conferences begun the following year, state supervisors of guidance and counselor trainers from colleges and universities differed with Myers; they concluded that clearer thinking would result if the word *guidance* were to be used as an *adjective*. One would then speak of a "guidance program," "guidance services," "guidance techniques," and a "guidance philosophy." They based their position on data obtained through several university counseling programs which offered evidence that the majority of students who request counseling have problems involving more than one "area" of guidance. If students' *problems* do not restrict themselves to one area, went the argument, why should we compartmentalize *guidance*?

Though our concept of guidance was greatly clarified in the 1940's, some confusion remained. During the 1950's we searched for explanations of this persistent confusion over a concept of guidance. Barry and Wolf (5) warned that "the issue of vocabulary should be of immediate concern to guidance-personnel workers because, without some clarification of terminology, the issues in other areas of the work cannot be resolved."

Kitson (27) had provided part of the answer earlier when he identified the great variety of individuals who, at one time or another, may claim to be doing guidance. It is logical to expect individuals with different types and levels of training and experience to interpret their "guidance" function in different ways.

Crow and Crow (13) suggested that the confusion existed because guidance, as interpreted, touches "every aspect of an individual's personality; physical, mental, emotional, and social. It is concerned with all of an individual's attitudes and behavior patterns. It seeks to help the individual to integrate all of his activities in terms of his basic potentialities and environmental opportunities." In other words, as guidance became concerned with the "whole pupil" and became increasingly integrated with the school curriculum, it became more difficult to define.

Froehlich (17) argued that the problem was rooted in the fact that both guidance workers and personnel workers had broadened the scope of their activities. "Inevitably this led to some overlap in functions and to confusion in terminology. Some writers have even used the terms 'guidance' and 'pupil personnel' interchangeably."

Smith (46) suggested that the confusion over a concept of guidance was typical of a new science.

> Since guidance services are among the more recent ones developed in education, the difficulties inherent in changing concepts and semantics plague many guidance workers and other persons. This fact is not one about which we should be apologetic. Similar difficulties are common to other professional fields during their early developmental periods. Time is the most prominent factor in the stabilization of points of view and the terms which describe them in any professional field. It is not to be expected that we should attain complete unanimity of viewpoint or terminology in any field of endeavor, including the exact sciences.[2]

Barry and Wolf (5) believed that the problem originated in the intangible nature of guidance concepts.

> Jargon poses problems for guidance-personnel workers that are not found in the special languages of some other groups. An em can be measured; a dislocated vertebra is a physical thing that can be X-rayed; a tort is an action. Most guidance-personnel concepts, however, cannot be demonstrated, pictured, acted out, or measured. As a result, terminology becomes more elusive of definition. The intangible nature of their work, however, requires guidance-personnel workers to be doubly careful that their langauge is clear, well defined, and understood by all members of their own group.[3]

All of these explanations are still pertinent and contribute to our understanding of the semantic tangle in which we still find ourselves. In brief, our troubles in definition have two major sources:

1. *The intangible nature of guidance* which (a) makes it difficult to measure and evaluate; (b) makes it difficult to separate from such

---

[2]From *Principles and Practices of the Guidance Program* by Glenn E. Smith. Copyright 1951 by the Macmillan Company. Used with their permission.
[3]Used with permission of Columbia University, Teachers College.

concepts as curriculum and education; and (c) allows a great many individuals, with a great variety of training and experience, to operate as "guidance specialists."

2. *The recency of the guidance movement* which has caused (a) theory to be at considerable variance with practice in many cases and (b) rapid change in our concepts of guidance; changes so rapid that some concepts presented in our texts ten to fifteen years ago are now outdated.

A Definition of Guidance

As we have seen, *guidance* means many things to many people. We still hear in some quarters such statements as "guidance is for specialists," "guidance is education," "guidance is teaching," and "the teacher is the key in the guidance program." In each of these statements there is an element of truth. But there is also an element of generalization and dogmatism that can be misleading. None of these views is comprehensive enough to indicate the basic principles of guidance.

Guidance is the process of helping individuals achieve the self-understanding and self-direction necessary to make the maximum adjustment to school, home, and community. In order to achieve this goal, a school guidance program must (a) make a systematic and comprehensive study of its pupils; (b) provide them with a wide variety of information about themselves and their educational, vocational, and social opportunities; (c) offer them the opportunity to receive individual assistance through counseling; and (d) render services of an informational, training, and research nature to the school staff, parents, and community agencies in order to help them meet the needs of these pupils. The tools and techniques used to provide these services may differ at the different levels of education and even between schools at the same educational level. However, these services will prove most effective if they involve the cooperative efforts of the entire school staff, and the understanding and support of home, church, and community agencies.

Guidance and Counseling

It is not uncommon to find the expression "guidance and counseling" or "counseling and guidance" in lay magazines and periodicals today. The term "guidance counselor" has been used just as frequently. Yet counseling represents only one of the services to be found in a guidance program. The counseling service has variously been called the *brains* of the guidance program and the *heart* of the guidance program. Regardless of the part of the anatomy it represents, it is still only a *part* of the total process. Dolph Camp (9) once said, "One may as well say that he was going to use his car and his car wheels as transportation as to use the term 'guidance and counseling.'" "Guidance counselor" is particularly redundant, for the implication seems to be that some counselors give guidance and some do not. If we must use the terms together, it would be more accurate to talk about "the counseling guidance worker," recognizing that some guidance workers in the schools may serve in a counseling capacity and some may not.

Guidance and Personnel Services

The term "personnel" appears to have originated with industry. "Personnel work" involved administrative activities related to the management of workers. It found its way to the college campus as "student personnel services," where it became associated with the administrative functions of the deans of men and women, the registrar, the director of housing, the director of admissions, and others. The term "pupil personnel services" is now being used in many elementary and secondary schools. Originally interpreted as largely an administrative function, involving such areas as attendance and truancy, "pupil personnel services" has, in the minds of some, become synonymous with "guidance services." However, most authorities give "personnel services" the broader connotation. Froehlich (17) identifies the three major categories of personnel services as (a) *child accounting and regulatory services,* involving admission and registration of pupils, the school census, attendance, work permits, truancy, discipline and pupil conduct; (b) *clinical services,* provided by members of non-educational professions in our schools; and (c) *guidance services.* Hatch and Stefflre (20) agree with this point of view, arguing that there are many activities designed primarily for the personnel function that are not considered guidance services. They place the following services under "pupil personnel services": (a) guidance services, (b) health services, (c) pupil accounting services, (d) special psychological services, (e) student activities, and (f) special group activities.

The author feels that "pupil personnel services" is a broader term than "guidance services" and constitutes a necessary addition to our vocabulary. Its use implies a "helping" philosophy in borderline administrative-personnel areas formerly considered purely administrative (such as the enforcement of compulsory attendance laws). However, terminology is not always indicative of philosophy. It would be unwise to assume that the use of either of these terms by a school gave evidence of their attitude toward "helping" students in these borderline administrative-personnel areas. (Pupil personnel services will be discussed in some detail in Chapter 7.)

Principles of Guidance

Principle 1: Guidance is for all pupils

All young people need help, not just those who are maladjusted. Practical considerations of time, space, staff, and budget have caused many school guidance programs to restrict their counseling service to referrals, potential dropouts, trouble-makers, and those students who request counseling. However, group procedures are usually an effective and economical method of giving *some* assistance to *all* students. In order to be consistent with our principles of democratic education and with what we have learned about individual growth and development, the guidance program should touch the lives of all the students in the school.

Principle 2: Guidance is for pupils of all ages

Some parents, teachers, administrators, and counselors conceive of guidance as solely a secondary school service. This attitude would appear to be in conflict with what we have learned about pupil growth and development. Students at certain ages tend to learn certain behavioral patterns and acquire knowledge about themselves and others. Since the process of acquiring these learnings is continuous, guidance, too, must be *continuous*. Guidance should begin prior to the youngster's entrance into school and continue after his graduation. It should be able to bridge the gap from one educational level to another and from one school to another. A career conference and a ninth-grade testing program are easily identified as guidance activities and may be of considerable value to students. Guidance activities are more easily identified in the secondary school than they are in the elementary school because of such factors as departmentalization of instruction and more extensive use of specialized personnel. Furthermore, high school students are able to express themselves more adequately regarding their own problems. This has resulted in a disproportionate number of "problem" studies on the high school level.

But similar studies on the elementary level by Hulslander (22) and others have invalidated any assumption that pupil problems begin only after they enter the ninth grade. Indeed, for some time, elementary teachers have observed confused and unhappy pupils who could be helped by the direction which a guidance program offers. Guidance is particularly valuable in lower grades because, there, the guidance worker can often make effective use of preventive measures. It is in the elementary school that pupils acquire values and form attitudes that will have a lasting effect upon their future behavior. It is at this point that problems often have their origin. It is here that the *preventive* aspects of guidance need to receive much attention. The need for remedial services at the secondary school level might be less pressing if we were to give greater attention to preventive measures at the elementary level.

If we agree that guidance is for pupils of all ages, then the character of guidance will be more *developmental, preventive,* and *continuous* than it will be *problem-centered, remedial,* and *sporadic.*

Principle 3: Guidance must be concerned with all areas of pupil growth

Guidance must be concerned with the whole pupil and be directed toward his physical, mental, social, and emotional growth. Man is holistic in nature; his behavior and growth cannot be fragmented and isolated. Up to the present time, many parents and teachers have equated *guidance* with *vocational guidance.* This misconception has been due to (a) the vocational origins of the guidance movement, and (b) current programs of federal assistance which emphasize more effective utilization of our manpower. Although vocational information, planning, and placement have been, and will remain, very important services in our school guidance programs, other services are of equal importance. Even a broader concept of vocational guidance, which would include the educational planning necessary to reach desirable vocational goals, would be inadequate as a concept of guidance services. Super (49) warns against this narrow interpretation of guidance.

> The psychology of learning and of development brings out the fact that guidance is not just a matter of matching youth and jobs. It is not just a process of helping people to understand their abilities and interests and to make decisions on the basis of the ways in which these personal characteristics relate to educational and vocational opportunities. It is, rather, a matter of guiding individual development. Guidance is not so much guidance in the making of a choice, nor even in the making of a series of choices, as it is the guidance of development. In this process, choices or

decisions must be made, but they are often choices of what to try in order to prepare for the making of a later choice, and it has been shown that the purpose of guidance in the junior high school and even in the first year or two of senior high school is most properly exploration rather than choice-making.

Principle 4: Guidance encourages self-discovery and self-development

Gardner Murphy (38) once said, "The giving of advice is a universal human weakness." We all enjoy telling others what to do. In addition, students themselves often consider it poor manners to take other than a passive role when consulting a guidance specialist. Is it any wonder that guidance has been used on occasion as an excuse for pushing, prodding, or manipulating students? However, the counselor who pushes, prods, or manipulates students errs in three ways:

1. *He shows little regard for the dignity and integrity of the individual's personality.*
2. *He encourages students to become more dependent rather than less dependent on others for help in problem-solving.*
3. *He confuses information-giving with the manipulation of student plans and goals.* Informational services are a recognized part of any guidance program. Information on scholarship applications, entrance examinations for college, employment interviews, and so forth can be of tremendous aid to students. But a competent guidance worker should be able to impart this information without assuming the role of a "manipulator," and without encouraging conformity in behavior.

It is difficult to understand why so many persons equate conformity and adjustment. The author knows of no reputable counselor or psychologist who has offered such an equation. In fact, in text after text it is clearly pointed out that conformity is only one form of adjustment to our society. Furthermore, self-adjustment or the ability to "get along" with one's self hardly bears the taint of conformity. McQuarry (35) feels that critics who equate adjustment and conformity usually object to guidance programs because they fear that individual initiative will be stifled, individuality will be considered maladjustment, with the resulting development of a society characterized by mediocrity. But if the goal of guidance is *self*-understanding, *self*-direction, and *self*-development, it would appear that guidance encourages individuality rather than conformity.

Every student has the freedom and the right to choose his own set of beliefs and behavioral patterns. Guidance should help the student to understand his behavior and assist him in facilitating changes. Through continual involvement in the process of guidance, the student becomes increasingly adept at self-understanding and at applying this knowledge toward the development of his talents or the resolution of his problems. In this sense, the effective guidance specialist is continually attempting to "drive himself out of business."

*Principle 5: Guidance must be a cooperative enterprise
involving pupil, parent, teacher, administrator,
and counselor*

The "team" approach to guidance implies continuous cooperation and communication between members of the team. While we look to the specialist for the professional leadership necessary to maintain effective guidance services, this does not relieve the parent, teacher, and administrator of the responsibility for dealing with pupil problems. Those who view guidance as the province of guidance specialists may do so out of ignorance, laziness, or insecurity. They may also be victims of a newly anointed specialist who wishes to impress others with his expertise. Parents, teachers, and administrators are all "specialists" in some aspect of child growth and development. It is the *parent* who is the primary educator of the child, who exerts the initial influence on his attitudes and behavior, and who, day by day and year by year, has the most uninterrupted view of his growth and development. Likewise, every *teacher* has some influence on the educational, vocational, and personal attitudes and choices of students. It is desirable that this influence be consciously and wisely planned. Otherwise, teachers, by accident or through indifference, might assume the manipulative role discussed previously. The *administrator,* as educational leader in the school and community, has the opportunity to encourage and support cooperation between in-school and out-of-school personnel in the identification, treatment, and prevention of pupil problems. Finally, it is the *pupil* himself who bears the major responsibility for his own growth and development. And, although he needs to be guided in his choices, the final decision and the responsibility for that decision will eventually rest in his hands.

Effective communication between these five members of the guidance enterprise will result in the discovery of (a) more "early-stage" problems and (b) conditions contributing to pupil problems, thus permitting greater emphasis on preventive rather than remedial measures.

Principle 6: Guidance must be considered as a major part of the total education process

Traxler (50) has said, "The practice of guidance is a whole process, as unitary as the lives of the individuals with which it deals. No school can successfully engage in a few selected aspects of guidance, because the personalities of individuals cannot be divided into compartments." Thus, guidance must not only be interwoven with the instructional program. It must be intertwined with attendance, extracurricular activities, disciplinary procedures, scheduling problems, and evaluation studies. It must be concerned with making maximum use of community resources. And it must be offered by individuals who are willing to play a leading role in improving school and community relations.

Principle 7: Guidance must be responsible both to the individual and to society

At one time, it was popular to identify the function of guidance as "assisting young people to move from *dependence* to *independence*." Today, we would undoubtedly phrase it differently. The function of, and challenge to, guidance might better be described as "assisting young people to move from *dependence* to *independence* to a recognition of our *interdependence upon one another*."

Mathewson (30) feels the problem is basically one of reconciling individual happiness with social good:

> Assertions have sometimes been made that, in stressing emotional well-being, feelings of adequacy, security, belonging, and the like, child-rearing principles of recent decades have contributed toward a broad social tendency to elevate individual impulses and desires and subordinate social need, obligation, and duty. On the other hand, it is contended that stress upon social conformity and obedience have led (in some countries) to the tyrannies which have made a nightmare of the modern world.
>
> The tightrope lying between the extremes becomes, as always, the difficult line of progress. Strategies of guidance or education which unduly exalt individual self-realization at the expense of social needs and values and, conversely, those which stress social demand at the expense of legitimate individual aspiration are equally defective. Although this may be less a matter of structure and strategy than of a state of mind pervading any guidance or educative process, it is true that one form of guidance may tend to overemphasize individual whim and caprice.

It seems obvious that individuals must recognize their interdependence upon one another, if our democratic society is to survive. *Freedom* can become *license* and *individuality* can become *anarchy*. Each day we give up some of our "freedom" and "individuality" by conforming to countless laws or customs involving the streets we cross, the car we drive, the clothes we wear. "If individuality is to be safe-guarded or preserved at all, a distinction has to be made between its social and its antisocial forms. For individual personalities will in the future be compelled to realize themselves along with, rather than over against, community of effort with others (41)." For this reason guidance must be concerned with helping young people develop the kind of independence which gives recognition to our responsibilities toward one another. The guidance worker, therefore, becomes responsible both to society and the individual. He strives to create among his students a satisfactory balance between individuality and conformity, between "inner-direction" and "other-direction," between independence and social responsibility. As Millet (37) has written:

> It is a unique characteristic of Western civilization that it has professed, if not always practiced, the proposition that man is both an individual and a social animal, that the two roles can be reconciled without the complete sacrifice of the claims of personality on the one hand or the contrary claims of society on the other. It is this single proposition which is the explosive, revolutionary ideal of our heritage.

Some elaboration on these principles of guidance may be found in Chapter 3 in connection with the discussion of necessary characteristics of the guidance program.

Summary

In this chapter, considerable attention has been given to a variety of views on guidance, particularly in regard to its definition and interpretation. The two major sources of our semantic troubles are (a) the intangible nature of guidance and (b) the recency of the guidance movement. Guidance is the process of helping individuals achieve the self-understanding and self-direction necessary to make the maximum adjustment to school, home, and community. In order to achieve this goal, a school guidance program must make a systematic and comprehensive study of its pupils; provide them with a wide variety of information about themselves and their educational, vocational, and social opportunities; offer them the opportunity to receive individual assistance through counseling; and render services of an informational, training, and research nature to the school staff, parents, and community agencies in order to help them meet the needs of these pupils. Today, guidance may be viewed as a synthesis of many services and functions. These services and functions are important throughout the student's school experience, but the emphasis placed upon each will vary as the student's current needs vary.

Seven general principles of guidance are:

1. Guidance is for all pupils.
2. Guidance is for pupils of all ages.
3. Guidance must be concerned with all areas of pupil growth.
4. Guidance encourages self-discovery and self-development.
5. Guidance must be a cooperative enterprise involving pupil, parents, teacher, administrator, and counselor.
6. Guidance must be considered as a major part of the total educative process.
7. Guidance must be responsible both to the individual and to society.

Bibliography

1. Arbuckle, Dugald S. *Counseling: Philosophy, Theory and Practice.* Boston: Allyn & Bacon, Inc., 1965. Chap. 1.
2. ————. *Guidance and Counseling in the Classroom.* Boston: Allyn & Bacon, Inc., 1957. Chaps. 1, 2.
3. ————. *Pupil Personnel Services in American Schools.* Boston: Allyn & Bacon, Inc., 1962. Chap. 3.
4. Barr, John A. *The Elementary Teacher and Guidance.* New York: Henry Holt and Company, 1958. Chaps. 1, 2.
5. Barry, Ruth and Beverly Wolf. *Modern Issues in Guidance-Personnel Work.* 2nd ed. New York: Columbia University, Teachers College, 1963. Pp. 45-6, 64 and Chaps. 1, 3, 4, 16.
6. Bennett, Margaret E. *Guidance and Counseling in Groups.* 2nd ed. New York: McGraw-Hill Book Company, Inc., 1963. Chaps. 1-3.
7. Berdie, Ralph F., Wilbur L. Layton, Edward O. Swanson, and Theda Hagenah. *Testing in Guidance and Counseling.* New York: McGraw-Hill Book Company, Inc., 1963. Chap. 1.
8. Byrne, Richard Hill. *The School Counselor.* Boston: Houghton Mifflin Company, 1963. Chaps. 1, 3.
9. Camp, Dolph. "Clarification of Concepts and Procedures," Luncheon address, National Association of Guidance Supervisors and Counselor Trainers, Chicago, April, 1953.
10. Cottingham, Harold F. *Directed Readings in Foundations of Guidance and Personnel Services.* Bloomington, Illinois: McKnight & McKnight Publishing Co., 1964. Chap. 1.
11. ————. *Guidance in Elementary Schools: Principles and Practices.* Bloomington, Illinois: McKnight & McKnight Publishing Co., 1956. Chap. 1.
12. ———— and William Hopke. *Guidance in the Junior High School: Principles and Practices.* Bloomington, Illinois: McKnight & McKnight Publishing Co., 1961. Chap. 4.
13. Crow, Lester D. and Alice Crow. *An Introduction to Guidance.* New York: American Book Company, 1951. P. 12.

14.   ———. *Organization and Conduct of Guidance Services*. New York: David McKay Company, Inc., 1965. Chap. 1.

15.   ———. *Readings in Guidance*. New York: David McKay Company, Inc., 1962. Chap. 3.

16.   Dietz, J. Walter. "Critical Issues in Guidance and Personnel," *Occupations*, 15, May, 1937, 692.

17.   Froehlich, Clifford P. *Guidance Services in Schools*. New York: McGraw-Hill Book Company, Inc., 1958. Pp. 7-8.

18.   Glanz, Edward C. *Foundations and Principles of Guidance*. Boston: Allyn & Bacon, Inc., 1964. Chaps. 1, 11, 14.

19.   Gordon, Ira J. *The Teacher as a Guidance Worker*. New York: Harper and Brothers, 1956. Chap. 1.

20.   Hatch, Raymond N. and Buford Stefflre. *Administration of Guidance Services: Organization, Supervision, Evaluation*. Englewood Cliffs, New Jersey: Prentice-Hall, Inc., 1958. Chaps. 1, 3.

21.   Hollis, Joseph W. and Lucile U. Hollis. *Organizing for Effective Guidance*. Chicago: Science Research Associates, Inc., 1965. Chaps. 1, 2.

22.   Hulslander, S. C. "Assisting Youth Adjustment in Elementary Schools." *Personnel and Guidance Journal*, XXXII:7, March, 1954, 392-4.

23.   Humphreys, J. Anthony, Arthur E. Traxler, and Robert North. *Guidance Services*. 2nd ed. Chicago: Science Research Associates, Inc., 1960. Chaps. 1, 2, 5.

24.   Hutson, Percival W. *The Guidance Function in Education*. New York: Appleton-Century-Crofts, 1958. Pp. 12-23.

25.   Johnson, W. F., *et al. Pupil Personnel and Guidance Services*. New York: McGraw-Hill Book Company, Inc., 1961. Chap. 1.

26.   Jones, Arthur J. *Principles of Guidance*. 5th ed. New York: McGraw-Hill Book Company, Inc., 1963. Chaps. 1-3.

27.   Kitson, Harry D. "Individualized Education: A Heart-to-Heart Talk with a Superintendent about 'Guidance,'" *Occupations*, 13, February, 1935, 411.

28.   *Manpower and Education*. Washington, D.C.: Educational Policies Commission, National Education Association of the United States and the American Association of School Administrators, 1956. Chap. 6.

29.   Martinson, Ruth and Harry Smallenburg. *Guidance in Elementary Schools*. Englewood Cliffs, New Jersey: Prentice-Hall Inc., 1958. Chap. 1.

30.   Mathewson, Robert Henry. *Guidance Policy and Practice*. 2nd ed. New York: Harper and Brothers, 1955. Pp. 22, 24.

31.   ———. *Guidance Policy and Practice*. 3rd ed. New York: Harper & Row, Publishers, 1962. Chaps. 2, 6, 8, 9.

32.   McDaniel, Henry B. *Guidance in the Modern School*. New York: The Dryden Press, 1956. Chap. 1.

33.   ———, *et al. Readings in Guidance*. New York: Henry Holt and Company, 1959. Chap. 1.

34.   McGowan, John F. and Lyle D. Schmidt. *Counseling: Readings in Theory and Practice*. New York: Holt, Rinehart & Winston, Inc., 1962. Chap. 1.

35.   McQuarry, John P. "Erroneous Concepts About Guidance," *Vocational Guidance Quarterly*, 7:1, Autumn, 1958, 23-5.
36.   Miller, Carroll H. *Guidance Services: An Introduction*. New York: Harper & Row, Publishers, 1965. Chap. 1.
37.   Millett, John David. *The Liberating Arts*. Cleveland: Howard Allen, Inc., 1957. P. 20.
38.   Murphy, Gardner. "The Cultural Context of Guidance," *Personnel and Guidance Journal*, XXXIV, September, 1955, 4-9.
39.   Myers, George. *Principles and Techniques of Vocational Guidance*. New York: McGraw-Hill Book Company, Inc., 1941.
40.   Ohlsen, Merle M. *Guidance Services in the Modern School*. New York: Harcourt, Brace, & World, 1964. Chap. 1.
41.   Otto, Max. *Science and the Moral Life*. New York: New American Library of World Literature, Inc., 1949. P. 35.
42.   Patterson, C. H. *Counseling and Guidance in Schools*. New York: Harper and Brothers, 1962. Chap. 2.
43.   Payne, Arthur F. *Organization of Vocational Guidance*. New York: McGraw-Hill Book Company, Inc., 1925.
44.   Peters, H. J. and Gail Farwell. *Guidance: A Developmental Approach*. Chicago: Rand McNally & Co., 1959. Chap. 1.
45.   Riesman, David, Nathan Glazer, and Reuel Denney. *The Lonely Crowd*. New Haven, Connecticut: Yale University Press, 1950. Pp. 82-5.
46.   Smith, Glenn E. *Principles and Practices of the Guidance Program*. New York: The Macmillan Company, 1951. P. 2.
47.   Stewart, Laurence and Charles Warnath. *The Counselor and Society: A Cultural Approach*. Boston: Houghton Mifflin Company, 1965. Chap. 2.
48.   Stoops, Emery and Gunner L. Wahlquist. *Principles and Practices in Guidance*. New York: McGraw-Hill Book Company, Inc., 1958. Chap. 1.
49.   Super, Donald. "Guidance in American Education: Its Status and Its Future," in Landy, Edward and Paul A. Perry, eds. *Guidance in American Education I: Backgrounds and Prospects*, 1964.
50.   Traxler, Arthur E. *Techniques of Guidance*. 3rd ed. New York: Harper and Brothers, 1966. Chap. 1.
51.   Tyler, Leona E. *The Work of the Counselor*. New York: Appleton-Century-Crofts, 1961. Chap. 1.
52.   Warters, Jane. *Techniques of Counseling*. 2nd ed. New York: McGraw-Hill Book Company, Inc., 1964. Chap. 1.
53.   Weitz, Henry. *Behavior Change Through Guidance*. New York: John Wiley & Sons, Inc., 1964. Chap. 4.
54.   Wrenn, Charles Gilbert. *The Counselor in a Changing World*. Washington, D.C.: American Personnel and Guidance Association, 1962. Chaps. 1-3.

2

The Development
of Guidance Services

The need for educational and vocational guidance is particularly
important in a society such as ours which operates on the principle of
self-determination, on the democratic concept that "every boy can
become President," subject only to the natural restrictions of ability
and maturity. Student conflicts and confusion are greater here than in
countries where a class society or family occupational traditions limit
the opportunities of youth. Guidance services arose to meet the needs
of students who must grow up and take their place as adults in an
advanced and complex society.

Factors Contributing to the Need
for Guidance Services

The factors contributing to the need for guidance services in this
country may be placed under five headings: (a) democracy, (b)

technology, (c) expansion of the educational program, (d) moral and religious conditions, and (e) socio-economic conditions.

Democracy

Our earliest secondary schools were highly selective. They were selective in that their tuition charges generally excluded all but the wealthy. They were selective because their curriculum was designed to prepare young men for a profession or for religious work. In either case, a reasonable amount of scholarly achievement was necessary. The future of the "gentlemen and the scholars" who attended these schools had been predetermined to a great extent. Consequently, early secondary education was limited to young men who had similar socio-economic backgrounds and similar (often predetermined) goals and who possessed a reasonably high degree of mental ability.

The decreasing selectivity of the secondary school during the nineteenth and twentieth centuries has already been well documented. As "equality of opportunity" became a reality, first our secondary schools, then our colleges and universities, and, finally, our industries and professions opened their doors to women. The advent of free, publicly supported education made it possible for the children of lower- and middle-class families to attend school.

Today, our schools contain pupils of every type of social, economic, racial, and religious background. Individual schools are faced with great differences in the mental capacity, social maturity, and interest patterns of their pupils. We have come to realize that equality of educational opportunity can only be realized through increased attention to individual differences. The problem is not merely one of giving each pupil academic challenges appropriate to his mental capacity. To insure equality of opportunity, our schools have been forced to accept the responsibility for helping each pupil plan and progress toward realistic educational and vocational goals. Confusion, in some quarters, between "equality of opportunity" and "equality of education" has only served to increase the difficulty of this task.

Technology

Hamrin (8) quotes from Benjamin Franklin's autobiography in order to illustrate how simple the process of job selection was in the eighteenth century. Franklin wrote that when the time came for him to be apprenticed, his father took him to see different men at work. They watched a bricklayer, a carpenter, a printer, and a cutler. Franklin decided to be a cutler, but an apprenticeship was found to be too costly for the family budget. So Franklin decided to become a printer and was apprenticed to his older brother. Today, it would take us at least a lifetime to make such a personal investigation of job opportunities. The world of work has expanded to include thousands of occupations. We have only to examine the listings in the *Dictionary of Occupational Titles* to realize the extent of this growth. The industrialization of our society and the advent of automation have been responsible to a large extent for this proliferation of jobs. But rapid growth and change in the pure and applied sciences have developed new frontiers of opportunity. Such booming fields as nuclear research and missile construction have created a whole new category of jobs unknown to us a few years ago. *Without the assistance of a well-trained guidance worker,* it is difficult, if not impossible, for students to match their interests and abilities with the ever-changing and expanding opportunities available to them in the world of work.

Expansion of the Educational Program

The expansion of our educational program has been three-dimensional. First, it has grown in *height* through a continual rise in the level of education achieved by the average student. This rise has been caused, in part, by the adoption of state compulsory education laws. However, we have also witnessed a great increase in the amount of training required for different types of work. While some of this training has been of the specialized, vocational variety, business and industry, as well as the professions, have gradually demanded a more adequate background of general education as a basis for employment or accreditation.

Increased *breadth* in our educational program resulted from the establishment of elective courses in our secondary schools. The Smith-Hughes Act accelerated this movement by providing government funds for vocational education courses. High schools began to offer a vast array of courses, sometimes divided into "programs" labeled "college preparatory," "commercial," "vocational," or "general." Increased breadth in our educational program was also achieved through the rapid growth of co-curricular activities. Yet, time limitations kept the student from taking advantage of all the courses and activities which were useful to him. He was forced to choose some subjects and reject others. Pupils began to require more and more help in choosing the school subjects and non-academic activities that would best prepare them for college or for a post-high-school job.

Increased *depth* in our educational program has resulted from our research in child growth and development. Our emphasis on "child study" has caused us to study the emotional, social, mental, and physical "ages" of pupils and their relation to learning, motivation, and adjustment. With the pupil replacing subject matter as the center of the learning process, his needs, interests, and problems became more important to us. Our philosophy of education had become, in a sense, a "guidance" philosophy.

One further development needs to be mentioned here. In a philosophical sense, we had become more concerned about the individual pupil. Practical considerations, however, tended to prevent us from applying this philosophy in the classroom. With schools rapidly increasing in size, partly due to the tremendous increase in enrollment and partly as the result of the trend toward school consolidation, the growth of "assembly line" education prevented the classroom teacher from giving adequate personal attention to pupils and their problems. The teacher began to require professional assistance in order to reach educational objectives.

Moral and Religious Conditions

As our population increased rapidly and as we moved from an agricultural to an industrial society, the population centers shifted from the country to the city. This urban population concentration brought with it attendant sociological problems. As people of different races, religions, and socio-economic standards began to live in close proximity, an alarming rise in juvenile delinquency, increased racial and religious tension and prejudice, and an accompanying decrease in the effectiveness of the home as a moral force caused major concern throughout the country.

We are making some progress in the fight against racial and religious prejudice. Our schools, through the development of a broad program of non-academic activities, appear to be taking positive action in offering constructive leisure time activities to students. But the breakdown of the home as a moral force constitutes a formidable problem. There is a general consensus that religious customs have changed—that young people are thinking for themselves and questioning religious dogma. Yet, many young people have been unable to find effective values to replace the ones which they reject. As a result, they have become confused about what is right and what is wrong. Today, when the percentage of both parents working is at an all-time high, help in answering these puzzling questions is not always forthcoming from the home.

While guidance workers are not in a position to deal directly with religious belief, it is possible for them to have a great effect on the moral and ethical values of students. Murphy (19) feels that a guidance worker cannot help conveying, directly or indirectly, to every client, the perspective in which his own life is lived.

> . . . it is not true that the wise man's sharing of a philosophy of life is an arrogant imposition upon a defenseless client. On the contrary, the risk of arrogance lies, I believe, in the technician's assumption that, by virtue of his skills, he can guide a whole person to move wisely in a complex and swiftly changing society. As we have noted, the young man and woman of today simply cannot be directed into paths guaranteeing a happy and effective life; they can only be assisted in developing into people with the maturity and the flexibility to solve new problems as these are presented.
>
> . . . it is often said that all philosophies are subjective and arbitrary, and that one system of values is as good as another. But if you believed that, you would not have chosen personnel and guidance as a way of life. Your experience, moreover, has shown you that some values, such as those of sympathy, tenderness, generosity, and self-control resonate to the deeper chords of human nature, and that they are for that reason intensely practical and dependable. Other values work badly, either because they cannot be solidly built into human nature or because they involve profound internal contradictions.[1]

Socio-Economic Conditions

A great variety of socio-economic factors also contributed to the need for guidance services. The great depression of 1929 was one of these. The "alphabetical" agencies of the 1930's, created in order to bolster a sagging economy, tended to bring the government into the guidance field. The *Civilian Conservation Corps* was established during this period in order to give unemployed young men a chance to do some constructive work. Work on projects such as dam construction, road building, and forest clearance was supplemented by counseling of an educational and vocational nature. *The National Youth Administration* went one step further—it provided testing and counseling services for young people interested in a job or further education, and then helped place these young people in a training situation compatible with their interests, abilities, and work experience. A Junior Division of the United States Employment Service was also organized during this depression period. Testing, counseling, and placement services for youth were initiated. Research stemming from

---

[1]Reprinted with permission of the *Personnel and Guidance Journal*.

these services provided the basis for an organizational framework to the world of work published under the heading *Dictionary of Occupational Titles.*

World War II brought the government still further into the guidance field. The immediate need for group and individual tests to select and place military personnel caused the government to enter into what amounted to a "crash" program of research on testing. With a tremendous number of "captive subjects" available in military installations throughout the country, psychologists and psychometrists found themselves in a virtual Utopia. They had an ample budget, a large, measurable population, and considerable freedom of operation. Research and measurement that normally might have required a decade or more for completion was accomplished in a two- or three-year period. Psychologists and psychiatrists also found a fertile field for counseling research. Battle fatigue, a real military problem during the war, began to be studied from the psychological as well as from the physical side. A high priority was given to research on leadership potential in order to improve selection procedures for officer training schools.

At the close of the war, testing and counseling programs were put into effect by the Veterans Administration to assist in the postwar adjustment of veterans. Most of these counseling centers were established on college and university campuses in order to provide counseling services for the vast number of veterans continuing their education under the G.I. bill. These centers were partially staffed with graduate students from the university who were completing an advanced degree in counseling or in clinical psychology. This arrangement had two beneficial effects. It provided excellent training and experience for these graduate counselors. Also, the large number of veterans returning for testing and counseling provided an excellent "sample" for further research in this area.

World tension has also contributed to our need for guidance services. Insecurities, created by such new developments as the hydrogen bomb, missile construction, and earth satellites, and compounded by changing or lost religious beliefs, have aroused serious personal and emotional problems in many of our young people. The advent of the *peacetime draft* caused many young boys of high school age to adopt a "live for today for tomorrow you may be drafted" philosophy.

Finally, as a result of improved methods of communication and transportation, our *pace of living* has quickened to the point where good mental health is something to be written about and sought after.

An attempt has been made to identify those factors which have contributed to the need for guidance services. These factors were not entirely unrelated to one another. The three-dimensional expansion of our educational program could not have been accomplished in a country founded upon aristocratic or totalitarian concepts. Democracy encouraged rapid technological progress and laid the groundwork for the aforementioned moral, social, and economic developments. War had an effect upon our moral values, and war today causes tension and insecurity.

The Origins of the Guidance Movement

It is not the purpose of this book to present a detailed account of the activities of our pioneers in the guidance movement. Brewer (3) and Reed (25) have presented well-documented and comprehensive accounts of these historical developments. Instead, the origins of the guidance movement will be identified in order to gain some appreciation of the issues and problems facing the guidance field today.

The Vocational Guidance Movement

Experimental work in vocational guidance appears to have begun as early as 1895 through the efforts of *George Merrill* at the California School of Mechanical Arts in San Francisco. Brewer (3) reports that Merrill's work was the first systematic attempt, under educational auspices, to provide specific guidance services for pupils. Merrill's plan provided for exploratory experiences in each of the trades taught by the school, and was accompanied by counseling, job placement, and follow-up of former pupils.

Frank Parsons and the Vocation Bureau of Boston are always mentioned in any discussion of the development of vocational guidance. This bureau, later to become part of Harvard University, was established with the help of Parsons in 1909. Its purpose was to assist young men to make vocational choices based upon their occupational aptitudes and interests. Parsons also established the first counselor-training program. Originating just nine months after the establishment of the Vocation Bureau, the program was designed "to fit young men to become vocational counselors and manage vocation bureaus in connection with Young Men's Christian Associations, schools, colleges, universities, and public systems, associations, and business establishments anywhere in the country." Seven years later, Brewer (3) points out, the School Committee of Boston adopted the first certification program for counselors. The requirements included (a) adequate study of education, and (b) experience in a vocational school or in a special vocational service as approved by the board of superintendents.

Credit must also be given to *Frank P. Goodwin* for organizing a city-wide guidance program for the Cincinnati, Ohio school system in 1911. The basic principles of this program would be acceptable to us today. As director of the Department of Civil and Vocational Service, Goodwin proposed six conditions which he regarded as necessary for successful vocational guidance in a large high school. Reed (25) reports them as: (a) the appointment of a director with time for supervision, (b) a school organization which permits the close personal contact of each pupil with at least one teacher of the right type, (c) the exercise of an intelligent and sympathetic helpfulness on the part of the teacher, (d) a logical analysis of the personal characteristics of each pupil, (e) an understanding of the relation of the school work to the life-career motive, and (f) the adaptation of school work to the vocational needs of the community.

From 1898 to 1907, as class counselor in Central High School, Detroit, Michigan, *Jesse B. Davis* spent most of his time in the educational and vocational counseling of eleventh-grade boys and girls. On becoming principal of the Grand Rapids, Michigan, High School in 1907, he began a school-wide program of (a) personality culture and character development, and (b) vocational information in connection with regular curriculum subjects. It should be pointed out that Davis was the first to stimulate the guidance movement from within the school system rather than from outside. As a result of this pioneering, he was appointed Director of Vocational Guidance for the city of Grand Rapids in 1913. Four months after his appointment, Grand Rapids schools established a centralized system of guidance.

Eli W. Weaver of the Boys High School of Brooklyn attracted national attention during the period 1908-1910 because of his efforts to organize guidance services in New York City schools. In a city school system handicapped by excessive decentralization, without official endorsement, and in the face of some dissension among his superiors, he laid the groundwork for the New York City Vocational Guidance Survey of 1911, organized a number of local agencies to deal with guidance and placement, and promoted the Second National Conference on Vocational Guidance held in New York City in 1912.

The Mental Hygiene Movement

The moving force behind the mental hygiene movement was *Clifford Beers,* a wealthy young man who became interested in problems of mental health as a result of confinement after a mental breakdown. In *A Mind That Found Itself,* he documented his experiences in a mental hospital. This book became influential in two ways. First, it aroused the public to the deplorable conditions existing in many of our mental hospitals. Second, it aroused interest in the problem of mental health itself. Beers helped found the National Committee for Mental Hygiene in 1909. Initially, this committee was organized to promote the impovement of services to the mentally ill. Advances followed Beers' pioneer work. Increased emphasis began to be placed upon the preventive aspect of mental health. Mental hygiene clinics were established. In 1922, Yale University became the first institution of higher education to establish a mental hygiene clinic.

The Child Guidance Movement

The child guidance movement began in 1909 with the establishment of a clinic by Dr. William Healy and his wife (also an M.D.) in Chicago, Illinois. This clinic was an outgrowth of their experiences in treating the physical illnesses of children (many from broken homes) who lived in one of the slum areas of Chicago. The Healys felt the need for a clinic which would treat the physical and psychological problems of children as related aspects of a total problem. With the financial backing of a wealthy widow, they established the clinic that, years later, was taken over by the state of Illinois to become known as the Illinois Institute of Juvenile Research. By 1914, over one hundred child guidance clinics had been established.

Personnel Work in Industry

Another influence on the development of our present guidance movement came about through the beginning of personnel work in industry. Dr. Munsterberg of Harvard University, on the basis of his work with a Boston streetcar company, pioneered in introducing the job-analysis technique to industry. Further impetus to the movement resulted from the development of group tests of mental ability. Short-form editions of these tests, such as the Wonderlic Personnel Inventory, enabled business and industry to become more objective in the selection of new employees with a minimum expenditure of time and energy. The Excess Profits Tax, placed on business and industry as an indirect result of World War II, also had a favorable effect on personnel work. Many industries started or expanded their own personnel services at this time, financing the program out of money that would otherwise have gone to the government in taxes. These three factors: the development of the job-analysis technique, the construction of "short-form" group tests of mental ability, and the Excess Profits Tax were mainly responsible for the growth of personnel work in industry.

The Testing Movement

The growth and development of standardized tests might be considered the fifth source of the guidance movement. The origin of the scientific measurement of intelligence is commonly attributed to the work of the French psychologist, Alfred Binet. His early work was stimulated by the need for identifying and assisting mentally retarded children. Nevertheless, his Intelligence Scale of 1905 and Terman's 1916 adaptation of the scale for American use were big steps forward in the development of measurement techniques that gave a greater degree of objectivity to the process of educational and vocational planning with *all* children and young adults. One of Terman's students at Stanford University, Arthur S. Otis, gave further impetus to the testing movement by preparing an intelligence test that could be administered to large groups of persons by relatively unskilled examiners. This test formed the basis for the *Army Alpha Examination* used in classifying thousands of soldiers in World War I. A great number and variety of tests, many of them poorly constructed and/or inadequately standardized, made their appearance in the decade immediately following that war. Today, the testing movement is approaching professional maturity as a result of (1) improved test development practices, (2) better safeguards on the proper distribution of tests, and (3) the large number of professional journals and yearbooks (such as Buros' *Mental Measurements Yearbook*) that offer vigorous and sophisticated criticisms of newly developed tests.

Dean of Girls Movement

One further development deserves mention here. Reed (25), in discussing the efforts of Superintendent Ella Flagg Young to establish vocational guidance in the Chicago schools, refers to a recommendation made by Superintendent Young to the Board of Education on January 22, 1913.

1. That the board accept the offer made by various organizations to extend the work in vocational guidance begun at the Lucy L. Flower High School to other schools of the city "subject to direction by the Superintendent of schools" and that Assistant Superintendent Roberts be in charge.
2. That women counselors be appointed in each "mixed" high school for the social guidance of girls. . . . The boys have a coun-

selor and a friend in the principal who directs and advises them
in affairs of personal and organized social nature arising outside
the classroom . . . the girls have no woman teacher to whom
they can go in similar circumstances.[2]

Superintendent Young recommended selection of a woman teacher
who would teach three regular classes and, under the direction of the
principal, give special attention to the organized social life of the
girls. She would be paid $300 extra for this responsibility. This recom-
mendation to the board, though not mentioned too frequently in our
literature, represented "pioneering" of a far-reaching nature.

State and National Organization of Guidance Services

While the *National Vocational Guidance Association* will be dis-
cussed more fully in Chapter 12, it merits comment here because,
through it, guidance work took on a truly national flavor. The First
National Conference on Vocational Guidance sponsored by the Boston
Chamber of Commerce in March, 1910 has already been mentioned. A
Second National Conference was held in New York City two years
later. At this time, plans were drawn up for the establishment of the
National Vocational Guidance Association. At the Third National
Conference held in Grand Rapids in October, 1913, NVGA was
founded, a provisional constitution was adopted, and its first officers
were elected. At this meeting, the three needs for guidance were
identified as: *economic*, the need for a better and more efficiently
selected body of employees in industry; *educational*, the need for wise
choices of educational programs by pupils; and *social*, the preserva-
tion of society.

In the two decades following the establishment of the National
Vocational Guidance Association, more and more programs of
guidance appeared in our city school systems, but organization on the
state and national level was lacking.

In 1933, the *National Occupational Conference* was founded in
order to provide an agency for clearing information and practice
concerning the problem of supplying vocational guidance to our
young people. The NOC continued to function until 1939; it sponsored the publication of several books in the guidance field, issued a
periodic annotated index of books and pamphlets called the *Occupa-*

---

[2]Proceedings of the Board of Education of the City of Chicago, 1911-1912,
p. 80.

tional Index, and performed various field services of a consulting and research nature. The heavy demand for its services undoubtedly encouraged the development of a guidance service in the United States Office of Education.

The President's Advisory Committee on Education, appointed in 1936, provided the first official recommendations for the organization of guidance services on a national level. In February, 1938, after eighteen months of study, the committee of educators recommended an expanded program of Federal Aid for Vocational Education. The committee specifically recommended an occupational service that would provide information on a national, state, and local basis regarding the number of recruits required annually in each of the major occupational fields, and the number in training for each occupation. They also recommended that a sound program of vocational education should include guidance and placement services as well as training services. Finally, they suggested that schools furnishing vocational education should cooperate closely with public employment offices in the initial placement and adjustment of those leaving the full-time school. As a result of this report, the *Occupational Outlook Service* was established in the Department of Labor in 1940. Except for a short period during World War II, it has provided schools with a wealth of information concerning occupational opportunities and requirements.

The recommendation of the President's Advisory Committee on Education was also directly responsible for the establishment of the *Occupational Information and Guidance Service* in the United States Office of Education in 1938. At the beginning, the OIGS was subsidized by funds drawn through the George-Dean Act. Money from the George-Dean Act was intended to subsidize vocational education only, but the Commissioner of Education gave a broader interpretation of the functions of the OIGS in a statement of principle issued in 1940. This interpretation also made it possible to use George-Dean Act funds for the establishment of guidance offices in state departments of education. Guidance thus joined agriculture, business education, homemaking, and industrial education as areas qualifying for federal aid through the Smith-Hughes Act of 1917 and the George-Dean Act of 1936. The men placed in charge of these guidance offices were given the title *Chief, Occupational Information and Guidance Service* or simply, *State Supervisor of Guidance.*

The *George-Barden Act* of 1946 broadened federal support of state and local guidance services. Like the Smith-Hughes and George-Dean Acts preceding it, the George-Barden Act designated funds for the promotion of vocational education. In the absence of any specific statements regarding the expenditure of funds, the United States Commissioner of Education ruled that they might be used for four different purposes:

1. *The maintenance of a state program of supervision.* This merely reaffirmed the commissioner's ruling of 1938.
2. *Reimbursement of salaries of counselor trainers.* The Smith-Hughes and George-Dean Acts had provided funds for salaries and travel expenses of teacher trainers in agriculture, home economics, and industrial education. The commissioner's ruling placed counselor trainers in this category. Today, a number of states use these funds to reimburse the salaries of counselor trainers associated with state colleges or universities.
3. *Research in the field of guidance.* Under this provision, funds may be used by the states to subsidize research activities in the field of guidance.
4. *Reimbursement of salaries of local guidance supervisors and counselors.* A number of states today have plans for reimbursing guidance workers in local schools. Other states have not made use of this provision.

While the George-Barden Act provided the real "breakthrough" in our attempts to organize guidance services on a state and national level, the active leadership of such men as Harry A. Jager should not be underestimated. Until his death in 1954, Jager, as Chief, Occupational Information and Guidance Service of the United States Office of Education, provided the guidance movement with the cohesion and "forward look" necessary for continued progress.

The National Defense Education Act of 1958

Between 1950 and 1955, a number of studies were sponsored by the United States Office of Education, the National Science Foundation, and the Committee on Financing Higher Education to determine the extent to which secondary school graduates with aptitude and interest for college failed to continue their education. The results of these studies were not encouraging. The surveys indicated that many superior students who graduate from high school do not go on to college. In addition, a substantial number of talented high school students drop out before graduation. One study, made under a grant from the National Science Foundation to the Educational Testing Service (35) investigated the college and career plans of 10,000 high school seniors from 478 representative high schools who were in the top 30 per cent of their classes. Of this group of superior students, 80 per cent of the boys and 70 per cent of the girls reported that they would like to go on to college. Of those who originally were not interested in continuing their education, four-fifths indicated that they would probably go on to college if they had scholarships. The report concluded:

> ... the fact that a very large number of able students without college plans would be willing to go on to college if given a scholarship surely indicates that many students do not have college plans simply because they have never been able to view college as being a reasonable prospect.... Given a way to pay their expenses, their plans apparently would readily change; given the assurance early in their school career that college was financially attainable, they might have included in their course work the science, mathematics and English needed to make it a reality. We believe that it is in the salvage of cases such as these that a large-scale scholarship program, combined with better counseling in the junior and senior high schools, could most effectively increase the proportion of able students going to college. The existence of such a scholarship program would make it possible for these high school counselors to demonstrate to the "No Interest" student that college is, in fact, a real possibility.[3]

A second study, made by the same group under a similar grant from the National Science Foundation (36), was based upon questionnaire returns from approximately 35,000 high school seniors in 516 representative high schools during the spring of 1955. This study concluded that approximately one-half of the top 30 per cent of the nation's high school graduates do not go on to college. It was estimated that over 60,000 highly able secondary school graduates with aptitude and interest for college failed to continue their education for financial reasons. Another group of similar size and ability who reported no college plans reported also that they had "not discussed going to college with their teachers or counselors."

A nation-wide study by the Office of Education (12), covering the period 1950-1954, indicated that approximately one-third of the students in the upper-half of high school graduating classes did not go on

---

[3]Used with permission of Educational Testing Service. See G. Stice, W. G. Mollenkopf, and W. S. Torgerson, *Background Factors and College-Going Plans Among High Aptitude Public High School Seniors.* A report of a study supported by a grant from the National Science Foundation (Princeton, N.J.: Educational Testing Service, August, 1956).

to college, and another sixth (16.5 per cent) continued only on a part-time basis.

A fourth study, sponsored by the Commission on Financing Higher Education (9), was based upon 1951 data of eighteen-year-olds and high school graduates. These conclusions were drawn: Of approximately 528,000 eighteen-year-olds in the top quarter of ability, one out of five dropped out of high school before graduation. Of the 422,000 who did graduate, 219,000, or 52 per cent, went on to college. Of the 203,000 superior graduates who did not go on, about three-fourths might have gone to college if they had been offered scholarships.

These and similar studies pointed toward three conclusions:

1. We needed improved testing of student aptitudes and improved cumulative records so that the potential abilities of students could be better identified at an earlier stage in their education.
2. We needed skilled counseling to encourage talented young people to stay in school, to work harder in academic courses, and prepare for college.
3. We needed a greater number of scholarships for those with great potential talent who were presently barred from college by its cost.

Committee hearings on a new education bill were held in the House of Representatives between August, 1957, and April, 1958, and in the Senate between January and March, 1958. Passage of a bill in each chamber in August, 1958, and subsequent conferences to effect a compromise, led to adoption of Public Law 85-864, signed by President Eisenhower on September 2, 1958, after approval (66-15) in the Senate and (212-85) in the House. The purpose of Public Law 85-864, entitled the National Defense Education Act of 1958 (24) was set forth as follows:

> The Congress hereby finds and declares that security of the nation requires the fullest development of the mental resources and technical skills of its young men and women . . . the defense of this Nation depends upon the mastery of modern techniques developed from complex scientific principles. It depends as well upon the discovery and development of new principles, new techniques and new knowledge. . . . We must increase our efforts to identify and educate more of the talents of our nation. . . . It is therefore the purpose of this act to provide substantial assistance in various forms to individuals and to states and their subdivisions

in order to insure trained manpower of sufficient quality and quantity to meet the national defense needs of the United States.

The bill in its original form contained ten sections or Titles. Title I stated the purpose of the act and defined certain words recurring frequently in the various other Titles. The remaining Titles provided for the following:

Title II—Loans to students in institutions of higher education.

Title III—Financial assistance to secondary schools for strengthening science, mathematics, and modern foreign language instruction.

Title IV—National Defense Fellowships for graduate students interested in becoming teachers in institutions of higher education.

Title V—Improvement of guidance programs in our secondary schools.

Title VI—Establishment of language institutes and research centers designed to improve and expand the teaching of modern foreign languages.

Title VII—Research and experimentation in more effective utilization of television, radio, motion pictures, and related media for educational purposes.

Title VIII—Establishment of area vocational education programs.

Title IX—Establishment of a Science Information Service and a Science Information Council.

Title X—Improvement of statistical services of state educational agencies.

The guidance section, known as Title V in the bill, had two parts. Part A authorized funds to assist state educational agencies in establishing and maintaining programs of testing, counseling, and other guidance services. States wishing to participate were asked to submit a plan to the United States Commissioner of Education setting forth:

1. A program for testing students in the public secondary schools, and if authorized by law in other secondary schools of such state, to identify students with outstanding aptitudes and ability, and the means of testing which will be utilized in carrying out such programs.

2. A program of guidance and counseling in the public secondary schools of such state, (A) to advise students of courses of study best suited to their ability, aptitudes and skills, and (B) to encourage students with outstanding aptitudes and ability to com-

plete their secondary school education, take the necessary courses for admission to institutions of higher education and to enter such institutions (24).

During the first fiscal year, federal funds were available to meet the total cost to participating states for carrying out their plans, but for the three succeeding fiscal years covered by the act, states were to match federal funds on a fifty-fifty basis. Private nonprofit secondary schools could obtain assistance under a state plan if the state educational agency was permitted by law to provide services to such schools. Where the state educational agency could not provide such services, the act stated that, "the commissioner shall arrange for the testing of such students and shall pay the cost thereof for the fiscal year ending June 30, 1959, and one-half the cost thereof for any of the three succeeding fiscal years out of State's allotment."

Part B of Title V authorized the Commissioner of Education to set up counseling institutes in colleges and universities for the purpose of improving the qualifications of personnel engaged in counseling students in secondary schools, or of teachers in secondary schools preparing to engage in such counseling. These institutes could be conducted as part of the regular school term or as a part of a summer session or summer quarter. Colleges and universities conducting these institutes were to be reimbursed for all expenses incurred during the program. Part B further provided that eligible students could receive a stipend at the rate of $75.00 per week for the period of attendance at such an institute, plus an additional $15.00 per week for each dependent.

The first of these special counseling institutes was held during the summer of 1959 at fifty colleges and universities whose proposals for such institutes had been approved earlier by the Commissioner of Education. These institutes were located at strategic points so as to serve a specified geographical area. A total of 2,210 counselors attended the fifty counseling institutes during the summer of 1959. (A complete report on the first fifty institutes has been compiled by Tyler (43). The largest institute to date has been held at Northwestern University in cooperation with the North Central Association of Colleges and Secondary Schools. One counselor from each of the 100 cooperating secondary schools in the Association's *Superior and Talented Student Project* attended this institute. However, institute enrollments have generally ranged from twenty to sixty students.

The National Defense Education Act was amended in 1964 and became known as Public Law 88-665. It provided for major changes in Titles II, III, IV, and V, and added a Title XI (Institutes for school library personnel; educational media specialists; elementary school teachers; and secondary school teachers of modern foreign language, reading, history, geography, English, and disadvantaged youth).

Modifications in Title V included the following:

> *Title V-A*: Provided for extension of the program to all elementary grades and to public junior colleges and public technical institutes.
>
> *Title V-B*: Enabled the Commissioner of Education to arrange, through grants or contracts, short-term or regular session institutes for advanced study, including the use of new materials.
>
> Extended the program to individuals who are engaged in counseling (as well as to teachers preparing to become counselors) in elementary or secondary schools or in institutions of higher education, including junior colleges and technical institutes.

It is still too early to judge the full impact of the National Defense Education Act of 1958 and its subsequent amendments. The variety of its provisions has made administration of the bill a rather complex and difficult task. Except for Title IX, which establishes a special service in the National Science Foundation, the act is administered, at the federal level, by the United States Office of Education. The U.S. Office of Education has greatly increased the size of its staff in order to fulfill these additional responsibilities. Opponents of federal aid to education have tended to regard this rapid increase in personnel as additional evidence that we are moving toward federal control of education. The danger of federal control of schools was considered by Congress prior to passing this legislation. The act states, "Nothing contained in this Act shall be construed to authorize any department, agency, officer or employee of the United States to exercise any direction, supervision or control over the curriculum, program of instruction, administration or personnel of any educational institution or school system." However, Little (14), in a survey sponsored by the U.S. Office of Education, reported sharp opposition to centralized control of all federal aid to education programs. Specifically, the following major criticisms of federal aid programs were made by university faculty members and administrators:

1. Restrictions on federal funds tend to increase the divisions between the strong and the weak universities, since twenty-five to fifty major schools receive the bulk of assistance.
2. Federal projects favor the *graduate* programs at the expense of the *undergraduate* programs.

3. Federal projects emphasize *research* and neglect *teaching*.
4. Federal projects inevitably discriminate against those areas not supported.
5. Some faculties working on these projects tend to favor the *project* rather than the *university*.
6. Some state and regional boards of education are bypassed by the direct cooperation between the government and the institution.

On the positive side, Title V of NDEA has served to focus attention on guidance services in our schools. All fifty states, the District of Columbia and three territories are participating in the Title V-A program. The Counseling and Guidance Branch of the U.S. Office of Education has added many specialists to its staff, thereby increasing its leadership potential for state and local programs of guidance. Four sections have been formed within the Counseling and Guidance Branch: (1) *Guidance Program Development*, (2) *Guidance Procedures and Techniques*, (3) *Occupational and Career Guidance*, and (4) *Counselor Preparation*. A brochure of the U.S. Office of Education (44) identifies the following changes as having taken place during the five-year period (1958-1963) immediately following the enactment of the National Defense Education Act:

A. The full-time equivalent of counselors increased 127 per cent from 12,000 to 27,180 and the ratio of full-time counselors to students dropped from 1 to 960 to 1 to 530.
B. Members of professional guidance staffs in state educational agencies increased from 99 to 257.
C. Under Title V-B, 29.7 million dollars were spent to support 416 counseling institutes. The total number of students receiving training in these short-term and regular-session institutes was 13,784.
D. Title V-A was a successful "pump-priming" operation. From 1958 to 1963 local school district expenditures for guidance services jumped from 5.6 to 127.1 million dollars.

Yet, a number of important questions remain to be answered. Have we improved counselor *quality* at the same time that we have improved counselor *quantity*? Are there not better ways to subsidize counselors-in-training than through special "institutes"? The issues raised by these and other related questions will be discussed in Chapter 13.

Recent Developments

White House Conference on Children and Youth

Twelve recommendations for citizen action in the area of guidance and guidance personnel were adopted in April, 1960, by the Golden Anniversary White House Conference on Children and Youth. Over 7,600 educational and youth leaders participated in this major conference which is held every decade. The American Personnel and Guidance Association and its participating members played an important role in the formation of the following twelve proposals for the future of guidance (46):

1. That guidance and counseling programs be strengthened, expanded, and coordinated at all levels; and that the role of the guidance and counseling program be clearly defined.

2. That guidance and counseling begin in the elementary school with educational and vocational planning based on early, continuous, and expanded testing and diagnostic appraisal of each child, in order to identify abilities, weaknesses and problems, mental, physical, and emotional.

3. That every secondary school have sufficient trained professional counselors to deal with adolescent problems; that each adolescent be counseled throughout the secondary years by the same staff adviser, acceptable to him; that school planning for adolescents be based on awareness of individual differences in skills and capacities; that community counseling services be made more widely available to youth and their parents; and that coordination between school and community services be emphasized.

4. That school resources for identification and guidance of the gifted, limited, and otherwise exceptional child, as well as for the average and normal youth, be expanded and improved.

5. That vocational counseling and guidance programs be provided with adequate financial support from Federal, State, and local sources; that school personnel, boards, and parents interpret to taxpayers the need for increased and improved guidance services; and that these services cooperate closely with Government, employment services, industries, labor unions, armed services, trade and service organizations, higher educational institutions, and other community groups.

6. That the qualified professional staff (of every school system) include educational and vocational guidance counselors, job placement counselors, physical health personnel, psychologists to assist in diagnosis and continued study of the children, and school social workers or visiting teachers to assist in the treatment of children with special problems.

7. That the ratio of students to elementary school counselors be 600 to 1.

8. That the number of students per counselor in secondary schools be decreased from the present ratio of 625 to 1, to 250 to 1.

9. That more adequate psychological and psychiatric services be provided for all school-age youth in a ratio of one specialist to 2,000 pupils.

10. That all States require the certification of guidance counselors and other specialized personnel.

11. That the qualifications for certification be continually reviewed and strengthened, in accordance with the latest research findings in the field; and that they recognize and give credit to appropriate training and work experience in lieu of classroom teaching.

12. That the training of guidance and counseling personnel for elementary and secondary schools, colleges, and community and professional agencies be intensified and improved to meet the demand; and that Federal funds for the education of school counselors be given only to institutions with professionally approved counselor education programs.

Identification and Education of the Academically Talented

Attempts to define and describe the importance of intellectual ability as a national resource were quite numerous during the 1950's. In 1951, the Commission on Human Resources and Advanced Training pointed out that only about 10 per cent of our country's young people who possessed an I.Q. of 110 or above actually went to college. Similar studies at this time revealed that only about 40 per cent of the top quarter of students who actually graduated from high school went on to college. In 1954, Wolfle (47) concluded that high school graduates in the top 20 per cent of their class had only a fifty-fifty chance of going to college. Later studies sponsored by the National Science Foundation and the United States Office of Education (12, 35, 36) uncovered evidence supporting Wolfle's conclusion. In reaction to these studies, a multitude of new scholarship and financial aid programs for superior students sprang into existence. A $20,000,000 grant by the Carnegie Foundation provided support for the National Merit Scholarship Program, organized in 1955 to engage "in the discovery, recognition and encouragement of exceptionally talented young people. Upon such unusual boys and girls—provided adequate education and training is given them—depends the future leadership and destiny of America (33)." In 1965, approximately 796,000 students in 17,607 high schools participated in National Merit examinations.

On October 4, 1957, the Russians put an earth satellite, Sputnik I, into orbit. After recovering from the initial shock caused by this scientific achievement in a country other than our own, we began to give increased impetus to our search for talent. A variety of studies, conferences, and reports were organized to consider the methods, techniques, and goals of identifying, motivating, and educating the academically talented student. Some of the more important projects are summarized here.

1. *The North Central Association of Colleges and Secondary Schools Project on the Guidance and Motivation of Superior and Talented Students* was initiated by a grant from the Carnegie Corporation in March, 1958. Ten conferences were held during the summers of 1958 and 1959. In addition, the Project, in cooperation with Northwestern University, sponsored a counseling institute under the provisions of the National Defense Education Act. Shertzer (32) has compiled and edited a report containing much of the discussion and research undertaken by this group.

2. *The National Education Association Invitational Conference on the Academically Talented Secondary School Pupil* was convened in February, 1958 with the aid of a grant from the Carnegie Corporation. Under the chairmanship of James B. Conant, 200 outstanding educators and laymen devoted two and one-half days to consideration of problems involved in finding and educating the academically talented pupil. The report (20) of this conference has been published by the National Education Association.

3. *Project Talent,* a national census of the aptitudes and abilities of high school students, is being conducted jointly by the University of Pittsburgh and the American Institute for Research, and is receiving major support from the United States Office of Education with assistance from the National Institute of Mental Health and the Office of Naval Research. The testing phase of the project was completed during the spring of 1960. Approximately thirty psychological, educational, and personal background measures were obtained from about 450,000 high school students. Each of the 1,357 schools in the sample filled out fifty pages of questionnaire material regarding the school, the guidance program, and the counselors. In addition to providing a national inventory of the talent potential in our high schools and furnishing data on guidance programs, services, and facilities currently supported by a representative sample of high schools throughout the country, the long-range objectives of Project Talent are to develop: (a) a set of standards for educational and psychological meas-

urement, (b) a comprehensive counseling guide indicating patterns of aptitude and ability which are predictive of success in various careers, (c) a better understanding of how young people choose their life work, and (d) a better understanding of the educational experiences which prepare students for their life work. Follow-up studies will be carried out by mailing questionnaires to each of the 450,000 students one, five, ten, and twenty years after they graduate from high school in order to provide insights concerning factors which were most effective in influencing the students' decisions to take advanced training in preparation for careers and to enter these fields, as well as information regarding success and satisfaction in their work. *Design for a Study of American Youth,* the first of a series of books reporting on this research, was published early in 1962. As later results are compiled, further reports will be published under the series title, *The Talents of American Youth.*

4. The recent activities and reports of *James B. Conant* have had considerable impact upon the thinking of educators and laymen alike. Among his recommendations (4) which have stimulated searching re-examinations of the high school curriculum are several which have direct implications for the school guidance program:

(1) *The Counseling System*—There should be one full-time counselor or guidance officer for every 250-300 pupils in the high school.

(2) *Individualized Programs*—It should be the policy of the school that every student have an individualized program; there would be no classification such as college-preparatory, vocational, or commercial.

(3) *Programs of the Academically Talented*—School policy should be adopted in regard to elective programs for the academically talented as a guide to counselors.

(4) *Highly Gifted Pupils*—Identification of this group, about 3 per cent nationally of the student population, should start in seventh or eighth grade.

(5) *Foreign Languages*—Guidance officers should urge the completion of a four-year sequence of one foreign language if the student demonstrates ability in handling foreign languages.

5. *The Special Studies Project of the Rockefeller Brothers Fund, Inc.* is an attempt to assess the major problems and opportunities which are likely to confront the United States over the next ten to fifteen years. Seven major areas of national concern are to be studied. The fourth of the series of reports published by participants in this

project is entitled *The Pursuit of Excellence* (27). The theme of this report appears in its foreword:

> There is no more searching or difficult problem for a free people than to identify, nurture, and wisely use its own talents. Indeed, on its ability to solve this problem rests, at least in part, its fate as a free people. For a free society cannot commandeer talent: it must be true to its own vision of individual liberty. And yet at a time when we face problems of desperate gravity and complexity an undiscovered talent, a wasted skill, a misapplied ability is a threat to the capacity of a free people to survive.[4]

Commission on Guidance in American Schools

As a result of a $50,000 grant by the Fund for the Advancement of Education to the American Personnel and Guidance Association early in 1960, a Commission on Guidance in American Schools was appointed to study and report on the role of school guidance in our society. The resulting report (48), entitled *The Counselor in a Changing World,* has provided impetus to the drive toward the professionalization of school counselors (see Chapter 12 for a more detailed account of this report).

Career Development Theory

Largely as a result of Donald Super's redefinition of the function of vocational guidance as that of developing and implementing a self-concept (37, 38), current professional literature is giving much more attention to theories of career development, particularly with respect to the Career Pattern Study at Teachers College, Columbia University (39, 40), the Career Development Studies at Harvard University (41), the work of Anne Roe (28, 29, 30), and the studies of women students at Vassar College (31).

New Educational Legislation

A wide variety of educational legislation has been enacted by Congress recently. These laws, together with the government's war on poverty (as represented by the Economic Opportunity Act of 1964), will have a tremendous, but as yet undetermined, impact on our schools. The following legislation will undoubtedly have considerable

---

[4]From *The Pursuit of Excellence—Education and the Future of America.* © Copyright © 1958 Rockefeller Brothers Fund, Inc. Reprinted by permisson of Doubleday & Company, Inc.

influence on the function of guidance in our schools and on the role to be played by the school counselor.

ELEMENTARY AND SECONDARY EDUCATION ACT OF 1965
(PUBLIC LAW 89-10)

Title I provides financial assistance to school districts for improvement of the education of children of lower income families. This Title is designed to encourage and support the establishment, expansion, and support of special programs, including the construction of school facilities.

Title II authorizes a five-year program to expand school library resources and instructional materials.

Title III provides funds to communities for supplementary education centers and services which would develop and establish exemplary education programs not normally available in most schools. These centers could include special guidance and counseling activities, remedial courses, continuing adult education, and other programs offering a diverse range of educational experiences to children and adults of varying talents and needs.

Title IV amends the Cooperative Research Act to allow utilization of noncollegiate research organizations and professional associations. The Title also accelerates the funding of regional educational laboratories.

Title V provides for the strengthening of state departments of education through long-range educational research and an interchange of personnel between states and the U.S. Office of Education.

HIGHER EDUCATION ACT OF 1965 (PUBLIC LAW 89-329)

Title I provides a five-year program of urban university extension and continuing education. The plan is for assistance through higher education in the solution of community problems in such areas as housing, poverty, government, recreation, employment, youth opportunities, transportation, health, and land use.

Title II provides a five-year program of college library assistance and library training and research.

Title III provides a five-year program to strengthen developing institutions by raising the academic quality of colleges that have a desire and potential to make a substantial contribution to the higher education resources of the nation.

Title IV provides a five-year program of student financial aids to make the benefits of higher education available to academically qualified students in need of financial assistance. The Title provides four types of assistance: (1) undergraduate scholarships to qualified high school graduates from low-income families; (2) insured reduced-interest private loans to both undergraduate and graduate students through approved commercial lenders and certain state and nonprofit private programs; (3) an expanded work-study program to provide part-time employment; and (4) extension and expansion of the National Defense Student Loan Program.

Title V provides for the establishment of a National Teacher Corps in order to strengthen the educational opportunities available to children in areas having concentrations of low-income families. The Title also provides a new graduate fellowship program for experienced teachers engaged in elementary and secondary education and for other experienced elementary and secondary school personnel serving in such ancillary fields as library science, educational media, guidance and counseling, and school social work.

Title VI provides financial assistance for the improvement of undergraduate instruction in selected subject areas in institutions of higher education.

The Concept of Guidance Services

There have been four stages in the development of our concept of *guidance services.* As we have seen in Chapter 1, our initial concepts of guidance equated it with *education* or with *good teaching.* The classroom teacher was held totally responsible for providing "guidance" services that would meet the pupils' special needs: intellectual needs would be met through the study of the curriculum, social needs would be met by sponsoring extra-class activities, and physical needs would be met by providing recess periods and activity programs. As we became aware of other pupil "needs," our concept of guidance broadened. By 1932, Brewer (2) appeared to be equating guidance with the whole of education when he argued that the ultimate goal of guidance was unified, integrated, harmonious personalities and that, consequently, pupils should be guided in *all* of their life activities.

The concept of guidance as consisting of *specialized services for pupils with serious problems* arose out of our gradual realization that the classroom teacher was ill-equipped, in terms of time and training, to deal with every type of pupil problem.

The concept of *guidance services for all pupils* developed as we recognized the desirability of making systematic studies of pupils in order to identify those who were likely to encounter future trouble. Guidance services were looked upon as *preventive* as well as *remedial*.

Our current concept of guidance services is usually characterized as being *developmental* or *integrative*. There are three dimensions to this concept:

1. *Longitudinal articulation*

    Guidance services should be *developmental* in the sense that they should be present in, and account for, each developmental stage of pupil growth. Data on pupils should be *cumulative*, and two-way communication should exist between personnel responsible for guidance services in adjacent *levels* of the educational process.

2. *Horizontal articulation*

    Guidance services should be *integrative* in the sense that they should operate in close conjunction with, rather than in isolation from, other specialized services. Data on pupils should be *exchangeable*, and two-way communication should exist between personnel responsible for pupil services in adjacent *areas* of the educational process (see Chapter 7).

3. *Articulation with other professions*

    Close communication and cooperation should also exist between school personnel administering and performing guidance services and personnel in professions not primarily concerned with the educational process. As we come of age as a profession, we will require the recognition and support of other professional personnel, particularly those in the medical and legal fields, if we expect to anticipate and provide for the individual needs of each pupil.

Summary

The guidance movement sprang from the philanthropic or humanitarian motives of individuals and agencies interested in giving our older youth help in choosing a satisfactory vocation. Nurtured by our democratic concept of equality of opportunity, motivated by our rapid technological progress, and molded by a host of moral, social, and economic factors, guidance has become a cohesive, continuous, and comprehensive movement that has caused great changes in our school system. Since its humble beginning, the *movement* has become a *profession*, with a profession's concern for the preparation, certification, and ethical standards of its workers. It has borrowed from related professions. It has appealed to teachers and specialists alike. It has filtered down to the elementary school program. It has acquired the firm moral and financial support of our state and national governments.

However, the profession still suffers from "growing pains." Many of our schools are faced with serious problems in establishing and maintaining effective guidance programs. And considerable conflict still exists concerning the *nature* of an effective guidance program and the *work* of the counselor in that program. But such conflict is to be expected. As Cremin (5) has phrased it: "Beyond any other individual in today's education system, the counselor incarnates the aims and ideals of progressivism. He is the most characteristic child of the progressive movement, and as such is heir to all its vigor and optimism, and all of its diversity and contradiction."

Bibliography

1.   Barry, Ruth and Beverly Wolf. "A History of the Guidance-Personnel Movement in Education." Unpublished doctoral dissertation, Columbia University, 1955.
2.   Brewer, John M. *Education as Guidance*. New York: The Macmillan Company, 1932.
3.   ———. *History of Vocational Guidance*. New York: Harper and Brothers, 1942.
4.   Conant, James B. *The American High School Today*. New York: McGraw-Hill Book Company, Inc., 1959. Pp. 45-63.
5.   Cremin, Lawrence A. "The Progressive Heritage of the Guidance Movement," in Landy, Edward and Paul A. Perry, eds. *Guidance in American Education I: Background and Prospects*. Cambridge, Massachusetts: Harvard University Press, 1964.
6.   Farwell, Gail·F. and H. J. Peters. *Guidance Readings for Counselors*. Chicago: Rand McNally & Co., 1960. Chap. 3.
7.   Glanz, Edward C. *Foundations and Principles of Guidance*. Boston: Allyn & Bacon, Inc., 1964. Chaps. 2, 3.
8.   Hamrin, Shirley A. *Guidance Talks to Teachers*. Bloomington, Illinois: McKnight & McKnight Publishing Co., 1947. Chap. 3.
9.   Hollinshead, Byron S. *Who Should Go to College?* New York: Columbia University Press, 1952.
10.   Humphreys, J. Anthony, Arthur E. Traxler, and Robert D. North. *Guidance Services*. 2nd ed. Chicago: Science Research Associates, Inc., 1960. Chaps. 3, 6.
11.   Hutson, Percival W. *The Guidance Function in Education*. New York: Appleton-Century-Crofts, 1958. Pp. 3-12.
12.   Iffert, Robert E. *Retention and Withdrawal of College Students*. Washington, D.C.: U.S. Office of Education, Dept. of Health, Education, and Welfare, Bulletin No. 1, 1958.
13.   Jones, Arthur J. *Principles of Guidance and Pupil Personnal Work*. 4th ed. New York: McGraw-Hill Book Company, Inc., 1951. Chaps. 1, 27.

14.   Little, J. Kenneth. *A Survey of Federal Programs in Higher Education*. Washington, D.C.: U.S. Office of Education, Dept. of Health, Education, and Welfare, Bulletin No. 50033, 1962.

15.   Martinson, Ruth and Harry Smallenburg. *Guidance in Elementary Schools*. Englewood Cliffs, New Jersey: Prentice-Hall, Inc., 1958. Chap. 2.

16.   Mathewson, Robert Henry. *Guidance Policy and Practice*. 3rd ed. New York: Harper and Brothers, 1962. Chaps. 3, 4.

17.   McDaniel, Henry B. *Guidance in the Modern School*. New York: The Dryden Press, 1956. Chap. 2.

18.   Miller, Carroll H. *Foundations of Guidance*. New York: Harper and Brothers, 1961. Chaps. 5, 6.

19.   Murphy, Gardner. "The Cultural Context of Guidance," *Personnel and Guidance Journal*, XXXIV:1, September, 1955, 4-9.

20.   N.E.A. Conference Report. *The Identification and Education of the Academically Talented Student in the American Secondary School*. Washington, D.C.: National Education Association, February, 1958.

21.   Parsons, Frank. *Choosing a Vocation*. Boston: Houghton Mifflin Company, 1909. P. 74.

22.   Patterson, C. H. *Counseling and Guidance in Schools*. New York: Harper and Brothers, 1962. Chap. 1.

23.   Pierson, George A. *An Evaluation: Counselor Education in Regular Session Institutes*. Washington, D.C.: U.S. Office of Education, Dept. of Health, Education, and Welfare, Bulletin No. 25042, 1965.

24.   Public Law 85-864. *The National Defense Education Act of 1958*. 85th Congress. H. R. 13247. Pp. 2, 3, 13, 14.

25.   Reed, Anna. *Guidance and Personnel Services in Education*. Ithaca, New York: Cornell University Press, 1944. Pp. 11, 17.

26.   *Report on the National Defense Education Act—Fiscal Year 1963*. Washington, D.C.: U.S. Office of Education, Dept. of Health, Education, and Welfare, Bulletin No. 10004, 1963.

27.   Rockefeller Bros. Fund Report. *The Pursuit of Excellence—Education and the Future of America*. Panel Report 5 of the Special Studies Project. Garden City, New York: Doubleday & Company, Inc., 1958.

28.   Roe, Anne. "A Psychological Study of Eminent Biologists" *Psychological Monographs*, 331:14:65, 1951.

29.   ———. "A Psychological Study of Eminent Physical Scientists." *Genetic Psychological Monographs*, 43:121-239, 1951.

30.   ———. "A Psychological Study of Eminent Psychologists and Anthropologists and a Comparison with Biological and Physical Scientists." *Psychological Monographs*, 352:2:67, 1953.

31.   Sanford, N., ed. "Personality Development During the College Years." *Journal of Social Issues*, Vol. 12, 1956, 3-70.

32.   Shertzer, Bruce, *et al. Working with Superior Students*. Chicago: Science Research Associates, Inc., 1960.

33.   Stalnaker, John. *Recognizing Exceptional Ability Among America's Young People, Fourth Annual Report*. Evanston, Illinois: National Merit Scholarship Corp., 1959.

34.   Stewart, Lawrence and Charles Warnath. *The Counselor and Society: A Cultural Approach.* Boston: Houghton Mifflin Company, 1965. Chap. 1.

35.   Stice, Glen, William G. Mollenkopf, and Waren S. Torgeson. *Background Factors and College-Going Plans Among High-Aptitude Public High School Seniors.* Princeton, New Jersey: Educational Testing Service, 1956. P. 115.

36.   Stice, Glen, William G. Mollenkopf, John W. French, M. Clemens Johnson, *et al. Background Factors Relating to College Plans and College Enrollment Among Public High School Students.* Princeton, New Jersey: Educational Testing Service, 1957.

37.   Super, Donald E. "Career Patterns as a Basis for Vocational Counseling." *Journal of Counseling Psychology*, Vol. 1, 1954, 12-20.

38.   ———. "Vocational Adjustment: Implementing a Self Concept," *Occupations*, Vol. 30, 1951, 88-92.

39.   ———, J. O. Crites, R. C. Hummel, H. P. Moser, P. L. Overstreet, and C. F. Warnath. *Vocational Development: A Framework for Research.* New York: Teachers College, Columbia University, 1957.

40.   ———, and P. L. Overstreet. *The Vocational Maturity of Ninth-Grade Boys.* New York: Teachers College, Columbia University, 1960.

41.   Tiedeman, David V. and R. P. O'Hara. *Career Development: Choice and Adjustment.* New York: College Entrance Examination Board, 1963.

42.   Traxler, Arthur E. *Techniques of Guidance.* Rev. ed. New York: Harper and Brothers, 1957. Chap. 1.

43.   Tyler, Leona E. *The National Defense Counseling and Guidance Training Institutes Program—A Report of the First 50 Institutes.* Washington, D.C.: U.S. Office of Education, Dept. of Health, Education, and Welfare, Bulletin No. 31, 1960.

44.   Warner, Ray. *Commitment To Youth.* Washington, D.C.: U.S. Office of Education, Dept. of Health, Education, and Welfare, Bulletin No. 25039, 1964.

45.   Warters, Jane. *High School Personnel Work Today.* New York: McGraw-Hill Book Company, Inc., 1956. Chaps. 1-3.

46.   "White House Conference Recommendations in Guidance," in the *Guidepost*, III, No. 1, 6. Appeared originally in the booklet *Recommendations, Composite Report of Forum Findings.* Washington, D.C.: White House Conference on Children and Youth, Department of Health, Education, and Welfare.

47.   Wolfle, Dael. *America's Resources of Specialized Talent.* New York: Harper and Brothers, 1954.

48.   Wrenn, Gilbert. *The Counselor in a Changing World.* Washington, D.C.: American Personnel and Guidance Association, 1962.

PART **2**

PROGRAM AND PERSONNEL

3

Guidance Programs Within Schools

Students are receiving *guidance* in a great many American schools today. However, the number of schools maintaining an *organized guidance program* is much smaller. It is important that we distinguish between guidance services that are offered on a spontaneous, spasmodic, or sporadic basis and those that are offered through a carefully planned and organized guidance program. The advantages of an organized guidance program may be summarized as follows:

1. An organized guidance program enables staff members to spend their time more efficiently in guiding students. Information about students is gathered and organized in a scientific manner. Teachers are given professional help in fulfilling their guidance responsibilities. Lines of communication between staff members are kept open. Overlapping of services is reduced, if not eliminated.

2. An organized guidance program helps the student receive an adequate balance of guidance services. For example, in a school where no organized guidance program exists, students might be tested quite extensively, yet receive little or no counseling. In another school, a great deal of time might be spent in gathering information about pupils, and little or no time spent in disseminating this information. More will be said about this point later in the chapter.

3. In a properly organized guidance program, staff members are aware of the advantages accruing to them through their participation in the program, are quite likely to think of themselves as part of a team, and are willing to engage in planning for additional services. An organized guidance program tends to improve and expand its services.

Necessary Characteristics of the Guidance Program

While each guidance program will have certain distinguishable features of its own, an effective guidance program generally possesses the following characteristics.

1. *It has developed gradually rather than being superimposed abruptly on school and staff alike.* An adequate program can only be developed through careful planning and concern for the interests and views of every staff member. Too often, the budget is the sole concern of those charged with initiating or developing a program. Money will buy materials and facilities, but it won't buy a program. Unless the cooperation and good will of the great majority of the staff is obtained during the planning stage, the program may never fulfill the purposes for which it was organized.

2. *It is idealistic in its announced goals and realistic in its current performance.* It has been said that a good leader stays in sight of his followers lest they lose sight of the direction he is taking. Similarly, the guidance program which attempts services that are beyond the experience and training of its staff members thwarts its own success. Students receive little benefit when guidance services are ineptly administered or when the staff members have become confused by and antagonistic toward the program. Progress toward achieving predetermined goals will proceed at a pace comparable to the growth in training and experience of the school staff.

3. *It fosters continuous communication among all members of the school staff.* Teachers and counselors are members of a smoothly func-

tioning team. Each teacher must be willing at all times to make properly documented referrals to counselors or to other staff members. The counselor, in turn, becomes a "teacher assistant" who is interested in helping students fulfill their classroom learning role more effectively. Both teachers and counselors recognize that easy and frequent communication among themselves, and with parents, prevents duplication of effort, thereby saving staff time. Such communication also helps to close the time-lapse between the incidence of a pupil problem and positive action by the staff to reduce or eliminate the problem.

4. *It has special facilities at its disposal.* Adequate space is provided for school records and other pupil data. The testing room or rooms are spacious, well-ventilated, well-lighted and are relatively free from outside distractions. There is at least one private interviewing room where pupil-counselor or parent-counselor conferences may take place. These facilities occupy as central a location as possible in the school building or school system.

5. *It is interwoven with the instructional program.* By furnishing data necessary to intelligent curriculum planning, the guidance program helps the school meet the educational and vocational needs of the pupils. By helping teachers understand their pupils and by helping pupils accept their role in the school situation, it helps to improve teacher-learner relationships. Further assistance to the instructional program is given by helping parents understand their children and the ways they might be assisted to learn more effectively in the classroom.

6. *It brings guidance services to every student, not just to those in distress.* While many programs are forced, at the outset, to restrict their services to a relatively small percentage of the pupils enrolled in the school or school district, an effective program will eventually reach all students.

7. *It plays an important role in the school's public relations program.* By offering a variety of services to students, parents, and other members of the community, it gives each group a better understanding of the purposes of the school and builds a closer working relationship between school and community.

8. *It is constantly engaged in a process of self-examination.* Through follow-up studies and other evaluative techniques, the program is engaged in a continuous effort to gather data concerning its strengths and weaknesses in order that appropriate changes in philosophy, program, or personnel may be made.

9. *It insures a balance in the services it offers pupils.* Hamrin (20)

has identified the following "balances" as desirable in a guidance program.

A. *A balance between services to the group and services to the individual.* Although frequently either group guidance or individual counseling is pursued to the exclusion of the other, both have contributions in a total guidance program, supplementing and extending each other.

B. *A balance between the use of the generalist and the specialist, the classroom teacher and counselor, the well-trained and the willing but less-trained.* The concept of the guidance team captures the ideal balance between generalist and specialist and makes clear the fact that both types of workers can contribute to the guidance activities.

C. *A balance between the use of objective and subjective devices and techniques in the study of an individual.* Even the results of the most careful objective measurements depend ultimately upon the subjective evaluation of the interpreter.

D. *A balance between the study of the individual and the counseling of the individual.* A guidance program that tests extensively and counsels briefly errs as much or more than the one which tests briefly and counsels extensively.

E. *A balance in the use of the various contributing disciplines.* Many disciplines have contributed to the profession of guidance, notably vocational guidance, mental hygiene, personnel work in industry, child guidance, measurement, statistics, social work, psychology and psychotherapy. Eclecticism is the key to the modern guidance program.

F. *A balance between the attitude-centered counseling and general clinical counseling.* The work of the non-directive counselor has served to emphasize the internal resources of the individual where often before only external resources had been considered. Both points of view have made a big contribution to present thought.

G. *A balance within an individual's school program.* A balance needs to be struck in each individual's school program between such so-called opposites as academic and non-academic courses, work and play, general and specialized education. Some adjustments need to be made in education for boys and girls for while they have many common educational needs they have some differentiated ones also.

H. *A balance between use of in-school and out-of-school resources.* While members of the community can and should contribute to a guidance program in matters of career information, work experience, agency resources, and home and school cooperation; school personnel can and should contribute equally.

I. *A balance among opportunities to think, feel, do*. Knowing is not enough; feeling and doing are important also, and opportunities to feel and to do ought to be offered equally with opportunities to learn. A balance should be kept in a testing program along the same line, including attitudes and skills as well as academic knowledge.

J. *A balance between the needs of the individual and the needs of society*. Unfortunately our educational system has encouraged the competitive system to the point where many people do not know how to work with people. Only by moving *with* people, and neither away from them nor against them, are the needs of society met as well as the needs of the individual.[1]

Basic Services of the Guidance Program

The services which are available to students, teachers, parents, and the community through the guidance program have been identified in a number of ways. Froehlich (16) lists them as (a) services to pupils in groups, (b) services to pupils as individuals, (c) services to the instructional staff, (d) services to the administration, and (e) research services. McDaniel (29) refers to the adjustive, distributive, and adaptive functions of guidance programs. Hamrin (19) discusses guidance services under the following headings: (a) pre-admission, (b) orientation, (c) learning more about students, (d) studying the school program, (e) assisting students to be well adjusted, (f) helping students plan wisely, (g) assisting students to bridge the gap, and (h) follow-up. In this text, guidance services have been discussed under four categories.

Student Appraisal Services

The various processes of acquiring information about students have been referred to both as *techniques* and as *services*. While the accumulation of information about students may represent a service to the school staff (in the sense that each staff member is saved the task of collecting this information entirely through his own efforts) it does not, in itself, represent a service to students unless it is used to facilitate self-understanding. One can still find schools with fairly extensive testing programs that make no attempt to share the test data with pupils, parents, or, in some cases, even with teachers. These schools are content to convert the test data into statistics that "prove"

---

[1]Reprinted by permission from the *Chicago Guidance Newsletter*, December, 1950, Chicago Public Schools.

the achievement level of their students is on a par with the published norms. It is difficult to see where the testing programs in these schools would constitute a service to pupils and parents. Therefore, it may be more accurate to refer to these information-gathering processes as *prerequisites* to the various guidance services offered by the school. Observation, anecdotal records, rating scales, self-report forms, autobiographies, sociometric devices, standardized tests, case conferences, and personnel records are the major tools and techniques used to gather data which can be used to assist students in the process of self-discovery and self-development.

The Counseling Service

Counseling is the most important service offered to pupils. It has been called the heart of the guidance program. Counseling services have exerted a strong influence on the lives of many students. For this reason, it is necessary that counseling be performed by professionally trained individuals. Many colleges and universities now have comprehensive counselor education programs that culminate in a practicum or internship similar to student teaching. Some student problems, primarily of an educational or vocational nature, may be handled by the beginning counselor or by one whose training is incomplete. Other problems, particularly of a personal or emotional nature, generally will require a much higher degree of counseling skill. Most states have now set up certification requirements for counselors. The problems of selecting, preparing, and certifying school counselors will be discussed in Chapter 12.

The counseling service is dependent upon adequate previous analysis of the individual student. Counseling a student without adequate background information on his home environment, health, academic record, abilities, interests, or personal traits is generally indefensible. While some of this information might be gained through the counseling interview, it can be gathered more objectively and in a more leisurely fashion prior to the interview, thereby saving counseling time for more important matters. It should be emphasized here that *counseling* and *interviewing* are not synonymous. Many interviews may be disciplinary in nature or may merely involve an exchange of information where no counseling is involved. On the other hand, counseling is a process that encompasses more than the relatively formal interview technique. It may involve telephone conversations and correspondence between the counselor and the counselee. It requires preparation on the part of the counselor prior to the interview and should include follow-up procedures after the interview has been terminated.

The counseling service is also dependent upon various informational services. Counseling and information-giving sometimes go hand in hand. Information about college scholarships, college entrance requirements, or job opportunities in the community may have to be given to a student as part of the counseling process.

Counseling is a very important guidance service; its success depends on the qualifications of the counselor and the adequacy of other guidance services in the school.

Informational Services

A great variety of informational services are offered through the guidance program. As part of the pre-admission or orientation program, pupils receive information before or upon entering the school with respect to school policies and regulations, school facilities and activities, and, on the high school level, courses and curricula. Guidance workers can assist students in making further educational or vocational plans by helping them to understand their interests and abilities, by furnishing them with information about college opportunities, and by giving them realistic occupational information. The students can be made aware of community surveys which reveal specific job opportunities. Counselors will obtain information from college admissions officers that will enable students to keep up-to-date regarding entrance requirements, entrance examinations, available scholarships, and application procedures. To facilitate the placement of students in a college or a job, counselors will also make data available to college admissions officers and employers. Finally, the guidance program can provide teachers with information on their pupils that will encourage the growth of good teacher-learner relationships.

Research and Evaluation Services

Research and evaluation services are vital to the guidance program for a number of reasons. First, research on employment trends, educational opportunities, cultural advantages, etc. in the community is necessary if the informational service available to students is to be accurate and effective. The community survey, available as an informational service, obtains its information through research projects. Second, research is necessary in order to acquaint teachers and administrators with the strengths and weaknesses of the curriculum or of other school activities. This may be accomplished through a survey involving teachers, students, parents, or a combination of the three groups. Or it may be accomplished through a follow-up study of high school graduates or dropouts. Third, the guidance program, itself, needs constant evaluation. While there are serious limitations to each of the various evaluative techniques, it is imperative that the guidance program be in a position to answer queries from teachers, administrators, parents, and community leaders regarding the value of the services it offers students. Furthermore, the improvement of these services is dependent upon a reasonably scientific analysis of the strengths and weaknesses of the current program.

In summary; the successful guidance program will offer four important and interrelated areas of service: (a) student appraisal, (b) counseling, (c) information, and (d) research and evaluation. Within each of these four areas lie additional and more specific services.

Organizational Patterns

There are three basic designs to guidance programs in our schools. In the first, guidance services are performed by all staff members as part of their regularly assigned duties. No time is specifically set aside for guidance. The program is "headed up" by the administrator as part of his regular administrative duties. There is no guidance specialist. The philosophy underlying this type of program may be summarized as follows: Guidance and education are synonymous, there is no need to distinguish between them through the manipulation of time or personnel. As one administrator has put it, "All our teachers are guidance specialists." While it would be desirable for all teachers to have this specialized training, such a development is not likely to occur in our lifetime. On the contrary, there is some evidence to indicate that a sizable percentage of teachers do not fully understand their guidance responsibilities. Labeling them as guidance specialists does not make them so.

The second pattern of organization structures the guidance program more clearly and devotes specific time to its services. A full-time guidance specialist, with no teaching responsibilities, administers the guidance program and is usually designated as director of guidance. In the larger secondary schools, several full-time counselors will share the responsibility for the guidance program.

1. The counselor may be given responsibility for the counseling of all pupils at a certain grade level—for example, the tenth-grade counselor.

2. He may be given responsibility for the counseling of all pupils of one sex at a certain grade level—for example, the junior-senior girls counselor.

3. He may be given responsibility for the counseling of a group of students from the time they begin their freshman year to the time they graduate as seniors. This "class counselor" or "horizontal" approach allows the counselor to establish rapport with students over an extended period of time. Yet, he remains a specialist in the sense that he is able to deal with the problems unique to a group on one grade level only.

4. The counselor may be assigned a certain number of students from each grade level. Advocates of this "vertical" approach argue that the counselor "turns over" only a fraction of his counselees each year. Therefore, he is not confronted with a completely new group of counselees each year or even every three or four years. However, each grade level has specific needs. Many of these needs are affected by *timing* throughout the course of the year. The danger in this approach is that, at certain *times* of the year, the counselor may give an inordinate amount of attention to a certain segment of his counselees (i.e. the college-bound senior).

5. Division of responsibilities may be in terms of areas of guidance services rather than groups of students. One counselor may be in charge of vocational guidance (the occupational files, the career conference, job placement); another counselor in charge of college planning (college entrance examinations, college catalogue file, scholarship applications); and another counselor in charge of the testing program. Under this arrangement, students often have the opportunity to choose their own counselor.

6. Counselors may or may not be assigned disciplinary responsibilities. Where disciplinary responsibilities are specifically assigned, counselors are often given the title of dean of boys or dean of girls. Discussion of the relationship between counseling and discipline may be found in Chapter 9.

On the elementary level, guidance specialists may have responsibilities to more than one school. A social worker and a reading specialist may divide their time between four or five schools in the same district. Some specialists are also being asked to play roles for which they have not been trained. The school nurse often finds herself playing the role of psychologist and social worker, the pediatrician doubles as psychiatrist, and the social worker is forced to serve as attendance officer, psychiatrist, or nurse. A director of guidance services for a district containing four or five elementary schools may also be a "jack-of-all-trades." Lacking adequate assistance, he is forced to become test administrator, counselor, teacher-advisor, student government sponsor, statistician, and record-keeper. In many instances, he is an ex-officio member of every school committee.

The demands on "administrator-counselors" on both the elementary and secondary levels have been well documented. Goldstein (18) found that many of the clerical duties counselors reported they were required to perform were of such a nature that they could have been handled more expeditiously and with less expense by a school clerk. Martyn (27) found that counselors in his sample spent as much as 80 per cent of their time on clerical duties. Even after eliminating such tasks as have "necessary counseling components," these counselors still spent 43 per cent of their time on other clerical tasks. Arnold (5) surveyed 126 counselors in Ohio and found that they gave more time to attendance, discipline, tardiness, and other chores than to counseling on personal, educational, and vocational problems. He concluded that counseling would be grossly inadequate if all counselors were burdened to this extent.

The problems of "administrator-counselors" appear to be due, in large measure, to their assignment of responsibility for both the *guidance* and the *regulatory* or *enforcement* phases of personnel services. Where the director of guidance serves in both a staff or consulting capacity and a line or administrative capacity, actual service to students usually suffers. Hatch and Stefflre (21) call this an "unexplained phenomenon" and go on to say:

> The personnel function may be thought of as having two major aspects, *service* and *enforcement*. . . . If the primary responsibility for the personnel function is assigned to one individual, it is only a short time until the enforcement aspects tend to consume most of his time. A case in point is the counselor with an additional assignment for pupil accounting. The accounting aspect soon shunts the counseling service aside and counseling is incidental to the activities of the counselor.

The third pattern of organization applies to the secondary level only and represents a compromise between the first two patterns. Generally known as the teacher-counselor plan, this pattern of organization appears to be declining in popularity. Guidance functions are assigned to selected teachers, who are released from classroom duties for a portion of each day. In many cases, these teachers are assigned as counselors to the same pupils they teach. While this arrangement allows counselor and pupil to maintain a continuous rather than a sporadic relationship, there are basic differences between the process of teaching and the process of counseling which the teacher may have difficulty in reconciling. A detailed discussion of these differences and their effect upon the teacher as a counselor may be found in Chapter 4.

There are, of course, variations to these patterns of organization. On the secondary school level, there may be a director of guidance who devotes full time to the administration and coordination of guidance services and to the counseling of students with serious problems. The remaining guidance services may be handled by a staff composed entirely of teacher-counselors. This arrangement provides a reasonable balance between the need for a professionally trained staff member who can handle serious personal problems and the need for easy communication between teacher and specialist.

A discussion of the merits and limitations of the homeroom program is beyond the scope of this book. However, as a vehicle for conducting various guidance activities, it has been the subject of considerable criticism. In theory, the homeroom can provide orientation and other group guidance services to small groups of pupils and, in the process, create better understanding and easier communication between teacher and specialist. In practice, critics charge, the homeroom is often ineffective for one of two reasons:

1. The non-guidance activities of the homeroom (taking attendance, reading announcements, etc.) gradually crowd out the guidance activities, particularly when the homeroom period is of short duration.

2. Instead of contributing *to* the guidance program, the homeroom tends to usurp the functions of the guidance program and provides an excuse for the assignment of testing and counseling responsibilities to teachers with full-time teaching loads who may have little or no training for these extra responsibilities.

It is undoubtedly true that the homeroom has been a valuable part of the guidance program in some schools. In other schools, the homeroom has reduced the effectiveness of the total guidance program.

Each of the organizational patterns mentioned above has its advantages and its disadvantages. What is workable for one school will not necessarily be workable for another. The size of the school, the training and experience of the staff, and the attitude of the community are among the factors that will influence the organization of the guidance program.

The Role of the Counselor in the Guidance Program

Some confusion over the counselor's role in the guidance program has resulted from (a) controversy over whether the counselor is primarily an *educator* or a *psychologist,* and (b) numerous surveys of counselor responsibilities that show a serious discrepancy between tasks that counselors *are* performing and the tasks these counselors feel they *should be* performing. School systems have made varied and rather flexible interpretations of the duties of individuals who bear the title of *school counselor, school psychologist,* or *psychological examiner.* At the present time, only twenty-five states maintain certification requirements that distinguish the school counselor from the school psychologist. The problem involves a rather serious difference of opinion regarding the type of training and experience that qualifies one as a specialist in pupil personnel services. Many administrators feel that the pupil personnel worker should have considerable teaching experience. Some professional psychologists, on the other hand, believe that the pupil personnel worker must be a trained clinical psychologist. This issue will be explored more thoroughly in Chapters 12 and 13.

Research by Arnold (5), Goldstein (18), and Martyn (27), mentioned earlier in the chapter, refers to the burdensome clerical and administrative duties often placed on counselors. Stewart (37), after summarizing these and similar studies, has proposed a Bill of Rights for School Counselors.

BILL OF RIGHTS FOR SCHOOL COUNSELORS

1. The right to a reasonable counseling load.
2. The right to favorable working conditions . . . office space, ample clerical help, and other material conditions.
3. The right to enough time to do his real job . . . to engage in counseling per se.
4. The right to a real opportunity to establish effective contact with parents, referral agencies, and other organizations in the community.
5. The right to sufficient time and the privilege of serving on curriculum and other critical committees.
6. The right to have an effective voice in determining guidance and counseling policy and practice.
7. The right to have reasonable time for research.

8. The right to a recognized professional status.
9. The right to remuneration commensurate with the training and responsibility involved.
10. The right to have the full trust and support of the administrators to make the above rights effective.

A more specific analysis of the roles of the elementary and secondary school counselor will be found in Chapters 5 and 6.

Initiating and Developing the Guidance Program

It is difficult to overemphasize the leadership function of the administrator during the initial stages of the development of the guidance program. This is a challenging task for any administrator. Unless he takes definite steps to "start the ball rolling," the numerous and varied responsibilities of the school staff and the skepticism of certain of its members tend to keep plans in the "some day we ought to" stage. Yet, too vigorous leadership can cause antagonism toward the guidance program before it is started. One of the administrator's earliest objectives should be the discovery of those staff members who are willing and able to play an active part in the development of the guidance program. Once these members are found, the administrator should begin to play a less active role.

Preparation

School and staff should be prepared for a long and slow period of development. Unfortunately, some schools have attempted to start guidance programs by devoting a few days to a special "guidance workshop" or by hiring new personnel. School X falls in this category. A director of guidance for school X was hired in June. During the summer months, the new director of guidance and the principal hammered out a "guidance program" for the coming school year. During the first week in September this program was presented to the school staff by means of a two-day teachers' institute. Teachers were assigned various guidance responsibilities. They were designated as "counselors" for certain students. Kits of test manuals and mimeographed articles on counseling were furnished to the staff at this time. Two days later the "guidance program" was set in motion. Is it any wonder that low staff morale, bitter controversy, and little "guidance" resulted?

Opinion surveys of teachers, students, and parents appear to be an excellent method of gaining a proper appreciation of the need for a guidance program. These surveys should provide answers to the following questions.

1. What guidance services currently exist and who is responsible for them?
2. What are the strengths and weaknesses of current guidance services?
3. What pupil needs are not being met? What additional guidance services are needed?
4. Are current members of the staff qualified to administer these additional services?
5. Are current members of the staff willing to administer these additional services?

Such a survey has a three-fold value: (a) it focuses attention on the major objective of a guidance program—meeting the guidance needs of the pupils, (b) it determines a "starting-point," and (c) it employs the psychologically sound principle of involving all interested parties in the planning phase of the guidance program.

Careful analysis should also be made of the school assets and liabilities. What portion of the school budget can be made (or will be made) available for the guidance program? Does the school possess adequate space and facilities for testing, counseling, records, etc.? What is the attitude of the community toward guidance services? Will the assistance of specialists from outside the school be available in planning the program? A school survey of this type is as necessary as the opinion survey.

Preliminary Meetings

Preliminary meetings to discuss the importance and need for a guidance program should bring together members of the board of education, representatives of the leading community-service agencies, parents, teachers, and, possibly, administrators from other schools who have recently set up their own guidance program. Information gathered from the above-mentioned surveys will serve as a starting point for the discussions. It is most important that all members present understand, as early as possible, the purposes of such a guidance program. Their natural concern for the welfare of their young people will cause them to be attentive and sympathetic toward a proposed program once its purposes are understood. Community-service organizations such as the American Association of University Women, the Rotary, Kiwanis, and Lions Clubs; church-supported youth agencies such as Y.M.C.A., Y.W.C.A., B'nai B'rith, and Catholic Youth Organization; and parent-teacher groups will be in a position to offer moral support, advice, and valuable publicity to the budding program.

Pre-Organization Committee

As an outgrowth of one or more of these preliminary meetings, a committee should be appointed to draw up further plans for getting started. This committee should be representative of the entire school staff and should, at the outset, include representatives from some of the community agencies mentioned previously. It should be made clear to all staff members that this committee is a temporary one and has only one function—to consider ways and means of initiating and developing the guidance program. While it is quite likely that one or more members of this temporary committee will eventually be appointed to a permanent guidance committee, any impression of permanence at this time may discourage other staff members from taking an active role in subsequent planning activities. The committee should include members who are skeptical about the program as well as those who are enthusiastic in their support. A "loaded" committee may not only alienate the skeptical but convince the balance of the staff that the pre-organization committee is, indeed, the guidance services committee of the future. The committee should keep the school staff, parents, and community representatives well informed of their progress in drafting further plans. This may be done through mimeographed communiques or additional staff meetings. At the same time, every effort should be made to insure two-way communication. Teachers, parents, and other interested persons should be invited, at frequent intervals, to make suggestions regarding future courses of action or to criticize the steps being undertaken by the committee.

The pre-organization committee may be said to have three tasks.

1. *It must determine the objectives of the guidance program.* These objectives must be consistent with the educational philosophy of the school and reflect the needs of its pupils, as determined by the preliminary survey. The completion of this task answers the question, "Why are we initiating this guidance program?"

2. *It must set up an organizational chart of the guidance program.* This chart will be supplemented by descriptions of the guidance services to be offered and the staff members who will have the responsibility for administering them. The completion of this task answers the question, "What will we do and who will do it?"

3. *It must set up plans for starting the guidance program.* These plans may provide for a full-fledged program from two to four years

after its inception but will almost always provide for a modest beginning. Whether this modest beginning will be made by (a) offering a minimum of services to *all* students in the school, or (b) offering more extensive services to a smaller number of students (the group to be determined by grade level, teacher referral, homeroom membership, or some other criterion) is a decision that the committee must make as soon as possible. The completion of this task answers the question, "How and when do we begin?"

As each of these tasks is completed, the committee submits its recommendations in the form of a report to the entire staff. An open discussion on the merits of the report should be held in order that the staff may have the chance to approve the report or request certain revisions before the committee begins its next task.

The Guidance Committee

When the pre-organization committee has completed the above tasks to the satisfaction of the staff, it has fulfilled the function for which it was designed. With the initiation of the guidance program, a permanent guidance committee should be formed. Undoubtedly, several members of the temporary committee will have gained knowledge and experience that will make them valuable members of the permanent committee. However, membership on the permanent committee should be determined primarily by the organizational pattern of the guidance program.

The formation of subcommittees promotes the high morale essential for effective operation of the program. Subcommittees both insure special attention to important aspects of the program and encourage active support, as all staff members can actually take part in the decisions which are made. Phases of the program that might become the immediate responsibility of a subcommittee include the *testing program* (materials, administration, scoring, interpreting, reporting, recording); *the records system* (materials, organization, clerical help); and *in-service education for teachers.* All aspects of the teacher's role in the guidance program, including in-service education, will be examined in Chapter 4.

The Community and the Guidance Program

The previous discussion has concerned itself, largely, with encouraging teacher support and participation in developing the guidance program. Mention was also made of the desirability of including pupils, parents, and other representatives of the community in the planning process. The distribution of the opinion survey directed at pupils and parents, discussed earlier in the chapter, is an excellent way to arouse their interest and support. Their enthusiasm will wane, however, unless they are furnished with periodic reports detailing the progress made in planning the program and the efforts being made to incorporate their suggestions and criticisms into a working program. Both pupils and parents must feel that the guidance program is *their* program, *their* service, *their* opportunity. Even after the program is in operation, parents should be encouraged to work more closely with counselors and teachers in understanding and helping their children. This may be done through displays of guidance materials, a P.T.A. program, a guidance workshop for parents sponsored by one or more members of the guidance staff, or a monthly newsletter to parents. The following letter (42) was the first of a series addressed to parents for the purpose of encouraging their participation in the testing phase of a new guidance program.

DEAR PARENTS:

"Why, how you've grown!" You've heard that said so often to your boy or girl that you've taken as a matter of course that he is taller (or heavier) than he was several months ago. Anyone can see the difference very quickly by merely looking at him. But have you "seen" the growth he has made in other ways—growth which can't be weighed by a machine or measured by a tape?

Growth in his ability to work using books, as well as in activities not involving books, is just as interesting to you as his "growing up" physically. This year your schools have continued their interest in promoting these desirable changes in him and have also begun a program attempting to measure the extent of the changes themselves.

As parents you will be interested in looking at this unusual "snapshot" of him. Tests measuring mental ability and reading achievement have been given during the present school year. In addition, the vocational interests and personal traits of every tenth grader have been inventoried. If you are curious about these scores, if you would like to discuss their meaning and how they are obtained, feel free to stop at the school whenever convenient. Our phone number is 239, if you would like to make an appointment. Miss Thompson has the records for the girls and I have them for the boys.

Very truly yours,
P. E. PEARSON
Dean of Boys

A special issue of a Parent's Bulletin may be devoted to answering questions about the school's guidance program. One such bulletin (34) devoted eight pages to answering the following questions:

1. What is counseling?
2. Why are counseling programs needed in the schools today?
3. What is the organization of the guidance departments in our high schools?
4. Does each student have a counselor?
5. What does the counselor do?
6. How does a student go about talking to his counselor?
7. Can a parent come in and talk with his child's counselor?
8. How do counselors work with teachers?
9. What part do school health services play in regard to the total guidance services?
10. What special services are offered by the guidance departments?
11. What standardized tests do our students take?
12. How are the results of standardized tests used in high school?
13. What information is available to students regarding schools and colleges?
14. Is there an opportunity for pupils to meet representatives of schools and colleges?
15. When should college applications be filed?
16. What are the student-parent responsibilities in regard to college applications?
17. How does a student obtain information as to sources of financial aid?
18. What information is provided those students seeking post-high school training other than college?
19. Does the guidance department have a placement service?
20. Is the guidance department concerned with former students?

While the cooperation and participation of the staff members, pupils, and parents are vital to the development of an effective guidance program, it would be unwise to neglect those citizens of the community who, while less concerned with the problems of the schools, have just as big a voice in determining school board membership, school tax rates and, indirectly, the programs and activities of the school. While it may be assumed that the inclusion of community representatives in the preliminary discussions resulted in some degree of publicity for the guidance program, good public relations demands that the community be given a comprehensive picture of the objectives, services, and personnel of the guidance program. This may be accomplished, for example, through a series of newspaper articles entitled "Know Your School," or through the publication of a special school bulletin. The guidance program, once it is in operation, will rely heavily on community cooperation. The success of its placement service will depend on the cooperation of business and industry. The success of its referral service will depend on the cooperation of religious leaders and service and professional agencies. The success of its information service will depend on the cooperation of a great variety of community organizations. To gain this cooperation, the guidance program must first be understood.

Summary

There is a distinction between a guidance *program* and the uncoordinated efforts of staff members to offer occasional guidance to their pupils. The types of services which an effective guidance program provides may be grouped under the following headings: (a) student appraisal, (b) counseling, (c) information, and (d) research and evaluation. There are three basic designs to guidance programs in our schools. In the first, guidance services are performed by all staff members as part of their regularly assigned duties. There is no guidance specialist. In the second, one or more full-time guidance specialists are given the responsibility for administering the program. In the third, "teacher-counselors" perform the major functions of the program during the portion of the school day when they are released from their classroom duties.

The administrator's role in the guidance program is primarily one of democratic leadership during the initial developmental stages of the guidance program and one of consistent support to the program once it has become adequately organized. The counselor's role is one of implementing the various services offered through the guidance program. In so doing, he is of assistance not only to pupils but also to teachers and parents.

The initiation and development of the guidance program involves careful and considered planning, participation by teachers, pupils, parents, and representatives of community agencies, and the sympathy, understanding, and cooperation of the entire community.

Bibliography

1.   Adams, James F. *Counseling and Guidance: A Summary View*. New York: The Macmillan Company, 1965. Chap. 4.
2.   Arbuckle, Dugald S. *Counseling: Philosophy, Theory and Practice*. Boston: Allyn & Bacon, Inc., 1965. Chaps. 2-4.
3.   ———. *Guidance and Counseling in the Classroom*. Boston: Allyn & Bacon, Inc., 1957. Chap. 9.
4.   Andrew, D., and R. D. Willey. *Administration and Organization of the Guidance Program*. New York: Harper and Brothers, 1958. Chap. 3.
5.   Arnold, Dwight L. "Time Spent by Counselors and Deans on Various Activities," *Occupations*, XXVII:6, March, 1949, 391-93.
6.   Barr, John A. *The Elementary Teacher and Guidance*. New York: Henry Holt and Company, 1958. Chap. 20.
7.   Barry, Ruth and Beverly Wolf, *Modern Issues in Guidance-Personnel Work*. 2nd ed. New York: Columbia University, Teachers College, 1963. Chaps. 5, 8-10.
8.   Blanchard, Howard L. and Laurence S. Flaum. *Guidance: A Longitudinal Approach*. Minneapolis: Burgens Publishing Company, 1962. Chaps. 12, 13.
9.   Boy, Angelo V. and Gerald J. Pine. *Client-Centered Counseling in the Secondary School*. Boston: Houghton Mifflin Company, 1963. Chaps. 2, 7.
10.   Cottingham, Harold F. *Directed Readings in Foundations of Guidance and Personnel Services*. Bloomington, Illinois: McKnight & McKnight Publishing Co., 1964. Chap. 8.
11.   ———. *Guidance in Elementary Schools: Principles and Practices*. Bloomington, Illinois: McKnight & McKnight Publishing Co., 1956. Chaps. 11-13.
12.   ——— and William Hopke. *Guidance in the Junior High School: Principles and Practices*. Bloomington, Illinois: McKnight & McKnight Publishing Co., 1961. Chap. 5.
13.   Crow, Lester D. and Alice Crow. *An Introduction to Guidance*. 2nd ed. New York: American Book Company, 1960. Chaps. 4-7.

14. ————. *Organization and Conduct of Guidance Services.* New York: David McKay Company, Inc., 1965. Chaps. 2-5, 8, 17-20.
15. Farwell, Gail F. and H. J. Peters. *Guidance Readings for Counselors.* Chicago: Rand McNally & Co., 1960. Chap. 7.
16. Froehlich, Clifford P. *Guidance Services in Schools.* New York: McGraw-Hill Book Company, Inc., 1958. Chaps. 2-5, 16.
17. Glanz, Edward C., *Foundations and Principles of Guidance.* Boston: Allyn & Bacon, Inc., 1964. Chap. 11.
18. Goldstein, H. A. "Job Analysis of Junior and Senior High School Counselors," *Industrial Arts and Vocational Education,* No. 39, 1950.
19. Hamrin, S. A. *Guidance Talks to Teachers.* Bloomington, Illinois: McKnight & McKnight Publishing Co., 1947. Chap. 7.
20. ————. "It's All in the Balance," *Chicago Guidance Newsletter,* December, 1950.
21. Hatch, Raymond N. and Buford Stefflre. *Administration of Guidance Services: Organization, Supervision, Evaluation.* Englewood Cliffs, New Jersey: Prentice-Hall, Inc., 1958. Chaps. 4-6, p. 126.
22. Hollis, Joseph W. and Lucile U. Hollis. *Organization for Effective Guidance.* Chicago: Science Research Associates, Inc., 1965. Chaps. 3-10, 13, 14.
23. Humphreys, J. Anthony, Arthur E. Traxler, and Robert North. *Guidance Services.* 2nd ed. Chicago: Science Research Associates, Inc., 1960. Chap. 16.
24. Hutson, Percival W. *The Guidance Function in Education.* New York: Appleton-Century-Crofts, 1958. Chap. 18.
25. Jones, Arthur J. *Principles of Guidance.* 5th ed. New York: McGraw-Hill Book Company, Inc., 1963. Chap. 10.
26. Loughary, John W. *Counseling in Secondary Schools: A Frame of Reference.* New York: Harper and Brothers, 1961. Chap. 5.
27. Marlyn, Kenneth A. Report on doctoral dissertation, Stanford University. *California Guidance Newsletter,* September, 1950.
28. Mathewson, Robert Henry. *Guidance Policy and Practice.* 3rd ed. New York: Harper and Brothers, 1962. Chaps. 10, 11.
29. McDaniel, Henry B. *Guidance in the Modern School.* New York: The Dryden Press, 1956. Chaps. 3, 4.
30. ————, *et al. Readings in Guidance.* New York: Henry Holt and Company, 1959. Chaps. 2, 4.
31. McGowan, John F. and Lyle D. Schmidt. *Counseling: Readings in Theory and Practice.* New York: Holt, Rinehart & Winston, Inc., 1962. Chap. 7.
32. Miller, Carroll H. *Guidance Services: An Introduction.* New York: Harper & Row, Publishers, 1965. Chaps. 2, 3, 11.
33. Ohlsen, Merle M. *Guidance Services in the Modern School.* New York: Harcourt, Brace & World, Inc., 1964. Chaps. 1, 16.
34. *Parents' Bulletin.* Township High School District No. 207, Des Plaines-Park Ridge, Illinois, November, 1965.

35.   Patterson, C. H. *Counseling and Guidance in Schools.* New York: Harper and Brothers, 1962. Chaps. 3, 16, 17.
36.   Roeber, Edward C., Glenn E. Smith, and Clifford E. Erickson. *Organization and Administration of Guidance Services.* New York: McGraw-Hill Book Company, Inc., 1955. Chaps. 2, 3, 5, 10.
37.   Stewart, C. C. "A Bill of Rights for School Counselors," *Personnel and Guidance Journal,* XXXVII:7 March, 1959, 500-03.
38.   Stoops, Emery and Gunner L. Wahlquist. *Principles and Practices in Guidance.* New York: McGraw-Hill Book Company, Inc., 1958. Chaps. 9, 11, 12.
39.   Traxler, Arthur E. *Techniques of Guidance.* New York: Harper and Brothers, 1957. Chap. 2.
40.   Warters, Jane. *High School Personnel Work Today.* New York: McGraw-Hill Book Company, Inc., 1956. Chap. 6.
41.   Wrenn, Charles Gilbert. *The Counselor in a Changing World.* Washington, D.C.: American Personnel and Guidance Association, 1962.

UNPUBLISHED MATERIAL

42.   Pearson, Paul. Counselor, Oak Park-River Forest High School, Oak Park, Illinois. (formerly Guidance Director, Monmouth, Illinois Public Schools.)

4

Teachers and the Guidance Program

An effective guidance program requires the cooperative effort of every teacher in the school. It is only through the teacher that the guidance program can maintain the continuity necessary to achieve its goals. Yet, many teachers who are anxious to accept their classroom responsibilities have difficulty in giving wholehearted acceptance to this point of view. They have been taught that the primary responsibility of the classroom teacher is to teach well. With so many demands being made on their time by reading specialists, health specialists, curriculum specialists, etc. they have become perplexed regarding the extent of their participation in the guidance program. Their perplexity leads them to ask a number of questions: What are the classroom teacher's specific guidance functions? To what extent have teachers been prepared to fulfill these functions? Are there times when a teacher's guidance responsibilities might interfere with teaching effectiveness? How can secondary school teachers give guidance to one hundred students, most of whom are not seen for more than fifty minutes each day? Are there limits to the teacher's role? What about students with serious maladjustments? Doesn't an elementary teacher have more time for guidance than a secondary teacher?

Confusion over the role of the teacher in the guidance program is due to a number of factors. Some teachers are more interested in subject-matter than in students. Some feel that they lack the proper personal characteristics; others feel that they lack the necessary training and experience. Some teachers have such heavy teaching loads that they cannot fulfill their guidance responsibilities. Some are taking an active role in the guidance program without realizing it. The size of the school and the number of specialists or specialized services available to students often determine the extent of the teacher's assigned responsibilities. Teachers frequently accept responsibilities beyond their training and experience simply because no qualified person is available in the school system. In such situations, teachers are likely to give more to the guidance program than they receive from it. As a result, their teaching effectiveness may be impaired. The opposite situation may also prevail. In some schools, specialized personnel perform many services for teachers but get little or no cooperation from them. This is not always the fault of the teacher. Some would like to cooperate but lack an understanding of what is expected from them.

In addition, some confusion results from the different roles to be played by the elementary and the secondary teacher. The general preparation of the elementary teacher is designed to place emphasis on "the whole child" or "the total development of the child," while the secondary teacher becomes more of a specialist in a subject-matter area. The elementary teacher, while working with a relatively small group of children for the entire school day, finds a flexibility to the curriculum that is conducive to the fulfillment of various guidance functions. The secondary teacher, while working with a large number of students, most of whom are with him for only a small part of each day, discovers that the compartmentalization of subject-matter forces him into a more structured, less flexible role in the classroom.

In the final analysis, however, confusion over the teacher's proper guidance function has stemmed from our inability to distinguish, in any precise manner, between *guidance* and *teaching*. Tiedeman and Field (27) have recently laid the groundwork for adequate differentiation between these two functions:

. . . teaching involves a communication of *others'* experiences—data and conclusions. Guidance, on the other hand, involves primarily an examination of the individual student's experiences—data and the *process of forming* conclusions about them. Teaching continually creates useful discontinuity by saying "Here are things you do not know, or know how to do." Guidance, on the other hand, deals with the individualized reduction of discontinuity:

1. by pointing out where discontinuity has (or has not yet!) come to exist;
2. by making it *not* seem undesirable or overwhelming, but useful; and
3. by making it more possible for the individual to choose actions designed to reduce (or establish and *then* reduce) such discontinuity.

It becomes clear that Guidance involves behavioral change, a change quite different from that necessarily induced by teaching.

Guidance Responsibilities of Teachers

There are a number of reasons why the classroom teacher must be considered an important guidance worker in the school. First of all, we have discovered that learning is most effective when the material to be learned is directly related to the immediate personal goals of the learner. Teachers who are concerned with the individual aspirations and problems of their students will, therefore, set up the most effective learning situations and, consequently, do a better job of teaching. In short, the guidance approach to pupils makes teaching more effective. Second, teachers who understand pupils and their problems are more sensitive to what is and what is not "going over" in the classroom. They are able to make a more effective contribution to program planning and curriculum revision. In addition, teachers have certain advantages over specialists in serving as guidance workers. They have already established a "helping" relationship with their students; therefore, the classroom represents a more natural counseling atmosphere than does the relatively strange office "down the hall." A teacher can observe his students more frequently than can other staff members. These observations may take place in a variety of situations—in the classroom, in the library, in the cafeteria, in the halls, in the auditorium, in the gymnasium, or on the playground. The teacher may see the pupil when he is alone or part of a group. Early and frequent observation gives the teacher an opportunity to apply preventive guidance, whereas the counselor may not hear about a problem until it has become serious enough to disturb the pupil, the teacher, or the parent. Finally, the teacher may get a "moving picture" of a problem as it develops, while other staff members may be dependent on secondhand summaries or recapitulations.

The guidance functions of the teacher may be categorized in different ways. McQueen (21) listed them as (a) understanding students, (b) helping students to develop healthy personalities, and (c) providing guidance and occupational information. Ohlsen (23) and Humphreys, Traxler, and North (15) have also listed these functions in some organized fashion. For purposes of this discussion, these guidance responsibilities will be grouped into the following areas: (a) developing a "helping" tension-free classroom atmosphere, (b) orientation, (c) studying pupils, (d) informal counseling, (e) supplying educational and vocational information, (f) promoting personal and social growth, (g) referral, and (h) cooperation with the guidance program.

Developing a "Helping," Tension-Free Classroom Atmosphere

The teacher who is interested in pupils, has respect for their classroom contributions, understands their problems of growth and adjustment, and helps them satisfy their basic needs, is meeting one of his most important guidance responsibilities. He will be able to provide a tension-free classroom climate that will facilitate the satisfactory social, emotional, physical, and intellectual adjustment of each pupil. Such an atmosphere is necessary if the teacher is to perform his other guidance functions in an adequate manner.

Orientation

Orientation is a responsibility that is often associated with school-wide activities of a group nature designed to acquaint the student with school facilities, time schedules, regulations, etc. However, orientation in the classroom should be a guidance responsibility of every teacher. The teacher should find ways of helping each student to know his classmates and to win a satisfying status within the group. The specific devices used to assist the class to get acquainted will be determined by such factors as the age of the pupils, their grades in school, and the size of the class. During the first few days of class, the teacher may find chance opportunities to mention various out-of-class activities of some of the pupils. As the year progresses, the students may be helped to know one another better by appointing them to small committees which change membership from time to time.

In summary, pupils need the security of knowing something about the teacher and his standards, the interests and plans of the other pupils in the room, and the classroom or library materials available to them. The sooner this knowledge is obtained, the more effective will be the learning situation.

Studying Pupils

Teachers are also fulfilling a guidance function when they study their pupils in some purposeful way. This can be accomplished by observing pupils in various activities in and out of the classroom; noting their patterns of behavior in group situations; and becoming aware of their interests, attitudes, values, work habits, etc. Teachers have the added responsibility of recording behavior which they consider to be significant. These anecdotal records may prove to be of great assistance in the guidance of these students at some later date. Additional information about students can be obtained through autobiographies, diaries, rating scales, questionnaires, standardized tests, parent-teacher conferences, home visits, talks with other teachers, and perusal of the school records. In the elementary school, the relationship of each pupil to other pupils can be ascertained through the use of sociograms and other group techniques. Each of these methods of studying pupils will be discussed in Chapter 8.

Informal Counseling

In most cases, teachers lack the training to deal with mentally disturbed children or those with deep-seated problems. This causes teachers to ask, "Should the teacher ever counsel?" The answer is that there are different levels of counseling. There will be times when counseling individual pupils will be within the scope of the teacher's professional competence. Problems that are not too serious may be alleviated through a type of "surface" counseling involving sympathetic attention, reassurance, and suggestions of a positive nature. By just being a good listener, the teacher may help to release tensions that are interfering with academic progress. Teachers have also found these "surface" counseling techniques to be effective in their conferences with parents. Thus, while it may not be accurate to state that every teacher is a counselor, every teacher will profit by the use of certain counseling techniques.

Supplying Educational and Vocational Information

An important guidance function of the classroom teacher is to provide information that will help students to make appropriate educational and vocational choices. On the elementary level, the world of work may be approached in a general way, without direct concern for the needs of the individual pupil. The teacher may describe areas such as transportation, protective services, danger and safety in order to introduce pupils to their vocational environment. On the secondary level, the teacher can bring out the educational and vocational implications of his subject. Students can be given help in making long-range educational plans if they decide to major in this area. Pupils can also be made aware of vocational opportunities in the community through field trips and talks by employers or their representatives.

Promoting Personal and Social Growth

Teachers have many opportunities for promoting personal and social growth in the classroom. Through curricular and co-curricular activities, they may assist students to gain some insight into their interests, aptitudes, and values. Teachers who are sensitive to the group structure of their classes are able to give certain pupils individual assistance in making a desirable social adjustment. By setting a good example, a teacher may instill proper attitudes toward work and study. Class projects may be set up to fight prejudice and build human understandings. Opportunities for promoting social growth will vary from class to class and from day to day. The study of mathematics or science in high school may not provide as convenient a vehicle for combating prejudice as a high school social studies unit or a fifth-grade unit on "people in other lands." Yet, the mathematics or science teacher's tolerance and objectivity toward each member of the class will be, in itself, a lesson against prejudice and discrimination.

Referral

Pupils with serious problems need prompt referral to a counselor or other specialist. Teachers must be able to recognize those students with serious problems and must know the proper person or agency to whom referral should be made. Students who exhibit these types of behavior usually require referral:

1. Sudden changes in behavior, such as from friendliness to hostility, extroversion to introversion, excellent achievement to poor achievement.

2. Abnormal behavior, such as day-dreaming, withdrawal from the group, depression, neglect of personal appearance, constant suspicion or fear, and extreme nervousness.
3. Weakness, lassitude, inactivity, or other evidence of poor health.

It is not difficult to make referrals in schools where a number of specialized services are available. But in schools without these services, the teacher must have knowledge of community resources, such as mental health clinics, family service agencies, medical centers, and religious organizations that will be equipped to handle these problems.

Cooperation with the Guidance Program

It is important that the teacher cooperate with the school administration and the guidance committee in carrying out policies considered essential to the development of guidance services. He should, first of all, make every effort to understand the values and purposes of the program. The teacher can also cooperate by exchanging information with his colleagues on the problems of individual pupils and by supporting any plan that has been developed to help students make a better personal, social, or educational adjustment.

Undoubtedly, there will be phases of the guidance program which the teacher would like to see changed. Criticisms and suggestions for changes should be made only through proper channels—staff meetings, letters to the guidance committee, talks with the guidance director—to avoid a negative influence on pupils and parents. By serving on the school guidance committee, the teacher can introduce his own plans for conducting various guidance services. Membership in such a committee allows him to suggest necessary changes in a professional manner and enables him to initiate action toward effecting such changes.

Limitations on Teachers as Guidance Workers

Although the teacher is an important member of the guidance team, there is some debate over whether *all* teachers can perform *all* of the aforementioned functions. There are obvious limitations to the guidance role of *any* teacher. Yet, some teachers have found it difficult to recognize and accept guidance responsibilities that are being fulfilled adequately by other teachers. In an attempt to distinguish between the *rationalizations* of a few teachers who wish to avoid guidance responsibilities and the practical *limitations* on all teachers as guidance workers, let us analyze five statements often heard in this connection.

1. *Teachers lack the time for guidance.* Unfortunately, there is much truth in this statement. Many teachers are given numerous clerical responsibilities, such as the recording of scores from standardized tests or the transcribing of school records. These routine tasks have dubious value for the teacher and are likely to limit his teaching effectiveness. Teachers may also be asked to contribute a disproportionate amount of time to the organization of a guidance program. After the guidance program has gone through its "shakedown" period, the time saved in the program should be equal to the time spent; otherwise, the guidance program is not functioning adequately and teachers are being imposed upon. However, teachers are being misled when they are told that an effective guidance program permits teachers to perform the same services in less time. It is more accurate to state that an effective guidance program allows the teacher to provide more adequate services in the same amount of time. Many of the teacher's guidance responsibilities are fulfilled by an *attitude* as well as an *act*. Where the responsibility is more of an attitude than an act, the question of time loses its importance.

2. *Teachers lack the training and experience for guidance work.* There is an element of truth in this statement, also. It is unfair to expect teachers to administer, score, and interpret standardized tests or be given counseling responsibilities if they have not had special training in these fields. However, the guidance responsibilities previously discussed involve the same type and degree of training and experience that is necessary for effective teaching. The skills necessary for the successful performance of these functions should have been obtained as part of the teacher's pre-service education. An in-service training program can provide the additional skills needed by those teachers who are given special responsibilities in the guidance program.

3. *Teachers lack the personality for guidance work.* This statement is misleading. The implication seems to be that the personality necessary for teaching is different from the personality necessary for guiding youngsters. Many teachers *do* lack the personal characteristics necessary for effective guidance, but one questions whether they have desirable personal traits for teaching. Are they not, instead, "getting by" with certain personal traits in the group teaching situation that become a more obvious liability when they attempt to help a pupil with a problem after class? Teachers who make this statement may be

confusing guidance with counseling. This statement might apply only to the responsibility for counseling itself, and even this application is subject to debate. The relationship between teaching and counseling will be discussed later.

4. *Teachers lack the schedule flexibility necessary to perform those guidance functions which are not an actual part of classroom teaching.* This is, perhaps, the most frequent problem that teachers encounter in guiding students. There are two aspects to this problem. We know that we will be most effective in working with the problems of others when we are alert and rested. Yet, the teacher often finds the opportunity for individual help limited to a brief "in-between-periods" talk with a pupil while both pupil and teacher are preparing for the next class. Or, he is forced to schedule a conference with a parent or student at the end of the school day when the onset of fatigue has diminished his alertness, his understanding, and his patience. When faced with fatigue or a crowded schedule, counselors or other staff members often find it possible to make some adjustment in their daily contacts with students. The teacher, committed to a rather inflexible schedule in the classroom, finds it difficult, if not impossible, to make such an adjustment. Secondly, the teacher cannot simply dismiss or ignore a class when he discovers that a pupil needs individual assistance of a non-academic nature. Effective counseling, even of the "surface" type, is rarely accomplished in front of thirty other children. While it may be true that the opportunity for help will still exist at the end of the class hour, the need for assistance may be less obvious to the pupil, and the teacher may have lost the "on-the-spot" advantage that is often so important.

To summarize, teachers' guidance functions which are *not* an actual part of classroom teaching fall in four main categories: (a) getting information about pupils, (b) contributing information about pupils to colleagues or to the school records, (c) referring special cases to the counselor or out-of-school agencies, and (d) counseling. We may conclude that the teacher's inflexible class schedule *may handicap but not prevent* the performance of the first three of these functions. The fourth function, that of counseling, will be discussed in the next statement.

5. *There are basic differences between the process of teaching and the process of counseling which the teacher will have difficulty in reconciling, even though the ultimate objectives of each role are similar.* The activities of the classroom teacher cannot be separated into those that deal strictly with teaching and those that are entirely counseling. Since the objectives are quite similar, it would be difficult

to say where teaching ends and counseling begins. However, there are some identifiable differences between the two roles.

There are three differences between teaching and counseling that appear to merit discussion. They involve *discipline, communication,* and *goals.*

1. *Discipline*—There are many who feel that it is impossible for a teacher to be an effective disciplinarian and an effective counselor at the same time. If we interpret discipline in the schools to include the maintenance of order and the enforcement of regulations, then most teachers have disciplinary responsibilities, in one form or another. Does the teacher with such responsibilities operate at a disadvantage in counseling? Many college personnel workers feel that "disciplinary counseling" can be very effective. However, there is considerable difference between the responsibilities of college personnel workers and those of the classroom teacher. The teacher must be conscious of his responsibilities to all members of the class. Any counseling or discipline conducted within or outside of the classroom must be accomplished with that point in mind. The welfare of a classroom group may demand that the teacher deal with the belligerent or defiant youngster more abruptly than would be necessary if the two were in a private office. There are times when such action is necessary in order to preserve the morale of the group. Yet, this may not be as beneficial to the youngster and may result in further loss of rapport between teacher and pupil. We must conclude that the disciplinary responsibilities of the teacher will handicap his effectiveness as counselor under certain conditions and with certain students.

2. *Communication*—Whether the teacher is democratic and diplomatic, or autocratic and dominant in fulfilling his leadership role in the classroom, he has the responsibility for initiating much of the verbal communication that takes place between himself and the students. He asks questions, he gives answers, he explains, he probes, he leads the discussion so that it stays pertinent to the topic at hand. The counselor's role is more one of listening and clarifying and, through an acceptant attitude, encouraging pupils to talk about themselves and their problems. The teacher uses his communication skills to lead a group. The counselor uses his communication skills to pass leadership to the individual. Some adjustment in communication techniques will be necessary if the effective teacher is to serve as an effective counselor. This adjustment will be easier for the democratic and diplomatic teacher-leader than for the autocratic and dominant teacher-leader.

3. *Goals*—The teacher has a number of goals or objectives in mind as he works with his students. These goals may have been set by the

school or by himself. They may have been influenced by parents, by the community, or by forces outside the community such as standardized college entrance examinations. But they are known to the teacher, and he constantly works toward their fulfillment. The counselor, on the other hand, would be making a serious mistake if he attempted to predetermine the goals of an interview. Even when a student has identified a problem, the counselor is unable to work toward a specific goal. Evidence indicates that the problem originally identified by a student or client is often not the real problem. Therefore, the counselor cannot plan precisely how the interview will proceed or where it will lead.

However, the roles of the teacher and the counselor are not unreconcilable on this point. The democratic teacher will set *flexible* goals and adapt them, somewhat, to the needs, interests, and abilities of the class. The counselor may be said to set flexible goals when he determines, prior to the interview, that he will more listening than talking, that he will be interested but objective, and that he will respect the confidences of the pupil. We must conclude that the democratic teacher who is willing to adapt his plans and goals to the needs and interests of his students may find it easy to make the transition to counseling.

In-Service Education for Teachers

Only a small percentage of the elementary and secondary teachers now serving in our schools have had formal training in the field of guidance. This fact is attributable, in part, to the recency of the guidance movement. It is also a reflection of the relative scarcity of guidance courses in our undergraduate teacher education programs. Miller (22) found a very small number of colleges and universities that allowed undergraduate students to enroll in guidance courses. Only the teacher who undertakes graduate study has the opportunity to specialize in guidance work. This means that an in-service education program will be necessary if teachers are to participate in the formulation and operation of a program of guidance services.

Determining Readiness for In-Service Education

There are a number of factors that help determine the extent of the staff's readiness for in-service education. The interest of the staff in guidance work, the extent of their participation in the existing guidance program, and the competencies which they already possess will help to determine whether an in-service program should be started in the immediate future. In addition, resources in and out of the school must be checked. Are there faculty members who will be willing to spend time and energy in planning such a program? Are there outside consultants available to organize and conduct a portion of the program? Are there funds available for the purchase of materials vital to the success of the program? Is there time available during the school day for at least a portion of this program? Regardless of the size or location of the school, these factors should be considered before making definite plans for an in-service program in guidance services.

Determining Needs for In-Service Education

A series of preliminary meetings will probably be necessary in order to explore and clarify the guidance needs of the school and staff. While a questionnaire may be the ideal device for obtaining opinions from students and parents regarding the value of guidance services already in effect, such a device used with teachers at this time might give some the impression that the dice were "loaded," that a program was being "pushed" by just a few members of the staff. Staff participation in any type of in-service program will be dependent on their becoming actively involved in the planning of the program as early as possible. The mere fact that an in-service program is desirable does not insure teacher participation. Some of the more common blocks to teacher participation are listed in the report of the Eighth National Conference of State Supervisors of Guidance Services and Counselor Trainers (16).

1. Teachers resent a program which will add to their already overloaded schedules. Careful scheduling on the part of the principal may reduce the number of preparations for a single teacher, thus giving time for in-service education. Again, records may be so inadequate and inaccessible that the teachers will not take the time to use them, even though they recognize their value. Revamping of the record system may provide additional teacher time for guidance work. There is little doubt that many teachers who begin an in-service education program with a keen desire to do something about it end up with a "what's the use?" attitude unless steps are taken by the administration to facilitate the teachers' work rather than add to it.

2. Many teachers are concerned about their jobs. This militates against a successful in-service program. Providing teachers with tenure, financial security, positive administrative leadership, and status in the community is a prerequisite to improved educational programs.

3. Many teachers are frustrated because they do not know what is expected of them. The need for a clear understanding of responsibilities and of administrative policy is an absolute necessity in getting the program under way.

4. Some schools have in-service programs because they think it is the thing to do. This is certainly not a valid reason, as has been pointed out previously. Teachers justifiably resent participating in such a program. They will, however, be more interested if the program is built on the felt needs of the staff and in an atmosphere of cooperative planning.

5. Schools frequently fail to provide time during the school day for staff members to participate in training programs. Although it is usually impossible to conduct in-service education entirely on school time, a compromise plan will frequently do much to create enthusiastic participation.

During the preliminary meetings these "blocks" will, presumably, be discussed and overcome. If they are dealt with in some satisfactory way, a preorganization committee may be appointed. This committee should represent all shades of opinion held by the various staff members, in order to avoid the impression of being "loaded." The committee may plan a tentative agenda of in-service sessions. It might wish to contact various out-of-school consultants to determine their availability. It may order information materials. In any case, the committee will keep the rest of the staff well informed on all action taken and will ask their help in surveying the guidance needs of the school.

Planning the In-Service Education Program

The following principles should be observed in planning the in-service program.

1. *The administration must take the responsibility for initiating and organizing the program.* Policies regarding salaries, guidance responsibilities, school time available for training functions, and the like should be made known to the staff as they relate to the proposed in-service program. The principal or superintendent should guarantee the necessary equipment and materials for the program.

2. *A majority of the staff should participate in the planning of the program.* No teacher should be forced to participate. But a program planned by a large percentage of the teachers has a greater chance of success than one dictated by a few.

3. *Regular school time should be used for the major portion of the program.* The whole purpose of school guidance services is

thwarted if in-service training for such services causes an immediate increase in the work responsibilities of the teachers. The result is likely to be apathy or even resentment toward the program.

4. *The in-service program should be continuous.* It begins perhaps with a preschool institute and continues throughout the year with interschool visitation, extension courses, informative bulletins, and professional conferences.

5. *Procedures for the revaluation of the program should be developed.* With a continuous in-service program, the needs of the staff and school will change. Periodic revaluation of the program will be necessary in order that necessary changes can be instituted.

Operating the In-Service Education Program

An in-service education program should proceed in three directions: one to include the entire staff, one to include departmental areas or special interest groups, and one for the individual teacher. There should be a core of generalized experiences for all staff members. The rest of the program should be built on the interests and needs of departments or individual teachers. The following methods of operating the in-service program are in effect in many schools:

Extension courses offered by colleges or universities—Schools in metropolitan areas often find it possible to cooperate with a nearby college or university in setting up a structured course in guidance. While these courses are not generally conducted on school time, they provide professional leadership and often award credit toward an advanced degree.

Workshops—An in-service workshop can be centered around a practical problem selected by the group rather than a series of general topics predetermined by a specialist not connected with the school. Its keynote is informality and flexibility. The Ohio Education Association (14) has suggested that a good workshop has the following characteristics:

1. It is concerned with the problems of the participants, not the problems of the leaders.
2. It is one where the participants come prepared to participate.
3. It is one in which the leaders are prepared to carry out their function in an efficient yet democratic manner.
4. It is one that uses democratic discussion and leaders who can bring into the open the points of view of the participants.

5. It is one in which the groups are small, yet kept informed of the activities of the other groups.
6. It is one that takes time to evaluate itself as it goes along and to improve its own procedures of working together.
7. It is one in which the final session commits itself to carry out the conference decisions back in the classroom or practical school situation.

Interschool visits—This is a convenient way for staff members to obtain first-hand experience by observing guidance in practice. Teachers often find it profitable to visit a grade level just below or above the one they are teaching.

Faculty meetings—The faculty meeting provides the opportunity to build a core of generalized experiences for all faculty members. More important, faculty meetings devoted to this purpose would be less inclined to get bogged down in committee reports and other activities requiring little teacher preparation or participation. The seven characteristics of a good workshop, mentioned above, are applicable also, in the main, to faculty meetings. A faculty meeting with these characteristics could become the most effective type of in-service program. It would also provide an answer to the often heard complaint that faculty meetings are a waste of time and administrator dominated.

Departmental meetings—In schools large enough to have subject-matter departments, meetings may be held to discuss the contributions of the department to the program of guidance services and the benefits the department may derive from the program.

Guidance Handbook—Some schools supply every teacher with a handbook containing the principles on which the school guidance program rests, the goals of the program, and the guidance responsibilities of the teacher. Information on the materials used in the guidance program (such as standardized tests, report forms, record folders) is included. Such a handbook needs annual revision in order to avoid being outdated.

Guidance Bulletins—Teachers tend to lose interest in a handbook if outdated material is allowed to accumulate. The resulting bulky document is left to gather dust on an upper shelf. Guidance bulletins tend to be less expensive, less time-consuming in their preparation, and more up-to-date. They are more likely to include humorous anecdotes, pictorial material, and practical problems that will attract the teacher's attention. The following examples were excerpted from bulletins prepared by the counselor in charge of the guidance program in the Monmouth, Illinois schools (31) several years ago. It should be noted that these excerpts contain simple, easy-to-read material which is equally applicable to the elementary and secondary teacher.

WHAT'S HAPPENING IN OUR GUIDANCE AND TESTING PROGRAM DURING THE MONTH OF OCTOBER

During the month of October, 1,025 students were tested in the elementary grades and in the high school. Quite a few of you will soon be subjected to that occupational disease known as "parent-tonitis." One of the first symptoms is the giving of tests. This is rapidly followed by an anxious relative of the patient inquiring as to the strength or weakness of his I.Q. A word concerning the proper bedside manner is in order. "Should parents be told a student's I.Q.?" You've all been faced with this question. The answer is *no* and *yes*. No, the parent should not be given an I.Q. score under any circumstances, for a variety of reasons. Yes, the parent should be given an indication of his child's I.Q., possibly in the form of a percentile ranking. I.Q's tend to be handled as gingerly as an ailing aunt who has a large sum of money. A single number indicating an I.Q. tells very little about a child. It is an approximation within a five to ten point variance that is affected by such factors as the child's physical condition, his susceptibility to tension, his previous experience with tests, etc. Intelligence has been defined as the ability to adjust to the environment or, as we have so often tested for it, the ability to succeed in school. While it is relatively constant, it works within the limits set by native endowment, growth and maturation, opportunities for new educational experiences, and the drives of the individual. Therefore, it is better to measure the various aspects of intelligence. We can, thus, determine the differences in ability between two children with an "average" I.Q. of 100.

A "percentile" is one of the handiest weapons we have in the fight to report scores professionally and honestly. A pupil's percentile ranking on a test shows the per cent of the pupils in a group that he equals or excels in score—or the per cent of pupils that are below him in score. If a pupil's percentile ranking is 85, it may be explained that his score equals or exceeds 85 per cent of the group upon whom the test was standardized.

Elementary School News

During October, group testing was completed in the first, second, third, and sixth grades. The remaining grades will be scheduled as soon as the balance of the tests are received. Individual testing will be scheduled during the first week in November.

A recent Purdue University study into the common problems of youth will be of interest to each of you. It is described at length in the S.R.A. Junior Inventory manual and can only be summarized here. Forty-five hundred pupils in grades four through eight were studied. The following findings were reported:

1. Educational guidance problems are already serious at the fourth-grade level. Many student dislikes of school have developed before the age of nine.

2. Personal and social problems that worry teenagers so much start early and become steadily more important, although major shifts in emphasis occur through the years.

3. Social class differences between children coming from poor home backgrounds and those from middle and upper groups are already clearly apparent by the fourth grade.

4. Students show a keen interest in jobs long before high school.

5. Attention to the interests of students can motivate them to do better school work.

This study reveals the need for guidance in the elementary school; it reveals the need for guidance services that will lead toward a better understanding of each individual pupil. Our group testing represents one of these services. After the testing is completed our real work will begin . . . *making use of test results.*

Secondary School News

During October, 433 ninth, tenth, and eleventh grade students were tested. The ninth-graders received the S.R.A. Reading Test and the S.R.A. Youth Inventory. The tenth-graders received the Kuder Preference Record—Vocational and the Kuder Preference Record—Personal. The eleventh-graders took the Illinois Statewide Testing Program.

A different emphasis is placed on counseling interviews each year of the pupil's high school life. Freshman interviews stress "getting adjusted" and are built around the S.R.A. Youth Inventory. Sophomore interviews emphasize vocational interests and the world of work. Both Kuder Preference Records are used as a point of departure. Juniors are encouraged to think more seriously of a vocational or educational choice. Aptitudes and abilities are considered as well as interest patterns. Seniors receive specific information on occupations, application procedures, specific job openings, etc.—or information on specific colleges, scholarships, entrance requirements, etc. Summaries of these interviews are filed and are available to help you understand your students. Test results are also available for the same reason. No scores are "secret." They may prove helpful in making your own work easier. Quite a lot of occupational and educational material is now available on loan. Why not drop around and see what's here?

WHAT'S HAPPENING IN OUR GUIDANCE AND TESTING PROGRAM DURING THE MONTH OF NOVEMBER

A teacher whom I admire very much defines the aim of guidance as "Helping Johnny see through himself and then helping Johnny see himself through." If the major aim of guidance is to help students in their development, why beat around intellectual bushes? We can best *promote* this development by giving the students their percentile scores for all tested factors of intelligences. Last month's discussion was concerned with presenting these scores accurately. In what ways can we create a better understanding of these scores? We can point out that intelligence is influenced by environment, that it is developing continually, even though heredity may set the extreme limits of development. (Do many of us struggle to those limits?) We might also remember that (a) every intelligence test contains an element of what has already been learned, (b) there are different kinds of mental ability or intelligence, and (c) there is some reason to believe that many of our better known tests are "culture-biased." Learning ability of other-than-middle-class students is often underestimated.

Further help to each of you can be supplied by our Visiting Counselor. Her busy schedule includes visits to the homes of students and maintaining continual contact with local community services. Referrals to the Visiting Counselor in no way reflect upon the ability of the teacher to handle a difficult situation. A room in which all students are equally understood has not yet been assigned. Her reports, especially in the social and emotional areas, will be of great value to you in understanding your students.

Let's look at Johnny again for a minute. He is under sixteen years of age. Which would be most helpful in predicting achievement, I.Q. or M.A.? I.Q. is a ratio which shows the rate at which a student is developing mental ability. M.A. indicates the level of ability (or intelligence) at a given time. For students under sixteen years there may be several cases where students have the same I.Q. but who have very different mental ages. This can be seen quickly in the comparison between Johnny and Bratilla. Johnny (sixth grade) has an I.Q. of 130 and a M.A. of fifteen years. Bratilla (second grade) has an I.Q. of 130 and a M.A. of ten years. What both of these students should be able to do can more quickly be seen by referring to their mental ages than to their I.Q.'s. An I.Q. should not be used in predicting achievement by itself any more than the type of glass used in car windows should be considered the sole basis for describing the car.

Elementary School News

The last group tests at the Junior High are scheduled for December fourth. The last classroom tests in the other schools are scheduled for December fourteenth. So the end of testing approaches and our real challenge begins—breathing functional life into the test results. More concerning this in the following bulletins.

Our program of individual testing has started. Tests can be given to small groups or to individuals, as you prefer. They will be administered, scored, and the results sent to you. With a minimum of effort you receive the maximum of information.

Secondary School News

While a scholarship may not be in everyone's future, there are many to choose from if a student is qualified. Many announcements concerning scholarships are posted in the Dean of Boys' office. When you're walking by, stop in for a minute and glance at them.

The Dean's List, beginning this month, is yet another attempt to solve the old question, "What can I do in high school to prepare the advanced student for college?" Suggestions from each of you will be welcome as the experiment progresses.

Other methods of operating the in-service education program includes *demonstrations* by outside consultants, *teacher-study groups* built around a specific guidance problem, *case conferences* devoted to the intensive study of an individual pupil, and the establishment of an *information center* or comfortable lounge for teachers that may be stocked with professional reading materials such as textbooks, pamphlets, standardized tests, test manuals, and case reports.

Revaluating the In-Service Education Program

The guidance in-service education program must be revaluated periodically in order that the needs of the staff and the school may be met. This revaluation may be made in three ways: (a) It may be evaluated in terms of its effect on the total guidance program. An analysis may be made of the changes that have taken place in the guidance program since the in-service program was instituted. (b) The approach may be through the formulation and use of a set of criteria designed to evaluate the in-service program itself. (c) Staff members who participated may be asked (preferably by means of an unsigned questionnaire) to give their opinion regarding the value of the program. It is probable that a combination of these approaches will produce the most effective results.

Summary

The teacher's role in the guidance program is extremely important. Teachers have certain advantages over specialists in performing some guidance functions; they are at a disadvantage in attempting to perform others. It is necessary that we distinguish between the rationalizations of a few teachers who wish to avoid guidance responsibilities and the limitations on all teachers in the performance of certain guidance functions. Some of the limitations may be removed through effective in-service education. An in-service education program will be most effective if the entire staff participates in the working out of procedures for initiation, organization, operation, and evaluation.

Bibliography

1. Arbuckle, Dugald S. *Guidance and Counseling in the Classroom.* Boston: Allyn & Bacon, Inc., 1957. Chaps. 3, 5.
2. ———. *Pupil Personnel Services in American Schools.* Boston: Allyn & Bacon, Inc., 1962. Chap. 4.
3. Association of Supervision and Curriculum Development. *Guidance in the Classroom.* Washington, D.C.: NEA, 1955. Chaps. 1, 2, 11.
4. Barr, John A. *The Elementary Teacher and Guidance.* New York: Henry Holt and Company, 1958.
5. Bennett, Margaret E. *Guidance and Counseling in Groups.* 2nd ed. New York: McGraw-Hill Book Company, Inc., 1963. Chap. 10.
6. Blanchard, Howard L. and Laurence S. Flaum. *Guidance: A Longitudinal Approach.* Minneapolis: Burgens Publishing Company, 1962. Chap. 1.
7. Crow, Lester D. and Alice Crow. *Organization and Conduct of Guidance Services* New York: David McKay Company, Inc., 1965. Chap. 6.
8. ———. *Readings in Guidance.* New York: David McKay Company, Inc., 1962. Chaps. 25, 29.
9. Froehlich, Clifford P. *Guidance Services in Schools.* New York: McGraw-Hill Book Company, Inc., 1958. Chap. 12.
10. Glanz, Edward C. *Foundations and Principles of Guidance.* Boston: Allyn & Bacon, Inc., 1964. Chap. 13.
11. Gordon, Ira J. *The Teacher as a Guidance Worker.* New York: Harper and Brothers, 1956. Chaps. 1, 7-9.
12. Hatch, Raymond N. and Buford Stefflre. *Administration of Guidance Services: Organization, Supervision, Evaluation.* Englewood Cliffs, New Jersey: Prentice-Hall, Inc., 1958. Chap. 4.
13. Hollis, Joseph W. and Lucile U. Hollis. *Organizing for Effective Guidance.* Chicago: Science Research Associates, Inc., 1965. Chap. 12.
14. *How to Organize an In-Service Workshop.* Columbus, Ohio: Ohio Education Association.
15. Humphreys, J. Anthony, Arthur E. Traxler, and Robert North. *Guid-*

ance Services. 2nd ed. Chicago: Science Research Associates, Inc., 1960. Chap. 17.

16.   *In-Service Preparation for Guidance Duties.* Washington, D.C.: U.S. Office of Education, Misc. 3314-17A, 1950. P. 10.

17.   Johnson, W. F., *et al. Pupil Personnel and Guidance Services.* New York: McGraw-Hill Book Company, Inc., 1961. Chap. 6.

18.   Kelley, Janet A. *Guidance and Curriculum.* Englewood Cliffs, New Jersey: Prentice-Hall, Inc., 1955. Chaps. 2-4.

19.   Martinson, Ruth A. and Harry Smallenburg. *Guidance in Elementary Schools.* Englewood Cliffs, New Jersey: Prentice-Hall, Inc., 1958. Chaps. 4, 8, 10, 13.

20.   McDaniel, Henry B., *et al. Readings in Guidance.* New York: Henry Holt and Company, 1959. Chap. 3.

21.   McQueen, Mildred. "The Teacher's Role in Guidance," *Science Research Associates Research Report.* Chicago: Science Research Associates, Inc., 1951.

22.   Miller, Frank W. "Counselor-Training Programs in Colleges and Universities." *Personnel and Guidance Journal,* XXXII:3, November, 1953.

23.   Ohlsen, Merle M. *Guidance Services in the Modern School.* New York: Harcourt, Brace & World Inc., 1964. Chap. 15.

24.   Patterson, C. H. *Counseling and Guidance in Schools.* New York: Harper and Brothers, 1962. Chap. 6.

25.   Peters, H. J. and Gail Farwell. *Guidance: A Developmental Approach.* Chicago: Rand McNally & Co., 1959. Chaps. 9, 17.

26.   Syracuse University, School of Education. *Guidance in the Age of Automation.* Syracuse, New York: Syracuse University Press, 1957. Chap. 11.

27.   Tiedeman, David V. and Frank L. Field. "Guidance: The Science of Purposeful Action Applied Through Education," in Mosher, Ralph L., Richard F. Carle, and Chris D. Kehas, eds. *Guidance: An Examination.* New York: Harcourt, Brace & World, Inc., 1965. P. 206.

28.   Traxler, Arthur E. *Techniques of Guidance.* New York: Harper and Brothers, 1957. Chap. 16.

29.   Willey, Roy DeVerl and Melvin W. Strong. *Group Procedures in Guidance.* New York: Harper and Brothers, 1957.

30.   ———— and Melvin Dunn. *The Role of the Teacher in the Guidance Program.* Bloomington, Illinois: McKnight & McKnight Publishing Co., 1964.

UNPUBLISHED MATERIAL

31.   Pearson, Paul. Counselor, Oak Park-River Forest High School, Oak Park, Illinois (formerly Guidance Director, Monmouth, Illinois Public Schools).

5

Role of the Elementary School Counselor

Guidance services in the elementary school have developed more slowly than similar services in the secondary school. This is generally attributed to (1) the vocational origins of guidance, (2) the difficulty in differentiating between teaching and guidance at the elementary level, and (3) the early development of other specialized services for elementary school pupils. However, as we have already noted, problems of pupils are not purely vocational; they do not suddenly begin upon entrance into the secondary school; and opportunities for preventative or developmental guidance are limited if we ignore these problems until the pupil is twelve to fourteen years old.

Need for Guidance Services in the Elementary School

Concern over the need for guidance services in the elementary school has been expressed recently by counselor educators (10, 30), by other educational leaders such as Conant (9), by committees representing professional organizations concerned with guidance services (2, 5), by state departments of education (8, 33), and by personnel representing the U.S. Office of Education (59). This need appears to have been well established through recent studies that have documented the problems of educational, emotional, social, and physical adjustment currently besetting sizeable percentages of our children at this age level. These adjustment problems have been related to such factors as class size, population mobility, working mothers, broken homes, emotional illness, delinquency, and dropouts.

Class size

Although 1,700,000 more children entered elementary and secondary schools in 1959-60 than during the year before, there was not a proportional increase in the number of qualified teachers (3). "Classes in elementary schools are now oversized, with too many temporary, inadequately prepared teachers. With this classroom situation, a withdrawn child may be overlooked or an aggressive child may cause excessive interruption of class work (59)."

Population mobility

One-fifth of the population moves each year from one home to another. In 1958, 12 million children were displaced, and had to adjust to new surroundings and make new friends (67).

Working mothers

Thirty per cent of mothers with children under 18 years of age are working and over 20 per cent of these mothers have children under the age of six (67). Some of these mothers have entered the labor market in order to raise the standard of living of their families. Others have taken jobs because they are the family's sole support. Regardless of the reason, many of their children suffer from lack of supervision and companionship and from a weakened family structure.

Broken homes

Thirteen per cent of our children under 18 years of age come from broken homes (67). Another 202,000 have been born out of wedlock (67). These children often have problems of a social or emotional nature that are more serious than the problems of those who suffer from lack of supervision and companionship.

Emotional illness

No reliable data exist on the prevalence of childhood psychiatric disorders. However, in 1955, 1,200 outpatient psychiatric clinics in the country reported that about 212,000 children under the age of 21 had been under diagnosis or care during the year (67).

Delinquency

In a sample of 500 persistent delinquents from the underprivileged areas of Boston, the average age at onset of maladapted behavior was somewhat over eight years, with almost half the group showing clear signs of anti-sociality at seven or younger, and nine-tenths at ten or younger (21). The implication is clear. The elementary school receives potential delinquents at a crucial age and is in an excellent position to apply preventive measures.

Dropouts

During the 1960's, some 7.5 million youngsters will drop out before high school graduation. About 2.5 million will not go beyond the eighth grade; two out of three will go no further than the tenth grade (61). "Problems which finally result in a dropout begin, and are quite overt, way back in the elementary grades. In fact, it is quite early in grade school that many of the potential dropouts begin to fall behind in their scholastic achievements and this results in ... retardation. ... These results suggest that perhaps some of our occupational education and guidance might begin much sooner than it does now (69)."

Stripling and Lane (64) are among those who have documented the recent, rapid increase of guidance services at the elementary school level. The government's interest in accelerating this trend gave impetus to the passage of the Elementary and Secondary Education Act of 1965 and resulted in the revision of Title V of the National Defense Education Act (see Chapter 2). However, there is a very real danger that we may move too fast in developing guidance services in elementary schools. Federal support programs often motivate administrators to hire personnel and establish services out of a quest for status, a desire for financial support, or simply because it "appears to be the current thing to do." A hastily established, unplanned program could prove to be so ineffective as to cause a community (or a school staff) to reverse its attitude toward these services.

The danger that we may move too rapidly in establishing elementary school guidance services is accentuated by the relative absence of research providing evidence of the value of these services. (See

Chapter 10 for a detailed account of the problems we face in evaluating guidance services.) It is relatively easy to document the adjustment problems of our elementary school children. However, it is not
easy to validate the assumption that elementary guidance services
will significantly reduce or alleviate these problems. Most research, to
date, has been designed to elicit opinions from parents, teachers,
counselors, and administrators about what elementary school counselors do (8, 48, 54) or should be doing (8, 27, 43, 58). These studies
are necessary but they give us little assistance if we are asked to
justify the need for elementary school guidance services.

The Elementary School Counselor

Debate over the elementary school counselor usually concerns his
title, his background and experience, his preparation, and his role and
function.

Title: Counselor or Consultant?

A variety of views prevail regarding the proper title to be given
the guidance specialist in the elementary school. The recent statement by the Joint ACES-ASCA Committee on the Elementary School
Counselor (5) indicates a definite preference for the term *counselor*.
A contrasting point of view is held by specialists in the U.S. Office of
Education. Smith and Eckerson (59) argue that it is more appropriate to use the term *guidance consultant*. More recently, the same
authors (60) have suggested that the term *child development consultant* be applied to counselors, social workers, and psychologists since
these three specialists are all currently working in programs labeled
"elementary school guidance." Koeppe (36) suggests that both *counselor* and *consultant* are appropriate: the former connoting a "generalist" who provides services to *all* pupils, the latter identifying a "specialist" who provides services to only *some* pupils. According to
Koeppe, the same school district might have one or more *elementary
school counselors* and one or more *elementary school consultants*.

Elementary school counselor has been employed in this chapter
since the title is traditional and parallels the title given to similar
personnel in the secondary school. However, the author feels that
consulting is, and will continue to be, a more important function than
counseling for these elementary school specialists.

Background: Is Teaching Experience Necessary?

The great majority of statements on elementary school counseling
emphasize successful teaching as a necessary prerequisite to success-

ful counseling. Representative of this point of view is the concluding statement in the report of the Committee on Guidance in the Elementary School of the American School Counselors Association (2):

> A teaching experience in the elementary school should be a basic qualification for appointment as an elementary school counselor. Such teaching experience must be of superior quality, and should probably extend over a period of five years.

However, a study by Stewart (63) caused him to question the value of teaching experience. Recruitment of personnel from fields other than teaching has been recommended by the White House Conference on Children and Youth (67) and by Eckerson and Smith (16). Trow (66) believes that a practicum experience for future elementary counselors can serve in lieu of classroom experience. More recently, the Joint ACES-ASCA Committee on the Elementary School Counselor (5) has issued a statement which includes the following cautious words:

> By *educationally oriented* we mean having a knowledge of the elementary school program, including curriculum, the learning process and school organization. We recognize the value of teaching experience in the elementary school but feel that knowledge of the school program and processes can also be gained through a planned program of experiences in the school as a part of the "counselor's" preparation.

It seems clear that this problem will remain controversial until we have evidence regarding the effectiveness of counselors with different types of backgrounds. We also need to remind ourselves that if it is indefensible to *require teaching experience* solely on the basis of past and present subjective judgments of educators in the field, it is equally, if not more, indefensible to *substitute other experience* solely on the basis of the subjective judgments of counselor educators and others who are not elementary school practitioners.

Preparation

In a recent study, Hill and Nitzschke (32) summarized information furnished them by 154 directors of master's degree programs in elementary school guidance and concluded:

> Preparation programs for guidance workers in elementary schools are as yet not well defined. Some of these programs make little, if any, differentiation between preparation for the elementary school and preparation for the secondary school. Very few universities have clearly planned programs for the preparation of guidance workers in elementary schools. ... It would seem that the time is

at hand for leaders in elementary education and in guidance to combine their judgments to formulate a clearer definition of "elementary school guidance."

There is growing recognition (5, 53, 59) that the elementary school guidance consultant needs a broadly based, multi-disciplinary background of preparation that includes work in the disciplines of anthropology, economics, education, philosophy, psychology, and sociology. The overlapping nature of the *experience* and *training* issues comes into focus at this point. To meet the needs of elementary school guidance, Patouillet (53) has proposed the utilization of persons who have already completed programs in guidance, psychology, or social work. Smith and Eckerson (59) have offered several arguments in support of this point of view:

1. The depth and emphasis of their preparation may serve the needs of certain schools more adequately than teaching experience plus courses in guidance.
2. Graduate programs for school social workers and school psychologists require two years beyond the bachelor's degree, while state certification for guidance personnel usually requires one year or less of graduate work.
3. Psychologists and social workers from our finest institutions can be employed if the requirements for guidance consultants are liberalized to include, in lieu of teaching experience, orientation in education or an internship in an elementary school setting.

It is apparent that the arguments over *experience and preparation* are due primarily to our lack of role definition. To what extent is the elementary guidance specialist a counselor? to what extent is he a consultant? and to what extent is he a coordinator?

Role and function

All authorities appear to agree that the elementary school counselor has three major roles: *coordinator, counselor,* and *consultant.* However, a review of the literature reveals substantial disagreement over which of these roles should be considered the primary one. Shertzer and Lundy (58) found that elementary principals viewed the counselor's role as being *coordinator, consultant,* and *counselor,* in that order of importance, after being told to use the term "elementary school counselor" as if it were synonymous with "a qualified school psychologist." Foster (19) found that five groups of educators (elementary teachers, elementary counselors, elementary principals, secondary counselors, counselor educators) all perceived *counseling* as the most important function performed by the elementary school counselor. A survey by the California State Department of Education (8) found that elementary principals and counselors in California schools were in substantial agreement that the major functions of elementary counselors were *counseling, teacher consultation,* and *parent consultation,* in that order of importance. Perrone and Evans (54), by contrast, reported that elementary counselors were *spending little time in counseling individuals and considerable time in various consulting activities.* Hill (31) and Stripling and Lane (64) describe the elementary school counselor as primarily a *resource person to teachers.*

A strong case can be made for the view of the elementary counselor as primarily a *consultant.* Smith and Eckerson (59) conducted an intensive review of 24 elementary school guidance programs selected as "outstanding" by state directors of guidance services. These 24 programs were found to have the following common features:

1. Guidance services are part of a broader program of services offered by the school system. They are usually called pupil personnel services.
2. The guidance program serves *all* children.
3. The guidance consultant is at the center of a guidance program which involves the entire school staff, and the teacher plays an essential role in the program.
4. The guidance consultant:
   (a) Tests and observes children who have learning difficulties, who are underachievers, who show signs of emotional disturbances, who need curricular advice or placement in special classes, and who are being considered for referral to other specialists.
   (b) Counsels children with minor personal troubles that interfere with school life.
   (c) Helps needy children obtain glasses, hearing aids, clothes, food and other essentials.
   (d) Consults with teachers, principal, and parents to help them understand normal children as well as children with problems.
   (e) Refers children needing intensive diagnosis and treatment to pupil personnel specialists and community agencies, and interprets their findings and recommendations to teachers and parents.
   (f) Provides inservice education for teachers. Through scheduled meetings and informal conferences relating to normal development and behavior in children, the guidance consultant aids teachers in meeting difficult classroom situations with understanding and composure.

Other subjects included in inservice training are: mental health, administration and interpretation of tests, maintenance and use of cumulative records, and techniques of interviewing.

(g) Develops group guidance programs in common personal problems, study habits, occupational orientation, and preparation for the secondary school.

(h) Interprets the guidance program to parent and community organizations.

(i) Conducts research and evaluative studies relative to the effectiveness of the guidance program.

On the basis of the functions performed by the guidance specialists in these 24 programs, Smith and Eckerson felt that it was most appropriate to refer to them as *guidance consultants.* "On the secondary level, the counselor's primary role is counseling—to help each student understand himself and make decisions relating to his education, vocation and personal problems. The *guidance consultant,* however, has a different role because (1) there is seldom a choice of courses in elementary schools; (2) vocational planning is not encouraged at this level, although occupational orientation usually is part of guidance; and (3) only a limited number of children in elementary grades have the maturity for the self-analysis and understanding needed for counseling on personal problems." Eckerson (15) has elaborated on this point of view by building her argument around the following premises:

1. Guidance for all children should be a fact rather than a theory.
2. Emphasis should be on development guidance.
3. Emphasis should be on prevention of problems.
4. A school's guidance program should begin where the needs are.
5. A counselor should help teachers understand the effect of their behavior on children.
6. Work with parents is vital to an elementary school guidance program.
7. The counselor should recognize the need for referral when necessary and prepare the appropriate persons.
8. Consultation is one of the counselor's ways of obtaining information.

Heisey (29) argues that the elementary school counselor must be primarily a *parent consultant* because (a) the parent is potentially the greatest agent of change in the child's environment, (b) the parent sustains more consistently over a longer period of time a more intense and concerted interest for the child, (c) primary value training should come from the home, (d) parents have the greatest storehouse of contributing data regarding a child, and (e) it will foster perpetual growth of the counselor's own skill in dealing with the areas with which parents are most concerned.

Both the Joint ACES-ASCA Committee on the Elementary School Counselor (5) and the Illinois State Department of Guidance Services (33) have issued statements that give more attention to the *counseling* responsibilities of the elementary school counselor. For example, the statement by the Illinois State Department of Guidance Services suggests that the elementary school counselor should "provide individual counseling to (a) help pupils and parents develop better understanding about the pupil's personal characteristics, (b) help pupils and parents develop better understandings about the pupil's potentialities, and (c) help pupils make a smooth adjustment to the particular school situation." It will be observed that this statement differs from the Smith and Eckerson statement as to the scope of pupil problems requiring individual counseling. Disagreement is also evident as to whether parents are *consulted* or *counseled.*

Finally, Koeppe (36) is representative of those writers who identify the elementary counselor as a professionally trained person whose major responsibility is *counseling* and who provides this service to *all* pupils. The rationale for this point of view appears to be built around the premise that guidance programs in the elementary school should be developmental rather than problem-centered. However, a number of writers, including the author, would question the assumption that a program of developmental guidance would require the *counseling* of *all* pupils.

Summary

We may summarize by stating that the elementary school guidance specialist serves as a *counselor, consultant,* and *coordinator.* The emphasis placed upon each of these functions will be determined by the following factors:

1. Counseling takes time. The amount of time that can be devoted to individual counseling varies with the number of children to be served, their age and maturity, and the extent of services available from other specialists.
2. Since no guidance program can expect to be successful without the enthusiastic support of the entire staff, it is apparent that the empathic specialist will allow his role to be shaped some-

what by the attitudes of the teachers and administrators in the
school.

3. The experience, training, and personal qualifications of the specialist will probably enable him to serve more effectively in one
   type of role than another.
4. The values and expectations of parents and other members of
   the neighborhood or community will become known to the
   specialist and will begin to condition his actions.

In the final analysis, however, it would appear that the specialist
will be more of a *consultant* than a counselor or coordinator. His role
must be more *preventative* than *remedial* in nature. He does less
schedule planning, career counseling, testing, and record keeping than
the secondary school counselor. Economy dictates that he spend more
time assisting teachers in preventing problems than in accepting
referrals for treatment. In this manner, he can contribute to the
welfare of a great many more children. Economy also dictates that he
spend considerable time consulting with parents in order that they,
too, may become more effective in preventing problems from reaching
a crucial stage. Finally, the greatest educational economy results
when teachers are freed from the distractions and pressures that
interfere with their main job of instruction. Every teacher will be
more effective in this job if he receives assistance in those activities
which contribute to the ability of each child to learn.

Bibliography

1. Adams, James F. *Counseling and Guidance: A Summary View*. New York: The Macmillan Company, 1965. Chap. 8.
2. American School Counselor Association. *Report of the Committee on Guidance in the Elementary School*, 1959.
3. *Annual Report, U.S. Department of Health, Education, and Welfare*. Washington, D.C.: U.S. Government Printing Office, 1960. Pp. 196-228.
4. Apostal, Robert A. "Objectives of Elementary Guidance." *The School Counselor*, Vol. 10, October, 1962, 23-26.
5. Association for Counselor Education and Supervision and American School Counselor Association. *Preliminary Statement: Joint ACES-ASCA Committee on the Elementary School Counselor*, 1965.
6. Buchheimer, Arnold. "Elementary Guidance, A Fragment of a Theory," *Elementary School Guidance and Counseling*, Vol. 1, No. 4, Fall, 1966.
7. Byrne, Richard H. *The School Counselor*. Boston: Houghton Mifflin Company, 1963. Chap. 12.
8. California State Department of Education, Bureau of Pupil Personnel Services. *Elementary School Counselors in California*. Research Brief No. 13. Sacramento: the Department, 1965.
9. Conant, James B. *The American High School Today*. New York: McGraw-Hill Book Company, Inc., 1959. Pp. 45-63.
10. Cottingham, Harold F. "National-Level Projection for Elementary School Guidance." *Personnel and Guidance Journal*, XLIV:499-502, January, 1966.
11. Crow, Lester D., and Alice Crow. *An Introduction to Guidance*. 2nd ed. New York: American Book Company, 1960. Chap. 13.
12. ———, eds. *Readings in Guidance: Principles, Practices, Organization and Administration*. New York: David McKay Company, Inc., 1962. Chaps. 10, 11.
13. Delacato, Carl H. *The Elementary School of the Future: A Guide for Parents*. Springfield, Illinois: Charles C. Thomas, Publishers, 1965.
14. Detjen, Ervis W. and Mary F. Detjen. *Elementary School Guidance*.

2nd ed. New York: McGraw-Hill Book Company, Inc., 1963. Chaps. 1-3, 14, 15.

15.   Eckerson, Louise O. "Consultation in the Counselor's Role: Invitation to Dialogue," *Elementary School Guidance and Counseling*, Vol. 1, No. 4, Fall, 1966.

16.   —— and Hyrum M. Smith. "Guidance in the Elementary School." *School Life*, May, 1962, pp. 13-16 and July, 1962, pp. 27-31.

17.   Farwell, Gail F. and Herman J. Peters, eds. *Guidance Readings for Counselors*, Nos. 59, 60, 61. Chicago: Rand McNally & Co., 1960.

18.   Faust, Verne. "Elementary School Counseling," *Developments in Counseling*. Tempe, Arizona: Bureau of Educational Research and Services, College of Education, Arizona State University, 1965.

19.   Foster, Carl M. "The Elementary School Counselor—How Perceived?" *Counselor Education and Supervision*, Vol. 6, No. 2, Winter, 1967, 102-107.

20.   Garry, Ralph. *Guidance Techniques for Elementary Teachers*. Columbus, Ohio: Charles E. Merrill Books, Inc., 1963. Chaps. 1-4, 11, 14, 17, 18.

21.   Glueck, Sheldon and Eleanor Glueck. *Predicting Deliquency and Crime*. Cambridge, Massachusetts: Harvard University Press, 1959. Pp. 114-115.

22.   Gowan, John Curtis and George D. Demos. *The Guidance of Exceptional Children*. New York: David McKay Company, Inc., 1965. Chap. 9.

23.   *Guidance 1964*. Department of Elementary School Principals, National Education Association, 1964.

24.   Harrison, Edna L. "The Counselor's Role in the Early Identification of Gifted Children." *Personnel and Guidance Journal*, Vol. 39, May, 1961, 735-738.

25.   ——. "The Elementary School Counselor and the Gifted Underachiever." *Personnel and Guidance Journal*, Vol. 41, April, 1963, 716-719.

26.   ——. "The Elementary School Counselor's Unique Position." *The School Counselor*, Vol. 11, December, 1963, 107-109.

27.   Hart, Robert N. "Are Elementary Counselors Doing the Job?" *The School Counselor*, Vol. 9, December, 1961, 70-72.

28.   Hatch, Raymond N. and James W. Costar. *Guidance Services in the Elementary School*. Dubuque, Iowa: William C. Brown Company, 1961. Chaps. 1-7.

29.   Heisey, Marion. "A Differential Approach to Elementary Guidance," *Elementary School Guidance and Counseling*, Vol. 1, No. 4, Fall, 1966.

30.   Hill, George E. *Management and Improvement of Guidance*. New York: Appleton-Century-Crofts, 1965. Chap. 3.

31.   ——. "The Start of a Continuous Program of Guidance in Elementary Schools," *Clearing House*, Vol. 38, 1963, 111-116.

32.   —— and Dale F. Nitzschke. "Preparation Programs in Elemen-

tary School Guidance," *Personnel and Guidance Journal,* XL:155-159, October, 1961.

33.   Illinois State Department of Education, Department of Guidance Services, *Guidelines for Elementary Guidance.* Springfield, Illinois: Office of the Superintendent of Public Instruction.

34.   Johnson, Walter F., Buford Stefflre, and Roy A. Edelfelt. *Pupil Personnel and Guidance Services.* New York: McGraw-Hill Book Company, Inc., 1961. Chap. 10.

35.   Knapp, Robert H. *Guidance in Elementary Schools.* Boston: Allyn & Bacon, Inc., 1959.

36.   Koeppe, Richard P. "Elementary School Guidance," in Beck, Carlton E. *Guidelines for Guidance: Readings in the Philosophy of Guidance.* Dubuque, Iowa: William C. Brown Company, 1966. Chap. 3.

37.   Koeppe, Richard P. "The Elementary School Counselor—What is He?" *The School Counselor,* Vol. 12, October, 1964, 11-13.

38.   Kowitz, Gerald T. and Norman C. Kowitz. *Guidance in the Elementary Classroom.* New York: McGraw-Hill Book Company, Inc., 1959. Chaps. 1-3, 6-16.

39.   Lee, J. Murray. "Is a Guidance Consultant Needed in the Elementary Schools?" *Illinois Guidance and Personnel Association Newsletter,* No. 10, 1964, 56-59.

40.   Lloyd-Jones, Esther. *Guidance in Elementary Education.* New York: Bureau of Publications, Teachers College, Columbia University, 1958.

41.   Martinson, Ruth and Harry Smallenburg. *Guidance in Elementary Schools.* Englewood Cliffs, New Jersey: Prentice-Hall, Inc., 1958. Chaps. 1, 2, 4-10, 13-16.

42.   McDaniel, H. B., J. L. Gilmore, J. E. Lallas, and James A. Saum. *Readings in Guidance.* New York: Henry Holt and Company, 1959, No. 3.

43.   McDougall, William P. and Harry H. Reitan. "The Elementary Counselor as Perceived by Elementary Principals," *Personnel and Guidance Journal,* XLII.348-354, December, 1963.

44.   Meeks, Anna R. "Elementary School Counseling." *The School Counselor,* Vol. 10, March, 1963, 108-111.

45.   ———. "Guidance in the Elementary School," *Journal of the N.E.A.,* Vol. 51, March, 1962, 30-32.

46.   ———. "What Can Be Done at the Elementary Level," in Miller, Leonard M., ed. *Guidance for the Underachiever with Superior Ability.* Washington, D.C.: U.S. Office of Education, Dept. of Health, Education, and Welfare, Bulletin No. 25021, 1961. Chap. 3.

47.   National Association of Guidance Supervisors and Counselor Trainers. *Report of the Committee on Training Counselors for the Elementary School,* April, 1960.

48.   Newman, William H. "A Full-Time Counselor in an Elementary School," *Elementary School Journal,* Vol. 56, 1956, 354-357.

49.   Nitzschke, Dale F. and George E. Hill. *The Elementary School Counselor.* Pupil Service Series, Center for Educational Research and

Service, College of Education, Ohio University, Athens, Ohio, 1964.

50.   Norris, Willa. *Occupational Information in Elementary Schools.* Chicago: Science Research Associates, Inc., 1963. Chaps. 1-4.

51.   Oldridge, Buff. "Two Roles for Elementary School Guidance Personnel," *Personnel and Guidance Journal,* Vol. 43, December, 1964, 367-370.

52.   Orgel, R. G. "Contemporary Views of Elementary School Guidance," *The School Counselor.* Vol. 8, October, 1960, 22-27.

53.   Patouillet, Raymond. "Organizing for Guidance in the Elementary School," *Teachers College Board.* Vol. 58, May, 1957, 431-438.

54.   Perrone, Philip A., and David L. Evans. "The Elementary School Counselor? Coordinator? Or What?" *Counselor Education and Supervision,* Vol. 4, Fall, 1964, 28-31.

55.   Peters, Herman L., Anthony C. Riccio, and Joseph J. Quaranta, eds. *Guidance in the Elementary School: A Book of Readings.* New York: The Macmillan Company, 1963. Nos. 1, 4, 6-8.

56.   Peters, Herman J., Bruce Shertzer, and William H. Van Hoose. *Guidance in Elementary Schools.* Chicago: Rand McNally & Co., 1965.

57.   Riccio, Anthony C. "Elementary School Guidance: Its Present Status," *Theory Into Practice,* Vol. 2, 1963, 39-44.

58.   Shertzer, Bruce and Charles T. Lundy. "Administrator Image of an Elementary School Counselor." *The School Counselor,* Vol. 11, May, 1964, 211-214.

59.   Smith, Hyrum M. and Louise O. Eckerson. *Guidance for Children In Elementary Schools.* Washington, D.C.: U.S. Office of Education, Dept. of Health, Education, and Welfare, Bulletin No. 25032, 1963.

60.   ————. *Guidance Services in Elementary Schools: A National Survey.* Washington, D.C.: U.S. Office of Education, Dept. of Health, Education, and Welfare, Bulletin No. 25045, 1966.

61.   *Social Dynamite. The Report of the Conference on Unemployed, Out-of-School Youth in Urban Areas.* Washington, D.C.: National Committee for Children and Youth, 1145 19th Street, N.W., 1961. Pp. 15-16.

62.   Stefflre, Buford. "Research in Guidance: Horizons for the Future," *Theory Into Practice.* Vol. 2, 1963, 44-50.

63.   Stewart, Lawrence H. "Teachers and Counselors Look at Students: Some Implications for Guidance Practice," *Personnel and Guidance Journal,* XXVII:565-568, 1957.

64.   Stripling, Robert O. and David Lane. "Trends in Elementary School Guidance," *National Association for Elementary School Principals Bulletin.* Vol. 63, 1964, 11-15.

65.   Thompson, Jack M. "Current Issues and Problems in Elementary School Guidance," *The School Counselor,* Vol. 13, December, 1965, 77-81.

66.   Trow, William C. "Diagnostician, Ed.S., and Ph.D. Programs for School Psychologists in Michigan," *American Psychologist,* Vol. 16, February, 1961, 84-85.

67.   White House Conference on Children and Youth. *Children in a*

Changing World. Washington, D.C.: U.S. Government Printing Office, 1960. Pp. 7-39.

68. Willey, Roy de Verl. *Guidance in Elementary Education.* Rev. ed. New York: Harper & Row, Publishers, 1960. Chaps. 1-11.

69. Wolfbein, Seymour L. "The Transition from School to Work," *Personnel and Guidance Journal,* XXXVIII:103, October, 1959.

6

Role of the Secondary School Counselor

A basic requirement of any successful business or educational enterprise is that every member of the organization understand (a) what he is expected to accomplish, and (b) how his accomplishments contribute to the major goals of the enterprise. There are two reasons why this requirement is of crucial importance to the secondary school counselor:

1. The school counselor's work brings him into close and continuous contact with a great variety of individuals (teachers, parents, administrators, other pupil personnel specialists, pupils, representatives of community agencies) whose cooperation is essential if a coordinated approach is to be taken in dealing with the educational, vocational, and personal needs of youth. A prerequisite to this cooperation is that these individuals have a

common and reasonably precise understanding of the counselor's role and function.

2. Other pupil personnel specialists, particularly the school psychologists and the school social workers, have identified their roles in considerable detail (see Chapter 7). It is apparent that the roles and functions of these other specialists overlap, to some extent, with the roles and functons that many counselors have assumed.

However, the proper role and function of the secondary school counselor in the total educational program remains a matter of considerable debate today. The resolution of this debate has been complicated by two factors: (a) the complex and intangible nature of counseling and guidance services and (b) the proliferation of forces, both internal and external, that operate on the secondary school counselor.

Reference has already been made to the first of these factors in earlier chapters. It is difficult to isolate the counseling function from attendant guidance services. It is likewise difficult to distinguish between those clerical and administrative activities which should be performed by counselors, and those activities which could be handled more expeditiously and with less expense by administrators and clerical workers. A great variety of surveys have been conducted in an effort to discover what counselors *are doing*. Studies by Arnold (4), Goldstein (16), and Martyn (24) mentioned earlier and by Fredericks (14), Tennyson (33), and the Ohio State Department of Education (27) reveal that counselors are asked to play many roles and fulfill many different responsibilities. These surveys also reveal considerable variation in counselor role and function from school to school and, occasionally, within the same school system. Hill (19) has summarized the conditions that make the counselor's task of role definition a difficult one:

1. The school counselor is a member of a new profession. He is currently experiencing what all new professions experience, lack of understanding as to his functions, lack of acceptance in some quarters, a seeming confusion which is both discouraging and hampering. Even some of his fellow counselors may seem to be lacking in understanding!

2. The school counselor belongs to a public service profession. He is a member of the school team which involves also teachers, supervisors, administrators, other pupil personnel workers. This team is under the general direction of a lay board of education. They all function in close relationship with parents and other citi-

zens. Thus many people get involved when it comes to defining the counselor's functions.

3. The school counselor's work, however it is currently defined, ends up being a complicated, demanding job. If he yearns to simplify it, he finds himself thwarted. This is perhaps just another way of saying that the counselor is in a professional position.

4. The school counselor is in a position which requires that he help young people predict both their own futures and the general future of their society. He walks a tightrope between unwarranted crystal ball gazing on the one hand, and laissez faire fact-distribution on the other hand. He finds himself pressed to predict when he knows the facts are inadequate and his responsibility is not well defined. Thus clarification of his functions is complicated both by the immature character of his tools and by the rapidity of social and economic change.

5. The counselor is engaged in a profession built upon a comparatively new ideal in human society, the ideal of the dignity, the worth, and the independence of each person. This ideal is not so tenaciously rooted in our American culture as we once thought. Attacks upon it currently are as vigorous as they have ever been since the founding of our republic. The counselor finds himself attempting to practice an ideal and also being called upon, in this practice, to defend the ideal. Thus clarification of his functions is further complicated by an ideological battle that forces the counselor to take sides, to stand up and be counted. Day by day he does this in his work, whether or not he is aware of it.

Conditions and Forces that Influence the Counselor's Role

The role and function of the secondary school counselor is presently molded (and distorted) by conditions within the school system and by forces outside the school system. Major *internal* determinants include the following:

1. Administrator attitudes;
2. Teacher attitudes;
3. Student attitudes;
4. Parent-community attitudes;
5. Salary schedules;
6. School size;
7. Counselor-student ratios;
8. Other pupil personnel specialists;
9. Organization of pupil personnel services.

The concepts of counselor role held by various school personnel have been examined in a variety of studies. Schmidt (30) compared the role concepts of 48 counselors with the role concepts held by their principals. Soldahl (32) compared role concepts of counselors with concepts held by counselor educators, teachers, and principals. Gilbert (15) found that sophomores and seniors in high school differed markedly in their concepts of ideal counselor role.

External factors or forces affecting the counselor's role and function include the following:

1. School counselors, through their local, state, and national organizations;
2. Counselor educators, through their local, state, and national organizations;
3. State departments of education, particularly those personnel charged with the responsibility of supervising guidance services and/or certifying guidance specialists;
4. Regional school accreditation associations;
5. Federal Aid to Education legislation;
6. The inter-disciplinary nature of counselor education programs in colleges and universities;
7. Statements by public figures representing education, government, business, labor, and the military services.

One mark of a profession is that its members have been given (or have taken) primary responsibility for determining their role and function. School counselors will not be accorded full professional status until they have assumed more leadership in the matter of role definition. The recent study of the American School Counselor Association is a step in the right direction.

Responsibilities of the Secondary School Counselor

The American School Counselor Association culminated two years of study on the role and function of secondary school counselors by preparing a report, officially adopted at the 1964 San Francisco convention of the American Personnel and Guidance Association, that contained two sections: a statement of policy for secondary school counselors, and a set of guidelines for the implementation of this statement of policy. This report (3) lists and describes in some detail ten professional responsibilities of the secondary school counselor. The report deserves careful attention since it was developed *by* secondary school counselors *for* secondary school counselors. Of roughly 2,900

ASCA members voting on this report, 80 per cent approved the statement of policy and 90 per cent endorsed the guidelines for implementing the policy statement.

1. *Planning and Development of the Guidance Program.* An effective guidance program in a school results from cooperative effort of the entire staff in planning and developing the program. Parents, pupils, and community agencies and organizations can also contribute toward these efforts. It is essential that the objectives of the program and procedures for meeting those objectives be clearly formulated.

In planning and development of the guidance program, the school counselor—

a. Assists in defining objectives of the program.
b. Identifies the guidance needs of pupils.
c. Assists in developing plans of action.
d. Coordinates various aspects of the program in a meaningful sequence of guidance services.
e. Assists in continued guidance program planning and curriculum development.
f. Evaluates the program and assists other members of the school staff in evaluating their contributions to guidance services.

2. *Counseling.* It is essential that the majority of a school counselor's time be devoted to individual or small-group counseling. In a counseling relationship the counselor—

a. Assists the pupil to understand and accept himself as an individual, thereby making it possible for the pupil to express and develop an awareness of his own ideas, feelings, values, and needs.
b. Furnishes personal and environmental information to the pupil, as required, regarding his plans, choices, or problems.
c. Seeks to develop in the pupil a greater ability to cope with and solve problems and an increased competence in making decisions and plans for which he and his parents are responsible.

3. *Pupil Appraisal.* The school counselor assumes the roles of leader and consultant in the school's program of pupil appraisal. In pupil appraisal the school counselor—

a. Coordinates the accumulation of meaningful information concerning pupils through such means as conferences with pupils and parents, standardized test scores, academic records, anecdotal records, personal data forms, records of past experiences, inventories, and rating scales.
b. Coordinates the organization and maintenance of confidential files of pupil data.

c. Interprets pupil information to pupils, parents, teachers, administrators, and others professionally concerned with the pupil.
d. Identifies pupils with special abilities or needs.
e. Takes advantage of available data-processing equipment for facilitating the processing and transmission of pupil data.

4. *Education and Occupational Planning.* In efforts to provide pupils and parents with an understanding of the pupil as an individual in relation to educational and occupational opportunities for his optimal growth and development and to promote self-direction of the pupil, the counselor—

a. Assists the pupil and his parents in relating the pupil's interests, aptitudes, and abilities to current and future educational and occupational opportunities and requirements, long-range educational plans, and choices.
b. Collects and disseminates to pupils and parents information concerning careers, opportunities for further education and training, and school curricular offerings. These activities should be provided through a carefully planned sequence and many include group and individual sessions with pupils and parents, special programs, provision of up-to-date educational and occupational files readily accessible to pupils, bulletin boards, guidance newsletters, and visits by pupils to educational institutions and business and industry.
c. Assists pupils and parents in understanding procedures for making applications and planning for financing the pupil's educational goals beyond high school.
d. Consults with school administrators and members of the school faculty relative to the curricular offerings which will meet the abilities, interests, and needs of the pupils.
e. Assists in the educational and occupational planning of pupils who have withdrawn or who have been graduated from the school.

5. *Referral Work.* The counselor has a major responsibility in making and coordinating referrals to both other specialists in pupil personnel services and public and private agencies in the community. Recognizing his own limitations to provide total service, the counselor—

a. Assists pupils and parents who need such services to be aware of and to accept referral to other specialists in pupil personnel services and community agencies.
b. Maintains a close working relationship in referrals to other specialists in pupil personnel services.
c. Identifies pupils with special needs which require the services of referral sources.
d. Identifies community referral agencies and their services.

    e. Assists in the development of referral procedures and in the maintenance of liaison and cooperative working relationships with community resources.

    f. Provides a follow-up referral of agency recommendations to help the pupil and/or his family work through the problems.

6. *Placement.* The counselor's role in providing placement services for individual pupils involves assisting them in making appropriate choices of school subjects and courses of study and in making transitions from one school level to another, one school to another, and from school to employment. Placement thereby involves the informational services of educational and occupational planning, pupil appraisal, and counseling assistance appropriate to the pupil's choices and progress in school subjects, extracurricular and community activities, and employment. In addition to these other types of assistance which aid effective placement, the counselor—

    a. Helps pupils and parents to make a long-range plan of study for the high school years and assumes responsibility for periodic review and revision of such plans according to need as shown by such factors as changes in the curriculum, pupil appraisal data, school achievement, the pupil's maturity, and new goals.

    b. Plans with administrators and teachers (1) to provide appropriate classroom placement for pupils with special abilities or disabilities and (2) to establish procedures for course selection by pupils and grouping of pupils.

    c. Helps furnish pupil data to the receiving school when a pupil transfers, obtains pupil data for new pupils, and gives individual pupil data to educational and training institutions, prospective employers, and employment agencies.

    d. Assists in giving pupils and parents an understanding of procedures for making applications and financial plans for attending educational or training institutions and for making application for employment.

    e. Confers with admissions personnel and personnel directors and visits educational and training institutions as well as businesses and industries applicable to pupils in his school.

7. *Parent Help.* The counselor holds conferences with parents and acts as a resource person on the growth and development of their children. Through individual or group conferences the counselor—

    a. Interprets the guidance and counseling services of the school.

    b. Assists parents in developing realistic perceptions of their children's aptitudes, abilities, interests, attitudes, and development as related to educational and occupational planning, school progress, and personal-social development.

c. Provides parents with information about school policies and procedures, school course offerings, educational and occupational opportunities and requirements, and resources that can contribute to the fullest development of their children.

8. *Staff Consulting.* The school counselor works closely with members of the administrative and teaching staffs to the end that all of the school's resources are directed toward meeting the needs of individual pupils. In staff consulting the counselor—

a. Shares appropriate individual pupil data with staff members, with due regard to confidentiality.

b. Helps teachers to identify pupils with special needs or problems and keeps teachers informed of developments concerning individual pupils which might have a bearing upon the classroom situation.

c. Participates in in-service training programs, staff meetings, and case conferences through which he discusses his own role, interprets a child-centered point of view, and encourages effective use of pupil data in teaching activities and guidance services given by teachers.

d. Assists teachers to secure materials and develop procedures for a variety of classroom group guidance experiences.

e. Provides materials and information concerning such matters as the characteristics and needs of the pupil population, pupil post-school behavior, and employment trends for use in curriculum study and revision.

9. *Local Research.* Research in guidance is concerned with the study of pupil needs and how well school services and activities are meeting these needs. The school counselor plays a role of leadership in determining the need for research, conducting or cooperating in research studies, and discussing research findings with members of the school staff.

The counselor conducts or cooperates with others in conducting studies in areas such as the following:

a. Follow-up of graduates or pupils who have withdrawn.

b. Relationship of scholastic aptitude and achievement to selection of courses of study, class placement, and post-high-school education and occupational placement.

c. Characteristics, as well as educational and guidance needs of the pupils.

d. The use of records and pupil personnel data.

e. Occupational trends in the community.

f. Evaluation of the school's counseling and guidance services.

10. *Public Relations.* The school counselor has a responsibility for interpreting counseling and guidance services of the school to members of the school staff, parents, and the community. All of his services in the guidance and counseling program have potential public relations value. In discharging his responsibility in public relations, the school counselor may—

a. Participate in programs of civic organizations and other community groups.
b. Prepare or furnish information for articles in school and community publications.
c. Assist in programs for presentation by radio or television.

Since the "grassroots" approach was employed in developing the ASCA statement, it must be regarded as an authoritative and realistic statement on the responsibilities of secondary school counselors. While the author feels that the "statement of policy" section tends to isolate the counselor from his guidance functions, he is in full agreement with the "guidelines" section in which these ten responsibilities have been delineated.

Legal Aspects of the Counselor's Role[1]

There are three principal ways in which a school counselor may become involved with legal issues: first, he may be called upon to testify in court as an "expert witness"; second, because of the intimate nature of the material revealed in the counseling relationship, he may feel obligated to establish his "professional immunity" (the right of privileged communication); third, the counselor may become involved in a civil law suit, where it is alleged that, by either omission or commission, the counselor must be held liable for the acts of a client.

The Counselor as an Expert Witness

McCary (25) has defined an expert witness as a person whose special training and experience in a certain field of knowledge qualifies him to present facts to the court in their search for the truth.

The essential knowledge . . . marks the witness as an expert [and] may . . . be derived from reading aloud, . . .from practice alone, or . . . from both. . . .while a court may decide that, for a particular subject of inquiry, the expert may have to be a member of a given profession, as a doctor, an engineer, or a chemist . . . a

---

[1]Much of the material appearing in this section has been adapted from an article (26) by Frank W. Miller and Richard J. Simpson.

specialist in a particular branch within that profession will not be required. In the interest of growth in law, therefore, it is fortunate that, to date, the tests with respect to a given expert's qualifications have not for the most part [become] crystallized in specific rules, but it is recognized that the matter is one for the trial judge's discretion.

The object of admitting the opinion of the expert into evidence is to inform the jury as to matters with which jurors would not be sufficiently familiar to draw their own inferences.

It should not be understood that, for the purpose of expressing an expert opinion, the witness must hold some form of academic degree, or be a graduate of an institution of higher learning but he should belong to the profession or calling to which the subject matter of the inquiry is related.

McCary concludes:

Once an adequate definition of a competent psychological expert has been established by legal authorities, the problems . . . will be much nearer to a solution. It would not seem . . . improper to suggest that the several states ought now [to] enact legislation providing for the certification or licensing of psychologists, specifying the minimal education and experience background to be required. By so regulating the practice, it would be possible to create a class from which the trial judge could pick an expert without being forced to prejudge the professional competence of the witness. So long as any person may call himself a psychologist, however, it is only natural to expect that there will be resistance to the proposal that the mantle of expert witness be granted to psychologists as a class.

McCary's concern over the ". . . adequate definition of a . . . psychological expert" is well-founded. It is quite interesting to note that definitions of the terms *psychology, psychologist,* and *psychotherapist,* do not appear in either *Words and Phrases* or *The Dictionary of Legal Terms.* Yet, both of these reference books are widely used by the legal profession.

The Counselor and Privileged Communication

At least one Supreme Court case exists where the presiding judge did insist that the psychological expert give complete answers to all questions. Although the expert sought to invoke privileged communication for himself, the judge denied the request. This is interesting because, in that state, the doctor-patient privilege had been previously upheld.

Cottle (10) has identified the many court decisions which have granted privileged communications to the psychotherapist. Two factors seem to operate as this privilege is obtained for psychotherapists: (1) the extreme difficulty in defining psychotherapy, and (2) the difference between the psychotherapist's approach and technique and those of the medical doctor.

Cottle quotes Dean Wigmore, a leading authority in the specialty field of Evidence Law, as outlining four conditions necessary for establishing a privilege against disclosure of communications:

1. The communications must originate in the confidence that they will not be disclosed.
2. The element of confidentiality must be essential to the full and satisfactory maintenance of the relationship between the parties.
3. The relationship must be one which, in the opinion of the community, ought to be fostered.
4. The injury . . . to the relationship by the disclosure of the communication must be greater than the benefit gained thereby for the correct disposal of the litigation.

Pierson (29) has presented a very general discussion of the admissibility of evidence through testimony of expert witnesses, giving major emphasis to actual cross-examination in the courtroom.

Hilton (20) has discussed the ethical conduct of the expert witness. He points out that the purpose of an expert witness in any legal proceeding is to assist the court and jury in their interpretation and understanding of technical evidence. "While an expert witness has never been clearly defined as an agent of the court, regardless of who calls him, he will do well to conduct himself as though he were." However, this author gives no direct attention to the function of the personnel worker as an expert witness.

Carter (8) has defined "immunity" as "an exemption from duties which the law generally requires individuals to perform," and has cited various cases where debate over professional immunity has arisen.

At the time of his writing (1954), Carter felt that counseling profession was suffering from a lack of statutory immunity normally granted to other professions which make use of highly personal information. It was his concern that counselors should know under what circumstances, and to whom, they may make use of privileged communications without being in danger of legal action for libel or slander. He concluded:

It may be reasonable to assume that the general principles of statutory law dealing with privileged communications will be applied to counseling if a case arises that is not within the letter but is plainly within the spirit of the law. It is nevertheless contended that guidance . . . is of the nature that it is in the best interest of the counselor, the counselee, and the public at large, that the profession be granted statutory immunity.

Wrenn (35) in discussing the various implications of handling confidential information which has been disclosed in the counseling relationship, makes a distinction between confidential notes and official office or institutional records. "The counselor may keep confidential notes on his clients in the form of personal memoranda and since these do not become part of the official records of the institution or of his office, they do not have to be released when the personnel records of an individual are taken into custody." It would appear, however, that such "informal" data may still be extracted in court when the counselor is placed under oath.

Bakken (6) has studied the legal foundations of the many aspects of student personnel services in state colleges and universities in the United States. In this comprehensive effort, Bakken found certain interesting facts about privileged communications.

Bakken notes from the *Iowa Law Review* remarks concerning the nature of professional relationships. These state that there are three conditions to be fulfilled under privileged communication: (1) There must be one who is legally a lawyer, a doctor, or minister; (2) The party must have been acting in an official capacity at the time the communication was made; and (3) The person making the communication must have regarded the professional man as his doctor, lawyer, or minister. Psychologists could be added to the list of professionals referred to above in those states which granted them privileged communication status. The *Iowa Law Review* article went on to say that some courts and most writers doubted the wisdom of the statutes on privileged communications and, consequently, would apply them very strictly. In his own research, Bakken found no doctor-patient privilege in England or in about half of the American states.

Basing an observation on court decisions to which Bakken refers, it appears that it is safe for a counselor to write letters of recommendation without fear of liability for libel or slander. Further, it appears safe for a counselor to communicate with parents about their children's condition without being subject to suit for damages.

Bakken found, as Wrenn has suggested, that data can be subpoenaed from a student's file, and data not entered officially could be obtainable only by placing the counselor under subpoena and questioning him in court.

Schmidt (31) has investigated professional recognition, privileged communication, libel, slander, the right of privacy, malpractice, and criminal liability as they relate to the counseling psychologist.

At the time of his writing, Schmidt found that "... there seem to be no cases on record involving a counselor in a litigation in which a question of privileged communication [is] involved."

Louisell (23) has documented the growing acceptance of the confidential nature of the work done by psychologists and counselors. He has also reviewed the matter of privileged communication:

> Counseling services, while action might be on a counselor-client or patient status, were not given privileged communication status except in six states (Arkansas, Georgia, Kentucky, Tennessee, New York, Washington) .... In all states except the six mentioned, counseling relationships, while professionally confidential, were not legally confidential.

Michigan and Indiana now have legislation which would appear to give the school counselor privileged communication status. Michigan's statute is particularly inclusive but has never been tested in court:

> No teacher, guidance officer, school executive, or other professional person engaged in character building in the public schools or in any other educational institution, including any clerical worker of such schools and institutions, who maintains records of students' behavior or who has such records in his custody, or who receives in confidence communications from students or other juveniles, shall be allowed in any proceedings, civil or criminal, in any court of this state, to disclose any information obtained by him from such records or such communications; nor to produce such records or transcript thereof. Provided, that any such testimony may be given, with the consent of the person so confiding or to whom such records relate, if such person be twenty-one years of age or over, or if such person be a minor, with the consent of his or her parent or legal guardian.[2]

The Counselor and Criminal Liability

Twenty-seven states have medical legislation which specifically applies or has been interpreted by courts to apply to the treatment of both physical and mental conditions. In these states, the psychological counselor is technically without legal right to practice. In nine states,

---

[2]Michigan Statutes Annual, Sec. 27, p. 934.

where restrictions in the treatment of "disease" may or may not be considered applicable to the treatment of mental ailments, the counselor was in a questionable position. Only in the remaining twelve states where medical practices laws were specifically inapplicable to the treatment of mental ailments or to the use of medical means of treatment, was the counselor secure with respect to the avoidance of criminal liability.

The Counselor and Civil Liability (The Wisconsin Supreme Court Case: A Much Needed Precedent)

That the Iverson case is in many ways a classic is a statement which needs little defense. Throughout the literature the statement recurs to the effect that no cases are on record in which legal aspects of the counselor-client relationship have been tested in court. The actual legal immunity of the counselor; that is, his right to privileged communication, has not been tried in the courts. Nowhere in the literature surveyed in connection with this article were cases found where school guidance and personnel workers appeared in court as expert witnesses.

General Background of the Case:

Dr. Ralph G. Iverson, a Professor of Education holding a Ph.D. degree, is the Director of Student Personnel Services, which services include guidance and counseling, at Stout State College, Menominee, Wisconsin.

Jeannie Bogust, the daughter of the plaintiffs, was a student at Stout State College. On November 11, 1957 she sought the services of the defendant in his official capacity as Director of Student Personnel Services. At this time, Dr. Iverson began administering aptitude, achievement, and personality tests to her, and interviewed her subsequently.

On April 15, 1958, Dr. Iverson suggested a termination of future interviews and it appears that the final interview took place on this date.

Forty-two days later, on May 27, 1958, Jeannie Bogust committed suicide.

Complaint as Alleged by Mr. and Mrs. Bogust:

The plaintiffs, Mr. and Mrs. Bogust, charged that Mr. Iverson was negligent with their daughter in that he:

1. Failed to secure or attempt to secure emergency psychiatric treatment after he was aware or should have been aware of her inability to care for the safety of herself;

2. Failed at all times to advise Mr. and Mrs. Bogust or contact them concerning the true mental and emotional state of their said daughter, thus preventing them from securing proper medical care for her;

3. Failed to provide proper student guidance.

The plaintiffs sought the following judgment against Mr. Iverson in their suit:

1. $3,500 for funeral expenses

2. $15,000 for general damages

3. For costs, disbursements, and attorney's fees of the action.

Defense in Behalf of Mr. Iverson:

Permission was granted by the Wisconsin State Supreme Court for briefs to be filed in behalf of Mr. Iverson by the American Personnel and Guidance Association, the National Education Association, and the Wisconsin Education Association. Each of these associations retained separate law firms to prepare their respective briefs.

In their case against Mr. Iverson, the plaintiffs, Mr. and Mrs. Bogust, asked the court to accept certain bare allegations as stating a necessary course of action based upon the existence of a legal duty (tort). The attorneys for the American Personnel and Guidance Association found that the plaintiffs were inclined to use assumptions as bases of fact. The amicus curiae brief of the American Personnel and Guidance Association pointed out that ". . . court needs no citation for the statement of law that assumptions are not facts." On this basis, then, the attorneys challenged or demurred against, the charges which the plaintiffs made.

The Judgment:

"Jeannie Bogust was, according to the complaint, suffering emotional disturbances when she first sought counseling from defendant. Defendant is a teacher, a professor of education. Nowhere is it alleged that he has had any education, training or experience in the medical field. No case has been cited to the Court which suggests that a teacher is an insurer or guarantor of the health, welfare or safety of his pupils. To hold that a teacher who has had no training, education or experience in medical fields is required to recognize in a student a condition, the diagnosis of which is in a specialized and technical medical field, would require a duty beyond reason. The Court feels that such a requirement is too high and that no duty can be spelled from such a situation. In the absence of duty there can be no liability."

It is apparent that a valuable precedent now exists whereby a counselor was not held civilly liable for the suicide of a client. However, since the counselor in this decision was not held responsible for the diagnosis and/or referral of his client, the value of the precedent is offset, to some extent, by an interpretation of counselor responsibility that is contrary to current professional opinion and state certification requirements.

Summary

The debate over the proper role and function of the secondary school counselor has been difficult to resolve. The major causes of this difficulty may be found in the complex and intangible nature of counseling and guidance services and the multitude of internal and external forces that influence the attitudes and actions of the counselor. School counselors are beginning to assume more leadership in determining their proper role and function. Such leadership is necessary if counselors are to be accorded full professional status.

Until full professional status has been attained, it is doubtful whether counselors will be given much recognition by courts of law, either as *expert witnesses* or as enjoying *privileged communication*. However, it appears that legal precedent has been established which protects counselors from being held responsible for the actions of their clients.

The primary function of the secondary school counselor is, of course, one of implementing the various services of the guidance program. In so doing, he has *service, referral, consultative*, and *supportive* roles to fulfill. Specifically, we may identify the counselor's role as one of:

1. Appraising student ability, achievement, attitudes, and needs;
2. Coordinating this data and supervising its maintenance through cumulative records;
3. Counseling with students;
4. Identifying students with special needs and referring these pupils to other specialists in pupil personnel services and to public and private agencies in the community;
5. Working with teachers on student problems;
6. Collecting, organizing, and maintaining information of an educational, vocational, and environmental nature;
7. Presenting this information to students individually, and through group procedures such as assemblies, homeroom programs, career conferences, and college days;
8. Encouraging and assisting in the in-service education of all staff-members;

9. Consulting with parents on pupil problems of mutual concern to school and home;
10. Serving in a public-relations capacity by maintaining close working relationships with various community agencies;
11. Working in close cooperation with other pupil personnel specialists in the school;
12. Implementing policies delegated by the administration and by appropriate faculty committees;
13. Planning and conducting research designed to improve (a) the total educational program and (b) guidance services available to students.

Bibliography

1. Adams, John F. *Counseling and Guidance: A Summary View*. New York: The Macmillan Company, 1965. Part 4, Chap. 1.
2. American Personnel and Guidance Association. "The Counselor: Professional Preparation and Role," *Personnel and Guidance Journal*, 42:536-541, January, 1964.
3. American School Counselor Association. *Statement of Policy for Secondary School Counselors and Guidelines for Implementation of the ASCA Statement of Policy for Secondary School Counselors*. Washington, D.C.: American Personnel and Guidance Association, 1964.
4. Arnold, Dwight L. "Time Spent by Counselors and Deans on Various Activities," *Occupations*, XXVII:391-93, March, 1949.
5. Association for Counselor Education and Supervision. *Standards for Counselor Education in the Preparation of Secondary School Counselors*. Washington, D.C.: American Personnel and Guidance Association, 1964.
6. Bakken, Clarence J. "An Analysis of the Legal Basis for Operating Selected Student Personnel Services in State Tax-Supported Four-Year Colleges and Universities in the United States." Unpublished doctoral dissertation, University of Denver, March, 1959.
7. Byrne, Richard Hill. *The School Counselor*. Boston: Houghton Mifflin Company, 1963, Chap. 13.
8. Carter, Thomas M. "Professional Immunity for Guidance Counselors," *Personnel and Guidance Journal*, 33:130-135, November, 1954.
9. Cottingham, Harold F. *Guidance in the Junior High School*. Bloomington, Illinois: McKnight & McKnight Publishing Co., 1961. Chaps. 1, 3, 5, 8-14.
10. Cottle, Martha O. "Witnesses—Privilege—Communications to Psychotherapists," *University of Kansas Law Review*, Vol. 4, May, 1956, 597-599.
11. Crow, Lester D. and Alice Crow. *An Introduction to Guidance*. 2nd ed. New York: American Book Company, 1960. Chaps. 14, 15.
12. ———, eds. *Readings in Guidance: Principles, Practices, Organiza-*

tion and Administration. New York: David McKay Company, Inc., 1962. Chaps. 11, 12.

13.   Farwell, Gail F. and Herman J. Peters, eds. *Guidance Readings for Counselors.* Chicago: Rand McNally & Co., 1960. No. 51, Chap. 8.

14.   Fredericks, J. R. "Concepts of the Role of the Counselor in Selected Secondary Schools as Held by the Counselor and Other Professional Personnel." Unpublished doctoral dissertation, University of Missouri, 1961.

15.   Gilbert, Norman S. "When the Counselor Is a Disciplinarian," *Personnel and Guidance Journal,* XLIII, January, 1965, 485-491.

16.   Goldstein, H. A. "Job Analysis of Junior and Senior High School Counselors," *Industrial Arts and Vocational Education,* No. 39, 1950.

17.   Gowan, John Curtis and George D. Demos. *The Guidance of Exceptional Children.* New York: David McKay Company, Inc., 1965. Chap. 11.

18.   Hatch, Raymond N., Paul L. Dressel, and James W. Costar. *Guidance Services in the Secondary Schools.* Dubuque, Iowa: William C. Brown Company, 1963. Chap. 1.

19.   Hill, George E. *Management and Improvement of Guidance.* New York: Appleton-Century-Crofts, 1965, Pp. 98, 109.

20.   Hilton, Ordway, "Ethics of the Expert Witness," *The Alabama Lawyer,* Vol. 17, October, 1956, 419-425.

21.   Johnson, Mauritz, Jr., William E. Busacher, and Fred Q. Bowman, Jr. *Junior High School Guidance.* New York: Harper and Brothers, 1961. Chaps. 1-10, 12.

22.   Jones, Arthur J. *Principles of Guidance.* 5th ed. New York: McGraw-Hill Book Company, Inc., 1963. Chap. 8.

23.   Louisell, David W. "The Psychologist in Today's Legal World," *Minnesota Law Review,* Vol. 39 (Part 1), 235-272; Vol. 41 (Part 2), 731-750.

24.   Martyn, Kenneth A. Report on doctoral dissertation, Stanford University. *California Guidance Newsletter,* September, 1950.

25.   McCary, J. L. "The Psychologist in Court," *Chicago-Kent Law Review,* Vol. 33, June, 1955, 230-240.

26.   Miller, Frank W. and Richard J. Simpson. "Some Legal Aspects of the Counselor-Client Relationship," *Counselor Education and Supervision,* Vol. 1, Fall, 1961, 19-29.

27.   Ohio State Department of Education and Ohio State University Research Staff. *Guidance in Ohio.* Columbus: Ohio State Department of Education, Division of Guidance and Testing, 1961.

28.   Peters, Herman J., *et al,* eds. *Counseling: Selected Readings.* Columbus, Ohio: Charles E. Merrill Books, Inc., 1962. Sec. I-No. 3, Sec. II-No. 6-9.

29.   Pierson, W. DeVier. "Evidence: Examination of Expert Witnesses," *Oklahoma Law Review,* Vol. 9, November, 1956, 425-437.

30.   Schmidt, Lyle D. "Concepts of the Role of Secondary School Counselors," Unpublished doctoral dissertation, University of Missouri, 1959.

31.   ———. "Legal Implications for Counseling Psychologists," *University Testing and Counseling Service Report No. 19*. Columbia: University of Missouri, February, 1959.

32.   Soldahl, Thomas A. "Secondary School Counselors Concept of Role in Relation to Personal Data and Psychogenic Needs," Unpublished doctoral dissertation, Kent State University, 1962.

33.   Tennyson, W. W. "Time: The Counselor's Dilemma!" *Personnel and Guidance Journal*, 37:129-135, October, 1956.

34.   Ware, Martha L., ed. *Law of Guidance and Counseling*. Cincinnati: W. H. Anderson Company, 1964.

35.   Wrenn, C. Gilbert, "The Ethics of Counseling," *Educational and Psychological Measurement*, Vol. XII, No. 2, Summer, 1952, 161-177.

7

Guidance Within Pupil Personnel Services

The need for a comprehensive and coordinated program of pupil personnel services to meet the problems and needs of school children has been recognized for some time. The ideal of equal educational opportunity cannot be attained unless specialized services are provided for children and youths who encounter difficulty in participating constructively in the school program. However, attempts by local school administrators to translate this recognition into action have been hampered by a general dearth of information relative to the scope of these services and to the organizational patterns and administrative practices which would insure their effective operation.

Most commonly included in pupil personnel services are the areas of *attendance, guidance, school health, school social work,* and *school psychological services.* Some school districts have also included *speech correction* and special programs for the *physically handicapped* and *mentally retarded* in their concept of pupil personnel services. However, this is not generally the case. "It is becoming increasingly accepted that special education programs provided for atypical or exceptional children—the physically handicapped, emotionally disturbed, and mentally retarded—children whose needs tend to differentiate them from the larger group of pupils in attendance at the public schools, should be classified as instructional rather than pupil personnel services (4)."

Guidelines for changing existing autonomous, provincial, and overlapping pupil services into a coordinated and effective program of pupil personnel services have been issued by the Council of Chief State School Officers (4). These guidelines also serve to identify the underlying principles that must be observed when guidance services are organized and administered:

1. Assignment and definition of administrative responsibility for pupil personnel services and the establishment of lines of communication and responsibility between this grouping of services and other areas of department or local school organization.

2. Definition of the specific functions of each service, including their relationship within pupil personnel services to other phases of the educational program and to referral resources and related agencies.

3. Development, within the staff of the total educational organization, of an understanding of the functions and contributions of pupil personnel services in relation to individual pupils and in support of the total instructional program.

4. Identification of the common characteristics in the professional preparation of various staff members in pupil personnel services—principles and techniques, study of human growth and development, the use of referral resources, and an orientation to the educational setting upon which the more advanced and specific preparations are built.

5. Development of a team approach to the several pupil personnel services involving activities such as the cooperative use of pupil records, case conferences, and in-service education of staff members.

All pupil personnel services should function to facilitate the progress and development of individual pupils. All staff members in pupil personnel services should function in cooperation with other school staff members in translating the work with individual pupils into action for broad educational planning.

The Role of the Administrator in Pupil Personnel Services

The superintendent must assume the responsibility for initiating, developing, and coordinating pupil personnel services, or he must delegate this responsibility. In some districts, the responsibility has been delegated to an assistant superintendent or another administrator as part of his overall function. In other districts, a Director of Pupil Personnel Services has been appointed. The report (8) of a U.S. Office of Education study of pupil personnel services in eight urban school districts states, "There appeared to be a relationship between delegation of responsibility and awareness of the need for changing the structure. In those school systems where the activities of the pupil personnel workers were coordinated and supervised by a full-time director of the program, superintendents were relatively satisfied with the current organizational structure."

The administrator's role in pupil personnel services is primarily one of *democratic leadership* during the initial developmental stages of the program and one of *consistent support* once the program has become adequately organized. It is more often lack of leadership than authoritarian direction that handicaps the budding pupil personnel program. The *leadership* function is fulfilled through:

1. Sponsoring a preliminary survey of the current educational, emotional, social, physical, and vocational needs of the pupil population;
2. Sponsoring a preliminary survey of existing school and community services, facilities, and resources in order to determine the nature and extent of the gap existing between pupil needs and existing school and community resources;
3. Determining, with the assistance of pupil personnel specialists, the type of administrative organization that will be most effective in meeting the particular needs of the school district;
4. Discussing budgetary requirements of the pupil personnel program with the board of education well in advance of the submission of the budget in order to insure approval of the additional expenditures;
5. Encouraging preliminary meetings of the school staff to discuss various approaches to the establishment of the pupil personnel program;
6. Selecting a pre-organization committee whose membership is acceptable to the faculty;

7. Cooperating with this committee in determining a plan of action;
8. Providing sufficient time so that the chosen plan of action can be carried out;
9. Selecting staff members who are interested, capable, and qualified.

It is the administrator who must encourage teachers to feel that they play a vital role in the program of pupil personnel services. It is important that *all* members of the staff accept each other as professional equals, and each as professionally competent in his own field. All specialized services must be identified and interpreted in terms of their relationship to the instructional program and to each other. The administrator's role in facilitating this *interior cooperation and communication* is crucial to the eventual effectiveness of the pupil personnel program.

The *support* function of the administrator is fulfilled through:

1. Providing the necessary space, facilities, equipment and supplies for the program;
2. Arranging in-service education activities for staff members;
3. Encouraging staff members to improve their professional competencies through participation in workshops and institutes, and by enrollment in pertinent additional graduate courses;
4. Encouraging the constant evaluation of the pupil personnel program and supporting changes that appear to be necessary as a result of such evaluation;
5. Reducing to a minimum the clerical and administrative responsibilities of pupil personnel specialists;
6. Continuously interpreting the pupil personnel program to the community.

Attendance Services

The primary objective of these services is to insure regular attendance of all school-age children who should be in school. A second concern is to see that all school-age children who are unable to participate in the regular school program because of mental, physical, or emotional handicaps are properly exempted, and are permitted to engage in educational programs appropriate to their needs.

Attendance personnel at local levels should be qualified to give leadership to a program designed to promote positive pupil and parent attitudes toward regular school attendance. They should also be able to assist teachers in the early identification of patterns of non-attendance indicative of inadequate pupil adjustment. They should be willing and able to take immediate action regarding problems of non-attendance, using a case-work approach, and obtaining the cooperation of parents, teachers, other pupil personnel workers, and appropriate community agencies. They should also be responsible for supervising the school's program of child accounting, including the school census, the issuance of employment certificates, and registers of attendance.

Some districts hire attendance officers. Other districts delegate attendance responsibilities to assistant principals, principals, assistant superintendents, non-professional staff members, and others.

Health Services

The objectives of the school health program are (a) to bring each child, through health services and counseling, into optimum condition to profit from the educational program; (b) to develop in each child a sense of responsibility for his own health, as well as the health of others; and (c) to gain an understanding of the principles upon which good health is based. Personnel in health services have the responsibility for initiating and implementing periodic health examinations for every child. They also have the responsibility for providing an adequate follow-up to these health examinations through the maintenance of health records and the proper dissemination of appropriate health information to other school personnel.

Continuing day-to-day health service is the responsibility of the school nurse, the dental hygienist, and (in larger school systems) the specialists in vision, hearing, and health. In smaller systems, this responsibility is generally shared by the school physician and school nurse.

Psychological Services

School psychological services function as an integral part of the total school program, in cooperation with all school personnel in order to achieve the mutual goal of providing each child with an opportunity for maximum learning, adjustment, and development in relation to his potentialities.

The school psychologist applies his specialized knowledge of human behavior and personality, child growth and development, learning processes, interpersonal relationships, and assessment techniques to the study of the individual child. He interprets his findings to other school personnel and cooperates with them in planning the best possible program for fulfilling the needs of each child. The major portion of his time is usually spent in the individual study of children having the following types of problems: mental and educational retardation, improper school placement, psychological difficulties due to physical handicaps, special types of learning difficulties, and inadequate adjustment to peer groups or to the educational environment.

According to the by-laws of the American Psychological Association, Division of School Psychologists, "a school psychologist is a psychologist, a major portion of whose work is (a) the application of clinical psychological techniques to children and adolescents presenting problems in school, or (b) the psychological supervision of psychologists doing such work." In 1955, this Association recommended a ratio of 1 school psychologist for every 3,000 pupils. A more recent statement from the Association recommends a ratio of 1 to every 2,000 students with a still lower ratio in rural areas where much time must be given to travel. It is difficult to determine the number of our school districts who employ school psychologists, since the roles of the school counselor and school psychologist often overlap and many states still do not distinguish between the two specialties in their certification requirements. However these recommended ratios, if observed, would limit the school psychologist to a few carefully selected individual cases. The major portion of his time would be devoted to serving as a resource person for other professional staff members.

Bower (1) identifies the following duties of the school psychologist:

Informs school personnel and parents regarding the special services he is prepared to render.

Accepts for study individuals referred to him by school personnel.

Studies the problems and potentialities of individuals referred to him, formulates procedures to be followed in the cases of individuals studied, and provides or helps to secure the treatment needed.

Confers with school personnel who are working with an individual studied regarding the results of the study, interprets his findings, recommends the treatment needed to correct the individual's difficulty, and suggests ways in which all can cooperate in giving the treatment.

Keeps informed regarding the various services available in the community that can be used in helping individuals to solve their problems and is prepared to secure the particular services for the individual who needs them.

Helps school personnel to understand the problems and needs that
children commonly have at different age levels.

Helps school personnel to understand the causes underlying various
kinds of behavior and methods of helping each child to develop
desirable behavioral patterns.

Helps members of the community to understand the causes underlying various kinds of behavior and to understand the intellectual
needs of children, youth, and adults.

Promotes and engages in the research that is needed to help each
child and youth to work successfully at a rate and at a level
commensurate with his potentialities.

A conference sponsored by the Public Health Service for the purpose of studying the functions, qualifications, and training of school
psychologists (generally known as the Thayer Conference) concluded
its study (7) by publishing a report that included the following statements:

While only the psychologist can perform some of his functions,
a large share of his contribution will be in the form of adding to
the resources that other school personnel will use. His aim is
neither to take over the functions of a classroom teacher nor to
endeavor to have the teacher take over the unique functions of
the psychologist.

Definition. The school psychologist is a psychologist with
training and experience in education. He uses his specialized
knowledge of assessment, learning, and interpersonal relationships
to assist school personnel to enrich the experience and growth of
all children, and to recognize and deal with exceptional children.

Functions. The school psychologist serves in an advisory capacity to school personnel and performs the following functions:

1. Measuring and interpreting the intellectual, social, and emotional development of children.
2. Identifying exceptional children and collaborating in the planning of appropriate educational and social placements and
programs.
3. Developing ways to facilitate the learning and adjustment of
children.
4. Encouraging and initiating research, and helping to utilize research findings for the solution of school problems.
5. Diagnosing educational and personal disabilities, and collaborating in the planning of re-educational programs.

Levels. Two levels of functioning and training are recommended. The position of *school psychologist* involves such broad comprehensive preparation at a high level that these responsibilities

can be met only with doctoral training or its equivalent. This training should consist of four years of graduate study, one of which should be a year of internship. The position of *psychological examiner* is considered essential. The training for this position should be a two-year graduate program, of which one-half year should be an internship. Such training should equip the examiner to perform many psychological services.[1]

Camp (2) found that only twenty-five states had certification requirements for school psychologists as of 1963.

Social Work Services

The school social worker, or visiting teacher, is another specialist who plays an important role in the school's guidance program. One of the most comprehensive descriptions of the functions and activities of the school social worker is contained in a report of the Committee on Credentials for Pupil Personnel Services of the California State Department of Education (3).

Functions of the School Social Worker

The service offered by the school social worker is a specialized form of social case work identified with an integral part of the program of the public school. It is a method of helping individual children with emotional conflicts which are interfering with their development and their use of the school and of increasing the value of the work of the classroom teacher. It involves the following as functions of the school social worker:

1. Help children, either individually or as part of a group, in an effort to assist them toward a better emotional development and to make use of the school.
   (a) Help children use special school services, such as health service, psychometric testing, special classes, home instruction, etc.
   (b) Help children use other community resources through referral or cooperative planning with other community social agencies.

2. Help parents, either individually or as part of a group, in order to improve parent-child relationships, school and home relationships, and home and community relationships.

3. Help teachers and other school personnel.
   (a) Help teachers to identify difficulty early through continued interpretation and awareness of children's needs (physical and emotional).

---

[1]Used with permission of the American Psychological Association.

(b) Increase understanding of the teacher's role in meeting the child's needs and the meaning of teacher-pupil relationships in the child's development.

(c) Assist teachers to develop classroom programs to meet children's needs consistent with general classroom goals and activities.

(d) Work with teachers and teacher groups toward continued improvement of curriculum, environment, teachers' working conditions, etc., for the purpose of providing children with satisfying school experiences.

4. Contribute toward the general program of the school.
   (a) Develop and plan with school personnel concerned the social worker's program in the school, and integrate it with other specialized services.
   (b) Provide leadership or participate in in-service training programs, workshops, lecture series, extension classes in the field of social and emotional development of children; and organize and/or conduct parent study groups.
   (c) Represent the school in various committees for community planning—case-study committee, guidance committee, welfare councils, coordinating councils.
   (d) Service as liaison agent between school and other community agencies concerned with welfare of children and families—probation office, county welfare, family and children's agencies, psychiatric clinics, law enforcement agencies.
   (e) Interpret program to community groups and individual citizens, parents, other educators, and community agencies.
   (f) Serve as consultant to research department in schools and perform special assignments such as cooperating in the development of special projects, conducting studies, etc.
   (g) Participate in school's curriculum development program.
   (h) Evaluate the school's program in terms of the child's social and emotional needs, directing attention to the use of resources to meet those needs.

5. Assist school in working closely with the home and the community.

6. Perform necessary administrative and supervisory duties.
   (a) Develop, plan, and evaluate school social work program with administrators.
   (b) Integrate program with all other school services.
   (c) Develop field training program and supervise student school social workers.
   (d) If head of department, plan meetings, assign work, organize staff development program, etc.
   (e) Conduct research studies as related to school social work.

(f) Collaborate with teacher training institutions in the development of training programs.

(g) In cooperation with the school personnel, develop procedures for referral, referral forms, and other necessary forms of interschool communications.

(h) Develop library for use of teachers and parents.

7. Participate in the training of teachers.

Activities Commonly Performed by the School Social Worker

The school social worker, in fulfilling the functions of the position, takes part in the following activities to assist pupil and teacher and to integrate the school's program for the individual pupil with that of the home and the community.

1. Serve pupils.

(a) Consult with teachers and those having immediate responsibility for the child in school. The purpose of such consultation is to gain an understanding of the child's difficulties and the best approach to treatment. Emphasis is placed on the teacher's role in meeting the child's needs and the meaning of teacher-pupil relationships in the child's development.

(b) Perform intensive case work with the child, either individually or as part of a group, in an effort to assist him toward a better emotional adjustment.

(c) Perform intensive case work with the parents, either individually or as part of a group, in order to improve the parent-child relationships.

(d) Interview children to prepare them to use other school services. This frequently involves working through resistance interpreting functions of other school personnel, etc.

(e) Interview parents and children for referral to other community agencies. This may involve a number of interviews helping the parent recognize his feelings about the child, his problem, developing understanding and a desire for help from the community agency involved.

(f) Act as consultant in in-service training programs and parent study groups in the field of the social and emotional development of children.

(g) Act as a representative of the school on various committees for community planning.

(h) Consult cooperatively with staff psychiatrists, clinical psychologists, deans, counselors, nurses, physicians, etc.

(i) Participate in the development and use of cumulative records.

(j) Observe children in classroom and on playground.

(k) Maintain social case records.

> (l) Participate in the development and maintenance of a li-
> brary in the field of special interest, making pamphlets,
> etc., available to parents and teachers.

2. Assist teachers.
   (a) Arrange for, conduct, and participate in individual and
       group conferences.
   (b) Collect and provide for use of teachers, books, periodicals,
       pamphlets, and other materials which may be of assistance
       in increasing their understanding of various types of emo-
       tional and behavior problems.
   (c) Add to teachers' understanding of children through indi-
       vidual interviews or group discussion in which dynamics
       of behavior and causative factors involved are interpreted.
   (d) Help the teacher to deal with problems through under-
       standing of her own strengths and a recognition of class-
       room and administrative limitations. This involves use of
       social case work skills in relieving pressures operating on
       teacher and clarifying her role in treatment.
   (e) Help teacher to differentiate between problems arising from
       natural developmental phases or temporary situations and
       those representing abnormal reactions to common situa-
       tions.
   (f) Help teachers to use the information in cumulative folder
       to (1) identify problems early or (2) increase understand-
       ing of child in classroom.
   (g) Help teachers use information on children and families
       professionally, guarding its confidential nature.
   (h) Help teachers understand emotional interactions and re-
       sponses—their own as well as those of children and parents.
   (i) Help teachers by contributing toward general school pro-
       gram.
   (j) Help teachers by assisting the school to work closely with
       the home and the community.

It is clear that the roles of the school social worker, or visiting
teacher, often overlap with those of the school counselor and school
psychologist. In the past, school social workers have been employed
more frequently at the elementary school level than at the secondary
level since (a) there appeared to be a greater need for preventive
work at the elementary level and (b) the secondary level was more
likely to have school counselors performing similar services.

Since school social workers have such diverse responsibilities, it is
difficult to determine minimum or maximum case loads. A survey of
thirty-nine large cities made in 1958 by the Toledo Council of Social
Agencies indicated that the most common ratio seemed to be 1

worker to every 2 or 3 elementary schools, or to 1 high school of 2,500 pupils. However, the ratio of pupils to school social workers ranged from a low of 793 to a high of 9,000 with a median of 3,212. Such large ratios are forcing the school social worker into more of a consultative role. We may expect to find that, in the future, social workers will be spending less of their time working with individual pupils and a great deal more of their time serving as consultants to classroom teachers, both on an individual basis and through a case conference approach aimed at facilitating the in-service training of classroom teachers. We may also expect to find social workers used more and more as consultants in curriculum planning, due to their extensive training in child development and their experience in recognizing and understanding child problems and needs.

At the present time, thirty states have special certification requirements for the school social worker. These requirements generally include a degree in social work and additional specialized training in education. However, certification requirements can hardly be considered standardized at the present time. Some states require a teaching certificate, and some do not. Some states require special clinical or social work experience, and some do not. This diversity in training requirements is even greater among our larger cities. Only five of the thirty-nine cities represented in the Toledo survey reported that a master's degree in social work was the basic requirement. All others reported the basic requirement to be state teacher certification, supplemented by specialized course work in child psychology, mental hygiene, counseling, etc. As of 1958, Phoenix, Arizona required its social workers to have one year of graduate training in social work, five years of social work experience, and an elementary teacher's certificate. Detroit, Michigan required a teaching certificate, three years of teaching experience, 30 hours of graduate study in social work, and 500 hours of field work. Rochester, New York required a master's degree in social work. Dayton, Ohio hired visiting teachers with no definite training requirements.

The present professional organization for these specialists is the National Association of Social Workers, formerly known as the American Association of Visiting Teachers and the National Association of School Social Workers.

Interprofessional Research Commission on Pupil Personnel Services

Early in 1961, the U.S. Office of Education sponsored a series of meetings of representatives from the national offices of 13 associations which supply and use pupil personnel services. These meetings led to the formal organization of the Interprofessional Research Commission on Pupil Personnel Services. In 1962, the Commission applied for and received a grant of more than $1.3 million from the National Institute of Mental Health to conduct a 5-year program of research and demonstration in pupil personnel services. The following statement, taken from the proposal for financial support of the Commission, describes its purpose:

> Within any one school, a child's symptoms of poor mental health may become the concern of the teacher, principal, school psychologist, school social worker, attendance coordinator, counselor, speech clinician, or school nurse, each working with little knowledge of what the others are doing. The aim of pupil personnel services in helping such a child is to provide a complete evaluation of the problem and the factors contributing to it, followed by a unified program in which school personnel and parents cooperate. Fragmented aid by many persons may result in no aid, or may even be detrimental to the child. The causes of trouble rather than its symptoms demand professional attention from both instructional personnel and specialists competent to assess the situation and make recommendations for the benefit of the child.
>
> The growth of pupil personnel services has been rapid but uncoordinated. Inasmuch as the services have been offered by school systems, community mental health clinics, public health departments, and other organizations, they have suffered from a lack of interprofessional communication which has resulted in some instances in unnecessary inefficiency and duplication. While excellent programs exist in some quarters, specialists have not generally understood fully the roles of other professional personnel, and children have not, as a rule, been the recipients of unified programs through cooperative planning. Since the child is a complex being, the services required for his effective development are multiple; they should be coordinated in such a manner as to make their maximum contribution.
>
> One of the aims of the Interprofessional Research Commission on Pupil Personnel Services is the 'Analysis and evaluation of organizational and administrative patterns of pupil personnel services; establishment of pilot demonstration centers to test and evaluate practices in pupil personnel organization and relationships.'

The Commission has identified the following areas as requiring research and demonstration:

> 1. Organization and administration of pupil personnel services for school systems of different sizes, with different personnel and student bodies.

2. Relation of pupil personnel services to instruction.
3. Effective mental health practices.
4. Identification of children in need of pupil personnel services.
5. Functions and program of pupil personnel services.
6. Evaluation of pupil personnel services.
7. Pupil personnel services and community relations.
8. Interprofessional relations.
9. Intraprofessional problems of recruitment, training, certification, and career development.

Associations represented on the Commission include the American Academy of Pediatrics, American Association of School Administrators, American Medical Association, American Nurses Association, American Personnel and Guidance Association, American Psychiatric Association, American Psychological Association, American School Health Association, American Speech and Hearing Association, Association for Supervision and Curriculum Development, Council for Exceptional Children, Department of Elementary School Principals, International Association of Pupil Personnel Workers, National Association of Secondary School Principals, National Association of Social Workers, and the National Education Association. It is probable that the newly-organized National Association of Pupil Personnel Administrators will be represented on the Commission in the near future.

Summary

Pupil personnel services generally include *attendance services, school health services, school psychological services, school social work services,* and *guidance services.* The superintendent must assume the responsibility for initiating, developing, and coordinating these services or he must delegate this responsibility. Professional organizations representing these services have not, in the past, coordinated their activities. Requirements for certification, both at the state and city levels, have lacked standardization. An Interprofessional Research Commission is currently engaged in securing data that will be used to effect improvements in the organization, administration, and coordination of pupil personnel services at the local, state, and national levels and in the recruitment, training, and certification of specialists representing these services.

Bibliography

1. Bower, Eli Michael. "The School Psychologist." *Bulletin of the California State Department of Education*, XXIV:12, November, 1955, 2-3.
2. Camp, Dolph. *Guidance Workers Certification Requirements*. Washington, D.C.: U.S. Office of Education, Dept. of Health, Education, and Welfare, Bulletin No. 14, 1960; Rev. OE-25005A, 1963.
3. Committee on Credentials for Pupil Personnel Services, California State Department of Education. "The Preparation and Training of Pupil Personnel Workers." *Bulletin of the California State Department of Education*, XXI:5, April, 1952, 27-30.
4. Council of Chief State School Officers. *Responsibilities of State Departments of Education for Pupil Personnel Services, A Policy Statement*. Washington, D.C.: the Council, 1960.
5. Crow, Lester D. and Alice Crow. *Organization and Conduct of Guidance Services*. New York: David McKay Company, Inc., 1965. Chaps. 4, 7.
6. Cunningham, Mary, ed. *Social Work in the Schools: Selected Papers*. New York: National Association of Social Workers, 1960.
7. Cutts, Norma E., ed. *School Psychologists at Mid-Century—A Report of the Thayer Conference on the Functions, Qualifications, and Training of School Psychologists*. Washington, D.C.: American Psychological Association, 1955. Pp. 30-31.
8. Fusco, Gene C. *Organization and Administration of Pupil Personnel Service Programs in Selected School Systems*. Washington, D.C.: U.S. Office of Education, Dept. of Health, Education, and Welfare, Bulletin No. 22, 1961; OE-23014, 1961.
9. Gottsegen, M. G. and Gloria B. Gottsegen, eds. *Professional School Psychology*, Vol. 1. New York: Grune and Stratton, 1960.
10. Hodges, Walter L. "State Certification of School Psychologists," *The American Psychologist*, June, 1960. Pp. 346-349.
11. Johnson, Arlien. *School Social Work: Its Contribution to Professional Education*. New York: National Association of Social Workers, 1962.

12.   Johnson, Walter F., Buford Stefflre, and Roy A. Edelfelt. *Pupil Personnel and Guidance Services*. New York: McGraw Hill Book Company, Inc., 1961. Chaps. 1, 6, 8, 9, 18.

13.   Landy, Edward. "Implementing Change in Programs of Pupil Personnel Service," in Landy, Edward and Arthur M. Kroel, eds. *Guidance in American Education II: Current Issues and Suggested Action*. Cambridge, Massachusetts: Harvard University Press, 1965.

14.   Loeb, Millicent X. "The Nurse in the School Counseling Program," in Rosencrance, Francis C. and Velma D. Hayden. *School Guidance and Personnel Services*. Englewood Cliffs, New Jersey: Allyn & Bacon, Inc., 1960. Pp. 169-175.

15.   Lundberg, Horace W., ed. *School Social Work: A Service of Schools*. Washington, D.C.: U.S. Office of Education, Dept. of Health, Education, and Welfare, Bulletin No. 15, 1964; OE-31007, 1964.

16.   Magary, James F. ed. *School Psychological Services: In Theory and Practice*. Englewood Cliffs, New Jersey: Prentice-Hall, Inc., 1966.

17.   Miller, Carroll H. *Guidance Services: An Introduction*. New York: Harper & Row, Publishers, 1965. Chap. 11.

18.   National Association of Social Workers. *Professional Qualifications for School Social Workers*. New York: the Association (Mimeo).

19.   Patterson, C. H. *Counseling and Guidance in Schools*. New York: Harper and Brothers, 1962. Chap. 16.

20.   Pearman, Jean R. and Albert H. Burrows. *Social Services in the Schools*. Washington, D.C.: Public Affairs Press, 1955.

21.   Peters, Herman J. and Bruce Shertzer. *Guidance: Program Development and Management*. Columbus, Ohio: Charles E. Merrill Books, Inc., 1963. Pp. 111-118.

22.   Quattlebaum, Virginia, ed. *School Social Work Practice*. New York: National Association of Social Workers, 1958.

23.   White, Mary Alice and Myron W. Harris. *School Guidance and Personnel Services*. Englewood Cliffs, New Jersey: Allyn & Bacon, Inc., 1960. Chaps. 5-7.

PART 3

SERVICES

8

Student Appraisal Services

An effective guidance program is concerned with developing pupils' potentialities to their optimum. This may be accomplished through counseling, providing pupils with a variety of informational services, making changes in the curriculum, or re-educating the community with respect to educational values. If the school is to perform this task in an adequate fashion, it must first gather a considerable amount of data on each pupil. What can he do? What has he done? What does he want to do? What are his mental, physical, social, and emotional limitations? What biological and environmental factors are contributing to his success or failure? These and many other questions must be answered before the pupil can be given adequate help.

Hoyt (30) identifies eight operational principles for programs of student appraisal:

Principle I: There is no single best appraisal method or procedure to be universally recommended.

Principle II: The effectiveness of student appraisal programs is directly related to the extent to which all professional staff members accept active roles in the program.

Principle III: To aim for complete understanding of students is both futile and foolish.

Principle IV: Understanding and helping students should be concurrent and not sequential operations.

Principle V: Student appraisal procedures involve both the study of students and the study of their environments.

Principle VI: The potential value of using appraisal procedures in combination is greater than the simple additive value of their respective individual potentialities.

Principle VII: Student appraisal procedures are not required in the same amount or to the same degree or necessarily for all students at the same time.

Principle VIII: The ultimate purpose of student appraisal procedures is increased student self-understanding leading to wiser student decisions.

Areas of the Individual Requiring Study

There are at least nine areas of individual development and activity which need to be studied by teachers and counselors in order that they may be of assistance to pupils. These nine areas are not entirely independent of one another. In some instances, they may be closely related. The counselor has the responsibility for selecting pertinent information from these areas. He attempts to fit together these relatively isolated items of pertinent information much as one fits together the pieces of a jigsaw puzzle. From this process he gains a picture of the pupil as a whole, and the forces or factors which cause him to perform and develop as he does.

Home and Environmental Conditions

Evidence, to date, supports the conclusion that home and neighborhood environment exert a strong influence in the development of individual attitudes, values, and habits. Consequently, information should be obtained regarding the occupation, health, education, and nationality of the parents and other members of the immediate family. In addition, information regarding neighborhood problems of a racial, religious, or social nature may provide further insight into the pupil's growth and adjustment.

Previous Educational Experience

A second area of information concerns the in-school and out-of-school educational experiences of pupils. Has the youngster been in many different schools? or has he spent his entire life in a single school system? Has he traveled extensively with his parents? and has this travel taken place during the school months or during the summer? How well has he done in his school work? What are his strengths and weaknesses? On the secondary level, there should be a complete record of courses taken by the student and his progress in these courses.

Health

Most of the information regarding the pupil's health will be gathered through periodic examinations conducted by the school physician. Information regarding illnesses or accidents occurring prior to the first physical examination can be obtained through questionnaires or interviews with parents. Because of his close association with pupils, the teacher is in a better position than either the doctor or the nurse to discover incipient illnesses. The teacher need not be a doctor and need not attempt to diagnose illnesses, but he should be alert for fatigue, lassitude, restlessness, tenseness, flushed cheeks, and pallor and refer pupils with these common symptoms of poor health for a check-up.

Abilities and Attitudes

A fourth kind of information needed for guidance is an appraisal of the abilities and aptitudes of each pupil. Most elementary and secondary schools now administer an intelligence or academic aptitude test to their pupils. Many elementary schools will administer two or three intelligence tests during a six- or eight-year period. With the growing popularity of academic aptitude tests that yield two, five, or seven different scores, the distinction between the terms "ability" and "aptitude" has become somewhat hazy. Scores on a twin-axis test of mental ability are now known as linguistic or language aptitude scores and quantitative or non-language aptitude scores. More recent test batteries that measure various factors of mental ability include "aptitude" in the title (for example, the Differential Aptitude Tests, the Multiple Aptitude Tests).

A picture of the pupil's mental ability will not be complete without some measure of reading speed and comprehension. Since his reading ability will have a significant effect upon the pupil's performance on the language portion of intelligence tests, an appraisal of mental ability without this information could be extremely misleading.

In the secondary school, special aptitudes in art, music, manual dexterity, etc. may be measured. Although these specific aptitude tests are not used extensively, they can provide an important link in the chain of information necessary to make future educational and vocational plans.

Interests

The relationship between what one is interested in doing and what one plans to do in the future seems obvious to the mature individual. Yet, again and again, we find youngsters in high school and even in college who are enrolled in a program or course of study which holds little interest or significance for them. Their plans have been determined by parental wishes, a friend's advice, the desire to make money, or disappointment over lack of achievement in another area. Youngsters can be helped to understand their interests through inventories such as the Kuder Preference Record—Vocational and the Strong Vocational Interest Blank. An early administration of such an inventory may serve to orient pupils to the world of work and help them understand the relationship between vocational interests and vocational goals. A later administration of an interest inventory may give them assistance in making further educational and vocational plans. Parents and teachers have often questioned the value of interest inventories. It is true that they have their weaknesses. But the interest inventory represents an advance over the interview as a technique of gathering information about pupil interests because (a) it is less time-consuming and (b) it is more objective. A competent counselor might spend a week in questioning a student regarding his interests. Yet, because of his greater knowledge of some vocational fields, he might question the student more specifically in these areas and thus gain a biased picture of the student's interests. Since interests are such a significant factor in educational and vocational success, it is important to consider all possible areas which might interest the student.

Leisure Activities

In addition to securing information regarding the educational and vocational interests of pupils, the school should keep a record of their activities in and out of school. While membership in certain clubs or participation in certain co-curricular activities may be due to social rather than vocational forces, it would be unwise to neglect this area of information. These co-curricular or leisure time activities may shed further light on the pupil's interest patterns. Is his interest in a vocational field largely theoretical? or is it buttressed by practical experience? Does this interest area represent a potential hobby or a future vocational pursuit?

Social and Emotional Adjustment

The pupil's lack of adjustment to his social environment or his inability to cope with himself may result in under-achievement, disciplinary problems, or even physical disabilities. The teacher should not be expected to perform diagnostic and remedial services for which he has not been trained. Nevertheless, he has a vital role to play in dealing with this problem. Through careful observation and accurate reporting he can contribute a wealth of worthwhile information about youngsters that will be beneficial to other teachers or to a specialist should referral be necessary. *Anecdotal records,* the teacher's written descriptions of pupil behavior, and *rating scales, autobiographies,* and *personality inventories* have been used to obtain this type of information. Further discussion of the value of these techniques will be made later in the chapter.

Work Experience

In the case of older pupils, summer or part-time work experience may furnish valuable clues to the educational, vocational, and social maturity of the student. Through the use of questionnaires and personal interviews, information should be obtained concerning the type and variety of jobs held, their duration, earnings, and the individual's attitude toward the work.

Plans and Goals

A final important area of information concerns the plans and goals presently held by the pupil and his parents. Many pupils have set goals for themselves which are inconsistent with their current performance and may be beyond their reach. Other pupils may have made plans which will not allow them to capitalize on their abilities and interests. An interview with a pupil and his parents often discloses a serious discrepancy between the goal which a pupil has set for himself and the goal which his parents have set for him.

Tools and Techniques of Appraisal

Studying the individual in the areas previously mentioned requires the use of a variety of tools and techniques. The following sections of this chapter will be devoted to a discussion of observation, anecdotal records, rating scales, self-report forms, autobiographies, sociometric devices, standardized tests and inventories, interviews, teacher-parent conferences, case conferences, and personnel records as devices for obtaining this information.

Observation

Teachers, counselors, and other staff members have always made casual observations of their pupils in and out of the classroom. Frequently, these observations are unplanned, haphazard, and inaccurate. They often spring from the teachers' desire to maintain order, prevent cheating on examinations, check lesson preparations, or insure quiet for study. Particularly in larger classes, teachers tend to focus their attention upon the "disturbing" or "disrupting" activities of a small minority. Yet, these teachers have been given the responsibility for the personal and social as well as the intellectual development of each youngster in the room. In order to fulfill this responsibility, the teacher must make adequate and systematic observation of pupil behavior. It is basic to every other technique of studying pupils. An anecdotal record can be misleading and actually damaging to a pupil unless it is based on accurate observation. Rating scales contain summarized observations. Observations made during an interview may give the counselor more significant information than he can gather from the comments of the pupil. During testing sessions, observation of the pupil at work may furnish important clues to the pupil's ability to concentrate, to do independent work, and to work under pressure.

Effective observation of others is a science as well as an art. The ability to make good observations improves through training and practice. At children's parties, it used to be popular to have the youngsters file by a table loaded with a large number of miscellaneous objects and then, in the next room, request them to write down all that they saw. The youngster correctly identifying the greatest number of objects on the table won the prize. If there were enough parties during the year, the children became quite adept at observing and recording the objects on the table. They were getting practice. The fortune teller's occasional successes are due to his ability to observe inconspicuous but telltale evidence of his client's past history or present status. He notices the smoothness or roughness of his client's hands, the ring mark on the third finger of the left hand, subtle variations in speech, facial complexion, or wearing apparel. He is able to place an aura of mysticism around his work because most of us have become somewhat jaded in our observations. We do not see things in detail and we do not notice exactly what happened. Evidence to support this statement may be obtained from any traffic court where auto accident cases are being decided. Impartial witnesses will be in direct disagreement over the position and speed of the cars, whether the cars were accelerating or decelerating, and whether the traffic light was red, green, or yellow.

While an understanding of the basic needs of individuals may serve to guide our observations and assist us in interpreting what we see, an understanding of the observer's possible influence on the observation is also necessary. It is easier to make accurate observations of preschool children than of older children because the younger children are less aware of being observed and are more likely to express their true thoughts and feelings. Knowledge of the observer's presence often causes pupils to exhibit atypical behavior. Furthermore, it is difficult for the observer to be completely objective in his observations. His background and training and personal biases may cause him to see only a part of the picture. The school doctor and nurse look primarily for evidences of illness. The physical education teacher gives primary attention to the acquisition of health habits and body coordination. The high school teacher of English looks for evidence of academic achievement in that field. The effective observer, therefore, is not merely one who has become practiced in observing every detail of a behavior incident. The effective observer also understands himself and the effect his background, training, and attitude will have upon the record he makes of the observation. While a balanced picture of a pupil will only be obtained if he is observed in a variety of behavioral situations, it is in the classroom that most observations take place. It is also the classroom teacher who will be most greatly tempted to notice "bad" or "disturbing" behavior. The following list by Strang (50) indicates some of the other kinds of behavior that may be observed in the classroom.

Observation of learning abilities
    Rapidity with which student comprehends printed material
    Rapidity, accuracy, and expression in oral reading
    Note vocabulary, ability to think independently about what is read, etc.
    Indication of ability in other subjects, as hesitancy or failure to attack problem in arithmetic

Kind and number of questions asked—relevant to the discussion; showing originality; showing grasp of subject; trivial or important

Kind of answers given—relevant; showing originality; showing grasp of subject

Eagerness to answer many questions versus a tendency to answer only when called upon

Deficiency in one or more skills as compared with the other students in the class

Observation of study habits during school periods

Conception of study as a process of memorizing

Record of attention and distraction (Morrison's technic)

Promptness in beginning to study

Persistence in work—for example, finishing the problem on which he is working rather than stopping the minute the bell rings

Use of bibliographical helps in reference work

Apparent lack of interest in school work

Cheating—copying children's papers on test or copying their homework

Inability to comprehend directions

Observation of personal characteristics

Physical defects—evidences of difficulty in vision or hearing; holding book or paper nearer to the eyes than twelve inches; evidences of malnutrition; poor posture, apparent fatigue, special deformities

Skill in social relations

Emotional control and responsiveness and behavior difficulties—temper outbursts, extreme aggressiveness, insistence upon holding center of stage; lack of usual inhibitions; interference of other behavior with class work; shyness, feelings of inferiority; marked self-consciousness, withdrawing behavior, sullenness, defiance, teasing and bullying, moodiness, marked overactivity, unpopularity with other children, apparently excessive daydreaming

Speech difficulties and language handicap

Unnecessary tardiness

Nervous habits—tic, etc.

"Queerness" in other ways—giving odd responses, being apparently unconscious of irrelevancy of his remarks

Inferior performance in motor skills[1]

Anecdotal Records

Recorded observations are known as *anecdotal records,* a term that apparently originated at the Rochester Athenaeum and Mechanics

---

[1] Used with permission of Harper and Brothers.

Institute, now known as Rochester Institute of Technology. Obviously, it would be impossible to record all observations. Yet, there are important reasons for recording incidents involving pupil behavior that seems significant to the observer.

Values of Anecdotal Records—We consider it unwise today for a wage earner to rely on his memory when making out his income tax return. It is quite possible that he will remember the more recent or the more unusual financial transactions of the past year while forgetting some of the earlier, more routine income or expenditures. In like fashion, the teacher or counselor is inclined to remember the most recent or most unusual behavioral incidents. Even if his memory serves him well, he is not likely to retain as comprehensive and accurate a picture of earlier incidents as he will of later incidents. Anecdotal records tend to reinforce (and sometimes correct) the observer's memory. In addition, anecdotal records, if properly maintained and summarized, can be helpful to all staff members. If there are a number of anecdotes on each pupil, if they describe his actions in a variety of settings, and if a number of observers have contributed to these anecdotes, the teacher or counselor can obtain a well-balanced, cross-sectional view of the pupil's behavior without the necessity of conducting an individual time-consuming investigation. Furthermore, if adequate clerical help is available, these records may be accumulated over a period of time in order to furnish a developmental picture of pupil growth. This developmental and cross-sectional picture is necessary if teachers are to gain insight into the ever-changing, exceedingly complex behavior of pupils. Finally, anecdotal records help teachers (a) obtain a better understanding of their pupils, (b) gain greater skill in identifying the causes of pupil behavior, and (c) develop improved techniques for dealing with pupil problems. Recording the observation helps the teacher to avoid snap judgments. It also motivates him to search for answers to three important questions: What? Why? How? What exactly took place? Why did it take place? How may I handle the situation most effectively?

Various experimental projects have reported the following changes in teachers as they acquired more training and practice in observation and anecdotal records:

1. The teachers became more objective in observing and reporting pupil behavior;
2. They became more specific in their descriptions of the behavioral incident;
3. They acquired deeper insights and became more cautious in drawing conclusions;

4. Their records became longer and more detailed;
5. The percentage of favorable reports increased as did the percentage of those reports that were neither wholly favorable nor unfavorable.

Characteristics of Good Anecdotal Records—A good anecdotal record is objective. Objectivity will be increased if: (a) the report is written by the actual observer, (b) it is written immediately after the occurrence of the incident, and (c) the specific description of the incident is kept separate from the observer's interpretations and recommendations. *The good anecdotal record is descriptive.* The setting or the background for the episode should be described, conversations should be recorded verbatim, and the actions of all participants described in the order in which they took place. *The good anecdotal record deals with a single situation.* Anecdotes should be as simple and brief as possible. In attempting to report on several incidents at once, the observer is likely to sacrifice clarity, accuracy, and even objectivity. *The good anecdotal record is selective.* It is not written about the unusual or atypical incident unless such an incident is relevant to the pupil's growth and development. On the other hand, routine incidents that have little significance are not worth reporting. The decision as to whether typical or atypical behavior is significant rests, of course, with the observer. That is why the most significant anecdotes are usually written by teachers with special training in guidance, psychology, or mental hygiene. Since the individual's behavior may be "typical" of him and "atypical" for his group, or vice versa, a good anecdotal report form will request this information of the observer.

*Limitations to Anecdotal Records—*Limitations to anecdotal records may be placed in two categories: (a) those involving inadequate training or practice on the part of the observer, and (b) those resulting from inadequate organization of the anecdotal record program. In the first category belong the following:

1. Unconscious bias on the part of the observer;
2. An incomplete observation with consequent distortion of behavior reported;
3. An inaccurate observation with consequent distortion of behavior reported;
4. An inconsequential or irrelevant observation;
5. An observation reported for the purpose of justifying the observer's own behavior or action.

These limitations are not insurmountable. They can be minimized if not eliminated through a sound in-service education program. However, the effectiveness of anecdotal records may also be limited by the manner in which they are organized and maintained. A workable plan for transcribing and summarizing the anecdotes must be devised before the writing of anecdotes is begun. When a sufficient number of anecdotes have been gathered on a pupil, a summary and interpretation should be prepared. This is *not* the task of clerical workers. Professional training is necessary in order to summarize and interpret anecdotal records in an accurate fashion. At the elementary level, one teacher will usually have contributed the majority of reports on a particular pupil and, therefore, is the logical one to summarize these reports. At the secondary level, where a greater variety of staff members may have contributed anecdotes, the summarizing should be done by the person most responsible for the guidance of the student, whether it be homeroom teacher, advisor, or counselor. The frequency with which summaries are made will depend largely on how quickly the reports accumulate on an individual. In any case, a summary should be made at least once a year. A copy of the report should be included in the cumulative record folder of every pupil. On the secondary level, the student's counselor should also receive a copy if a different staff member made the summary.

Debatable Points—

1. *Should teachers be required to write a certain number of anecdotal records per week or month?* Those arguing for quotas and time limits assert that, if contributions of anecdotes are made on a purely voluntary basis, teachers will vary tremendously in the degree to which they participate in the program, and there will be a tendency for the reports to decline both in quantity and quality as the enthusiasm engendered by the in-service program wears off. They feel that teachers, being human, will need continual external motivation to perform this task satisfactorily. They recognize that class size varies markedly with each school system, and that it is difficult to set up a quota that will be fair to all teachers. However, they feel that teachers within a given school will be in a position to set their own quotas after participation in an experimental or in-service program.

Those in favor of a voluntary system of reporting observations argue that teachers (or any other person) can no more be forced to observe than they can be forced to learn. Motivation for observing and reporting must come from internal rather than external forces.

Since the reports will be time consuming, this group feels that forcing teachers to meet a quota every week or month will result in (a) resentment toward the administration; (b) hurried, inaccurate observations being made just before the "deadline"; (c) reporting obvious or nuisance situations that thrust themselves upon the teacher but are not necessarily significant; and (d) reducing the length and descriptiveness of the anecdotes in order to save time.

2. *Should observations be systematic or spontaneous?* Should a specific time be set aside each day for observing pupils? Should the teacher's attention be focused on only one or two pupils each day to insure that an equal number of anecdotes will be written on each pupil in the room? Will such a practice help teachers make more effective observations of their pupils? or will it cause them to miss significant behavior of other pupils in the room? The advocates of systematic obervation point out that the pupil should be observed in many different situations—in class and out-of-class, in school and out-of-school, playing and working by himself, playing and working with others. They do not feel that this many-sided view of the pupil can be obtained without some predetermined "plan of attack" by each teacher and without some coordination of these individual plans by someone on the school staff.

The opponents of a heavily structured program of observation agree that the efforts of the teaching staff must be coordinated if anecdotal records are to be an effective tool for gathering data on pupils. However, they feel that a "plan of attack" that chooses certain pupils or certain class periods for observation is unrealistic and unnecessary. If Mary and John are chosen to be observed on Thursday, is it not possible that their behavior will be less significant than their Wednesday or Friday behavior? Is it not possible that the homeroom period selected for observation on Monday will produce fewer worthwhile anecdotes than the study hour or the lunch hour? The opponents of a structured program doubt whether it is possible for any teacher to observe Mary and John and be oblivious to the significant behavior of Susan and Tom who are seated a few feet away. Finally, they are unworried about the possibility that some pupils will be reported on more frequently than others. They argue that the lack of anecdotes on one pupil may be as significant as a large number written on another pupil.

Should teachers be given a minimum number of anecdotes to write per week? Should the anecdotes be the result of systematic or spontaneous observation? No decisive answer to these questions can be given. If the members of a school staff use the experimental, open-minded approach to the development of an anecdotal record program, they will develop procedures that will be most satisfactory for their own school situation.

Rating Scales

The rating scale is another tool that may be used in reporting observations. Whereas the anecdotal record is used to report a single incident, the rating scale is used to record the observer's general estimate of the pupil. "Rating scale" is defined here as a tool used by one individual to describe, classify, rate, or judge another individual. When an instrument is used by an individual to describe, classify, rate, or judge himself, it is usually called a "test," an "inventory," or a "self-report form." These instruments will be discussed in another section of the chapter.

Types of Rating Scales—Rating scales have been classified in many different ways. As early as 1933, Weiss (57) placed rating scales in two groups—those involving *scoring methods* and those involving *ranking methods*. Freeman (21) supports this classification. Warters (56), however, feels that some of the newer and superior scales are designed primarily to help teachers study and describe pupil behavior rather than to evaluate or measure it. Therefore, she places rating scales in four groups—those involving *scoring methods, ranking methods, graphic scales,* and *check lists or behavior descriptions*. Since some scales may be used in two or three different ways, it is difficult to classify them. However, most present-day scales may be described as primarily *quantitative, descriptive,* or *graphic*. In the quantitative scale, the size of the number checked or circled by the rater indicates the degree to which the pupil possesses a trait or attitude. Thus, on a ten-point scale, a *1* would indicate an absence of the trait, a *5* or *6* would indicate an average amount of the trait and a *10* would indicate that the trait was present in the pupil to a great degree.

EXAMPLE

(if the pupil excels circle *10*, if very deficient circle *1*)

Cooperation	1	2	3	4	5	6	7	8	9	10
Industry	1	2	3	4	5	6	7	8	9	10
Initiative	1	2	3	4	5	6	7	8	9	10

The descriptive scale allows the rater to place a check mark in the space before a phrase which best describes the pupil.

EXAMPLE

Cooperation _____Cannot or will not work with others

_____Occasionally works with others, but not very effectively

_____Works well with some pupils, will not work
with others
_____Usually works well with others
_____Works very well with others

Industry   _____Does very little
_____Does what he is told to do but no more
_____Always does what he is told to do, occasion-
ally does more than is asked
_____Works harder than most pupils
_____Very hard worker, is always looking for more
to do

Initiative   _____Must always be given directions
_____Must be given directions to get started, in
areas of interest will sometimes plan further
activities
_____Plans and executes activities in areas of in-
terest, must be given direction in other
areas
_____Plans most activities but occasionally needs
help in executing them
_____Can plan and execute his own activities with-
out help from others

The graphic scale allows the rater to make even finer distinctions. In the following example, checks may be placed at any spot along the continuum.

EXAMPLE

Cooperation

Will not work with others	Seldom works with others	At times difficult to work with	Usually congenial and cooperative	Always cooperates very well with others

Industry

Does little or nothing	Needs constant pressure	Needs occasional prodding	Works harder than most	Very hard worker

Initiative

Always needs direction	Usually needs direction	Needs direction in some areas	Needs occasional supervision	Works well when left alone

Uses of Rating Scales—As a tool for gathering data on pupils, the rating scale is simpler and less time consuming than the anecdotal record. Less training is needed by the teacher. Yet, its standardized format allows comparisons to be made between one pupil and another. While these are rather dubious values, they indicate why rating scales have enjoyed some degree of popularity. Like anecdotal records, they are probably most useful in helping teachers to become observant of pupil behavior and more accurate and analytical in their judgments. For this reason, the descriptive or graphic type of rating scale would appear to be preferable to the quantitative type.

Limitations of Rating Scales—The validity and reliability of ratings have been the subject of controversy for some time. The following limitations have been consistently identified by research workers:

1. *Ratings depend on the attitudes and personal bias of the rater.* While the opinion of the rater about the person being rated may be of some significance, the subsequent confusion of the reader over whether the rating was based on objective evidence or subjective opinion reduces its value. Since a biased rater may be consistently biased, this subjectivity factor will not necessarily show itself after successive administrations of the rating scale.

2. *There are no commonly accepted definitions of the intangible qualities that frequently appear on rating scales.* Even when the rater makes a conscientious attempt to report only what he has seen, his interpretation of the meaning of "honesty," "cooperation," or "initiative" makes his rating subjective.

3. *There is a tendency to rate the specific traits of an individual on the basis of the rater's general impression.* This tendency, frequently referred to as the "halo effect," usually develops when the rater is more familiar with certain traits of the individual than he is with others. He permits his rating of known traits to affect his rating of other traits on which he has little or no information. "Halo effect" may be reduced by (a) limiting the traits to be rated to the most essential five or six, (b) rating one trait for all members of a group before rating any individual on the next trait, and (c) varying the arrangement of the rating descriptions so that the least or most desirable descriptions do not always fall in the same spot on the scale.

4. *Rating scales are usually so heavily structured that the rater has little opportunity to add explanatory comments to his ratings.* An explanation of *why* a certain rating had been made would appear to be more significant than the rating itself. Unfortunately, only a few scales make provision for this type of comment.

Each of these limitations can be reduced to some extent. The element of subjectivity can be minimized by having the same pupil rated by a variety of experienced persons under different conditions, and by helping the raters reach general agreement on the definition of interpretation of the intangible traits listed on the scale. Procedures for reducing "halo effect" have already been mentioned. Space for explanatory comments on the scale would make ratings more significant by (a) allowing raters to offer a reason for their rating and (b) allowing the rater to describe the circumstances under which he acquired his information.

Self-Report Forms

In a broad sense, all instruments which use the student as the source of information about himself may be considered as "self-report forms." However, some distinction is usually made between tests and questionnaires. Symonds (51) differentiates between the two by defining a *test* as an instrument containing questions sufficiently difficult to reveal the ability of the person taking the test, and by defining a *questionnaire* as an instrument containing questions so simple and easy that the respondent can understand and answer truthfully. In a test, Symonds says, the issue is whether a person *can answer* the questions, whereas in a questionnaire it is whether he *will answer* truthfully.

A test may also be defined as any instrument which measures in a quantitative fashion and which yields data that furnishes a basis for comparing one individual with other individuals or groups. Using this definition, inventories designed to study and measure interests and personality traits would be classified as tests (and will be interpreted as such in this chapter).

In this section we are concerned with (a) those instruments that ask the individual to rate himself on a number of traits, attitudes or abilities; and (b) those instruments asking for factual information. In general, *self-ratings* have been rather low in validity and reliability. While they have some value in helping pupils understand the traits and characteristics which they possess and which will be related to their future success and happiness, the data obtained can hardly be accepted by teachers or counselors without further corroboration. However, self-rating can be quite effective as a means of arousing a pupil's interest in his abilities and traits and, thus, it may serve as good preparation for counseling.

Self-report forms that request information from pupils with respect to home and family background, health, tentative educational and vocational plans, work experience, interests and hobbies, or most liked and least liked school subjects are usually identified as *personal data blanks*. They represent a quick and easy way to obtain a great deal of information about the pupil. The counselor is able to study this data prior to an interview and, as a result, may be able to spend more time on counseling and less on "information-getting." The personal data blank may also be used to gather information about the characteristics or unique features of a group of pupils. This is an acceptable practice as long as *group* data obtained in this way will not be used for *individual* counseling. As Rothney and Roens (47) point out, guidance workers should be "aware of the danger of being misled by common generalizations which tend to make them think in terms of *group* characteristics at the time that they should be concerned about *particular* characteristics of the individual with whom they are to work."

Personal data blanks requiring the pupil to identify his problem areas are usually known as *problem check lists*. Since these problem check lists are most frequently used to assist teachers in gaining a better understanding of a pupil's social and emotional adjustment, they will be treated as one type of personality inventory and will be discussed later in the chapter.

The Autobiography

The autobiography is another convenient means of securing information about pupils. It may be either *structured* or *unstructured*. If a structured autobiography is desired, students are given explicit instructions regarding the type of information desired and how this information might be organized. The unstructured autobiography is obtained by merely requesting students to write about themselves. The structured autobiography covers all areas of the pupil's life in some logical order, thereby making it complete and well balanced. Yet, the unstructured autobiography may furnish greater insights into the pupil's plans and problems. The skilled counselor or teacher can observe a number of important factors from it—what the pupil considers to be of greatest importance, what he wants and does not want known about himself, how he would like and not like to be perceived, any dangerous fantasies which he may entertain, etc.

Values of the Autobiography—Since the autobiography can be used as an English assignment, it serves a dual purpose. Teachers can learn about the problems, attitudes, and aspirations of their pupils while appraising their progress in grammar and literary composition. In addition, counselors obtain information on these pupils that may prove valuable at some later date. Secondly, the autobiography is likely to give the pupil a better understanding of himself. As he writes about himself—his hopes and fears, his likes and dislikes—the pupil often gains insight into why he is as he is, where he is going, and why he is going there. Finally, an autobiography often helps to release tension in the writer. Many of us have "poured out our troubles" in a conversation with a friend; the same therapeutic effect may be achieved by writing about them. The autobiography will be most valuable as a cathartic device if students are given sufficient time to complete the assignment.

Limitations of the Autobiography—There are a number of factors which may affect the pupil's ability or desire to write accurately about himself. He may accidentally or deliberately distort the facts even when he is convinced that his writing will be kept confidential. Or, he may feel that the autobiography is primarily a literary composition and sacrifice accuracy for literary style. He may treat it as "just another assignment" and restrict himself to a very mechanical, barren outline of his earlier years. His inability to write well may limit his self-analysis and cause some of his statements to be misinterpreted. He may distort his abilities and interests in order to obtain greater recognition from the teacher. He may even derive satisfaction from overstating his problems or exaggerating escapades. For these and other reasons, autobiographical information provided by the pupil must be verified through other sources of data. "The subjectivity of the autobiography is both a strength and a weakness. It is a strength in that it enables a student to relate something as he wishes to relate it. In so doing, it serves as a cathartic and/or self-evaluative purpose. It is a weakness in that the material presented may be distorted or superficial (46)."

Interpretation of the Autobiography—Fortunately, there are clues that assist us in the proper interpretation of an autobiography. *Omissions* of important data may indicate pupil rejection of that experience or period in life. He may write with *intense feeling* about certain events, yet write in a rather blasé fashion about other events normally of greater importance. The use of *superlatives, absolute statements,* or *undue repetition* may indicate deliberate or unintentional *fabrication.* His *vocabulary* may give some indication of his background and environment. The *length* of the document may give some indication of his interest and/or fluency in writing. The *organization* of the document may shed some light on the events the pupil feels were of greatest importance. Even the *physical appearance* of the manuscript may furnish some important clues to the student's habits or behavior. The following excerpts from an autobiography (25) include the identification of some of these clues in the margins.

Selection of Topic (starts with problem)	Last year I flunked two of my courses because I was very ill during most of the year. This made me feel very bad, and I want you to know that this past year has been one of the unhappiest years of my life.
Distortion of Fact	I wouldn't tell this to anyone else but I have thought many times recently of quitting school because of being sick.
Variation of Feeling from Preceding Paragraph	Well, anyway, I was born on October 1, 19___, and was the first child that my mother and father had. My mother's name is Mary and my father's name is George.
Omission of Sister's Name	I also have two brothers, Bill and George Jr. I don't guess that we are much different from any other family in this town except that my mother does not have a car to carry us kids to school in.
Unusual Vocabulary Distortion of Fact	We live in a large ten-room house over on the other side of town which is one of the most expensive houses in the area. Most of the kids from my neighborhood go to this school.
Inconsistency from Central Theme	My father works late every night and once last year was arrested when he came home drunk and tried to beat up Mom and us kids. However, Daddy is sober most of the time and really a very nice fellow.
Level of Understanding	I sometimes think that the reason he drinks is that we have had many doctor bills during the past ten years and he finds it hard to get a good job because he has had no special training for any kind of work. Then, too, my mother always bosses and nags him a lot.

| Variation of Feeling from Preceding Paragraph | My mother is one of the most wonderful, exciting and beautiful women you have ever seen. |
| Inconsistency with an Earlier Description of the Mother | We always have such gay times together. She always makes me feel so happy and gay when I am with her. |

Tentative analysis of autobiographies in this manner should be followed by checking these clues against the data to be found in the cumulative record folder. Only in this manner can the autobiography serve as an effective tool for gathering information on pupils. "Teachers and counselor cooperation in examining and interpreting selected autobiographies might well serve as a beginning of the continual use of the case conference method in the school setting (46)."

Sociometric Devices

Sociometry is the process of determining natural groupings and patterns of association among the members of a group by asking pupils to reveal their personal feelings for others. While sociometric techniques were devised primarily to study the social structure of a group, teachers have found them useful in gathering information about the "popularity" or social adjustment of individuals within the group. If the teacher has a specific goal in mind (for example, organizing committees), she may wish to devise her own sociometric question or questions. If she wishes to gather additional data on the emotional dvelopment or social adjustment of individual students in the room, she may rely on one of several instruments devised for this purpose: the "Guess Who" test, the Ohio Social Acceptance Scale, the Classroom Distance Scale, the Friendship Target, the Syracuse Scales of Social Relations or the Who's Who In My Room.

Regardless of whether the questions originate with the teacher or appear in printed form, the validity of the test results will depend on (a) the manner in which the teacher has prepared the pupils for this experience and (b) the technique used to administer the question or questions. Since sociometric techniques are measures of opinion rather than measures of personality, the validity of the data cannot be determined by the criteria we use with respect to ability or aptitude tests. The following precautions need to be observed if the teacher is to gain the most assistance from the sociometric process:

1. Members of the group should know each other rather well.
2. Teacher-pupil rapport must be excellent.

3. Pupils must feel that the information will be treated confidentially.
4. Pupils must feel that the teacher is trying to help them.
5. The word "test" should be avoided; its use may cause some students to try to give the "right" answers rather than the "correct" ones.
6. Clear questions must be asked.
7. Questions must apply to only one situation and the pupils must understand this.
8. Pupils must understand how the results are to be used.
9. The results should be used as soon as possible and the pupils should be aware that they are being used.
10. The entire process should be completed as casually as possible.

Results may be recorded in tabulated form so that a numerical score can be given each pupil in terms of his selection or rejection by other members of the group. These scores may be ranked in order if it seems desirable. However, a graphic method of organizing and presenting the data is generally considered more desirable. This graphic presentation or *sociogram* can be constructed to indicate the extent to which factors such as sex, race, religion, and socio-economic status determine relationships within the group. Group leaders and isolates can be determined very easily. However, it is important to remember that the results may apply to only one situation. The leaders in one situation might not be the leaders in another.

Figure 1 illustrates a type of sociogram which makes it possible to place students on the chart at meaningful positions which are indicative of their social acceptance. Based on a statistical formula called the *dual deviation technique* developed by Thorpe, Whitson, Baron, and Adams (52), this sociogram shows the social score and first choice of each pupil in a seventh-grade class. The triangle symbols for boys are placed on the left side of the chart, and the circle symbols for girls on the right side. Arrows are drawn to indicate each student's preference or first choice as expressed in the sociometric test. The symbol for each pupil is placed on the chart at a specified distance (determined by his social score) from the heavy circle denoting "average" social acceptance (a social score of 0). Thus Pupil 1, with a social score of −10, is plotted on the circle labeled − 10. Pupil 18, with a social score of 16, is plotted near the center of the diagram, on the circle representing 16. The value of this type of sociogram is that it shows both the social status of each pupil (based on all choices) and the individual relationships within the group (based on the direction

FIGURE 1

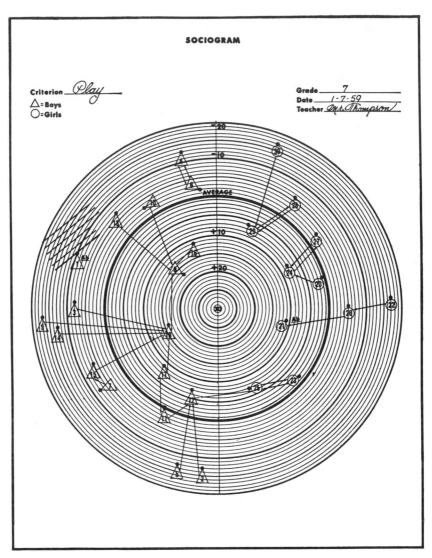

Reprinted by permission from Studying Social Relationships in the Classroom: Sociometric Methods for the Teacher *by Louis P. Thorpe, Milo E. Whitson, Denis Baron, and Georgia Sachs Adams, copyright © 1959 by Science
Research Associates, Inc.*

of the first choices of each member of the group). When a sociometric
study of this group is repeated, changes in the social position of
individual pupils will be noticed quite easily.

Psychological Tests

Since the beginning of the measurement movement, psychological tests have been used to collect information about pupils. Their employment in educational settings has increased at a phenomenal rate. Among the reasons for this rapid growth are the following:

1. The development of *group tests,* beginning with the work of Otis and Scott in constructing the *Army Alpha* for use with World War I draftees;
2. The growth of *test publishing companies* whose *major* function was the development of standardized tests;
3. The increase in numbers of students desiring to enter institutions of higher education and the selection problems facing these institutions as a result of this increase;
4. The increased cost of higher education, the resulting increase in scholarship awards at the federal, state, local and university levels, and the need for efficient and equitable procedures for determining the recipients of these awards.

A thorough discussion of psychological testing requires a book in itself. The reader who wishes comprehensive, up-to-date treatment of this field is referred to the work of Anastasi (2), Buros (8), Cronbach (12), Freeman (21), and Remmers, Gage, and Rummel (45) listed in the bibliography. The discussion of testing in this chapter is limited to identifying types of psychological tests and their advantages and limitations as devices for gathering information on pupils.

Since tests are generally easy to buy, administer, and score, they have been used in many schools as the principal technique of gathering data on pupils. In some schools, testing is the *only* technique which is used. In these schools, "testing" has become synonymous with "guidance." However, other techniques frequently yield better results in gathering data and facilitating teacher understanding of pupil behavior. Tests can make a valuable contribution to the *total* program of studying pupils if they are administered and interpreted properly by staff members who understand their strengths and weaknesses and who regard them as a means to an end rather than an end in themselves.

Psychological tests may be classified in a number of ways. We may distinguish between (a) *individual* and *group* tests, (b) *speed* and *power* tests, (c) *paper-and-pencil* and *performance* tests, and (d) *language* and *non-language* tests. It has also been customary to classify tests according to the aspects of behavior they are attempting to measure. Thus, tests have been identified as measuring *intelligence, aptitude, achievement, interest,* and *personality.* However, these categories are somewhat oversimplified and outdated. The following excerpts from Test Service Bulletin Number 51 (59) of the Psychological Corporation point out the difficulties teachers and counselors face in distinguishing between tests of intelligence, aptitude, and achievement.

> Let us look at the basic characteristics of achievement tests, intelligence tests, and aptitude tests. By definition, an achievement test measures what the examinee has learned. But an intelligence test measures what the examinee has learned. And an aptitude test measures what the examinee has learned. So far, no difference is revealed. Yet three of the traditional categories into which tests are classified are intelligence, aptitude, and achievement. Now these categories are very handy; they permit publishers to divide their catalogs into logical segments, and provide textbook authors with convenient chapter headings. Unfortunately, the categories represent so much over-simplification as to cause confusion as to what is being measured. What all three kinds of tests measure is what the subject has learned. The ability to answer a proverbs item is no more a part of the examinee's heredity than is the ability to respond to an item in a mechanical comprehension test or in a social studies test. All are learned behavior.
>
> Moreover, all are intelligent behavior. It takes intelligence to supply the missing number in a number series problem. It also requires intelligence to figure out which pulley will be most efficient, or to remember which president proposed an inter-American doctrine. We can say, then, that an intelligence test measures intelligent behavior, an aptitude test measures intelligent behavior and an achievement test measures intelligent behavior.
>
> Finally, all three types of tests measure probability of future learning or performance, which is what we generally mean when we speak of "aptitude." In business and industry, the chances that an employee will profit from training or will perform new duties capably may be predicted by scores on an intelligence test, by scores on one or more specific aptitude tests, or by some measure of the degree of skill the employee already possesses. Similarly, test users in the schools know that an intelligence test is usually a good instrument for predicting English grades, a social studies test is often helpful for prediction of future grades in social studies, and a mechanical comprehension test is likely to be useful in predicting for scientific or technical courses. So, intelligence tests are aptitude tests, achievement tests are aptitude tests and aptitude tests are aptitude tests.
>
> On what basis are the types to be differentiated? One possible basis is that of content. Quite often, we can look at the subject

matter of a test and classify the test as achievement or intelligence or aptitude. But content is not a sure guide by any means.

Let us take a specific item. A student is taught to multiply $(x - y)$ by (x). If he demonstrates that he can perform this operation correctly, we accept this item as an achievement measure. Next, without specific formal instruction, he is asked to multiply $(p + q)$ by $(p - q)$, and again answers correctly. Is this achievement? The mathematics teacher would say it is. Is it aptitude? Certainly the ability to perceive the analogy between the taught and untaught algebraic problems is indicative of future learning ability in algebra. Is it intelligence? The demonstrated ability to generalize is clearly symptomatic of intelligence.

The same point can be made with regard to entire subtests. In the *Metropolitan Achievement* series there is a Spelling test; one of the *Differential Aptitude Tests* is also a test called Spelling. Tests of arithmetic comprehension may be found in most achievement batteries; one of the subtests in each of the *Wechsler Intelligence Scales* measures arithmetic comprehension. What does all this mean? Have we demonstrated that the authors of these tests are confused, or is our classification system less neat and simple than it appears to be on the surface?

We believe the classification system is at fault. The teacher who has taught pupils how to solve arithmetic problems is perfectly justified in claiming that the pupils' performance on tests in these abilities represents achievement—both hers and theirs. At the same time, the learning of the skills and appreciations by the pupils is evidence of intelligence. Furthermore, the possession of the skills and of the ability to learn demonstrates the possession of aptitude for further learning in those same school subjects, and probably in other subjects as well. For example, scores on the *DAT* Spelling Test provide excellent prediction of success in learning stenography.

It would appear, then, that test content is not entirely adequate to discriminate among intelligence, achievement, and aptitude testing. Can we use process to discriminate among them? Shall we say that achievement is measured when the subject is tested for recall of what he has been taught, and that intelligence is shown in the ability to generalize from facts?

Every modern educator and every modern test constructor would reject such classification outright. Rare is the teacher who will admit her students are merely memorizing facts; rare is the curriculum which is not aimed at developing the ability to generalize, to apply learned principles in new situations. Furthermore, inspection of the items in some of our most highly regarded intelligence tests will reveal many items which are as direct questions of fact as any to be found in the least imaginative achievement tests. Processes of recognition, recall and rote repetition may be distinguishable from processes of generalization, appreciation, and problem solving—but apparently they are not satisfactory for distinguishing between intelligence and achievement.

If test content will not serve, nor test process, what will successfully discriminate intelligence or aptitude from achievement measures? A logical candidate would seem to be function. What are we trying to accomplish with the test scores? How are the results to be used? What inferences are to be drawn concerning the examinee? If a test's function is to record present or past accomplishment, what is measured may be called achievement. If we wish to make inferences concerning future learning, what is measured is thought of as aptitude. One kind of aptitude test, usually some combination of verbal and numerical and/or abstract reasoning measures, is sometimes called an intelligence test; more properly, in educational settings, it is called a scholastic aptitude test.

Whether achievement, intelligence or differential aptitude tests should be used depends on the functions to be served. The test user should ask "what inferences do I want to make; what information do I need to make those inferences?" The user who answers those questions will show intelligence, achievement of proficiency in test usage, and special aptitude for further advances in psychometrics.

The recent growth of *differential aptitude batteries* is due, in part, to the recognition that "intelligence tests" did not provide enough information on pupils in terms of their educational and vocational potential. These batteries have utilized the latest developments in factor analysis to enable teachers and counselors to obtain a "profile" of pupil abilities. This "profile" ordinarily includes measures of verbal and numerical aptitude as well as other aptitudes or abilities of a more specialized nature. In order to distinguish between these differential aptitude batteries and the earlier omnibus style "intelligence tests," the latter are now usually referred to as *general classification tests*. They still constitute one of the largest groups of psychological tests and are generally used to identify the intellectually retarded and gifted children; to assist in the diagnosis of academic failure; and to assist in the proper placement of pupils in a grade, room, or section. Differential aptitude batteries, on the other hand, are generally used where a broader scope of ability testing is necessary in order to assist the student in his educational and vocational planning.

The measurement of interests by means of *interest inventories* is a comparatively recent development. While interests may be identified by (a) observing behavior of students, (b) asking students about their interests, and (c) making a record of the activities of students, it is generally recognized that these techniques can supplement but not replace the data obtained through an interest inventory. It is difficult to observe students so continually and so intensively that an accurate picture of a student's total pattern of interests can be obtained. And there are at least two reasons why stated or claimed interests may be unreliable. First, as Darley and Hagenah (16) have emphasized, "claimed interests emerge from different causal factors—factors more associated with prestige, family pressures, aspirational level, and misconception of the world of work—than do measured interests." Secondly, both Nunnally (41) and Cronbach (12) have pointed out that young people are usually quite unaware of the specific activities entailed in different occupations and that individuals' stated preferences for occupations are often prompted by glamorous stereotypes. Finally, lack of participation in an activity does not prove the absence of an interest. The multiplicity of clubs and activities available to pupils in large schools today forces them to restrict their participation in such a way that some interests may be ignored, either because of financial problems or lack of time. Conversely, participation in an activity may be due to social pressures rather than interest.

Interest inventories, themselves, have certain limitations: (a) it is impossible to list *all* the activities and occupations on an inventory; (b) students are often forced to choose between two interests when *both or neither* are liked; (c) most inventories do not allow the pupils to express their *degree* of interest in an area or activity; (d) students may make different interpretations of the word or words describing an occupation (*actress* may be variously interpreted as *movie, legitimate theatre, television,* or *burlesque*); (e) students, without being aware of it, may allow factors other than interest to influence their choices; and (f) students may have little or no information about certain areas—choices made here may reflect *curiosity* rather than interest. In view of these and other limitations, data from interest inventories should be supplemented by other methods of identifying interests.

The appraisal of personal adjustment through the use of *personality inventories* has been the subject of considerable controversy in recent years. Personality inventories tend to fall into four categories:

1. Paper-and-pencil measures of personal adjustment (*California Test of Personality, Mental Health Analysis, Bell Adjustment Inventory*);
2. Paper-and-pencil measures of personal traits or values (*Allport-

Vernon-Lindzey Study of Values, Kuder Preference Record—
Personal, Thurstone Temperament Schedule);
3. Problem check lists (*Mooney Problem Check List, S.R.A. Youth*
Inventory);
4. Projective-type tests (*Rorschach, Thematic Apperception Test*).

Projective tests have been used, primarily, to identify deviate behavior and are, therefore, in the province of the clinical psychologist. The remaining types of personality inventories may all prove useful to the counselor if he uses them with caution. None of these instruments is refined enough to allow the counselor to make accurate quantitative comparisons between individuals regarding some trait or area of personality. But, if the teacher or counselor has good rapport with the student and the student *wants* help with a personal problem, the personality inventory can help identify the *area* where the problem of maladjustment exists. Interviewing techniques may then be used to determine *what* the problem is and *why* it exists.

The *problem check list* has been used effectively to furnish leads for group discussion of personal or social problems. The administration of the problem check list in the homeroom, for example, can furnish the homeroom teacher with a list of topics for discussion that will be of greatest interest to the group. The problem check list has shortcoming: *all* problems may not be included, the *intensity* of problems checked is undetermined, only consciously felt problems will be expressed, and it is difficult to phrase problems in language that is meaningful to all. Yet, this type of instrument appears to offer greater promise than the inventories that measure in a quantitative fashion. Fick (20) made an intensive study of questionnaires, inventories, and check lists and found that the check list was most valuable and practical when used: (a) to facilitate counseling, (b) to make group surveys, (c) to provide a basis for orientation and discussion programs, (d) to increase instructor understanding in any teaching situation, and (e) to conduct research on the problems of people. He found that the *Mooney Problem Check List* and the *S.R.A. Youth Inventory*, in particular, had the following advantages over twenty-one other personality inventories: (a) wider coverage of problems; (b) identification of actual problems rather than "scores"; (c) convenient grouping of problems by areas, for easy, quick review; and (d) rapid and easy administration and tabulation.

Values of Tests—

1. *Tests provide information on achievement and intelligence which, in conjunction with other data, allow new pupils to be placed*

in an appropriate grade or group. Early and proper placement of these pupils will insure continuity in the learning process without loss of time or pupil morale. Without this testing several weeks would elapse before a teacher, using other techniques, could acquire the same information.

2. *Tests are generally more objective and more accurate predictors of performance than are people.* As Drasgow (18) says: "... tests are validated and cross-validated, people are not; tests have known validities and reliabilities, people do not; predictions are made from tests with regression equations and known *beta* weights; what is your *beta* weight? In a word, tests are standardized and people aren't. Our attempts to 'standardize' personnel can be seen in our variegated graduate training program. No wonder tests predict better!" The recent emphasis on scholastic aptitude test scores as important criteria for admission to college is the result of numerous studies showing the value of such tests in predicting college success.

3. *Tests provide a basis for a cumulative record of pupil progress or achievement.* Without the quantitative data we obtain by testing, we would find it difficult to determine, in any accurate fashion, the year-to-year progress made by pupils in various subject-matter areas and the changes that have taken place in their interest patterns. Comparing pupils' mental ability or achievement with the mental ability or achievement of other pupils within the same age or grade group would be equally difficult. Determining the pupils who were working up to their capacity and those who were not would be largely a matter of guesswork.

4. *Tests help to identify pupils who need special attention.* The talented students who could profit from enriched classroom assignments and a special program of courses are often neglected because of the teacher's failure to recognize their superior ability. A good test of mental ability would identify these pupils. Pupils who are in need of remedial help may be identified through achievement testing. Pupils who appear to lack motivation for academic work may be given more effective help as a result of the measurement and understanding of their interest patterns. Pupils who have serious personal problems may be identified through measures of personal adjustment or problem check lists.

Limitation of Tests—The major limitations of psychological tests as tools for gathering information on pupils are of three types: (a) those inherent in the tests themselves, (b) those caused by the variety of factors which may influence test performance, and (c) those resulting from improper interpretation of test scores.

1. *Tests provide inexact and limited measurement.* Since the beginning of the measurement movement, great progress has been made in improving and standardizing psychological tests. Probably no other technique of studying pupils has been subjected to such careful scrutiny. A vast array of studies has been devoted to determining the validity and reliability of specific tests, yet much research remains to be done. This task is complicated by the yearly appearance of new tests, some of them inadequately standardized or validated, yet all neatly packaged and vigorously advertised. Even the best tests give us an approximate rather than an accurate measure of a pupil's ability, knowledge, skill, or interests. Many of our best tests place considerable emphasis on speed. Emphasis on speed gives great advantage to youngsters whose responses are quick. Other youngsters may score rather poorly on speed tests yet do well on power tests.

A pupil from an enriched cultural environment with a good understanding of language usage and a background of books appears to have an advantage over other, less fortunate pupils when achievement or intelligence is being measured. Early research conducted by Davis and Eells at the University of Chicago indicated that many of our best known intelligence tests were "culture-biased." Davis and Hess (17) argue that these tests "pose academic problems, the kind which are taught in the average classroom and which do not stem from real-life situations at all, but from a highly traditional, unrealistic middle-class culture. The cultural group which all present I.Q. tests favor is the middle class." However, the *extent* of this culture-bias is still to be determined. Davis and Eells, in experimenting with what were considered culture-fair tests, obtained results that were not much different than those obtained by the so-called culturally-biased tests.

Finally, the relatively artificial testing situation does not always furnish us with an accurate index of the pupil's ability to *apply* the knowledge or skill he reveals. For example, a vocabulary test measures a pupil's ability to *recognize* words, but rarely his ability to *use* them.

The following monologue, author unknown, provides some humorous illustrations of the difficulties we sometimes encounter in attempting to isolate and measure the factor of intelligence.

The Voice of the Low I.Q.

Yeah, I'm in the special class this term. Sure, I like it all right; we have lots of fun and the work's got some sense to it. I can do it. Why did I get put there? Well I ain't so sure. The report said I had a low I.Q., but nobody noticed it till last spring when I couldn't get along in Miss Brown's class. She gave me the test and when I handed in my paper she looked at it and said, "Just what I thought. I knew he didn't belong in here."

Yeah, it was something they call an Intelligence test. It was awful funny. At first I thought it was a joke but it turned out it wasn't. You had to put crosses on pictures and circles around 'em and lines under 'em and dots over 'em till I sorta got mixed up so I just drew a line right through the middle of all of 'em. There was sentences to write YES or NO after; sentences like this: "A carpenter builds houses." I wrote NO because my old man's a carpenter and he ain't built a house in four years. He's workin' on the railroad track. The boy that sat next to me put NO on every other sentence and then filled the rest up with YES. He got a swell mark. I read so slow I only got four done before the time was up. I get so tired of bein' hurried up all the time.

A tree, a fish, a cake of ice.—Look at this. It was so funny I tore out the page and kept it. See three pictures—a tree—a fish—and a cake of ice. I'll read what it tells you to do. "John is ten years old and his sister is eight. If John is not Mary's brother draw a line from the fish to the cake of ice. If Mary and John are twins write your middle name under the tree and if you have no middle name put zero there. If they are not twins print your last name on the tree. If Mary is younger than John write the Roman number eight in the upper left hand corner of the paper but if John is older than Mary draw a cat in the lower right hand corner. If they both go to school write your full name at the bottom of the paper." I'm never sure just how to spell my name so I didn't even try this one.

Miss Brown didn't like it because I always asked a lotta questions. She thought I was being fresh but I wasn't. There's a lotta things I want to know about. I never got mad when she asked me questions all the time. I answered 'em. I've got lots of answers—but they always seem to fit the wrong questions. Anyway, everything's changin' all the time so what's the use of learnin' a lotta things today when maybe they won't even be true by tomorrow? I know heaps of things Miss Brown don't know—like where to find birds' nests and how to fix a leaky pipe and what the baseball scores are. She has to send for the janitor when the lights go out or a window shade tears. I can do lots of things if I don't have to read how in a book first.

Sure, I'm glad I'm in the special. I get lots more attention. Seems like if you're awful smart or awful dumb they do a lot for you in school. But I heard the school Psychologist—that's a man that comes in just before promotion time and tells the teachers why they're not promotin' us—he told Miss Brown it was account of my grandfather and the rest of my ancestors. She said wasn't it

kinda late to do anything about that now, and he said it WAS but
I must have the proper training so I'd be a good ancestor.

Gosh, I don't want to be no ancestor. I'm goin' to be a
plumber.

2. *Test performance may be influenced by a variety of factors.*
Test performance may be influenced by (a) unusual or adverse
testing conditions involving lighting, acoustics, temperature, humidity,
interruptions, the size of the group being tested, or the length of the
testing period; (b) worry, anxiety, excitement, or other temporary
emotional conditions experienced by the pupil; (c) hunger, fatigue, or
other aspects of the physical condition of the pupil; (d) the pupil's
test sophistication or previous experience with similar tests; (e) the
degree to which the pupil is motivated to perform to capacity or to
answer questions honestly; (f) the pupil's reading and writing skills;
and (g) the ability of the examiner to establish rapport and to
administer the test without modifying the test instructions or the time
limit. Some of these factors are difficult, if not impossible to control.
We are unable to measure the courage, aspiration, or determination
that pupils bring to the testing situation, their ability to concentrate
on the task at hand, or their ability to work independently, without
getting help from others. Yet, these unmeasurable factors will not only
affect test performance but will be important determinants of the
pupils' future educational and vocational success.

3. *Many errors can be made in test interpretation. Errors will be
made in interpreting test scores unless there is a thorough understanding of the test, its validity, reliability, and the nature of the group on
which norms were established.* Without this understanding, (a) the
interpreter is likely to place too much faith in the test results and
draw unwarranted conclusions regarding the exactness of the test
scores; (b) improper norms may be used; and (c) results are likely to
be interpreted with too much subjectivity, since statistical data on
the test's adequacy as a predictive instrument are not likely to
be known by the interpreter. *Errors will probably be made in interpreting test scores unless there is a thorough understanding of child
growth and development.* Scores are likely to be interpreted with
finality, and past performance interpreted as indicative of future
performance. The "norm" may be interpreted as satisfactory for everyone, regardless of mental capacity. *Errors may also be made in
interpreting test scores unless there is a thorough understanding of the
individual pupil and the effect such factors as his home environment,
his vocabulary and reading ability, and his social adjustment may
have had on his test scores.*

The Interview

Interviews may be conducted for several purposes to "get acquainted" with the pupil, to obtain information, to give information, or for counseling. Seldom, if ever, does an interview serve one purpose or function exclusively. In the "get-acquainted" interview, the interviewer will undoubtedly obtain considerable information from the pupil. The counseling interview usually furnishes the interviewer with additional information. The information-getting interview may, likewise, have some counseling value but, as the name implies, its primary purpose is to obtain information from the pupil that would be difficult or impossible to obtain in another way. This type of interview is easier to conduct than a counseling interview, where the counselor has a more sensitive and dynamic role to play. But, in common with other types of interviews, it is necessary for the interviewer to develop a friendly relationship with the pupil prior to and during the interview. Through the homeroom and other group meetings, and at the beginning of the interview, pupils may be informed of the need for gathering certain information. If they understand the use that will be made of this information and have confidence in the interviewer, they usually cooperate and give the desired information.

Teacher-Parent Conferences

Interviews with parents may be held in the school or in the home. In either case, obtaining information becomes a "two-way street." Parents can furnish teachers with information that will prove useful in understanding a youngster's behavior at school. On the other hand, the teacher can often help parents achieve a better understanding of their own child. Interviews in the home are desirable for two reasons: (a) the teacher obtains a first-hand impression of the pupil as a member of a family unit, and (b) parents generally talk more freely in familiar home surroundings than they do in the relatively unfamiliar school environment. From the home visit, the teacher or counselor may often gain a better understanding of parental concerns and hopes for their child, parental attitudes toward the teachers and the school, parental techniques for managing children, personal relationships in the home, and the customs, manners, and habits which members of the family observe as part of the daily routine. Yet, few school systems have encouraged their teachers to become well acquainted with their pupils' families. A home visit is more time-consuming for the teacher than a school conference, and schools rarely make provision for this extra time to be taken from the regular school day. Some teachers argue that an announced visit rarely provides the visitor with a normal or typical view of the home situation, while an unannounced visit often arouses resentment in parents that deprives the interview of much of its value.

Teacher-parent conferences are held more frequently in the school than in the home. The teacher finds the school conference more convenient than the home visit and has, close at hand, tests, papers, drawings, etc. that are of interest to the parent. Reference to these materials often accelerates the process of establishing a friendly, cooperative relationship. The school conference has one major weakness as a technique of gathering data on pupils. The parent usually comes to the conference to listen, rather than talk. During the course of the conference it is often difficult for the teacher to make the transition from the primary role of *information-giver* to *information-getter.*

Ample time should be allotted for each of these conferences. They will prove more effective as devices for building better teacher-parent and teacher-pupil understanding if they are scheduled over a period of several weeks rather than crammed into "Visitation Day" or "Parents Night." The following suggestions for parent conferences were prepared by the staff of the Curriculum and Guidance Department of School District No. 102, LaGrange, LaGrange Park, and Congress Park, Illinois.

SUGGESTIONS FOR PARENT CONFERENCES
I. *Introduction*

Parent conferences may well be the springboard for even better relationships between home and school. In order to serve this intended purpose, thoughtful planning and a voluntary approach are necessary.

The more teachers and parents understand each other's personalities the better the child is understood by both. Parents and teachers can reach mutual understandings without implying that they must see eye to eye on everything. Children are more relaxed and learn easier when their teachers and their parents know and understand each other.

Teachers' and parents' evaluations and discussions at the Planning Committee as well as the Administrative Council suggested sufficient value gained to warrant the continuation of parent conferences, with some justifiable modifications. In Grades 1-6 (self-contained) the classroom teachers are responsible for arranging for the conferences. In Grades 6-8 (departmental) the content-area teachers may arrange the conferences as needed. The homeroom teachers should be informed of the conferences in advance so that other members of the staff may be included, if desired.

II. *Planning for the Conferences*
1. Read and reread all data in the cumulative folder, but do not have the folder out during the conference.
2. Think through carefully the child's pattern of growth.
3. Anticipate some of the questions the parents may ask.

III. *Suggested Topics for Discussion*

In preparation for the conference choose topics from the following list, remembering that certain areas are more informative. Do not at any time have this list before you during the conference.

Home
1. In what activities does he engage and what is his reaction toward them?
2. What are his hobbies and special interests?
3. What responsibilities has he assumed and what is his reaction to them?
4. How does he use his leisure time when he is alone?
5. What is the child's place in the family?
6. What are his ambitions? Do the parents' wishes concur?

School
1. What does he think about school life?
2. How has he accepted activities with his peers?
3. What responsibilities has he accepted in the classroom?
4. What are his academic strengths and weaknesses?
5. What seems to be his behavior pattern?
6. On what problems, if any, need the home and the school work specifically?

IV. *Physical Set-Up*
1. Sit beside the parent at the desk or the reading table to give less formal atmosphere.
2. Avoid having the desk *between* you and the parent.
3. Avoid note-taking during the conference.

V. *Human Relations*
1. Put the parent at ease by creating a friendly atmosphere. (A smile and a handshake do wonders.)
2. Be relaxed yourself; be prepared and unhurried.
3. Be a sympathetic, interested, and courteous sounding-board!
4. Keep up a *two*-way conversation.
5. Let the parent know that you like his child, even though you may not approve of all the things he does.

VI. *The Conference*
1. Be willing to learn from the conference. (Can you tact-

fully discover more about the child's interests, his out-of-school activities, his friends, his feelings, his habits, his health, his problems?)

2. Concentrate on constructive comments, recognizing the child's good qualities.
3. Use a vocabulary parents can understand.
4. Use samples of the child's work, if you wish.
5. If comparisons are made, use the child's own achievement as a basis.
6. Be objective and withhold judgment.
7. Try to get suggestions from the parent by asking leading questions.
8. Try not to be overly surprised at anything unusual or shocking the parent may reveal.
9. Avoid criticizing other people.
10. Ask the parent to visit classes.
11. Plan a follow-up *if* the parent expresses the desire. (If deemed necessary, refer to the counselors through your principal.)

VII. *Record Keeping*

Following the conference, record meaningful notes for future use in preparing comments for the cumulative folder and/or for the report card.

VIII. *District Planning*

1. Announce to the parents at Parent Nights, explaining fully the purpose and the plan of our parent conferences.
2. Plan to have the initial conferences throughout the first three quarters, leaving the last quarter for conferences regarding summer remedial work, retention, and the like.

Case Conferences

Case conferences are of two types: (a) those held regularly by staff specialists in guidance of psychology for the purpose of studying the records of an individual pupil, pooling their own information, and arriving at a mutually agreed upon course of action; and (b) those conducted for the same purpose but attended by *all* staff members, teachers and specialists alike, who are directly concerned with the case or who have information to contribute. The second type of conference may also serve as an in-service education activity and may be opened to staff members not directly concerned with the case. The case conference is not primarily a technique for gathering data on pupils but one of coordinating and interpreting data already gathered. However, as data on a pupil are coordinated and interpreted, many of the participants and/or observers will gain new information on the pupil and new insight into the causes of his behavior. The primary obstacle to a more frequent use of the case conference technique is the amount of time required for such a conference and the difficulty in scheduling it at a time when all staff members who are directly concerned with the case find it possible to attend.

Personnel Records

The term "personnel records" is usually interpreted to include all the records of a school that are employed for the purpose of organizing, preserving, and accumulating information about individual pupils. Among the types of personnel records that are easily identified are health records, reports to parents, test records, pupil program and course-of-study cards, transcripts of credits, and cumulative records. Many other types of routine forms, passes, and permits might also be interpreted as part of the personnel-record system.

Most valuable of all the types of personnel records are the instruments used to synthesize and centralize the significant information gathered on pupils through the use of the various tools and techniques just discussed. These instruments, usually identified as *cumulative records,* will either house other types of records such as the health record or will contain a summary of data to be found on other records. A comprehensive cumulative record system is indispensable to a school guidance program. Since these instruments not only preserve, accumulate, and centralize information on pupils, but also offer teachers at each grade level information on pupils obtained at previous grade levels or by special staff members, cumulative records may be included in the list of appraisal techniques available to school staff members. Information on the individual's home and environmental background, previous educational record, health, abilities and aptitudes, interests, leisure activities, social and emotional adjustment, work experience, and plans and goals may be obtained from properly maintained cumulative records.

A personnel-record system contains many types of records and performs many valuable services. It furnishes data important to the administration of the school, it provides the basis for follow-up studies and other types of research, and it enables placement officers to furnish college officials and personnel managers with valuable information on prospective students or employees. But these purposes must not be allowed to usurp the primary function of a record system. *The primary purpose of establishing a record system should be to improve the instruction and guidance of each individual pupil.* The cumulative record, which Peters and Farwell (44) call "the vehicle for the pupil inventory service," should be as free as possible of items not related to this central purpose.

Establishment and Developing a Record System—Warters (56) lists the following guiding principles in the establishment and development of a record system:

> 1. The development and revision of record forms for use in a particular school should be a cooperative project.
> 2. The faculty should start with simple records that all its members can use so that they may progress smoothly and steadily toward use of more comprehensive records.
> 3. Usable items that will actually be used are the ones to be included in the record forms adopted.
> 4. Certain questions regarding practical details should be considered before the first supply of record forms is prepared.
> 5. The adoption of the cumulative record form agreed upon should be considered tentative.
> 6. Revision, like the development of record forms, should be a cooperative undertaking.[2]

A program of teacher education in the establishment and development of a record system is desirable and should begin with a careful re-examination of the school's philosophy and objectives. After this has been accomplished, the faculty should be ready to discuss and decide (a) *why* records are important to the school, (b) *what* types of data they want to include in the records, (c) *how* they will use the records, (d) *who* will have access to the records, and (e) *where* the responsibility lies for their organization and maintenance. A definite plan should be formulated for collecting and recording the information to be included in the records.

Maintaining a Record System—Hatch and Dressel (26) identify the following problems in maintaining a record system:

> The issues regarding records can be clarified by considering a series of records and providing opportunity to mention and indicate ways to combat the more common objections or criticisms of cumulative records.
> 1. Uniformity vs. individuality
> It may seem contradictory, but the record system which has its origin in concern about individual differences must achieve a degree of uniformity by providing the same general types of

---

[2]By permission from *Techniques of Counseling*, by Jane Warters. Copyright, 1954. McGraw-Hill Book Company, Inc.

information on all students and a standard form for organizing it. Failure to provide such uniformity makes the records so difficult to use that they will be of little practical value. This consideration effectively rules out a system based entirely on accumulating isolated bits of information in a folder and suggests the need for a printed form involving a planned organization of common items of information.

2. Objectivity vs. subjectivity

Many traits and behaviors of students can be reported only on a subjective basis, but objectivity represents a goal toward which everyone contributing to records should strive. The more subjective items which inevitably partake of the personality of the reporter should be identified as written by the reporter.

3. Accessibility vs. restrictivity

Records which are to be helpful to teachers in understanding students must be readily accessible to them. The intermediation of a clerk, counselor, or principal will result in disuse. Likewise, each student through a teacher or counselor should have ready access to his own record but certainly not to that of other students. The implication of such accessibility is that certain highly confidential materials will not become a part of the permanent record system but will remain in the personal file or mind of the person receiving the information. Accessibility also requires some weighing of possible misuse by an unwise teacher against the disuse resulting from restrictivity. While such misuse is to be avoided, restrictions which will eliminate it will also greatly reduce the effectiveness of the record system.

4. Continuity vs. irregularity

Records to which items are contributed only at specified times or at highly irregular intervals are unlikely to represent a sufficiently broad sample of student behavior to be truly helpful in understanding a student. Such practice undermines their usefulness and will probably result in ultimate abandonment because the system is worthless.

5. Simplicity vs. complexity

Some median position on this alternative must be the goal. Simplicity must be sought only in so far as it is consistent with the range and kind of evidence collected. Hence, the achievement of simplicity becomes mainly a matter of careful organization of the record and of the reporting forms so as to minimize both the clerical work and the process of interpretation. Preprinted items which can be checked rather than blanks requiring the writing of a complete answer, for example, are simpler for the student to fill out and, because of the standardization, are more easily grasped by one referring to them. Such convenience must be weighed against the probable loss in individuality of response.

6. Benevolence vs. malevolence

This issue involves an in-service training program with teachers. Many teachers are primarily conscious of undesirable behaviors and are, therefore, inclined to report only these. Subconsciously these teachers may view the record as a disciplinary device or as a way to relieve their own aggressions. Clearly, the association of records with discipline will destroy much of their value in the guidance of students.

7. Utility vs. curiosity

A frequent objection to record systems is that the request for and filing of information involves an invasion of privacy. This objection goes hand in hand with a natural concern about who uses records and for what purposes. Most humans do have considerable curiosity with respect to the private lives of others. Casual chatter about humorous or unusual items on the record is to be avoided; for each such comment encourages more like it, resulting in an ultimate letdown in ethics and probable student and parental rebellion against the system. The earlier cautions with regard to the legality and wisdom of including certain types of information in the file should be kept in mind.

8. Commission vs. omission

Records are likely to show more of what a student has done than of what he has omitted to do. Thus, the student who makes a nuisance of himself by violent handwaving in a desire to recite may energize the teacher to a report.

The student who never volunteers may be overlooked, although the absence of any item on the record would seem to imply normality in this respect. The absence of certain types of behavior is just as significant a thing to report as the presence of others.[3]

A practical problem in the maintenance of records involves the degree of participation expected of teachers, counselors, and clerical workers. Since the size of the school (and the school budget) will have considerable effect upon the amount of clerical help available, the most effective method of operation will vary from school to school. However, the following points should be kept in mind when dealing with this problem:

1. The process of collecting and reporting all kinds of information on students is a time-consuming one for teachers. Their clerical

---

[3]R. N. Hatch and P. L. Dressel, *Guidance Services in the Secondary School* (Dubuque, Iowa: William C. Brown Company, 1953), pp. 60-63. Used with permission of the publisher.

work should be reduced to a minimum through (a) the judi-
cious use of printed report forms and (b) the employment of
experienced clerical help to record the information on the
cumulative record.

2. Since the collection and recording of information on students is
considered an invasion of privacy by some parents, every effort
should be made to insure that the material in the records is
treated as professionally and as confidentially as possible. Confidential information obtained during counseling with the student
or his family should remain in the counselor's files rather than
be placed in the cumulative record. A note in the record will
suffice to identify the location of this material if it is needed by
professionally responsible persons. Clerical workers should not be
permitted to interpret record material to parents and should be
impressed with the dangers of "gossiping" about items appearing in the records.

3. The clerical staff should be given printed directions for recording the different types of information. This will (a) reduce
the danger of information becoming "garbled" during the tran-
scription process and (b) insure standardized recording
procedures that will enable teachers and counselors to obtain
information quickly and easily.

4. Quite often, subjective data need to be summarized and/or
interpreted before being placed in the cumulative record. This
should be the responsibility of the counselor rather than the
clerical staff.

Teachers frequently report that the cumulative records in their
school are seldom used. There are many possible reasons for the
existence of such a situation. The staff may not have been given
a chance to plan the record system and, consequently, may
neither understand nor support the program. The records may
not be easy to read or interpret. The central record office may
not be easily accessible. An investigation by Kaczkowski (36)
indicates that schools have made little or no attempt to integrate or synthesize the important data on each student. Possibly
staff members simply find it too difficult and time-consuming to
obtain what they want from the records.

Types of Cumulative Records—Traxler (54) traces the development of modern personnel records from early school records and
reports on the origin of cumulative records. Warters (56) discusses

recent trends toward expanded and more uniform records. A review by Kaczkowski (36) of seventy cumulative records from large metropolitan school districts and from schools recommended by state departments of public instruction reveals that the *typical* record was constructed of manila tagboard, was 9½ by 11½ inches in size, and was buff colored. Records were of the *card, folder, envelope,* and *booklet* type, with the *folder* type predominating.

The cumulative record *card* has the very serious disadvantage of lacking adequate space to accommodate the multiplicity of information that many schools have found necessary to gather on their students.

The cumulative record *folder* has four sides instead of two available for recording information and can also serve as a container for additional material. However, the folder must be removed from the file and enclosures must be removed from the folder in order to read the information recorded on the inner side of the folder. This disadvantage has led many schools to adopt a combination *card* and *folder* system. In this system, the folder itself is either entirely blank or the inside area is left blank. The cumulative record card and other material can be withdrawn and replaced at any time. This system can be effective if enclosures do not become too numerous and if they can be maintained within the folder in some organized fashion. Some schools have found it profitable to keep the cumulative record card and the folder in separate files.

The cumulative record *envelope* will generally hold more material than the folder type and will hold it more securely. The contents are usually identified on the front of the envelope. Schools with a great variety of printed forms and records often find the envelope more satisfactory than the folder.

The cumulative record *booklet* provides more material than can be reported through use of any of the other types. The Guidance Services Department of Evanston (Illinois) Township High School has developed a Student Personnel Folder that contains twenty-two pages of material. Included in the booklet are a three-page personal data blank, a two-page program and grade record, a four-year subject elections plan, an entrance test information sheet, the Career Testing Battery, a four-year activities plan, a two-page activity record, four pages devoted to the pupil's future educational and vocational plans, and several pages for counselor notes. The cumulative record booklet has these advantages over the other types of records: (a) a very large quantity of material can be maintained in an organized fashion, (b) easy removal and addition of pages makes frequent revision possible, and (c) pagination and indexing greatly simplifies the task of the reader.

Other Records—A great variety of forms is required for the administration of a guidance program in any large school system. The following types of personnel records are frequently found in these schools:

1. Elementary School Registration Card
2. Health Record Card
3. Family Census Card
4. Pupil's Excuse for Absence or Tardiness
5. Elementary School Report Card
6. Perfect Attendance Certificate
7. Elementary School Certificate
8. Transfer Record
9. Scholarship Certificate
10. High School Registration Card
11. Classification-Personal Data Card
12. Test and Personal Data Card
13. High School Library Reading Record
14. Student Pass
15. High School Report Card
16. Student Program Card
17. Request for Counseling Form
18. Counseling Summary Card

The counseling summary card represents a rather recent development in personnel records. As personnel records have expanded, it has become increasingly difficult for counselors to remain well acquainted with the material in the records. Counseling summary cards allow counselors to keep themselves "up-to-date" on their students with a minimum of time and energy. Figure 2 represents the counseling summary card developed by Lelia L. Teague, Counselor at the Clayton, Missouri, High School.

Summary

In order to provide effective services for pupils, a guidance program must first gather a considerable amount of data on each pupil. Areas of the individual requiring study include home and environmental conditions, previous educational experience, health, abilities and aptitudes, interests, leisure activities, social and emotional adjustment, work experience, and plans and goals. The tools and techniques

Figure 2

COUNSELING SUMMARY CARD

THE SCHOOL DISTRICT OF CLAYTON
CLAYTON, MISSOURI

Last Name	First Name	Middle Name	Address	Telephone	Elementary School	Birth

Family	Occupation	Education	Birth	Health
Father:				
Mother:				

Siblings: ______ Birth ______ : ______ Birth ______ : ______ Birth ______ : ______ Birth

Educational Plans:	(9)	(10)	(11)	(12)
" "	(9)	(10)	(11)	(12)
" "	(9)	(10)	(11)	(12)
Vocational Plans:	(9)	(10)	(11)	(12)

ACADEMIC ACHIEVEMENT

Grade 9	S 1	S 2	Cr.	Grade 10	S 1	S 2	Cr.	Grade 11	S 1	S 2	Cr.	Grade 12	S 1	S 2	Cr.
Class Rank															
Attendance															
Counselor															

MENTAL ABILITY

Date: Test:	% ile N	C		% ile N	C		% ile N	C		% ile N	C

ACHIEVEMENT

Date:	Test:	N	C	Date:	Test:	N	C	Date:	Test:	N	C	Date:	Test:	N	C

READING

Date:	Test:	N	C	Date:	Test:	N	C	Date:	Test:	N	C	Date:	Test:	N	C

APTITUDE

Date:	Test:	N	C	Date:	Test:	N	C	Date:	Test:	N	C	Date:	Test:	N	C

N - %ile National Norms; C - %ile Clayton Norms

Figure 2 (continued)

SPECIAL TESTS							
Grade 9 Date: Test:	Zile	Grade 10 Date: Test:	Zile	Grade 11 Date: Test:	Zile	Grade 12 Date: Test:	Zile

INTEREST

Date: Test:		Date: Test:		Date: Test:		Date: Test:	

PERSONALITY

Date: Test:		Date: Test:		Date: Test:		Date: Test:	

ACTIVITIES
(Offices)

WORK EXPERIENCE

AWARDS

necessary for gathering this data include observation, anecdotal records, rating scales, self-report forms, the autobiography, sociometric devices, psychological tests, the interview, teacher-parent conferences, case conferences, and personnel records.

Bibliography

1.   Adams, James F. *Counseling and Guidance: A Summary View*. New York: The Macmillan Company, 1965. Chap. 6.
2.   Anastasi, Anne. *Psychological Testing*. 2nd ed. New York: The Macmillan Company, 1961.
3.   Arbuckle, Dugald S. *Counseling: Philosophy, Theory and Practice*. Boston: Allyn & Bacon, Inc., 1965. Chap. 5.
4.   ———. *Pupil Personnel Services in American Schools*. Boston: Allyn & Bacon, Inc., 1962. Chaps. 7, 8.
5.   Berdie, Ralph F., Wilbur L. Layton, Edward O. Swanson, Theda Hagenah. *Testing in Guidance and Counseling*. New York: McGraw-Hill Book Company, Inc., 1963. Chaps. 5-8, 15.
6.   Blanchard, Howard L. and Laurence S. Flaum, *Guidance: A Longitudinal Approach*. Minneapolis: Burgens Publishing Company, 1962. Chaps. 4-6.
7.   Boy, Angelo V. and Gerald J. Pine. *Client Centered Counseling in the Secondary School*. Boston: Houghton Mifflin Company, 1963. Chap. 6.
8.   Buros, Oscar K., ed. *The Fifth Mental Measurements Yearbook*. Highland Park, New Jersey: The Gryphon Press, 1958.
9.   Byrne, Richard Hill. *The School Counselor*. Boston: Houghton Mifflin Company, 1963. Chaps. 8, 9.
10.   Cottingham, Harold F. *Directed Readings in Foundations of Guidance and Personnel Services*. Bloomington, Illinois: McKnight & McKnight Publishing Co., 1964. Chap. 3.
11.   ——— and William Hopke, *Guidance in Junior High School: Principles and Practices*. Bloomington, Illinois: McKnight & McKnight Publishing Co., 1961. Chaps. 6, 7.
12.   Cronbach, Lee J. *Essentials of Psychological Testing*. 2nd ed., Part II. New York: Harper and Brothers, 1960.
13.   Crow, Lester D. and Alice Crow. *An Introduction to Guidance*. 2nd ed. New York: American Book Company, 1960. Chap. 8.

197

14.   ———. *Organization and Conduct of Guidance Services*. New York: David McKay Company, Inc., 1965. Chaps. 9, 10.

15.   ———. *Readings in Guidance*. New York: David McKay Company, Inc., 1962, Chaps. 39-41.

16.   Darley, J. G. and Theda Hagenah. *Vocational Interest Measurement*. Minneapolis: University of Minnesota Press, 1955.

17.   Davis, Allison and Robert Hess. "How Fair is an IQ Test?" *The University of Chicago Magazine*, January, 1951.

18.   Drasgow, James. "To Test or Counsel?" *The Vocational Guidance Quarterly*, 7:4, Summer, 1959, 252.

19.   Farwell, Gail F. and H. J. Peters. *Guidance Readings for Counselors*. Chicago: Rand McNally & Co., 1960. Chap. 5.

20.   Fick, Reuel L. "The Problem Check List: A Valuable Approach to Counseling," *Occupations*, March, 1952.

21.   Freeman, Frank S. *Theory and Practice of Psychological Testing*. New York: Henry Holt and Company, 1950.

22.   Froehlich, Clifford P. *Guidance Services in Schools*. New York: McGraw-Hill Book Company, Inc., 1958. Chap. 9.

23.   Gardner, Eric F. and George G. Thompson. "Measuring and Interpreting Social Relations," *Test Service Notebook, Number 22*. Yonkers-On-Hudson, New York: World Book Company, 1959.

24.   Glanz, Edward C. *Foundations and Principles of Guidance*. Boston: Allyn & Bacon, Inc., 1964. Chaps. 6, 8, 9.

25.   Guidance and Counselor Training Staff, Department of Administrative and Educational Services, College of Education, Michigan State University. *The Anecdotal Record and The Autobiography*. East Lansing, Michigan: Michigan State University, 1957.

26.   Hatch, R. N. and P. L. Dressel. *Guidance Services in the Secondary School*. Dubuque, Iowa: William C. Brown Company, 1953. Pp. 60-3.

27.   ——— and James W. Costar. *Guidance Services in the Secondary Schools*. Dubuque, Iowa: William C. Brown Company, 1963. Chaps. 2, 3, 7.

28.   ———, and Buford Stefflre. *Administration of Guidance Services: Organization, Supervision, Evaluation*. Englewood Cliffs, New Jersey: Prentice-Hall, Inc., 1958. Chap. 5.

29.   Hollis, Joseph W. and Lucile U. Hollis. *Organizing for Effective Guidance*. Chicago: Science Research Associates, Inc., 1965. Chaps. 11-16.

30.   Hoyt, Kenneth B. "Methods of Individual Appraisal," *Individual Appraisal in Student Personnel* (Monograph). Pittsburg, Kansas: Kansas State College, June, 1962.

31.   ———. "The Student Autobiography—A Neglected Tool in Guidance," *The School Counselor*, IV:3, March, 1957, 54-8.

32.   Humphreys, J. Anthony, Arthur E. Traxler, and Robert North. *Guidance Services*. 2nd ed. Chicago: Science Research Associates, Inc., 1960. Chap. 7.

33.   Hutson, Percival W. *The Guidance Function in Education*. New York: Appleton-Century-Crofts, 1958. Chaps. 11-13.

34.   Johnson, W. F., *et al., Pupil Personnel and Guidance Services*. New York: McGraw-Hill Book Company, Inc., 1961. Chaps. 13-15.

35.   Jones, Arthur J. *Principles of Guidance*, 5th ed. New York: McGraw-Hill Book Company, Inc., 1963. Chaps. 4-6.

36.   Kaczkowski, Henry R. "The Current Status of Cumulative Records," *The Vocational Guidance Quarterly*, 7:4, Summer, 1959, 211-213.

37.   Mathewson, Robert Henry. *Guidance Policy and Practice*. 3rd ed. New York: Harper & Row, Publishers, 1962. Chap. 12.

38.   ———, *et al. Readings in Guidance*. New York: Henry Holt and Company, 1959, Chaps. 5-7.

39.   McGowan, John F. and Lyle D. Schmidt, *Counseling: Readings in Theory and Practice*. New York: Holt, Rinehart & Winston, Inc., 1962. Chap. 11.

40.   Miller, Carroll H. *Foundations of Guidance*. New York: Harper and Brothers, 1961. Chap. 9.

41.   Nunnally, Jum C., Jr. *Tests and Measurements*. New York: McGraw-Hill Book Company, Inc., 1959.

42.   Ohlsen, Merle M. *Guidance Services in the Modern School*. New York: Harcourt, Brace & World, Inc., 1964. Chaps. 6-9.

43.   Patterson, C. H. *Counseling and Guidance in Schools*. New York: Harper and Brothers, 1962. Chap. 9.

44.   Peters, H. J. and Gail Farwell. *Guidance: A Developmental Approach*. Chicago: Rand McNally & Co., 1959. Chaps. 5-8, p. 129.

45.   Remmers, H. H., N. L. Gage, and J. Francis Rummel. *A Practical Introduction To Measurement and Evaluation*. 2nd ed. New York: Harper & Row, Publishers, 1965.

46.   Riccio, Anthony C. "The Status of the Autobiography," *Peabody Journal of Education*, 36, July, 1958. Pp. 33-6.

47.   Rothney, John W., and Bert A. Roens. *Counseling the Individual Student*. New York: The Dryden Press, 1949. P. 86.

48.   Stewart, Lawrence and Charles Warnath. *The Counselor and Society: A Cultural Approach*. Boston: Houghton Mifflin Company, 1965. Chaps. 7-8.

49.   Stoops, Emery and Gunner L. Wahlquist. *Principles and Practices in Guidance*. New York: McGraw-Hill Book Company, Inc., 1958. Chaps. 2, 3.

50.   Strang, Ruth. *Counseling Technics in College and Secondary School*. Rev. ed. New York: Harper and Brothers, 1949. Pp. 49-50.

51.   Symonds, P. M. *Diagnosing Personality and Conduct*. New York: Appleton-Century-Crofts, 1931. P. 122.

52.   Thorpe, Louis P., Milo E. Whitson, Denis Baron, and Georgia Sachs Adams. *Studying Social Relationships in the Classroom: Sociometric Methods for the Teacher*. Chicago: Science Research Associates, Inc., 1959.

53.   Tolbert, E. L. *Introduction to Counseling*. New York: McGraw-Hill Book Company, Inc., 1959. Chaps. 3-6, 8.

54.   Traxler, Arthur E. *Techniques of Guidance*. New York: Harper and Brothers, 1957. Chaps. 4-10.

55.   Tyler, Leona E. *The Work of the Counselor*. New York: Appleton-Century-Crofts, 1961. Chaps. 5-9.

56.   Warters, Jane. *Techniques of Counseling*. 2nd ed. New York: McGraw-Hill Book Company, Inc., 1964. Chaps. 2-7, pp. 252-54.

57.   Weiss, L. A. "Rating Scales," *Psychological Bulletin*, 30, March, 1933. Pp. 186-7.

58.   Weitz, Henry. *Behavior Change Through Guidance*. New York: John Wiley & Sons, Inc., 1964. Chaps. 5, 6.

59.   Wesman, A. G. "Aptitude, Intelligence and Achievement," *Test Service Bulletin*. No. 51. New York: The Psychological Corporation, December, 1956.

60.   Zeran, F. R. and A. C. Riccio. *Organization and Administration of Guidance Services*. Chicago: Rand McNally & Co., 1962.

9

The Counseling Service

The counseling service has previously been identified as only one of several services of the guidance program. A sound counseling service cannot operate in isolation from other guidance services. The manner of its functioning within the guidance program will depend, to a great extent, upon several factors: (a) the degree to which the school defines or interprets counseling as a professional service, (b) the orientation and qualifications of those designated as counselors, and (c) the support and cooperation of the administration and the rest of the school staff.

Chapters 5 and 6 were concerned with the role of the counselor *in the total educational program.* This chapter deals with the role of the counselor *in counseling,* beginning with a review of some of the early approaches to counseling, continuing with some present-day interpretations and definitions of counseling, and concluding with a discussion

of some of the issues and problems that arise when we provide
counseling services in our schools.

Historical Perspective—Early Approaches to Counseling

An early definition of counseling equated it with teaching. Arbuckle (5) insisted that "the teacher *can* function as a counselor, in
many modern schools he *is* functioning as a counselor, and if our
children are to undergo the educational experiences that should be a
part of their living in a democratic society, then he *must* function as a
counselor." Pierson and Grant (61)strongly opposed this conception
of counseling and asserted that such an argument is comparable to
insisting that teachers, since they observe the health of students, en-
force attendance laws, and keep petty cash accounts, must function as
physicians, lawyers, and accountants. An interpretation of counseling
that equates it with teaching clearly decentralizes the counseling
service and implies that the "non-teaching counselor" would be occupied, to a large extent, with (a) administering and coordinating the
counseling service and (b) organizing and administering a program of
in-service education in counseling for the teaching staff.

While Arbuckle insisted that the teacher *must* function as a counselor (he no longer holds this point of view) other writers interpreted
counseling as a function that *may* be performed by teachers and
others not specifically trained for counseling. McKinney (51) has
said, "Teachers, ministers, social workers, personnel officers, lawyers,
doctors, parents, recreational workers, nurses—all sorts of specialists
and experts counsel constantly." In 1951, Wrenn (93) made no direct
mention of training when he argued, "Counseling is a personal and
dynamic relationship between two people who approach a mutually
defined problem with mutual consideration of each other to the end
that the younger, or less mature, or more troubled of the two is aided
to a self-determined resolution of his problems." Two years earlier,
Williamson and Foley (90) had stated that "counseling has been
defined as a face-to-face situation in which by reason of training, skill,
or confidence vested in him by the other, one person helps the second
person to face, perceive, clarify, solve, and resolve adjustment problems." These definitions did not resolve the problem of the *type* and
degree of participation by teachers in the counseling service. Schools
subscribing to the philosophy that counseling may be done by one with
"training, skill, *or confidence* vested in him by the other" or by one who
is older, more mature, or less troubled would be expected to support a
partly decentralized counseling service where specially selected

teacher-counselors and/or homeroom teachers supplement the work of the full-time counselor.

A third definition of counseling restricted it to a relationship between a client and an individual with professional training in this field. Pepinsky and Pepinsky (60) offered the following definition:

> The term *counseling relationship* refers to the interaction which (a) occurs between two individuals called "counselor" and "client," (b) takes place within a professional setting, and (c) is initiated and maintained as a means of facilitating changes in the behavior of the client. . . . The counseling relationship develops from the interaction between two individuals, one a professionally trained worker and the other a person who seeks his services. . . . To speak of the counseling relationship is to say that two persons, and no more than two, stand in this relationship, and in this relationship only, to each other.

Schools supporting this viewpoint would insist that staff members designated as counselors have professional training in the techniques of interviewing, educational and psychological testing, the use of career information, and the use and coordination of school and community resources.

A final definition of counseling made no attempt to restrict counseling to a person-to-person relationship. By 1951, Froehlich (32) had become the most outspoken proponent of what he termed "multiple-counseling." He insisted that it differed from teaching, group guidance, and group psychotherapy and that, under certain conditions, it could be as effective as individual counseling. It is obvious that a school's adherence to the "multiple counseling" concept would cause substantial changes in the organization and program of its counseling service.

The publication of Carl Rogers' book, *Counseling and Psychotherapy,* in 1942, marked the beginning of a debate over counseling theory that is still alive today, despite considerable change in its nature and intensity. The opposing groups became identified as "directive" and "nondirective" or as "clinical" and "client-centered" counselors. Counselors of both persuasions considered these labels to be misleading, but they have not entirely disappeared from counseling literature. A third theory of counseling, known as the "eclectic" approach, developed sometime later among personnel workers who recognized values in both the directive and nondirective approaches and felt that counselors should be flexible enough to employ different counseling approaches. The approach to be used would be determined by the nature and extent of the client's problem. These three points of view will be discussed briefly in order to gain some appreciation of the effect each might have on a school counseling service. However, it is important to remember that (a) *we are examining these points of view from the standpoint of historical perspective,* (b) counseling theory cannot be viewed today as being of three distinct types, (c) there are common elements in all systems of counseling, (d) the personality of the counselor will have considerable effect upon the counseling techniques he employs and the relationship he maintains with counselees, and (e) the personality of the counselor may not always be in harmony with the theoretical approach to which he is oriented.

Client-Centered Counseling

The chief exponent of the *client-centered* approach to counseling has been Carl Rogers. In 1945, Rogers (64) defined client-centered counseling as a "definitely structured relationship, highly permissive in nature, in which the client finds an opportunity to explore freely and without defensiveness, his difficulties and the emotionalized attitudes which surround them." *A basic tenet of client-centered counseling is that the initiative must rest with the client.* He must decide for himself if he is in need of help, he must seek that help, and he must accept the responsibility for solving his problem. *A second major tenet is that every individual has a tremendous capacity for adaptation and readjustment, a strong drive toward maturity and independence.* The counselor must depend on this force, not upon his own influence, for therapeutic change. The counselor's role becomes one of structuring and reflecting feeling, creating an atmosphere of security in which the client is free to talk about his problems in his own way, at his own pace, and for his own purposes. The client is under no compulsion to reveal himself except through his own inner tensions. As his feelings are reflected, the client learns to know his problems, to accept them, to gain insight into why he has them and to evaluate accurately his need and goals. Rogers (65) listed the following steps in nondirective or client-centered counseling:

1. *The individual comes voluntarily for help.* In cases where students were referred to the counselor by some other individual, client-centered counseling would require that a permissive relationship be set up that would enable the student to make his own decision regarding whether or not to continue with the interview situation.

2. *The counseling situation is defined.* The client is encouraged to accept the responsibility for working out the solution to his

problem. This responsibility can hardly be encouraged unless the counselor has faith in the individual's ability to help himself once he has freed himself from the forces impending his natural drive toward adjustment, maturity, and independence.

3. *The counselor encourages free expression of feelings regarding the problem.* By displaying a friendly, interested, receptive attitude, the counselor enables the client to express his feelings of hostility, anxiety, concern, guilt, and indecision and to experience, thereby, some relief from the tension and pressure that he felt before.

4. *The counselor accepts, recognizes, and reflects these negative feelings of the client.* By responding to the feelings underlying the client's words rather than to the intellectual content, the counselor helps the client to understand and accept these negative feelings.

5. *Full expression of negative feelings is followed by faint and tentative expressions of positive feelings.*

6. *The counselor accepts, recognizes, and reflects these positive feelings of the client.*

7. *The period of release or free expression is followed by a gradual development of insight.* The client understands and accepts his problem as he begins to understand and accept himself.

8. *As the client recognizes and accepts emotionally as well as intellectually his real attitudes and desires, and as he comes to a clearer understanding of the causes of his behavior and gains a fresh perception of his life situation, he perceives the decisions that he must make and the possible course of action open to him.*

9. *The client begins to translate insight into action.*

10. *Further growth takes place with further achievement of insight.*

11. *There is increasingly integrated positive action.*

12. *The client feels a decreasing need for help and recognizes that the counseling must end.* He terminates the counseling relationship.[1]

This chronological presentation of the client-centered process leaves no doubt that diagnosis becomes the responsibility of the client, not the counselor. It is the client who must dominate the counseling process. As Rogers (66) said: "The function of responsible integration of knowledge, the evaluation of self, the function of responsible choice, of planning, of taking action—all of these evaluative

---

[1]Used with permission of Houghton Mifflin Company.

activities are lodged with the client, and he is respected as the person upon whom they rest."

Criticisms of the Client-Centered Approach—Certainly the client-centered philosophy, as expressed by Rogers, can be helpful to teachers, counselors, and others who have frequent contact with students and their problems. But before examining the major contributions of the client-centered school of counseling, it seems necessary to identify the criticisms leveled against this approach. Thorne (76) mentioned seven inadequacies which can be summarized as follows:

1. The client's evaluation of himself is accepted at face value without reference to the objective facts in the case.
2. The client may only scratch the surface of his problem and, unaided, never get to the underlying motives and roots of the difficulty.
3. The nondirective counselor often fails to follow up significant leads that the client gives him.
4. The nondirective counselor may refrain from giving information and advice when it might help the client move forward to a better adjustment.
5. In his efforts to remain neutral, the inexperienced nondirective counselor often fails to meet the client's expectation of what counseling should be; the result is client dissatisfaction and resentment.
6. Case history data are neglected; this makes adequate diagnosis impossible.
7. The nondirective method is too often used exclusively when other methods would be more effective.

With respect to Thorne's last criticism it is interesting to note that Rogers does not like to identify the client-centered approach as a "method." In *Client-Centered Therapy* (63) he says:

> There has been a tendency to regard the nondirective or client-centered approach as something static—a method, a technique, a rather rigid system. Nothing could be further from the truth. The group of professional workers in this field are working with dynamic concepts which they are constantly revising in the light of continuing clinical experience and in the light of research findings. The picture is one of the fluid changes in a general approach to problems of human relationships, rather than a situation in which some relatively rigid technique is more or less mechanically applied.[2]

---

[2]Used with permission of Houghton Mifflin Company.

In an attempt to relate the client-centered technique to school counseling, Strang (75) identified the following situations in which the approach would not appear to be workable:

1. When the counselee becomes more and more confused, more and more impatient with the nondirective approach.

2. When the counselee says, "I see what I ought to do but I just don't do it."

3. When he is under great stress and needs reassurance, suggestions, and other "palliative techniques" to get past the crisis.

4. When the counselee is a compulsive neurotic whose thoughts go round and round in a closed circle.

5. When the counselee is depressed and cannot get out of this state by himself.

6. When the counselee is a person with a very low I.Q. who lacks ability to make a self-analysis.

7. Whenever the interview reaches a point at which the resources of the counselee are obviously inadequate—when he lacks information or the power of analysis. To facilitate progress in such cases, especially in the short contact, the counselor provides help over and above the client's own resources.

8. When there is extreme disparity between the client's aspirations and his potential.

9. When verbal communication is very difficult for the counselee. If the counselor persists in expecting this kind of counselee to talk freely, he loses rapport, or even creates an argumentative atmosphere or a clash of wills, as in the following instance:

Student: What do you want me to do now?
Counselor: I'm not particular; anything you want to tell me
Student: I'd rather answer questions. I can answer questions better than I can start a conversation.

In this case the counselor finally suggested that the interview be used to develop the counselee's conversational ability. The counselee then began to talk about current events, books he had read, and other intellectual topics out of line with the direct purpose of the counseling. For this student, who needed social experience, such a use of the interview time may have been a sound investment when the more vital nondirective method failed.[3]

Boy and Pine (15) have made an excellent case for client-centered counseling in the secondary school. However, most counselors would agree that there are practical limitations to the employment of this approach in our schools. *Time* is an important limitation. Rogers

---

[3]Used with permission of Harper and Brothers.

(63) has pointed out that fifteen years ago, client-centered counseling tended to average five or six interviews each, and rarely to run longer than fifteen. Today, cases average fifteen to twenty interviews, and fifty or one hundred interviews are not unusual. Current responsibilities assigned to many school counselors make it impossible for them to employ the client-centered approach to any great extent without seriously jeopardizing the balance of the school counseling service. *Referrals* constitute a second limiting factor. Many counselors are involved, to varying degrees, in the interpretation of school regulations and the disciplinary measures caused by infractions of these regulations. Client-centered counselors, operating in such a situation, might find these responsibilities a serious handicap in their efforts to establish permissive relationships with students. The third practical limitation to the employment of the client-centered approach in school counseling is *the heavy incidence of problem situations that center around effective study habits, choosing a college, choosing a vocation, applying for a scholarship, etc.* These problems usually require a certain amount of giving and receiving information that may or may not be considered counseling but still consume a large portion of the counselor's time.

Contributions of Client-Centered Counseling—Client-centered counseling has made three major contributions. First, it forced a reappraisal of the *personality vs. skill* issue. It reminded counselors that rapport is not a one-way street. The whole concept of "acceptance" and "permissiveness" is based on respect for the client as a person and a recognition of his right to agree or disagree, cooperate or not cooperate, be friendly or unfriendly, change or not change. It further reminded counselors and others who found themselves in a "helping" relationship that skill in "helping" was no substitute for a sincere *desire* to help others and a pervasive *faith* in the ability of individuals to help themselves. Second, client-centered counseling focused attention on a common weakness of human beings in our society; the urge to preach, to give advice, to do things *to* and *for* the individual. Rogers and his followers were not the first to deplore "expertizing" and the counselor's undue concern for the solution of problems rather than the counseling process itself. But the client-centered approach has helped teachers and counselors realize that the counseling process is a learning process, that the most effective "learning" in counseling is self-initiated learning, and that, consequently, the *process* of counseling deserves more emphasis than the *outcome*. Finally, through their extensive recording and reporting of counseling interviews, the client-centered group must be given considerable credit for instituting a type of research methodology that has enabled us to make a more scientific analysis of the counseling process and a more objective evaluation of its effect on the client.

Clinical Counseling

E. G. Williamson, Dean of Students at the University of Minnesota, has been the leading advocate of a school of counseling that was variously labeled as *clinical, directive,* and *counselor-centered.* While Williamson and his group referred to themselves as clinical counselors, Froehlich (31), Shostrom and Brammer (68), and others characterized this approach as directive or counselor-centered. There is some justification for the use of the terms "directive" and "counselor-centered" if we refer to the earlier writings of the men in this group. Williamson, in his book, *How To Counsel Students* (89), wrote, "Ordinarily, the counselor states his point of view with definiteness, attempting through exposition to enlighten the student." Darley (24) stated that "the interview seems somewhat similar to a sales situation, since the counselor attempts to sell the student certain ideas about himself, certain plans of action, or certain desirable changes in attitudes." Bingham and Moore (11) identified the three major functions of counseling as (a) to give information, (b) to secure information, and (c) to influence or motivate the student. However, subsequent statements by these men reflected considerable change in viewpoint. Darley's brochure, *The Interview in Counseling* (25) published in 1946, included this statement: "Whenever the interviewer starts to impose his ideas on the client, it would be well for him to beware of his own inclinations to dominate." And Williamson's current position is more accurately reflected in these words (26):

> This is what I am arguing for, as an explicit responsibility of the counselor: to help the student become more sophisticated, more matured in understanding the value options that he faces and to identify clearly those that he prefers. The search is the important educational experience—not a control of behavior, a rigging in favor of one choice or the other, even though the counselor may have his personal preference.... We need to invent new ways of helping him continue his search for values because he will not understand himself until he more clearly perceives his own implicit value orientation. I fail to see how he can achieve self-understanding until his commitments to value systems determine his behavior, and surely such is our objective in counseling.... In vocational guidance we have operated for a long time on our implicit value commitment as counselors that a

student is not really making a "good" choice unless the choice is based upon demonstrated possession of sufficient aptitude and interests. This value orientation of counselors has proved to be highly successful in helping students make more satisfying and adequate choices. I use it to illustrate the fact that it has been possible to bring value orientation into counseling without denying the student his own precious right of self-determination.[4]

The clinical counselor does not accept the thesis that every individual has, within himself, the resources necessary to solve his problems. The clinical counselor feels that (a) many students are too immature to engage in self-diagnosis, to arrive at self-understanding, and to engage in self-planning unaided by an older or more experienced person; (b) other students, having been told what to do all their lives, are unwilling to accept the responsibility for making their own decisions; and (c) some problems are too complex to be solved by the most mature and the most willing students unless they receive some assistance. As Williamson (88) phrased it: "The history of pedagogy, as well as that of therapy, indicates that some types of direct assistance from outside the individual's human capacities seem to be needed to achieve inner growth."

The clinical counselor also feels rather strongly that complete freedom of choice cannot be allowed students in our schools. The immature student is not always able to make the wisest, even a wise, decision. Where a student is engaged in making a decision that might be against the best interests of the community, the school, other students, or might be contrary to his own best interests, the counselor has the obligation to assist in, or even control, the decision-making process. *Counselors have an obligation to society as well as the individual.* Williamson, again was the spokesman for this point of view (26):

> I believe counselors are not in the business of aiding students to develop just any and all kinds of individuality for which they have potential. We are rather, as educators, in the business of helping students to become individuals with some similar but not identical patterns of individuality. We are helping them avoid self-destructive and anti-social forms of individuality, and to achieve, paradoxically, fullest freedom through effective membership in groups, to achieve a community of individuals, interdependent, and with high social idealisms.

---

[4]From *Counseling Points of View,* edited by Willis E. Dugan (No. 3, Modern School Practices Series). University of Minnesota Press. Copyright 1959 by the University of Minnesota.

Williamson (87) identified six steps in counseling: (a) analysis, (b) synthesis, (c) diagnosis, (d) prognosis, (e) treatment, and (f) follow-up.

(a) *analysis*—the collection of data about the counselee and his environment from a variety of sources.

(b) *synthesis*—the selection of the pertinent data, the summarization and organization of this data in order to gain a picture of the student's strengths and weaknesses, adjustments and maladjustments.

(c) *diagnosis*—the formulation of conclusions regarding the nature and the cause of the student's problems.

(d) *prognosis*—the prediction of the outcome of various courses of action by the counselee.

(e) *treatment*—counseling that may include some or all of the following procedures: (*i*) establishing rapport with the student, (*ii*) interpreting the collected data to the student, (*iii*) advising or planning a program of action with the student, (*iv*) assisting the student in carrying out the plan of action, and (*v*) referrals to other counselors for assistance in diagnosing or counseling.

(f) *follow-up*—the determination of the effectiveness of counseling: (*i*) did the student carry out his plan of action?, (*ii*) was it successful? and (*iii*) if not successful, what might be done to alter or improve the plan of action?[5]

Eclectic Counseling

Eclectic counseling has been described as *selective* counseling. Its advocates believed that there were strengths and weaknesses in both the clinical and client-centered positions and that neither position allowed the counselor the flexibility necessary to counsel most effectively. They pointed out that (a) no two problems or situations are identical; (b) problems rarely restrict themselves to one area; and (c) the emphasis frequently shifts from one problem area to another, often during the same interview. Consequently, the counselor must select the approach which is most appropriate to the immediate problem and be ready and willing to change his approach at any time. Thorne (78) felt that it was possible for a counselor to alternate between clinical and client-centered approaches *within the same interview* without disrupting, or disrupting for long, the permissive relationship he had established with the client. "The client will usually accept anything which is done within reason providing it is done

---

[5]By permission from *Counseling Adolescents*, by E. G. Williamson. Copyright 1950. McGraw-Hill Book Company, Inc.

tactfully and in nonthreatening manner. . . . The critical factor is not what method is used but rather the skill with which it is used."

Current Approaches to Counseling

As counseling has gained increased professional stature, counseling theory has become more closely intertwined with learning theory and personality theory. Consequently, the old labels of "directive," "non-directive," and "eclectic" are appearing less frequently in the current literature on counseling theory. As early as 1954, Pepinsky and Pepinsky (60) placed counseling theories into five major categories: the trait-and-factor centered approach, the communications approach, self-theory, the psychoanalytic approach, and the neobehavioral approach. More recently, Patterson (59) has suggested the following categories as a means of organizing and identifying current points of view or approaches to counseling:

1. *Rational approaches to counseling,* including Williamson's clinical counseling, Thorne's personality counseling, and the rational psychotherapy of Albert Ellis.
2. *Learning theory approaches to counseling,* including Rotter's social learning approach, Phillips' interference theory approach, and the conditioned response theories of Dollard and Miller, the Pepinskys, Salter and Wolpe.
3. *Psychoanalytic approaches to counseling,* including Bordin's psychological counseling and Alexander's psychoanalytic therapy.
4. *Perceptual-phenomenological approaches to counseling,* including Rogers' client-centered therapy, Kelly's psychology of personal constructs, and Grinker's transactional approach.
5. *Existential psychotherapy,* including Frankl's logotherapy.

What is Counseling?

Having identified early and current approaches to counseling, we must now (1) attempt to define counseling and (2) distinguish it from psychotherapy. It would be difficult enough to define *any* activity involving two individuals who associate with one another purposefully in order to facilitate behavioral changes in one of them. In the case of counseling, the difficulty is compounded by two major factors:

1. *Various authorities who attempt to define counseling do so from the standpoint of their own field of interest and/or their own academic orientation.*

Hahn (37) has suggested that there are three major groups who are interested in and support counseling: (a) those who are concerned about *social welfare,* such as Coombs, Rogers, and others in the phenomenological school; (b) those who are more *medically oriented,* such as Thorne; and (c) those who are primarily concerned with *student personnel administration* and who have a great interest in *measurement,* such as Strong and Williamson.

Likewise, a report (2) by the American Psychological Association, Division of Counseling Psychology, points out that three specialties have now merged in counseling psychology: *vocational guidance, psychometrics,* and *personality development.* It is easy to understand why specialists in each of these areas would view counseling somewhat differently.

2. *Theories of counseling cannot be clearly separated from theories of learning, theories of personality, or general theories of behavior.*

Patterson (59) states the problem as follows:

> Counselors deal with behavior. The fact that they work with clients who exhibit behavior which is more or less disturbed, abnormal, or unsatisfactory in some respects, either to themselves or to society or to both, does not change the fact that it is behavior with which the counselor is concerned. Moreover, the aspect of behavior which is the primary focus of the counselor falls in the area of personality in its individual and social aspects. In addition, the goal of counseling is the changing of behavior or personality in some respect or to some extent. Different approaches to counseling vary in the specific nature and extent of behavior change toward which they are directed, but all accept behavior change of some kind, including changes in attitudes, feelings, perceptions, values, or goals, as the objective of counseling. Since learning may broadly be defined as change in behavior, then counseling is, of course, concerned with learning and thus with theories of learning. In fact, it is difficult to distinguish between theories of learning, theories of personality, and theories of counseling. All are concerned with behavior and are thus theories of behavior.

Counseling as a Learning Process

If there is one point on which all counselors appear to agree it is that counseling represents a learning situation. Rogers (63) Williamson (87), Thorne (78), Pepinsky and Pepinsky (60), and Lloyd-Jones and Smith (46) are among the writers who have stressed the close relationship between counseling and learning. Since learning is a two-way street, it follows, then, that both the counselor and the student are engaged in learning from each other.

Why Must the Counselor Be a Learner?—(a) Since no two problems or students are the same, the counselor must learn to use the tools that will work best for that particular situation. (b) Since very few problems restrict themselves to one area (and the emphasis often shifts from one area to another as the problem develops), the counselor learns to "shift gears" from one counseling approach to another. (c) Since no two counseling situations are the same, the counselor can profit by experience but should never copy previous procedures. Therefore, the counselor must constantly study and improve his techniques. *His learning is continuous.*

In What Ways Does the Counselor Become Involved in the Learning Process?—There are many areas in which the counselor becomes a learner. At least four areas are easily identified:

1. *Improving and expanding procedural techniques.* The counselor constantly learns better ways of preparing for an interview, a more satisfactory method of explaining testing procedures, a more diplomatic technique of acquainting the student with his own responsibility for solving his problem, a more casual style of note-taking, etc.

2. *Establishing rapport.* The counselor learns new techniques of developing a satisfactory counseling relationship with the student. He learns more effective ways of establishing an atmosphere of frankness and honesty, of mutual trust and cooperation. Leona Tyler (82) has written that years ago, when she was in the course of an interview with a person who was, for some reason, hard to talk to, she used to say to herself, "He must like me. Whatever else happens by the time the hour is over, he must like me, at least a little." She reports that she has *learned* to put it a little differently today. Now she says, "We must like each other." She has learned that the salesman approach, or that of the popularity seeker, is not conducive to the establishment of a good client-counselor relationship.

3. *Communicating more effectively.* The counselor learns to be a person with many vocabularies or vocabulary levels. He does not expect the student to adjust to "counselor language." He learns to appreciate the degree to which nonverbal communicaton such as the crinkled nose, the set of the mouth, the shrug of the shoulders, the frown, or the relaxed position of the body can affect the student's trust and frankness. Routh (67) says, "The importance of all kinds of nonverbal communication should not be underestimated. While a

counselor should work with a client within the bounds of an emotionally supporting relationship in an atmosphere that is permissive and
client-centered, still, he should realize that the client is reading his
every act, and developing his own set of feelings and attitudes.
Gestures and mannerisms, then, are capable not only of producing
feelings, but counter-feelings as well."

4. *Becoming more sensitive to student attitudes and feelings.* The
counselor, through his experiences with students, learns to be more
alert for the moment when the student is ready to "get down to
business." He learns to distinguish between the conversational pauses
which might be embarrassing to the student and those where counselor comment might interrupt an important train of thought. He becomes sensitive to the proper moment for beginning the termination
of the interview.

In What Ways Is the Student Engaged in Learning?—First of all,
the student is engaged in learning about himself. Through the counselor's interpretation of test results, he learns about his strengths and
weaknesses, his abilities, aptitudes, interests, and personal traits.
Through his own verbal expressions of his problem to the counselor,
he clarifies his own self-concept. He learns to understand the relationship between his problem and his self-concept. He learns to understand
the relationship between his problem and other factors in his environment.

Second, the student learns about the counselor. He discovers that
the counselor listens more than he talks. He discovers that the counselor does not become excited or dismayed over the story that he
unfolds. He learns, gradually, that the counselor is to be trusted with
personal problems, that he does not betray confidences. He discovers
that the counselor does not intend to tell him what to do.

A third area of learning for the student is in self-expression. The
counselor encourages this self-expression because he knows that it is a
good way of releasing tension and has therapeutic qualities. Equally
important, the counselor knows that self-expression leads, frequently,
to greater self-confidence.

Finally, the student learns to solve his own problems with less and
less help from the counselor. However, this type of learning seems to
take place only after the student has engaged in the other types of
learning. When the student learns to understand himself and his
relationship with the counselor, when he learns to understand his
problem and its underlying causes, when he learns to express himself

and to have confidence in himself, he is able to attain greater independence in problem-solving.

The concept of counseling as a learning situation deserves considerable attention for two reasons. (a) It represents a theoretical position that appears to be acceptable to the different schools of counseling. (b) It represents a theoretical position that can most readily be related to the classroom experiences of teachers and teacher-counselors. In the words of Traxler (81): "This view of counseling will remove much of the vagueness and mystery from counseling activities and will naturally and inevitably lead to the integration of these activities with the instructional program of the institution."

Counseling as Assistance in Choice-Making

Many counselors also agree that counseling represents a situation where one person helps another to choose a course of action ... and follow it. The following definitions are illustrative of this point of view:

> Counseling is a purposeful, reciprocal relationship between two people in which one, a trained person, helps the other to change himself or his environment.—Shostrom and Brammer (68)

> A counselor's task is helping the student to examine and analyze his own problem; to gather, evaluate, and organize pertinent data in regard to it; to think through the probable consequences of various possible solutions; to choose and try out the solution that seems to fit the known facts and needs most adequately; and to modify his plan of solution when it proves to be out of harmony with the facts and needs of the situation.—Traube (80)

> Counseling is one kind of psychological helping activity, the kind that concentrates on the growth of a clear sense of ego identity and the willingness to make choices and commitments in accordance with it.—Tyler (85)

> Counseling is a form of interviewing in which the client is helped to understand himself more completely in order to correct an environmental or adjustment difficulty.—Wolberg (91)

Counseling as Personality Development

Bordin (14) is, perhaps, most representative of those counselors who define counseling in terms of personality development. "The psychological counselor is a psychological practitioner who aids people with these problems of behavior in which the critical issues have to do with their emotions and motivations. . . . Counseling . . . involves interactions . . . where the counselor . . . has taken responsibility for making his role in the interaction process contribute positively to the other person's personality development."

Counseling as Role Clarification

Tyler (84) is representative of those theorists who suggest that one of the major purposes of counseling is to help an individual understand or clarify one of his role commitments and carry it out more successfully.

It is well to remember that agreement over *what* counseling is or does in no way reflects agreement over *how* it should be used to change behavior. We may agree that counseling is a learning process, but we are still in disagreement over how counseling facilitates learning and how learning occurs. We may agree that counseling involves personality development, but we are still in disagreement over how personality development is furthered.

Counseling and Psychotherapy

The difficulties associated with defining counseling are obviously still with us when we attempt to distinguish between counseling and psychotherapy. In addition, some authorities feel that such a distinction is unnecessary. Still others feel that such a distinction is impossible. Hahn (37) makes an excellent summation of the problem:

> I know of few counselors or psychologists who are completely satisfied that clear distinctions (between counseling and psychotherapy) have been made. . . . Perhaps the most complete agreements are: (1) that counseling and psychotherapy cannot be distinguished clearly, (2) that counselors practice what psychotherapists consider psychotherapy, (3) that psychotherapists practice what counselors consider to be counseling, and (4) that despite the above they are different.

Several attempts have been made to place counseling and psychotherapy on a continuum and to identify the two ends of such a continuum. For example, Brammer and Shostrom (16) identify the counseling end of this continuum with such terms as "educative, supportive, situational, problem-solving, conscious awareness, and emphasis on normal" and characterize the therapy end by using terms such as "reconstructive, depth emphasis, analytic, focus on unconscious and emphasis on neurotic or other emotional problems." However, Patterson (59) regards a distinction in terms of severity of disturbance as artificial since "so-called counselors practice psychotherapy while psychotherapists practice counseling; for it is clear that a therapist cannot and does not make a determination that the client, after a period of psychotherapy, is now functioning at a minimal 'normal' level and should therefore be transferred to a counselor for help beyond this point. In any case, the counselor or psychotherapist takes a client where he is and allows him to go as far as he can go or desires to go."

Since the school counselor presently averages about one year of graduate work (and no more than half of that is psychological in nature), it is important that he be alerted to his limitations as a therapist. Counselors who "do too much" are as much of a problem to the profession as counselors who "do too little." Stefflre (72) suggests that there are five major differences between counseling and psychotherapy that school counselors need to recognize:

> 1. Counseling tends to be concerned with instrumental behavior, with role problems, with situations, with choices which must be made, and with actions which must be taken. Goals of counseling are more limited than those of psychotherapy, but this does not mean that these limited goals are unimportant or that changes in immediate behavior may not have lasting global effects.
> 2. Counselors deal primarily with normal individuals. (The distinction between "normal" and "neurotic" is as fraught with difficulties, of course, as the distinction between counseling and psychotherapy.)
> 3. The practitioner of counseling may be trained at the doctoral level with a two-year internship as would be his counterpart in clinical psychology. Many counselors, however, are trained at less than a doctoral level or at the doctoral level but with relatively little psychology and little or no formal supervised internship. These people because of the prestige rank of psychology and because of their own confused role concepts may quickly come to think of themselves as psychotherapists. Although they have difficulty making the distinction, there is no reason why more objective observers should.
> 4. The setting in which counseling takes place is most apt to be an educational setting or a community agency, although counselors may work in a medical setting or in private practice.
> 5. The methods used will indicate that counseling shows more concern than psychotherapy with present events than those of the past, more concern with cognition than with effect, more concern with clarity than with ambiguity.

Since there is no clear and precise "point of no return" which marks the passage of counseling into psychotherapy, it behooves the school counselor to have his own goals clearly in mind before he enters into a counseling relationship.

Goals of Counseling

Much of the confusion over the role and/or goals of the school counselor is related to the fact that the school counselor has (or should have) more than one goal in mind as he proceeds with counseling. Byrne (17) has suggested that counseling goals fall logically under three headings: ultimate, intermediate, and immediate. The *ultimate* goals of a counselor are philosophical goals and receive their substance from the counselor's views of universal man and of the nature of life. *Intermediate* goals hinge on students' decisions and planning needs, or on courses of action that they must take to remedy fairly immediate problems. *Immediate* goals are represented by the counselor's interviewing techniques, his purpose in saying what he is saying, or in doing what he is doing. The counselor then uses immediate goals as a means of working toward intermediate goals. These intermediate goals should be consistent with, rather than disruptive of, the counselor's ultimate goals.

We have only to add that the counselor's immediate and intermediate goals will undergo constant change; his ultimate goals should remain relatively constant.

Counseling and Discipline

Most authorities in the field of guidance agree that secondary school counselors should not be charged with the responsibility for the administration of punishment. Erickson (28), while indicating that counselors can be helpful in disciplinary cases, cautions, "Counselors should not become known as the disciplinarians of the school or they will lose their counseling relationship to pupils." Smith (69) emphasizes the importance of constructive relationships and stresses that "the disciplinary function is sometimes the greatest obstacle to effective counseling relationships. Indeed, this function has led directly to the complete breakdown of the counseling service in some instances." Counselors should work with discipline cases, Sorenson (70) advocates, but they must not punish behavior. Nugent (54) conjectures that the practice of assigning counselors as disciplinarians is inconsistent with counseling theory because of (a) the need to preserve the uniqueness of the counselor's role within the school (everyone else has disciplinary responsibilities), (b) the importance of a non-threatening relationship to the individual student, and (c) the importance of maintaining a non-threatening counselor image to the total student body. Byrne (17) notes that "the counseling relationship is a non-judgmental one because the counselor is in a non-judgmental role—he is perhaps the only non-judgmental person the counselee has met or will ever meet." Zeran (94) argues against the counselor's responsibility for the administration of restrictive procedures because "one's effectiveness as a counselor is negated if he takes on administrative responsibility; the individual will not reveal confidences important in resolving his problems if his image of the counselor contains the threat of disciplinary action." Mathewson (48) feels that the function of the counselor in discipline is to appraise and evaluate, and even attempt to adjust, but not to regulate, behavior. "Supervision and enforcement of necessary social regulations for the common good in school is an administrative function. It is an administrative, not a guidance, responsibility to deal with infractions of such regulations." O'Donnell (55) contends that any referral of a discipline problem to the counselor is doomed to failure. Fullmer and Bernard (33) warn that the counselor should not impose discipline, for he hopes that ultimately his counselee will be self-determining—that he will develop inner controls. If the counselor imposes discipline, he is, in effect, denying an occasion for these controls to develop. Cortale (18) states, "Discipline should be handled by the administration." And Dugan (27) concludes, "While the school counselor should be in close touch with the principal on every discipline case, his role is one of interpretation, follow-up, and counseling; not the role of determining the punishment or enforcing the penalty."

An opposing point of view has been expressed by Fritzemeier (30) who argues that counselors who assume disciplinary responsibilities and prepare pupil programs perform a greater service to the school than counselors who do not assume these duties. Opstad (57) feels that many teachers look upon counselors as mere "hand-holders" because of the "sometimes frantic scurrying of counselors to avoid situations of a disciplinary nature." And Stefflre (71) suggests that we are having second thoughts on the matter of keeping the counselor clean of all contact with discipline:

> Why? Because in practice, all of the students who need help desperately, all the hoods, pre-dropouts, the trouble-makers, now talk to the administrator, who is trained in administration. The students with the delicate problems, like "Should I take French this semester or next semester?" get to talk with a counselor, who has had a year's training in getting ready to help them with such earth shaking decisions. So, perhaps we are not making the best

use of counselors if we insist that they have nothing to do with discipline and attendance.

Gilbert (34) compared students' perceptions of counseling relationships in schools where counselors *had* responsibility for discipline with students' perceptions in schools where counselors *did not have* this responsibility. He found that good communication, student and counselor security, and student responsibility for directing counseling are characteristic of counseling relationships with counselors who have *no* responsibility for discipline more so than with counselors who *have* assigned disciplinary responsibility. He also found that students who were counseled by counselors who had *no* responsibility for discipline described their *actual* counseling relationships more like their *ideal* counseling relationships than did students counseled by counselors who *were* assigned disciplinary responsibilities.

Unfortunately, studies of this nature are extremely difficult to locate in the literature. We must reluctantly conclude that research, to date, has been unable to prove or disprove the validity of assigning disciplinary responsibilities to counselors. Until such research is available, the proliferation of opinion currently being offered on this issue will confuse many secondary school counselors. Counselors and administrators will have to determine their own rationale for the practices they will be employing. The following statements are intended to serve as a base upon which such a rationale might be developed.

1. Research suggests that the administration of punishment is most effective when it is accompanied by (a) an explanation of the purpose of the punishment, and (b) an attempt at rehabilitation. It appears, then, that punishment in the school would generally be more effective when administered by an individual who had a counseling background and/or a counseling point of view. *Generalization: Discipline, accompanied by counseling, is the highest form of discipline.*

2. Research suggests that the most effective relationship between counselor and client is a non-judgmental one. Yet, the administration of punishment automatically requires a judgment by someone or some group in the school. *Generalization: Counseling, accompanied by punishment, is the most difficult form of counseling.*

3. The author's experience leads him to believe that there are *some* individuals with extensive backgrounds of training and experience who have personality patterns that allow them to serve effectively in both capacities.

4. The counselor's training and experience make him the most logical (and logically the most effective) staff member to assume leadership in the following aspects of any disciplinary situation:

a. *the investigative aspect*, or the deliberate and systematic search for causes of behavior;

b. *the interpretive aspect*, or the purposeful attempt to counsel students whose behavior has been punished.

Counseling and Confidentiality

Confidentiality in counseling refers to the obligation of a counselor not to reveal information acquired about a student during the course of a counseling interview. There are two main reasons for respecting such confidences. First, divulging confidential information violates the student's confidence and may cause the student (and other students) to believe that the counselor is one who should never be trusted. The second reason has to do with the professional aspects of his position. Simply stated, it is that the counselor should maintain confidentiality because it would be unethical not to do so. One reason involves *counselor role*, a topic already discussed in earlier chapters. The other reason relates to *counselor ethics*, a subject that is discussed further in Chapter 12. However, we need to remind ourselves that today's school counselor is faced with a panorama of problems concerning confidentiality. He is often torn between principles and practicality, ethics and expediency, rules and reasonableness. He has ethical guidelines to help him (see Part Five, Code of Ethics), but he knows also that the actions he takes will be influenced to some extent by the student's age, the regulations of the school, the expectations of the community, and his own legal immunity from testimony in a court of law (see Chapter 6).

Issues in Counseling

A review of past and current issues in counseling leads us to the following conclusions:

1. *Issues that troubled us twenty years ago do not appear to be of major concern today.*
2. *Current issues appear to be more clearly delineated than those of twenty years ago.*

Blocher (13) has identified those issues that once troubled us and which he now terms as false or "illusional." (1) Should counseling be "directive" or "non-directive"? (2) Should counselors "diagnose"? (3) Should counseling be personal-emotional or informational-didactic? Byrne (17) and Stefflre (72) are among those who have discussed today's issues in a detailed, organized, and definitive fashion. It is not our purpose to examine these issues in detail. However, the following represent some of the questions which, to date, we have been unable to answer:

1. *To what extent do individual differences between clients (students) determine the effectiveness of counseling technique?* What is the relationship between (a) counseling technique and (b) client personality, maturity, and experience?
2. *What is the precise nature of the counselor's responsibility to society?* In what ways should this responsibility be allowed to affect the counselor's relationship with his counselee?
3. *What is the relationship between client attitude and counseling effectiveness?* Is counseling equally effective with students who are referred to the counselor and those who approach him voluntarily? What values does the student gain from "disciplinary counseling"?
4. *Is counseling developmental, educational, and preventive in nature? or is it adjustive, therapeutic, and remedial in nature?*
5. *Is counseling liberating or conditioning by nature?* Recognizing that counselors cannot avoid influencing clients, what is their proper role in value orientation?

Counseling Services in Schools

The development of an effective counseling service requires more than adequate facilities and trained personnel. An effective counseling service is dependent upon the continuing support of the administration, the wholehearted cooperation of the staff, and pupil understanding of the purposes and scope of the service. The support of the administration will be reflected in the school budget. The U.S. Office of Education (86) has recommended a maximum ratio of one counselor for every 300 students at the secondary level and one counselor for every 600 pupils at the elementary level. Froehlich (31) feels that a more effective ratio might be one counselor for every ten teachers. He feels that this plan has two distinct advantages:

> First, regardless of the demands for lighter teaching loads or budget reduction, a constant portion of the available resources is devoted to the guidance program. . . . Second, it tends to encourage teacher support of the guidance program. The counselor's

load is proportional to that of the teachers. When larger enrollments increase the teachers' load, they also add to the counselors'
work. Teachers are not as likely to feel that the counselor is
"getting off easy." They will feel, rather, that the counselor is a
regular member of the team.

An adequate pupil-counselor or teacher-counselor ratio does not
insure adequate staffing for the counseling service. Counselors have
reported that a large portion of their time is taken up with clerical
and administrative tasks that could and should be handled by other
members of the school staff (see Chapter 3). A counselor working
under these conditions will not have time to provide effective counseling services for 300 students. Consequently, a counselor-pupil ratio of
300 to 1 must be considered *a guide* rather than *an answer* to the
problem of maintaining counseling services in the schools.

Organized counseling services are rarely found in our smaller
schools. These schools usually lack the qualified personnel and the
facilities necessary for the proper maintenance of such services. They
rely, instead, on informal conferences between staff members and
students.

Almost every school is forced to place some limitation on its
counseling services. First, while it is desirable that every student be
included in the guidance program of the school, it is unrealistic to
expect that every student will receive individual counseling. Many
students will receive the help they need from the classroom, the
homeroom, or other group guidance activities. Second, some students
who receive individual counseling will need to be referred to other
specialists within or outside of the school.

While most schools recognize the necessity for providing counseling services for all students who request help, it is obvious that each
school must work out its own program of counseling services. In
addition to providing services for the self-referrals, schools may be
found today that give special attention to counseling one or more of
the following groups: the psysically handicapped, the scholastically
delinquent, the potential dropouts, high school freshmen, high school
seniors, college planners, disciplinary cases, pupils from broken
homes, and students who are transferring to or from another school.

Summary

The role of the counseling service within a school guidance program will be determined by the degree to which the school interprets
counseling as a professional service, by the orientation and qualifica-

tions of those designated as counselors, and by the amount of support and cooperation given the program by the administration and the school staff. There are, of course, many types and levels of helping relationships involving students, parents, teachers, health workers, coaches, and administrators. To identify them all as counseling relationships is confusing and, in the final analysis, undermines attempts to professionalize school counseling services. In view of the widespread use of the term "counselor" in our society today (investment counselor, loan counselor, insurance counselor, rug and carpet counselor . . . even cemetery counselor), it is doubtful whether a substantial segment of the public considers counseling a professional service. However, it is not enough to deplore the loose usage of the term "counselor" in the business world. Our own frequent reference to "guidance and counseling" and the "guidance counselor" has helped to create the impression that the two concepts are almost identical and that one who is equipped to *guide* is also equipped to *counsel*.

Counseling may be conceived of as a learning process, in which both the counselor and the client assume "learning" roles. The concept of counseling as a learning process offers a possible meeting ground upon which most of the current issues in counseling may be debated. These issues appear to be more clearly delineated than they were some years ago. However, the resolution of these issues must await additional experimental research, particularly with respect to counseling relationships, process, and outcomes.

All students in *every* school do not need individual counseling. However, counseling services should be available to all students who request help. The argument that counseling must be defined in terms of current practice in our schools is as stultifying as the argument that space travel must be defined in terms of current practice. We have many professional counselors in our schools today. Many other individuals are attempting to counsel without adequate professional training. No greater challenge faces the guidance movement today than the increased professionalization of counseling services in our schools.

Bibliography

1.   Adams, James F. *Counseling and Guidance: A Summary View.* New York: The Macmillan Company, 1965. Chap. 1, Nos. 1, 3, 5, 6; Chap. 5.
2.   American Psychological Association. "The Current Status of Counseling Psychology." A report of a special committee of Division 17 of the American Psychological Association, 1961.
3.   Andrew, D. and R. D. Willey. *Administration and Organization of the Guidance Program.* New York: Harper and Brothers, 1958. Chap. 10.
4.   Arbuckle, Dugald S. *Counseling: Philosophy, Theory and Practice.* Boston: Allyn & Bacon, Inc., 1965. Chaps. 10-12.
5.   ————. *Guidance and Counseling in the Classroom.* Boston: Allyn & Bacon, Inc., 1957. Chaps. 4-7.
6.   ————. *Pupil Personnel Services in American Schools.* Boston: Allyn & Bacon, Inc., 1962. Chap. 5.
7.   Barr, John A. *The Elementary Teacher and Guidance.* New York: Henry Holt and Company, 1958. Chaps. 4-5.
8.   Barry, Ruth and Beverly Wolf. *Motives, Values and Realities.* New York: Teachers College Press, Teachers College, Columbia University, 1965.
9.   Bennett, Margaret E. *Guidance and Counseling in Groups.* 2nd ed. New York: McGraw-Hill Book Company, Inc., 1963. Chaps. 4-7.
10.   Berdie, Ralph F., Wilbur L. Layton, Edward O. Swanson, and Theda Hagenah. *Testing in Guidance and Counseling.* New York: McGraw-Hill Book Company, Inc., 1963. Chaps. 9, 11, 12.
11.   Bingham, W. V. and B. B. Moore. *How to Interview.* New York: Harper and Brothers, 1941.
12.   Blanchard, Howard L. and Laurence S. Flaum. *Guidance: A Longitudinal Approach.* Minneapolis: Burgess Publishing Company, 1962. Chap. 11.
13.   Blocher, Donald H. "Issues in Counseling: Elusive and Illusional," *Personnel and Guidance Journal,* XLIII, April, 1965, 796-800.

14. Bordin, Edward S. *Psychological Counseling*. New York: Appleton-Century-Crofts, 1955. P. 3.
15. Boy, Angelo V. and Gerald J. Pine. *Client-Centered Counseling in the Secondary School*. Boston: Houghton Mifflin Company, 1963. Chaps. 3-5, 8-10.
16. Brammer, Lawrence M. and Everett L. Shostrom. *Therapeutic Psychology*. Englewood Cliffs, New Jersey: Prentice-Hall, Inc., 1960. P. 6.
17. Byrne, Richard Hill. *The School Counselor*. Boston: Houghton Mifflin Company, 1963. Chaps. 3-5, 7, 10, 11.
18. Cortale, Michael J. "Counselors and Discipline," *Personnel and Guidance Journal*, XXXIX, January, 1961, 349-351.
19. Cottingham, Harold F. *Directed Readings in Foundations of Guidance and Personnel Services*. Bloomington, Illinois: McKnight and McKnight Publishing Co., 1964. Chaps. 5-6.
20. ———. *Guidance in the Junior High School: Principles and Practices*. Bloomington, Illinois: McKnight and McKnight Publishing Co., 1961. Chap. 8.
21. Crow, Lester D. and Alice Crow. *An Introduction to Guidance*. 2nd ed. New York: American Book Company, 1960. Chap. 10.
22. ———. *Organization and Conduct of Guidance Services*. New York: David McKay Company, Inc., 1965. Chaps. 11, 12, 14.
23. ———. *Readings in Guidance*. New York: David McKay Company, Inc., 1962. Chaps. 27, 33, 34.
24. Darley, J. G. *Testing and Counseling in the High School Guidance Program*. Chicago: Science Research Associates, Inc., 1943. P. 169.
25. ———. *The Interview in Counseling*. Washington: Retraining and Re-employment Administration, Department of Labor, 1946. P. 9.
26. Dugan, Willis E., ed. *Counseling Points of View*. Proceedings of the Minnesota Counselors Association Midwinter Conference, 1958. Minneapolis: University of Minnesota Press, 1958. Pp. 3, 7-9.
27. ———. "The Counselor and His Relationships," *Bulletin of National Association of Secondary School Principals*, XXXV, 1951, 55-67.
28. Erickson, C. E. *A Practical Handbook for School Counselors*. New York: The Ronald Press, 1949. P. 185.
29. Farwell, Gail F. and H. J. Peters. *Guidance Readings for Counselors*. Chicago: Rand McNally & Co., 1960. Chap. 7.
30. Fritzemeier, L. H. "Pupil Programs, Discipline, and the Counselor," *Bulletin of National Association of Secondary School Principals*, XLVII, 1963, 40-47.
31. Froehlich, Clifford P. *Guidance Services in Schools*. New York: McGraw-Hill Book Company, Inc., 1958. Pp. 58-59, Chaps. 6-8, 10.
32. ———. "Stars, Parsons, and Clients," *Personnel and Guidance Journal*, XXXVI, September, 1957, 10-16.
33. Fullmer, Daniel W. and Harold Bernard. *Counseling: Content and Process*. Chicago: Science Research Associates, Inc., 1964. Chaps. 4-7.
34. Gilbert, Norman S. "When the Counselor is a Disciplinarian," *Personnel and Guidance Journal*, XLIII, January, 1965, 485-491.

35.   Glanz, Edward C. *Foundations and Principles of Guidance.* Boston: Allyn & Bacon, Inc., 1964, Chaps. 5-7.

36.   Hadley, John M. *Clinical and Counciling Psychology.* New York: Alfred A. Knopf, Inc., 1961.

37.   Hahn, M. E. "Conceptual Trends in Counseling," *Personnel and Guidance Journal,* XXXI, 1953, 231-235.

38.   Hatch, Raymond N., Paul L. Dressel, and James W. Costar. *Guidance Services in the Secondary Schools.* Dubuque, Iowa: William C. Brown Company, 1965. Chap. 5.

39.   Hollis, Joseph W. and Lucile U. Hollis. *Organizing for Effective Guidance.* Chicago: Science Research Associates, Inc., 1965. Chap. 17.

40.   Hulslander, Stewart C. and Charles E. Scholl. "U.S. School Principals Report Their Counselor Needs," *Vocational Guidance Quarterly,* VI, Autumn, 1957, Chap. 5.

41.   Humphreys, J. Anthony, Arthur E. Traxler, and Robert North. *Guidance Services.* 2nd ed. Chicago: Science Research Associates, Inc., 1960. Chaps. 8-15.

42.   Hutson, Percival W. *The Guidance Function in Education.* New York: Appleton-Century-Crofts, 1958. Chaps. 15-16.

43.   Johnson, W. F., *et al. Pupil Personnel and Guidance Services.* New York: McGraw-Hill Book Company, Inc., 1961. Chap. 16.

44.   Jones, Arthur J. *Principles of Guidance.* 5th ed. New York: McGraw-Hill Book Company, Inc., 1963. Chaps. 9, 11-14.

45.   Katz, Martin. *Decisions and Values—A Rationale for Secondary School Guidance.* New York: College Entrance Examination Board, 1963. Chaps. 1-3.

46.   Lloyd-Jones, Esther and Margaret R. Smith, eds. *Student Personnel Work as Deeper Teaching.* New York: Harper and Brothers, 1954.

47.   Loughary, John W. *Counseling in Secondary Schools: A Frame of Reference.* New York: Harper and Brothers, 1961. Chaps. 4, 6, 7.

48.   Mathewson, Robert Henry. *Guidance Policy and Practice.* 3rd ed. New York: Harper and Brothers, 1962. Chap. 13.

49.   McDaniel, H. B., *et al. Readings in Guidance.* New York: Henry Holt and Company, 1959. Chaps. 8-10.

50.   McGowan, John F. and Lyle D. Schmidt. *Counseling: Readings in Theory and Practice.* New York: Holt, Rinehart & Winston, Inc., 1962. Chaps. 5, 6, 8-10, 12.

51.   McKinney, Fred. *Counseling for Personal Adjustment.* Boston: Houghton Mifflin Company, 1958. P. 20.

52.   Miller, Carroll H. *Guidance Services: An Introduction.* New York: Harper and Row, 1965. Chaps. 5-10, 12.

53.   Miller, Frank W. "High School Counseling and the Learning Process," *The High School Journal,* XLI (May, 1958), 347-50.

54.   Nugent, Frank A. "High School Counseling and Discipline: A Theoretical Clarification," *Counselor Education and Supervision,* III, Fall, 1963, 44-49.

55.   O'Donnell, Robert J. "Guidance and Discipline—Never the Twain. . . ?" *Bulletin of National Association of Secondary School Principals,* XLVI, November, 1962, 51-53.
56.   Ohlsen, Merle M. *Guidance Services in the Modern School.* New York: Harcourt, Brace, & World, Inc., 1964. Chaps. 3-5.
57.   Opstad, Paul E. "The Role of the Counselor in Discipline," *Education,* LXXXI, December, 1960, 210-212.
58.   Patterson, C. H. *Counseling and Guidance in Schools.* New York: Harper and Brothers, 1962. Chaps. 8, 13-15, 7.
59.   ———. *Theories of Counseling and Psychotherapy.* New York: Harper & Row, Publishers, 1966. Pp. 2-7.
60.   Pepinsky, Harold B. and Pauline N. Pepinsky. *Counseling: Theory and Practice.* New York: The Ronald Press, 1954. Pp. 171-172.
61.   Pierson, George A. and Claude W. Grant. "The Road Ahead for the School Counselor," *Personnel and Guidance Journal,* XXXVIII, November, 1959, 207-210.
62.   Rogers, Carl R. "The Attitude and Orientation of the Counselor in Client-Centered Therapy," *Journal of Consulting Psychology,* XIII April, 1949, 134-5.
63.   ———. *Client-Centered Therapy.* Boston: Houghton Mifflin Company, 1951. Pp. 5-6, 8, 10.
64.   ———. "Counseling," *Review of Educational Research,* XV, 1945, 155-63.
65.   ———. *Counseling and Psychotherapy.* Boston: Houghton Mifflin Company, 1942. Chap. 2.
66.   ———. "Divergent Trends in Methods of Improving Adjustment," *Harvard Educational Review,* XVIII, Fall, 1948, 209-219.
67.   Routh, Thomas A. "The Importance of Body Language in Counseling," *Vocational Guidance Quarterly,* VI, Spring, 1958, 134-5.
68.   Shostrom, Everett L. and Lawrence M. Brammer. *The Dynamics of the Counseling Process.* New York: McGraw-Hill Book Company, Inc., 1952.
69.   Smith, G. E. *Principles and Practices of the Guidance Program.* New York: The Macmillan Company, 1951. P. 29.
70.   Sorenson, A. G. "On the Functions of a School Counselor," *Journal of Secondary Education,* XXXVI, 1961, 89-91.
71.   Stefflre, Buford. "Issues in School Guidance: Varying Perceptions of Administrators, Counselors and Counselor Educators," *The Teachers College Journal,* XXXVI, March, 1965, 195-200.
72.   ———, ed. *Theories of Counseling.* New York: McGraw-Hill Book Company, Inc., 1965. Chaps. 2, 5, 6, 8.
73.   Stewart, Lawrence and Charles Warnath. *The Counselor and Society: A Cultural Approach.* Boston: Houghton Mifflin Company, 1965. Chaps. 11, 12.
74.   Stoops, Emery and Gunnar L. Wahlquist. *Principles and Practices in Guidance.* New York: McGraw-Hill Book Company, Inc., 1958. Chap. 6.

75.   Strang, Ruth. *Counseling Techniques in College and Secondary School.* Rev. ed. New York: Harper and Brothers, 1949. Chap. 5.

76.   Thorne, Frederick C. "A Critique of Nondirective Methods of Psychotherapy," *Journal of Abnormal and Social Psychology,* XXXIX, October, 1944, 459-70.

77.   ———. "Critique of Recent Developments in Personality Counseling Theory," *Journal of Clinical Psychology,* XIII, 1957, 234-44.

78.   ———. *Principles of Personality Counseling.* Brandon, Vermont: *Journal of Clinical Psychology,* 1950. P. 124.

79.   Tolbert, E. L. *Introduction to Counseling.* New York: McGraw-Hill Book Company, Inc., 1965. Chaps. 1, 2, 7, 10-13.

80.   Traube, M. R. *Pupil Personnel Work. V. Counseling Services,* in *Encyclopedia of Educational Research.* New York: The Macmillan Company, 1950. Pp. 930-938.

81.   Traxler, Arthur E. *Techniques of Guidance.* New York: Harper and Brothers, 1957. Chaps. 15, 16, 20; p. 310.

82.   Tyler, Leona E. "The Initial Interview," *Personnel and Guidance Journal,* XXXIV, April, 1956, 466-69.

83.   ———. *Techniques of Counseling.* 2nd ed. New York: McGraw-Hill Book Company, Inc., 1964. Chaps. 17-19.

84.   ———. *The Work of the Counselor.* New York: McGraw-Hill Book Company, Inc., 1959. Chaps. 2-4, 10-12, 14.

85.   ———. "Theoretical Principles Underlying the Counseling Process," *Journal of Counseling Psychology,* V (1), 1958, 3-8.

86.   Warner, Ray. *Commitment to Youth.* Washington, D.C.: U.S. Office of Education, Dept. of Health, Education, and Welfare, Bulletin No. 25039, 1964.

87.   Williamson, E. G. *Counseling Adolescents.* New York: McGraw-Hill Book Company, Inc., 1950. Pp. 101-26.

88.   ———. "Directive versus Nondirective Counseling," *California Journal of Secondary Education,* XXV, October, 1950, 332-36.

89.   ——— *How to Counsel Students.* New York: McGraw-Hill Book Company, Inc., 1939. P. 136.

90.   ——— and J. D. Foley. *Counseling and Discipline.* New York: McGraw-Hill Book Company, Inc., 1949. P. 192.

91.   Wolberg, Lewis R. *The Technique of Psychotherapy.* New York: Grune and Stratton, 1954. P. 12.

92.   Wrenn, C. G. *The Counselor in a Changing World.* Washington, D.C.: American Personnel and Guidance Association, 1962. Chaps. 5, 6.

93.   ———. *Student Personnel Work in College.* New York: The Ronald Press, 1951. Chaps. 7-11.

94.   Zeran, Franklin, *et al. Guidance: Theory and Practice.* New York: American Book Company, 1964. P. 215.

95.   ——— and A. C. Riccio. *Organization and Administration of Guidance Services.* Chicago: Rand McNally & Co., 1962. Chap. 5.

10

Information Services

The educational, occupational, and social-cultural opportunities available to our young people become more varied and complex each year. One of the most important functions of guidance is to help young people become acquainted with these opportunities as they exist in the school, in the community, in institutions of higher education, and in the world of work.

Schools are striving to meet this responsibility. Yet smaller schools often lack the facilities and personnel necessary to acquire and disseminate this information. Large schools, particularly those in metropolitan areas, may attempt to acquire and distribute this information through a variety of services involving many members of the school staff. However, these services often overlap and/or fail to provide certain types of information.

Centralization and coordination of information services become the most effective means of helping schools meet this responsibility. Where there is a central agency for collecting and disseminating information, there is likely to be less overlapping in services and fewer areas of opportunity which are overlooked. Coordination is best achieved where one person is in charge of heading up the information services. One approach, for large schools with extensive informational services, would involve the establishment of an office of information and the appointment of a director of informational services. Another approach, perhaps more feasible for smaller schools, would involve the delegation of these responsibilities to a member of the current guidance staff. The person in charge of "heading up" the school's program of information services would be responsible for:

1. Planning and coordinating the articulation and orientation program;
2. Acquiring, organizing, housing, and distributing prepared materials of an occupational, educational, and personal-social nature;
3. Planning and coordinating all procedures for distributing information to groups;
4. Organizing and administering the placement program.

Discussion of information services in this chapter will be organized around these functions.

The Articulation and Orientation Program

Articulation and orientation may be thought of as taking place at three different times: preceding entrance to the new school, during the first week in the new school, and during the first term or semester. Pre-entrance activities are primarily concerned with (a) creating attitudes favorable to the new school and (b) giving pupils and parents general information about school personnel, activities, facilities, courses, and curricula. The most concentrated orientation should take place during the first week of school. It is at this time that students must be provided with specific and detailed information concerning school regulations, time schedules, room locations, special fees, fire drills, luncheon arrangements, and so forth. Attention must also be given to various aspects of the pupil's personal and social adjustment to a new environment. This becomes the major purpose of orientation activities during the first term or semester.

On the following pages, various techniques and activities useful in articulation and orientation services will be discussed. It is not to be expected that all of these techniques will be appropriate or feasible in every school. However, it would be possible for a school to build an adequate orientation service by instituting a selected number of these procedures.

Visitation to "Sending" Schools

Visits to the "sending" schools by personnel from the "receiving" schools constitute one of the articulation devices in common use today. This program may be organized in a variety of ways. At North Chicago Community High School, North Chicago, Illinois, counselors begin the program by meeting with the eighth-grade teachers of the districts from which the high school draws its students. The school's program is explained to these teachers in order to obtain their criticism and support. At a later meeting, counselors discuss school activities, courses, and curricula with all eighth graders and their parents. Part of this meeting is devoted to a question-and-answer session regarding the contents of the *Student Handbook,* which students and parents have been asked to read prior to the meeting. Still later, the various high school departments present their course offerings at a series of meetings held in each grade school. Students learn exactly what is taught in the various subject matter areas. A final visit to each grade school is made by the counselors after completion of the eighth-grade testing program. Using test data and the recommendations of the eighth-grade teachers, counselors help each pupil arrange a course program for their first semester in high school.

The visitation program of Woodruff High School, Peoria, Illinois, is somewhat simpler. An initial visit by the freshman counselor is devoted to collecting data on the incoming pupils from their cumulative records. Early in April, the freshman counselor and the Dean of Girls visit each of the feeder schools to register pupils in their first semester courses. Prior to this meeting, each pupil had filled out a "Tentative Schedule Card" with the help of his teacher. The counselor discusses this tentative schedule of courses with each pupil before actual registration is completed.

Visitations to "Receiving" Schools

Visits to the "receiving" school by pupils and their parents represent a second articulation-orientation approach. These visits may be scheduled when school is in session, on the weekend, or in the evening. Visits may be made by pupils in groups or individually. In some cases, high school students serve as hosts or conduct part of the program. At Woodruff High School, Peoria, Illinois, two orientation meetings are scheduled each year. At an evening meeting for students and their parents, various members of the school staff discuss the organization of the school, attendance regulations, disciplinary procedures, guidance services, and extra-curricular activities. The evening closes with a tour of the building and refreshments served in the cafeteria. The second orientation meeting takes place on the morning before the opening of the new school year. Members of the Student Council serve as hosts and as discussion leaders in the informal group sessions that follow a general assembly and a tour of the building. At the end of the morning, all students reassemble in the auditorium to view two films: *Making the Most of High School* and *High School: Your Challenge.*

At some schools, an entire day is devoted to orientation procedures. Freshman Day at North Chicago Community High School, North Chicago, Illinois, includes introduction of the teaching staff, a brief talk by the principal, assignment to homerooms, registration for courses, and a tour of the building. Students also follow a shortened schedule of class periods in order to become familiar with the building and classrooms, to meet their teachers, and to receive initial assignments.

The Student Handbook

The student handbook can be one of the most effective orientation devices. It has the advantage of being useful to students prior to their entrance into the new school, during their first week in school, and during the entire first year. Many student handbooks contain information useful to students throughout their four-year program. However, the handbook will not be effective as an orientation device unless it is revised often enough to reflect current activities, committees, publications, awards, services, traditions, and regulations. Furthermore, its organization, style, and appearance must attract student attention.

The topics included in student handbooks vary considerably. However, the following outline is representative of the better handbooks. It summarizes the contents of *The Pilot,* student handbook of Evanston Township High School, Evanston, Illinois.

> Greetings from the Superintendent-Principal
> History of Evanston Township High School
> School Calendar
> Activities Calendar
> Organization of Evanston Township High School
>   Division System
>   Facilities

Guidance Services
Student Council
Homeroom Councils
Daily Schedule
Student Regulations
Graduation Requirements
Spring Trips
Financial Obligations
Student Activities
 Clubs, such as Future Teachers of America, Debate Club, Chess
  Club
 Publications, including the school paper, yearbook, and handbook
 Miscellaneous activities, such as cheerleaders, musical groups,
  Interclub Council, and Magazine Sales Campaign
 Eligibility for Student Activities (participation, candidates for
  office)
Floor Plan of Evanston Township High School
Health and Athletics
 Girls' Physical Education, tournament winners, field day
 Swimming Pool, health and safety rules
 Boys' Physical Education, interscholastic sports, intramural pro-
  gram
Individual Honors
 Scholarship awards, such as college and university scholarships,
  scholarship medals, pins, and trips
 Activity and service awards, such as writing contests, Kiwanis
  Career award, Boys' State, Girls' State, Evanston League of
  Women Voters Citizenship Award, American Legion Medal
 Sports awards, such as Dads' Club Awards, Tom Boswell Trophy
Directory
Index
Evanston Township High School Songs[1]

Special Meetings

During the first semester, various types of group and individual meetings may be arranged for orientation purposes. The *homeroom* has been widely used as a vehicle for conducting group orientation activities for new students. It is essential to the effective functioning of homeroom orientation programs that all homeroom teachers participate in the development and revision of materials to be used.

Counselors at many schools arrange *get-acquainted interviews* with new students after the school year has begun. At these meetings,

---

[1]Courtesy of Evanston Township High School.

students are invited to ask questions about the school and staff that have not been answered to date. These interviews are particularly valuable for late enrollees and transfer students who have missed the earlier orientation activities.

Films for the Orientation Program

Films and film strips are an important source of educational, vocational, and personal-social information. If the school budget permits, a library of guidance films should be started. These films should be housed in the central guidance office unless the school maintains a separate department of audio-visual aids. The major sources of audio-visual materials are listed in the bibliography at the end of the chapter. However, the following films are particularly suitable for group orientation activities:

High School: Your Challenge (Coronet Films) 1¼ reels, 13½ minutes. Color $125 or B & W $68.75. Approximate rental fee, $3.50.

Learning to Study (Encyclopaedia Britannica Films) 14 minutes. B & W $75.00. One to three day rental, $3.00

Making the Most of School (Coronet Films) 1 reel, 11 minutes. Color $90.00 or B & W $45.00. Approximate rental fee, $3.50.

Making Friends (Encyclopaedia Britannica Films) 11 minutes. Color $120 or B & W $60.00. One to three day rental, color $4.00; B & W $2.50.

Belonging to the Group (Encyclopaedia Britannica Films) 16 minutes. B & W $90.00. One to three day rental, $3.50.

Everyday Courtesy (Coronet Films) 1 reel, 11 minutes. Color $100 or B & W $55.00. Approximate rental fee, $3.50.

Developing Responsibility (Coronet Films) 1 reel, 11 minutes. Color $100 or B & W $55.00. Approximate rental fee, $3.50.

How Friendly Are You? (Coronet Films) 1 reel, 11 minutes. Color $100 or B & W $55.00. Approximate rental fee, $3.50.

Sources of Information

An important consideration in the development of the information service is the selection of prepared materials of an occupational, educational, and personal-social nature. A wide variety of materials is available to the guidance worker. Free and inexpensive materials can be obtained from educational institutions, governmental agencies, business and industrial organizations, trade associations, private publishers, and many other groups and organizations. In addition, materials can be obtained from professional guidance services and audio-visual distributing centers at a reasonable cost. However, this material must be selected carefully, particularly if there is limited housing space in the school, in order to insure a balanced library of information that is accurate and up-to-date. The following types of materials are available to the guidance worker:

Occupational

1. Occupational abstracts, bulletins, and pamphlets
2. Books on one or more occupations
3. Posters, charts, graphs, and pictures
4. Filmstrips, films, phonograph records, tapes
5. Professional journals
6. Occasional articles from general periodicals

Educational

1. College and university catalogues
2. Directories of institutions of higher education
3. Directories of private schools
4. Directories of technical schools
5. Directories of correspondence and home study schools
6. Directories of business and professional schools
7. Books on choosing, planning for, or adjusting to college
8. Directories of scholarships, fellowships, and loans
9. Accreditation association reports and bulletins
10. Films
11. Posters, charts, graphs, and pictures
12. Booklets on study-habits, note-taking, preparing for examinations and writing themes or term papers

Personal-Social

1. Booklets on personal and social adjustment
2. Booklets on personal appearance
3. Films
4. Posters, charts, graphs, and pictures

In addition to this prepared material, valuable information can be obtained through community surveys, contacts with local employment agencies, and continuous communication with employers in local business and industrial organizations.

Disposition of Prepared Materials

Once materials have been selected and ordered, arrangements can be made with professional guidance services and other publishing companies to receive new or supplementary material on a monthly, quarterly, or semi-yearly basis. However, a chaotic situation will soon prevail unless a plan is devised for the systematic disposition of this material. The facilities in each school will help to determine the nature of the plan to be devised. The following suggestions may be appropriate for most schools:

1. A special section of the school library may be devoted to books, college catalogues, directories, and other bound material that contains educational, occupational, or personal-social information.
2. An occupational file of loose materials and small pamphlets may be located in the school library or in a central guidance office.
3. Display cases and bulletin boards in the corridors, library, classrooms, and guidance office may be used to display posters, charts, graphs, and pictures.
4. Departments in the larger secondary schools may wish to house and present information pertaining to educational and vocational opportunities in certain fields.
5. Clubs and organizations within the school may wish to collect and house educational and vocational materials relating to their own special areas of interest.

Since college catalogues and occupational information become obsolete rather quickly, some provision needs to be made for screening existing materials on a periodic basis. Limited housing facilities in many schools require the elimination of obsolete material in order that new material can be stored. A more important reason for the periodic review of informational materials is the need for eliminating the possibility that students will obtain inaccurate or misleading information from outdated material.

Sources of occupational, educational, and personal-social information are listed in the bibliography at the end of this chapter.

Presenting Information to Groups

A variety of group procedures has been employed to disseminate information to students. While such methods are not a complete substitute for individual contacts, they have been popular for three reasons:

1. They are more economical and less time-consuming than individual approaches.

2. Students have the opportunity to exchange ideas and to interact with one another.
3. Much of the information has general value for all the pupils in the group.

These are valid reasons provided that individual counseling is available to those students whose needs are not completely met through group procedures. However, it is difficult to schedule group activities so that they present a continuous program of information for all students. In addition, there is some disagreement over whether the dissemination of this information is the primary responsibility of the instructional staff or the guidance staff. Consequently, considerable debate has raged over the merits of a vocations or "career planning" course as compared with the career conference or vocations day organized and administered by the guidance staff.

A number of surveys have been conducted on the methods used to disseminate occupational information in high schools. Rimel (32) obtained questionnaire responses from 327 small high schools and found that the following methods were being used (listed here in order of frequency):

Films
Unbound current vocational file
Occupations course
Supervised excursions
Library reading list on occupations
Career or college days
Bulletin board displays
Outside speakers at assemblies
Occupational units in social studies classes
Vocational emphasis in subject fields
School paper covering vocations

Kinker and Fox (22) surveyed 253 high schools in the midwest and found that occupational files were used in 62 per cent of the schools; industrial visits were conducted by 36 per cent; vocations were studied through homerooms and classrooms by 35 per cent; and occupations courses were offered by 24 per cent of the schools in the study. A survey of 408 Minnesota high schools by Kaupp (21) revealed that occupational briefs and pamphlets were used by 301; displays of current materials by 289; occupations correlated with subject-matter by 285; occupations course or units by 278; audio-visual materials by 233; field trips by 196; files of unbound materials by 189; career days by 148; and community occupational surveys by 62 schools.

Guidance Courses

The guidance course is a group instructional activity separate and distinct from any other course of instruction. Guidance courses vary widely as to specific purpose and the length and frequency of instructional periods. Such courses may be called *vocations, occupations, orientation, career planning, guidance, social living, life adjustment,* or *psychology* courses. They will generally include units on (a) self appraisal and understanding, (b) educational planning, and (c) vocational planning. However, some courses will concentrate on only one of these areas. Evidence concerning the value of such courses has been somewhat scanty. Cuony and Hoppock (10) found that a group of students who have completed a high school course in job finding were more satisfied with their jobs and earned more money one year after graduation than a comparable group of students who had not taken the course.

Career Days

The career day or career conference has been as controversial a guidance activity as the organized guidance course. While this activity brings the community into the school and is an excellent aid to good public relations, its value for the pupil is debatable. Most of the criticism, however, has not been of the activity itself, but of the manner in which it is conducted. Occupational representatives are often selected by the company or organization rather than by the school. Some are biased in their presentations; others are unable to present their information in an adequate manner. The time set aside for the group meetings is often inadequate. Group meetings sometimes fail to end on time, thereby causing students to be late for the following meeting. Some groups become too large for the classrooms in which the meetings are scheduled, thus causing additional loss of time while new rooms are being located. Most of these recognized limitations to career conferences can be eliminated through careful planning. Roeber, Smith, and Erickson (33) have developed a twelve-point check list that serves as an excellent guide for a career-conference planning committee.

Most career conferences afford students the opportunity to hear a keynote speaker at a general session and to attend two group meetings of their choice. Some schools require attendance at these meetings; some do not. North Dallas High School, Dallas, Texas, requires all sophomores, juniors, and seniors to attend the Career Day activities. North Chicago Community High School, North Chicago, Illinois, restricts its programs to juniors and seniors. The latter school actually schedules *two* career days. On *Industry Day*, representatives from fourteen local industries are invited to the school to discuss the hiring policies and available jobs at their respective companies. Freshman and sophomore students are dismissed for the afternoon in order to provide sufficient space for the group meetings. On *Career Day*, speakers representing the ten major occupational fields present information on the various jobs within each occupational field, with emphasis on the requirements for entrance, the nature of the work, and the employment outlook. For those students who are seriously considering a specific occupation, interviews are arranged with a specialist from that area.

Field Trips

The field trip represents another type of group instructional activity that helps to develop better understanding and cooperation between school and community. While field trips are often scheduled in conjunction with a course or a unit of work, they may be arranged by the guidance staff if the main purpose of the trip is to give students a better picture of vocational opportunities in the community. Most employers and plant managers are happy to schedule such tours. They realize that many of their potential employees are currently enrolled in the local schools.

Many school systems hold an annual one-day meeting called Business, Industry, and Education Day. B-I-E Day may be summarized as a field-trip day for the school staff instead of the students. It is hoped that, by this means, the school staff will be in a better position to relate their areas of instruction to immediate and long-range vocational opportunities.

College Days

Many schools hold another type of workshop for students, which can be organized much as career days are organized. This type of workshop, usually known as "college day," furnishes information to all students who are interested in continuing their education. Admissions representatives from colleges, universities, and other types of post-high school institutions conduct group meetings for students interested in attending their school. In many instances, it is possible for the college representative to schedule individual conferences with students. It is common practice for schools within the same geographical area to cooperate with one another in scheduling dates for their college days. By arranging these activities on consecutive days, a group of schools can attract a larger number of college and university representatives.

Pre-college days are scheduled at some schools. This activity is usually devoted to speeches and group discussions on such topics as "Should I go to college?" "How is college different from high school?" and "Choosing the right college." Students are usually given suggestions as to the type of questions they might ask institutional representatives on college day.

The New York State Association of Deans and Guidance Personnel has published a report (31) which suggests procedures for organizing a college day. Portions of this report are presented here.

A. *Pre-college day plans*
   1. The program should be planned to meet the needs of the students in a particular school or schools, and include those students who are planning to attend college.
   2. The program should be held at a time when interested high school students and their parents will find it easy to attend.
   3. The guidance department of the high school should enlist the cooperation of the administration and the faculty in the planning stage so as to insure maximum efficiency of the actual program. English classes and social studies classes can cooperate by having students write themes as a result of investigations of admissions practices in several colleges, program of studies, what is expected of a student in college, what should a student expect of college, what is college, and so forth.
   4. It is considered good practice for the guidance department to hold assemblies or classes prior to the college day to acquaint the student with procedures to be used during the actual program, preliminary instruction of the conduct of the college day, what questions should be asked, and so forth.
   5. Whenever joint participation of two or more schools in a county, city or other local area is practicable, the schools should meet jointly in a centralized place. Preliminary details should be jointly planned so as to insure uniformity.
   6. Announcements of the date for the college day program should be mailed to the colleges a few months in advance. In addition to giving the time and place of the meeting, the

type of meeting should be included. Information concerning transportation and hotel accommodations should also be included.

7. As early as possible, the students should be canvassed to determine their first, second, and third choices in colleges, and the invitation list made up as a result of this survey. It is considered good practice to invite only those colleges for which five or more students have shown a preference, and the names should be sent to the college with the original or subsequent announcement. Invitations to other colleges should be extended but they should be informed as to the interests of the students.

8. Students should be encouraged to become well acquainted with the literature of the colleges *prior* to the college day program. If this material is not available, the students should write to the admissions office.

9. On-campus representation by the college should be provided. Less-informed alumni representatives seem to do more harm to the college than good.

B. *Conduct of the college day*

1. Whenever possible, each college representative should be assigned an individual room to conduct his conference. When this is not possible, preference should be given to those who may expect a large number of participants.

2. Closer unity between the high school and the college is undoubtedly accomplished by a college day program; therefore, the time should be allowed before the program for an informal meeting of the college representatives and the high school guidance personnel.

3. It is considered good practice to have guides in the hall to meet college representatives, parents and visitors, and show them to rooms. A printed or mimeographed program giving the list of the colleges represented, room assignments, and names of the representatives is desirable.

4. Assemblies during the college day program are discouraged. If a school finds that it needs one, it should be limited to thirty minutes, and should be largely for "kick off" and explaining procedures. They have an advantage as to providing a gathering place so that all are present to start the real business of the day.

5. There should be at least two, and no more than three sessions, of not less than thirty minutes each during which college representatives may talk to students. The students should be expected to remain in the room for the entire period, and not leave before some pre-arranged signal, such as a bell sounding at the end of the period. If it is considered

essential, a "free period" might be scheduled at the conclusion of the regular program to allow students to return to a
particular college representative or be allowed to vagabond
into new rooms.

6. It is preferable to have only juniors and seniors meet with
   college representatives.

7. Each college representative should arrange his time schedule
   during the day for maximum effectiveness. Perhaps the first
   ten and not more than fifteen minutes might be directed
   toward general remarks about the college by the college
   representative; the remainder of the period should be given
   to the students for their questions.

C. *Post college day activities*

If the college day program is to be effective as a counseling
technique, some provisions should be made to integrate this
with the other guidance programs of the school, and follow-up
should be encouraged. These suggestions are offered:

1. Follow-up assemblies or guidance sessions, with individuals
   or groups, are encouraged to discuss the topics presented
   during the college day conference.

2. Students should be encouraged to write to the college representatives with whom they visited for aditional information which may be needed. The correspondence should
   mention that the student discussed his plans with the college
   representatives during the college day conference.

3. Students should be encouraged to visit the campuses of their
   interest with their parents. They should, however, be urged
   to write ahead.

Some schools prefer to invite their graduates currently enrolled in
college to return for the college day program. However, it is usually
difficult to obtain a representative number of these former students
since their own academic responsibilities curtail their off-campus trips.

Presenting Information Through Regular Classes

Every school subject has some educational and vocational significance. Every teacher should be willing and able to relate his subject
to the world of work. The presentation of this type of information
through units on transportation, protective services, and so forth; or
carefully planned around a guidance unit.

In the primary grades, occupational information is generally
related to the home, family, and community and can be introduced
through units on transportation, protective services, and so forth; or

can be developed **through** such discussions as "What does Daddy do?" In the intermediate grades, the social studies curriculum provides the logical framework for studying the life and work of employed adults in various regions of the country. At the secondary school level, it is common practice to set up special guidance units in social studies or English classes. At North Chicago (Illinois) Community High School, vocational information is presented through freshmen social studies classes and junior English classes. Four weeks, or twenty class periods, are devoted to vocational topics in the freshman social studies classes. During this period the following activities take place:

1. An interest inventory is administered and interpreted to all students.
2. A trip to the library is scheduled to enable students to become familiar with the filing system for all occupational materials.
3. Four films and six film strips are shown.
4. Vocational charts and posters are displayed.
5. Lectures and discussions are conducted.

Two weeks, or ten class periods, are devoted to vocational topics in the junior English classes. During this period, lectures and discussions are devoted to the subject matter preparation necessary to qualify for various jobs and the techniques for securing these jobs. Another interest inventory is administered and interpreted to all students. Once again, use is made of films, film strips, vocational charts, and posters.

Presenting Information Through Special Classes or Groups

Group instructional activities may also be conducted through the *homeroom,* through *special assemblies,* and through *group meetings* dealing with planning and adjustment topics. The homeroom provides a natural setting for group work. It has already been identified as a widely used vehicle for conducting group orientation activities. Unfortunately, many schools give the program an inadequate amount of time and direction. It is not uncommon to find homeroom periods of ten to fifteen minutes duration devoted almost exclusively to checking attendance and reading announcements. Ohlsen (28) has reported on a junior high school that was dissatisfied with its homeroom program. The committee that was appointed to develop an improved homeroom plan made the following recommendations:

1. The homeroom should be staffed by teachers who volunteer for the duty.

2. Those teachers who volunteer for homerooms should be assigned a proportionately lighter teaching load.

3. Pupils should indicate their first and second choices for homeroom teachers and first choices should be honored wherever possible.

4. Wherever possible, a pupil should take two of his courses with the homeroom teacher.

5. Pupils' daily schedule should be arranged so that they spend three periods, preferably three *consecutive* periods, with their homeroom teacher.

6. The principal should permit teachers to have two homeroom groups, one in the forenoon and one in the afternoon.

7. The principal should provide a training program for homeroom teachers.

In recognition of the limited contacts between students and their homeroom teachers in the daily fifteen-minute period, some schools have set aside an additional class period for homeroom activities. These "special" homerooms are often scheduled at the beginning of the school year. To provide a minimum of interference with regularly scheduled classes, these meetings are carefully spaced during the year and occur at different class periods. In schools that do not have a homeroom program, these special meetings may be organized according to grade level.

Some schools prefer to schedule special meetings or assemblies as the need arises. At these schools, the regular class periods may be shortened for the day to permit the inclusion of an extra period. A special assembly for juniors and seniors may be called a few days prior to a career conference in order to acquaint all students with the procedures to be followed during the conference. Special meetings or assemblies may also be scheduled on short notice when it is discovered that a prominent speaker can fit the school into his itinerary.

Placement Services

Placement may be defined as that part of the information service which assists students to carry out their educational and vocational plans. Placement services may be said to consist of (a) the acquisition, organization, and maintenance of information concerning job vacancies, scholarship competitions, college registration procedures, and so forth; (b) the distribution of this information to individual pupils; and (c) other procedures designed to facilitate the pupil's entrance into the job or educational program of his choice.

Job Placement

In many schools, staff members have accepted the responsibility for placing their students in part-time or summer jobs. Some staff members have maintained contacts with employers in order to help students find jobs of a more permanent nature. It is not unusual to find teachers or departmental chairmen in the areas of business education or industrial education giving considerable attention to the placement of their own students. Coordinators of diversified occupations or office occupations and distributive education teachers may be released from a portion of their teaching responsibilities in order to function as part-time placement officers.

However, the proper coordination of job placement procedures usually cannot be effected without the services of a full-time placement officer or the establishment of a placement committee. Where it is impractical to employ a full-time placement officer, a placement committee should be formed. Such a committee would normally include members of the guidance staff and representatives from the industrial education and business education departments. One of the first tasks of this committee would be to inform staff members of their placement responsibilities and to encourage them to volunteer for specific placement duties.

Humphreys, Traxler, and North (18) offer the following suggestions for organizing and operating a job placement service:

1. Determine the kinds of positions and the kinds of registrants that the office will handle.

2. Publicize the office's services among present and former students and among prospective employers.

3. Set up a filing system that classifies available jobs and that has cross references to these jobs.

4. Establish cooperative relationships with prospective employers. To do this, a placement officer can write brief to-the-point letters to employers. Or even better, he can telephone them. Or, best of all, he can visit and talk with them. By knowing employers personally, the placement officer is best able to develop cooperative working relationships.

5. From employers, obtain notices of their job vacancies and their specifications for these jobs. For each notice, make out a card and place it in the employers' card file.

6. Interview and register job-seekers. Secure as complete information as possible concerning the qualifications of each registrant. This information should include vital data (birth date, place of birth, sex, etc.); school record (major and minor fields and academic marks); offices held in school or community organiza-

tions; hobbies and other interests; and work experiences. The registrant should supply most of these facts when he fills out his biographical form.

7. Organize an efficient filing system of registrants' data. This system should include a registration or applicant's card and file folder for each registrant. This folder should hold copies of the registrant's biographical form.

8. Secure definitive statements from the references listed by each registrant.

9. Check up on the accuracy of the information given by each registrant on his registration card and on his biographical form.

10. For a vacant position announced by an employer, select the registrants to be recommended by the placement office. To do this, a placement officer should carefully screen all registrants; he should then recommend as candidates only those registrants who appear to meet the qualifications specified by the employer. If the placement office recommends an unqualified person, this action may bring disappointment to the candidate and may alienate the employer.

11. Notify registrants of job vacancies and secure their approval before recommending them for these jobs.

12. Send to the prospective employer a copy of each recommended candidate's biographical form. Include a covering letter. In some cases, this letter may present the highlights of a candidate's qualifications.

13. Later, check with the prospective employer to find out (a) whether he offered the job to the recommended candidate and, if he did so, (b) whether the candidate accepted that job.

14. Record the results of a job application in the employers' card file and in the candidates' card file. In the active sections of these files, respectively, put the cards of unfilled vacancies and of unplaced candidates.

15. At the end of each academic year, prepare a summary report of the work of the placement office. In this report, include the number of registrants placed according to types of positions, the number of notices of job vacancies received, and the like. Give copies of this report to the school's administrative head and other staff members, to present and former students, to the parents of students, and to the press.

16. From time to time, conduct follow-up studies to evaluate and to improve the services of the placement office. These studies may include two types of questionnaires—one to be filled out by former students; the other, by their employers.[2]

[2] Reprinted by permission from *Guidance Services* by J. Anthony Humphreys, Arthur E. Traxler, and Robert D. North. Copyright 1960 by Science Research Associates, Inc.

Central High, Sioux City, Iowa, started its placement service by obtaining a list of employers from the classified section of the telephone directory and from the help-wanted column of a local newspaper. Letters listing available students were then sent to each employer. A copy of this letter was also published in the monthly publication of the Credit Bureau and the local Associated Retailers group. When appointments were made for job interviews, cards of introduction were sent to prospective employers a few days before the interview. This businesslike approach allowed both student and employer to begin the interview with greater confidence.

The Long Branch (New Jersey) High School has experimented with a "try-out" job orientation program which represents a unique departure from the traditional job placement service. By special arrangement with employers in the area, each student is given a chance to try several different after-school, weekend, or summer jobs before he graduates from high school. In this way, he gains (a) varied work experience and (b) increased confidence and competence in his job application techniques. This latter service is often overlooked by job placement programs. Yet, schools have as much responsibility for orienting their students to "job-getting" procedures as they have for assisting them to find employment. This responsibility can be fulfilled through conferences with students, through the acquisition and use of booklets and films dealing with the job interview, and by asking employers for their cooperation in identifying the reasons why students were or were not hired as a result of their job interviews. In the latter case, students can be informed of their mistakes and will have a chance to modify their approach at the next interview.

Educational Placement

A generation ago, our high schools did not have to worry about the educational placement of their graduates. Many colleges and universities were operating at less than capacity and were begging for students. But the days are gone when one could mutter with some degree of truth, "If the check is good and the body is warm, he's in." Most good colleges are overcrowded today; some of them are rejecting three or four applicants for every applicant they accept. Every year, more and more youngsters plan to extend their education beyond high school. There is every indication that young people (and their parents) are beginning to consider at least two years of college a socio-economic necessity. In the next decade, college enrollments are expected to double in size. Newly established community colleges, junior colleges, and extension divisions will reduce some of the pressure on the top-rated colleges and universities by accepting some students who are rejected elsewhere. But the better institutions of higher education will still be forced to deny admission to many qualified applicants. Under these circumstances, college planning should begin in the seventh or eighth grade in order that pupils will be able to make maximum use of the school's college preparatory program. Educational placement, likewise, has become more than a brief service for students in their senior year. It is, rather, a continuous program designed to (a) inform the student of additional educational opportunities that are compatible with his abilities, interests, needs, and goals and (b) help him gain admittance to the institution of his choice. These responsibilities will usually be met in the following ways:

1. Planning and administering the college day program;
2. Assisting students to plan a program of study that will be in accord with college admissions requirements;
3. Obtaining and circulating information on college scholarships, educational contests, and other awards which provide financial aid to potential college students;
4. Obtaining and circulating information concerning college scholarship and college-admissions testing programs;
5. Processing college admissions and scholarship applications, writing letters of recommendation, and gathering additional data as requested by the training institution;
6. Conducting follow-up studies of all graduates who have continued their education beyond high school;
7. Working with all of the local scholarship groups who want help in setting up scholarship awards and help in the selection of deserving students;
8. Developing and managing a community scholarship fund through which all students, parents, and other interested members of the community may contribute.

The rapid growth of college scholarship and college-admissions testing programs during the past few years has made educational placement a more complex process than it was formerly. Most schools have assumed the responsibility for informing eligible students and their parents of the time, place, cost, and purpose of each of these test batteries. Dr. Arthur Ryden, District Director of Guidance and Testing for the three Niles Township High Schools, Skokie, Illinois, schedules a series of evening meetings with parents in order to acquaint them with this information. He distributes and discusses the following "Testing Calendar" at these meetings:

TESTING CALENDAR FOR NATIONAL TESTING PROGRAMS

PRELIMINARY SCHOLASTIC APTITUDE TEST (PSAT)

of the College Entrance Examination Board

TEST DATE	OPENING DATE FOR REGISTRATION	CLOSING DATE FOR REGISTRATION	TESTING TIME	FEE
October 23	September 13	September 24	2½ hours	$1.00

AMERICAN COLLEGE TESTING (ACT)

TEST DATE	OPENING DATE FOR REGISTRATION	REGISTRATION DEADLINE*	TESTING TIME	FEE
November 13	September 1	October 16	3½ hours	$4.00
February 19	November 15	January 22		
April 23	January 24	April 2		
June 25	April 25	June 4		
August 6	June 6	July 16		

*No registrations or changes of registrations guaranteed after this date.

COLLEGE ENTRANCE EXAMINATION BOARD (CEEB)

TEST DATE	PENALTY DATE*	ABSOLUTE CLOSING DATE	TESTING TIME	FEE
December 4	November 6	November 20	3+ hours	$4.50 (SAT)
				$6.75
January 8	December 4	December 18		(ACHIEV)
March 5	February 5	February 19		$2.00
May 7	April 9	April 23		(WRITING
July 9	June 11	June 25		SAMPLE)

*$2.50 penalty fee after closing date.

NATIONAL MERIT SCHOLARSHIP QUALIFYING TESTS (NMSQT)

TEST DATE	OPENING DATE FOR REGISTRATION	REGISTRATION DEADLINE	TESTING TIME	FEE
February 26	December 13	January 12	3+ hours	$1.00

NATIONAL EDUCATIONAL DEVELOPMENT TESTS (NEDT)

There is a Fall and Spring testing schedule. Niles Township High Schools will use the Spring testing schedule.

SPRING TESTING SCHEDULE — February 28 through March 5.

ADVANCED PLACEMENT PROGRAM EXAMINATIONS (APP)

TEST DATE	OPENING DATE FOR REGISTRATION	REGISTRATION DEADLINE	TESTING TIME	FEE
Week of May 16 May 20	March 23	April 13	4+ hrs. per ea. test	$5.00 registration fee, plus $10.00 for each test

Summary

Information services play an important role in the school's guidance program. It is the function of the articulation and orientation program to acquaint pupils with the educational and social-cultural opportunities that will be available to them within the school. In order to furnish students with adequate information concerning their out-of-school opportunities, prepared materials of an occupational, educational, and personal-social nature must be acquired, organized, housed, and distributed. Information can be disseminated through school subjects, field trips, homerooms, assemblies, group meetings, special conference programs, or through an organized guidance course. Placement services are designed to facilitate the student's entrance into a specific job or educational program by (a) furnishing him with information concerning job-getting techniques, job vacancies, scholarship competitions, and so forth; and (b) distributing pupil data to prospective employers, college admissions officers, and officials of other training programs. The centralization and coordination of information services is difficult to achieve unless responsibility is delegated to one individual.

Bibliography

1.　Andrew, D. and R. D. Willey. *Administration and Organization of the Guidance Program*. New York: Harper and Brothers, 1958. Chap. 9.
2.　Arbuckle, Dugald S. *Pupil Personnel Services in American Schools*. Boston: Allyn & Bacon, Inc., 1962. Chap. 9.
3.　Baer, Max F. and Edward C. Roeber. *Occupational Information*. 2nd ed. Chicago: Science Research Associates, Inc. 1958.
4.　Bennett, Margaret E. *Guidance and Counseling in Groups*. 2nd ed. New York: McGraw-Hill Book Company, Inc., 1963. Chaps. 8, 9.
5.　Berdie, Ralph F., Wilbur L. Layton, Edward O. Swanson, and Theda Hagenah. *Testing in Guidance and Counseling*. New York: McGraw-Hill Book Company, Inc., 1963. Chap. 10.
6.　Blanchard, Howard L. and Laurence S. Flaum. *Guidance: A Longitudinal Approach*. Minneapolis: Burgens Publishing Company, 1962. Chap. 10.
7.　Cottingham, Harold F. *Directed Readings in Foundations of Guidance and Personnel Services*. Bloomington, Illinois: McKnight & McKnight Publishing Co., 1964. Chap. 4.
8.　———— and William Hopke. *Guidance in Junior High School: Principles and Practices*. Bloomington, Illinois: McKnight & McKnight Publishing Co., 1961. Chaps. 9-11.
9.　Crow, Lester D. and Alice Crow. *Readings in Guidance*. New York: David McKay Company, Inc., 1962. Chap. 48.
10.　Cuony, E. R. and Robert Hoppock. "Job Course Pays Off," *Personnel and Guidance Journal*, XXXII:7, March, 1954, 389-91.
11.　Farwell, Gail F. and H. J. Peters. *Guidance Readings for Counselors*. Chicago: Rand McNally & Co., 1960. Chap. 6.
12.　Ginsberg, Eli. "Guidance In A Dynamic Economy," in Landy, Edward and Paul Perry, eds. *Guidance In American Education I: Backgrounds and Prospects*. Cambridge, Massachusetts: Harvard University Press, 1964.

13.   Glanz, Edward C., *Foundations and Principles of Guidance.* Boston: Allyn & Bacon, Inc., 1964. Chap. 10.

14.   Hatch, Raymond N., Paul L. Dressel, and James W. Costar. *Guidance Services in the Secondary Schools.* Dubuque, Iowa: William C. Brown Company, 1963. Chap. 4.

15.   Hollis, Joseph W. and Lucile U. Hollis. *Organizing for Effective Guidance.* Chicago: Science Research Associates, Inc., 1965. Chaps. 15, 18, 19.

16.   Hoppock, Robert. *Group Guidance—Principles, Techniques and Evaluation.* 2nd. ed. New York: McGraw-Hill Book Company, Inc., 1964.

17.   Hughes, Everett C. "The Study of Occupations," in Merton, Robert K., Leonard Broom, and Leonard S. Cottrell, Jr., eds. *Sociology Today.* New York: Basic Books, 1959.

18.   Humphreys, J. Anthony, Arthur E. Traxler, and Robert North. *Guidance Services.* 2nd ed. Chicago: Science Research Associates, Inc., 1960. Chaps. 7, 9, 12-14.

19.   Isaacson, Lee. *Career Information in Counseling and Teaching.* Boston: Allyn & Bacon, Inc., 1966.

20.   Johnson, W. F. *et al. Pupil Personnel and Guidance Services.* New York: McGraw-Hill Book Company, Inc., 1961. Chap. 17.

21.   Kaupp, L. E. *An Evaluation of Guidance Services in Minnesota High Schools Based upon the State Seven-Point Guidance Program.* Unpublished Ph.D. thesis, University of North Dakota, 1954.

22.   Kinker, H. R. and W. H. Fox. "A Study of High School Guidance Services in Six-State Area," *Bulletin of the School of Education.* No. 28. Indiana University, 1952.

23.   McDaniel, Henry B. *Guidance in the Modern School.* New York: The Dryden Press, 1956. Chaps. 11, 12, 15.

24.   Miller, Carroll H. *Foundations of Guidance.* New York: Harper and Brothers, 1961. Chap. 8.

25.   ————. *Guidance Services: An Introduction.* New York: Harper & Row, Publishers, 1965. Chap. 4.

26.   Norris, Willa. *Occupational Information in the Elementary School.* Chicago: Science Research Associates, Inc., 1963.

27.   ————, Franklin R. Zeran, and Raymond N. Hatch. *The Information Service In Guidance.* Chicago: Rand McNally & Co., 1960.

28.   Ohlsen, Merle M. *Guidance Services in the Modern School.* New York: Harcourt, Brace & World, Inc., 1964. Chaps. 10-12.

29.   Patterson, C. H. *Counseling and Guidance in Schools.* New York: Harper and Brothers, 1962. Chaps. 10, 11.

30.   Peters, H. J., and Gail Farwell. *Guidance: A Developmental Approach.* Chicago: Rand McNally & Co., 1959. Chaps. 9, 17.

31.   "Report Suggesting Procedures for Organizing a College Day," *The Guidance Point of View.* New York Association of Deans and Guidance Personnel, March, 1954.

32.   Rimel, Evelyn G. *Guidance Practices in the Smaller High Schools of*

the United States; Their Present Status and Proposals for More Effective Implementation. Unpublished Ph.D. thesis, Syracuse University, 1952.

33.   Roeber, Edward C., Glenn E. Smith, and Clifford E. Erickson. *Organization and Administration of Guidance Services.* New York: Mc-Graw-Hill Book Company, Inc., 1955. Chaps. 8, 9.

34.   Stewart, Laurence and Charles Warnath. *The Counselor and Society: A Cultural Approach.* Boston: Houghton Mifflin Company, 1965. Chap. 6.

35.   Stoops, Emery and Gunner L. Wahlquist. *Principles and Practices in Guidance.* New York: McGraw-Hill Book Company, Inc., 1958. Chaps. 4, 5, 7.

36.   Tiedeman, David. "The Cultivation of Career in Vocational Development Through Guidance-in-Education," in Landy, Edward and Arthur M. Kroll, eds. *Guidance In American Education II: Current Issues and Suggested Action.* Cambridge, Massachusetts: Harvard University Press, 1965.

37.   Tolbert, E. L. *Introduction to Counseling.* New York: McGraw-Hill Book Company, Inc., 1959.

38.   Traxler, Arthur E. and Robert D. North. *Techniques of Guidance.* 3rd ed. New York: Harper & Row Publishers, 1966. Chaps. 3, 20.

39.   Zeran, F. R. and A. C. Riccio. *Organization and Administration of Guidance Services.* Chicago: Rand McNally & Co., 1962. Chaps. 3-4.

Sources of Educational Information and Financial Aid

1.   *A Guide to Member Colleges of the Association of College Admissions Counselors.* Evanston, Illinois: Association of College Admissions Counselors, 1963.
2.   *Approved Technical Institutes.* Washington: National Council of Technical Schools, 1957.
3.   Astin, Alexander W. *Who Goes Where To College.* Chicago: Science Research Associates, Inc., 1965.
4.   Bellman Publishing Company, P.O. Box 172, Cambridge 38, Massachusetts. *Scholarships, Fellowships, and Loans News Service.*
5.   Bowles, Frank H. and Richard Pearson. *Admission to College: A Program for the 1960's.* College Entrance Examination Board, 1962. (% Educational Testing Service, P.O. Box 592, Princeton, New Jersey.)
6.   Brownstein, Samuel C. *College Bound.* Great Neck, New York: Barron's Educational Series, Inc., 1957.
7.   ——— and Mitchell Weiner. *How to Prepare for College Entrance Examinations.* Great Neck, New York: Barron's Educational Series, Inc., 1957.
8.   Burckel, Christian E. *The College Blue Book.* 10th ed. Yonkers, New York: C. E. Burckel and Associates, P.O. Box 311, 1962.
9.   Cartter, Alan M. *American Universities and Colleges.* 9th ed. Washington, D.C.: American Council on Education, 1964.
10. Cass, James and Max Birnbaum. *Comparative Guide to American Colleges.* New York: Harper & Row Publishers, 1964.
11. Chronicle Guidance Publications, Moravia, New York. Monthly publication of *Student Aid Bulletin: Announcement of Scholarships Available to Entering College Freshmen.*
12. *College Admissions Data Service, 1964-65.* Cambridge, Massachusetts: Education Research Corp. (Published annually.)
13. *College Board Score Reports.* College Entrance Examination Board,

1963. (% Educational Testing Service, P.O. Box 592, Princeton, New Jersey.)

14.   *The College Board Today, 1964-65.* New York: College Entrance Examination Board, 1964. (% Educational Testing Service, P.O. Box 592, Princeton, New Jersey.)

15.   *The College Booklet, 26th edition, 1964-65.* Chicago: The Adult Education Council of Greater Chicago, 1964.

16.   *The Cost of Four Years of College.* New York: Life Insurance Agency Management Association, New York Life Insurance Company, 1963.

17.   *Description of the College Board Achievement Tests.* College Entrance Examination Board. (% Educational Testing Service, P.O. Box 592, Princeton, New Jersey.)

18.   *Description of the College Board Scholastic Aptitude Tests.* College Entrance Examination Board. (% Educational Testing Service, P.O. Box 592, Princeton, New Jersey.)

19.   Diamond, Esther, ed. *Preparing Students for College.* Chicago: Science Research Associates, Inc., 1959.

20.   *Directory of Sources for Higher Education Planning.* Chicago: Science Research Associates, Inc., 1965.

21.   *Educational Directory, Part III—Higher Education.* Office of Education, U.S. Department of Health, Education, and Welfare. Washington, D.C.: Government Printing Office. (Published annually.)

22.   *Facing Facts About College Admissions.* The Prudential Insurance Company of America, Box 36, Education Department, Newark 1, New Jersey, 1962.

23.   Feingold, Norman. *Scholarships, Fellowships and Loans.* (4 vols.) Boston: Bellman Publishing Company, 1962.

24.   Fine, Benjamin. *Barron's Profiles of American Colleges.* Great Neck, New York: Barron's Educational Series, Inc., 1964.

25.   ——— and Sidney Eisenberg. *How to Get Money for College.* Garden City: New York: Doubleday & Company, Inc., 1964.

26.   Fleming, Alice. *Complete Guide to the Accredited Correspondence Schools.* Garden City, New York: Doubleday & Company, Inc., 1964.

27.   Gleaser, Edmund J. and Alice M. Carroll, eds. *American Junior College.* 6th ed. Washington, D.C.: American Council on Education, 1963.

28.   Hill, Alfred T. *A Directory of Small Colleges.* Washington, D.C.: Council for the Advancement of Small Colleges, Inc.

29.   Karl, S. Donald. *The College Handbook.* New York: College Entrance Examination Board, 1963. (% Educational Testing Service, P.O. Box 592, Princeton, New Jersey.)

30.   Lehman, Ellem M., Shirley J. Ramsay, and Joe Jefferson. *A Handbook for the Counselors of College Bound Students.* Evanston, Illinois: Association of College Admissions Counselors, 1964.

31.   Lovejoy, Clarence E. *College Guide.* 6th ed. New York: Simon and Schuster, Inc., 1961-62.

32.   ———. *Vocational School Guide.* New York: Simon and Schuster, Inc., 1963.

33.   ———. *Lovejoy's Scholarship Guide.* New York: Simon and Schuster, Inc., 1964.

34.   *Manual of Freshman Class Profiles.* College Entrance Examination Board, 1964 ed. (% Educational Testing Service, P.O. Box 592, Princeton, New Jersey.)

35.   Miller, A. E., and Betty I. Brown. *National Directory of Schools and Vocations.* 2nd ed. North Springfield, Pennsylvania: State School Publications, 1963.

36.   *Post-High School Educational Opportunities in Illinois.* Office of the Superintendent of Public Instruction, Springfield, Illinois.

37.   Sargent, Porter. *Junior Colleges and Specialized Schools and Colleges.* Boston: Porter Sargent, 11 Beacon St., 1959.

38.   Splaver, Sarah. *Your College Education—How to Pay for It.* New York: Julian Messner—Division of Pocket Books, Inc., 1964.

Sources of Occupational Information

1.   Baer, Max F. and Edward C. Roeber. *Occupational Information.* Chicago: Science Research Associates, Inc., 1964.

2.   Bellman Publishing Company, 83 Newbury St., Boston, Massachusetts. *Vocational and Professional Monographs.*

3.   B'nai B'rith Vocational Service Bureau, 1424 16th St., N.W., Washington 6, D.C. *Occupational Bibliographies, Career News,* and *Occupational Orientation Charts.*

4.   Brancke, S. Dolores, ed. *Handbook of Job Facts.* Chicago: Science Research Associates, Inc., 1959.

5.   *Charm* magazine, 575 Madison Ave., New York 22, New York. *Fact Sheets* (occupational information and bibliographies for women).

6.   Cohen, Nathan M. *Vocational Training Directory of the United States.* Arlington, Virginia: Potomac Press, 1958.

7.   *Counseling and Employment Service for Youth.* Bureau of Employment Security. Washington, D.C.: U.S. Government Printing Office, 1962.

8.   *Counselor's Guide to Occupational and Other Manpower Information —An Annotated Bibliography of Selected Government Publications.* Department of Labor. Washington, D.C.: U.S. Government Printing Office, 1964.

9.   *Dictionary of Occupational Titles.* U.S. Department of Labor, Bureau of Employment Security. Washington, D.C.: Government Printing Office, 1965.

10.   Forrester, Gertrude. *Occupational Literature—An Annotated Bibliography.* New York: H. W. Wilson Co., 1964.

11.   *Glamour* magazine, 420 Lexington Ave., New York, New York: *Fact Sheets* and reprints of articles on women's occupations.

12.   Hoppock, Robert. *Occupational Information.* New York: McGraw-Hill Book Company, Inc., 1964.

13.   Institute for Research, 537 S. Dearborn St., Chicago, Illinois. *Career Research Monographs and Career Charts.*

14.   *Job Guide for Young Workers, 1963-64 edition.* U.S. Department of Labor, Bureau of Employment Security—U.S. Employment Service. Washington, D.C.: U.S. Government Printing Office, 1963.

15.   Lifton, Walter M., *Guide to the Use of Widening Occupational Roles Kit.* Chicago: Science Research Associates, Inc., 1962.

16.   ————, ed. *Keys to Vocational Decisions.* Chicago: Science Research Associates, Inc., 1964.

17.   *Mademoiselle* magazine, 575 Madison Ave., New York, New York. Reprints of articles on women's occupations.

18.   *Manpower and Training Trends Outlook Programs.* Department of Labor. Washington, D.C.: U.S. Government Printing Office, 1962.

19.   *Manpower Developments and Training Act: A Report and Evaluation of Research, Trainees, Training Programs, and Training Activities.* Secretary of Labor. Washington, D.C.: U.S. Government Printing Office, 1963.

20.   *Manpower Report of the President and a Report on Manpower Requirements, Resources, Utilization and Training.* U.S. Department of Labor. Washington, D.C.: U.S. Government Printing Office, 1963.

21.   Murphy, James M., compiler. *Directory of Vocational Training Sources.* Chicago: Science Research Associates, Inc., 1964.

22.   Occupational Index, Inc. New York University, Washington Square East, New York 3, New York. *Occupational Abstracts.*

23.   *Occupational Outlook Handbook.* Bulletin No. 1255. U.S. Department of Labor, Bureau of Labor Statistics. Washington, D.C.: U.S. Government Printing Office, 1963.

24.   *Occupational Outlook Quarterly.* U.S. Department of Labor, Bureau of Labor Statistics. Washington, D.C.: U.S. Government Printing Office.

25.   Ottley, William H., ed. *Career . . . the Annual Guide to Business Opportunities.* New York: Career, Inc., 1960.

26.   Reference Library. The Quarrie Corporation, 35 E. Wacker Drive, Chicago, Illinois. *Vocational Monographs.*

27.   Science Research Associates, Inc., Chicago 10, Illinois. *Occupational Briefs, American Job Series, Jobs in Action* picture series, *Life Adjustment Booklets,* and *Guidance Index* (occupational bibliography).

28.   *Seventeen* magazine, 11 West 42nd St., New York, New York. Reprints of articles on women's occupations.

29.   Splaver, Sarah. *Your Career If You're Not Going to College.* New York: Julian Messner—Division of Pocket Books, Inc., 1963.

30.   *Training for Jobs in Redeveloped Areas.* U.S. Department of Labor: Office of Manpower, Automation, and Training. Washington, D.C.: U.S. Government Printing Office, 1963.

31.   Vocational Guidance Manuals, Inc., 45 W. 45th Street, New York 19, New York. *National Vocational Guidance Manuals.*

Sources of Information on The Military Services

1.   *Army Occupations and You.* Department of the Army, Office of the Adjutant General, Washington 25, D.C. Rev. 1959.
2.   *Careers for Women in the Armed Forces.* Women's Bureau, Department of Labor, Washington 25, D.C., 1960.
3.   *Careers in the Medical Services of the U.S. Armed Forces* (women). Women's Bureau, Department of Labor, Washington 25, D.C., 1960.
4.   *For You—An Officer's Career in the U.S. Armed Forces* (Women). Department of Defense, Defense Advisory Committee on Women in the Services, Washington, D.C., 1960.
5.   Harwood, Michael. *The Student's Guide to Military Service.* Manhasset, New York: Channel Press, 1963.
6.   *Information on Regular NROTC: How to Go to College and Start a Navy Career.* U.S. Navy Recruiting Station, 631 E. St., N.W., Washington 4, D.C. (Reprinted annually.)
7.   *It's Your Decision—A Booklet for High School Students.* Department of the Army, Office of the Adjutant General, Washington 25, D.C.
8.   *Jobs For You—U.S. Marine Corps* (women). U.S. Marine Corps recruiting stations.
9.   *Military Guidance in Secondary Schools: Suggestions for Principals, Teachers, and Counselors.* Department of the Army, Washington, D.C.
10.   *Pathway to Maturity: A U.S. Army Booklet for Parents.* Department of the Army, Washington, D.C.
11.   *Pocket Guide to Air Force Opportunities.* U.S. Air Force recruiting stations.
12.   *Reserved For You.* Department of the Army, Office of the Adjutant General, Washington 25, D.C.
13.   *The Secret of Getting Ahead for High School Graduates.* Department of the Army, Office of the Adjutant General, Washington 25, D.C.
14.   *This. . . . Is How It Is.* U.S. Army recruiting stations.
15.   *U.S. Air Force Information Kit.* U.S. Air Force recruiting stations.
16.   *U.S. Air Force Occupational Handbook.* Headquarters, U.S. Air Force, Washington 25, D.C., 1959-60.
17.   *U.S. Navy Enlisted Occupational Handbook.* U.S. Navy recruiting stations.
18.   *U.S. Navy Occupational Handbook for Women.* U.S. Navy recruiting stations.
19.   *U.S. Marine Programs.* U.S. Marine Corps recruiting stations.
20.   *Where the Leaders Are.* Army Opportunities, Box 1040, Westbury, New York, 11591.

Sources of Life Adjustment Materials

1.   Billett, Ray O. and Yeo, J. Wendell. *Growing Up.* 2nd ed. Boston: D. C. Heath and Co., 1958.

2.   Ochsner, Alton, M.D. *Smoking and Your Life*. New York: Julian Messner—Division of Pocket Books, Inc., 1964.
3.   Row, Peterson and Co., 1911 Ridge Avenue, Evanston, Illinois. *Way of Life Series*.
4.   Sakol, Jeanne. *What About Teen-Age Marriage?* New York: Julian Messner—Division of Pocket Books, Inc., 1964.
5.   Science Research Associates, Inc., Chicago 10, Illinois. *Junior Life Adjustment Booklets* (for upper elementary and junior high school pupils) and *Life Adjustment Booklets* (for high school pupils).
6.   West, Ruth. *The Teen-Age Diet Book*. New York: Julian Messner—Division of Pocket Books, Inc., 1964.

Sources of Audio-Visual Materials

1.   Association Films, 347 Madison Ave., New York 17, New York.
2.   *Blue Book of 16 MM Films*. Educational Screen, 64 E. Lake St., Chicago, Illinois.
3.   Carl Mahnke Productions, 215 E. 3rd St., Des Moines, Iowa.
4.   *Coronet Films Catalog*. Coronet Instructional Films, 65 E. South Water St., Chicago 1, Illinois.
5.   *Educational Film Guide*. H. W. Wilson Co., 950 University Ave., New York 52, New York.
6.   *Educators Guide to Free Films* and *Educators Guide to Free Slide-films*. Annual ed. Educators Progress Service, Randolph, Wisconsin.
7.   *Encyclopaedia Britannica Films Catalog*. Encyclopaedia Britannica Films, 1150 Wilmette Ave., Wilmette, Illinois.
8.   *Films on Vocations*. Educational Film Library Association, Inc., 345 E. 46th St., New York 17, New York.
9.   *Ideal Pictures Educational Film Catalog*. Ideal Pictures, 58 E. South Water St., Chicago 1, Illinois.
10.   Institute of Life Insurance, Educational Division, 488 Madison Ave., New York 22, New York.
11.   Jam Handy Organization, 2821 E. Grand Blvd., Detroit 11, Michigan.
12.   *McGraw-Hill Films Catalog*. Text-Film Dept., McGraw-Hill Book Company, Inc., 330 W. 42nd St., New York 36, New York.
13.   Science Research Associates, Inc., Chicago 10, Illinois.
14.   Society for Visual Education, 1345 W. Diversey Blvd., Chicago, Illinois.
15.   *Young America Films Catalog*. Young America Films, 18 E. 41st St., New York 17, New York.

11

Research and
Evaluation Services

Guidance services cannot continue to grow in effectiveness unless they are subjected to a variety of research and evaluation procedures. Research is necessary for (a) the continued improvement of the guidance program; (b) the continued support of the guidance program by the school and the community; and (c) the continued school staff understanding of the contribution of guidance functions to the instructional program, extra-school activities, and administration. The counselor's fluid time schedule, his unique relationship with students, and his (generally) better research background make him the ideal person to provide leadership in stimulating, initiating, administering, and interpreting *all-school research studies* as well as studies evaluating some specific guidance or counseling service. Peters (36) suggests the following necessary research competencies of the school counselor:

1. Experience in developing, identifying and resolving questions about the guidance function.
2. Knowledge of different types of research and the inherent demands of each for rigorous, reputable accomplishment.
3. Understanding of implications for one's school guidance program from research reports in appropriate journals.
4. Ability to assess student educational development in the local school against a backdrop of national information.
5. Ability to determine discrepancy between student potential and performance and its possible significance.
6. Ability to analyze guidance test data and record data.
7. Skills to conduct research relevant to achievement, study skills, career thinking, personal development and follow-through studies.

This chapter is concerned with research procedures that will (a) help to develop a curriculum that meets the needs of the students, (b) help teachers improve classroom procedures, and (c) enable the guidance program to function more effectively.

School Surveys

School surveys may focus their attention on pupils, teachers, parents, administration, facilities, or upon relationships between two or more of these groupings. Typical of school surveys which would focus attention on pupils are the following:

1. Preparing a composite picture of the student population, grade by grade, in terms of age, sex, race, religion, family background, socio-economic status, etc.;
2. Preparing a composite picture of the student population, grade by grade, in terms of abilities, aptitudes, achievement, interests, and other data obtained through the testing program;
3. Comparing an entering class of first-graders, seventh-graders, or freshmen with all previous entering classes in terms of level of intelligence or achievement;
4. Comparing the intelligence or achievement of transfer students with that of the school population;
5. Identifying the gifted and retarded students or those with special problems;
6. Identifying the under- and over-achievers through analysis of test scores and grade averages;
7. Studying the effectiveness of the remedial reading program by means of before-and-after testing of the pupil's reading speed and comprehension.

There is a definite need for more study of different phases of the school's program. Attention needs to be given to the degree of effectiveness of classroom teaching procedures, special remedial or accelerated programs, extra-class activities, and orientation procedures. Roeber, Smith, and Erickson (37) feel that the following areas need examination by means of the school survey approach:

1. To what extent do the orientation activities in a sending school prepare pupils for optimum adjustments to the receiving school?

2. To what extent do orientation procedures in the receiving school supplement those of the sending school and lead to optimum adjustments for all pupils?

3. To what extent does the reading readiness program in the first grade prepare pupils for learning the necessary reading skills?

4. To what extent are pupils reading up to their level of ability? To what extent are they achieving in other skills?

5. To what extent are extraclass activities achieving their objectives?

6. To what extent do curricular or extraclass placements meet the real needs of the pupils?

7. To what extent do pupils use test and other data in developing self-concepts?

8. To what extent do pupils at any school level feel that they are a part of the school's social climate?

9. To what extent are pupils using the counseling service? In what ways did the pupils become acquainted with this service?

10. To what extent are pupils going to individuals outside the school for assistance with their planning problems?

11. To what extent are pupils transferring skills, understandings, and appreciations to living outside the school?

12. To what extent are pupils oriented to each subject by the teacher of that subject?

13. To what extent are pupils able to adapt skills and understandings learned in one school to learning experiences expected by another school?

14. To what extent are pupils who transfer from one school system aided in their adjustments to the new school situation?

15. To what extent are teachers adapting classroom activities to the individual differences of the pupils?

16. What are the causes for pupils dropping school or considering such a step?

17. To what extent are various group procedures, such as career conferences, work-experience programs, or enrollment procedures in homerooms, attaining their objectives?[1]

The list of possible surveys is almost endless. The alert guidance worker will also recognize the value of surveying certain situations or conditions outside the school environment. It is generally agreed that the school, as a community agency, should gear its program to the needs of the community. Consequently, surveys of home conditions, youth-serving agencies, and recreational facilities outside the school may discover information that will help develop a curriculum that meets the needs of its students in a more effective manner.

Follow-Up Studies

Follow-up studies provide a means of gathering two types of information of value to the school: (a) information on the kinds of occupational, educational, and training opportunities which former pupils have found to be desirable and profitable; and (b) information which allows us to appraise and evaluate the experiences which former pupils had while in school.

Baer and Roeber (2) offer a detailed account of the step-by-step procedure to be followed in conducting follow-up studies of school-leavers. Roeber, Smith, and Erickson (37) caution against a hurried approach to follow-up studies and identify seven problems that require attention before such a study is begun: (a) determining readiness and insuring committee participation, (b) establishing leadership, (c) recognizing the complexity of the planning process, (d) developing effective techniques for obtaining information, (e) determining the role that can be played by pupils within the school, (f) making provision for recording the follow-up study, and (g) making provision for establishing the follow-up study on a year-to-year basis. Such an undertaking requires the cooperation of the entire school staff. This cooperation will usually be forthcoming when the objectives of the follow-up study have been determined by the staff, rather than by a single individual or a small group. The staff must determine *what* information it is seeking, the *purpose* in seeking it, and *how* this information is to be obtained.

---

[1]By permission from *Organization and Administration of Guidance Services*, by Edward C. Roeber, Glenn E. Smith, and Clifford E. Erickson. Copyright 1955. McGraw-Hill Book Company, Inc.

Objectives of the Follow-Up Study

The general objectives of the follow-up study may be placed in six categories:

1. Curriculum revision;
2. Improvement of the guidance program;
3. Identification of graduates and dropouts in further need of help;
4. Intensive study of a special group of students;
5. To obtain information that will be helpful to the students;
6. To obtain information that will be useful to the staff in gaining a better understanding of their students.

The general objectives of the follow-up study can be broken down into a number of specific objectives which reveal more clearly the kinds of information that should be sought from former pupils. Smith (38) lists the following specific objectives of a follow-up study:

1. To determine the holding power of the school.
2. To discover grade levels at which most drop-outs occur.
3. To learn why pupils leave school before graduation.
4. To seek information which will provide clues for identifying potential drop-outs.
5. To determine the mobility of former pupils.
6. To determine the percentage of drop-outs and graduates who seek further training after leaving school, and whether the secondary schools should provide training of the kinds pupils seek later.
7. To determine the percentage of pupils who enter college, and what colleges.
8. To determine the percentage of former pupils who enter employment immediately after leaving school.
9. To evaluate the effectiveness of the school's placement activities.
10. To discover employment opportunities for young workers in the local community.
11. To discover the barriers to employment and occupational adjustment encountered by former pupils.
12. To obtain the opinions of former pupils concerning the efficacy of the guidance program.
13. To obtain opinions concerning needed modifications of the curriculum in light of the experiences of former pupils.
14. To compare the occupational stability and adjustment of graduates and drop-outs.
15. To compare the occupational interests of former pupils with those expressed by them before leaving school.

16. To identify former pupils who need further counseling to aid them in making more adequate personal, educational, or occupational adjustments.

17. To identify former pupils for whom the school might offer additional education, training, or other needed services.[2]

Techniques of the Follow-Up Study

The majority of follow-up studies have been conducted by distributing questionnaires. A few studies have used the interview as the data-gathering tool. Still other studies have made use of standardized tests. But the questionnaire continues to be the easiest and simplest method of acquiring a large amount of information in a short period of time. In addition, pupils in school can perform most of the tasks required in the questionnaire type of follow-up study. An English class can assist in setting up the instructions, smoothing out the mechanics of expression, etc. A business education class can work on the layout and printing problems. A mathematics class can tabulate the responses and determine percentages. These tasks will provide valuable learning experiences for the students and, at the same time, prepare them for future follow-up studies in which they will be the major sources of information. However, the questionnaire approach can yield inconclusive or misleading data if certain precautions are not observed. The following points should be considered before devising the questionnaire:

1. The organization, content, length, and appearance of the questionnaire will have considerable effect upon the percentage of responses obtained from graduates or dropouts. The highest percentage of returns may usually be expected from a questionnaire that is (a) short, (b) simply organized, and (c) printed rather than mimeographed. Questions should be stated briefly and clearly and should, if possible, require little writing by the respondents. Questions which might cause embarrassment to the respondent should be avoided. Respondents should be allowed to remain anonymous if they do not wish to identify themselves.

2. To insure the greatest percentage of responses, arrangements should be made to follow up the original questionnaire with a personal letter, urging that the questionnaire be completed and returned to the school. Ideally, three follow-up letters should be sent at intervals of ten days to two weeks. An interview is an excellent means of securing

---

[2]From *Principles and Practices of the Guidance Program* by Glenn E. Smith. Copyright 1951 by The Macmillan Company. Used with their permission.

information from those individuals who, for some reason, failed to answer the questionnaire after receiving the follow-up letters. However, these interviews require careful planning and should only be attempted by an experienced interviewer.

3. Questionnaires should be devised so that the responses may be easily tabulated. Check marks and ratings are tabulated more easily than answers in the form of statements, suggestions, or criticisms. However, the essay-type response can yield valuable information. Descriptive statements should be encouraged by providing space for additional comments. The best questionnaires usually yield qualitative as well as quantitative data.

4. Caution should be used in interpreting data obtained from a questionnaire when either (a) less than 100 per cent of the school-leavers were contacted or (b) less than 100 per cent of the school-leavers responded. There is some evidence that significant differences often exist between respondents and non-respondents with regard to their attitude toward the school, their satisfaction with the school's program of educational services, or their satisfaction with their present educational or vocational environment. Where respondents have identified themselves, some attempt can be made to determine the adequacy of the sample. Respondents and non-respondents can be compared with respect to variables which might influence their responses. In addition, individual responses may be interpreted in conjunction with the school record of each respondent.

Characteristics of the Successful Follow-Up Study

The successful follow-up study will be planned carefully by a committee that is representative of the entire school staff. It will be planned so that the results will be of value to both the individual and the school. Adequate publicity will be given to the study prior to its inception. The planning committee will determine (a) the objectives of the study, (b) the techniques to be used in gathering data, (c) the role to be played by pupils within the school, (d) the manner in which data are to be tabulated, and (e) the procedures for recording and reporting results, before beginning the study. The study will include *all* school-leavers, not just a portion of them. Every effort will be made to insure returns from close to 100 per cent of this group. When responses do not approximate 100 per cent, the data will be interpreted with caution. The comments of individual respondents will be viewed in the light of the record they made while attending school. It will be recognized that follow-up studies conducted on a year-to-year basis will provide more valuable data than sporadic attempts at follow-up by allowing the school to determine *trends* in the responses or reactions of school-leavers. Traxler (44) suggests the following additional characteristics of a follow-up plan:

1. It begins before the students leave school.
2. Each class is followed up for at least five years.
3. A representative sampling of each group is interviewed in order to obtain more extensive and detailed information than can be included in a questionnaire.
4. Responsibility for making follow-up studies is decentralized so that each class adviser follows up his own classes as they leave school.
5. The adviser's analysis of the data is made available to other school functionaries and is combined with those of other advisers in order to give a complete picture for the school system.
6. Conclusions concerning causal relationships are drawn with caution.
7. The significant items from each individual's return are transferred to his cumulative record.
8. The follow-up plan is coordinated with a post-school counseling service.
9. So far as possible, the cooperation of lay citizens is obtained in collecting, studying, and using the follow-up data.[3]

Evaluating Guidance Services

One of the most challenging tasks facing guidance workers today is the evaluation of the actual effects of guidance services upon the lives of pupils. In the past, guidance programs have had the benefit of relatively few evaluative studies to point out strengths and weaknesses. In addition, the majority of the few studies made have dealt with only single aspects of the total guidance program. Schools have been forced to depend upon studies of specific guidance techniques for help in assessing the benefits and limitations of a total program of guidance. In a 1945 publication, Wrenn and Darley (48) described the situation in these words:

> When one looks for studies of counseling that fall within the scope of even a liberal definition of evaluation, the cupboard is found to be almost bare. There are many descriptions of counseling programs and many statements of the expected outcomes but little evidence of what has actually taken place in terms of stated criteria.

---

[3]Used with permission of Harper and Brothers.

Some progress in the development of evaluative criteria and techniques has been made since 1945. At the same time, guidance workers are being asked, with greater frequency, to furnish evidence of the value of guidance services for pupils. With the advent of federal aid to school guidance services through the National Education Defense Act of 1958, some concern has been expressed over whether the American taxpayer will be content with current explanations of the value of guidance procedures. As Humphreys and Traxler (22) have phrased it: "No matter how good these procedures and devices appear to be in and of themselves, their values can be judged only in the light of their proved contributions to guidance."

Stefflre (39) concludes that counseling research is still far from providing us with definitive answers to the questions relating to the effectiveness of guidance and counseling services:

> The present relationship between research and practice in counseling is much like the relationship between research and practice in other areas of education. If we did in the name of counseling only those things which research has proved to be worth doing, we should have a good deal of free time on our hands.
>
> Present knowledge in counseling can be divided into three categories. There is a very small category of knowledge which we know to be true as a result of sound research evidence. There is an extremely large category of "knowledge" which we "know" from common sense or scholastic revelation; such knowledge may be said to be a part of the "conventional wisdom." Finally, there is a category of knowledge, which is growing rapidly, that indicates what we do not know! Well-designed research in counseling typically results in transferring "knowledge" from the second category to the third one. The most common conclusion reached as a consequence of carefully designed research in counseling is the verdict "Not proved."

Major Obstacles to Evaluation

There are five major stumbling blocks to evaluating guidance services:

1. *Guidance workers in the schools often lack the time, training, and/or facilities necessary to conduct research studies of this type.* The area of *research procedure* is a relatively recent addition to many of our programs of counselor preparation. The great majority of research articles appearing in our professional journals are contributed by college and university personnel or by graduate students reporting on their thesis or dissertation investigations.

2. *Many outcomes of guidance are intangible and are, therefore, exceedingly difficult to evaluate.* How does one measure the *confidence* built in a boy as he gains an understanding of his problems and how to deal with them? How does one measure the *release of tension* experienced by a girl as she is given the opportunity to talk about her problems with a competent, sympathetic counselor?

3. *Many outcomes of guidance cannot be determined for a long period of time.* We tend to measure only intermediate outcomes of guidance. It may be ten or fifteen years before a student reaches his vocational goal or resolves a personal problem. Yet many of our guidance workers are under considerable pressure to produce immediate results, in order that next year's school budget will make adequate provision for maintaining or expanding current guidance services.

4. *Even intermediate outcomes of guidance are measured by criteria that lack validity.* Few studies have been directed thus far at the validation of criteria themselves. Criteria that have been used include (a) vocational choice, (b) job satisfaction, (c) appropriateness of vocational choice, (d) change in client attitudes or feelings, and (e) client satisfaction with counseling. Criteria of "success" and "satisfaction" are difficult to define. Even when they have been defined (at least to the research worker's satisfaction), they are difficult to measure without relying on the subjective judgment of the counselor, the client, individuals who know the client, or the research worker himself.

5. *There are many variables outside the control of the guidance program which may influence the student's adjustment or development.* His educational development may be affected by financial pressures, family responsibilities, academic load, or the personal impression he makes on the instructional staff and on his peer group. His vocational adjustment may be affected by his geographic location, current supply and demand of workers in his job area, influential friends and relatives, his socio-economic status, his race and/or religion, family and financial pressures, his level of aspiration, and the personal relationships existing between himself, his employer, and his fellow workers.

Methods of Evaluation

Evaluative research has been categorized by a number of writers. Travers (43) placed all studies in two categories: (a) experimental designs, and (b) survey designs. Roeber, Smith, and Erickson (37) feel that "case-study designs" constitute a third type. Perhaps the most comprehensive review of evaluative research has been made by Froehlich (16) under the following headings:

1. *External criteria* or the do-you-do-this? method.
2. *Follow-up* or the what-happened-then? method.
3. *Client opinion* or the what-do-you-think? method.
4. *Expert opinion* or the "information please" method.
5. *Specific techniques* or the little-by-little method.
6. *Within-group changes* or the before-and-after method.
7. *Between-group changes* or the what's-the-difference? method.

Hahn and MacLean (18) place considerable emphasis on counselor self-evaluation since, as they point out, it is the counselor himself who must blend the information which comes from all of the other methods. They propose the following classification of evaluative methods:

1. Generalized program evaluations.
2. Evaluation of specific counseling tools and techniques.
3. Evaluation by counselees.
4. Evaluation by problem type.
5. Evaluation by faculty.
6. Evaluation by administrators.
7. Evaluation by other counseling specialists.
8. Evaluation by measurement of group changes.
9. Evaluation through long-range and follow-up studies.
10. Counselor self-evaluation.

More recently Peters (36) has suggested the following classifications:

1. *Historiographic* research.
2. *Survey—descriptive* research.
3. *Longitudinal* or *developmental* studies.
4. The *case study* method.
5. The *experimental* method.

Some overlapping occurs in any classification of evaluative studies. The following categories will serve to identify the major types of evaluative research and the limitations to be found in each type: (a) two-group experiment, (b) single-group experiment, (c) evaluation by clients, (d) follow-up studies, (e) judgment by experts, and (f) counselor self-evaluation.

The Two-Group Experiment—The most highly controlled experimental approach to evaluating guidance services involves the use of two matched groups, one designated as the control and the other as the experimental group.

However, research workers face major problems in equating two groups. It is difficult to match individuals trait for trait, ability for ability, attitude for attitude, so that two strictly comparable groups are obtained. Moreover, factors of motivation, concentration, independence, and emotional maturity may have as much or more effect upon student success as age, sex, intelligence, or socio-economic status. For example, there is some evidence that unless members of both groups are unaware that an experiment is being conducted, individuals in an experimental group become more highly motivated and "succeed" or "change" to a greater extent than individuals in a control group. This particular problem has been minimized by setting up a two-stage experiment in which the control group in the first stage of the experiment becomes the experimental group in the second stage and vice versa. Measurement of differences between the two groups is undertaken at the beginning of the experiment, at the end of stage one, and at the end of stage two. Although this is one means of accounting for motivation, scientists working in this area have generally found it extremely difficult to treat subjective factors in a quantitative manner.

There are also practical limitations to setting up a two-group experiment in the school. Aside from the ethical question raised by withholding guidance from one group of students in the school, even for a short time, the two groups cannot be isolated from one another and might well influence each other. It is possible to set up matched groups in two schools. However, such a step introduces a number of new variables. Students in the two schools would be likely to receive different educational opportunities and would be subject to the influence of different staff members.

The Single-Group Experiment—A simpler experimental design involves the study of changes that take place within a single group as a result of contact with a guidance tool, procedure, or service. This group is measured, according to some objective standard, immediately before and immediately after participation in the activity to be evaluated. The control group, with its attendant problems, is eliminated. However, the nature of the design prevents proper assessment of the extent to which measured "changes" are due to factors outside the guidance activity.

Evaluation by Clients—A simple and direct approach to evaluation may be made by obtaining the opinions of students who have participated in the guidance services. However, the student's satisfaction or dissatisfaction with guidance services may or may not be an accurate reflection of their value for him. Some opinions are more emotional than rational. When student opinion is elicited during or immediately after counseling, the warm relationship existing between counselor and student tends to exert a positive influence on the student's judgment. Miller (32) found that student satisfaction with a counseling process was significantly higher immediately after the termination of counseling than it was one month later. Similarly, some opinions are more definite and specific than others. Yet, we tend to place the same value on the opinion of the uninformed student as on that of the well informed. Winslow (47) developed a semi-structured interviewing technique to determine whether students were basing their opinions on generalized feeling or upon the recall of specific instances.

Client satisfaction with counseling may also be affected by his earlier attitudes toward his problem and his need for counseling. Do self-referrals evaluate their counseling more highly than do teacher-referrals? Is there a relationship between student participation in the counseling process and student satisfaction with the outcome? Likewise, to what extent does the downgrading or upgrading of the student's educational and vocational aspirations affect his opinion of the counseling he has received? Research is needed to determine the extent to which client opinion is influenced by these and other factors.

Follow-Up Studies—The follow-up study has been extensively used in evaluating guidance services, with the majority being conducted for the purpose of determining the accuracy and effectiveness of counseling.

The difficulties involved in obtaining an adequate sampling of responses from former students have been identified earlier in the chapter. These difficulties have raised serious objections to the use of follow-up data as the only basis for evaluating a guidance program. There is, however, an additional limitation to the follow-up method of evaluation. It is impossible to separate the factors within a guidance program from the factors outside the guidance program which, over a period of time, influence the students' development, achievement, adjustment, or success. The longer the interval of time between counseling and follow-up, the greater the possibility that outside influences have been responsible for certain changes taking place in the individual. Yet, if the time interval is shortened, we increase the possibility that the data obtained will represent intermediate or incomplete outcomes of counseling. In brief, follow-up procedures are a relatively easy way to obtain information that may be used as a basis for evaluating a guidance program or individual guidance techniques. However, this data must be interpreted with caution. It is advisable to supplement the follow-up study with other evaluative methods.

Judgment by Experts—Another approach to evaluating guidance services requires the professional judgment of experts who are not associated with the guidance services they are evaluating. Berdie (5) used five experienced counselors to judge the adequacy of the counseling received by a group of pre-college men. The identities of the clients and the original counselors were unknown to the judges. The judges supported the vocational diagnosis of the original counselor 84 per cent of the time. While impartial evaluation may be expected from qualified "outsiders," these individuals may be unfamiliar with the guidance services and the educational setting in which they function. This lack of information would seriously impair the validity of their judgment.

Counselor Self-Evaluation—Judgment by experts may also take the form of counselor self-evaluation. Through the use of checklists such as may be found in the *Criteria for Evaluating Guidance Programs in Secondary Schools, Form B* (12), counselors are able to compare their staff, facilities, variety of services and organizational plan with predetermined standards. Yet, there are several difficulties inherent in this form of evaluation:

1. It is difficult for counselors to make an unbiased evaluation of their own services.
2. In judging the merits of a program through a study of its organization, personnel, and procedures, only a partial evaluation is being made. A study of the external aspects of the guidance program fails to extract the qualitative values of the services involved.
3. It is often unfair to compare one guidance program with another, or with an "average" or "ideal" program. Differences in student population and school size must be considered. An activity or procedure which is essential to one program may not be essential to another.

It is apparent that there is no *one* best method of evaluating guidance services. Perhaps more attention should be given to the refinement of existing methods than to the search for a superior method of evaluation. Perhaps more time should be spent in evaluating specific techniques than in appraising a total program. Roeber, Smith, and Erickson (37) point out that "evaluation may be so complex that it does not lend itself to a global approach but rather to a planned increment-by-increment attack." As long ago as 1938, Kitson and Crane (25) offered a similar warning:

> The chief difficulty, however, is that the ultimate values of vocational guidance lie in the spiritual realm and so cannot be reduced to quantitative expression. Measurement is applicable, however,

in studying the efficacy of means for attaining the ends. One technique can be compared with another and in this way measurement can help us in making our work more effective. In view of all the limitations attending investigations in this extremely complex field, perhaps investigators should be advised to cease seeking an ultimate 'evaluation' of vocational guidance and set the more modest aim of experimenting with various techniques for the performance of simple functions which can be controlled.

Suggestions for the Evaluation of Guidance Services

Evaluating the effectiveness of guidance services is an extremely difficult task. Adequate criteria for evaluation have not been developed. Human behavior which results from, or is affected by, guidance services constitutes the evidence for which we are searching. But criteria used to measure changes in human behavior (such as school grades and vocational success) have generally been lacking in validity and, in some cases, have been incompatible with the generally recognized goals of guidance. Furthermore, all methods of evaluation have their limitations. Guidance workers, who are often handicapped by a lack of research time, training and/or facilities, are handicapped still further by being forced to use evaluative methods that are open to criticism. Yet, we must have evidence of the value of guidance services in order to insure the growth of existing school guidance programs and to accelerate the introduction of guidance programs into other schools.

Stefflre (39) suggests six ways that research needs to be used in order to aid guidance practices and, in turn, the total educational activity of the school.

1. We need, as a profession, to come to some agreement with regard to what we mean by such terms as "counselor," "pupil personnel services," "therapy," and "guidance." Until we have done this job of thinking through and defining, it seems unlikely that we will make any significant progress in research in this field.

2. We need much research that is local and descriptive. That is, we need much study of the process of counseling rather than of an ultimate product. Such studies are best done by local school counselors and do not involve any ultimate proof of the value of their work but rather describe for us what they are doing.

3. We need to recognize that knowledge of human behavior is not confined to the quantitative sciences. Too many counselors, like other workers in education, have blinded themselves to the humanities as a way of understanding behavior.

4. We must recognize that along with a human need to "know," we have an equally human need "not to know." Some of our most supersophisticated research designs grow out of the latter need. The insistence on complete randomization when we know that it is impossible to achieve, the use of very involved statistical manipulations for data which do not merit such careful treatment, the obsession with assumptions underlying statistics when their violation sometimes does not really alter the conclusions—all are evidences of our need not to know. Such a need, perhaps stemming from the guilt of some unresolved academic voyeurism, needs to be brought out into the open and clarified if we are going to make progress in research in counseling. Absolute, ultimate answers—free from the pedant's attack—will not soon be found in counseling research.

5. We must be more concerned about illuminating ends and less concerned about examining means. We cannot expect any dramatic breakthrough in guidance, or for that matter in education, until we have thoroughly thought through what it is we are trying to do. We could make a plea, then, for less correlation and more conceptualization.

6. In some cases, we ought to delay research and substitute demonstration projects. In elementary school counseling, for example, it seems that there is no general agreement as to what the program should involve. Since we know very little about the field, perhaps our "research" should deal with the evolving of theory rather than its testing.

The following additional suggestions are offered with the intention of stimulating guidance workers to make renewed and continual efforts at evaluating their programs or themselves.

Evaluative Research Takes Time and Planning— A well-defined and meaningful study may take as much time to plan and organize as to implement. The following steps are essential to a sound evaluation study: (a) choose the objective, (b) define the objective in terms of pupil behavior, (c) determine the criteria for measuring this pupil behavior, (d) plan the evaluative design, (e) collect the data, (f) analyze the data, (g) draw conclusions, and (h) check and reanalyze the data for verification. The planning phase of the study should include an investigation of previous studies of a similar nature. Provision should also be made for the collection of as much data as possible concerning pupil problems, counselor activities, and the services of the program, even if no immediate evaluation study is planned in all of these areas. This data may be invaluable later in helping to determine the objectives, the criteria, and/or the design of the study.

Evaluative Research Requires the Development and Use of Multiple

Criteria—A combination of criteria should be used in all efforts of evaluation. Value judgments based upon a single criterion are likely to be inaccurate or inadequate. Multiple criteria may be used in a series of planned and interrelated studies as well as in a single study. By this procedure, schools with limited resources can attack the evaluation problem in a piecemeal fashion. In these cases, value judgments should be withheld until they can be based upon several criteria.

Evaluative Research Requires Flexibility in Approach—Since all methods of evaluation have serious limitations, the use of a combination of methods will minimize these limitations through "cross checking" of data. Miller (32) used a combination of experimental design and survey approach to evaluate a counseling procedure. The experimental design involved a single group of students whose self-understanding and vocational plans were measured immediately before, immediately after, and one month after counseling. The survey approach was used to obtain qualitative and quantitative judgments regarding the value of the counseling from these students and their parents. In an attempt to reduce the subjectivity inherent in personal judgment, the following steps were taken:

1. Client opinion was measured (a) immediately after, (b) one month after, and (c) one, two, and three years after the completion of the counseling procedure.
2. Immediately after completion of counseling, counselors rated each of their clients with respect to their *concern over the counseling,* and their *elation or disappointment over their test results,* in order to determine what, if any, influence these factors had on client opinion.
3. The evaluator's judgments were made through a study of the clients' case reports and were then verified or modified by checking the data obtained through the experimental portion of the study.

Opportunities for "cross checking" data were numerous in this study. Comparisons could be made between qualitative and quantitative responses, client opinion and parent opinion, client opinion and measured changes in behavior, "concerned" clients and "unconcerned" clients who "upgraded" clients and "downgraded" clients, and between clients who had recently completed counseling and those who were a year or more removed from the counseling procedure.

Progress in Evaluation Rests Upon Coordination of Effort—An increased effort needs to be made to share the results of evaluative studies. While it is not possible to find a publisher for every research report, a summary of results can be mimeographed and made available to all interested co-workers. In the past, counselors have been reluctant to publish or distribute results of studies which have not yielded significant information. Yet, this information is necessary if we are to improve the validity of our criteria and the effectiveness of our evaluative designs. Our efforts at evaluative research need coordinating if we are to make substantial improvements in our guidance services. This coordination can begin at the local level. However, leadership in this area must be forthcoming from our state and national agencies and from our professional organizations.

Summary

Research and evaluation services of school guidance programs consist of three types: (a) school surveys, (b) follow-up studies of graduates and dropouts, and (c) evaluative studies of the guidance program. These three services overlap to some extent.

The first two services are necessary if we are to adapt the educational program to the needs of the students. Studies will be most effective if the entire school staff participates in formulating objectives and appraising the results. If these studies are conducted on a year-to-year basis, a picture of changing school conditions can be obtained.

Guidance services must be subjected to scientific evaluation if they are to make an effective contribution to the educational program and to pupil adjustment. Guidance workers must produce evidence of the value of these services if school guidance programs are to continue to receive the support of the public. However, there are a number of obstacles to successful evaluation which can only be overcome through the intensified efforts of individual research workers and the coordination of these efforts at the local, state, and national level.

Bibliography

1.   Andrew, D. and R. D. Willey. *Administration and Organization of the Guidance Program*. New York: Harper and Brothers, 1958. Chap. 13.
2.   Baer, Max F. and Edward C. Roeber. *Occupational Information*. 2nd ed. Chicago: Science Research Associates, Inc., 1958. Chap. 10.
3.   Barr, John A. *The Elementary Teacher and Guidance*. New York: Henry Holt and Company, 1958. Chap. 18.
4.   Barry, Ruth and Beverly Wolf. *Modern Issues in Guidance-Personnel Work* 2nd ed. New York: Columbia University, Teachers College, 1963. Chap. 11.
5.   Berdie, Ralph F. "Judgments in Counseling," *Educational and Psychological Measurement*, IV, Spring, 1944, 35-55.
6.   ———, Wilbur L. Layton, Edward Swanson, and Theda Hagenah. *Testing in Guidance and Counseling*. New York: McGraw-Hill Book Company, Inc., 1963. Chap. 14.
7.   Blanchard, Howard L. and Laurence S. Flaum. *Guidance: A Longitudinal Approach*. Minneapolis: Burgens Publishing Company, 1962. Chap. 14.
8.   Boy, Angelo V. and Gerald J. Pine. *Client-Centered Counseling in the Secondary School*. Boston: Houghton Mifflin Company, 1963. Chap. 11.
9.   Callis, Robert. "Counseling," *Review of Educational Research*, XXXIII, 1963, 184-5.
10.   Cottingham, Harold F. *Directed Readings in Foundations of Guidance and Personnel Services*. Bloomington, Illinois: McKnight & McKnight, Inc., 1964. Chaps. 7, 9.
11.   ———. *Guidance in Elementary Schools: Principles and Practices*. Bloomington, Illinois: McKnight & McKnight, Inc., 1956. Chaps. 10, 15.
12.   *Criteria for Evaluating Guidance Programs in Secondary Schools, Form B*. Misc. 3317. Office of Education, Division of Vocational Education. Washington, D.C.: Occupational Information and Guidance Service, January, 1949.
13.   Crow, Lester D. and Alice Crow. *Organization and Conduct of*

Guidance Services. New York: David McKay Company, Inc., 1965. Chaps. 13, 15-16.

14. ————. *Readings in Guidance.* New York: David McKay Company, Inc., 1962. Chap. 5.

15. Farwell, Gail F. and H. J. Peters. *Guidance Readings for Counselors.* Chicago: Rand McNally & Co., 1960. Chap. 10.

16. Froehlich, Clifford P. *Evaluating Guidance Procedures: A Review of the Literature.* Misc. 3310. Washington, D.C.: Office of Education, Federal Security Agency, January, 1949.

17. ————. *Guidance Services in Schools.* New York: McGraw-Hill Book Company, Inc., 1958. Chap. 15.

18. Hahn, Milton E. and Malcolm S. MacLean. *General Clinical Counseling in Educational Institutions.* New York: McGraw-Hill Book Company, Inc., 1950. P. 375.

19. Hatch, Raymond N., Paul L. Dressel, and James W. Costar. *Guidance Services in the Secondary Schools.* Dubuque, Iowa: William C. Brown Company, 1963. Chap. 6.

20. ———— and Buford Stefflre. *Administration of Guidance Services: Organization, Supervision, Evaluation.* Englewood Cliffs, New Jersey: Prentice-Hall, Inc., 1958. Chaps. 5, 7-8.

21. Hollis, Joseph W. and Lucile U. Hollis. *Organizing for Effective Guidance.* Chicago: Science Research Associates, Inc., 1965. Chaps. 20-21.

22. Humphreys, J. Anthony and Arthur E. Traxler. *Guidance Services.* Chicago: Science Research Associates, Inc., 1954. P. 36.

23. Humphreys, J. Anthony, Arthur E. Traxler, and Robert North. *Guidance Services.* 2nd ed. Chicago: Science Research Associates, Inc., 1960. Chaps. 10-11.

24. Jones, Arthur J. *Principles of Guidance.* 5th ed. New York: McGraw-Hill Book Company, Inc., 1963. Chap. 15.

25. Kitson, Harry D. and Margaret Cranc. "Measuring Results of Vocational Guidance: A Summary of Attempts, 1932-1937," *Occupations,* XVI, June, 1938, 837-42.

26. Loughary, John W. *Counseling in Secondary Schools: A Frame of Reference.* New York: Harper and Brothers, 1961. Chap. 8.

27. McDaniel, Henry B. *Guidance in the Modern School.* New York: The Dryden Press, 1956. Chaps. 13, 16.

28. ————, et al. *Readings in Guidance.* New York: Henry Holt and Company, 1959. Chap. 14.

29. Martinson, Ruth and Harry Smallenburg. *Guidance in Elementary Schools.* Englewood Cliffs, New Jersey: Prentice-Hall, Inc., 1958. Chap. 15.

30. Miller, Carroll H. *Foundations of Guidance.* New York: Harper and Brothers, 1961. Chap. 11.

31. ————. *Guidance Services: An Introduction.* New York: Harper & Row, Publishers, 1965. Chap. 15.

32. Miller, Frank W. "Evaluating a Guidance Procedure," *Journal of Educational Research,* XLVI, September, 1952, 61-9.

33.   Ohlsen, Merle M. *Guidance Services in the Modern Schools.* New York: Harcourt, Brace & World, Inc., 1964. Chap. 17.
34.   Patterson, C. H. *Counseling and Guidance in Schools.* New York: Harper and Brothers, 1962. Chap. 18.
35.   ———. "Program Evaluation," *Review of Educational Research,* XXXIII, 1963, 222.
36.   Peters, Herman. "The School Counselor as a Researcher," *The School Counselor,* II, March, 1964, 165-70.
37.   Roeber, Edward C., Glenn E. Smith, and Clifford E. Erickson. *Organization and Administration of Guidance Services.* New York: McGraw-Hill Book Company, Inc., 1955. Chaps. 9, 11.
38.   Smith, Glenn E. *Principles and Practices of the Guidance Program.* New York: The Macmillan Company, 1951. Pp. 309-10.
39.   Stefflre, Buford. *Theories of Counseling.* New York: McGraw-Hill Book Company, Inc., 1965. Pp. 265-72.
40.   Stewart, Lawrence and Charles Warnath. *The Counselor and Society: A Cultural Approach.* Boston: Houghton Mifflin Company, 1965. Chap. 10.
41.   Stoops, Emery and Gunner L. Wahlquist. *Principles and Practices in Guidance.* New York: McGraw-Hill Book Company, Inc., 1958. Chaps. 8, 14.
42.   Tolbert, E. L. *Introduction to Counseling.* New York: McGraw-Hill Book Company, Inc., 1959. Chap. 13.
43.   Travers, Robert M. W. "A Critical Review of Techniques for Evaluating Guidance," *Educational and Psychological Measurement,* IX, Summer, 1949, 211-25.
44.   Traxler, Arthur E. *Techniques of Guidance.* New York: Harper and Brothers, 1957. Chap. 17. Pp. 297-8.
45.   Tyler, Leona E. *The Work of the Counselor.* New York: Appleton-Century-Crofts, 1961. Chap. 13.
46.   Warters, Jane. *High School Personnel Work Today.* New York: McGraw-Hill Book Company, Inc., 1956. Chap. 12.
47.   Winslow, J. T. "A Study of the Guidance Program of 'A' High High School," Columbia, Missouri: College of Education, University of Missouri, 1952. (Mimeographed.)
48.   Wrenn, C. Gilbert, and John G. Darley. "Evaluating the Effectiveness of Counseling," *Frontier Thinking in Guidance.* Chicago: Science Research Associates, Inc., 1945. P. 51.
49.   Wrenn, C. Gilbert. *The Counselor in a Changing World.* Washington, D.C.: American Personnel and Guidance Association, 1962.
50.   Zeran, F. R., and A. C. Riccio. *Organization and Administration of Guidance Services.* Chicago: Rand McNally & Co., 1962. Chaps. 6-7.

PART **4**

ISSUES

12

Guidance as a Profession

A professional has been described as "an individual who ... performs tasks that are of more than usual difficulty, requiring a long period of preparation and education, resulting in the attainment of a high degree of skill and knowledge (19)." A profession is usually characterized as a field which (a) maintains adequate standards of preparation or training for its members, (b) licenses or certifies individuals who have successfully completed the prescribed preparation or education, (c) supports continuous research designed to improve the quality of the services it offers the public, and (d) enforces ethical standards of performance on the part of its members. The implementation of these objectives is usually accomplished through one or more professional organizations and one or more professional journals.

At the present time, it is debatable whether guidance can be considered a profession. As Pierson and Grant (35) phrase it, "the objectives of the guidance movement in education have remained so general and so comprehensive during the past fifty years that guidance is still mainly a point of view, a pervasive influence, a belief in the importance of individualized education."

Tiedeman and Field (43) feel that the current status of guidance is that of a technology rather than a profession since "the current practice of guidance stems from the traditional desires of educational authorities and practitioners to make *teaching* more powerful without limiting the authority of *teachers*. This role of *aiding* teachers is necessarily based upon the assumption that the teacher is in a position superior to that of the counselor. Such a relationship further implies that the counselor is necessarily a technician; his theory that of a technology."

Many individuals, with varying degrees of training and a wide variety of responsibilities, call themselves counselors or guidance workers. Certification requirements for school counselors in most states are quite modest, yet a substantial number of those individuals who are called guidance specialists or school counselors do not even meet these requirements. Johnson (24) has suggested that we are on thin ice when we indicate that the requirement for the achievement of "professional" status is the completion of several courses, sometimes taught by individuals whose own professional status is doubtful, and often completed in institutions which have little or nothing in the way of a counselor education program. In addition, our professional organizations have been criticized (10) as lacking unity and direction. Pierson and Grant (35) draw the conclusion that "personnel and guidance workers must face the unhappy fact that so far they have been unable to distinguish themselves from the amateur."

On the more positive side, the field of guidance is receiving increased recognition as a vital educational movement. The federal government is now extending financial support to guidance services in our schools. The American Personnel and Guidance Association, through its various committees, is engaged in establishing or raising professional standards in such areas as membership, ethics, training, certification, research, and publications. More adequate communication is being established between those individuals who have the responsibility for *educating* guidance specialists, those who *certify* guidance specialists, those who *administer* guidance services, and those individuals who are *performing* guidance services.

This chapter is concerned with the organizations, ethical standards, educational programs, certification requirements, research, and publications which will be instrumental in the continued professionalization of guidance services.

Professional Organizations

American Personnel and Guidance Association, Inc.

The American Personnel and Guidance Association, Inc. is a scientific and educational association dedicated to the advancement of the discipline of guidance and personnel work. Founded in 1952, APGA brings together eight guidance and personnel associations whose histories extend back to the beginning of the organized guidance movement early in this century. These associations each represent specialized interests in the guidance and personnel field.

Together they span personnel and guidance work in elementary and secondary schools, in higher education, and in community agencies; also, they encompass many personnel interests in government, business, and industry. Graduate students are eligible for membership in each Division of APGA.

APGA attempts to promote and stimulate the exchange of professional experience through national, regional, state, and local meetings. APGA represents personnel and guidance services on several national and international committees and boards. Active relationships are maintained with the National Education Association, the U. S. Office of Education, the U. S. Department of Labor, the American Council on Education, and other national and international groups. APGA constantly keeps abreast of matters of national policy which affect the discipline of counseling. When appropriate, and upon request, the Association has submitted statements to the national legislative bodies on such matters.

APGA is continually engaged in projects of special interest to the membership. For example, a national conference was held on "Guidance and New Educational Media" under a contract with the U. S. Office of Education. The Fund for the Advancement of Education of the Ford Foundation supported a major study by the Association on "The Role of Guidance in American Schools." The project, directed by Dr. C. Gilbert Wrenn, culminated in a major APGA publication— *The Counselor in a Changing World.*

The book, *Guidance for the Academically Talented Student,* was the result of a joint conference with the National Education Association's project on "The Academically Talented Student." Similar efforts have been carried out under sponsorship of the U. S. Steel Foundation, the Kiplinger Foundation and the American Child Guidance Foundation. The outcome of most of these projects is a major publication, available at special rates to the membership.

Ten times a year, September through June, each member of APGA receives the Association's official publication—the *Personnel and Guidance Journal.*

The *Journal* seeks to help personnel and guidance workers in all settings by keeping them informed of developments in the field. It serves a teaching function by publishing articles dealing with significant practices in personnel and guidance work, current problems in the field, trends in training personnel and guidance workers, and theory and research that give promise of practical application.

The *Journal* also brings to the members of APGA news of the Association, its branches and divisions, its people, policies, and events. An annual feature in the January issue is a survey of financial aids to graduate students in guidance and personnel work.

APGA also publishes a newsletter, the *Guidepost,* which serves as a source of topical news for the members. It covers a variety of pertinent subjects, including a news roundup of current congressional legislation and discussion of special projects in the field.

APGA provides its members with publications which serve their needs and interests. These publications are created to stimulate closer understanding of the theory, philosophy, and practice which are the foundation of today's guidance and personnel movement. These publications, which are unique to APGA, serve the specialized interests of the membership. The Association publishes educational and occupational information for counselor and student use in career and college planning. A Membership Directory is also published biennially and is made available to the membership at a reduced price.

Descriptions of the eight divisions of the American Personnel and Guidance Association follow.

Division 1
AMERICAN COLLEGE PERSONNEL ASSOCIATION
(ACPA)

Organized in 1924, the Association adopted its present title in 1931 and adopted its present charter in 1937. Its purpose is to provide for the cooperative association of those engaged in college student personnel service and their administrators. Also included are related areas such as teaching, administration, and research at the college level; and personnel work in industry, government, or a public agency. Publication: *Journal of College Student Personnel* (Bimonthly).

Division 2
ASSOCIATION FOR COUNSELOR
EDUCATION AND SUPERVISION (ACES)

With the adoption of a new constitution in 1961, increasing attention is being given to problems of counselor education and counselor supervision at state and local levels.

With the rapidly expanding demand for school counselors in recent years, ACES has become more and more concerned with the problem of preparation, placement, certification, and evaluation of counselors in the public schools.

In conjunction with Division 5, ACES has developed a national cooperative study of counselor education standards. Publication: *Counselor Education and Supervision* (Quarterly).

Division 3
NATIONAL VOCATIONAL
GUIDANCE ASSOCIATION (NVGA)

Established in 1913, NVGA is an association concerned with education and vocational counseling and career development. Included are persons in public and private schools, colleges, in industry and government, in private counseling centers and social agencies—all those actively engaged in vocational and educational counseling and student personnel work.

NVGA attempts to meet the current challenge for effective guidance, counseling, selection, retention, placement, and follow-up. It as important factors in dealing with many of the most crucial social and economic issues facing America. Publication: *Vocational Guidance Quarterly.*

Division 4
STUDENT PERSONNEL ASSOCIATION
FOR TEACHER EDUCATION (SPATE)

Founded in 1931, the Association is concerned primarily with students planning to enter teaching—their admission, orientation, guidance, counseling, selection, retention, placement, and follow-up. It includes those teaching in the guidance and personnel area and those engaged in personnel services in education at the counseling or supervision level. Publication: *Student Personnel Association for Teacher Education Journal* (Three times per year).

Division 5
AMERICAN SCHOOL COUNSELOR
ASSOCIATION (ASCA)

Since 1952, the Association has been active in fostering a close relationship among guidance counselors at all school levels.

ASCA has completed a study on "The Role, Function and Conditions of Work of the School Counselor." This subject was studied by counselors in all 50 states and territories of the United States. Over 9,000 members of ASCA contributed to the overall picture of today's school counselor and established a model for the future. Publication: *The School Counselor* (Quarterly).

Division 6
AMERICAN REHABILITATION
COUNSELING ASSOCIATION (ARCA)

Formed in 1957 in response to the steady increase in rehabilitation counseling in recent years, the Association adopted its present title in 1962. It is comprised of those engaged in any aspect of rehabilitation counseling, such as service, administration, teaching, or research.

The objective of ARCA is to foster the development of rehabilitation counselors to enable them to provide better services in the rehabilitation of the handicapped. Publication: *Rehabilitation Counseling Bulletin* (Quarterly).

Division 7
ASSOCIATION FOR MEASUREMENT AND
EVALUATION IN GUIDANCE (AMEG)

Constituted in 1965, AMEG's purpose is to provide leadership in measurement and evaluation in guidance and personnel work. Included are persons engaged in teaching, research, administration, interpretation, and related activities in personnel and guidance aspects of evaluation and measurement.

AMEG strives to provide a forum for the discussion of ethical, social, and technical problems related to measurement and evaluation in guidance, including the opportunity for communication between the producers and the consumers. Publication: *Newsletter* (Quarterly).

Division 8
NATIONAL EMPLOYMENT COUNSELORS ASSOCIATION
(NECA)

The National Employment Counselors Association (NECA) became Division 8 of the American Personnel and Guidance Association by vote of the 1966 APGA Senate at the APGA Convention in April.

Professional and regular membership in NECA is open to those who are engaged in administering, planning, and conducting employment counseling programs and related research. It is also open to those who help prepare counselors. Those who have an interest in the aims and objectives of NECA are invited to become associate members. Publication: *Journal of Employment Counseling* (Quarterly).

The National Association of Social Workers

The National Association of Social Workers (NASW) became a national professional organization on October 1, 1955, when several related organizations terminated their separate activities to work together as one united group. These parent organizations were American Association of Group Workers, American Association of Medical Social Workers, American Association of Psychiatric Social Workers, American Association of Social Workers, Association for the Study of Community Organization, National Association of School Social Workers, and Social Worker Research Group.

The Association recognizes and carries out a two-fold responsibility: (1) to promote activities appropriate to strengthening and unifying the social work profession as a whole, and (2) to promote the sound and continuous development of the various areas of social work practice whereby the profession contributes to the meeting of particular aspects of human need. To these ends NASW designs a program to attain its several objectives and organizes and uses its resources to consistently maintain a sound balance and integration of its general and special activities.

NASW is composed of more than 27,000 individual members who are organized in 155 chapters located in each state and in Puerto Rico. A master's degree from an accredited school of social work is required for membership in the Association.

Association chapters are local bodies created upon the initiative of members in states, localities, or regions, subject to the approval of the Board of Directors. By pooling the experience of members, the chapters serve as two-way avenues for the development and exchange of local and national thinking, planning, and action within the scope of Association purposes.

A biennial assembly attended by delegates chosen by each chapter provides the chief means of formulating membership opinion on national issues. The program is carried out nationally through sections created by the Delegate Assembly and through commissions and committees established by the Board of Directors of the Association.

The results of commission and committee study are submitted to the membership for approval either at the Delegate Assembly or by direct mail vote. In 1960, the Delegate Assembly approved a plan for nation-wide certification of social workers effective in 1961.

NASW regularly publishes *Social Work,* its official quarterly journal; the *NASW News,* a quarterly membership bulletin; and the bi-monthly *Personnel Information.* The Washington office periodically publishes a *Report from Washington* when Congress is in session. In 1961, the Association issued the second edition of the *Social Work Year Book,* published under its auspices. The *Year Book* is now issued every three years. For the first time, in 1960, the Association also published its *Directory of Professional Social Workers.* NASW also publishes monographs, pamphlets, and special program materials.

NASW and APGA share many interests in common. School social workers who are members of NASW work side by side with APGA members in the schools, and there are joint professional projects. Psychiatric social workers are particularly close to those engaged in personnel and guidance activities. For the last few years, NASW has joined with other social work organizations in operating a booth at the APGA Convention, stressing social work as a career but also serving as a contact point between social workers and APGA members.

NASW has its headquarters at 95 Madison Avenue, New York 16, New York.

The National Association of Women Deans and Counselors

The National Association of Women Deans and Counselors (founded in 1916 as the National Association of Women Deans) is not affiliated with the American Personnel and Guidance Association. However, since many of its members belong to one or more divisions of APGA, the association schedules its annual convention to coincide with the time and place of the APGA convention. Its membership consists of women who are engaged in guidance and personnel work in colleges and secondary schools.

National Association of Pupil Personnel Administrators

Organized in 1966, the National Association of Pupil Personnel Administrators gives representation to the increasing number of specialists who are administering and coordinating pupil personnel services in elementary and secondary school districts. Although it is not affiliated with the American Personnel and Guidance Association, most of its members belong to one or more of its divisions.

Ethical Standards

Concern over ethical standards for guidance workers was first expressed by members of the National Vocational Guidance Association in the late 1930's. It was recognized that, in the absence of legal support, persuasion and professional example would have to serve as the major tools for the encouragement of good guidance practice and the elimination of malpractice. NVGA published the first directory of approved vocational counseling agencies in 1950. The services of these agencies had been examined by a committee of NVGA and found to be professionally competent. This pioneering work of NVGA was continued by the American Personnel and Guidance Association and resulted in the establishment of the American Board on Professional Standards in Vocational Counseling in 1957. Late the next year, this board published the first *Directory of Vocational Counseling Services.* However, it soon became apparent that the use of the term "vocational" was too limiting and that the functions of the Board should be expanded. In 1961, in recognition of this expanded scope and function, and with the approval of the American Personnel and Guidance Association, the Board changed its name to the American Board on Counseling Services, Inc. A new set of criteria for approval of counseling services was adopted by the Board in March, 1962.

Each agency seeking approval must submit extensive information about its practices and the professional background of its personnel. It also is visited by two members of the counseling profession who are appointed by the Board to serve as an evaluation team. If all the criteria are met, the agency (or individual) is approved and listed in the published *Directory of Approved Counseling Agencies,* a biennial publication (2). The current directory lists one hundred and seventy-seven approved agencies in thirty-seven states, Puerto Rico, Canada, and the District of Columbia. Since the number of approved agencies is only a small proportion of the agencies that offer counseling to the public, the American Board on Counseling Services sees its mission as not only that of approving or disapproving applying agencies, but also of conducting a broad educational program that will encourage other agencies to improve their services and to apply for the board's approval.

School counselors should be familiar with ethical standards developed by the National Education Association (34), the American Psychological Association (6), and the American Personnel and Guidance Association (3). Ethical standards for members of the American Personnel and Guidance Association were adopted in 1961 and were supplemented in 1965 by an Ethical Standards Casebook (4). This casebook, developed by the Association's Ethical Practices

Committee, contains a minimum of four illustrations for each of the 56 statements appearing in the APGA code. However, it is doubtful whether any code can be devised that can cover all possible situations faced by personnel workers in various settings, both in and out of school. Instead, it sets broad guidelines and establishes a general pattern of behavior. The counselor must still use sound judgment in applying these guidelines to each specific ethical problem that he encounters.

Selection of School Counselors

Crissey (17) has pointed out that the selection of persons to engage in any occupation should follow a certain logical pattern:

1. *Job Analysis.* This should be studied in sufficient detail to provide guides for selection and training and for ultimate job placement and evaluation.

2. *Recruitment.* Identification of persons who might conceivably do the job well.

3. *Selection.* Screening preliminary to training should be followed by screening during training.

4. *Training.* A program of training realistically related to the occupation should be provided. This may, in certain jobs, be done during preliminary learning on the job. In other jobs pre-employment training may be adequate, while in still others this will need to be supplemented by on-the-job training.

5. *Placement.* The most suitable position for the worker must be found. In some work, especially professional work, this will require attention to the appropriateness of a candidate's qualifications to highly variable job situations.

6. *Follow-up and evaluation.* The selection, training, and placement procedures should be tested and necessary readjustments made.[1]

It is doubtful whether any profession has been very successful in employing these procedures. Hill and Green (22) remind us that guidance, as other professions, has the problem of planning selection procedures which are realistically geared to a great diversity of functions. The problem facing the counselor educator and others concerned with the selection of guidance personnel is complicated by at least five major variables:

---

[1]From Orlo L. Crissey, "Personnel Selection," *Current Trends in Industrial Psychology* (Pittsburgh: University of Pittsburgh Press, 1949). Used with permission of the Director, University of Pittsburgh Press.

1. The responsibilities of guidance personnel vary from school to school and region to region.

2. The guidance worker is expected to be a very versatile individual, one who possesses a wide variety of skills, understandings, interests, and attitudes.

3. There is considerable variation in the degree to which the definition or description of a guidance position is indicative of the demands that are made of the guidance worker.

4. We are forced to prepare and select workers for a hierarchy of guidance positions. Yet we are not in agreement as to how these positions relate to one another. Various terms such as school counselor, guidance specialist, school psychologist, personnel worker, and counseling psychologist have been used to identify these positions.

5. Counselors work with a wide variety of clients. Their personal traits and attitudes and "style" of counseling will be more acceptable with some clients than with others.

Criteria for Selection

Desirable qualifications of counselors have been identified in terms of traits, attitudes, knowledges, skills, competencies, and interests. Attempts to develop criteria for the selection of counselors have been made (a) through job analysis surveys of counselors in the field; (b) through opinion surveys conducted to determine what high school students, college students, teachers, administrators, and counselors regard as the necessary competencies and qualities of counselors; and (c) through reports by committees of experts representing various professional organizations.

Analysis of these reports reveals that three types of criteria are invariably recommended as characteristic of the competent counselor: (a) personal qualifications, (b) training, and (c) experience. *Personal qualifications* generally recommended as necessary include scholastic aptitude sufficient to successfully complete a program of graduate work in guidance; interest in working with people; ability to work with people; and various qualities of personality, such as flexibility, tact, capacity to inspire confidence, a sense of humor, freedom from withdrawing tendencies, and freedom from annoying mannerisms. *Teaching experience and non-educational work experience* have usually been recommended, although there is increasing debate over the value of these experiences for the counselor. It is questionable whether workers who have drifted from job to job before entering the guidance field have acquired experiences which will assist them in their work. It is possible that some kinds of work experience are actually detrimental to effective counseling. In any event, the *quality* of the experience rather than the *quantity* of the experience should receive primary consideration. A *supervised counseling experience* or *internship* is also recommended. The master's degree, with the major emphasis of study being in *counselor education,* is usually considered to be the minimum amount of training that should be required for counselors. The training requirement will be discussed later in the chapter.

Surveys of Counselor Selection

Surveys of counselor selection have been confined largely to studies of the procedures used by colleges and universities in the selection of graduate students for their counselor education program. Keppers (26) found that approximately one-half of the institutions supporting counselor education programs did not employ selection procedures other than those employed with *all* applicants for graduate work. Studies by Keppers (26), MacMinn and Ross (27), Miller and Cox (31), and Santavicca, Richards, and Adman (37) furnish evidence that *grade average in undergraduate work* is employed most frequently as a criterion for selection of counselor-trainees. *Teaching experience, undergraduate preparation in the areas of education and psychology, and scholastic aptitude test scores* are the other criteria that are most frequently employed in the selection of graduate students for the counselor education program. The most frequently used tests of scholastic aptitude are the Graduate Record Examination and the Miller Analogies Test. However, Poirier (36) canvassed 116 counselor educators and state supervisors of guidance and discovered that only a minority of the group claimed knowledge of tests that would aid in the selection of candidates for counselor education programs.

While most institutions reported that the *personal qualifications* of the applicant were considered in the selection process, only a few institutions attempted to measure personal traits or personal adjustment through the administration of tests or inventories. Most counselor education programs assessed personal qualifications of applicants through the use of the interview or by requiring references or recommendations. Miller and Cox (31) found that many counselor education programs have established procedures that encourage trainees to engage in continuous evaluation of their own personal qualifications as they progress through the program.

It is generally agreed that the selection of counselors should be a *continuous process,* rather than an *event.* Such a process would begin prior to the candidate's application for admission to the counselor education program and continue through his placement in a school. The report of the Committee on Counselor Education Standards of the Association for Counselor Education and Supervision (9) suggests the following standards for the selection and retention of counselors:

1. *The institution has a procedure for identifying and selecting candidates for counselor education.*
   a. The counselor education staff has cooperatively developed criteria and procedures relating to selection, retention, endorsement and placement.
   b. The criteria used for selection are consistent with the philosophy and objectives of the institution's counselor education program.
   c. Information about the counselor education program and about state counselor certification is available to the candidates.
   d. Qualified candidates may be drawn from various undergraduate fields and from various occupations.
      (1) Candidates who have been teachers have demonstrated superior competence as teachers.
      (2) Candidates from fields other than teaching demonstrate their understanding of the secondary school and their competence to perform guidance and counseling functions in secondary schools by completing courses and supervised experiences planned for this purpose.
   e. Members of the counselor education staff are available to confer with prospective candidates.
2. *The institution follows a defined procedure for the selective admission of candidates to the program of counselor education.*
   a. The candidate is assessed with respect to:
      (1) Capacity to do graduate work.
      (2) Familiarity with the objectives of the program.
      (3) Potential for developing effective relationships with youth, teachers, administrators and parents.
      (4) Potential for engaging in research.
   b. The counselor education staff admits to the program only those candidates who meet the requirements established for admission to study in counselor education. These requirements may be in addition to those established by the institution for admission to graduate study.
   c. Decisions with respect to admission to the counselor education program are made by the staff (or by a committee) and not by any one staff member.
3. *The institution administers a planned program of selective retention, designating points within the program for evaluation*

of progress and informing of procedures for selective retention.

a. The counselor education staff has the responsibility of denying continuation in the program to any candidate whose level
of academic performance and/or personal characteristics do
not adequately meet institutional or professional standards.

b. Each counselor candidate is encouraged to enter into a
program of self-evaluation related to his retention in the program. To assist him in his growth in self-understanding, a
counseling service separate from the counselor education
program is available to him.

c. When appropriate, cooperating school counselors and state
supervisors and administrators are consulted concerning decisions about retention of candidates.

d. Decisions with respect to retention or dismissal of a candidate are made by the staff (or by a committee) and not by
any one staff member.

Preparation of School Counselors

Recommendations for the preparation of school counselors have
generally come from two organizations:

AMERICAN PSYCHOLOGICAL ASSOCIATION (APA)
Division 17—Division of Counseling Psychology
AMERICAN PERSONNEL AND GUIDANCE ASSOCIATION (APGA)
Division 2—Association for Counselor Education and
Supervision (ACES)
Division 3—National Vocational Guidance Association
(NVGA)
Division 5—American School Counselor Association
(ASCA)

Six recent reports by these organizations have special significance
for those who are concerned with the preparation of school counselors:

1. *The Scope and Standards of Preparation in Psychology for
School Counselors,* APA-Division of Counseling Psychology (7).
This report states what counseling psychologists believe to be the
necessary role of *psychology* and *psychologists* in the preparation of
school counselors and expresses the concern that too many school
counselors have had an inadequate psychological orientation.

2. *The Professional Preparation of Counseling Psychologists: Report of the 1964 Greyston Conference,* APA-Division of Counseling
Psychology (42).

This conference endorsed the statements of Division 17 of APA concerning standards of training (1952), practicum training (1952), definition of counseling psychology (1956), internship standards (1960), and status of counseling psychology (1961). The report is significant since, at many institutions, the training of persons for the allied discipline of counseling psychology overlaps with the preparation of school counselors.

3. *The Counselor in a Changing World,* C. *Gilbert Wrenn, ed.,* APGA-Commission on Guidance in American Schools (46).

This report deals with the social changes anticipated in the next twenty years, the impact these changes will have upon the function of counseling, and the significance of these changes in determining the qualifications and professional education of school counselors. It recommends a two-year graduate program that would include the following:

1. One major core in psychology, including developmental and child psychology, personality growth and dynamics, and group psychology.
2. A second major core in the study of societal forces and culture changes involving the graduate areas of sociology, anthropology, economics, and international relations. This core could be based upon undergraduate preparation in any of the natural sciences, social sciences, or humanities. The relation of the undergraduate program to the graduate years in the liberating and scientific disciplines is given further attention in the later section on "Teaching Experience." Depending upon the strength of the undergraduate program in the social sciences and psychology, *from one-third to one-half* of the total graduate program should be devoted to these two major core areas.
3. An understanding of the basic educational philosophies and school curriculum patterns.
4. Provision for the essential applied or technique courses in counseling, measurement, educational and occupational information, etc., to the extent of *not more* than one-fourth of the total graduate program. The preparation for psychological appraisal would stress research knowledge of the tests used and attention to life history analysis. In the area of occupational information, emphasis would be placed on the psychological factors entering into vocational choice and the differential meaning of occupational information to each student. There can, of course, be no substitute for a *rigorous study of the world of occupations* as they exist today and as they are

projected into the immediate future. Educational information would examine ways in which counselors would determine the distinctive intellectual and social climate of the school to which the student might transfer.

5. Supervised experience in both individual counseling and planned group situations to the extent of *not less* than one-fourth of the total graduate program. The supervision would be by a combination of graduate school staff and well-qualified counselors in the school who were carefully selected and appointed as part of the graduate school team. The goal would be paid internships on an academic-year basis.

6. An elementary understanding of research methods and designs, including an introduction to electronic computer programming and the outcomes to be expected from computer use.

7. Introduction to the problems of ethical relationships and legal responsibilities in counseling.

4. *Statement of Policy for Secondary School Counselors,* APGA-American School Counselor Association (8).

This report is the culmination of a two-year study of the role and function of the school counselor and includes the following section on Professional Preparation:

PROFESSIONAL PREPARATION

There is no single best program for developing the school counselor competencies listed above. Counselor education programs vary in nature from institution to institution, and will continue to vary as counselor educators and supervisors experiment with new methods and procedures in their attempts to develop increasingly stronger programs. The school counselor endorses and strongly encourages the continued search for improved preparation programs. Thus, he views the professional preparation criteria listed below as appropriate at this time, realizing that changes in knowledge and conditions will inevitably result in criteria modifications.

1. School counselor education is graduate education and should result in the counselor receiving as a minimum (a) a master's degree in counseling from an accredited institution, and (b) appropriate professional certification as a counselor from the state in which he is employed.

2. It is conceivable and reasonable that more than one level of certification can exist. It is conceivable and reasonable that more than one level of professional preparation and certification should exist. The two-year program of graduate study for counselors, including supervised counseling and pupil personnel services experiences in a school setting, is recognized as a desirable goal.

3. School counselor certification should represent legal profes-

sional status in a state and should have as one requirement the endorsement of the counselor education program in which the counselor obtained his preparation.

4. School counselor education programs should include the following components:

a. A core of professional study consisting of the following elements: (1) developmental and educational psychology, (2) counseling theory and procedure, (3) educational and psychological appraisal, (4) group theory and procedures, (5) the psychology and sociology of work and vocational development, (6) the functions and methodology of research, and (7) the legal and professional ethics of counseling and education.

b. Provision for developing a background in the humanities and the social, behavioral, and biological sciences according to the particular needs and developmental status of each counselor candidate. School counselor candidates lacking a broad undergraduate background in the physical and natural sciences, the behavioral sciences, and the humanities should correct such deficiencies in addition, rather than in lieu of, the graduate-level education referred to here.

c. Supervised experiences such as laboratory, practicum, and internship work.

d. Provision for developing a working understanding and appreciation of the school's curriculum and the psychological and sociological climate of in-school learning situations.

5. School counselor education programs should continue to develop and refine selection procedures reflecting the philosophical ideas stated earlier and be consistent with the intellectual and emotional prerequisites implied in the counselor competencies listed.

6. School counselor education programs should be systematic, yet planned individually in regard to each candidate's particular background and needs.

7. School counselor education does not terminate with the completion of a formal program, but continues throughout the career of the counselor. Therefore, counselors have a responsibility to plan, implement, and participate in in-service and other post-certification programs and study designed to maintain and promote professional competency.

5. *Standards for Counselor Education in the Preparation of Secondary School Counselors,* APGA-Association for Counselor Education and Supervision (9).

This report is the culmination of a five-year study of counselor education and presents standards to be used on an experimental basis for a three-year period for institutional self-evaluation. The portion of the report dealing specifically with the program of studies in a counselor education program is presented here.

SECTION II. CURRICULUM: PROGRAM OF STUDIES AND
SUPERVISED EXPERIENCES

A. General Program Characteristics.

1. *The institution provides a graduate program in counselor education, based primarily on the program of studies and supervised practice outlined in B and C below. The institution provides a minimum of one year of graduate counselor education. In order to fulfill the requirements of the studies and supervised practice detailed in B and C below, the institution provides at least one additional year of graduate study in counselor education either through its own staff and facilities or through cooperative working relationships with other institutions which do have at least a two-year program of counselor education.*

    a. The opportunity for full-time study in counselor education is provided throughout the academic year.

    b. Flexibility is provided within the curriculum to allow for individual differences in competencies and understandings developed prior to entering the institution's counselor education program.

    c. The organized curriculum for the program is published and is available for distribution to prospective students. This description includes information relating to the institution's requirements for full-time study.

2. *There is evidence of quality instruction in all aspects of the counselor education program.*

    a. Syllabi or other evidences of organized and coordinated instructional units of the curriculum are available.

    b. Appropriate resource materials are provided.

    c. Responsibilities are assigned to or assumed by staff members only in those areas for which they are professionally qualified by preparation and experience.

    d. Provisions are made for periodic evaluation by students, staff, former students, and employers of all aspects of the counselor education program, such as course content, methods of instruction, and supervised experiences both on and off campus.

    e. Evaluation is followed by appropriate revisions and improvements, if indicated.

3. *Planned sequences of educational experiences are provided.*

    a. A sequence of basic and advanced graduate courses and other associated learning experiences is defined and provided.

b. The program provides for the integration of didactic instruction, seminars, and supervised experiences in counseling and other related guidance services throughout the sequence.

c. Prerequisites are identified.

4. *Cooperation exists among staff members directly responsible for the professional education of counselors and representatives of departments or schools offering courses in related fields.*

a. Cooperative working arrangements are in existence.

b. Staff members from related areas meet with the counselor education staff for planning, implementing, and evaluating the counselor education program.

c. Course work in other areas is identified for the counselor candidate with respect to its appropriateness for graduate credit or for background work.

d. There is evidence of interdisciplinary planning with respect to both student and staff participation in designing, conducting, and evaluating research.

5. *Within the framework of the total counselor education program, there are available curriculum resources as well as procedures that make it possible for the counselor candidate to develop understandings and skills beyond the minimum requirements of the program.*

a. Elective courses are available.

b. Staff time is provided for the supervision of individual study in the areas of counselor education.

c. Advisers make counselor candidates aware of such opportunities.

6. *The counselor education staff encourages the spirit of inquiry and the production and use of research data.*

a. The statement of objectives of the program reflects an awareness of the role of research in the work of the counselor and the competencies to be developed.

b. Instructional procedures make frequent use of, and reference to, research findings. Areas in which research is needed are identified.

7. *Opportunities for self-evaluation and the further development of self-understanding are provided for the counselor candidate.*

a. Opportunities are provided through such activities as laboratory experiences, supervised counseling, and self-analysis through tape recordings and/or video tapes.

b. Opportunities for improvement of interpersonal relationships are provided through small group activities.

c. Counseling services provided by persons other than the

counselor education staff are available to students in
counselor education.
B.   Program of Studies.
   1. *Opportunities are provided for the development of under-
      standing and competencies in the following:*
      a. The foundations and dynamics of human behavior and
         of the individual in his culture.
      b. The educational enterprise and processes of education.
      c. Professional studies in school counseling and related
         guidance activities:
         (1) Philosophy and principles underlying guidance and
              other pupil personnel services;
         (2) The nature and range of human characteristics and
              methods of measuring them in individual appraisal;
         (3) Vocational development theory;
         (4) Educational and occupational information, its na-
              ture and uses;
         (5) Counseling theory and practice;
         (6) Statistics and research methodology, independent
              research and familiarization with data processing
              and programming techniques;
         (7) Group procedures in counseling and guidance;
         (8) Professional relationships and ethics in keeping with
              the APGA Ethical Standards;
         (9) Administration and coordination of guidance and
              pupil personnel services;
        (10) Supervised experience (see C below).
C.   Supervised Experiences.
   1. *Supervised experiences in counseling and other guidance
      activities are provided as an integral part of the total coun-
      selor education program.*
      a. Settings in which such experiences are provided are
         appropriate for the preparation of secondary school
         counselors.
      b. These supervised experiences, including both observation
         of and work directly with secondary school age youth,
         frequently are provided in the actual school situation.
      c. Opportunities are provided for working under supervision
         with parents and with a variety of school and commu-
         nity agency personnel.
      d. All such experiences are conducted under established
         ethical policies.
      e. Primary responsibility for all supervised experiences is
         assigned to counselor education staff members, qualified
         as stated in C, 3a below, [p. 306]; secondary school

counselors and advanced graduate students may be assigned subsidiary responsibilities.

2. *Three aspects of supervised experience are recognized in the counselor education program: laboratory experiences, practicum experiences, and internships.*
   a. *Laboratory experiences are provided in the first and second years.*
      (1) Opportunities are provided for both observation and participation in activities related to the total guidance program, *e.g.*, role-playing, listening to tapes, testing, organizing and using pupil personnel records, working with professional personnel, preparing and examining case studies, and using educational and occupational information materials.
      (2) Laboratory experiences appropriate to the counselor candidate's needs are a continuing part of the counselor education program. Plans and procedures adopted by the staff clearly describe the integration of such experiences.
   b. *Practicum experiences are provided in the first and/or second years.*
      (1) Practicum consists of counseling and small group work, both under supervision.
      (2) Practicum is conducted in settings which are appropriate for the preparation of secondary school counselors, and which include young people with a variety of educational and vocational potential.
      (3) Practicum includes opportunities for continuing experiences in a series of counseling relationships with each of several secondary age youth.
      (4) A stated number of hours is spent by each counselor candidate in actual counseling relationships. This does not include time required for preparation and for supervisory consultations.
         (a) Counselor education students completing the two-year program spend 60 hours as a minimum.
         (b) Students in counselor education who complete a one-year program for certification spend 30 hours as a minimum.
      (5) Opportunity is provided within the total work load for staff to supervise practicum experiences.
      (6) Media such as tape recorders, television and one-way vision screens are utilized in the supervision of the practicum activities.

(7) Practicum provides for a growth experience which is spread over a period of time.

(8) Supervised experiences are provided as an integral part of courses throughout the counselor education program of the student.

c. *Internship may be provided.*

(1) Internship is an advanced level of on-the-job supervised experience offered in a school setting.

(2) It is under the systematic supervision of qualified members of *both* the school staff and the institution's counselor education staff.

(3) It is normally a paid experience.

(4) Opportunities are provided for the counselor candidate to share responsibilities in all phases of the school guidance program.

3. *A well-qualified staff with adequate time allocated to supervision is provided.*

a. Members of the on-campus staff responsible for supervision

(1) Have earned advanced degrees (preferably the doctorate) from accredited institutions.

(2) Have had experience in counseling and related guidance activities with secondary age youth.

b. Secondary school staff members who supervise counselor candidates concurrently with the institution's staff, should have at least two years of graduate work in counselor education or have equivalent preparation developed through long-term service and professional activity.

c. Doctoral students who supervise practicum experiences as a part of their preparation are under the supervision of staff members with appropriate advanced degrees and experience.

d. The counseling practicum is virtually a tutorial form of instruction; therefore, the supervision of five students is equivalent to the teaching of one three-semester-hour course. Such a ratio is considered maximum.

e. Supervision of internship is provided regularly by the cooperating secondary school staff, and adequate staff time is allowed both for day-to-day supervision and for weekly supervisory conferences.

f. Supervisors from the institution's staff have internship consultations and supervision assigned as part of their total work load.

g. Time is allocated by the school system for secondary school staff members to assist in supervision of laboratory practicum and internship experiences.

4. *Appropriate facilities, equipment, and materials are provided for supervised experiences in both on- and off-campus settings.*

6. *The Counselor: Professional Preparation and Role. A Statement of Policy,* APGA-Committee on Professional Preparation and Role (5).

This inter-divisional committee report deals with counselors without regard to the particular setting within which they work. The portion of the report dealing specifically with counselor preparation is presented here.

COUNSELOR PREPARATION

Counselor education programs should be planned to promote excellence in counseling by preparing counselors who are able to perform effectively their appropriate role in our society. Programs should be related to the tasks to be performed—to the professional role of the counselor in the setting in which he is likely to work. They should provide the knowledge upon which effective counseling procedures are based and enable the counselor candidate to use this knowledge skillfully.

1. Counselor education should be designed to achieve carefully formulated goals based on a philosophy which reflects the highest level of professional knowledge and social concepts.

2. The counselor education staff should be concerned with the task of continually evaluating the program and searching for more adequate methods of counselor preparation. The curriculum should be sufficiently flexible and dynamic to permit revisions and adjustments as required by increasing professional knowledge or by changes in the professional responsibilities of counselors

3. The curriculum of the counselor education program should assure that essential content and experiences are included in each candidate's program, should provide increasingly for integration of learning, and should avoid duplication of content. Each candidate's program of courses should constitute a planned sequence spiraling toward progressively more advanced work. Programs should recognize individual differences among counselor candidates (their ability, goals, educational background, and experience), and should challenge each person individually.

4. Counselor education should provide experiences which are planned to contribute to the counselor candidate's growth in self-understanding.

5. The counselor education program should assure that each counselor candidate has a background (undergraduate or graduate) in the humanities and in the social, behavioral, and biological sciences that helps him understand individuals, their behavior and

adjustments; the nature of the environment and its impact on the individual, including the forces that affect his personal and vocational life; and the counselor's role in a changing culture.

6. There should be provisions to promote the integration of studies in related disciplines with the professional studies in counseling in such a manner that these related studies will make meaningful contributions to the competence of the counselor.

7. The program should provide for such specialized study related to the setting in which the counselor will work as is needed to enable him to function effectively within that employment environment and to perform such duties in addition to counseling as may be an appropriate part of his professional role.

8. There should be a year-round program of counselor preparation that makes possible full-time graduate study. There also should be opportunities for additional continuing education of practicing counselors.

9. A program of counselor preparation which would meet the principles listed above as well as provide the professional studies described below would consist of a minimum of two years of graduate study, a substantial portion of which should be in full-time graduate study.

Professional Studies in Counseling. To achieve the quality of professional preparation necessary for counselors, the following are recognized as essential aspects of professional studies in counseling.

1. Professional study in counseling should provide counselors with a knowledge of counseling theory and practice; group procedures; testing and other methods of psychological and educational appraisal; the cognitive and emotional processes of growth, change, and adjustment; the social, educational, and work environment; economic, psychological, and sociological aspects of work and vocational development; statistics; research methodology; legal responsibilities and professional ethics.

2. Essential in the core of counselor preparation is supervised experience such as laboratory work, counseling practicum, and internship.* Criteria for practicum and internship settings should

---

**Laboratory experiences* include activities such as testing, analysis of case records, observation of interviews, role playing, working with occupational and educational materials. They may be self-contained or integrated with classroom instruction.

Counseling practicum is defined as actual supervised counseling experience, with the counselor candidate handling counseling cases and group situations under systematic and continuing individual supervision and evaluation. The practicum may be provided in a campus counseling center or in an off-campus setting.

Internship is defined as on-the-job experience under systematic supervision and evaluation. It may be a paid assignment and is usually a full-time activity serving as an extension of practical experience beyond the counseling practicum.

include quality of professional supervision and of learning opportunities plus their applicability and adequacy for the employment setting in which the counselor candidate expects to work. The candidate should work with a variety of counselees appropriate to his eventual employment under conditions that protect the interests of the counselee as well as contribute to the competence of the counselor candidate.

Experiences should include related tasks that are judged to be a part of the counselor's role in that setting. There should be provision for assistance to the counselor candidate in integrating theory and practice. The experiences and the time allotment should be sufficient to enable him to grow personally and professionally, to develop an appropriate level of counseling skill, and to acquire a more meaningful understanding of the nature of the counseling relationship.

3. Counselor preparation should emphasize philosophy, theory, and scientific knowledge as well as specific techniques and procedures in a manner that assures understanding and mastery of counselor functions and that helps the counselor candidate to learn to adapt his professional self-concept and his professional skills to a variety of work situations. Learning experiences should encourage creative thinking and inquiry; the ability to use research and evaluation as a professional tool; and a recognition of the need for continued professional growth.

Instructional Conditions. Counselor education programs must be part of strong graduate schools or divisions and have appropriate facilities.

1. Courses in counseling should be taught by faculty members who have had relevant experience and whose professional preparation includes an appropriate doctoral degree. Additional criteria should include involvement in research and a relationship of responsibility to the profession. Staff members should have an understanding of the employment settings in which their students will work and of counselor roles in those settings. Faculty members should be adequate in number and have the variety of specializations needed to offer the necessary courses.

2. Faculty members teaching courses in related disciplines to counselor candidates should be well qualified in their respective fields.

3. The counselor education staff should have sufficient time for their professional responsibilities including time for careful supervision and evaluation of each candidate, as well as for research and professional leadership. The practicum load should be weighted in recognition of the fact that this is virtually a tutorial form of instruction.

4. Practicum and internship should be provided in settings

that offer a competent staff and adequate facilities as well as
appropriate counseling and other learning experiences. Supervisory
staff in the off-campus setting should have a meaningful relationship to the counselor preparation program and its staff.

5. A strong program of counselor education requires adequate
facilities including physical facilities for practicum, testing laboratories, private offices for staff members, seminar rooms, library
materials, secretarial assistance, and research aid.

Financial Support for Counselor Candidates. Meeting society's
need for qualified counselors requires support in the form of
stipends, graduate assistantships, fellowships, and scholarships in
sufficient numbers and amount to make it possible to attract and
hold potentially able persons.

CONCLUDING STATEMENT

The maximum development of the potential of all individuals, for
their own satisfaction and for the benefit of society, requires that
effective and extensive counseling services be provided by qualified,
competent counselors. The American Personnel and Guidance
Association believes that the policies here outlined will contribute
to this objective, and that the concerted efforts of the profession
will make possible the realization of the quality of counselor preparation and performance envisioned in this statement.

These reports are not in complete agreement with respect to the
length and type of preparation needed by school counselors. They
reflect, in part, the current debate over the proper function of
guidance services in our schools (see Chapter 13). They also reflect
the differences in background of those individuals who claim a share
of responsibility for determining the nature and extent of the school
counselor's preparation. The major areas of disagreement are reflected in the following questions.

1. Should we prepare guidance *generalists* or counseling *specialists?*
   a. What percent of a school counselor's time should be spent
      in counseling?
   b. What should school counselors know about curriculum, ad-
      ministration, and community relations?
2. How closely related are *counseling* and *teaching?*
   a. Should school counselors be required to possess a teaching
      certificate?
   b. Should school counselors be required to have teaching ex-
      perience?
3. Should a specific *amount* of preparation be required of school
   counselors?

a. Is it possible for school counselors to be qualified to fulfill their assigned responsibilities on the basis of one year of graduate study?

b. If not, what are the practical alternatives?

4. Should one *discipline* be allowed to dominate the preparation of school counselors?

a. If so, which one?

b. If not, how may we develop programs of a true interdisciplinary nature?

5. Is *part-time study* less effective than *full-time study* in the preparation of school counselors?

6. To what extent does the graduate student who is preparing for school counseling need *counseling* himself?

a. Is it possible for a counselor educator to be the *counselor to* as well as the *supervisor of* graduate students?

b. How can we facilitate self-analysis and introspection in our future school counselors when they face the rather rigid hurdles of grades, course credits, and degrees?

While there are still areas of disagreement regarding the preparation of school counselors, it is clear that counselors will require background preparation of an interdisciplinary nature if they are to be adequately prepared for the broad areas of responsibility traditionally assigned them. Even though the great majority of counselor education programs are located in schools or departments of education, it is imperative that a close working relationship be maintained between the areas of education, psychology, sociology and the other social sciences. In the past, this has not always been the case. Interdepartmental bickering has prevented the establishment of an effective, well-balanced counselor education program. It is encouraging to note that an Interdisciplinary Committee on Pupil Personnel Services has been established by our various professional organizations. It is to be hoped that this committee will assume leadership in exploring the desirability and feasibility of joint training programs for school psychologists, school social workers, school counselors, and other pupil personnel specialists.

Certification of School Counselors

Counselor certification requirements have changed substantially during the past decade. According to the latest survey (39), forty-eight states (all but Michigan and Washington) have now established certification requirements for guidance personnel. However, only a few states have set forth separate requirements for elementary school counselors. Guidance officers in states requiring the certification of counselors report three major benefits resulting from such a program:

1. Certification provides status for the individual who meets the requirements and provides motivation for others seeking to meet the requirements.
2. Administrators are able to select and employ counselors with greater confidence.
3. State certification has a stimulating effect on counselor education programs that may not be realistic or up-to-date in certain content areas.

However, disagreement exists concerning the extent to which certification should be a seal of approval or a device for raising professional standards. Eleven states have a single certificate for all school counselors, twenty-seven states maintain two levels of certification, and ten states provide three levels of certification. In the states having two- and three-level plans, the upper levels of certification serve both as a seal of approval for a small number of counselors and as a device for raising the professional qualifications of counselors possessing the minimum amount of preparation.

A lack of standardization among state certification requirements also exists with respect to (a) the title of the certificate, (b) the amount and type of preparation and experience required for the various certificates, and (c) the certifying procedure itself.

Titles of Certificates

Among the titles used to identify the certificate are: General Pupil Personnel Services Credential, Provisional Counselor's Certificate, Standard Counselor's Certificate, Professional Counselor's Certificate, Guidance Counselor's Professional Standard Certificate, Director of Guidance Professional Standard Certificate, Director of Student Personnel Services Certificate, Supervisor of Guidance Certificate, Teacher-Counselor Certificate, Vocational Counselor's Certificate, Class AA Secondary School Counselor's Certificate, Two-year Temporary Certificate, Certificate of Guidance, Standard Pupil Personnel Certificate, and Permanent Certificate.

Preparation and Experience Required for Certification

All forty-eight [certifying] states currently require the *teaching certificate* as a prerequisite to certification as a counselor. Forty-five states require from *one to three years of teaching experience* as a prerequisite to certification. Twenty-two states require *one year of accumulated work experience* as a prerequisite to certification.

The number of states requiring various types of preparation (and counseling experience) for Provisional (P), Standard (S), and Professional (PRO) certification are given in Table I. *Provisional* certificates are generally for the individuals who devote less than half of their time to guidance services. *Standard* certificates are generally for individuals who devote from half to all of their time to guidance services. *Professional* certificates are generally for individuals who serve as supervisors, directors, and coordinators of guidance services.

TABLE 1
State Certification Requirements for Counselors*

Requirement	No. of States		
	P	S	Pro
1. Counseling experience	0	0	10
2. Master's degree	8	28	17
3. Content areas			
Principles and practices of guidance	22	43	22
Analysis of the individual	20	38	21
Occupational and educational information	18	41	22
Counseling techniques	22	40	21
Tests and measurements-research methods	17	32	18
Organization and administration of guidance	11	31	18
Group guidance	6	17	15
Supervised practicum	12	31	19
Mental hygiene	3	8	7
Related psychology courses	4	7	6
Related sociology courses	0	2	3
Social case work	0	1	4
Vocational education	1	1	4
Labor and industrial relations	0	0	2
School administration	0	0	5
Economics	0	1	4
Curriculum construction	1	1	2

Certification Procedures

Primary responsibility for the certification of school counselors rests with the various state departments of education. In some states, however, the training institutions are beginning to play an influential

*Data contained in Table 1 was obtained through a survey conducted by Skill and Gorman of De Paul University, Chicago, Illinois and represents certification requirements as of 1965.

role in the certification process. The ACES report, *Standards for Counselor Education in the Preparation of Secondary School Counselors* (9), mentioned earlier, supports institutional endorsement of candidates for counselor certification and proposes the following guidelines:

1. *The institution endorses successful candidates for certification and employment.*
   a. A statement of policy relating to the institution's procedure for formal endorsement has been adopted by the staff and approved by the proper administrative authority.
   b. Each candidate is informed of procedures for endorsement for certification and employment.
   c. The counselor education staff participates in this endorsement procedure.
   d. Endorsement is given only on the basis of evidence of proficiency. This implies that the candidate has completed a substantial part of his graduate work in counselor education, including supervised counseling experience, at the endorsing institution, and that his personal growth is considered to have been satisfactory.

2. *The institution provides a placement service.*
   a. Placement service organization and procedures are consistent with established principles of student personnel work.
   b. Provision is made for the participation of personnel from the state department of education and cooperating schools in the placement of candidates and their induction into the profession.
   c. Students are assisted as needed in the preparation of placement papers.
   d. Staff members utilize individual professional relationships to assist in the placement of their graduates.
   e. Assistance is provided in the evaluation of job opportunities and in the selection of positions appropriate to the individual's qualifications.
   f. The placement service provides continuing assistance to the candidate throughout his professional career.

3. *The institution maintains a program of research designed to evaluate its selection, retention, endorsement and placement procedures.*
   a. School counselors, administrators, and state department of education personnel, when appropriate, participate in the planning and execution of the follow-up program and other evaluative procedures.
   b. The program of evaluation and follow-up includes early leavers as well as those who complete the program.

    c. Evaluation is followed by appropriate revisions and improvements.

Certification of Other Pupil Personnel Workers

According to the latest survey (15), twenty-five states now have certification requirements for *school psychologists, counseling psychologists,* or *psychometrists.* Six states (Minnesota, New Mexico, Oklahoma, Utah, Washington, and Wisconsin) now have certification requirements for *school social workers.* Three states (Indiana, Minnesota, and Washington) now have certification requirements for *school nurses.*

Research and Publications

While there are many professional journals in the fields of education and psychology, the individual who is interested in research on counseling, measurement or some other phase of guidance work will find the greatest number of pertinent articles in the *Journal of Counseling Psychology, Educational and Psychological Measurement, The Personnel and Guidance Journal, Counselor Education and Supervision, The School Counselor,* and *The Vocational Guidance Quarterly.* The last four have already been referred to as publications of the American Personnel and Guidance Association and its divisions. However we will continue to be lacking in objective evidence upon which to base many of our guidance practices until guidance specialists on the elementary and secondary school levels are willing and able to devote more time to conducting and publishing research on their own programs State guidance offices could improve the current research situation by conducting an annual survey of research studies undertaken by elementary and secondary schools within their state. Mimeographed lists of these research studies, distributed to all schools within the state, would facilitate an interchange of data between schools and accelerate research efforts.

The following topics are suggestive of the type of research still needed in various areas of guidance. No attempt has been made to compile a complete list of research needs.

    1. *Definition and Description of Personnel Workers' Jobs*
        a. What would be the findings from job analyses of guidance personnel who handle administrative duties? non-administrative duties? non-guidance duties? What proportion of time is spent in the counselor's various tasks?
        b. What is the social, economic, training, and experience status

of the school counselor as compared to other school personnel? What is the effect of such status on the work of the
counselor?

c. What is the counselor's role as viewed by school administrators, teachers, and students? To what extent do these individuals view the counselor as a supervisor of guidance services? a colleague? an influence on the educational program?
etc.

d. What similarities and differences are there in the definition
of duties of directors of guidance, counselors, school psychologists, teacher-counselors, and other personnel workers in
schools? How do these definitions compare with each other
when they are made by administrators, teachers, counselor
educators and by the guidance personnel themselves?

e. What are the crucial differences between personnel workers
who work most effectively with people and those whose most
effective work is in research?

2. *School Guidance Programs*

a. How effective are various guidance programs in rural areas
in terms of efficiency of operation, extent and quality of services provided, and economy? Are some patterns of organization and operation superior to others when employed by rural
schools?

b. What are minimum acceptable standards for the program of
services offered by the guidance section of a state department of education? What relationships should exist between
school guidance programs and state guidance services?

3. *Counseling Services*

a. What are appropriate and usable criteria for evaluating personal and educational-vocational counseling?

b. What are the correlations between various "immediate" criteria for the effectiveness of counseling and "long-range"
criteria of effectiveness?

c. What are the relative merits of group guidance and individual counseling as measured by such factors as number of
contacts per counselee, ratings of effectiveness of contacts by
counselees, time spent in counselor preparation for contacts,
types of topics and problems discussed voluntarily by counselees, etc.?

4. *Effects of Counselor Education and Experience*

a. What overt and covert behavioral changes occur when teachers or guidance workers receive additional training? What is the nature and extent of the change in their self-concepts?

b. Are there significant differences between counselors judged more successful and less successful in regard to amount and type of teaching and non-teaching experience?

Summary

Guidance is having difficulty achieving full professional status for three reasons:

1. Guidance has been given an ancillary rather than a central role in education. The guidance specialist continues to be regarded as a "teacher-aide."
2. Guidance continues to "borrow" principles from the various behavioral sciences. These disciplines remain artificially separated from one another, thus making it impossible to develop an integrated science (which Tiedeman and Field [43] call "the science of applying behavioral sciences").
3. The amount and type of preparation required of guidance specialists varies substantially from state to state. Furthermore, the stated requirements are not uniformly enforced.

Guidance will achieve wider recognition as a profession when it is successful in (a) building and maintaining adequate programs of preparation for *all* guidance specialists, (b) restricting certification to those individuals who have successfully completed these programs of preparation, and (c) stimulating research of a more valid and comprehensive nature that will result in the continuous improvement of guidance services. Cooperative action by the American Personnel and Guidance Association, the National Association of Social Workers, and the American Psychological Association should be encouraged in order that agreement may be reached regarding the nature and extent of the responsibilities of school counselors, school psychologists, and school social workers. The interrelatedness of pupil personnel service activities and functions makes it imperative that these three groups take joint action in the further professionalization of guidance services.

Bibliography

1.   Adams, James F. *Counseling and Guidance: A Summary View*. New York: The Macmillan Company, 1965. Chaps. 1 (#2), 8 (#6).
2.   American Board on Counseling Services. *Directory of Approved Counseling Agencies*. Washington, D.C.: American Personnel and Guidance Association, 1965.
3.   American Personnel and Guidance Association. "Ethical Standards," *Personnel and Guidance Journal*, 40:206-209, October, 1961.
4.   ————. *Ethical Standards Casebook*. Washington, D.C., 1965.
5.   ————. "The Counselor: Professional Preparation and Role," *Personnel and Guidance Journal*, 42:536-541, January, 1964.
6.   American Psychological Association, "Ethical Standards of Psychologists," *American Psychologist*, 14:279-282, 1959.
7.   American Psychological Association, "The Scope and Standards of Preparation in Psychology for School Counselors," *American Psychologist*, 17:149-152, 1961.
8.   American School Counselor Association. *Statement of Policy for Secondary School Counselors and Guidelines for Implementation of the ASCA Statement of Policy for Secondary School Counselors*. Washington, D.C., 1964.
9.   Association for Counselor Education and Supervision. *Standards for Counselor Education in the Preparation of Secondary School Counselors*. Washington, D.C., 1964.
10.   Barry, Ruth and Beverly Wolf. *Modern Issues in Guidance-Personnel Work*. 2nd ed. New York: Columbia University, Teachers College, 1963. Chap. 6.
11.   Bennett, Margaret E. *Guidance and Counseling in Groups*. 2nd ed. New York: McGraw-Hill Book Company, Inc., 1963. Chap. 10.
12.   Berdie, Ralph F., Wilbur L. Layton, Edward O. Swanson, and Theda Hagenah. *Testing in Guidance and Counseling*. New York: McGraw-Hill Book Company, Inc., 1963. Chap. 13.

318

13.   Boy, Angelo V. and Gerald J. Pine. *Client-Centered Counseling in the Secondary School.* Boston: Houghton Mifflin Company, 1963. Chap. 12.

14.   Byrne, Richard Hill. *The School Counselor.* Boston: Houghton Mifflin Company, 1963. Chaps. 14, 15.

15.   Camp, Dolph. *Guidance Workers Certification Requirements.* Washington, D.C.: U.S. Office of Education, Department of Health, Education, and Welfare, Bulletin 1960, No. 14, Rev. OE-25005A, 1963.

16.   Cottingham, Harold F. *Directed Readings in Foundations of Guidance and Personnel Services.* Bloomington, Illinois: McKnight & McKnight, Publishing Co., 1964. Chap. 10.

17.   Crissey, Orlo L. "Personnel Selection," *Current Trends in Industrial Psychology.* Pittsburgh: University of Pittsburgh Press, 1949.

18.   Crow, Lester D. and Alice Crow. *Organization and Conduct of Guidance Services.* New York: David McKay Company, Inc., 1965. Chap. 1.

19.   Farwell, Gail F. and H. J. Peters. *Guidance Readings for Counselors.* Chicago: Rand McNally & Co., 1960. Chap. 10.

20.   Glanz, Edward C. *Foundations and Principles of Guidance.* Boston: Allyn & Bacon, Inc., 1964. Chaps. 17, 18.

21.   Hatch, Raymond N. and Buford Stefflre. *Administration of Guidance Services.* Englewood Cliffs, New Jersey: Prentice-Hall, Inc., 1958. Chap. 3.

22.   Hill, George E. and Donald A. Green. "The Selection, Preparation and Professionalization of Guidance and Personnel Workers," *Review of Educational Research,* 30:115-130, April, 1960.

23.   Humphreys, J. Anthony, Arthur E. Traxler, and Robert North. *Guidance Services.* 2nd ed. Chicago: Science Research Associates, Inc., 1960. Chap. 17.

24.   Johnson, Walter. "The Counselor and His Professional Education," *Personnel and Guidance Journal,* XXXVII:9, May 1959, 694-5.

25.   Jones, Arthur J. *Principles of Guidance.* 5th ed. New York: McGraw-Hill Book Company, Inc., 1963. Chap. 15.

26.   Keppers, George L. *Survey of Current Practices in Selecting Candidates for Graduate Work in Guidance and Counseling.* University of New Mexico, 1959.

27.   MacMinn, Paul and Roland G. Ross. *Status of Preparation Programs for Guidance and Student Personnel Workers.* Washington, D.C.: U.S. Office of Education, Department of Health, Education, and Welfare, Bulletin 1959, No. 6, 1959.

28.   Mathewson, Robert H. *Guidance Policy and Practice.* 3rd ed. New York: Harper and Brothers, 1962. Chap. 14.

29.   McDaniel, Henry B. *Guidance in the Modern School.* New York: The Dryden Press, 1956. Chaps. 17, 18.

30.   McGowan, John F. and Lyle D. Schmidt. *Counseling: Readings in Theory and Practice.* New York: Holt, Rinehart & Winston, Inc., 1962. Chaps. 2, 13, 15.

31.   Miller, Frank W. and Richard Cox. *Current Trends in Counselor*

Selection and Training Among Schools Located in the North Central States. Evanston, Illinois: Northwestern University, 1959.

32.   Murphy, Gardner. "The Cultural Context of Guidance," *Personnel and Guidance Journal,* XXXIV:1, September, 1955, 4-8.

33.   Patterson, C. H. *Counseling and Guidance in Schools.* New York: Harper and Brothers, 1962.

34.   Perry, C. "A Code of Ethics for Public School Teachers," *Annals of the American Academy of Political Science.* 297:76-82, 1955.

35.   Pierson, George A. and Claude W. Grant. "The Road Ahead for the School Counselor," *Personnel and Guidance Journal,* XXXVIII:3, November, 1959, 207-10.

36.   Poirier, Benson B. *Factors in the Selection and Training of Guidance Counselors for Secondary Schools.* Unpublished master's thesis, University of Wyoming.

37.   Santavicca, G. Gene, Margaret Richards, and Ann Adman. *A Summary of A Study Concerning Supervised Experience and Selection of Counselor Trainees.* Oxford, Ohio: Miami University, 1958.

38.   Schwebel, Milton. "Some Ethical Problems in Counseling," *Personnel and Guidance Journal,* XXXIII:5, January, 1955, 254-9.

39.   Skill, Thomas E. and William Gorman. *The Certification and Recognition of Guidance Personnel in the United States in 1964-65.* DePaul University, 1965.

40.   Stewart, Lawrence and Charles Warnath. *The Counselor and Society: A Cultural Approach.* Boston: Chaps. 14-15.

41.   Syracuse University, School of Education. *Guidance in the Age of Automation.* Syracuse, New York: Syracuse University Press, 1957. Chaps. 4, 5.

42.   Thompson, Albert S. and Donald Super, eds. *The Professional Preparation of Counseling Psychologists. Report of the 1964 Greyston Conference.* New York: Bureau of Publications, Teachers College, Columbia University, 1964.

43.   Tiedeman, David V. and Frank L. Field. "Guidance: The Science of Purposeful Action Applied through Education," in Mosher, Ralph L., Richard F. Carle, and Chris D. Kehas. *Guidance: An Examination.* New York: Harcourt, Brace & World, Inc., 1965.

44.   Warnath, Charles F. "Ethics, Training, Research: Some Problems for the Counseling Psychologist in an Instructional Setting," *Journal of Counseling Psychology,* III:4, 1956, 280-5.

45.   Warters, Jane. *High School Personnel Work Today.* New York: McGraw-Hill Book Company, Inc., 1956. Chap. 14.

46.   Wrenn, Charles Gilbert. *The Counselor in a Changing World.* Washington, D.C.: American Personnel and Guidance Association, 1962. Chap. 7.

47.   Zeran, F. R. and A. C. Riccio. *Organization and Administration of Guidance Services.* Chicago: Rand McNally & Co., 1962. Chap. 10.

13

Current Issues in Guidance

In the preceding chapters of this book, discussion has centered around the major aspects of guidance services: terminology, principles, history and development, organization and administration, personnel, tools and techniques. In this final chapter, current issues in guidance will be examined. Since guidance and education are so closely interrelated, it is not surprising that these issues parallel several of our broader educational controversies. What is the function of education? What is the scope of education? What are the implications of federal aid to education? What competencies should we expect of our educational personnel? These and other challenging questions of a general educational nature have perplexed our society for many years and loom in the background as we debate the issues currently confronting the guidance movement. No attempt will be made in this chapter to settle these issues. Their eventual resolution will be accomplished through research and practical experience rather than by the pronouncements of individuals in the field.

Issue 1—The Function of Guidance

We have seen that there is both confusion and disagreement with respect to the nature and function of the services which guidance should offer through the school. This should not cause too much surprise. The normal "growing pains" of a young profession are aggravated by the accelerated pace at which our world is changing. As our world changes, so our childrens' needs change. As our childrens' needs change, so our educational goals must change. Consequently, the function of guidance within the educational setting must be subject to continuous reappraisal and review. This would be unsettling enough if we had an "anchor point," a strong foundation of professional theory. Without such a foundation the task of determining function assumes awesome proportions. No wonder Barry and Wolf (6) have characterized today's guidance workers as "less confident, more defensive, and a little more limited in their outlook than were their earlier counterparts."

Mathewson (27) has summarized the forces influencing the growth and unity of the guidance movement in the following way:

> On the one hand are many influences making for unparalleled growth of the movement:
>
> Economic demands for more effective matching of talents and tasks and for maximum development and utilization of human resources.
> Cultural needs for capable and cooperative citizens to insure democratic survival.
> Rapid change in a complex technological society with commensurate individual confusion and uncertainty requiring aid in planning and direction.
> More varied and extensive forms of educational and vocational opportunities available to more and more youth.
> Federal financial aid for training guidance counselors.
>
> Poised against these favorable factors, however, are some seriously obstructive forces:
>
> Divisive professional outlooks and commitments that may not be readily reconcilable and which may weaken national unity.
> Unfavorable and somewhat antagonistic settings for the practice of guidance in some school systems.
> Inadequate professional standards of training and practice in some areas.

Lack of a well-defined and widely accepted professional function.

Absence of a strong foundation of professional theory and related practices.

Figure 3 represents one way of diagramming the forces or "divisive professional outlooks" which have created confusion and disagreement with respect to the nature and function of guidance. Without question, *intellect, manpower,* and *adjustment* represent forces that have had, and will continue to have, a profound effect upon school guidance services. Yet, most crucial to the ultimate determination of the guidance function is the nature of the relationship between guidance and value orientation.

FIGURE 3

THE FUNCTION OF GUIDANCE

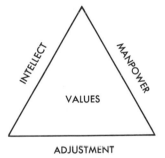

Guidance and Intellectual Development

Should guidance services be directed primarily toward furthering the academic and intellectual development of pupils? Since the nature and activities of the guidance program will be partially determined by the school's philosophy of education, we might also ask: To what extent should our schools be directly concerned with the personal-social development of pupils? Rickover (42) is typical of those who have linked our concern for the pupil's personal-social development with what they consider to be declining standards of academic performance in our schools. They urge the elimination of "frills and fads" (that is, direct concern for the personal-social development of the pupil) from our school programs and ask that increased attention be given to the teaching of the "basic disciplines."

However, others have argued that society is not well served by an educational program that emphasizes intellectualism at the expense of other types of individual growth and development. Kluckhohn (22) phrases this argument in the following manner:

> Our educational system has recently been built upon a kind of watery intellectualism. We have too often naively assumed that, if people were "well informed" and taught to reason in accord with accepted canons of logic, their characters would take care of themselves and they would automatically acquire the point of view requisite in the citizen of a great society. . . .
>
> Psychiatrists are agreed [however] that the elimination of social disorganization, as well as of personal disorganization, can be furthered only by more consistent educational practices both in the home and in the school, because automatic actions based on the habits of early life are the most stable.

And Wriston (55) has this to say:

> Education . . . is the life-long process of growth—physical, mental, moral, aesthetic. It is not primarily training, though training is part of it. Central are the stimulation and the discipline of the individual. This does not require every individual to be a scholar.

Guidance and Manpower Utilization

To what extent should factors such as national necessity overshadow an individual's freedom of choice? *What role can and should guidance play in the effort to utilize our manpower more effectively?* The language of the National Defense Education Act of 1958 left no doubt that Congress viewed manpower utilization as *one* of the functions of guidance, if not the most important one. Under Title I, Section 101, "Findings and Declaration of Policy" (40) it was stated, "We must increase our efforts to identify and educate more of the talent of our nation. This requires programs that ... will correct as rapidly as possible the existing imbalances in our educational programs which have led to an insufficient proportion of our population educated in science, mathematics, and modern foreign languages and trained in technology." Likewise, Title V-A, Section 503 of the act (40) required any state desiring financial reimbursement under Title V to set forth a program of guidance in the public secondary schools which was designed "to advise students of courses of study best suited to their ability, aptitudes, and skills, and to encourage students with outstanding aptitudes and ability to complete their secondary school education, take the necessary courses for admission to institutions of higher education, and enter such institutions." This type of statement merits criticism on two counts:

1. *The use of phrases and terms such as "advise", "encourage", and "correct as rapidly as possible" gives a directive connotation to the process of guidance which is at variance with the philosophy of most personnel workers and inconsistent with our principles of democratic education.*

James B. Conant, in his *Education in a Divided World* (10) writes on this subject:

> . . . really effective counseling is the keystone of the arch of a widespread educational system dedicated to the principle of equality of opportunity. A democracy, unlike a totalitarian state, cannot force its youth into what the authorities consider the appropriate groove of advanced education. In this republic of free men, no official can decree what line of study must be pursued. How is the sorting process to be accomplished? The answer is by the democratic method of enlightenment and persuasion.

The problem we face can be stated very simply. *How can guidance match individuals and occupations most effectively without undermining the individual's freedom of vocational choice?* The problem of matching men and jobs is a knotty one. Many individuals have made, and will continue to make, poor vocational choices, even when they have been made aware of their strengths and limitations, and of the vocational opportunities which would allow them to make maximum use of their interests and abilities. However, the advantages of preserving the individual's freedom of choice have been well stated by Hancher (17):

> Knowing that motivation is a powerful force in the learning process, guidance and counseling should be utilized to enable a student to appraise himself and his abilities and to make wise choices of his curriculum and his career. *But neither guidance nor admissions systems are infallible, and the best system is to allow all well-motivated and reasonably intelligent youth an opportunity to succeed.* What would our modern guidance and admissions systems have had to say of Churchill, Darwin, Newton, Einstein and other stubborn nonconformists? *The proof of ability is the trial of it—and there is less rebellion and frustration, bitter though they may be, toward the attempt that fails than there is toward the social order which denies the individual's right even to make the attempt.*

Wriston (55) speaks of the "distortion" of the educative process that can result if so-called "manpower analyses" are given too much importance:

> Whenever counseling and curriculum stress vocation primarily, they underestimate needs just as vital, though not statistically conspicuous. The nation needs philosophers, poets, artists, critics and a thousand other sorts of people—in numbers which 'manpower analyses' can never estimate.

2. *The view of guidance function as one of encouraging "students with outstanding aptitudes and ability" to plan for and enter higher education broadens the schism that already exists between vocational guidance and vocational education.*

The schism between *vocational guidance* and *vocational education* began years ago when the secondary school contained two curricula, general and vocational, that were considered separate and distinct from each other. The former was considered as preparation for higher education and the professions, the latter was regarded as a repository for the delinquent, for the "dropout" from the general curriculum, and for those who lacked the means of financing four additional years of education. Vocational education was called "manual training" and represented an inferior form of instruction. The assumption was usually made that students in this program required little guidance since (a) they had already lost (or given up) the opportunity for professional preparation, (b) their period of training was relatively short and intensely practical, and (c) requirements for entrance into a trade were well known and rarely changed.

The government has been generous in providing financial assistance to vocational education. Due to the Smith-Hughes Act, various New Deal legislative actions and amendments, the National Defense Education Act, the Vocational Act of 1963, and recent antipoverty legislation, annual Federal appropriations for vocational education now amount to approximately two-thirds of a billion dollars. However, most of this money has been used to develop training programs *outside* the regular educational system (i.e. manpower development and training programs, Opportunity Industrialization centers, Office of Economic Opportunity feeder systems, the Neighborhood Youth Corps programs), thus perpetuating the schism between general education and vocational education.

Fortunately, we are becoming aware of the problems (*social, economic,* and *political* as well as *educational* and *vocational*) resulting from such a schism. Cremin (11), Feldman (13), Hoyt (20), and Shoben (45) are among those who have warned that changes in counseling and curriculum are urgently needed. We need a coordinated curriculum in our elementary and secondary schools where vocational and general education supplement and reinforce each other. We also need counselors who recognize that occupational choice *results from* rather than *determines* the student's total life-style.

Guidance and Personal Adjustment

There is a growing tendency, particularly at the secondary level, to identify the school counselor as a specialist who deals with problems of personal adjustment. Aside from the practical problem of preparing enough of these specialists (which would appear to involve a minimum of two years of graduate study—see ACES statement, Chapter 12), there is the question of whether guidance should be limited to certain specialized functions, or whether it should be identified in much broader terms. As Ratigan (41) has phrased it, "The trend toward specialization involves the school counselor in one of the paradoxes that plague the profession. The guidance movement, intent on the consideration of individual differences and the unique personality, was conceived as a counteracting force to the assembly-line system of mass production in education that tended to produce specialists and render the entire process impersonal, with the individual learner reduced to a number or name in a roll book. But now the school counselor, as the leading expert in guidance, finds himself a specialist in combating the evils of specialization, a contradiction that bears watching and that points toward more training in the humanities rather than in the technologies because, essentially, guidance is the business of helping man reach full development as a human being."

It is difficult to understand how a school counselor can spend more than 50 per cent of his time in individual counseling of *any* kind without neglecting other supportive guidance services. Counseling, in isolation from pupil appraisal, information, and research services, would be charlatanry! As Barry and Wolf (6) conclude, "Guidance-personnel work has not in the past concentrated solely upon counseling activities, and it is questionable whether it should do so in the future." Hill (18) makes a strong plea for the "general practitioner" in guidance:

> The issue here is not so much whether all the services usually listed in a guidance program need to get done, but whether these are seen as the responsibility of several different specialists rather

than of a general practitioner in guidance. The issue is resolved easily in small schools where limited staff permit only one or two counselors in a school system. In larger schools specialization of function becomes more possible, and perhaps more feasible. With specialization of pupil personnel functions, however, who is to provide the integration of service, the close-at-hand relationship with teachers, which the practical and pressing needs of the school would seem to require? Is it not possible that the school counselor, even in large schools, will always be needed who is a generalist, a person broadly trained, a person easily accessible, a person providing leadership for the breadth and developmental character of the guidance effort that the children need? It is the conviction of this author that, as in the field of medicine, in the field of guidance there will continue to be need for general practitioners as well as for specialists. The general practitioner should be the school counselor on the local building staff. He should be a cooperative colleague of teachers, administrators, school psychologists, school health workers, and school social workers. His functions will involve counseling with pupils, consulting with teachers, parents and other community workers, conducting group guidance programs, developing the school's resources of educational and occupational information, providing leadership in research and evaluation, conducting the placement and follow-up services of the school, leading in the school's program for studying and understanding its children, and providing his fair share of help in the ongoing efforts of the staff to improve the total school program.

It is important to remember that the law does not regard the school counselor as a specialist in personal adjustment. It has not given him "expert witness" status; it has not generally granted him immunity from testimony, and, in the only pertinent Supreme Court decision, it did not recognize his responsibility for identifying abnormal behavior (see Chapter 6).

Guidance and Values

Most authorities agree that guidance should serve both the *individual* and *society*. They further agree that it is difficult, if not ultimately impossible, to benefit one without benefiting the other. If it is also assumed that the schools should accept a major share of the responsibility for the personal-social development of the individual (and some educators as well as laymen would not so agree), guidance is faced with still another problem. *What sort of balance should be sought between the encouragement of individual aspirations, creativi-*

ty, and leadership on the one hand, and emphasis on social conformity and group living on the other? Riesman, Glazer, and Denny (43), in their discussion of "other-directedness" among young people, offer evidence to indicate that we have, perhaps, overemphasized social conformity at the expense of individuality and leadership. Lynes (24) and Whyte (51) also support the contention that creativity and individuality are fast disappearing from the American scene.

Mathewson (26) suggests that there are three main areas in which guidance is faced with the problem of reconciling individual and social good:

1. *Social adjustment of individuals to normal and necessary social regulations.* This is not the denial of individual good but the guarantee of individual good through the reinforcement of the very social regulations that permit freedom by discouraging individual anarchy. The practical problem is, of course, to educate youth so that they may perceive this truth, accept it, and live by it.

2. *Optimum development of favorable social attitudes and habits of responsibility, cooperation, feeling, and mutual respect.* Such attitudes and dispositions transcend mere obedience to regulations and partake of the quality of spontaneous, emotionally rooted behavior essential to happy, gracious, and strong family, community and national living. They are essential attributes of the moral strength of any society; through them are ideals and values implemented; without them a nation degenerates into barbarism. Yet they cannot be too rigidly "taught" in school; they must be "caught" by example and perceived through significant experience.

3. *Personal aspiration, economic demand, and social necessity.*
The world is not the individual's oyster; he must come to some kind of terms with it. This coming to terms may be the essence of orientation through guidance rather than forcible orientation through failure in the market place. The social necessity of any given family may require that an individual give up his personal aspiration for a larger good. He may thereby gain in character but will lose his chance to fulfill a personal ambition. But beyond all these considerations is the great overwhelming necessity, that may exist for decades to come, for individuals to delay, or even thwart, their individual aspirations in service to country. This may be seen not as an unavoidable personal "sacrifice" but in its larger aspects as an opportunity, even a privilege, of living for a great cause, even greater than that of our own country. Only thus may the individual avoid the bitterness of frustration and enjoy the calm and strength of fulfilling a value greater than himself.

The "Rockefeller Report" on Education (44) takes the same stand, after noting that some of our more discerning critics are becoming uneasy about the current aspirations and values of Americans and the growing cult of self-gratification.

> People who live aimlessly, who allow the search for meaning in their lives to be satisfied by shoddy and meretricious experiences have simply not been stirred by any alternative meanings—religious meanings, ethical values, ideals of social and civic responsibility, high standards of self-realization.
>
> This is a deficiency for which we all bear a responsbility. It is a failure of home, church, school, government—a failure of all of us.
>
> In the context of the present discussion, there should be a general recognition that development of the individual's potentialities occurs in a context of values. Education is not just a mechanical process for communication to the young of certain skills and information. It springs from our most deeply rooted convictions. And if it is to have vitality both teachers and students must be infused with the values which have shaped the system.

Getzels (15) and Spindler (46), in distinguishing between *emergent* and *traditional* values, have rather effectively destroyed the argument that *all* values change and that one system of values is as good as another. And Murphy (34) directly challenges those who still argue that value orientation is somehow inconsistent with good counseling:

> . . . it is not true that the wise man's sharing of a philosophy of life is an arrogant imposition upon a defenseless client. On the contrary, the risk of arrogance lies, I believe, in the technician's assumption that, by virtue of his skills, he can guide a whole person to move wisely in a complex and swiftly changing society. As we have noted, the young man and woman of today simply cannot be directed into paths guaranteeing a happy and effective life; they can only be assisted in developing into people with the maturity and the flexibility to solve new problems as these are presented.
>
> . . . it is often said that all philosophies are subjective and arbitrary, and that one system of values is as good as another. But if you believed that, you would not have chosen personnel and guidance as a way of life. Your experience, moreover, has shown you that some values, such as those of sympathy, tenderness, generosity, and self-control resonate to the deeper chords of human nature, and that they are for that reason intensely practical and dependable. Other values work badly, either because they

cannot be solidly built into human nature or because they involve profound internal contradictions.

The simple truth is that counseling, no matter how "scientific" it purports to be, has a value system built into it. *Counselors, consciously or unconsciously, communicate values to clients.* Under these circumstances, is it not more professional (and honest) for the counselor to become aware of his own values, how he came to possess them, and how he communicates them to clients?

Ratigan (41) comes to the same conclusion when he argues that counseling is still an art, rather than a science:

> Every counselor faces another paradox of his own profession when he tries to follow the behavioral scientists in the belief that human behavior is caused and therefore can be predicted and controlled. If this is not so, then why is he wasting his time at impossible tasks? If this is so, then he is toiling hopelessly in a culture opposed to his efforts, a culture dedicated to the proposition that men are free and responsible for their actions rather than the captive victims of predestination.
>
> The above paradox may be resolved by paraphrasing a message of Christ, Himself called Counselor: 'Render unto Science the things that relate to Science, but to Art the things that relate to Art.' Although scientific behaviorism is useful as a guideline to school counselors, counseling at the secondary level remains an art, with human *values* and intangible verities still the heart of what takes place between the counselor and counselee.

There is general agreement that guidance must be concerned with furthering intellectual development, utilizing our manpower more effectively, and assisting with personal adjustment. Disagreement is over the *priority* to be assigned these three functions. *But if we agree that "development of the individual's potentialities occurs in a context of values (44)," then it is in the area of value orientation that guidance finds its major function—and its challenge.*

Issue 2—The Scope of Guidance

Guidance has frequently been defined, but rarely delimited. As a result, confusion over the scope of guidance exists in our schools, in our counselor education programs, and in our professional organizations.

1. The term "guidance" has been applied to a wide assortment of unrelated school activities, including assembly programs, homerooms, individual testing, attendance, and other pupil accounting services,

in-service education for staff members, chaperoning dances, sponsoring clubs, conducting field trips, home visitation, and many more.

2. Individuals who claim to be performing guidance services include superintendents or principals, assistant superintendents or assistant principals, directors of guidance, counselors, psychologists, career teachers, visiting teachers, advisors, deans of boys and girls, attendance directors, and classroom teachers.

3. Guidance "specialists" report that they are required to perform many tasks of an administrative or clerical nature and are often forced to spend more time on problems of attendance, tardiness, discipline and record-keeping than on appraisal or counseling activities.

Support personnel in guidance have existed for some time in the sense that secretarial and clerical personnel have learned to assume many clerical aspects of a counselor's job. Recently, we have witnessed a growing interest in defining and training support (or subprofessional) personnel in guidance, and employing them for specific duties and roles. If we are to move in this direction, it will be necessary for us to classify the various guidance duties as either *professional* or *support* functions. It will also be necessary to establish systematic short-term training programs for support personnel. It is generally agreed that the establishment of sub-professional personnel in guidance would enable many counselors to make more extensive use of their professional competencies. However, it is questionable whether, operationally, guidance duties can always be separated into professional and support functions. And, if these duties cannot always be separated, would support personnel be encouraged to perform functions beyond their range of competency, thus weakening the total counseling profession?

In summary, our schools, counselor education programs and professional organizations must reach greater agreement regarding the scope of guidance if we intend to (a) discourage unqualified individuals from performing guidance services, (b) relieve guidance workers of burdensome administrative and/or clerical tasks, and (c) achieve full recognition as a profession.

Issue 3—The Coordination of Guidance

Since 1943, Congress has passed a series of acts which have made provision for federally-supported counseling and guidance services for a large number of our citizens. Among the more important of these legislative enactments were (1) the Vocational Rehabilitation Act (1943) and its subsequent amendments; (2) the "GI Bills" of World

War II, Korea, and the Cold War; (3) the National Defense Education Act (1958) and its amendments; (4) the Area Redevelopment Act (1961); (5) the Manpower Development and Training Act (1962); (6) the Vocational Education Act (1963); (7) the Economic Opportunity Act (1964); (8) the Elementary and Secondary Education Act (1965); and (9) the Higher Education Act (1965).

As a result of this legislation a number of different government agencies, under widely varying guidelines and regulations, are attempting to provide guidance services to (a) all elementary, secondary, and vocational school students; (b) all junior college, college, university and technical institute students; (c) all disadvantaged youth and adults; (d) all vocationally handicapped civilians; (e) all veterans, disabled and non-disabled, together with the orphans of veterans and the children of disabled veterans; and (f) all persons occupationally displaced by industrial, technological or sociological changes. The effect has been to create vague and contradictory images of counselor education and counselor function and responsibility.

It has been proposed that a national commission on counseling and guidance be established for the purpose of coordinating all federal agency activities in this field. Opponents of this proposal argue that such a commission would result in increased bureaucracy, regimentation, and mediocrity in counseling and guidance. It appears that the need for coordinating federal agency activities will become more acute as current legislation is broadened and extended. Therefore, the commission proposal merits serious and immediate attention.

Issue 4—The Background and Qualifications of School Counselors

The fourth major issue facing guidance concerns the background and qualifications of those who would serve as school counselors. It would appear that our disagreements and/or confusion over the *function* and *scope* of guidance must be resolved before we can properly determine the competencies needed by the school counselor. In addition, the lack of valid criteria for predicting counseling effectiveness and the absence of objective tools for measuring personal qualities make it extremely difficult to assess these competencies, even after we have determined what they should be. Some reference has already been made in Chapter 12 to current disagreement over the background and qualifications of school counselors. However, the following questions warrant additional comment:

1. *Is personality or technique of primary importance?* The difficulties involved in making an adequate assessment of the personality of
prospective guidance workers have caused counselor education programs to place heavy emphasis on the acquisition of subject matter
and the development of technical skills. Yet, does not this heavy
emphasis on subject matter and skills cause the prospective counselor
to lose some of the concern for human nature and human society
which originally motivated him to enter the guidance field? Murphy
(34) has expressed some uneasiness over this subject-matter emphasis:

> We see everywhere in clinical psychology today the drive for
> the so-called raising of standards. This is often an excuse for piling
> more and more courses on students who are already worried to
> death by the sheer amount of stuff they are supposed to master
> and by the limited possibilities of warm relationships with their
> teachers and with one another during this long and difficult
> period of training. It seems to me that many clinicians have
> learned very little about keeping their own house in order. They
> force their students into savage competitive relations with one
> another, keep them under continuous strain, give them the
> economic and narcissistic rewards of grades and part-time work;
> yet keep remote from them and as far as they can, keep them
> from warm fellowship with one another. Are the personnel and
> guidance people better off, in the matter of applying what they
> know about the cultural and personal context in which guidance
> can be really effective?
>   The basic issue, as I see it, is personality versus technique. Of
> course, some would ask me not to draw the issue so sharply. They
> would say it is not personality and technique, but personality
> exhibited through technique. I would like to agree with this; but
> there are very definite limitations on the amount of time we can
> give to choosing those who are to serve in guidance roles, and we
> are giving so little time to studying them as people, largely
> because we are giving so much time to studying their special
> skills. . . .
>   There is just not enough attention being given to personality
> and interpersonal relationships, and a major reason is that so much
> attention is given to technical craft skills. If you wish, I will
> restate the point in the following way: the skills should be ways
> of strengthening the personality and the interpersonal relation-
> ships. The skills should be ways of enabling the guide to function
> more humanly, more informally, more warmly, more effectively,
> through understanding the person more fully that he is guiding.
> Skills from this point of view can be taught, if there are the

teachers who are sensitized to such issues, and students who are allowed to develop as people, and not simply as students who earn A's in courses.

I think, perhaps, the most important issue today is this concept of self-realization. . . . The point that I would stress is that self-realization on the part of the person guided is likely to be feasible only if there is a lot of self-realization on the part of the guide. This means, of course, ego-involvement; it means feeling fully and deeply absorbed in the tremendous human importance of what one is doing. . . . Your clients often learn, not by being told, but by getting the feeling. A great deal of what you communicate to your client is not what you say, but what you are. One learns to deploy one's feelings toward people in a rich way, just as one learns to deploy muscular contractions in a particular way when one learns cabinet-making or surgery. . . . [Counselors] must be selected for personality range and depth in the first place, and given as much range and depth as the years of their training will permit. The quality of the job can be no better than the quality of the people who are holding the job.

Adequate attention can be given to counselor personality if:

a. Admission to the counselor education program is based upon a variety of selection devices, including interviews, references, tests, and biographical data, and not solely on the basis of scholastic aptitude and previous experience.

b. The supervisor-trainee ratio is small enough to permit adequate observation of the prospective counselor's relationships with other students and with members of the faculty.

c. The counselor education program culminates in a practicum or internship experience where adequate staff and facilities are available for observing and recording the trainee's ability in counseling situations.

d. Staff members in the counselor education program recognize that the trainee's attempt to understand his own self concept as it influences his relationships with others is at least as important as his verbalized acceptance of the theories and techniques of counseling and his skill in employing these techniques.

If we expect our trainees to go into the schools as warm, outgoing, secure, sensitive counselors, then counselor educators ought to be as sensitive to the insecurities and frustrations of their trainees as they would be to students with whom they were counseling. Preparing effective counselors appears to be more a matter of developing a warm, secure, and wise personality than of teaching techniques or of learning tricks of the trade.

2. *Do counselors need teaching experience and/or preparation?*
The relationship between teaching and counseling has been the subject of discussion for many years. In recent years, the discussion has
become more heated. Three major reports (1, 5, 54) have recommended that alternatives to the teaching requirement should be explored. And a host of writers have expressed their own points of view
on this subject. Since, as Cohen (9) phrases it, "the evidence of either
position seems based on untested assumptions rather than on empirical data," it seems logical here to further identify the problem rather
than to add one more point of view that is lacking in supportive
evidence.

Discussion usually centers around three questions: (a) Do counselors with a teaching background have a better relationship with the
teaching staff? (b) Do counselors with a teaching background have a
greater commitment to education? and (c) Does the imposition of
the teaching requirement limit our source of counselors, both quanti-
tatively and qualitatively?

Hudson (21) may be considered representative of those who argue
that a teaching background is of great importance in developing
harmonious relationships with the teaching staff:

> If teaching makes one a better teacher, so does it make one a
> better counselor, for the counselor and the teacher are both
> educators. . . . Since most of his duties involve working directly
> with students and with teachers, the counselor who has been a
> successful teacher will have a greater understanding of students
> and a greater appreciation of the classroom teacher's point of
> view than the counselor who has not taught. . . . A counselor
> without teaching experience is likely to be looked upon with
> suspicion as a person who does not know what teaching entails
> and who thus cannot appreciate the complexities of a teacher's
> job.

On the other hand, Stewart and Warnath (47) believe that the
teaching experience is detrimental to the establishment of good relationships with the teaching staff. "Frequently teachers report that they
do not make use of the counselor because he is essentially just a
teacher like themselves."

Hoyt (19) is the most articulate spokesman for those who argue
that commitment to the objectives and goals of education is more
likely to be found in the counselor who has been a former teacher:

> Such a career commitment consists of more than an understanding
> of and appreciation for the goals and objectives of educators. It
> involves PERSONAL ACCEPTANCE of dedication to the goals

of education on the part of the counselor. It means that the counselor must regard himself as an educator and not simply as one who wants or is willing to work with teachers. The counselor shouldn't content himself with understanding educators; he should be one.

Opponents to the teaching requirement reply that motivations *other* than commitment to education may be involved when a teacher decides to seek formal training as a counselor. They suggest that some teachers enter counseling (a) for financial gain, (b) as a stepping stone to administration, and (c) out of disappointment with teaching.

With respect to the question of whether the teaching requirement unduly limits our supply of counselors, Cohen (9) produces evidence to reinforce the commonly held notion that teaching frequently attracts less talented individuals. And Stewart and Warnath (47) have protested that recruitment of counselors solely from the ranks of teachers shuts off new ideas from the guidance field. "Perhaps recruiting from many related areas will provide some of the cross-fertilization of ideas which is so urgently needed."

Issue 5—Programs of Counselor Education

Considerable attention has already been given (see Chapter 12) to the problems associated with establishing adequate programs of preparation for school counselors. Reference was made to current arguments over (a) whether we should be preparing *guidance generalists* or *counseling specialists,* (b) the *breadth* and *depth* of preparation that should be required, (c) the effectiveness of *part-time* study versus *full-time* study, and (d) the role to be played by the various academic disciplines. Several additional questions deserve attention here.

1. *Should we restrict enrollment in our counselor education programs to individuals who have expressed a commitment to school counseling?* If not, how can (or should) we accommodate those individuals who have other goals (i.e., classroom teachers, subprofessional or support personnel, school psychologists, school social workers, counselors for the handicapped)? Should differentiation be made in terms of breadth or depth of preparation, or both? Are there values in having individuals with different backgrounds and different goals share experiences in the same basic courses?

2. *Is the further standardization of counselor education programs desirable and/or necessary?* Counselor education programs have been found to vary significantly in regard to content, resources, and objec-

tives. There appears to be general agreement that minimum standards for counselor education programs need to be established. Yet, the prospect of enforcement of minimum standards by some sort of external accrediting agency touches three sensitive "institutional nerves":

   a. the desire to preserve *institutional autonomy* and to resist attempts by outside agencies (governmental and otherwise) to control or regulate specific educational programs;
   b. the recognized need for continuing research through *experimental and innovative programs* that might represent a departure from previously conceived standards;
   c. the concern for meeting *local and state educational needs* (and state counselor certification requirements) which vary greatly from state to state.

3. *Are the Counseling and Guidance Training Institutes, supported by the National Defense Education Act, the most effective means of supplementing the regular on-going counselor education programs supported by many of our colleges and universities?* These institutes, provided through Title V-B of the Act, were discussed briefly in Chapter 2. McCully (28) and Tyler (49) have reported on the apparent outcomes of the fifty institutes conducted during the summer of 1959. More recently, Pierson (38) has evaluated regular session institutes. All three reports have identified a number of significant positive outcomes of the institute experience.

On the other hand, Tyler (49) gave recognition to several possible negative effects of these institutes on the regular counselor education programs, the most obvious being the competition for staff and facilities in a university where an institute is located. Is it possible for both programs to operate on the same campus in isolation from one another without one suffering from a shortage of qualified faculty members or from a shortage of space and equipment? Patterson (37) has spoken most eloquently for the "loyal opposition" in expressing concern over the effect these institutes are having on the participating students, the institute staff, and the regular, on-going counselor education programs of the institutions involved (see Part Five). And members of the APGA Professional Preparation and Standards Committee have recently expressed concern over far-reaching changes in the new U.S. Office of Education Guidelines for NDEA Institute proposals which now (a) permit Counseling and Guidance Institutes to be conducted at institutions that do not ordinarily offer graduate instruction in counseling and guidance; (b) do not require that the institute program offer graduate credit; (c) do not require that participant eligibility be based upon possession of, or preparation for, state counselor certification; and (d) allow participants to be persons from other professional specialties whose duties include counseling and guidance.

As a result of the number and variety of criticisms that have been directed at the NDEA Institute program, it would appear that every effort should be made to expand fellowship programs operating under provisions of the National Defense Education Act or the Higher Education Act.

Summary

Current issues in guidance are of five types: (1) those that are concerned with the *function* of guidance, (2) those that involve the *scope* of guidance, (3) those relating to the *coordination* of guidance, (4) those connected with the *background* and *qualifications* of school counselors, and (5) those associated with the establishment and maintenance of adequate *programs of preparation* for school counselors. These issues are closely interrelated with several of our major educational controversies. As educators and laymen make future decisions in the area of educational philosophy, these issues may be modified or redefined. However, the complexity and importance of guidance in the medium of education makes it imperative that the final resolution of these issues be accomplished through the objective analysis of practical experiences and the application of carefully designed research procedures. School counselors will not be accorded full professional status until they have assumed more leadership in examining, defining, and resolving these issues.

Bibliography

1.　American Personnel and Guidance Association. "The Counselor: Professional Preparation and Role," *Personnel and Guidance Journal*, XXXXII: 536-541, January, 1964.

2.　Arbuckle, Dugald S. *Counseling: Philosophy, Theory and Practice*. Boston: Allyn & Bacon, Inc., 1965. Chaps. 6-9.

3.　————. "Counseling: Philosophy or Science," *Personnel and Guidance Journal*, XXXIX:11-14, September, 1960.

4.　————. "Five Philosophical Issues in Counseling," *Journal of Counseling Psychology*, V:211-215, Fall, 1958.

5.　Association for Counselor Education and Supervision. *Standards for Counselor Education in the Preparation of Secondary School Counselors*. Washington, D.C.: American Personnel and Guidance Association, 1964.

6.　Barry, Ruth and Beverly Wolf, *Modern Issues in Guidance-Personnel Work*. 2nd ed. New York: Columbia University, Teachers College, 1963. Chaps. 1, 3, 7, 15-16.

7.　Carter, Thomas M. "Professional Immunity for Guidance Counselors," *Personnel and Guidance Journal*, XXXIII:130-135, November, 1954.

8.　Chennault, Joann. "Professional Standards and Philosophical Freedom: A Peaceful Coexistence," *Counselor Education and Supervision*, III:8-12, Fall, 1963.

9.　Cohen, Nancy. "Must Teaching be a Prerequisite for Guidance?," *Counselor Education and Supervision*, I:69-71, Winter, 1961.

10.　Conant, James. *Education in a Divided World*. Cambridge, Massachusetts: Harvard University Press, 1958.

11.　Cremin, Lawrence A. "The Progressive Heritage of the Guidance Movement," in Landy, Edward, and Paul A. Perry, eds. *Guidance in American Education I: Backgrounds and Prospects*. Cambridge, Massachusetts: Harvard University Press, 1964.

12.　Crow, Lester D. and Alice Crow. *Readings in Guidance*. New York: David McKay Company, Inc., 1962. Chaps. 10, 21-22.

13.   Feldman, Marvin J. *Making Education Relevant.* Ford Foundation, Office of Reports, 477 Madison Avenue, New York, New York, 1966.
14.   Ferree, George. "Psychological Freedom as a Counseling Objective," *Counselor Education and Supervision,* III:13-18, Fall, 1963.
15.   Getzels, Jacob. "The Acquisition of Values in School and Society," in Chase, Francis S. and Harold Anderson, eds. *The High School in a New Era.* Chicago: University of Chicago Press, 1958.
16.   Greene, Maxine. "Values and the Schools," in Landy, Edward and Arthur Kroel, eds. *Guidance in American Education II: Current Issues and Suggested Action.* Cambridge, Massachusetts: Harvard University Press, 1965.
17.   Hancher, Virgil M. "The Challenge We Face," *Educational Record,* January, 1959. Pp. 11-19.
18.   Hill, George E. *Management and Improvement of Guidance.* New York: Appleton-Century-Crofts, 1965. Chap. 14, pp. 438-439.
19.   Hoyt, Kenneth. "Guidance: A Constellation of Services," *Personnel and Guidance Journal,* XXXX:690-697, April, 1962.
20.   ———. "Needed Counselor Competencies in Vocational Aspects of Counseling and Guidance," in McDaniels, Carl, ed. *Vocational Aspects of Counselor Education,* Washington, D.C.: The George Washington University, 1965.
21.   Hudson, George. "Counselors Need Teaching Experience," *Counselor Education and Supervision,* 0:24-27, Spring, 1961.
22.   Kluckhohn, Clyde. *Mirror for Man.* New York: McGraw-Hill Book Company, Inc., 1949.
23.   Litwack, Lawrence, Judy Holmes, and Janice O'Hern. *Critical Issues in Student Personnel Work: A Problems Casebook.* Chicago: Rand McNally & Co., 1965. Chaps. 1-3.
24.   Lynes, Russell. *The Tastemakers.* New York: Harper and Brothers, 1949.
25.   *Manpower and Education.* Washington, D.C.: Educational Policies Commission, National Education Association of the United States and the American Association of School Administrators, 1956. Chap. 6.
26.   Mathewson, Robert H. *Guidance Policy and Practice.* Rev. ed. New York: Harper and Brothers, 1955. Chaps. 2, 5, 6, 9, 10, 16-18.
27.   ———. *Guidance Policy and Practice.* 3rd ed. New York: Harper & Row, Publishers, 1962. Chaps. 7, 9, 14-16.
28.   McCully, C. Harold. *NDEA Counseling and Guidance Training Institutes: Implications for Counselor Education.* Mimeographed report of address before the National Association of Guidance Supervisors and Counselor Trainers, APGA Convention, Philadelphia, Pennsylvania, April, 1960.
29.   McDaniel, Henry B. *Guidance in the Modern School.* New York: The Dryden Press, 1956. Chap. 18.
30.   ———, et al. *Readings in Guidance.* New York: Henry Holt and Company, 1959. Chap. 15.

31.   McGowan, John F. and Lyle D. Schmidt. *Counseling: Readings in Theory and Practice.* New York: Holt, Rinehart & Winston, Inc., 1962. Chaps. 3-4.

32.   Moore, Gilbert. "A Negative View Toward Therapeutic Counseling in the Public Schools," *Counselor Education and Supervision,* I:60-68, Winter, 1961.

33.   Mosher, Ralph L., Richard F. Carle and Chris D. Kehas. *Guidance: An Examination.* New York: Harcourt, Brace & World, Inc., 1965.

34.   Murphy, Gardner. "The Cultural Context of Guidance," *Personnel and Guidance Journal,* XXXIV:4-9, September, 1955.

35.   Noble, F. C. "The Two Year Graduate Program in Counselor Education: A Re-examination," *Counselor Education and Supervision,* IV:160-162, Spring, 1965.

36.   Nugent, Frank A. "A Rationale against Teaching Experience for School Counselors," *The School Counselor,* 13:213-215, May, 1966.

37.   Patterson, C. H. "The NDEA and Counselor Education," *Counselor Education and Supervision,* III:4-7, Fall, 1963.

38.   Pierson, George A. *An Evaluation: Counselor Education in Regular Session Institutes.* Washington, D.C.: U.S. Office of Education, Department of Health, Education, and Welfare, Bulletin No. 25042, 1965.

39.   Polmantier, Paul and Lyle D. Schmidt. "Areas of Preparation for School Guidance Workers," *Personnel and Guidance Journal,* XXXIX:45-46, September, 1960.

40.   Public Law 85-864. *The National Defense Education Act of 1958.* 85th Congress. Pp. 2, 11.

41.   Ratigan, William. "The Place of Counseling Theory in High School Programs," in Stefflre, Buford, ed. *Theories of Counseling.* New York: McGraw-Hill Book Company, Inc., 1965.

42.   Rickover, Hyman. "Education for All Children," in Crow, Alice and Lester D. Crow, eds. *Vital Issues in American Education.* New York: Bantam Books, 1964. Pp. 63-72.

43.   Riesman, David, Nathan Glazer, and Reuel Denney. *The Lonely Crowd.* New Haven, Connecticut: Yale University Press, 1950.

44.   Rockefeller Bros. Fund Report. *The Pursuit of Excellence—Education and the Future of America.* Panel Report Five of the Special Studies Project. Garden City, New York: Doubleday & Company, Inc., 1958. Pp. 48-49.

45.   Shoben, Edward Joseph, Jr. "Guidance: Remedial Function or Social Reconstruction?" *Harvard Educational Review,* XXXII:430-433, 1962.

46.   Spindler, George. *Education and Culture.* New York: Holt, Rinehart & Winston, Inc., 1963. Chap. 7.

47.   Stewart, Lawrence and Charles Warnath. *The Counselor and Society: A Cultural Approach.* Boston: Houghton Mifflin Company, 1965. Chap. 3.

48.   Super, Donald E. "Guidance: Manpower Utilization or Human Development?" *Personnel and Guidance Journal,* XXXIII:8-14, September, 1954.

49.   Tyler, Leona. *The National Defense Counseling and Guidance Training Institutes Program—A Report of the First 50 Institutes.* Washington, D.C.: U.S. Office of Education, Department of Health, Education, and Welfare, Bulletin No. 31, 1960.
50.   Weitz, Henry. *Behavior Change Through Guidance.* New York: John Wiley & Sons, Inc., 1964. Chap. 10.
51.   Whyte, William Jr. *The Organization Man.* New York: Simon and Schuster, Inc., 1956.
52.   Wilkins, William D. and Barbara J. Perlmutter. "The Philosophical Foundations of Guidance and Personnel Work," *Review of Educational Research*, 30:97-104, April, 1960.
53.   Williamson, E. G. "Value Options and the Counseling Relationship," *Personnel and Guidance Journal*, XLIV:617-623, February, 1966.
54.   Wrenn, Gilbert. *The Counselor in a Changing World.* Washington, D.C.: American Personnel and Guidance Association, 1962.
55.   Wriston, Henry M. "The Challenge of Being Free." Adventures of the Mind Series. *The Saturday Evening Post*, December 10, 1960.
56.   Yates, J. W. and Lyle D. Schmidt. "The Counselor's Self-Concept," *The Vocational Guidance Quarterly*, VII:151-154, Spring, 1959.

Attaining the Promise
of Guidance for All

Kenneth B. Hoyt

The topic, "Attaining the Promise of Guidance for All," was chosen to represent three basic themes that, when played together, unite in a chorus of challenges for each of us in guidance. Beginning with individuals, we will turn to the guidance movement intended to serve them, and finally the organization that represents this movement in society. The first of these themes, concerning the individuals guidance seeks to serve, will be discussed as the question, *Is Guidance For All?* The second theme is represented by the guidance and counseling movement and will be discussed as the question, *In What Ways Should We Change?* The third and final theme is represented by the first letter of each key word in the title of this presentation—Attaining the Promise of Guidance for All—i.e., APGA, and will be

Reprinted by permission of the author and *Personnel and Guidance Journal,* XLV, No. 6 (February, 1967), 624-630.

Kenneth B. Hoyt, Professor of Education and Head, Division of Counselor Education, University of Iowa, Iowa City.

discussed as the question, *What Is Ahead For APGA?* In discussing each of these questions, major attention will be concentrated on the theme it represents. At the same time, some overlap with the remaining two themes will be attempted.

Is Guidance for All?

There is probably no more popular assertion in our field than that which states that the guidance and counseling movement represents a developmental process intended to be applicable and helpful to all persons. By this, we mean, of course, that the *opportunity* for guidance and counseling should be made available to all. That is, it seems apparent that no societal service is to be forced upon anyone. If we are to continue picturing guidance services as holding positive potential for all, there are some very hard and eminently practical issues to be faced.

The first such issue has to do with the phony finality of guidance services as they exist in specific settings at the present time. The increasing complexity of society is making it more and more difficult to assert that guidance is ever complete for any individual. Counselors in any setting must become more concerned about the *timeliness* of guidance services they offer and less concerned about the *timeless* effects resulting from the provision of such services. That is, if counselors devote part of their efforts to producing effects pervasive throughout the lives of those they serve, they must, it seems to me, devote at least equal effort to producing positive effects, timely and appropriate in the life of the individual as he exists *now*. To recognize the incompleteness of guidance in a particular setting at a particular time is not to deny the professional responsibilities of counselors in that setting. Rather, it is to allow counselors to accept responsibilities that, in fact, they may be able to meet.

The phrase "Guidance for All" has been applied most often in the school setting as meaning "all students in a school." Both the inadequacy and indefensibleness of such a meaning should be readily apparent now. If guidance is for all, we must include persons of all ages who are out of school as well as in school. We must recognize that the need for guidance, like the need for education, cannot in these times be restricted to a particular period in time in the life of the individual. Is guidance for all?

The second issue involved here stems from our phobia for forming phrases to represent those guidance is intended to serve. At this convention [of the American Personnel and Guidance Association, 1966], we have heard sessions involving guidance of such persons as the gifted, the slow learner, the physically handicapped, the college-bound, the culturally disadvantaged, the economically depressed, the unemployed, and the veteran. Special legislation has been enacted calling for guidance and counseling of persons in each of these classifications. What about guidance of persons who belong in none of them? It sometimes strikes me as odd that a person in this society should be handicapped by the fact that he is not. How do we justify guidance services to persons in any of these categories designed to help him become equal with others when our entire movement is dedicated to the promotion of inequality—to increasing rather than decreasing individual differences?

When we form phrases to represent certain parts of the total population guidance is to serve, it is important to recognize that our reasons for doing so are based on a desire to maximize individuality through more adequate understandings of such persons. The two basic errors to be avoided are: (a) the error of assuming that individual differences among those in any classification will be less than those existing between such individuals and other persons; and (b) the error of regarding our goal as one of eliminating differences among persons in various classifications. To the extent that classifications are used primarily for purposes of increasing our understanding and perspective, they can be very useful indeed. When they are used to restrict or artificially simplify our views regarding individuals, they are self-defeating to the basic goals and objectives of guidance.

In spite of such inherent weaknesses in classification systems, it would appear that there is little likelihood of their being eliminated. They do have some value if used to increase our understanding. Moreover, they seem to have strong emotional appeals to those in positions of legislative influence. As a consequence, many have argued that we should continue to support categorical federal legislation aimed at providing guidance and counseling services to those in separate classifications. Such persons contend that, by pursuing such a course, guidance services will eventually be made available to all. It seems obvious that, in spite of all the guidance legislation enacted in the last 20 years, we are still very far from having exhausted the possible categories of persons to whom guidance might be made available. When we view guidance legislation, can we say guidance is for all?

The third issue to be considered by those who assert that guidance is for all has to do with personal value systems of the recipients of guidance. That personal values must be considered here seems obvious in that the basic concepts of guidance are, themselves, values that we prize highly. The most basic of these values—including those concerned with the dignity and worthwhileness of the individual, the freedom of each individual to lead his own life, the acceptance of personal responsibility by individuals, and the desire to become a "better" person in ways that are personally meaningful to the individual—are among those we have chosen to call "human values." So long and to the extent such values are translated in terms of goals and objectives for guidance, we are on safe grounds in sounding our slogan of "Guidance For All."

But what happens when guidance is pictured in terms of more limiting goals and objectives? I am particularly concerned now with what many refer to as the "bread and butter" parts of guidance—i.e., educational and vocational guidance. Here, it seems we assume those who are recipients of guidance services hold personal values peculiar to only part of society. For example, they are hopefully persons who have a basic belief in the value of education, in the desirability of seeking work, in planning ahead towards goals that are more than immediate, and in wanting to make decisions based at least in part on rational understandings of themselves and their opportunities. What are counselors to do when they encounter prospective clients who appear not to hold such values? Can we really believe in the right of the individual to lead his own life and, at the same time, seek to impose such values on those who seem not to hold them when they come to us? Do we really mean that only those individuals whose personal values are like ours are free to lead their own lives? Do we mean that counselors should ignore those whose values are not like ours? Is guidance for all?

At this point, it seems reasonable for me to assume that at least a fair minority of this audience would expect my answer to this question to be "No." Those who would hold such an expectation are wrong. My personal feeling is that guidance, as it exists today, is not and has not been an opportunity for all. I feel equally strongly that there are positive steps to be taken in this society towards attaining the promise of guidance for all. At this time, I would like to turn to a discussion of some of those steps to be discussed under the general question of "In What Ways Should We Change?"

In What Ways Should We Change?

While I have no illusions that the opportunity for guidance will be available to all in the near future, I am convinced that this represents a desirable goal towards which to head. At this time, I would like to outline in specific fashion certain ways in which I feel our movement should be changing. Some will disagree with the desirability of the goal. Even more will disagree with some of the specific suggestions I am about to make. I welcome such disagreement because, to me, there are advantages in adversaries who help clarify issues, point out errors in judgment, and bring in new dimensions thereby contributing in valuable ways to the wisdom of our decisions.

First, I feel we should seek to clarify the meaning of such terms as "counselor," "counseling," and "guidance" in ways that will differentiate counselors as an occupational group from those in other helping occupations. That this task has not yet been accomplished even within the group of persons carrying the title of "counselor" is obvious. It is even more obvious that there is much to do before members of other helping occupations can agree to the kinds of distinctions some of us have already tried to draw. Not all persons in need of help in solving their problems can be expected to find the counselor to represent the one helping occupation ideally prepared to serve them. There are some things best done by counselors and other things best done by persons in other helping occupations. Counselors, as an occupational group, should be distinguishable from other helping occupations in terms of some unique *combination* of professional attitudes, job functions, and job competencies. Until we take this step, counselors will continue to be asked to accomplish tasks they are not prepared to do and, equally serious, our own movement will have no clear-cut means of protecting the professional meaning of the terms and titles we use. We cannot assess either our progress towards or the reasonableness of the goal of guidance for all until this step has been taken.

Second, assuming we can arrive at some agreement regarding terminology and meaning, we should be moving towards recognition of commonalities that exist among counselors in various work settings. To take this step would lead toward two related, very important directions for change. The first is greater professional communication among counselors in various settings which should not only rid each of us from some of the provincialism accumulating in a particular setting but should also help us work more effectively together in the continuing interest of those we serve. If we assume that counselors will tend to remain in the settings where they are employed, we must certainly assume that the clients they serve will not. The professional growth of individual counselors, the improvement of the guidance movement, and the continuing needs of persons for guidance services makes this step necessary.

The second direction for change growing out of this step is a movement towards establishment of the provision for a common core of counselor education. The spotty and inconsistent categorical federal support for counselor education that currently exists must be supplemented both by expansion of categorical support and by a new type of support for counselor education—support for a common core of graduate work to be taken by all prospective professional counselors regardless of the work setting towards which they are headed. We cannot make concerted progress towards the goal of guidance for all until we have taken this step against professional isolationism which currently exists within the guidance movement.

Third, as we move towards recognizing our commonalities, we must simultaneously move towards emphasizing differences among professional counselors in various work settings. It is time that concepts of career development be applied to counselors as well as by counselors. A prospective counselor must be prepared to answer, in sequence, two questions : (a) Why do you want to become a counselor? and (b) Why do you want to become a counselor in *this* setting? The first of these will be expected to be answered in terms of goals and objectives of the guidance movement while the second must be answered in terms of goals and objectives of the setting in which the counselor is employed. These two sets of goals must be compatible if counselors are to function effectively in ways that are professionally satisfying to them. Those counselors who would profess to be equally happy in any kind of setting (e.g., school, employment service, vocational rehabilitation, etc.) cannot logically expect that those who employ them will be equally happy about finding counselors with such a point of view. We should be moving towards helping prospective counselors acquire both some kind of identification with and special competencies for working effectively in particular settings. Accomplishment of this goal demands that some attention be given to it in the counselor education program. This means that, in addition to a common core of counselor education courses, we should expect to find certain special courses—illustrated at least by seminar and practicum experiences—designed for purposes of accomplishing this goal. Furthermore, it means that counselors in particular work settings must be able to recognize and accept the goals and objectives of the setting in addition to the specific goals and objectives of the guidance movement. Attaining the promise of guidance for all within any given setting demands that this be accomplished.

Fourth, we must recognize that to deal only with commonalities and differences as they exist among counselors in various work settings is not enough. In addition, we must concentrate on further differentiation in guidance methods and materials appropriate for performance of various specialized guidance functions. Specialization in counselor function on the job has always been more pronounced than specialization in counselor education—and should probably continue to be so. We are today not nearly so well prepared in either methods or materials to help the unemployed older worker in vocational counseling as we are to help the college-bound high school senior. Because within-group differences in clients may be greater than between-group differences among those from different populations (e.g., the high school senior, the culturally disadvantaged, the older worker) does not mean that between-group differences are nonexistent. Assuming all counselors are clear on the goals, objectives, and basic methodology of guidance, we should expect to find wide variations in specific methods and materials helpful in guidance of specific individuals. For example, it seems to me we can never hope to attain the goal of guidance for all if we persist in the almost blind worship of the magical power of the one-to-one relationship represented by what goes on in a counselor's office. Perhaps the most effective guidance we could provide for certain individuals demands a set of methods and materials that include no semblance of the one-to-one counseling relationship as we now know it. Attaining the promise of guidance for all demands that we be both willing and able to experiment with a wide variety of guidance methods and procedures—some of which have not yet been even conceived, let alone tried and tested for effectiveness.

Fifth, the continuing shortages of qualified professional counselors demand that we be willing to think creatively and productively with respect to levels of preparation for those who work in the guidance field. The tremendous demands currently being made of our field make it mandatory that we continue to raise our standards for professional preparation and that we take a multi-level approach to standards for professional counselors. These same demands make it simultaneously apparent that we seek to develop concepts and occupational descriptions for support personnel in the guidance field.

The basic strategy for change being proposed here is one of seeking to protect and increase preparation standards for professional counselors through the establishment and operations of an occupational classification system built on a kinds and levels framework for the guidance and counseling movement. There are too many settings calling for guidance services at the present time for us to insist that positions be filled only by counselors who have met the APGA goal of a minimum of two years of graduate education in our field. These positions will be filled with or without our cooperation. If systems can be established that include the presence of various kinds of guidance support personnel working under the direction and supervision of professionally educated counselors, we can protect and improve our standards of counselor preparation and, more impoitant, be assured that true guidance services are being provided. If we do not now quickly move in this direction, many thousands of individuals will be subjected to activities labeled as "guidance and counseling" which, in fact, are not, and progress towards attainment of the goal of guidance for all will be drastically reduced.

What is Ahead for APGA?

As the final theme concerned with attaining the promise of guidance for all, I would now like to turn to the question, "What is Ahead for APGA ?" It should be obvious from discussion of the preceding two themes that I feel APGA should devote serious attention to meeting each of the challenges posed by their discussion. In approaching this theme, then, I am not so much concerned about further discussion of goals as I am with ways of accomplishing our objectives through professional association activities. My feelings are my own and are not intended to reflect the thinking of the APGA Executive Committee, Executive Council, or Senate.

There are, in my opinion, only two basic reasons why any individual should choose to belong to APGA. These are : (a) in order to enhance his own professional growth and competence; and (b) in order to help support the guidance and counseling movement as part of our society. These two reasons for affiliating with APGA underlie all that I wish to say here. So far as I am concerned, the APGA Membership Committee and its divisional and state affiliates should devote major attention to providing information to members and prospective members that will allow individual counselors to view themselves and APGA in light of these two basic purposes. I have a strong feeling that the majority of practicing counselors—i.e., those who do *not* belong to APGA—have not rejected APGA so much as they have never had a real opportunity for making choices with respect to membership. Likewise, I am convinced that many of our current members would find it difficult to justify in specific fashion why they continue to pay their dues. It seems odd to me that a *guidance* association should support *recruitment* campaigns in order to secure new members. Why can't we use a guidance approach?

The first and foremost function of APGA must be to speak for the guidance and counseling movement as part of society. It is becoming increasingly clear that counselors in various settings and performing a variety of functions with different levels of effectiveness are bound together by common concerns, common goals and objectives, and common problems that must become the concerns, goals, and problems of the American Personnel and Guidance Association. There is, for example, no practicing professional counselor in the United States who could be said to be unaffected by the CAUSE I and CAUSE II programs operated under auspices of the U.S. Department of Labor in the summers of 1964 and 1965. Similarly, legislation creating counseling positions and current attempts to fill such positions in widely varying work settings hold action implications for the entire guidance movement and for many thousands of practicing counselors from a wide variety of work settings employed in the United States. For example, the school counselor can no longer—if, indeed, he ever could—legitimately contend that what happens to counseling in the public employment service or in vocational rehabilitation is none of his concern. The same could be said for counselors in any other setting.

Perhaps the strongest set of reasons for stressing the need for unity represented by APGA lies in the continuing guidance needs of persons in this society discussed earlier. The relatively small contribution made by any single counselor in any single setting towards helping individuals lead more satisfying and productive lives is becoming increasingly obvious. Counselors who are concerned about clients must surely realize that the counseling help they are able to extend to many clients will be but a small part of the total guidance help that a client can expect to receive from a community of counselors at various times in his life. A professional concern for clients should, by itself, be sufficient reason for affiliation with and support of APGA.

When such concern for clients is added to concerns over common professional terminology, standards and content of counselor education, patterns of occupational classifications of counselors, ethical standards, the concern of the guidance movement for human rights, and an ever increasing amount of federal legislation calling for the establishment and operation of programs of guidance and counseling services, the need for solid professional unity among all who deserve the title "counselor" seems very clear.

APGA does represent the guidance and counseling movement in our society. There are two operational differences between practicing counselors who belong as opposed to those who do not belong to APGA: (a) those who belong have something to say through their votes and expressed opinions about what the guidance movement says to society while those who fail to belong do not; and (b) those who belong have, through their financial, professional, and personal efforts, given a voice to the guidance movement in our society while those who fail to belong continue to ignore their professional responsibilities for providing this voice and determining what it will say.

The prime benefits to individual APGA members, then, lie in actions that APGA takes in representing the guidance and counseling movement in our society. To be sure, individual members can and do grow professionally through such APGA activities as committee work, convention attendance, and the reading of APGA professional publications. But, as one big, national group, it seems clear to me that these individual growth benefits are secondary in importance to the benefits gained from having a strong, national voice in society.

This paper has repeatedly emphasized commonalities that exist among professional counselors. It has also emphasized that differences among counselors from different work settings and performing different specialized guidance functions co-exist with all of the commonalities that bind counselors together in one occupational classification system. To speak in a clear and firm voice with respect to concerns, goals, and problems unique to a particular work setting or a particular guidance function is as important as to emphasize commonalities. This is why the current eight APGA Divisions—five of them setting-oriented and three function-oriented—exist. To speak only in terms of concerns common to all counselors would leave us silent on crucial issues affecting probabilities of professional success existing among counselors in particular settings and/or performing particular functions. Those who want to devote their entire energies to providing counselor perspective regardless of work setting or job functions run the risk of becoming operationally ineffective in any work setting or in performing any job function.

If we *claim* our rights as a part of society through APGA, we must also *earn* those rights through the proven effectiveness of guidance services represented in our eight divisions. Any APGA division could exist to some extent (although not well) without APGA, but APGA can never exist without its divisions, for it is from the application of guidance in particular work settings and with respect to particular guidance functions that the bona fide claims of APGA find their basis for existence. If APGA represents guidance as a set of beliefs we hold, the divisions of APGA must surely represent guidance as a set of specific competencies we possess and professional activities in which we engage.

Some have said that too many APGA divisions exist at present. In my opinion, quite the opposite is true. I believe APGA should seek to encourage the formation of still more divisions. Others have said that we should settle on a divisional organizational structure which is either setting- or function-oriented but not struggle with a combination of both. I believe, as new divisions are added, we should give equal priority to those oriented around setting and those oriented around function. Both are needed if this movement is to help attain the promise of guidance for all. Sometimes divisions themselves change their basic reasons for existence as is true of ACES which, with its new constitution, has now changed from a setting-oriented to a function-oriented division. If certain members of ACES choose to retain a setting orientation, they can do simply by establishing yet another APGA division.

The individual APGA member has more to gain in terms of personal professional growth through the state branches, state divisions, and local chapters of APGA than through the parent organization. It is through participation in activities of such local and state groups that most of our individual members gain prime operational identification with the profession and individual insights that help them perform more effectively in their work setting. In the long run, the strength of the APGA can be no greater than the cumulative professional voices of its individual members. Now that APGA state branches have been established in over 40 states, it is time that our major attention be directed towards encouraging still smaller parts of these state branches and to helping each of these smaller parts of APGA function effectively. If this can be accomplished, we will have not only optimal provisions for assisting in the professional development of individual members, but also a logical and orderly means by which communication can be established and maintained between individual APGA members and APGA as a single national organization. Such close communication is essential for the identification of problems, for making local, state, and national decisions, and for implementing the decisions reached at each level.

Summary

This presentation began with a title that referred to the goal of attaining the promise of guidance for all. In the first of its three themes, I attempted to raise certain questions regarding desirability of this goal through considering individuals guidance may be asked to serve. I concluded that, at present, it would be very difficult to pretend that guidance is, in fact, for all. At the same time, I repeated my basic belief in the value of the availability of guidance for all as a long-range goal towards which we should strive. Following this, I outlined five directions for change which I feel should be acted upon by the guidance movement if we are to make positive progress towards attainment of this goal. Finally, I tried to present a picture of the American Personnel and Guidance Association, both as a single, strong, national organization and as a collection of smaller parts, each of which must function effectively if the total APGA is to realize its full potential in helping attain this goal.

At several points in this presentation, I raised issues without resolving them. This is because I don't know how they should be resolved. At other times, I raised issues having only two primary sides and stated that they should be resolved by embracing both sides. When I chose this course of action, I was trying to act on the basis of knowledge, not ignorance. That is, it truly seems to me that many of the problems we face are of a "both-and" rather than an "either-or" variety.

In all of my remarks, I have tried to keep some focus and some perspective on the individual who is the recipient of guidance services.

The Progressive Heritage of the Guidance Movement

Lawrence A. Cremin

It is now almost twenty years since the psychologist, Lawrence K. Frank, first published his intriguing little essay, "The Historian as Thera-pist."[1] In it, Frank pleaded for historians who would serve society much in the fashion of psychoanalysts, clearing away distorted versions of the past so that men would be freed to contend more effectively with the problem of the present.

Reprinted by permission of the author and the publishers from *Guidance in American Education I,* Edward Landy and Paul A. Perry, eds. Cambridge, Massachusetts: Harvard University Press, pp. 11-19. Copyright 1964 by the President and Fellows of Harvard College.

Lawrence A. Cremin, Frederick A. Bernard Professor of Education and Chairman, Department of Social and Philosophical Foundations of Education, Teachers College, Columbia University.

---

[1]The essay is reprinted in Lawrence K. Frank, *Society as the Patient.* New Brunswick: Rutgers University Press, 1948, pp. 298-307.

Frank's proposals, of course, raise all sorts of difficulties for any historian who would take them seriously, notably in their subtle invitation to read the problems of the present into the story of the past. And yet, I would suspect my students and I had something of Frank's "therapeutic" goal in mind as we set out in the early 1950's to write a history of the progressive education movement. We wanted to do away with the cartoons and caricatures that had long dominated pedagogical discussion, and to substitute a clear and accurate account of what progressive education had really meant in the American tradition. Our goal, to be sure, was to discover the facts; but we also wanted to report those facts in such a way as to enable contemporary educators to respond more intelligently to the situations in which they found themselves.

I sketched some of our findings two years ago in a book called *The Transformation of the School*, and would like to use those fingings as a basis for my remarks. Perhaps I might summarize them in seven brief propositions:

First, what Americans refer to as *progressive education* began not in 1919 with the founding of the Progressive Education Association, but rather in the 1890's as the educational phase of the broader progressive movement in American life and thought.

Second, progressive education was not a single movement but rather a congeries of separate—frequently contradictory—movements, each seeking to contend in its own way with the central educational problem of the early twentieth century: how to adapt the popular school system to the needs of a democratic-industrial civilization.

Third, these movements enjoyed widespread support from businessmen, labor leaders, rural publicists, clergymen, academics, and social workers; they were not dreamed up and put across by a conspiracy of professional educators.

Fourth, these movements influenced all levels of education, public as well as private, rural as well as urban, southern as well as northern, western as well as eastern.

Fifth, John Dewey was the hero of the progressive education movement, not because he created it singlehandedly, but rather because he saw it whole; he was able to weave the *social reformism* of the urban settlement workers, the *individualism* of the Rousseauan pedagogues, and the *scientism* of the university psychologists into a reasonably consistent view of education. Seen in this light, the genius of *The School and Society*, the first great manifesto of the movement, and of *Democracy and Education,* its most comprehensive theoretical statement, resides less in their complete originality than in their synthetic character.

Sixth, the rise and fall of the movement was a political phenomenon comprehensible in political terms; progressive education collapsed as an organized movement in the 1950's partly because of internal dissension and partly because the political coalition supporting it in the schools dissolved.

Seventh, although the organized movement is dead, the ideas and ideals of the progressive era retain a distinctive relevance for our own time; but they need searching reappraisal and substantial restatement to render them intellectually tenable and politically viable.

II

Needless to say, the effects of the progressive revolution I have described here are everywhere with us: in the architecture of schools, in the arrangement of classrooms, in the programs of students, and in the attitudes of teachers. Nowhere are the effects more apparent, however, than in the work of the guidance counselor. (Beyond any other individual in today's education system, he incarnates the aims and ideals of progressivism. He is the most characteristic child of the progressive movement, and as such is heir to all of its vigor and optimism, and all of its diversity and contradiction.)

Consider, for a moment, the legacy of diversity and contradiction. The fact is that each of the principal facts of progressive education is reflected in a particular way in the early development of the guidance movement. The social reformism of the urban settlement workers, for example, is patently involved in the beginnings of vocational counseling during the first years of the present century. One need only recall that the work of Frank Parsons and Meyer Bloomfield emerged as part of the program of the Civic Service House, a Boston settlement. It was Parsons' idea that a Vocation Bureau attached to the settlement could be of substantial assistance to young people, especially those of limited means, in helping them arrive at wise, well-founded occupational choices. And he saw wise, well-founded occupational choices as the foundation of useful and happy lives.[2]

The key to Parsons' ultimate goal, of course, lay in his notion of "the useful and happy life." Parsons, a significant figure in the history of American reform, believed not only that vocational counseling would lead to greater individual fulfillment, but that people suited to their jobs would tend to be active in the creation of a more efficient and humane industrial system. Intelligently practiced, the craft of vocational guidance would serve not only the youngsters who sought counsel, but the cause of social reform as well. Thus did the earliest, and to date the most stubbornly central, thread of the guidance movement connect with the broader progressive program.

In like manner, the effort to individualize education—which had always been the essence of the new pedagogy—was at the heart of what came to be known as "educational guidance." In 1908, the very year Parsons and Bloomfield opened the Vocation Bureau in Boston, a young teacher named Jesse B. Davis organized a program of vocational and moral guidance in the schools of Grand Rapids, Michigan. His efforts included not only job

---

[2]See Parsons' first and only report as Director of the Vocation Bureau, reprinted in John M. Brewer, *History of Vocational Guidance*. New York: Harper, 1942, pp. 303-308. See also Frank Parsons, *Choosing a Vocation*. Boston: Houghton Mifflin, 1909.

counseling, but counseling with respect to courses and extra-curricular activities as well.[3] Six years later, Truman Lee Kelley wrote a Ph.D. dissertation at Teachers College, Columbia University entitled *Educational Guidance,* in which he urged the need for general counseling programs that would aid youngsters in their choice of studies. The concept broadened steadily during the 1920's, especially under the influence of the child guidance clinics pioneered by the National Committee for Mental Hygiene. By 1932, Professor John Brewer of Harvard was advancing a conception of guidance that came close to being synonymous with the whole of education. Pupils, Brewer argued, should be guided in *all* of their life activities; the ultimate goal of guidance was unified, integrated, harmonious personalities.[4]

Finally, the effort to develop a science of education, also at the heart of the progressive movement, was reflected in the spirited interest in tests and measurements that grew up in the United States shortly after the turn of the century. By the time of World War I a variety of intelligence and aptitude tests were already in fairly general use in the schools; and the wartime work of the Army Committee on Classification of Personnel (mainly in developing and administering the Army Alpha and Beta tests) really made testing a household notion throughout the country. Needless to say, the possibility of precise instruments for measuring and predicting achievement proved a boon to counselors, who were ever eager to make their work more scientific; and the tests rapidly became a standard counseling device. Thus the idea developed of the guidance worker as a trained professional, wise in administering and interpreting scientific instruments for the prediction of vocational and educational success.

Now, my effort here has not been to sketch a history of the guidance movement; that has been done elsewhere and well.[5] Rather, I have attempted to document the close and inextricable tie between the guidance movement and the broader progressive movement of which it was part. Both movements have had a heritage of diversity; and both have had a heritage of contradiction. Just as various schools of progressives began to argue among themselves during the 1930's and 1940's over whether teachers ought to "build a new social order" or "develop the whole child' or "apply scientific techniques in the classroom," so did various schools of counselors argue the merits of vocational versus educational guidance, of systematic testing versus non-directive interviewing. One need only follow the long and tedious discussions over what kind of organization should represent guidance workers and what it should be called, to grasp the significance of these differences.

---

[3]Davis describes his program in *Vocational and Moral Guidance.* Boston: Ginn, 1914.

[4]John M. Brewer, *Education as Guidance.* New York: Macmillan, 1932.

[5]The best history to my knowledge is the unpublished doctoral thesis of Ruth E. Barry and Beverly Wolf at Teachers College, Columbia University, entitled "A History of the Guidance-Personnel Movement in Education" (1955).

More important for our purposes, perhaps—and here I'm reminded of Lawrence Frank's plea with which I began—these differences and contradictions continue to affect the practice of guidance today; they are inherent in the very assumptions the counselor brings to his work. Permit me to illustrate with a few questions that might well come up in the day-by-day activities of any high-school counselor. How much social reformism, for example, of the sort implicit in Parsons' notion of vocational guidance, is the counselor going to permit himself in advising minority-group youngsters with respect to vocations from which they have traditionally been excluded? How much does the counselor's commitment to individual fulfillment in such cases ultimately conflict with his commitment to social reform? Or again, to what extent does the commitment to individual fulfillment in counseling lower-class children conflict with the knowledge that middle-class values are generally more appropriate to white-collar or professional occupations?[6] Or again, to what extent does the commitment to a notion of individuality lead the counselor to skepticism concerning scientific test data?[7] Universities, after all, are constantly taking chances on highly motivated youngsters who do poorly on every conceivable predictive measure. Or again, to what extent does a counselor support a personal sense of vocation where the market seems to call for different aptitudes (there's the old saw about Einstein doing poorly in school mathematics), or indeed, where there is little or no market for such a vocation. How much does "realism" about the job market sometimes fly in the face of the deepest meanings of vocation?

One could go on with such questions, but perhaps my point has been made. My concern is not with the dozens of decisions a counselor has to make every day in the very nature of his work. It is rather with the contradictory values and loyalties he brings to his work as heir to a contradictory heritage. Ultimately, it is only as he becomes aware of these contradictions that he can really enter upon the difficult task of resolving them; and it is only as he resolves them that he can eventually overcome the confusions they inevitably generate.

III

One other problem derives from the progressive heritage of the guidance movement: it concerns the need for a searching reappraisal of progressive doctrine to separate those notions that are still tenable from those that are not. In the extent to which progressivism has become the "conventional wisdom" of our time, it is increasingly prone to obsolescence. As John Kenneth Galbraith pointed out some years ago, the ultimate enemy of the

---

[6]Edgar Z. Friedenberg states the problem poignantly in "An Ideology of School Withdrawal," *Commentary*, Vol. XXXV (1963), pp. 492-500.

[7]There is a considerable body of literature on this problem, varying in character all the way from John Hersey's mordant novel, *The Child Buyer* (New York: Knopf, 1960), to Robert L. Thorndike's scholarly treatise, *The Concept of Over and Underachievement* (New York: Teachers College, Columbia University, 1963).

conventional wisdom is not so much ideas as the march of events. The conventional wisdom accommodates itself not to the world it is meant to interpret, but rather to the public's view of that world. And since the public tends to prefer the comfortable and familiar, while the world moves on, the conventional wisdom is ever in danger of obsolescence.

The implications for guidance are profound. It is no news that the movement has entered a period of vigorous expansion, aided in large measure by the federal government's financial assistance and Dr. Conant's moral assistance. Yet at this very time, some of the most fundamental assumptions of the movement, insofar as they derive from the progressive tradition, stand in need of drastic reformulation. Put another way, contemporary guidance theory is shot through with terms and concepts handed down from the progressive era that are now anachronistic in their meanings. Let me cite three by way of example.

First, the concept of *education*. As I read the contemporary guidance literature—and I admit to oversimplifying here to make my point—I come away with the notion that the counselor is dealing with a changing individual who is growing up in a changing world that has a changing occupational structure. Yet in all of this, the agencies of education somehow remain constant. The point, of course, is that this is simply not true. The structure of education is changing more rapidly in our time than at any other in history; witness the rapid rise of public social and recreational facilities, of quasi-public social service organizations, of teaching programs in business and industry, and most important, perhaps, of the mass media of communication, notably television.[8] All of these institutions educate, and as the counselor considers the range of educational possibilities open to his clients, he must bear them all in mind.[9] Few of these institutions existed during the formative period of progressivism, and hence the progressives thought almost exclusively in terms of an expanding *school*. To do so today is plainly anachronistic. An exciting case in point, by the way, is New York's Higher Horizon's program, in which counselors have turned to all of the city's educational resources—museums, parks, concert halls, theatres, libraries, zoos, and aquaria—in their effort to raise the intellectual sights of slum children.

A second progressive holdover I find in the guidance literature is a concept of *community* that almost always implies locality. Now, the commu-

---

[8]There is a good deal of literature on this subject, but it is scattered through journals in a dozen different fields. A useful synthesis is Margaret Mead, "Thinking Ahead: Why Is Education Obsolete" *Harvard Business Review,* Vol. XXXVI (November-December, 1958), pp. 23-30.

[9]The counselor must also bear in mind the continuing educational influence of these institutions. Note, for example, Harris Dienstfrey's incisive remarks on the vocational models offered youngsters by such television dramas as "The Defenders," "The Nurses," "Ben Casey," "Naked City," and others, in "Doctors, Lawyers & Other TV Heroes," *Commentary,* Vol. XXXV (1963), pp. 519-524. Note also the magnificent Jules Feiffer cartoon in *The New Republic* for May 18, 1963, which says more about the educational impact of television than many a learned essay.

nity in turn-of-the-century America *was* the locality, and the early progressives—except for the more far-sighted among them—had every right to assume that most people would spend their adult lives in the communities into which they were born. Indeed, many progressives, especially rural publicists concerned with the flight of farm youngsters to the city, took this goal as not only probable but eminently desirable. Much of what we know about contemporary America indicates that this is no longer so. Consider a passage from a recent report of the United States Census Bureau:

> About 35.5 million, or 20.0 percent, of the 177.4 million persons 1 year old and over who were living in the United States in March 1961 had moved at least once since March 1960. Although this overall mobility rate has reflected to some slight extent some of the postwar changes in business conditions, it has remained relatively stable in the 14 successive surveys conducted since 1948. . . .
> Of the 35.5 million persons 1 year old and over who were living in a different house in March 1961 from that in 1960, about 24.3 million, or 13.7 percent of the total population 1 year old and over, had moved within the same county; 5.5 million, or 3.1 percent had moved between counties in the same State; and 5.8 million, or 3.2 percent, had moved between States. In addition to these persons who moved within the United States, about 0.6 percent of the 1961 population had been living abroad in 1960. . . .[10]

Given these statistics, it is simply erroneous to assume that most graduates of a local high school are going to remain in the local community for the rest of their lives, and hence ought to be trained with reference to the occupational structure of that community. Today, the counselor must think in terms of a national—indeed, international—community if young men and women are to be prepared realistically for the world in which they will undoubtedly live.

A third anachronism from the progressive era that suffuses the literature of guidance is a particular notion of *vocation*. Based on the situation that prevailed in the first years of the present century, too many counselors have continued to assume that choice of occupation plays *the* determinative role in the development of adult character. Yet, as I read the sociology of occupations today, we seem to be moving into a period in which, paradoxically, occupation will probably play an ever more central role in the lives of those who enter the professions, but a less and less central role for those who enter the trades—witness the recent victory of the New York electricians' union in winning a five-hour basic work day.[11] If this be the case, the

---

[10]*Current Population Reports: Population Characteristics*, Series P-20, No. 118, August 9, 1962, p. 1. There are no accurate statistics on the mobility of the American population at the turn of the century; the earliest Census Bureau statistics refer to the period between 1935 and 1940.

[11]A useful summary of recent work on the sociology of occupations is Everett Cherrington Hughes, "The Study of Occupations" in Robert K. Merton, Leonard Broom, and Leonard S. Cottrell, Jr., eds., *Sociology Today*. New York: Basic Books, 1959, pp. 442-458.

counselor will have to develop a much broader concept of vocational choice, one concerned with total life-style rather than merely with occupation. Here, I find myself much in agreement with the arguments of my colleague Edward Joseph Shoben, Jr. in a recent essay in the *Harvard Educational Review*.[12] Dr. Shoben proposes that the counselor assist the youngster not merely in choosing a vocation, but in the whole process of choosing the personal models he takes for himself, or, if we use the Socratic terminology, in the process of learning to live the examined life. Incidentally, I might add that if the counselor is to play this role, he will have to prepare himself for it with a good deal more humanistic study than is currently present in most guidance curricula.

In connection with Dr. Shoben's proposal, I might also remark on one other educational change of extraordinary significance: the contemporary curriculum reform movement. You are all no doubt aware of the excitement generated by recent curriculum revision in mathematics and the natural sciences; and you are no doubt equally aware of the effort to extend this revision into the social sciences and humanities. This is not the place to debate the merits of the new reforms; suffice it to say they have produced some striking results that are patently here to stay. But they have also raised some thorny problems, one of which is a growing specialization, and consequent fragmentation, in the curriculum. Now, it may be that such specialization is unavoidable, given the nature and rapid expansion of knowledge in our time; I for one have not yet made up my mind on the matter. But I do know that as specialization moves down into the elementary and secondary schools, the role Dr. Shoben asks the counselor to play becomes all the more important. Ultimately, the counselor may end up as one of the few professionals primarily responsible for seeing the child's education whole.

One final comment, really in the nature of a postscript. Insofar as guidance is the child of the progressive movement, it is also heir to the characteristic vigor and optimism—some would say utopianism—of that movement. And this, too, has raised problems. After all, the counselor has dedicated his life to taking some of the waste, the accident, and the needless inefficiency out of the difficult business of becoming an adult. Yet however much he achieves his goal, he is ever doomed to a measure of failure. As Morris R. Cohen once remarked in a critique of John Dewey's perennial optimism: "So long as human beings lack omniscience they will lack omnipotence and will therefore have to face insuperable difficulties and evils."[13] The failure to recognize this, I would suspect, is the original sin of pride.

---

[12]Edward Joseph Shoben, Jr., "Guidance: Remedial Function or Social Reconstruction?" *Harvard Educational Review*, Vol. XXXII (1961-62), pp. 430-443.

[13]Morris R. Cohen, *Studies in Philosophy and Science.* New York: Holt, 1949, p. 169.

Some years ago, Ruth Barry and Beverly Wolf observed the following about the literature they had read in connection with their history of the guidance movement:

> The guidance and personnel literature indicates that personnel workers are also unrealistic about their own work. Personnel work has had its successes and presumably its failures, but the literature would lead a reader to believe that no program or no aspect of a program had ever failed. Mathematically, the odds against 100 per cent success in personnel work are infinite; yet, apparently no one ever fails in personnel work. Writers admit that a guidance program could be better, but never was it unsuccessful. . . . By refusing to recognize failure, personnel work creates a myth, an impossible ideal, a stereotype, which does not fool the public, but may mislead individual workers in the field. By reinforcing stereotypes, personnel work tacitly promises that it can be all things to all people and that each personnel worker can be everything to each individual student.[14]

I'm afraid I, too, come away with much the same impression. Somehow the guidance literature seems to promise that with more money, more personnel, and more effort, counselors could usher in some sort of utopia. I think counselors would do themselves and the public a great deal more good if they simply promised that they would try to make life a bit more planful, a bit more intelligent, and a bit more humane.

---

[14]Ruth E. Barry and Beverly Wolf, *Op Cit.*, p. 441.

Interferences to Guidance Program Development

Herman J. Peters

Why do guidance programs fail? Why are guidance programs ineffective? Comparatively, much has been written about the developmental factors necessary in organizing and administering a guidance program. Little has been written on interferences to guidance program development.[1] If one looks at the usually mentioned deterrents, he will find that, at times, those factors which promote guidance functions in one place may be factors which inhibit guidance program development in another setting. Perhaps this is due to the difficulty in analyzing interfering factors. However, one must be alert to truly basic interferences in order to take action to minimize

Reprinted by permission of the author and *Personnel and Guidance Journal*, XLII, No. 2 (October, 1963), 119-124.

Herman J. Peters, Professor of Education, the Ohio State University, Columbus.

[1]Guidance program development and guidance programming will be used interchangeably throughout this paper. Either terminology implies a dynamic on-goingness of process rather than a series of static discrete, albeit related, events.

their influence on effective guidance program development and management.

Usually "lack of" may be the general rubric for categorizing deterrents
to effective guidance program development. Lack of leadership, lack of
facilities, and lack of money are representative of these blocks. However,
there are more serious impeding interferences which are the basic blocks;
"lack of" may be a rationalization for a basic discrepancy between philosophy and practice. There is more to interference in guidance programming
than a differential between what is needed in the way of staff, facilities, and
materials, and what is on hand. Lack of staff, facilities, materials and
money are symptoms rather than causes. Too often there is quick retreat to
a listing of these factors as the basic deterrents. These merely reflect much
deeper roadblocks to effective guidance programming.

The importance of guidance programming must not be misconstrued as
a plea for rigorous uniformity or singularity of structural design. It may be
argued that adequate structure facilitates function. However, it may also be
shown that unilateral program design may stifle program growth because of
a dominant or rigid one-type program. Then, too, some "leaders" take refuge
in diversity as a pseudo-democratic approach to let each go his unique way
to the fullest. This is as deadly as autocracy. Thus, here and throughout
this paper in each factor analyzed, there is always need for the reader to be
cognizant of the need for an exquisite balance in the implementation of a
factor—neither emphasizing one extreme nor the other. What are some basic
interferences to guidance program development and management?

Theory Aversion

One basic interference to guidance program development and management is theory aversion. Guidance workers and school counselors, in particular, have given little thought to guidance theory. Sensitive to helping others,
loaded with endless clerical duties, human "brush-fire" extinguishers deluxe,
training-technique oriented, the school counselor has had little time to
reflect on the "why" of what he is doing. However, if sound theory precedes
sound practice, the conceptualization of the guidance function becomes the
imperative. A consideration of the nature of the pristine theory of the
guidance function will serve the counselor well in his work with his
superiors, peers, and counselees. He will know why he moves in the
direction that he does.

Stroup [10] indicates that, in the past, the student personnel worker has
been relatively unconcerned and inactive in theory and concept formulation.
He cites three reasons for this state. First, the personnel function operates in
the practical day-to-day concerns. The pre-requisite time for theory development and conceptualization seems to be lacking. Rather, the custodial
function had taken priority in the attention of personnel workers. Guidance
work is essentially an applied field of work gaining strength from a variety
of disciplines. Guidance workers' interest in persons tends to relegate to the
background those activities associated with theory development. He goes on

to point out a number of possible avenues for theory development for the guidance program. These are really directional signs. Each proposal would necessitate considerable analysis.

The first type of theory looks to the social context of guidance for meaning. The second type, ontological theory, emphasizes the reality testing approach. The third, mystic theory, is based on intuitive descriptions, hunches, and imaginative possibilities. His fourth, anthropologic theory, is concerned with a focus on man as the center of guidance conceptualization. The fifth, historical theory, is concerned with justification in what has happened.

The proper place of theory in guidance programming must be considered. Conceptualization is difficult. However, the aversion to theory has the resultant effect of continuing guidance as a diffuse unmanageable amorphous set of functions. This weakens the possibility for communicating to school staff and patrons the purposes inherent in the guidance point of view. Stroup's ideas may give us a start in the proper direction.

Neglect of Differential Premises

Differential premises result from goals attuned to different kinds of pupil populations. Differential premises in guidance programming may be in order. Resultant from differential premises, variations in guidance programs would be expected. In a recent study of guidance in Ohio secondary schools, it was noted that:

> It seems necessary that a state-wide representative conference should be held to clarify the nature and purpose of guidance in the twentieth century. This does not mean that there should be one philosophy or one point of view. Better, it should be recognized that there are a number of points of view toward guidance. It is necessary for the procedures, techniques, and tools to be consonant with the objectives of the guidance program. No one statement seems to be representative of a group or a section or region of the State. There are many avenues for guidance and of these one must be selected for the individual school [6. p. 3].

Inconsistencies in guidance programs seemed to result, in part, from discrepancies between stated program premises and program practices. Interference to guidance programming results from this discrepancy. The unrelatedness of purpose and technique can cause frustration and loss of interest by the school staff.

Therefore, it becomes necessary that organizers and developers of school guidance programs carefully decide on their basic premise, albeit not an exclusive one, for school programming. Following this decision, each staff should determine what specific guidance procedures are needed for the implementation of this selected premise. Further, each staff should determine what general guidance procedures should be emphasized to implement the particular premises chosen. This is in contrast to the oft-imitated plan of using a one-type published standard for developing a particular guidance program. If a school merely copies a program, there will have to be changes almost immediately if the program is to be congruent with pupil needs in that school. Prior care of defining premises and subsequent-follow-through with functions flowing out of the premises should lead to a guidance program in greater harmony with pupil needs. The urgency of a clearly stated set of premises for guidance programming is illustrated in the following brief from a particular guidance project. Although reported for a delinquency project, it seems to indicate that the school staff ought to consider its actual concern in terms of services to meet that concern.

> Since the school appears to be more concerned about these disturbed children than anyone else, the question might be raised whether the school should in the future, offer a clinical or therapeutic service. This is the question that should be examined very critically. These children are problems to the school, but they are not problems of the school. In physical illnesses the school offers nothing beyond first aid and turns the responsibility for "major surgery" over to the family and the community. The same should probably apply to mental and emotional illnesses [*4, pp. 158-159*].

Guidance Unawareness

Public unawareness of the guidance program and its purposes is a cause for interference to its development. For too long, guidance workers have assumed that their publics understand the nature and purposes of the guidance function. Recent meetings with industrial and businessmen, parents, and antagonists of guidance programs indicate that there is a long road ahead for assisting these "taxpayers" to become aware of the meaning and nature of professional guidance. In a recent statewide study of guidance in Ohio [*6*] it was discovered that the two least favored groups in terms of receiving information about the guidance program were school boards and the community. This weakness was also reported by Pruett in a study of Indiana city public secondary schools [*8*].

Awareness means more than periodic brochures, television programs, or PTA meetings on guidance. It means a continuous well-organized plan of information dissemination and opportunity for patron reaction. It should be kept in mind that too often the public relations approaches indicate, albeit unintentionally, that this is the best guidance program that our school can develop. What really should be indicated is that this is the best program under these circumstances. Then it should be indicated what constitutes possibilities for improvements.

Failure to Consider Value Differentials of Staff

Interference to guidance programming may come from differences in basic values held by school counselors and their principals. This value differential entwined with other job differences offers a subtle complexity which could lead to program interference.

In a study of counselor-principal preferences based on the Edwards Preference Scale, statistically significant differences were found in several preference areas. Counselors adhered to actions based on preferences for exhibition, affiliation, and intraception. Principals scored high on manifest needs in the areas of deference, order, aggression, achievement, and endurance.

These differences imply variations in direction of one's behavior in the accomplishment of his duties. The dimensions and their impact need to be researched. Perhaps the counselor becomes a person different from teacher and administrator. The discovery of these differences will alert each to the necessity of a consideration of them when determining the direction of guidance programming. The subtleties of communication may be more properly located in value differentials than in variations in professional terminology [5].

Legitimate Disorder Misinterpreted

Weber stated ". . . orientation to the validity of an order means more than the mere existence of a uniformity of social action determined by custom and self-interest." Too often in large school systems, custom and self-interest are rationalizations for omission of much needed leadership in guidance programming. The director of guidance leans on the crutches of "building autonomy," "rights of principals," and "cultural needs in a particular school." He leans on these for fear, so he says, of upsetting the local domain of the principal and staff. The director becomes a sort of "reconnaissance man," "information specialist on guidance for the superintendent," and a human placebo for disgruntled counselors pleading for active leadership. Thus, this situation becomes one of the major deterrents to effective guidance program development. The director of guidance must give continuing active professional guidance leadership.

The heading of "Legitimate Disorder" does not imply disobedience or evasion. It does mean that there are several patterns of order in guidance programming. To be sure, the school counselor owes obedience to his building principal. However, if he is to be professionally competent he needs the leadership from and professional obedience to the guidance director. This duality of allegiance may cause momentary problems in school. These may be worked out with the guidance director. He is an official staff member of the superintendent's office. The misunderstandings that may arise from time to time because of a director's properly aggressive leadership are of far less risk than a laissez-faire or anarchistic approach under a pseudo-democratic guise.

Weber states there are three pure types of legislative authority. These authorities are based on rational grounds, traditional grounds, and charismatic grounds. The traditional grounds of building autonomy must be blended with the rational grounds of professional guidance leadership. Beyond the scope of this paper is a full discussion of the myth of complete principal autonomy, similar to the myth of student government. Each is a qualified privilege, not an absolute one. The directors of guidance need to take visibly more active leadership in promoting guidance in the schools for which they *are* responsible *[11]*.

Threat of Program Change

One of the characteristics of the guidance function is its amenability to cultural change. The very essence and purpose of being for the guidance function is to act as a stabilizer, as a gyroscope, for the individual in a sea of change. Interference to guidance programming may come from an overt or covert resistance to change on the part of the staff.

The principle that there is a need for a well-designed program may be misinterpreted as a basis for continuing indefinitely that same program. A fundamental principle of guidance programming is that each year an appraisal should be made to determine modifications and changes in guidance activities. Changing conditions will necessitate variance in many aspects of the guidance program. Because implementation of change is often enervating, the staff may take refuge in continuing unchanged that which functioned in the past.

Threat to Personal Security

Thomas proposes that "the human wishes have a great variety of concrete forms but are capable of the following general classifications:

1. The desire for new experience
2. The desire for security
3. The desire for response
4. The desire for recognition"

Interference to guidance programming occurs in some cases because school counselors tend to dislike the desire for new experiences. Because guidance is based on change, the dislike for new experience offers a contradiction for school counselors. "The desire for security is opposed to the desire for new experience. . . . The desire for new experience implies, therefore, motion, change, danger, instability, social responsibility." The counselor likes some change, but this is always in rivalry with his desire for security and a greater certainty of the other two wishes. His understanding of himself in these desires will make for more realistic involvement in the ever-changing guidance scene.

Marginality in Professional Commitment

The concept of marginality in deviant behavior is a contribution of Park and Stonequist. "Its original meaning describes an enduring conflict between broad role commitments associated with incompatible collective memberships" *[7, p. 709]*. The broad role commitment and security therein of a counselor to his former teaching role often interferes with his newer dedication to counseling. This conflict is furthered by the part-time educational preparation approach to guidance work of the counselor. He never really leaves the teaching role to be completely immersed in the guidance function. The National Defense Education Act Academic Year Institute concept has served as a means for a clean break between one's teaching role and his new commitment to counseling. This should not be interpreted to mean that the school counselor should not arise out of the teaching ranks. What is meant is that he needs to be in guidance fulltime in his preparation study so as not to see it as a marginal activity. Marginality by definition implies another central purpose. If guidance duties are marginal in prospect, then there is apt to be interference to guidance programming in the daily action of one's guidance duties.

Lack of Depth in Counseling

Despite other interferences, the school counselor attempts to live his guidance commitment, once this is made. Outwardly he is very much ego-involved. The trouble arises, conscience-wise, when he has to decide whether he will counsel in depth or superficially. Too often, school counselors handle the educational programming of pupils in a mechanistic manner. Many times these educational concerns of pupils are opportunities for developmental counseling. Many counselors handle these educational concerns on a superficial level because of unwillingness, through fear and uneasiness, to involve themselves in a more meaningful interview situation. This is not to imply that the counselor should go beyond his competencies. However, it does seem to be an interference to guidance programming when a counselor does not activate a spark for better development of a pupil. This requires the counselor's artistry and understanding of the full significance of what can take place in the true counseling session as contrasted to a conference on one's time schedule.

Inattention to the Changing Adolescent

The ever-changing manner of adolescents gives rise to a subtle interference to guidance programming—the assumption that today's adolescents are no different than in yesteryear. A continuing study of adolescents, locally and regionally, is necessary if a guidance program is going to be useful to its customers [3]. Coupled with the general cultural change, changes in adolescent behavior present a real challenge for effective guidance programming. Coleman's analysis of social climates in high schools emphasizes the need for continuing research on adolescents [2]. The nature of the contemporary adolescent is a key factor in guidance program development.

Summary

The interferences to guidance programming given in this paper need to be studied by each staff as it examines its progress in guidance program development and management. Approximately 20 years ago, guidance workers were concerned with the reasons for guidance program failure. Representative of this concern at that time were reports by Chisholm [1] and Strang [9]. Each indicated a "lack of" basis for guidance program difficulty. This paper has attempted to alert the reader to more basic interferences to effective guidance programming. Common to both eras is Chisholm's counsel that,

> One final conclusion concerning the present investigation is worthy of emphasis. A knowledge of the handicaps that are standing in the way for a better program of secondary education should form the foundation for a constructive effort to provide youth adequate educational experiences. This above all: the handicaps to guidance should be looked upon merely as stumbling blocks standing in the way temporarily rather than as legitimate excuses that relieve the schools of their inherent responsibility [1, p. 31].

REFERENCES

1. Chisholm, Leslie L. Major handicaps interfering with guidance. *Sch. Rev.*, January 1946, *54*, 24-31.
2. Coleman, James S. *Social climates in high schools.* Washington, D.C.: U.S. GPO, 1961.
3. Gallup, George, & Hill, Evan. "Youth" the cool generation. *The Saturday Evening Post, 234*, (51), 63–80.
4. Kvaraceus, William C., Director. *Delinquent behavior.* Washington: National Education Association, Juvenile Delinquency Project, 1959.
5. Meek, Harry R. A comparison of manifest needs of secondary school counselors and principals. Unpublished master's thesis, The Ohio State Univ., 1961.
6. Peters, Herman J., et al. *Guidance in Ohio.* Columbus: Heer Printing Company, 1961.
7. Pitts, Jesse R. "Introduction," in Talcott Parsons, *et al., Theories of society.* New York: The Free Press of Glencoe, 1961.
8. Pruett, Rolla F. *Organization and administration of the guidance program in the city public secondary schools of Indiana, 1959–60.* Indianapolis: Department of Public Instruction, December 1961, 6, (6).
9. Strang, Ruth. Why guidance programs fail and succeed. *Educ. Dig.*, May 1940, *5*, 9–11.
10. Stroup, Herbert. Theoretical constructs in student personnel work. *J. higher Educ.*, June 1957, *28* (6), 319-326.
11. Weber, Max. Legitimate order and types of authority, in Talcott Parsons, *et al., Theories of society.* New York: The Free Press of Glencoe, 1961.

A Focus for Public School Guidance Programs: A Model and Proposal

Merville C. Shaw

John K. Tuel

This article represents an attempt to provide an adequate theoretical
basis for the development of guidance programs. Three important questions essential to any planning of guidance programs are discussed: (1)
scope of responsibility, (2) developmental timing, and (3) focus of
guidance activity. A model is proposed in an attempt to conceptualize
the relationship between these three important questions of emphasis.
The basic problem of the purpose of guidance programs is discussed, and
a proposal relevant to the model and the assumed purposes is made. The
proposed objective focuses on the environment of the learner, in an effort
to prepare him to actively and effectively appropriate and apply new
knowledge and skills. The implications that such an objective has for the
role of the guidance specialist, as well as for education in general, are
discussed.

Reprinted by permission of the authors and *Personnel and Guidance Journal,*
XLIV, No. 8 (April, 1966), 824-830.
Merville C. Shaw and John K. Tuel, Chico State College, Chico, California.

The theoretical literature dealing with the problem of appropriate goals for guidance services and the means of *effectively* implementing these goals reveals a state of active and healthy controversy. Three interrelated and essentially unresolved dilemmas are inherent in most such discussions of the guidance function. The *first* is, what will be the scope of responsibility envisioned by the program? Will the guidance program actively attempt to reach and help all of the children in the system, or only a part? A *second* question is one of timing. At what point in a child's personal development will guidance efforts be introduced? The *third* question is one of focus. Will the guidance efforts be aimed directly at the individual, or will such services be rendered indirectly through dealing primarily with the significant people in this environment?

Guidance for Whom?

The problem of whether guidance services are intended only for a small (and presumably deviant) segment of the population, or whether they are for the benefit of all or nearly all of the student population is, in the last analysis, a value judgment. Certainly a case can be made for dealing with almost any segment of the population, but the strongest position would seem to be that a guidance worker's services should be for all children. Ethical and psychological considerations combine to make this the most compelling of the available choices. From the ethical point of view it can hardly be argued that guidance services are only for a restricted number of children in the schools. Psychologically, it is generally agreed that all children, in the normal course of development, need assistance in learning how to deal effectively with learning problems, interpersonal and intrapersonal problems, and in making appropriate decisions. There does appear to be a consensus among those who have expressed written opinions on this problem that guidance services should be rendered to the larger rather than the smaller segment of the student population.

Guidance When?

Theoretical discussions bearing on the question of when guidance services should intervene in a child's educational career have been overridden by the weight of actuality. Historically, guidance services were introduced at the secondary school level and have largely continued to receive emphasis at that level. It has been suggested that preventive intervention at an earlier date might reduce problems at higher academic levels, but in actual practice guidance at the elementary school level appears to deal mainly with already existing problems. The importance of guidance at the elementary school level was further undercut by the original National Defense Education Act, which limited federal support of guidance to the secondary level. The recent change in this law broadening such support to include the elementary years may well provide the stimulus for more active investigation of the effectiveness of guidance services during the earliest school years. In the meantime, decisions related to where guidance emphasis should be placed appear to be dictated more by history than by the potential effectiveness of such services.

Guidance How?

If it is a consensus, as it seems to be, that guidance services are intended for all children, a logical question might be, "How can such services be rendered effectively? Under current conditions, the direct approach to individual students is hardly possible. The 300 to one counselor ratio recommended by Conant (1959) is not a reality in any but a few schools, and even if it were the rule rather than the exception, to what extent could the school guidance specialist effectively offer his services to the total student body on an individual basis? It is necessary to recognize that students' lives are seldom altered by relatively brief individual contacts with even the most skillful of guidance specialists. This being the case, different ways to reach students must be found.

A Model

Part of the current confusion appears to stem from the lack of an adequate model that would assist in conceptualizing the various options open to guidance workers. The accompanying diagram illustrates how six procedural options (not mutually exclusive) may be derived from the various possible answers to those three questions. Because of the interdependence of the scope and timing questions already noted above, it is possible to resolve the three questions in two dimensions: "Time Phase" and "Level of Focus." The vertical dimension, Level of Focus, expresses the fact that attention may be focused on either of two levels: (1) the extra-personal or environmental level (indirect focus) and (2) the intra-personal level (direct focus). With direct focus, guidance activities concentrate on the individual child, whether it be to train him for mental health or to treat his incipient or already developed pathology. As with medicine, this has been the apsect traditionally emphasized in guidance programs. Conversely, with indirect focus, individual therapeutic contact with the child receives less emphasis and, in its stead, efforts are put forth to improve his external environment, primarily by working through the persons who help to determine it, for example, his parents and teachers.

The horizontal dimension of the diagram corresponds to the time phase of personality development. Guidance efforts may be directed toward (a) general prevention, (b) selective prevention, or (c) diagnosis and remediation. In general prevention, the program is aimed at the entire population and must, in terms of content, have a general and comprehensive emphasis. Selective prevention implies early identification and special treatment of those individuals predicted, according to specified criteria (for example, tests, teachers' observations), to have a high probability of developing pathology (Bower, 1958). Diagnosis and remediation is the usual post-facto

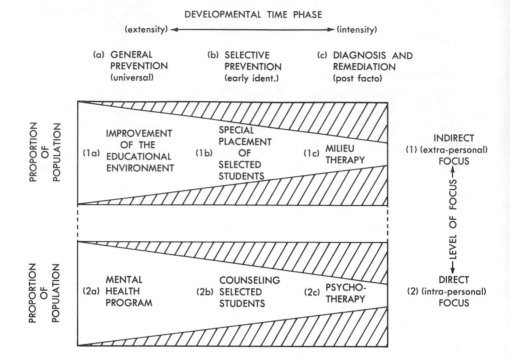

Figure 1. Procedural options for guidance programs—a model comprising three dimensions: (1) *developmental time phase* at which intervention is initiated, (2) *proportion of population* treated, and (3) *level of focus* at which treatment is aimed. Shaded areas represent proportions of population *not* reached by a given program.

approach of treating the pathology only after it has developed to a point where it is easily recognizable or can no longer be tolerated.

With indirect focus, general prevention (1a) could concentrate on improvement of the general educational environment. Selective prevention (1b) could involve special placement or milieu therapy of selected students. For example, children so selected could be placed in a special classroom with a particularly understanding teacher, or even in certain cases, in another home with foster parents. Such techniques have been used with potential dropouts and delinquents. Diagnosis and remediation (1c) would include individual milieu therapy. Examples would again include special classroom and home placement, but at a later point in the time phase of the developing pathology.

With direct focus, general prevention (2a) might be accomplished through a mental health program such as that developed by Ojemann (1959). Rather than direct manipulation of the environment, the emphasis of such a program is on training groups of students to understand the causes of behavior and thus improve their self-understanding and interpersonal relations. Selective prevention (2b) at this level is usually attempted through early identification and individual counseling with selected students. Diagnosis and remediation (2c), of course, implies conventional counseling and psychotherapy.

Certain generalizations may be made about the two dimensions and their interrelationships. Obviously, the later the time phase, the more intensive must be the treatment, but the smaller will be the proportion of the total population afforded such treatment. As one moves up the developmental scale, the emphasis of the form of intervention changes from one of breadth to one of depth. It is also a generally accepted principle that the later the time phase of treatment, the more difficult it is to completely eliminate the symptoms and after-effects of the pathology. On the other hand, the earlier the intervention takes place, the less special provision may be made for individual differences.

It is apparent that the relationship between the focus and time phase dimensions is not orthogonal. Thus, the difference between the focus levels appears to be least at the early (preventive) end of the time phase dimensions. The preventive phase would also seem to correlate more highly with indirect focus and the diagnosis and remediation phase with direct focus. To the extent that such correlation obtains, the diagram tends to misrepresent the true relationship of the two dimensions.

A Proposal

Utilization of the model makes it simpler to examine issues relative to the effective implementation of guidance programs and makes clearer the kinds of decisions necessary to the planning of sound programs. There is another issue, however, which has not yet been discussed and which is only implicit in the dimensions dealt with by the model. This is the problem of the purposes or objectives of guidance programs.

The Problem of Purpose

It is in relation to the basic purposes of guidance programs that guidance professionals have shown the greatest laxity. It seems generally true that present programs reflect lack of purpose. Many things are being done; tests are given, group guidance classes conducted, educational objectives are discussed with students, diagnoses are made, and yet, all is not well. Guidance programs are too frequently seen as unrelated to education by both educators and laymen. Guidance workers are over-involved in nonguidance activities (Gibson, 1962), and students do not see the role of the guidance professional as it is seen by the counselor himself (Heilfron, 1960; Roberston, 1958; Barahal & Brammer, 1950). Furthermore, different kinds of educational specialists do not conceptualize the guidance specialist's roles as guidance people themselves conceive of them (Pierson & Grant, 1960; Leton, 1959; Grant, 1955).

In order to intelligently examine what the objectives of guidance services might (or should) be, it is necessary to examine briefly the purposes of education itself. There are three basic general responsibilities of education that most persons would agree on even though there would doubtless still be disagreement about their relative places in the hierarchy of purposes. The first of these purposes is the *transmittal of knowledge and skills.* This purpose encompasses the historic and generally accepted role of education and few, if any, would deny that it occupies a central place in almost any philosophy of education. A second purpose which has gained prominence in more recent times stresses the *preparation of the learner* to actively and effectively appropriate new knowedge and skills. Still a third purpose, closely related to the second, focuses on the preparation of the learner to effectively *apply* his skills to practical problems, problem solving, or new learning situations. The overall responsibility that will find general agreement is, thus, that education must provide a situation or atmosphere in which the skills and knowledges deemed by society important to learn can be adequately learned in such a way that the student can put his knowledge to effective use. There may be more disagreement about the second and third postulated purposes than there is about the first, but in the light of a growing and irrefutable body of knowledge bearing on the conditions necessary to learning, both in the learning environment and the learner himself, and our growing belief that many who appear to learn are not able to make effective use of their knowledge, we cannot ignore these important objectives.

The Appropriate Focus

A question that now becomes appropriate is, "What unique contribution can be made to these goals by the well-trained guidance specialist?" The first goal, dealing with the transmittal of skills and knowledge, is primarily the province of the classroom teacher, although the guidance specialist also has some responsibility in this area. In the course of his contacts with teachers, parents, administrators, and children, he will invariably be called upon to behave in relation to this goal, but this is not primary function nor his *unique* contribution to the educative process. It seems obvious that it is in connection with the second and third proposed objectives that the guidance professional has the most to offer. Thus, the teacher can be viewed primarily (but not solely) as the conveyor of information, while the guidance specialist fulfills his role by facilitating and enhancing the ability of the students both to appropriate knowledge and to make effective use of it. He will thus be concerned with the overall *learning environment* and with personality characteristics of the learner that promote or interfere with learning and the learner's ability to make maximum use of material which he has already learned. Succinctly stated, the basic purpose of the guidance specialist is to maximize the learning of all students and to enable them to use their learning effectively.

The Unresolved Dilemma

At this point, four problems have been raised; (1) the question of *who* receives guidance services; (2) the issue of *how* such services can be effectively carried out; (3) the problem of *when* guidance intervention should occur; and (4) the clarification of *why* guidance services are maintained. It has been suggested that counseling services are for all children, and that this judgment in turn raises the serious question of how limited numbers of guidance personnel can effectively reach them. It has been pointed out that most guidance programs, while keeping their personnel fully occupied, reflect a general lack of purpose and a rationale for purpose has been suggested.

The most important issue requiring further discussion at this point is the problem of how the postulated purpose of guidance services can be met for all (or nearly all) students. The direct approach (e.g., individual counseling of students) has been ruled out as ineffective in reaching any significant number of students. Since the guidance worker's basic objective is to appropriately affect the learning environment (in terms of the present framework), and since he is trained primarily as a specialist in human behavior, it seems logical that his *primary* function in the school system would be to work with and through those people who most directly influence the child's learning environment, i.e., parents and teachers.

Implications

This will be a difficult kind of position for traditionally trained counselors to accept, and there is not room to discuss the problems of implementation in sufficient detail, but certain implications arise from acceptance of the following ideas: (1) that the guidance specialist is responsible for services to all students, (2) that his purpose is to enhance the learning environment, and (3) that to do this effectively he will do less direct work with students and more with teachers and parents. (Note that in terms of the diagram, we are talking about option 1a).

There are two implications which bear mention. The first of these is that it is now possible to think of the major objectives of both elementary and secondary school guidance in similar terms. Heretofore, there has been a frenetic attempt to formulate the objectives and practices of the embryonic art of elementary school guidance. The main result of this in practice, to date, appears to be that the methods and techniques of secondary school guidance, with all their lack of unifying philosophy, are being imposed on the elementary school. The only outcome can be the same confused and essentially purposeless jumble of "services" currently being rendered by secondary schools. If the currently proposed basic objectives of counseling services are accepted it will be possible to think, plan, and act in terms of unified objectives regardless of what academic level is under consideration.

A second implication of the proposed model lies in the relationship of the guidance specialist to the rest of the school staff. Two kinds of situations, each unhealthy for the maximum effectiveness of guidance programs, frequently characterize the relationship of the guidance staff to other members of the faculty.

In the first case, the guidance specialist is perceived as a quasiadministrative functionary by both teaching and administrative faculty. Unfortunately, guidance workers have often rightfully earned this dubious distinction by their frequent and unprotesting acceptance of administrative responsibilities. (Parenthetically, it can be said that such responsibilities are frequently assigned by administrators and accepted by counselors because neither is quite sure what the guidance staff *should* be doing with its time). The variety of administrative tasks dealt to guidance specialists is varied but often includes discipline (in the narrow sense of the word), work related to attendance and tardiness, maintenance of cumulative folders and files of various types, evaluation of teaching personnel to extracurricular functions, public relations, and so forth. Is it any wonder that teaching faculty often do not perceive guidance specialists as being related in any direct way to the education of children, or that many lay persons regard guidance services as a frill or fad?

The second situation that distinguishes the association of guidance workers with their administrative and teaching colleagues is typified by the actual physical separation of such services from the vicinity of the classroom. This tendency can be seen both in large metropolitan centers with a great many resources, and in smaller school districts that combine with each other to establish "guidance centers" which may be completely removed, not only from the school, but possibly from the district as well. It is difficult for teachers to understand how a function completely removed from the physical school plant can have much impact on what goes on in the classroom, or how it can be of assistance to any great number of students. They do not know the personnel involved except at a distance and thus do not regard them as co-workers. Conversely, the guidance specialist working under such conditions cannot know the strengths and weaknesses of the teachers who make referrals, hence his recommendations tend to be of the cookbook variety. In addition, there sometimes exists a tendency on the part of the members of such a staff to regard their responsibilities in a more impersonal light than is desirable, an attitude which cannot help but be perceived by both faculty and students served. Finally, feedback when it occurs is likely to be through written rather than verbal communication, further divorcing guidance activities from the school-learning process.

Implementation of the proposed focus in school guidance work would put the guidance staff where it belongs—back into the school and into the center of the learning process. The administrative responsibilities of guidance personnel would be minimized, and it would be possible to demonstrate to the teaching faculty that guidance workers have a direct contribution to make to the education of children and that they can provide real assistance to the classroom teacher. It does not seem unrealistic to suppose that a guidance staff could make such a significant contribution to the school that it would no longer be viewed primarily as an obstacle in the way of achieving a more desirable student-teacher ratio, as it is in many places where teaching positions are reduced by the number of counselors on the staff.

Summary

Four major dilemmas inherent in any theoretical discussion of guidance programs were postulated. A two-dimensional model was proposed, the focus dimension having two levels—direct focus and indirect focus, and the time-phase dimension exhibiting these phases, general prevention, selective prevention, and diagnosis and remediation.

A proposal permitting the effective implementation of guidance services and relating guidance to the generally accepted purposes of education was made. In terms of the available procedural options, this purpose can best be implemented by ultilization of guidance procedures that aim primarily at the improvement of the learning environment for all students. Acceptance of this particular purpose and mode of implementation appears to have desirable implications, but will necessitate a radical rethinking of the role of the public school guidance specialist.

REFERENCES

BARAHAL, G. D., & BRAMMER, L. M. What do freshmen think of their high school counseling. *Calif. J. of Sec. Ed.* 1950, 25, 328–331.

BOWER, E. M. A process for early identification of emotionally disturbed children. *Bull. Calif. State Dept. Educ.* (Sacramento) 1958, 27, (6).

CONANT, J. C. *The American high school today.* New York: McGraw-Hill, 1959.

GIBSON, R. L. Pupil opinions of high school guidance programs. *Personnel Guid. J.,* 1962, 40, 453–457.

GRANT, C. W. How students perceive the counselor's role. *Personnel Guid., J.,* 1954, 32, 386.

HEILFRON, MARILYN. The function of counseling as perceived by high school students. *Personnel Guid. J.,* 1960, 39, 133–136.

LETON, D. A. Concepts which school social workers hold of school psychology; report of a questionnaire study. Report to Committee on Relationship to Social Work, Div. 16, American Psychological Association, 1957.

OJEMANN, RALPH H. *Developing a program for education in human behavior.* Iowa City: State Univ. of Iowa, 1959.

PIERSON, G. A., & GRANT, C. W. The road ahead for the school counselor. *Personnel Guid. J.,* 1960, 38.

ROBERTSON, M. H. Comparison of counselor and student reports of counseling interviews. *J. counsel, Psychol.,* 1958, 5, 276–280.

Values and our Youth

Gordon W. Allport

One aim of education is to make available the wisdom of the past and present so that youth may be equipped to solve the problems of the future. If this is so, then we have good grounds for a feeling of consternation concerning the adequacy of our present educational procedures. The reason is that in the immediate future, the youth of today will have to live in a world very unlike the world of the past from which our store of wisdom has been drawn.

Some Prospects

Think of the vastly changed nature of life in the future, for which we have little relevant wisdom from the past to call upon:

Reprinted by permission of the author and *Teachers College Record*, Vol. 63, 1961, 211-219.

The late Gordon W. Allport was Professor of Psychology, Harvard University.

1. The new generation of students will have to face an ever increasing domination of life by science, by technology, and by automation. (One thinks of the story of two cows grazing along the roadside. An immense milk truck passes with the painted legend: Pasteurized, Homogenized, Vitamin B Added. One cow turns to the other and says, "Makes you feel inadequate, doesn't it?")
2. The new generation will have to recognize the impossibility of living any longer in a state of condescension toward the colored peoples of the world (about three-quarters of the world's population). Centuries of comfortable caste discrimination and segregation are from here on impossible to maintain.
3. The coming generation will have to deal with a population explosion whose predicted magnitude staggers our imagination.
4. It will need a completer understanding of world societies and their marked differences in values. In the past, we could be politely ignorant of such places as Africa, Latin America, and Asia in a way that is no longer possible.
5. It will have to create a world government or, at least, an effective confederation to forestall the threat of thermonuclear war.
6. As if a planetary world view were not difficult enough to achieve, the coming generation may have to develop an interplanetary point of view. (I find this prospect especially alarming because we seem to be solving the problems of outer space before those of the inner space of mind, character, and values.)

It is no wonder that this preview of problems confronting our youth throws us educators into a state of self-scrutiny bordering sometimes on panic. Where can youth find the needed equipment? Are they sound enough in mind and morale?

Sometimes our dismay finds an outlet in gallows humor. They tell of the benevolent lady who saw a depressing specimen of the very young generation sprawled on the curb of a city street, swilling down cans of beer. Greatly shocked, she asked, "Little boy, why aren't you in school?" "Cripes, lady," he replied, "I'm only four years old."

And they tell the story of the London bobby. London police, we know, are well trained for social work, even for psychotherapy. This bobby's beat was Waterloo Bridge. He spotted a man about to jump over and intercepted him. "Come now," he said. "Tell me what is the matter. Is it money?" The man shook his head. "Your wife perhaps?" Another shake of the head. "Well, what is it then?" The would-be suicide replied, "I'm worried about the state of the world." "Oh, come now," said the bobby. "It can't be so bad. Let's walk up and down the bridge here and talk it over." Whereupon they strolled for about an hour discussing the state of the world, and then they *both* jumped over.

Humor helps us put our dilemma into sane perspective, but it does not solve the problem. The vague apprehension we feel has led to certain empirical studies of the values of today's youth, with results, alas, that are not reassuring.

Assessing Values

Not long ago, Professor Phillip Jacob undertook to survey (5) all available studies concerning the values held by college students. He found a marked uniformity among them. Fully three-quarters of the students were "gloriously contented, both in regard to their present day-to-day activity and their outlook for the future." Their aspirations were primarily for material gratifications for themselves and their families. They "fully accepted the conventions of the contemporary business society as the context within which they will realize their personal desires." While they will not crusade against segregation and racial injustice, they will accept non-discrimination when its comes as a "necessary convention in a homogenized culture." They subscribe to the traditional virtues of sincerity, honesty, and loyalty, but are indulgent concerning laxity in moral standards. They normally express a need for religion, but there is a hollow quality in their beliefs. They do not desire to have an influential voice in public policy or government. Their sense of civic duty stops at the elementary obligation of voting. They predict another major war within a dozen years, but they say that international problems give them little concern and that they spend no time on them. Only a minority value their college education primarily in terms of its intellectual gains. They regard it as good because it gives them vocational preparation, social status, and a good time. Such is the flabby value-fibre that Jacob discovers among college students of today.

The picture becomes more vivid when viewed in cross-national perspective. James Gillespie and I, in a comparative study (3) of the values of college youth in 10 nations, asked students to write their autobiographies of the future ("My life from now until the year 2000") and also gave them an extensive questionnaire. The instrument was translated into nine different languages.

In comparison with youth of other nations, young Americans are delightfully frank and open, unsuspicious and cooperative. Their documents had no literary affectation (and, I may add, little literary quality). But the most important finding was that within these 10 nations, American students were the most self-centered, the most "privatistic" in values. They desired above all else a rich, full life for themselves, and showed little concern for national welfare or for the fate of mankind at large. The context of their outlook was private rather than public, passive rather than pioneer. The essential point is made clear by two excerpts, the first drawn from the autobiography of a Mexican girl, 18 years of age, and the second from a Radcliffe student of the same age:

> Since I like psychology very much, I wish, on leaving this school, to study it, specializing in it and exercising it as a profession. I shouldn't like to get married right away, although like any woman I am desirous

of getting married before realizing all my aspirations. In addition, I should like to do something for my country—as a teacher, as a psychologist, or as a mother. As a teacher, to guide my pupils in the best path, for at the present time they need solid bases in childhood in order in their future lives not to have so many frustrations as the youth of the present. As a psychologist, to make studies which in some way will serve humanity and my beloved country. As a mother, to make my children creatures who are useful to both their country and all humanity.

Now follows the Radcliffe document. Its flavor of privatism is unmistakable:

> Our summers will be spent lobster fishing on the Cape. Later we'll take a look at the rest of the country—California, the Southwest, and the Chicago Stockyards. I want the children, when they get past the age of ten, to spend part of the summer away from home, either at camp or as apprentices to whatever profession they may show an interest in. Finally, I hope we will all be able to take a trip to Europe, especially to Russia, to see what can be done about Communism.

Many critics have called attention to the same American value predicament. Our current social pattern, they say, is almost completely geared to one objective alone, namely a profitable, expanding production. To insure expanding production, there must be more and more consumption. Hence comes the expensive glamor of our advertising and its control of our mass media. The sole objective seems to be to stimulate the accretion of goods. Sel-respect and status, as well as comfort, are acquired in this way. Someone has called our national disease "galloping consumption." Half a century ago, William James saw the peril and was much worried by what he called "the American terror of poverty." He saw there was truth in the jibes that other countries direct at our "materialism."

Hope in Uneasiness

Now a high standard of living is not in itself an evil thing. All the world wants what we already have. But the singleminded pursuit of production and consumption has brought a dulling of other values. One consequence is symbolized by the scandal of rigged quiz programs. These were in the service of advertising, which in turn was in the service of a profitable expanding economy. Another consequence is the accumulated froth of our TV, radio, and movies. Another is the widely discussed conformity of the organization man, as well as the futile rebellion of the beasts. An especially peppy critic, Paul Goodman (4), has shown that the starved lives of juvenile delinquents and of young people caught in the organizational grind are at bottom much alike. Both are attracted to the cult of easiness and aspire to nothing more than amiable mediocrity. Both styles of living fail to prepare youth for the problems that lie ahead for themselves and for the nation.

A somewhat vulgar story seems to me to summarize all this mordant criticism. Moses, a stalwart leader of the old school, said to the Israelites in Egypt, "Load up your camels, bring along your asses, and I'll lead you to the promised land." By contrast, the modern American prophet seems to urge, "Light up your Camels, sit on your asses, and I'll bring you the promised land."

All this familiar criticism is irritating; yet the fact that it flourishes is a hopeful sign. We suspect it may be too harsh. I am inclined to think so. It is rash indeed to indict a whole generation. At worst, Jacob's gloomy picture held for three-quarters of the college students studied, but not at all for a vital and far from negligible minority. And even though the gloomy generalizations have some truth in them, are the assets given fair attention? I myself have some favorable impressions, although one man's view is not reliable. But youth today appears to enjoy a certain freedom and flexibility that was not common in the more rigid days of our parents and grandparents. I even have the impression that there is less neuroticism among students now than among those of a generation ago. What is more, young people, I find, are not blind to the world changes that are occurring. Their apparent repression of the challenge is due largely to their bewilderment concerning proper paths to take. (And one has the feeling that our own statesmen in Washington are no less bewildered.) All in all, these are hopeful signs that should not be overlooked.

Values and the School

Another hopeful sign is the fact that many teachers are asking, "What can we do to be helpful?" They know, and we all know, that the ability of the school to give training in values is limited. For one thing, the home is vastly more important. A home that infects the child with galloping consumption, that encourages only canned recreation and has no creative outlets, can only with difficulty be offset by the school. Another limitation lies in the fact that the school is ordinarily expected to mirror current social values and to prepare the child to live within the existing frame. It is an unusual school system and an unusual teacher who even *wish* to transcend the current fashions of value.

But assuming that we have an unusual school system and an unusual teacher, what values shall they elect to teach? If they do not choose to follow the prevailing fashions, what standards shall they follow? The ancient Romans were fond of asking, "Who will judge the judges?" and "Who will guard the guardians?" Can the guardians turn perhaps to standard discussions of "the aims of education"? Such discussions are numerous, abstract, and often dull. Their weakness, I feel, is their effort to formulate absolute goals, vistas of abstract perfection. The result is often a series of platitudes or generalizations so broad as to be unhelpful. Of course we want to develop "good citizenship"; we certainly want to "free the child's intellect." These and all other absolutes need to be reduced to concrete, stepwise processes before they can guide us in the strategy of teaching values.

The teacher must start with the situation as he or she finds it and in concrete instances sharpen the value-attributes of the lesson being taught.

To a considerable extent, these value-attributes can be drawn from the codified wisdom of our nation. We cannot neglect the value of profitable production and high living standards, for all our vocational and professional education contribute to this end. But the codified wisdom of our unique society extends far beyond the obsession of today. Our values include also such matters as respect for civil liberties. Does the school accent this value? They include approval for individual initiative, for philanthropy, for compassion. And they imply much concerning civic duties that are the reciprocal of civic rights. What must we do to deserve our precious cornucopia of freedom? Vote? Yes. But voting does no good unless the voter is informed above the sterotyped level of the mass media. He must also pay taxes willingly. Do schools and colleges teach the young to pay a glad tax? I wonder. To me the most disturbing finding in *Youth's Outlook on the Future* lay in the elaborate talk about one's right to a rich, full life and in the almost total silence regarding one's duties.

I am saying that in the first instance teachers should choose the values they teach from the whole (not from a part) of our American ethos. Deep in our hearts we know, and most of the world knows, that our national values, derived, of course, from Judeo-Christian ethics, are about the finest mankind has yet formulated. In no sense are these values out of date, nor will they go out of date in the world of tomorrow. Yet many of them are badly rusted. Unless they are revitalized, however, our youth may not have the personal fortitude and moral implements that the future will require.

The Larger Anchor

Excellent as the American Creed is as a fountainhead of values, it does not contain them all. It says nothing explicitly, for example, about intellectual curiosity. And yet surely schools exist to augment this value. The most severe indictment of our educational procedures I have ever encountered is the discovery that a sizeable percentage of graduates of our colleges after completing their formal education never afterward read a single book.

There are other important values that are not spelled out in our American Creed. I am thinking of those details of human relationships that make all the difference between boorishness and brotherhood in the human family. As our population increases, it becomes more and more important to teach the elements of the new science of human relations which go far toward smoothing the roughness of common life by leading us to respect effectively the integrity of the other fellow. I recall a teacher of English whose class was studying *The Merchant of Venice*. She turned a wave of incipient anti-Semitism in her class to a sound lesson in values. Shylock, she explained, was like the resentful, self-seeking portion of every person's nature. We are all potential Shylocks. But while self-love is prominent in all of us, we are so constructed that it need not be sovereign in our natures.

To return for a moment to the relation between home and school—the former, as I have said, is far more important. Recognizing this fact, some people say, "Well, let's leave the teaching of values to the home and to the church. Schools can't do much of anything about the matter."

This position is untenable. If the school does not teach values, it will have the effect of denying them. If the child at school never hears a mention of honesty, modesty, charity, or reverence, he will be persuaded that, like many of his parents' ideas, they are simply old hat. As they grow toward adolescence, children become critical of the teaching of both parents and the church. They are in a questioning stage. If the school, which to the child represents the larger outside world, is silent on values, the child will repudiate more quickly the lessons learned at home. He will also be thrown onto peer values more completely, with their emphasis on the hedonism of teen-age parties or on the destructiveness of gangs. He will also be more at the mercy of the sensate values peddled by movies, TV, and disc jockeys. What is more, some homes, as we have said, give no fundamental value training. In such a case, it is *only* in the school that the child has any chance at all of finding ethical anchorage.

This brings us to the hardest question: How does the teacher, the instructor, the professor, handle his assignment in the classroom? How is it possible to teach values, including the value of intellectual curiosity?

The Meaning of Value

Before tackling this question, we must pause to define what we mean by value. You will recognize that I am using the term psychologically, not in its objective philosophical sense. Values, as I use the term, are simply *meanings perceived as related to self*. The child experiences value whenever he knows that a meaning is warm and central to himself. Values, to borrow Whitehead's term, are "matters of importance" as distinct from mere matters of fact.

So much for definition. Now the hard-pressed teacher is given a solid substantive curriculum to teach. The curriculum in its original state consists of mere matters of fact. And on the number of facts absorbed the pupil's standing depends. It takes virtually all of a teacher's time to convey factual information and grade the pupil on his achievement. There is little time left to transmute these matters of fact into matters of importance, let alone teach all of the moral and social values we have thus far been discussing.

The curriculum itself is not, and should not be, a direct aid. Prescribed instruction in values would be laughed out of court. We have recently been bumped by Sputnik headforemost into core subjects. Get on with science, mathematics, language! Away with courses in folk-dancing, personal adjustment, and fudge-making! I agree that value-study has no place in curriculum planning, but not because it is a frivolous subject—rather, because it is a subject too hard and too subtle for curriculum makers.

Education for values occurs only when teachers teach what they themselves stand for, no matter what their subject is. If I were to write a treatise on the teaching of values, I would give most of my emphasis to the moral pedagogy that lies in a teacher's incidental comments, to the *obiter dicta*. The hard core is central, but the hard core has a penumbra of moral significance. I mentioned the teacher of English who made a value-lesson out of Shylock. I recall also my college professor of geology who paused in his lecture on diatom ooze to say to us, "Others would not agree with me, but I confess that whenever I study diatoms, I don't see how anyone can doubt the existence of God because the design and behavior of these protozoa are so marvelous." Is it not interesting how we all recall the *obiter dicta* of our teachers, the penumbra of value they point out to us, surrounding the hard-core data? We remember them better than the subject matter itself.

Why does the student remember them so well? No current theory of learning seems able to tell us. I suspect it is because values, being matters of importance to the self, are always warm and central and ego-involved and therefore claim priority on our attention. The child, being value-ripe, cannot help being impressed when the teacher betrays excitement and enthusiasm for a mode of thought or for the content of the subject being studied. True, the youngster does not, and should not, adopt the teacher's values ready-made; but the teacher's self-disclosure leads the student to self-discovery.

What wouldn't we give if we could develop intellectual ardor in every child for hard core subjects? Why is it that for most pupils arithmetic, spelling, physics, remain forever dull matters of fact and never become a meaning perceived as related to the self? One reason, I think, is that the weary teacher fails to convey his own sense of the importance of the subject to the student. If he did so, he would, as I have said, at least fix attention upon the value-potentiality of the subject.

Another reason perhaps is that not all of a teacher's *obiter dicta* are wholesome. Some, indeed, may be deeply damaging, though the teacher may be innocent of any such intent. Sometimes we hear incidental (but still attitude-forming) remarks like this one: "All right now, children. You have had a good time playing at recess; now settle down to your English lesson." Play is recognized as a matter of joyful importance. English, the teacher is saying in effect, is a mere routine matter of fact.

Values and Learning

I think our educational psychology has been mostly wrong about the process of learning—or perhaps not so much wrong as woefully incomplete. At the beginning of his learning career, a young child cannot, of course, be expected to feel adult enthusiasm for the intellectual content of his studies. He does his work in the first instance to avoid a scolding or because he has a habit of obeying instructions. Soon he finds added incentive. The teacher— really in the role of mother—gives praise and love ("Susan, I am proud of you"). There is a great deal of such dependency in the learning situation. Love and social reward (as well as some fear of punishment) sustain the processes of attention and retention. When the child puts forth intellectual effort, he does so in order to obtain a gold star, commendation, or other symbols of love.

All these incentives are extraneous to the subject matter. The youngster does not learn it because it is a matter of importance. When he leaves school or college, he loses these extraneous supports. He finds his love relations directly; they are no longer a reward for intellectual effort. Hence, intellectual apathy sets in, and, distressing to say, no further books are read.

In such a case as this, intellectual curiosity was never tied to independence, only to extraneous supports. At some point in the schooling—and the earlier the better—intellectual activity should become not a second-hand but a first-hand fitting to the sense of self. At the beginning, all learning must be tied, perhaps, to specific reinforcements; but if the dependency is long continued, authentic curiosity fails to develop.

It would be going too far to put the blame for intellectual apathy onto our current teaching of educational psychology. Yet I am inclined to feel somewhat punitive about this matter. Psychology has not yet settled down to the problem of transforming matters of fact—whose acquisition current learning theories explain fairly well—into autonomous matters of importance—which they do not explain at all.

Our emphasis has been on learning by drill and by reinforcement. Such "habit acquisition" receives all the emphasis. But the learning theory involved postulates a continuing dependency relation (extraneous reinforcement). When the relation terminates, the habits of study simply extinguish themselves. I am surprised, therefore, that stimulus-response psychologists do not see this consequence of their own theory. Insofar as teachers employ an educational psychology of this order, they are not likely to break the dependency relation, which belongs properly only to the earlier stages of schooling.

Matters of importance, I strongly believe, are not acquired by drill or by reinforcement. They are transformations of habits and skills from the "opportunistic" layer of personality into the ego-system itself *(1)*. Once inside the ego-system, these habits and skills turn into true interests and utilize the basic energy, the basic spontaneity, that the organism itself possesses. They are no longer sustained as "operant conditionings" by outside rewards. The interest, now being the very stuff of life itself, needs no outer supports.

Functional Autonomy

I have called this process of transforming means into ends, of changing extrinsic values into intrinsic values, *functional autonomy*. Concerning this concept, I am often asked two questions: How do you define "functional autonomy, and how does functional autonomy come about"?

For a definition, I offer the following: Functional autonomy refers to any acquired system of motivation in which the tensions involved are no longer of the same kind as the anetecedant tensions from which the acquired system developed.[1] To answer the question of how functional autonomy comes about requires a more extended and technical discussion. I can only hint at the direction of my answer. Neurologists are gradually discovering a basis for what I would call "perseverative functional autonomy." I refer to the "self-sustaining circuits," "feedback mechanisms," and "central motive states" that are now commonly recognized to exist in the nervous system. This line of discovery, I find, provides a partial answer to the question. But I believe we have to go further and call on the concept of self. Values, we have said, are meanings perceived as related to the self. Functional autonomy is not a mere preseverative phenomenon; it is, above all, an ego-involved phenomenon. Besides admitting an opportunistic layer to personality, which is the exclusive concern of most current theories of learning, we have no choice but to admit also a "propriate" layer. It is in this layer that all matters of importance reside.

The goal of the educator, then is to shift the content of the subject he teaches from the opportunistic (matter of fact) layer to the propriate. But there is no sure-fire, mechanical strategy to use. The best general rule, one that John Dewey saw clearly, is to strive ceaselessly to integrate routine matters of fact into the growing experience system of the child himself. It would take a long treatise to specify various detailed strategies of teaching that help achieve this goal.

Let me focus on only one aspect of this topic, upon a common mistake that teachers make. I myself am a continual offender. It is to present students with our own carefully thought out conclusions when they themselves lack the raw experience from which these conclusions are fashioned

This particular error is inherent, for example, in the lecture system. Instead of lecturing on comparative religion, for instance, it would be much better to require all students to attend services of worship that are unfamiliar to them. If raw experience is present, then perhaps a lecture may be effective. Much of the intellectual apathy we complain about is due to our fault of presenting conclusions in lieu of first-hand experience. To us, our well-chiseled conclusion, summing up a long intellectual struggle with a problem of knowledge or of value, seems like a beautiful sonnet. To the student, it may be gibberish.

The fallacy of giving conclusions holds both for subject matter and for values. A lad of 15 cannot profit from the fully fashioned philosophy of life of a man of 50. To register at all, a statement about values must fall precisely on his present growing edge.

Teaching, then, is not the art of offering conclusions, however hard won and valid they may be. No teacher can forcibly enter the students' proprium and plant a functionally autonomous motive. He can at best open channels

---

[1]If this definition seems too technical to be immediately helpful, see Ch. 10 of *Pattern and Growth in Personality (2)* for a more extended treatment of functional autonomy.

of experience and, by his *obiter dicta,* sometimes lead the student to see the value-potential in the experience.

The theory of personality that we need to guide a more fully developed educational psychology will teach us something important about our basic verb "to educate." It will show us that only at the outset of learning is it a transitive verb. By drill, by reward, by reinforcement, the teacher does indeed educate the child—in matters of fact. But true maturity comes only when the verb is reflexive. For in matters of importance, where values lie, the growing individual alone can educate himself.

REFERENCES

1. Allport, G. *Becoming.* New Haven: Yale Univer. Press, 1955.
2. Allport, G. *Pattern and growth in personality.* New York: Holt, Rinehart, & Winston, 1961.
3. Gillespie, J., & Allport, G. *Youth's outlook on the future.* New York: Random House, 1955.
4. Goodman, P. *Growing up absurd.* New York: Random House, 1960.
5. Jacob, P. *Changing values in college.* New York: Harper, 1957.

Consultation in the Counselor's Role: Invitation to Dialogue

Louise O. Eckerson

The ACES-ASCA Joint Committee on the Elementary School Counselor presented a report to the parent boards and to the general guidance public at the APGA Convention in Washington in April 1966. Understandably, there was practically unanimous acceptance of the three-pronged role: counselor, consultant, and coordinator.

The emphasis of this article will be on the rationale for consultation rather than on consulting techniques for the valid reason that I do not know much about the latter. Armed with concepts gleaned from reading, listening, logic, imagination, and hearing myself talk, I will attempt to agitate a friendly argument with persons better qualifed to expound on the subject

Reprinted by permission of the author and *Elementary School Guidance and Counseling*, Vol. 1, No. 4 (Fall, 1966), 5-8.

Louise O. Eckerson, Specialist, School Personnel Services, Office of Education, Department of Health, Education, and Welfare, Washington, D.C.

than I am. It is my intent to be provocative, to arouse assent and dissent, and to stimulate future articles on consultation written especially by counselors. To this end, the time is ripe for dialogue.

To begin with, I will reveal my biases. I believe that consultation is the most important though not the only aspect of the role of the elementary school counselor. His selection for graduate work should give weight to his potential for this role. His preparation should highlight it, and he should be permitted to devote much of his time in the elementary school to consultation with teachers, parents, principal, and pupil personnel specialists. My argument is based on the following premises:

Guidance for All Children Should be a Fact Rather than a Theory

Children in toto can be reached only through emphasis on consultation. This argument holds even if a counselor is responsible for as few as 300 children because no counselor can effectively work individually with 300 youngsters, their teachers, and parents. Of the many pilot programs in elementary school guidance which I have observed and read about, most have a counselor-pupil ratio of 1-600 or more. Many programs involve one counselor for over 1,000 children. In such schools an emphasis on counseling is inevitably an emphasis on remedial guidance affecting relatively few children.

To help all children, one must work through teachers and parents, individually and in groups. Group consultation organized for various numbers, for diverse purposes, and for the consideration of normal or abnormal behavior has the potential of helping all children. We have only begun to tap this guidance medium. Spreading the guidance gospel through group consultation with adults may reduce the number of children who would otherwise need individual attention at a later date.

Emphasis Should be on Development Guidance

The goal of guidance encompasses positive measures to enrich everyday experiences of children, beginning with the earliest possible influence which the school can exert. In the upper grades, individual and group counseling of children may open the door to personal development, but in K through 3, the sharing of observations and mutual decision-making with significant adults must provide the means to maximum development of children. Experiences, stimulation, attitudes, values, health factors, and physical surroundings which determine a young child's progress depend on adults.

The counselor's greatest contribution is in assisting parents and teachers in providing home and school environments conducive to optimum and total growth. Somehow, hopefully, counselors will find some time to influence the environment of children during the years when they develop most rapidly—from birth until preschool classes. Retardation which begins even before

Head Start programs may be reversed or slowed down through consultation with parents of very young children.

Emphasis Should be on Prevention of Problems

True prevention is maximum development. The counselor should begin with an awareness of conditions and situations at home and in the classroom that commonly give rise to problems. Some learning difficulties can be anticipated and therefore forestalled by manipulating factors in the child's world. A counselor needs to become familiar with effective procedures and exert imagination to conceive of new ways to help parents share in arousing curiosity, motivating, and building within a child a self-image of which he is proud. These evidences of a rich childhood should not be left to chance and hope, especially among low-income groups in which stimulation is often lacking.

Large numbers of children experience crises which are built into many families and can be anticipated, or immediately recognized and handled with insight and a sense of what is appropriate. Thus, traumatic experiences of a child may be cushioned when his family moves to a new neighborhood, or is rocked by mental illness, divorce, loss of income, or a new baby. Likewise, preparation may be made at school to counter the effects of initial reading difficulty, leaving and entering a new school, advancing to a new grade, and myriad new school practices being ushered in with widespread changes in education. Through consultation, a counselor may help parents and teachers anticipate and lessen difficult hurdles for children.

A School's Guidance Program Should Begin Where the Needs Are

Experimentation is essential to change, and although educators seek validation of innovations before they are widely introduced, the school community will often experience some suffering in the initial stages. There is need for a close and continuing look at what new materials, techniques, and organizational patterns do to children. Instead of evaluating a program by soliciting reactions from only teachers and parents, perhaps one should ask the children, even very young children, if they like the new look. Perhaps the counselor is the best qualified person in the school to examine the effect of new procedures on children—their self-image, their morale, as well as their enthusiasm to learn independently and seek original ways of thinking. Likewise, the counselor may well focus a critical eye, on numerous traditional practices, and ask if these ways of doing things have any relation to underachieving, leaving school, mental illness among adolescents, juvenile delinquency, etc. It may just be that some procedures have been perpetuated because they seemed good for school staff or parents rather than for children! Maybe some changes are long overdue.

It is probable that an elementary school counselor with a two-year graduate program behind him and a large block of preparation in psychology (we are looking toward the future now) will be the logical person in a school to initiate critical thinking and research to determine wherein the old is beneficial or detrimental to children, and what should be substituted. A few problem areas for study might include: the plight of little boys in schools dominated by female values, the self-image of pupils in the low ability track, school entrance policies, grading, and the reporting of grades.

Thus, the counselor should become a change-agent, a provocateur, a disturber of the peace. With consideration for feeling of defensiveness long engendered by the school establishment, the perceptive counselor will move slowly into discussions of change, helping school staff in self-analyses of classroom procedures, of school policies, and of system-wide educational philosophy. Two-way consultation with all adults interested in improving education for children would be the beginning of a continuing inquiry into what is happening to those for whom the schools exist.

A Counselor Should Help Teachers Understand the Effect of their Behavior on Children

The quality and amount of interaction between a teacher and the children in her classroom determine in large part the degree of learning. By bringing research and classroom observation to bear on improving teacher-pupil interaction, a counselor may help a teacher understand what effect his behavior has on children, the extent to which his pupils are learning to think or to absorb facts, and the educational values which are being built into children as a result of the typical school day.

The teacher can play a key guidance role only if helped when necessary to sharpen the techniques of classroom guidance. That the techniques often need sharpening is indicated by the incidence of nonreaders, withdrawn and aggresive children, and countless other problems related to living in a restless, competitive, and emotion-laden society. Sometimes consultation to this end may rightly move into a counseling relationship with the teacher, with the counselor constantly aware of his professional limitations in the area of personal counseling.

Work with Parents is Vital to an Elementary School Guidance Program

There is a fine line between consulting with and counseling a parent. Both techniques can be successfully used by a skilled and sensitive counselor. Most parents would rather view the meeting of minds as a consultation in which both parties contribute to the understanding of a child and the solution of his problems. However, the need for a counseling relationship of one or a few sessions may be rewarding when a parent is harassed, frightened, and confused about his child—or expects too much or too little from him. Thus, counseling may be in order when a parent-counselor meeting centers around a child's problem. When a counselor sees parents individually or in groups to study normal child development, the process usually consists of consultation.

The Counselor Should Recognize the Need for Referral When Necessary and Prepare the Appropriate Persons

Consultation is usually the machinery through which teachers, parents, principals, and pupil personnel specialists communicate with each other when a child is referred for help beyond that which the counselor can give him. The exchange of pertinent information and the coordination of the process of referral involves consultation. The effective nature of the communication and the terminology used varies with the involved adults, for there is no one technique of consulting any more than there is one technique of counseling. The role of coordinator, therefore, is implemented through consultation.

Consultation is One of the Counselor's Ways of Obtaining Information

Consultation should always be a two-way street. Usually, the counselor as a behavioral scientist is long on the giving end, interpreting child behavior to those who are responsible for children. However, in order to understand the behavior of any particular child the counselor must also listen. He must gather data, observations, voiced impressions, and subtly expressed attitudes from others and integrate them with what the counselor has gleaned from observing and testing the child. The counselor needs to cultivate the art of obtaining as well as giving information that throws light on why a child behaves as he does. Such information may reveal why a teacher or parent behaves as he does, and why a child reflects the same behavior or reacts against it.

On this pregnant note I rest my case for consultation.

A Differential Approach to Elementary Guidance

Marion Heisey

Elementary guidance is in its infancy if indeed it is even yet through the labor pains of birth. Much theoretical writing and ambitious thinking has been done to activate potential adherents for the elementary guidance band wagon. However, one of the structural weaknesses in the movement behind elementary guidance is the premise that this school personnel worker will be all things to all people. He serves as a modifier for the residual left over from the school psychologist, social worker, visiting teacher, and other specialists. If it were not an indictment against the proponents of professionals who attempt to define the functions of elementary guidance, one would be tempted to say that the specialist working in this area would need at

Reprinted by permission of the author and *Elementary School Guidance and Counseling*, Vol. 1, No. 4 (Fall, 1966), 18-21.

Marion Heisey, Director, Elementary Guidance, Kent State University, Kent, Ohio.

least three Ph.D. degrees in order to fulfill his expected role. It is the position of this writer that it will be necessary to delimit the services rendered by this specialist so that one service will be done well rather than many services done poorly. It is the tenet of this paper that the elementary counselor's area of specialization most fruitful in terms of greatest value to the child will be the role of serving as a parent consultant. Granted, as time permits he will function in other areas such as teacher consultation, testing, and individual or group child counseling, but these areas will represent a lower order of importance.

What support can be given to this position? On what basis can we say that teacher consultation or individual child counseling is less important than parent consultation? First of all, we must remember that the teacher is a co-worker with the counselor and in most cases is an individual who is thoroughly trained with much experience in the understanding of child learning and behavior. With this in mind, it is important to recognize the tremendous resources which the teacher has to contribute in the solving of her own classroom problems. The classroom teacher is doing this daily, and only with the more persistent cases will she need the assistance of the counselor.

It is also important for us to recognize that for an elementary counselor to work with a single child or even a group of students we are operating on the assumption that the child has the capacity and the insight to resolve his adjustment problems through his own resources. Although this author does not underestimate the potential of the child to assist himself in this process, it is nevertheless presumptuous to think that maximum change can be brought about through this approach alone.

We come then to the basic proposition of this paper. The home and the parents are the primordial constellation with the greatest influence, the greatest potential, and with the greatest intensity of personalized interest for the child's welfare. I would like to suggest five reasons why the elementary counselor should be a specialist in parent consultation and function with the greatest emphasis in this area. First, the parent is potentially the greatest agent of change in the child's environment. Hopefully the elementary counselor will serve as a resource to parents not only for corrective behavior but also for guidance and direction in normal developmental concerns. Many times a parent is aware of developing behavior patterns which as yet have not developed into serious problems, but have the potential for doing so. Many times the parent feels inadequate in knowing the best approach to use in implementing behavior change. And yet, because the parent is in the pivotal position of effecting, implementing, and enforcing necessary changes in the child's style of behavior, preventive techniques would be used if the parent had a capable and reliable resource to assist him. Although the institutions of the school and the church are powerful environmental contributors in a child's life, yet the critical variable and most potent element in the control of the child's environment is the parent himself. Although the teacher and the counselor do have significant contact with the child during a significant portion of the day, they provide more structure and greater limitations in stimulus-response relationships.

The second reason for the counselor to serve primarily as a parent consultant is because the parent sustains more consistantly over a longer period of time a more intense and concerted interest for the child. Because a child "belongs" to a set of parents there will be fruitful results in working with parents. Parents are interested in their children. Parents do want the best for their offspring. Parents will sacrifice to no end for the sake of their own flesh and blood. In marital difficulties a common response from either one or both parents is, "I will do anything for my children." Intense interest, concern, and motivation are pre-requisites to the success of any undertaking and generally speaking this triumverate exists with parents. The teacher can give only divided attention in her attempt to give positive direction or correction to a child. The church has a very limited contact with the child, and although important shaping takes place in the church, the contact with any one child during the week may be three or four hours at the most. Although a parent may feel discouraged and defeated with his or her approach to child rearing, the child's presence day after day is a continual reminder of the parent's need to give positive guidance and training, thereby keeping the spark of concern and interest alive and readily accepting whatever resources is available.

The third reason is that primary value training should come from the home. The counselor can serve as a resource in helping parents to implement their own value teaching. Although many philosophers and educators of the day decry the concept of value influence, educators are like the proverbial blind leading the blind if they do not recognize that they are in fact communicating and teaching values in our system of education. All parents and all teachers have values and they are communicated to the child either overtly or covertly. Parents are anxious for the school to be supporters of their own values, and since values are relative and arbitrary with many people, it should become the responsibility of the school to assist the parent in the implementing and teaching of their values to their own children.This may occur by the counselor serving as a resource to parents in helping them clarify and interpret their values to their children. One parent may seek help in getting a child to get up to go to church on Sunday morning, and another parent may seek help in getting a child to get up and mow the lawn on a Sunday morning. These parents have different values and the task of the counselor becomes that of helping the parent to understand principles of motivation and causation of behavior rather than passing judgment on which parent's values should or should not be accepted. Although parenthetically, it is this writer's position that the counselor has the prerogative to share his own values with a parent who is confused in his value system. Ambiguous or nebulous values communicate frustration to the child.

A fourth reason parents should receive a priority of the counselor's time is because the parents have the greatest storehouse of contributing data regarding a child. There is no merit in quantitative data as it stands alone, but the counselor is in a position to help the parent sort through voluminous mental files and select appropriate information bearing on a child's unique development. The school may have the child in classes for six years or more and never know that a traumatic separation from the mother occurred at age three because of infectious hepatitis. Or the school may never know that at age four a child suffered from terrifying nightmares for eight months as a result of a narrow escape from death when the family's home burned down. These situational events have an impact on the child's life which may affect attitudes and behavior at school, years after the events occur. The parents can relate from an observational viewpoint sibling relationships and parent-child interaction. As the parent and counselor explore together the possible ramifications of these situational events, the well trained counselor can selectively identify significant data in helping the parents to understand their child more objectively. The wealth of information which any parent has about his own child is like the proverbial alphabet of twenty-six letters. What is done with this alphabet depends upon which letters are selected and how they are pieced together into a meaningful pattern. This wealth of knowledge and information which the parent holds can be selectively chosen and pieced into a meaningful pattern so the child may be guided more appropriately. Since the counselor is an outside party and can evaluate all incoming data somewhat objectively he may be in a better position to evaluate a problem or situation than is the parent. What may seem like stubbornness and rebellion to the parent when a child refuses to learn to tie his shoe, may be interpreted by the counselor as further evidence of poor coordination which should be investigated. A parent is often blinded by the emotional overtones of any given incident and thereby unable to evaluate it objectively.

The fifth supporting reason for the elementary counselor to spend a priority of time with parents is that it will foster perpetual growth of the counselor's own skill in dealing with the areas with which parents are most concerned. The counselor can collate materials, review research, and make data available to parents which will help them to better understand their children. He will serve to provide continuity in understanding the child's development from one grade to another and will be the child's advocate through these transition years. The counselor will have had the necessary background to help the parent and the teacher understand pertinent data. There is also value in the kind of comprehensive knowledge which the counselor accumulates regarding a family constellation. As the counselor begins to understand the total picture of sibling relationship and parent attitudes and values, it makes it possible for the counselor to function in more depth with any particular family.

Very briefly we will mention the areas where the counselor should be able to serve as a real resource to parents. 1) *Learning difficulties*—he should be sufficiently familiar with the dynamics of various kinds of learning difficulties that he will be able to help the parent understand causes for the child's difficulties and make appropriate referrals when necessary. 2) *Adjustment problems*—he should sufficiently understand child behavior so that he may help the parents to implement techniques for adequate adjustment to a variety of problems. 3) *Emotional problems*—the counselor should be able to interpret symptoms of emotional problems so the parents and counselor together can explore the dynamics of what is causing a particular behavior. 4) *Child rearing practices*—through wide reading as well as through training the elementary counselor should be able to give sound advice on child rearing practices. Every parent at times faces problems in child rearing that are baffling. The counselor should be able to share knowledge and insight which will be of value to parents. 5) *Growth and development*—at every stage of child growth there are different physiological and psychological developmental patterns. The counselor should be sufficiently schooled in this area to serve as a resource to parents in helping them understand patterns of growth and what the expectations of the parents should be.

Although the material presented in this paper is not foreign to the area of elementary guidance, it does emphasize the neglected service of the counselor's involvement with parents. If more time will be spent in working with individual, small groups, and large groups of parents, more immediate and permanent effects on the child will be the result.

Can The Counselor Function as an Effective Agent of Change?

Donald Blocher

The school counselor is faced increasingly with the challenge of effecting change in educational institutions. Students, parents, and writers, both professional and popular, see the counselor as a person who can actually change the educational environment. The need for dramatic change in American education seems so overwhelmingly apparent that it would be difficult to cast any sophisticated argument against it. A great many of the cases which are continually referred to counselors in hope of some kind of remediative or palliative treatment are themselves simply products of the gross imperfections in the social systems represented by the school and community.

Reprinted by permission of the author and *The School Counselor*, Vol. 13, No. 4 (May, 1966), 202-205.

Donald Blocher, Associate Professor of Education, University of Minnesota, Minneapolis.

A central thesis of my own approach to counseling is that the counselor's primary professional responsibility is to facilitate human development. We know that development represents an interaction process between the individual with his own inherent dispositions and his environment, particularly that part of his environment which we call society and culture.

In their attempts to intervene in the transactional process between the individual and society, educators, physicians, judges, social workers, and other professional persons almost invariably assume that their intervention must be addressed solely to the individual. They tend to assume that it is always the individual who must be changed, adjusted, or manipulated to bring him into conformity with the unquestioned and unquestionable demands of groups, institutions, or other socially sanctified components of the culture.

Nearly thirty years ago Lawrence Frank, in an article entitled "Society As the Patient," summed up the cultural myopia of the helping professions in these terms:

> In every department and aspect of our social life we find the same pattern of thought about our society: that our social ills come from individual misconduct that must be corrected and punished so that these supposed social forces and social laws can operate without hindrances, thereby solving our social problems. . . .
>
> If then, we abandon this social mythology, as a growing number of individuals are urging, what have we as an alternative? . . . The conception of culture and personality, emphasizing the patterned behavior of man toward his group and toward other individuals offers some promise of help, for it indicates at once that our society is only one of numerous ways of patterning and organizing life and that what individuals do for good or evil is in response to the cultural demands and opportunities offered them. [2]

Unfortunately in the nearly thirty years which have intervened since these words were written, the promise which Frank saw has not been fulfilled. Education, as a social institution, has been particulary slow to adjust itself to the needs and demands of developing individuals and has instead settled back comfortably within the mythology of its own omniscience and moral rectitude.

In only one area of social welfare of which I have become aware have thorough and systematic attempts been made to abandon the myth of social inviolability and to attempt to conceptualize human problems within the model advocated by Frank thirty years ago. The area of which I speak is the movement called milieu therapy or sometimes social psychiatry which has already demonstrated its usefulness in mental health settings throughout the country. Characteristically, however, we are behind several European countries in this approach.

The concept of milieu therapy seems to me to offer a useful model from which education can learn. Cohen [1] writes of the hospital as a "therapeutic instrument" in which patterns of human relationships, physical environments, and interactions with the large society are consciously and systematically attuned to the treatment needs of patients.

In a similar vein, the counselor is interested in creating the school as a "developmental instrument" attuned to the developmental needs of youth. Goldsmith, Schulman, and Grossbard in an article on milieu therapy with disturbed children stress the point that a clinical process such as psychotherapy cannot be integrated into an environment which is alien to it. They say:

> To achieve a schematicized environment which can be consistent and therapeutic in all its aspects, there must first and foremost be a common denominator in the functioning of all staff—clinical and non-clinical—beginning with the acceptance of a common formulation for the treatment of those disturbed children. The common bond, the thread which runs through the institution, must be the understanding of the nature of the child. It is this understanding which extends the clinical process into all aspects of the environmental setting. This understanding creates identification, sympathy and tolerance. It permits individualization in the handling of children by all concerned. It is this which creates the basic milieu for and of therapy. [3]

The creation of a *developmental* milieu for clients is one of the goals of the counselor. The developmental milieu may not be quite the same as the therapeutic milieu, but it, too, would seem to rest on the common denominator of understanding human development. Unless the developing individual can exist in a melieu within family, within school, and within community where some rather high degree of understanding of developmental needs and processes can be found, much of the work of the counselor will be hopelessly difficult.

Can the counselor operate as an effective agent of change to produce this kind of developmental milieu? I raise a number of questions about this role for the counselor not to be a voice of doubt, but to focus upon some real considerations which must be faced before we can glibly undertake this role for the counselor as we have glibly taken on so many others in the past.

1. *Is the counselor qualified by training background and experience to be an effective agent of change?* To be such an agent the counselor, I believe, must be a behavioral scientist in the best sense of the term. He must be able to view human behavior as phenomena, phenomena that are potentially understandable and modifiable. He cannot be merely shocked, or frightened, or angered by behavior. He must also be able to get outside the cultural cocoon which encapsulates most members of a society to view human behavior and human institutions objectively and cross-culturally. These requirements, I believe, mean that the counselor must heve a broad and rigorous background in fields such as anthropology, sociology, political science, economics and social psychology (particularly group dynamics), as well as a thorough grounding in humanities.

I am afraid that at the present time neither most counselors nor most counselor education programs stack up very well on these criteria.

2. *Does the role of the counselor permit him to operate as an effective agent of change?* The counselor's primary role in the school is as a helping person. His effectiveness depends largely on being perceived as such a

person by parents, students, teachers, and administrators. One of his greatest assets is that because he is perceived as a helping person, the counselor has access to a great deal of "feedback" from people about how their needs are being met or not met that is available to no one else.

The counselor who is openly and strongly committed to controversial changes may no longer be perceived as a helping person, at least by many to whom such changes may be disturbing and threatening. The "boat-rocker" often is not seen as a helping person even when the boat may need rocking very badly.

3. *Is the counselor's position in the organization of the school such that he can become an effective agent of change?* The counselor is typically neither fish nor fowl insofar as his organizational relationships in the school are concerned. He is typically not a full-fledged administrator with well-defined responsibilities, nor is he viewed strictly as a teacher who operates without administrative authority or responsibility. The concept of staff roles in educational organizations is presently so poorly developed that the counselor must operate in a virtual organizational "no man's land." For the counselor to operate directly and consciously as a change agent in the school can lead to threat-inducing situations for both administrators and teachers.

One of the real enigmas to me is why those that consistently urge change in education have bypassed the school administrator, who is the only person in the school vested with the authority and responsibility to promote valued change.

Has the school administrator lost his identity as the educational leader? Has he become so identified with buses, buildings, and bands, that he is not identified with pupils, parents, and programs? Has the school administrator been so laden down with such a diversity of tasks that a leadership vacuum is forming under the increasing demands of a kaleidoscopic culture? Milieu therapy models would suggest that schools might be moving closer to the hospital model in which the administrator is essentially the office manager and the responsibility for professional treatments—the dominant mission of the organization—rests finally in the hands of the active practitioners rather than the professional administrator?

This movement, indeed, may already be underway. Perhaps counselors should continue to play quasi-administrative roles and concern themselves more and more deeply in curriculum, pupil grouping, and the many other areas in which vital changes are needed. Such is the challenge thrown out by Shoben when he says:

> . . . willy-nilly, the school represents a society-in-little. The challenge
> before it is whether it can transform itself into a developmentally pro-
> ductive one on an articulate and informed basis and, by a regular and
> planful process of self-appraisal, maintain itself as a true growth-enhanc-
> ing community. In such an effort to sharpen the impact of the school
> and to give it greater cogency for individual students, guidance workers
> can play a key role, forging in the course of it, a genuine new profes-
> sion for themselves. [4]

If this is the challenge which counselors wish to undertake, they must accept it with a clear vision of the demands which it will place upon them as individuals, with awareness of the scope of preparation which it will require, and with knowledge of the new organizational relationships which will inevitably emerge from it.

REFERENCES

1. Cohen, R. *The hospital as a therapeutic instrument,* in Milton, O. *Behavior disorders, perspectives and trends.* New York: J. B. Lippincott, 1965, pp. 290-298.
2. Frank, L. Society as the patient. *American J. School.* 1936, *42,* pp. 335-344, also in Vinacke, W. Edgar and Wilson, Warner R. *Dimensions of social psychology.* Chicago: Scott, Foresman, 1964, p. 50.
3. Goldsmith, J. Schulman, R. & Grossland, H. Integrating clinical processes with planned living experiences. In Gorlow, Leon & Katkovsky, Walter (Ed.) *Readings in the psychology of adjustment.* New York: McGraw-Hill, 1959, p. 483.
4. Shoben, E. J. Jr., Guidance: remedial function or social reconstruction? *Harv. educ. Rev.* Guidance—an examination (A special issue), 32, No. 4. Fall 1962, p. 442.

The School Counselor and Religious Liberty

Claud C. Crawford

There are certain aspects of the school counselor's role and function which are very pertinent to the traditional belief in religious liberty. It is the purpose of the writer to examine this state of affairs and to propose steps which will assure religious liberty in the work of the school counselor.

One of the functions of a counselor which is relevant to religious liberty is his involvement in moral concerns. Since the counselor's function is generally recognized as including both therapeutic and preventive counseling, then we must be saying (whether we say it covertly or overtly makes no difference) how the counselee "ought" to regard others and himself. If we counsel or teach, we cannot escape the responsibility or fact of the teaching of morals.

Reprinted by permission of the author and *Counselor Education and Supervision*, VI, No. 3 (Spring, 1967), 208-209.

Claud C. Crawford, Professor of Education, Hope College, Holland, Michigan.

A second function of the counselor is his involvement in religious concerns. Religion may be defined as a philosophy of life to which one is committed. Assuming the validity of the definition, are we in fact imparting some philosophy of life in the schools and are we advocating commitment? Calia has stated:

> The heretofore forbidden areas of values, philosophy of life and purpose should be considered the vital but hardly exclusive province of the effective counselor. The fine points of dogma, doctrine or theology need not concern nor deter the general counselor as long as he operates within the dictates of the cultural core. (1)

Gardner Murphy writes, ". . . it is not true that the wise man's sharing of a philosophy of life is an arrogant imposition upon a defenseless client;" he argues rather that such activities give ". . . clients a sounder, as well as a richer, life." (3) Williamson has stated that each person ought to ". . . add to the search for job competence and the full understanding of one's self-concept a full commitment to value systems which are growth producing, both to the individual and to his associates as an additional dimension of the adequate personality." (5) Such statements give credence to the practice of religious indoctrination by not only the counselor but also the educator.

If religious indoctrination is an essential aspect of education and counseling then what are some of the religions found in the schools today? One of these religions is materialism. We cover bulletin boards with the statistics about how much more one can earn by going to college. Educational planning is all too frequently made solely on the basis of its potential earning power.

Another religion which may be found in the schools is nationalism. It has a religious service in the pledge of allegiance. Its importance was reflected in a recent issue of the *Saturday Review* where Melman stated that "two-thirds of America's technical researchers now work for the military." (2)

Other powerful religions in the public schools are the religions of Naturalism, Subjectivism, and Relativism. Their dogmas include such things as: the only reality is Nature; there are no objective truths—everything is relative (save the absolute of relativism itself); everything one thinks and believes is only subjective; and truth is only a subjective phenomenon. Lastly there are the theistic religions which have already had their share in educational issues.

What remains to be considered is the question of what to do if the argument is valid. First, religion must remain in the schools. If the schools could become truly irreligious institutions, i.e., where they would be "commitmentless" environments, it would be disastrous. Trueblood has said, "Men can be deprived of much and bear it, but that of which they cannot be permanently deprived is a sense of meaning in their lives." (4)

Second, if religious liberty is to be functional in the public schools, all religions must be welcome and free to speak. Recently, there was a speaker at the University of Tennessee who spoke of religion in the school without naming it as such. When questioned in private with regard to this point the answer was, "Sure, but why call it that?" This may sound valid, but if a theist talks this way it is always called "that." The speaker's position necessarily results in a denial of religious liberty. Perhaps it should be pointed out that there is a difference between teaching religion and conducting a religious worship service. I agree that religious worship services should be kept out of the public schools, but the teaching of religion, at least its fundamental tenets, is another matter.

Third, since counseling is a private confidential relationship, the religious persuasion of the school counselor needs to be known to the students and the community ahead of time. Perhaps this could best be implemented by a written statement of his philosophy. Such a statement might embody definitive statements on such subjects as the nature of man, the nature of good and evil, the nature of the "good life," and the process of therapy, since these are all crucial concepts related to the counseling process. This presupposes the counselor can write his philosophy. If my observation of counselor education programs and counselors is typical, this is probably not the case. I would suggest then, the following:

1. That counselor educators write and make public their philosophical (i.e., religious) orientations.

2. That college students in counselor preparation be given time all through their preparation to develop, modify, and state definitively their philosophy, and that its acceptable writing be one condition for graduation and certification.

3. That the public schools insist that one condition for employment of a school counselor be his willingness to make public his written philosophy. The schools, however, must be careful to maintain religious liberty by not having the counselor's particular religious persuasion a criterion for employment.

In a powerful institution, such as the public schools, religous discrimination becomes a very serious matter. It is my contention that the above suggestions can assure religious freedom—the *status quo* discriminates. I recognize that the above suggestions present some serious problems. More serious, however, are the problems if nothing is done.

REFERENCES

1. McDaniel, Henry P. with G. A. Shaftel. *Guidance in the Modern School.* New York: The Dryden Press, 1957.
2. Melman, Seymour. "Behind the mask of success," *Saturday Review,* July 31, 1965, *46*, 8–10, 29.
3. Murphy, Gardner. "The cultural context of guidance," *Personnel and Guidance Journal,* September, 1955, *34*, 4–9.

4. Trueblood, David Elton. *General Philosophy*. New York: Harper & Row, 1963.
5. Williamson, E. G. "Value commitments and counseling," *Teachers College Record*, May, 1961, 42, 602–08.

Administrative Deterrents to Guidance Program Development

Bruce Shertzer

Shelley C. Stone

The school-guidance movement is in a hurry. Events within the past five years—space satelites, burgeoning enrollments, school reorganization, education as national defense—have accentuated the need for guidance and subsequently forced increases in guidance personnel and services in a manner unequaled in the fifty-year history of the movement. Shifts in emphasis resulting from these and many other events raise a singularly important and disturbing question regarding the relationship between administrators and guidance personnel: Can and will administrative leadership be exerted to facilitate and implement the stated goals of a specialized service within the schools? It is assumed that guidance services are an integral part of the total school program and therefore share the common goals of the educational enterprise. This is to say that guidance services and

Reprinted by permission of the authors and *Theory Into Practice*, II, No. 1 (February, 1963), 24-42.

Bruce Shertzer and Shelley C. Stone, Purdue University, Lafayette, Indiana.

personnel are *not* ancillary, expendable parts of a luxurious educational program, but rather, that they make necessary contributions to student learning and development.

The tasks confronting the school administrator who is committed to individualization within a broadening spectrum of pupil diversity are multiplying and becoming more complex. That administrators need to examine guidance-program developments thoroughly is patently clear. Kehas highlighted this need when he noted that "The emphasis on guidance programs and services, the great growth in recent years has been 'topsy-like' and situationally determined reflecting no clear program, direction or tendency of growth."[1] A *number* of factors have contributed to this chaotic state of affairs. A review of *some of the administrative deterrents* to purposeful guidance development may help reveal how past administrative behavior has set the pattern for the present lack of effective guidance direction and design. It also may be useful to those concerned with the challenge of today and the promise and the menace of tomorrow.

This article may be viewed as a somewhat critical presentation. The criticism stems from frustration born of a sincere commitment to the field coupled with the unpleasant experience of placing competent, dedicated counselors in intolerable situations marked by many restricting and disabling conditions. No doubt some will argue that we have been unnecessarily harsh with administrators. A number of nonadministrative factors contribute to the failure of guidance programs; however, this article is concerned primarily with administrative deterrents. What will be said is not wholly applicable to all schools, but the caricature fits many and parts of it may apply to all.

The careful reader will note that the discussion of each deterrent contains some positive alternative courses of action. It cannot be claimed that the alternatives are easy. But it can be claimed legitimately that progress and the eventual realization of any promise that these services hold depends upon the awareness of positive courses of action or other constructive alternatives. Persistence in past detrimental actions can produce no gains and, in fact, can seriously incapacitate a worth-while school service.

Deterrent number one lies in the failure to program guidance services adequately despite the recent stimulus of financial aid. Before the advent of the National Defense Education Act of 1958, guidance was overwhelmed by extremes in numbers—i.e., too few counselors, too many pupils, and consequently unrealistic pupil-counselor ratios. As a result, only marginal services were rendered. The windfall of aid from Title V of the NDEA should have produced fresh and imaginative approaches capitalizing upon the main strength of guidance by affording counselors time with the individual. But too many administrators seemed bound to conventional approaches which dictated service to large groups simultaneously. Solutions to old

[1]Kehas, Chris D. "Towards the Development of Theory in the Administration and Organization of Guidance Services," *Counselor Education and Supervision,* Winter, 1961, *1*, 100-101.

educational problems were forced upon new problems, whether the solutions were applicable to guidance or not. Thus, the primary strength of guidance, that of individualization, was rendered ineffectual.

Many administrators had long used the dollar shortage as an excuse for an inability to provide comprehensive guidance services. When NDEA funds were made available, too often the money was used for the questionable extension of certain services rather than for the improvement of the entire program. No clearer illustration exists than that of equating good guidance with extensive, unnecessary testing. Vast amounts of money were poured into stockpiling tests and the overtesting of student populations with little or no consideration given to the *use* of test results. This occurred despite the commonly accepted principle that a good testing program is a minimal testing program with a specific end in view: the application of test results so as to achieve better understanding of students and the evaluation of school programs in light of student needs. Money, therefore, should be used to acquire qualified personnel who will help promote this objective.

Deterrent number two lies in the proclivity of some administrators to play at strategy for the sake of strategy. It is known that practitioners of modern educational administration are seldom free agents. Only infrequently can they pursue educational strategy with any certainty that their public will react as they hope and plan it will. Factions within the total public invariably disagree. Often the cumulative impression left with the administrator who attempts to judge the public's mood is that it is skeptical, indifferent, and apathetic. To gain their ends, some educational administrators rely on the questionable practice of manipulating socially significant word-symbols in such fashion as to evoke the desired emotional response needed to produce support for administrative decisions. Brickell has called attention to this:

> The great significance of administrative initiative is heavily disguised. Phrases like "democratic administration," "the team approach," "shared decision-making," and "staff involvement" are commonplace. Behavior to match them is rare. The participation patterns in widespread use are very often little more than enabling arrangements, organized after an administrator has decided the general direction (and in some cases the actual details) of an instructional change. The control center of the school, as things are managed today, is the administrator.[2]

What is striking is that adroit administrators, in an effort to justify the need for guidance programs, find it expedient to appeal for public support not in the logical terms of the educational imperatives but rather in nonlogical terms such as the superiority of "our school" over "their school." A Machiavellian-like approach, while frequently effective, harms the very service it seeks to nurture. The result of this type of appeal is that little attention is given to a guidance design based upon the actual educational

---

[2]Brickell, Henry M. "The Dynamics of Educational Change," *Theory Into Practice,* April, 1962, *1*, 82-83.

and psychological needs of students in the local school. The energy spent on marshaling support for a program in name only can far better be expended in formulating a reasoned statement of objectives and purposes. This more positive approach could be effective with the public and at the same time would produce a policy framework to provide internal direction and structure to the guidance program.

Deterrent number three may be termed the misery of the impotent. In the past, administrators have been quick to assign, and counselors have been content to accept, clerical and administrative duties, such as taking attendance, scheduling, assigning discipline penalities, and doing substitute teaching. Knapp and Denny point out that it is not uncommon for studies to show that:

> . . . counselors are often a disgruntled lot due to an excess of quasi-administrative duties with a corresponding neglect of guidance and counseling. Such studies are of value as they focus attention on real problems, but much more must be done with the actual use of counseling time.[3]

Administrators usually base their requests for counselors on the argument that they are needed to provide individual counseling relationships for students. However, once hired, the counselor is too often used as a jack-of-all-trades operating in quasi-administrative areas. This places crippling limitations on the performance of appropriate counselor duties. If an administrator hires a counselor to do one thing, loads him down with a second and a third and a fourth set of tasks, he is unable, or at least unlikely, to perform his proper assignment. Counselors must share the blame with administrators for this situation. Many studies which decry the abuse of the counselor's time and skills[4] reflect the counselors' inability to communicate effectively what they are realistically able to do and ideally should be doing. Chenault and Seegars state:

> Principals indicate that counselors should play more of a decision-making, leadership role while counselors suggest that they, the counselors, should lean more toward impartial observation and understanding.
>
> Principals have much more strongly emphasized the qualities of aggressiveness and firmness . . . while counselors have indicated that principals should be more forceful and willing to accept responsibility. . . .
>
> With such findings in mind, certain types of conflicts between counselors and principals become more readily explainable. Although principals and counselors may be aware of the role differences expected in their jobs, principals frequently complain that counselors "do not accept

[3]Knapp, Dale L., and Denny, Earl W. "The Counselor's Responsibility in Role Definition," *Personnel and Guidance Journal*, September, 1961, *40*, 50.

[4]Martyn, Kenneth A. "We Are Wasting the Counselor's Time," *California Journal of Secondary Education*, November, 1957, *32*, 439-41; Purcell, Florence E. "Counseling Assignments and Efficiency," *Vocational Guidance Quarterly*, Spring, 1957, *5*, 111-13; Tennyson, Willard W. "Time: The Counselor's Dilemma!" *Personnel and Guidance Journal*, October, 1958, *37*, 129-35.

the responsibility necessary for their place in the administrative pattern," and counselors often state that principals "are not tolerant of the counseling function."[5]

Effective counselor communication with administrators is espcially needed because students' and parents' perceptions of the guidance services are frequently cast in the image the administrator projects. The counselor who is required to function as an administrative assistant, or who permits himself to be used in this way, will inevitably be seen by students and parents as no more than this. In most cases, students do not bring problems to an administrator; to the degree that a counselor functions as an administrator, he is rendered impotent as a counselor.

Deterrent number four is found in the controversies that now exist among counselor educators. Such questions as whether teachers should be the source of supply for counselors, how much emphasis should be given to psychology within the counselor-training program, what is the job and role of counselors, what are the services to be offered—to cite but a few—cloud the programing of guidance services. This deterrent is mentioned, not to point to a weakness among counselor educators, but because such debate is frequently misunderstood by administrators and used by them to postpone guidance planning and development. The administrator who views these controversies as evidence of weakness and confusion misunderstands the premises underlying counselor preparation. There is a continuous need for improvement and change in preparation to meet changing demands. The modifications brought about by such discussions ultimately will produce better personnel capable of rendering better guidance services. Examination of the history of the guidance movement supports the contention that counselor educators can be expected to build preparation programs based upon the realities of the public-school setting. However, this cannot and should not be interpreted to mean that they will merely maintain the status quo. Movements afoot in counselor training indicate that the counselor prepared in the next decade will differ from the counselor of the past decade. He will be better trained, more professional, more of a specialist in those areas pertinent to school guidance programs. The astute administrator will keep pace with these changes by encouraging corresponding growth and modification of job assignment and services offered. This can be done best by discussing with the counselor what he is best equipped to do and then permitting him to assume appropriate responsibilities.

Deterrent number five is the notable absence of research in guidance-program development and management. Three years ago, Dugan, in reviewing educational research, stated: "Previous reviews have noted the paucity of substantial research relating to the problem of guidance policy, staff qualification and relationships, budget, facilities, and counselor du-

---

[5]Chenault, Joann, and Seegars, James E., Jr. "The Interpersonal Diagnosis of Principals and Counselors," *Personnel and Guidance Journal,* October, 1962, *41,* 121.

ties."[6] The basic organizational patterns; program and personnel co-ordination, articulation, and supervision; staff functions and relationships; and physical facilities—all need immediate research attention. Guidance supervisors and school administrators must move in the direction of merging the principles and premises of guidance with those of organization and administration. The development and management of programs should flow simultaneously from guidance theory and from theory in educational administration. Perhaps it is premature to suggest that decisions be based on theory since neither area is noted for a well-developed theoretical base. Because of this lack of a systematic theoretical framework, a pragmatic approach is the only approach currently available. If it is true that we are in the unhappy and unscientific position of basing our activities upon trial and error methods, it is essential that we recognize that trial and error does not mean trial alone.

If the trial and error approach is the only feasible way, it is incumbent on those who employ it to scrutinize thoroughly its results. The tendency in the past has been to adopt practices because of expediency, economy, and emotionality. All too often such practices are maintained and defended, whether of value or not, because of an aversion to change and a failure to examine their results. The important point here is that many things work, but that some things may work better than the practices we now employ. If we never look, if we never test in the true sense of pitting methods against each other, if we never try new approaches, obviously we see no errors. Our first try becomes our last and only try. We remain complacent, happy—and maybe, less effective.

Deterrent number six has been the inadequate physical facilities and budget typically assigned to guidance services. Counseling space is often considered last, if at all, in guidance design. Counselors across the country have reported the dismal experience of moving from classroom to classroom to perform counseling duties and their feeling of achievement when they have finally been awarded the janitor's renovated supply closet for a private office. Despite the progress made in ascertaining what facilities are needed, where they should be located, and how they should be arranged and equipped, administrators seemingly find it difficult to provide minimally adequate facilities even in newly constructed or remodeled buildings. Students need privacy if counselors are to establish a helping relationship with them. Two observations are significant when one reviews the few studies dealing with guidance budgets.[7] First, very few schools have adequate

---

[6]Dugan, Willis E. "The Organization and Administration of Guidance Services," *Review of Educational Research,* April, 1960, *30,* 105.

[7]Crosby, Joseph W. *The Cost of Guidance Services in Selected High Schools.* Los Angeles: California Test Bureau, Report E, January, 1956; Palm, Harold. "High School Guidance: What Does It Cost Today?" *Vocational Guidance Quarterly,* Spring, 1961, *9,* 169-72; Wellman, Frank. "The Cost of Guidance Services," *Guidance Service Newsletter,* Columbus, Ohio: State Department of Education, January, 1957, *10,* 10.

guidance budgets or even approach the rule of thumb that schools should devote five per cent of the total budget to guidance. Second, not only do some administrators fail to provide a satisfactory financial base, but many have little knowledge of the actual amount of their total budget devoted to guidance.

It would be possible to argue convincingly that all of the deterrents mentioned above have their origins in the problem of finances. By its very nature, guidance is expensive since it does, or should, deal primarily with the individual student. The sooner administrators face up to this and make available adequate financial provisions, the sooner schools will stop having guidance programs in name only. A faltering administrative commitment unsupported by dollars and cents is frequently worse than no program at all.

The seventh and most telling deterrent to effective guidance-program development and management lies with those who foster the mistaken, shortsighted, and unrealistic notion that guidance can be all things and do all things for everyone. Within recent years, many local, state, and national groups have exerted simultaneous demands upon the schools to salvage the dropouts, redirect the delinquent, identify and nurture both ends of the ability continuum, and help the emotionally disturbed. In addition to these specific demands, and sometimes as a reaction against them, others have restressed the more general goal of developing the potentialities of *all* pupils. In an effort to satisfy everyone, administrators, as well as overeager guidance personnel, have responded to these public concerns by glibly citing the mere existence of guidance services in the schools. By so doing, they have implied to a naive public that guidance solves each and every educational difficulty and remedies every real or imagined community ill.

The easy answer that guidance programs and personnel are the magic solution to these diverse problems is absurd. Such social symptoms are a result of pervasive sociological, economic, emotional, and moral disharmonies in our culture. Consequently, they must be understood and dealt with in a broad context. To see them merely as isolated problems to be solved by guidance personnel alone is inappropriate. While guidance services may be *one* useful agent in the alleviation of some of these problems, such services are obviously inadequate cure-alls and often come too late to perform a prophylactic function.

Those administrators who are tempted to invoke the name of guidance as a quick answer to these problems would be better advised to use the opportunity to request support for the complex of specialists required to remedy society's mistakes. Unfortunately the same administrator who is somewhat cautious about making unfounded claims for his instructional program, frequently portrays his counselors as combination messiahs-magicians-pied pipers. Such claims condemn guidance personnel to failure. It is little consolation to say that it was impossible to succeed.

These deterrents have been cited to illustrate that in too many schools the gap between the administrators' verbal commitments to guidance and the living, working realities in program management is indeed great. Because of this discrepancy, some have grave doubts as to the eagerness of school administrators to risk tackling these problems. Clearly there is a need to face these problems honestly. To do so, administrators need most of all to become the realists that they so often formally proclaim themselves to be. There is a decisive urgency to reconsider the guidance function in their schools. We have every reason to believe that present problems can and will be met by forward-looking administrators. The current general concern with these problems argues well that we may expect better results in the future.

The Pupil Behavioral System

Herman J. Peters

To facilitate an individual's full development within the realities of a changing society—which is one of education's greatest challenges—requires a new look to evaluate the effectiveness of instruction, the educational plant operation, and what has been called "pupil personnel services." My special concern is with the last of these three.

The central goal of any pupil personnel program should be to facilitate learning opportunities for the pupil. However, the present pupil personnel system emphasizes a personnel approach—fit the pupil to the school—rather than a merger of the two *with the pupil as the dominant consideration* in the educational process. I propose that there is a need for a new approach.

The pupil personnel services system provides no systematic approach.

Reprinted by permission of the author and *Theory Into Practice*, IV, No. 4 (October, 1965), 146-152.

Herman J. Peters, Professor of Education, The Ohio State University, Columbus.

Rather, its role has evolved by performing a series of activities ranging from checking attendance to helping the dissonant pupil to record keeping. Of course, these are necessary activities, but as a basis for unified activity they provide an incidentalistic approach with all of the conflicts inherent in such sporadic efforts. A ramification of the problem of record keeping is that recorded information seems to be used only to confirm and to fix the present place of the pupil instead of serving as a point of departure to suggest action to move him forward.

Implicit in the system is an attempt to order the heterogeneity of the school program, and this in itself is not bad. However, the ordering usually ends as an attempt to subdue the pupils and keep them from "rocking the boat," so that, in numerous instances, the pupil personnel program operates only as the arm of the school to keep things in order.

The focus has been and has continued to be on troubled students. Because of this, the present system has developed a defensive posture as it has attempted to eliminate negative factors through therapeutic means. Too often the use of a service such as counseling simply gets the pupil ready to return to the same situation which created the need for counseling in the first place. Then, after numbers of pupils have exhibited a particular cluster of traits, the school staff beings to establish a means to remedy the problem. Rare is the program which is preventive and then developmental. The present system of pupil personnel services grew out of needs, usually desperate needs of pupils. However, these needs require a priori consideration before learning can ever hope to be fully effective.

A new approach must be established that will take up the offensive for pupils in a positive, developmental manner. It is such an approach as this that I propose for a new program to be called the Pupil Behavioral System. The Pupil Behavioral System will emphasize normality, i.e., the point of view that a pupil is normal if he can participate in the regular classroom. Positive emphasis will direct the effort to prevent a pupil's problems from becoming engulfing and self-defeating; problems and vulnerabilities are recast in terms of strengths.

A monitor for rather than after the facts, the Pupil Behavioral System implies an alertness for possible indicators to avenues for fuller development. Monitored data will be perused not only for the unsuccessful experiences of learning that may be reflected but also for the successful. As an agent of change, the System will stress a school program that is flexible to meet pupil needs it will discover. It will provide a point of reference to assess the suitability of the instructional program for pupils of today—and what other pupils are there?

The Pupil Behavioral System will pursue its goals in terms of the following objectives:

To provide an opportunity in the educational program for a pupil to view himself and to be viewed in his totality, unhampered by the instructional or administrative division of the school.

To guide the pupil to the maximum of his current strengths, based on the knowledge substance of child or adolescent development.

To help the pupil in forming a positive relationship between his developmental capacities and his environmental conditions so that the optimal exercise of his abilities will occur.

To challenge the pupil and school staff of the school system to consider whether the current academic program is the most effective that can be pursued.

To assist the pupil and school staff to perceive individuality not only in terms of the differences themselves but also in terms of the profoundly unique differences occuring as a person acts in his totality with the environment.

In consideration of these objectives, the Pupil Behavioral System necessitates new statements of the basic concepts of authority, focus, structure, substantive bases, and staff. Following is a brief discussion of each that evolves out of a basic proposition in each area.

Authority

Proposition One: The Pupil Behavioral System will function as an independent, autonomous division of the school system.

Of course, implementation of such a proposal necessitates an acknowledging of the functioning of the Pupil Behavioral System as an integral part of the total educational program but identifiably distinct from the instruction and educational plant divisions.

When the duties of the counselor include taking attendance, administrative duty, and some substitute teaching, doubt may arise in a pupil's mind concerning who really evaluates, judges, or keeps confidences. Such a situation strains any guidance relationship for its maximum impact. If the staff members in the schools are to be professionally responsible, then they must be removed from a line relationship to the principal and be directly responsible, instead, to the chief administrative officer in charge of the Pupil Behavioral System. They must not be contained within the efforts of the administration to maintain discipline nor of instruction to determine subject matter.

The traditional system of building autonomy will be blended with the rational grounds of professional pupil behavioral leadership. The staff member will respect the principal's authority, but he will seek the leadership and follow the professional decisions of his director who will be situated as a member of the superintendent's office. The director of the system will take visibly more active leadership to promote his work in the schools for which he is responsible.[1] Wary of upsetting the local domain of the principal and instructional staff, the director of the pupil personnel services system too

---

[1]Peters, Herman J. "Interferences to Guidance Program Development," *Personnel and Guidance,* October, 1963, *42,* 121-22.

often functions only as an information specialist on guidance for the superintendent. Weber stated ". . . orientation to the *validity* (italics mine) of an order means more than the mere existence of a uniformity of social action determined by custom and self-interest."[2] The responsibility of one's professional commitment must take precedence over the authority of hierarchy of formal structure and be coordinated with the authority of sanctions which persists in the total school organization. "The argument is for a functional allocation of authority in school systems, for a division of authority based on competence and expertise rather than on some unexamined notion of authority based on ultimate responsibility."[3]

Focus

Proposition Two: The Pupil Behavioral System will establish practices that are developmentally focused and proceed on knowledge of child and adolescent behavior, reflecting mental, social, emotional, and physical growth, with particular emphasis on the appraisal of the impacts of home, school, and community on the growing personality.

The pupil behavioral program will follow the example set by the federal labor department in its evaluative techniques—attention is to the panorama of life, including the vital influence of socioeconomic changes on the individual.

In the present guidance program, pupils are assessed and predictions follow that are almost entirely on the basis of past records, tests, and events. So much is focused on testing for college, and unfavorable results are interpreted as personal failure by the child. Emphasis needs to be given to all possible activities for living—available data will be used to determine developmental possibilities for the future, rather than merely to validate expectations of the past.

The Pupil Behavioral System will give consideration to those behaviors related to educational progress, career development, and personality fulfillment. It will include such related functions as health, sociology of one's living, individual psychology, learning transactions, peer relationships, and career bases. A key function of the Pupil Behavioral System will be to act as an agent of change, bringing in and making use of new variables to promote continuous growth: the pupil's present level of growth and maturity, his new perceptions, new demands, and new possibilities for behavior in the culture.

It is grossly unfair to judge a pupil from the narrow, restrictive framework of past knowledge alone—for he is an energy system capable of much change.

---

[2]Weber, Max. "Legitimate Order and Types of Authority," in *Theories of Society*, Talcott Parsons, editor. New York: Free Press of Glencoe, Ill., 1961, pp. 229-35.

[3]Kehas, Chris D. "Administrative Structure and Guidance Theory," *Counselor Education and Supervision*, Spring, 1965, p. 148.

Structure

Proposition Three: The Pupil Behavioral System derives its structure from responsibility inherent in the nature of the program to examine and work with pupils as they perceive and are perceived as individuals; it includes policy definitions, resources mobilization, and executive responsibility to activate its areas of function: appraisal, sociology, individual differences, and experiencing.

Policy is based chiefly on the thesis that the purpose of the Pupil Behavioral System is to act as a radar alert system to potential and recommend possibilities for its realization. Resources comprise human, technical, and physical assets of the school and community.

The pupil behavioral program would be of equal stature, authority, and responsibility with the divisions of instruction and of educational plant operation in the school system. While the educational plant operation shares definite lines of operation with instruction and vice versa, the Pupil Behavioral System, by the nature of its concern for the pupil, will operate as a more flexible system of relationships with these other major areas. Within the Pupil Behavioral System, the separate functions, i.e., appraisal, sociology, individual differences, and experiencing would be coordinated and would extend vertically.

The diagram by Weitz indicates the areas of the program's mutual concern with instruction.[4] The distinguishability of the primary functions of pupil behavioral work and those of instruction is often confused with

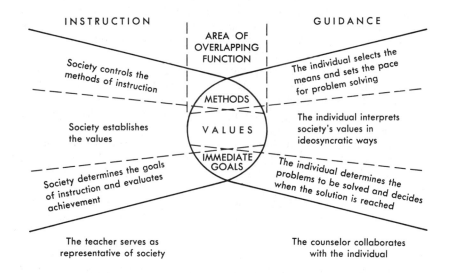

INSTRUCTION — GUIDANCE

AREA OF OVERLAPPING FUNCTION

Society controls the methods of instruction

The individual selects the means and sets the pace for problem solving

METHODS

Society establishes the values

The individual interprets society's values in ideosyncratic ways

VALUES

IMMEDIATE GOALS

Society determines the goals of instruction and evaluates achievement

The individual determines the problems to be solved and decides when the solution is reached

The teacher serves as representative of society

The counselor collaborates with the individual

---

[4]Weitz, Henry. *Behavior Change through Guidance.* New York: John Wiley and Sons, Inc., 1964, p. 63. (The diagram is reproduced with the permission of John Wiley and Sons, Inc.)

uniqueness and it is assumed that the primary functions occur only in one place but not in the other. As the Weitz diagram indicates, there are areas of overlap; and, if each respective staff member performs his primary function well, any secondary functions will not lead to duplication of effort but to a coordinated approach for total pupil development.

Substantive Base

Proposition Four: The Pupil Behavioral System relies in its substantive base on the behavioral disciplines: psychology, sociology, education, anthropology, economics, and certain aspects of health.

A pupil relates to, acts upon, and reacts to events—his life is a continuous series of transactions. The classroom situation itself presents a series of transactions in a relatively limited and predetermined direction of the subject matter. In contrast to current emphasis on the psychology of differences, the Pupil Behavioral System would provide a more encompassing transactional base which would transmit the information gained from viewing pupils from the vantage points of other behavioral disciplines, as well. It would, therefore, serve in assisting both the pupil and the teacher to make classroom situations more meaningful.

The pupil behavioral staff member would be able to interpret the sociology of the pupil's culture to open new ways of presenting subject matter, understanding the pupil's actions and ractions to learning subject matter, and using motivational schema for arousing the pupil's interest.

Staff

Proposition Five: The Pupil Behavioral System will encompass a staff of at least seven members, who will be prepared in a core of similar study in the last two years of their baccalaureate program and the first year of their two-year master's program. The second year of their graduate work will provide specialization in a particular phase of pupil behavioral work. A master's degree will be an employment requirement. Pupil behavioral preparation will use the resources of many areas and provide an interdisciplinary approach to understanding pupil behavior as an ever changing aggregate of developmental phenomena throughout all of the school years, with particular reference to school learning situations.

Understanding the impingements on children and youth in a synecological manner requires staff who have worked with children in a variety of situations. Preparation for pupil behavior staff would include experimental work with children and adolescents in youth groups, settlement houses, camps, and schools; microcounseling and guidance experiences would also be provided in many situations. Teaching experience per se would not be required—it offers only one limited situational opportunity.

Depending on the size of the system and characteristics of the pupil population, pupil behavioral staff members would work in one of the areas given below that is consistent with their competencies. In any one area, if demanded by local pupil needs, a staff member might focus his efforts on a particular set of pupil characteristics within that area—for example, one staff member might work exclusively on a program for the emotionally disturbed. In addition, according to pupil needs a number of staff might work in each area—for example, a counselor would be assigned to one hundred pupils. Each of the main areas would include a research staff whose work would be coordinated.

The minimum number of individual staff members planned in the Pupil Behavioral System are named and discussed below.

The *Pupil Behavioral Appraisal Analyst* would work in measurement, appraisal, and evaluation and be housed in central offices with an appropriate number of field representatives (one for each 5,000 students) and electronic equipment. The staff would monitor, analyze, alert, teach, and research other pupil behavioral staff and instructional personnel and would provide individual and group testing. However, each pupil behavioral staff member would be competent to use instruments relative to or overlapping in this area.

The *Pupil Behavioral Sociologist* would work with community agencies, parents, and concerns indigenous to the environmental impact on pupils. The staff would monitor, analyze, alert, teach, and research. The number of staff members would be dependent on the size and needs of the school system, but there would be at least one in each system.

One *Pupil Behavioral Counselor* would be in each school building to work with every one hundred pupils at all grade levels. A counselor could probably see about ten pupils a day in order to allow for some counselor-pupil contact at least every two weeks. As needed, there may be pupil behavioral counselors working at large to provide guidance for a special and timely need, e.g., to think through final stages in the moving of a pupil to an area technical school.

The *Pupil Behavioral Physical Consultant* would work with the medical personnel and specialists in speech and hearing identification and analysis, physically handicapped identification and analysis, as well as work with the developmental health concerns of the normal pupil.

The *Pupil Behavioral Mental Health Consultant* and his staff would have the responsibility for all pupils and those identifiable with particular concerns such as the emotionally disturbed and would work with specialists as needed.

The *Pupil Behavioral Information Specialist* would work with a myriad of information concerning educational and vocational choice.

The *Director for Pupil Behavioral Program Development* would be the head of the entire staff. In a large system, each staff member would be responsible to him through his area divisional head for the smooth functioning of the total system.

Efforts with exceptional children will encompass the various areas, the same as for all pupils. Except in rare instances, exceptional children should be considered normal pupils who have very limited but significant interferences to learning. Pupil behavioral effects and instructional processes for such children are related and must be, if pupils are truly the focus of our work; however, the educational effort to implement and complement the pupil behavioral staff work with exceptional children would be properly housed under instruction.

> It is becoming increasingly accepted that special education programs provided for atypical or exceptional children—the physically handicapped, emotionally disturbed, and mentally retarded—children whose needs tend to differentiate them from the larger group of pupils in attendance at the public schools, should be classified as instructional rather than pupil personnel services.[5]

In any one system the number of pupils with a particular set of characteristics, such as defective vision or retarded mentality, may necessitate special attention of a staff member. But, except for those relatively few who are at considerable variance with normality, it is far better to think and work in terms of individualizing education for all pupils—to continue to segment, categorize, and label every distinguishable group of pupils is to do them a disservice. A label is difficult to remove.

Conclusion

The Pupil Behavioral System reveals its major differences from present practices in the areas of authority, clarification of staff assignments, clearer articulation through all the grades, and emphasis on development rather than therapy. It focuses on pupil behavioral functions and allows the counselor to counsel—without forcing him to be an administrative assistant or teacher as well—and it clarifies the testing program for guidance purposes.

The pupil behavioral system staff would monitor pupil data and assign it to the relevent administrators and teachers. Individually and in groups, it would interpret meanings and suggest possible action to assist pupils' learning and total development with administrators and teachers—and, as appropriate, with the pupils themselves.

Through direct relationship with pupil behavior system staff or through a respresentative for a common concern, teachers would use initiative in the mutual approach to assisting pupils. By emphasizing their primary duties while working with the entire educational staff, they would create a more harmonious system of educational accomplishment. In-service education in proper use of the Pupil Behavioral System as an ongoing practice would reduce the discontinuity resultant from staff changes.

---

[5]Fusco, Gene C. *Organization and Administration of Pupil Personnel Service Programs in Selected School Systems.* Washington, D.C.: U.S. Government Printing Office, 1961, p. 1. *See* also, Council of Chief State School Officers, *Responsibilities of State Departments of Education for Pupil Personnel Services.* Washington, D.C.: the Council, 1960, p. 2.

For the Pupil Behavioral System to work effectively, coordination of its efforts internally and externally within the school system is important. A schoolwide coordinating committee of staff from administration, instruction, extraclass activities, and the pupil behavioral program should be formed to synchronize the actions of each of these areas of the educational system.

A well-organized, functional Pupil Behavioral System would be given *primary* consideration in the development of the total school program. In this connection, the role of the superintendent arises for consideration in such a change in the organization of the system. "The new concept of the superintendency," says Edwin A. Fensch, "envisions the central staff administrator of a school system as a team effort. . . . The primary mission of the team captain becomes that of coordinating the technical talents of his assistants toward a common goal."[6]

Effective functioning of the program will create no special financial problems. For some school systems, the cost of the Pupil Behavioral System would be no more than their current pupil personnel programs. The cost would increase as staff-pupil ratios would become more and more favorable; however, as in other areas of life, the question arises whether we can *afford* the cheap model. As Samler states in proposing a school program for improving pupils' self-understanding, ". . . such a program will cost money. But money is easier to come by than comfort. It is not really a problem. If we want this kind of program badly enough, we will provide the money. What we need to start with is the interest and conviction; ways to finance it will be found."[7]

If schools and school staff are to be as flexible as they expect their pupils to be, they will need to change. Entrenched methods, outdated organizational patterns, and resistant staff cannot long hold the line against inevitable change. The time is coming when we will have to choose between a remodeled, yet essentially the same, pupil personnel approach and a new, flexible system that will help take each child as far as he is capable of going—the Pupil Behavioral System.

---

[6]Fensch, Edwin A., and Wilson, Robert E. *The Superintendency Team.* Columbus, Ohio: Charles E. Merrill Books, Inc., 1964, p. 14.

[7]Samler, Joseph. "The School and Self-Understanding," *Harvard Educational Review,* Winter, 1965, *33,* 68.

Culture-Fair Testing

Anne Anastasi

The title of my talk illustrates one of the "Innovations in Testing" with which this panel is concerned. Had the organizer of this program been less sophisticated and up-to-date than she is, I might have been asked to talk about culture-free tests. This more traditional title would have provided me with a convenient opening sentence, in which I could have disclaimed the existence of any such tests. At that point either I could have sat down or I could have proceeded to talk about something else. But no such easy solution is open to me now.

I shall approach my topic from several angles, including rationale, varieties, universality, factorial composition, and validity. First we may ask, "What is the current *rationale* of culture-fair tests and how does it differ from that of the older 'culture-free' approach?" When psychologists began

Reprinted by permission of the author and *Educational Horizons*, Fall, 1964.
Anne Anastasi, Professor of Psychology, Fordham University, New York.

to develop instruments for cross-cultural testing some fifty years ago, they hoped it would be at least theoretically possible to measure hereditary intellectual potential independently of the impact of cultural experiences. The individual's behavior was thought to be overlaid with a sort of cultural veneer, whose penetration became the objective of culture-free testing.

Subsequent developments in genetics and psychology have demonstrated the basic fallacy in this concept. We now recognize that hereditary and environmental factors interact at all stages in the organism's development, from conception to death, and that their effects are inextricably intertwined in the resultant behavior. For man, culture permeates nearly all environmental contacts. Since all behavior is thus affected by the cultural milieu in which the individual is reared and since psychological tests are but samples of behavior, cultural influences will and should be reflected in test performance. It is therefore futile to try to devise a test that is *free* from cultural influences. The present objective in cross-cultural testing is rather to construct tests that presuppose only experiences that are *common* to different cultures. For this reason, such terms as "culture-fair," "culture-common," and cross-cultural" are gradually replacing the older "culture-free" label.

It follows that there can be many *varieties* of culture-fair tests—as many varieties as there are parameters along which cultural groups differ from each other. A well-known example of such a parameter is language. If the cultural groups to be tested speak different languages, we need a test that requires no use of language on the part of either examiner or subjects. This type of test is illustrated by the *Army Group Examination Beta* and the *Pintner Non-Language General Ability Test*. It is also illustrated by some of the earliest individual performance tests, such as those developed by Knox during the early part of this century to test immigrants at Ellis Island. The *Knox Cube Test,* later incorporated into the *Pintner-Paterson Performance Scale, the Arthur Point Scale of Performance Tests,* and the Wechsler scales, originated in that project.

Another type of culture-fair test is the non-reading test, which calls for extensive use of spoken language by the examiner, but no reading by the subject. Illiterates, persons with inadequate schooling, and those with special reading disabilities are among the groups for which this type of test is culture-fair. A relatively recent example of such tests is provided by Flanagan's *Tests of General Ability,* or TOGA. Extending from the preschool to the adult level, this test demands good understanding of spoken English and considerable information specific to the modern American culture; but it requires no reading. Another example is the nonverbal part of the *Lorge-Thorndike Intelligence Tests.* Many individual performance tests also fit into this category.

Cultures and subcultures frequently differ in the emphasis they place upon speed. Not only the tempo of daily life, but also the motivation to hurry and the value attached to rapid performance vary widely among national cultures, among ethnic minority groups within a single nation, and between urban and rural subcultures. Accordingly, cross-cultural tests have often—though certainly not always—tried to rule out the influence of speed by allowing long time-limits and giving no premium for faster performance.

Still other parameters along which cultures differ pertain to test content. Most non-language and non-reading tests, for example, call for items of information that are specific to certain cultures. Among the culturally linked objects in such instruments as the Army Beta and other non-language tests may be found violin, postage stamp, gun, pocketknife, telephone, piano, and basketball player. A reservation Indian in the United States or an Australian aborigine would lack the experiental background to respond correctly to such items. It was chiefly to control this type of cultural parameter that the classic "culture-free" tests were first developed. Currently available examples include the *Leiter International Performance Scale, the IPAT Culture Free Intelligence Test,* and Raven's *Progressive Matrices.* In all these tests, the attempt was made to include only content common to a wide variety of cultures. The *Davis-Eelts Games* represent an attempt to control content parameters with regard to socioeconomic classes within the urban American culture. Thus in this test, the authors tried to employ only items that would be as familiar to lower-class as to middle-class children in American cities.

The examples cited suffice to show that culture-fair tests have been devised with reference to several specific purposes and for use with specific groups. To be sure, the classical "culture-free" tests, such as the Leiter, IPAT, and *Progressive Matrices,* were developed with very broad objectives in mind. Moreover, the original concept of a "culture-free" test carried strong implications of *universality.* No available test, however, can be accepted as universally applicable or equally "fair" to all cultures. Although less restricted than other tests, cross-cultural tests are never completely unrestricted in their cultural reference. Any test tends to favor individuals from the culture in which it was developed. The mere use of paper-and-pencil or the presentation of abstract tasks having no immediate practical significance will favor some cultural groups and handicap others. Pictures are likewise unsuitable in cultures unaccustomed to representative drawing. A two-dimensional reproduction of an object is not a perfect replica of the original; it simply presents certain cues that, as a result of past experience, lead to the perception of the object. If the cues are highly reduced, as in simplified or schematic drawing, and if the necessary past experience is lacking, the correct perception may not result. Cultural differences in emotional and motivational factors may also influence test performance. Examples include intrinsic interest of test content, rapport with the examiner (who may be a member of another culture), drive to do well on a test, desire to excel others, and past habits of solving problems individually or cooperatively.

Obviously no single test can control all these cultural parameters. Even if it were possible to construct a test that included only content and functions common to all cultures and to so manage its administration as to admit only emotional and motivational variables shared by all mankind, the usefulness of the resulting test might be questionable. Its universally culture-fair residue of behavior would probably prove to be so minute and trivial as not to be worth measuring.

Paradoxical as it may seem, the culture-fairness of a test is itself culturally limited. In other words, a given test may be culture-fair when applied to groups A and B, but heavily culture-bound when used in comparing groups B and C. An entirely different test may be culture-fair in the comparison of groups B and C. This limitation in the applicability of culture-fair tests may be illustrated with the verbal-nonverbal dichotomy into which intelligence test content is often classified. It is commonly assumed that nonverbal tests are more nearly culture-fair than are verbal tests. This assumption is obviously correct for persons who speak different languages. But for groups speaking a common language, whose cultures differ in other important respects, verbal tests may be less culturally loaded than tests of a predominantly spatial or perceptual nature.

Cultural factors may influence relative performance on verbal and nonverbal tests in a number of ways. Interests, value systems, work habits, problem-solving attitudes, or emotional insecurity arising from cultural conditions may foster or retard the development of specific aptitudes. When the *California Test of Mental Maturity* was given to university students in Ceylon, the Ceylonese greatly surpassed the American norms on the language part while falling far below the norms on the non-language part. This difference is the reverse of what might have been expected in a bilingual population such as the Ceylonese. The investigator attributed these results to the value systems of the upper-class Ceylonese culture, which included rejection of manual tasks and attachment of high prestige to verbal scholarship. The nature of the Ceylonese educational system, with its emphasis upon feats of memory and upon learning by precept and rote, was also cited as a possible contributing factor.

As a result of a somewhat different combination of cultural pressures, Jewish groups tested in America usually perform much better on verbal tests than on tests involving concrete objects, spatial relations, and numerical problems. These results have been corroborated in several studies, employing a variety of tests and extending from the preschool to the college level. This intra-individual difference between verbal and nonverbal performance has also been found to increase with age. The traditional emphasis in most Jewish families on formal education and abstract intelligence has often been mentioned in explanation of such findings.

Still another example is provided by studies of American Negroes, who generally perform more poorly on perceptual and spatial tests than on most types of verbal tests. One explanation proposed for these differences centers around problem-solving attitudes. Insofar as the social environment of the American Negro has traditionally encouraged attitudes of passive compliance rather than active exploration, it would be more conducive to rote verbal learning than to perceptual manipulation of stimuli and problem solving.

Here then are three groups—two of them bilingual and one with a relatively poor educational background—which for very different reasons perform better on verbal than on nonverbal tests. These findings challenge the common belief in the greater culture-fairness of nonverbal tests and suggest that the problems of cross-cultural testing are too complex to be solved by a single, all-purpose type of test.

At this point we may well ask: "When is a culture-fair test not culture-fair?" The answer is: "When it fails to control *relevant* cultural parameters." It follows that in choosing a culture-fair test, we must take into account the cultural similarities and differences between the particular groups to be tested, as well as the specific cultural parameters controlled by each test.

There is still another important way in which culture-fair tests differ from each other, namely in their *factorial composition*. In their individual efforts to rule out language, reading, or other culturally biased content, test constructors have followed a variety of paths and have produced tests measuring widely different intellectual functions. When psychometricians regarded all intelligence tests as measures of Spearman's *g*, specific test content was a matter of indifference. But later research with the techniques of factor analysis has demonstrated that the aptitudes measured by different item types or different content may be quite distinct.

Non-language and other cross-cultural tests differ from one another in the extent to which they draw upon spatial and perceptual functions, as contrasted with symbolic manipulation of concepts and abstract relations. The latter functions resemble more closely those required in traditional verbal tests of intelligence. To be sure, the substitution of pictorial for verbal content may itself alter the nature of the test. At the same time, we cannot indiscriminately group together all pictorial or non-language tests. Some, like the Pintner Non-Language Test, concentrate on spatial and perceptual factors to the almost complete exclusion of other factors. Other non-language tests utilize item types calling primarily for ideational or symbolic responses as illustrated by Raven's *Progressive Matrices*.

Although all these tests may yield similar-sounding "intelligence quotients," their similarity is deceptive. The differences in the intellectual functions sampled by different culture-fair tests of intelligence, as well as in their proportional coverage of these functions, provide one more reason for evaluating each test individually, in the light of specific testing purposes and needs.

A final question concerns the *validity* of culture-fair tests. Whether we are interested in predictive validity in the narrow sense or in concurrent, construct, or even content validity, we always want to be able to generalize beyond the test itself. We give a test so that we may draw some conclusion about what this individual will do in *other* situations. Therefore, whether the elimination of cultural differentials from a test will raise or lower its validity depends upon the *breadth* of the cultural differential.

For example, if a test item requires the interpretation of a proverb familiar to children in one cultural group but not in another, its inclusion would probably lower the validity of this test against most criteria. On the other hand, if one group performs more poorly on certain items because of inadequate facility in the use of English, the inclusion of these items would probably not reduce the validity of the test for certain purposes. In this case, the same factor that lowered the test score would also handicap the individual in his educational and vocational progress and in many other activities of daily life. Similarly, slow work habits, emotional insecurity, low achievement drive, lack of interest in abstract problems, and many other culturally linked conditions affecting test scores are also likely to influence the relatively broad area of criterion behavior.

To be sure, these cultural handicaps are remediable—many within the individual's own lifetime. Others, such as the brain damage resulting from improper maternal nutrition or other inadequacies of prenatal environment, may require more than one generation for their elimination. But cultural handicaps cannot be remedied by removing cultural differentials from test scores while leaving them in the criterion behavior that the tests are designed to predict. This ostrich-like approach only evades the problem.

The purpose of tests is to show what the individual is able to do at the time of testing. Tests are not designed to show the causes of behavior or the origins of individual differences in performance. To identify causal factors, we need to investigate the experiential backgrounds of the individuals or groups tested. Nor can tests be used as instruments of social reform. To compensate for a cultural handicap, we need remedial programs directed toward the individual as well as toward society. Masking the handicap by the use of a culture-fair test is no solution.

To summarize: culture-fair tests endeavor to utilize what is common in the experimential backgrounds of different cultural groups. They include many varieties of tests, each eliminating one or more parameters along which cultures differ, such as language, reading, speed, or culturally loaded content. The culture-fairness of any test is not universal but must be evaluated in terms of the cultural differentials of particular groups. Culture-fairness depends upon the control of relevant cultural parameters. Culture-fair tests also differ among themselves in factorial composition, or in relative coverage of different intellectual functions. While an IQ on one such test may be largely a measure of abstract reasoning, on another it may depend chiefly on spatial and perceptual aptitudes. Finally, whether or not cultural differentials should be eliminated from a test depends ultimately upon the effect their elimination will have upon the test's validity for specific purposes.

Change in Values: A Goal In Counseling

Joseph Samler

It seems a safe statement in an otherwise hazardous paper that psychologists are no longer defensive about being concerned with values. Hobbs' summary is only the most recent in a series of essays on ethics, values, science, and psychology (1959). In her presentation of concepts of positive mental health, Marie Jahoda devotes a brief section to the value dilemma (1958). In the last three years, Williamson has written a number of articles on values and counseling. Patterson's chapter on Values and Psychotherapy in his current Counseling and Psychotherapy (1959) cites 52 references to pertinent literature. Wrenn's contributions and Meehl's great clarity on this problem are well known. The current puzzling courtship of religion by psychotherapy (or the other way around) is a related phenomenon.

Reprinted by permission of the author and *Journal of Counseling Psychology*, Vol. 7, No. 1 (Spring, 1960), 32-39.

Joseph Samler, Vocational Rehabilitation and Education Service, Veterans Administration.

On the Derivation of Values

We are at the core, here, of man's search for meaning in life, of his attempt to provide structure where in fact none may exist. Out of this overwhelming need, answers inevitably arose. For millenia they came from the wisdom and intuition of the noblest (a most value-laden term) among us.

The second Isaiah and the other Hebrew prophets, Jesus, the deeply perceptive poets, novelists, playwrights and our modern-day moral leaders, supplied the need out of their own deep feeling and identification with humankind. The nature of the values thus adduced is well known. They are absolute and final and not readily subject to question. They are an integral part of given institutions and to question them is to attack the institutions. Since this not infrequently brings personal guilt and anxiety into play, it is done at some hazard.

As against values thus derived, and in spite of the unnerving cold shower Hobbs' clarity provides, is the method of science. Its disadvantages in the field of values are clearly evident. Out of the scientific-instrumental approach flow values which are relative by definition, take context into account, represent stages in progress, and are, therefore, open-ended. They are necessarily partial, tentative and qualified. Wheelis' (1958) informed exposition of the etiology of these different value systems warrants the attention of all who are concerned with this problem.

Hobbs' (1959) conclusion (which sounds somehow regretful) seems to be that psychology, as a science, has no major contribution to make to value organization. But psychology is *not* any other science; it is the *science of man,* the *science of human behavior.* Also courage can be taken from his statement that he is as yet highly tentative about some of his formulations and that he is not yet able to let the problem alone. "For a science of man," Ashley Montagu cites Julian Huxley as saying, "the problem is not whether or not to have anything to do with values, but how to devise methods of studying them and discovering how they work."

There is another aspect of this general problem that does not relate to choice between traditional and scientifically derived value systems. Maslow probably has been most articulate about it, although he is joined by others. This point is that the prime disease of our time is valuelessness. It is a state variously described as amorality, rootlessness, emptiness, alienation, hopelessness, the lack, in short, of something to believe in and be devoted to. We are confronted with a vacuum in values which must be filled. The point of view is that traditional values have failed and in Maslow's terms, we "need a validated, usable system of human values that we can believe in and devote ourselves to because they are true rather than because we are exhorted to believe and have faith" (1959).

Three Basic Propositions

Yet with all of the disadvantages of the scientific method in the derivation of values granted, a number of points remain stubbornly in mind: That for the first time in the history of man there is a systematic means of exploring his needs and their fulfillment; that its appeal is widespread and has captured the interest and devotion of highly intelligent and creative workers; that its methodology is increasing in its sophistication; and that there is already a body of substantive information about the nature and condition of man.

Therefore, the first in a series of propostitions:

1. *Man's increasing scientific knowledge about himself should supply the basic data for derivation of his values.*

Obviously we lack the tightly designed researches with findings validated at high levels of confidence, but we are not without theoretical contributions out of which we can identify necessary lines of research and testable hypotheses. The contributions by psychological workers are too well known to cite extensively, but they should be called to attention even if only to remind ourselves that we are least of all without such ideas.

The characteristics of Erich Fromm's productive personality are very much in point here as in his formulation of human needs in society. Sullivan's mature personality belongs here. Probably there would be a certain amount of difficulty in living in a world of Goldstein's and Maslow's self-actualizing people, but their validity and force are indubitable. Sorokin and Ashley Montagu and Shoben have contributed in this area. Of very great interest is Maslow's well known hierarchy of needs with its strong instinctoid overtones. Needs, it may be granted, are without undue difficulty translatable into values, also capable of hierarchial ordering.

With these contributions in mind, it is possible to offer, however tentatively, a second proposition:

2. *The theoretical models of the psychologically healthy person, his orientation to himself and others, the choices he makes, and his criteria for making these choices, offer us meaningful material for value determinations.*

A third proposition reaches for even if it does not quite grasp the horn of another dilemma:

3. *Values should be subject to explicit examination as criteria for choice, as determinants of behavior.*

Here I have learned from John E. Smith's discerning essay on Jacob's study (1958), and it is congruent with our current professions relative to mental health, specifically with the importance of bringing unconscious motivation into awareness. Smith's emphasis is on the critical response which requires a standard or criterion in accordance with which the actual judgment or evaluation is made.

We have a choice of a kind here. If we do not examine our value predispositions, or indeed our valuelessness, our beliefs and behavior must flow from our present value orientation which exists at various levels of awareness and clarity and understanding. All of this affects our ability to move toward or away from them.

Thus far this paper (1) urged the need for values derived from man's increasing knowledge about himself, at least as a goal if not as an immediate program, (2) called attention to theoretical models of the well-functioning individual and (3) made Smith's point that in final analysis, values must stand as the referent points, as the criteria for choice. All of these have pertinence in considering the particular enterprise, the learning task we call counseling.

Values and the Counseling Task

It is hardly news that we have yet to define clearly and cleanly the job of counseling, its distinguishing characteristics relative to psychotherapy, or the appropriate range of effort in such specific goals as vocational counseling or marriage counseling. But it can be agreed that in some measure *personality appraisal, evaluation of misperception, examination of self-acceptance, resulting change of behavior, acceptance of responsibility,* and *assumption of independence* are common to all counseling tasks. Differential goals are also, of course, to be noted, e.g., *reduction in guilt, acceptance of appropriate feelings of dependence,* and *the experience of feeling.*

Whatever the true nature of these tasks, it seems quite a circumspect statement that the counselor plays a central role in them. For some workers in therapy and counseling he is clarifier of feelings, for others teacher and mentor, for still others a vehicle for safe reliving of the past and its examination. He is other things still, depending on what one feels actually takes place in the consulting room, and of course, the nature and cause and effect of behavior change in counseling or therapy are still largely unknown. Probably it is these different and partial theoretical views of counseling interaction that compel us to assign differing behavior to the counselor. The fourth proposition is based upon the idea now gaining increasing acceptance that as Sullivan's participant observer, as himself his most useful tool, the counselor is in effect an instrument which itself must be calibrated.

4. *The counselor's values must be held in awareness.*

In his usual comprehensive fashion C. H. Patterson (1959) has pulled together the literature on this problem. As against a previously adopted fancied neutrality, he cites theory and research relative to the impossibility of keeping the therapist's values out of his work. The evidence indicates that the influence can be unintended and quite below awareness levels. Logic compels us to the same conclusion, for to say that the counselor manifests no values is to require that he have no feelings and whatever great drama this may be it is not counseling. The unreality of such a devastating neutrality requires no comment. The least we can learn from this is that the counselor's awareness of his values is of prime importance.

The impression is gained in moving among professional colleagues and in reading that this need for search of self is accepted readily enough. It seems to be, in fact, the preferred style but whether this is only the cut of cloth or really integrated personality style is an open question. To be sure, life is a great teacher and the practicum leader's comments on taped interviews may go some distance, but it is doubtful that much light is shed in the dark area of unconscious motivation by these means. Yet how many counselors have been subject to the systematic and painful and enriching (and expensive) experience of truly investigating their behavior and its motivation, that is to say their values? The point that short of analytic procedures, we have been remiss in investigating and putting into effect systematic self-exploration methods, is defended elsewhere (Samler, 1959).

The point comes home in its specifics. Williamson points out in a recent article (1959) that in vocational counseling the counselor takes for granted that choice of occupation should reflect the individual's optimum potential, that interests should be capitalized, that university training is the *summum bonum,* and that job stability is much to be preferred to job hopping, which at times in fact is seen as a clinical symptom. The point Dean Williamson makes is that these values which determine base counselor attitudes and behavior probably are quite out of the counselor's awareness.

It seems useful to note that these are relatively "safe" value areas. That is, we do not deal here with the counselor's own deeply rooted value system relating to this regard for himself, the nature and extent of his guilt, his strong feelings of dependence and so on, although connections there may be. Yet these value assumptions also are in quite a mysterious and unlighted area.

Like the aprocryphal story of the paranoid patient who was advised he could continue in his delusions if only he kept his mouth shut, it may be possible to have behavioral change without fundamental change in values, but this is hardly an acceptable counseling goal. It is only making the obvious explicit to say that behavior constitutes a reflection, sometimes twisted and distorted as in peculiar mirrors, of values. How is it possible, for instance, to divorce values from Tyler's description of counseling which reads in part "a process by which each person can be helped to develop and understand his own characteristic life pattern, his own identity," or from the core of Super's statement relative to vocational counseling—"helping a person develop and accept an integrated and adequate picture of himself and his role in the world of work."

The next proposition, therefore, is that,

5. *Values are at the heart of the counseling relationship, are reflected in its content, and affect the process.*

It is clear that the very availability of counseling has deeply imbedded in it a particular value orientation. *All* counseling by definition is for the benefit of the counselee (with society's needs in mind, to be sure) and, therefore, the behavior, attitudinal set and basic relationship of the counselor to his client is characterized at least by interest, probably by concern, and possibly by a form of love. The need for respecting the client is a counseling byword. As silent preceptor, advocate of a particular way of relating to others, and as a respecting and expert helper, the counselor at the very least affects client attitudes. The literature is abundant on this point.

The counseling process as such is aimed at providing insight, changing behavior, and the exercise of choice along lines leading to more adequate functioning and greater comfort in living in terms of specified values. In vocational counseling, Super's phrase in his definition "helping the individual develop and accept an adequate picture of himself," is value loaded, as are other personality oriented counseling definitions. If the counselor functions along these lines he is inevitably, one way or another, addressing himself to the client's values. This is perhaps best illustrated by the studied observation not of a psychologist, but by the economist, researcher, and general gad-fly Eli Ginsberg (1951). In assessing the situation of vocational counseling he and his colleagues point out that:

> The connection between occupational choice process and work satisfaction is not contained in the specific decision which the individual reaches, but in how he clarifies the goals and values which are associated with the satisfactions he seeks in work. This clarification is an essential part of his occupational decision making, for he cannot make a choice without determining, at least preliminarily, what he wants to get out of work. If he fails to clarify his goals and values and fails to crystallize his choice, it is more than likely that his work experience will prove frustrating. Not knowing what he wants from work, he will be unable to choose from among such alternatives as he may have. *True crystallization and specification cannot take place until a clarification of goals and values has been made.* (Italics supplied)

Equally significant is understanding of the differential value systems of occupations. Here our colleagus in related fields have contributed heavily to understanding of social, class, and occupational expectations, roles, and their related values. It is difficult to conceive of counseling related to psychological realities which does not take these data into account.

We need not deal with the problem only on presumptive grounds. In his 1958 APA paper in this area, Paul Meehl, without offering his own support, cites workers (e.g., Wolpe, Herzberg, Maeder, Phillips, Frankl, Ellis, Thorpe) who, in his words "not only permit but who encourage a detailed consideration of value problems. These practitioners prefer not to treat the patient's value-orientation as merely a symptom or derivative of something else . . . but rather conceive that a patient's value orientation may itself be one of the important determiners of his unhappiness."

On Teaching Values

Proposition 6. *"Intervention" by the counselor in the client's values is an actuality and should be accepted as a necessary part of the process.*[1]

Almost the question answers itself. If the counseling task is in a context of values, and if counseling goals must explicate and integrate them, then

---

[1]Intervention is too coarse a term for what is intended; it is offered as a close approximation.

the counselor's activity in this area should be taken for granted. But I doubt that many will be satisfied with this abstraction. Specifics may help:

Given a highly talented 17-year-old youngster in educational and vocational counseling from a lower socio-economic stratum, I submit that the counselor assumes a given attitude set. This has to do with the client's self-actualization to be sure, and will allow for unique solutions. But for the generality of cases, the desirability of college will be very much in his mind. He has set a goal, tentative to be sure, for the youngster—it is obviously value oriented. I submit that the counselor will work toward that goal for and with the youngster.

Given impulsive and acting-out behavior with another client of whatever age, the role of the worker and his goals for the client are quite clear—more rational behavior and repression of some impulses.

One can list a set of troubles, the therapies of choice and their underlying value orientation:

for the demanding and infantile—assumption of responsibility;
for the vocationally disoriented—assumption of a working role congruent with the picture the client will develop of himself;
for the guilt-ridden—tolerance for himself and life's reality;
for the unloved and unloving—self-acceptance and kindliness;
for the achievement and power-ridden—appreciation of the rich resources in human beings;
for the highly controlling—reduction of anxiety and a more trusting and optimistic outlook.

The point I am making is that these goals in terms of change in client behavior and the accompanying assumption of congruent values, are clearly in the minds of the workers, and that they will address their efforts toward these ends.

In an oft-quoted article Gardner Murphy (1955) also addressed himself to this central issue. To the dilemma of activity relative to client values, Murphy's answer is unequivocal and along three lines. He feels that the counselor "cannot help conveying directly or indirectly to every client what he himself sees and feels, and the perspective in which his own life is lived." Second, "it is not true that the wise man's sharing of a philosophy of life is an arrogant imposition upon a defenseless client." Third, in addressing himself to our work he says "it is often said that all philosophies are subjective and arbitrary, and that one system of values is as good as another. But if you believed that, you would not have chosen personnel and guidance as a way of life. Your experience, moreover, has shown you that some values, such as those of sympathy, tenderness, generosity, and self-control resonate to the deeper chords of human nature, and that they are for that reason intensely practical and dependable."

In the Meehl's paper referred to before (1958), the therapists he cites, he states, "are willing to step into a pedagogical role and engage in direct behavioral retraining. Some would pay only incidental attention to cognitive issues; others view cognitive clarification—including persuasion and intellectual argument—as fundamental to the therapeutic process." Those who heard this thoughtful paper will recall that he goes on to say

> In the course of ordinary secular psychotherapy there occur, from time to time, exchanges between patient and therapist which are not defensive intellectualizations but which (whatever they may be called within the therapist's preferred theoretical scheme) are, in their actual verbal structure, rather like a segment out of one of the Platonic dialogues. I suspect that one reason why so many therapists are skittish about getting involved in this kind of thing is that they lack talent and training for the Socratic dialogue; and that this deficiency, together with their own personal ambiguity about the value-question, makes them feel unsafe if they treat any such material in its own right, rather than as a derivative calling for a psychodynamic interpretation at some other level.

It is of the greatest possible interest that the same point is made in very much the same way by Allen Wheelis (1958) in the rich context of his novelette-essay-autobiography.

Beyond a Single Technique

Proposition 7. *Promotion of given values and counseling technique are now seen as constituting an indissoluble unit. They should be regarded as separable.*

It seems to me that the actuality of counselor intervention in client values is beyond dispute. While such intervention is now accomplished through *a basic relationship technique,* it does not follow that this must be our only means. Even if methods determine ends it is still for consideration whether these are immutably the only proper means at our disposal.

We know that in their behavior, defenses, and values, human beings change least of all by exhortation, but this does not mean that the person to whom high achievement or power is a prime value and a way of maintaining self-respect, should not change; it only means that exhortation will not work with him. We have found that it is possible for people to learn to be loving, to like people (a value), but only by living through the *experience of themselves being loved,* being allowed suspiciously to test the lover-therapist in a thousand different ways. We have changed a value, in awareness, with full intention of doing so, but we have done it in a very particular way.

To the client who for the best of reasons has put a tight lid on his feelings, and is defended by intellect and emptiness, the therapist may sometimes want to say "try feeling, only the learning is painful," but he will not, because it will not work. But the encouraged experience, as it were, of *creeping up on feeling,* can work. The value is identified and sought out, change is encouraged, but again, the way of achieving it is very particular.

Probably the examples can be multiplied many times. There is a cause and effect relationship between the experience of being accepted and feeling the concern of another and increase in self-esteem, but it should not follow that this is the only way of achieving the desired effect in change in values. One is a very special kind of learning, a particular rich experience, but it is still a technique, and it should be seen as such. I keep on wondering whether if we deny the goal (specified change in values) and emphasize the means (our present relationship techniques), we are not selling ourselves short on the possibility of finding *other* ways of helping.

This proposition is based in part on the discerning discussion by Meehl and McClosky (1947) of the relationship between ethics and technique in therapeutic work. It is tempting to cite any number of sharp and clear paragraphs in this discussion. It is required reading for all of us concerned with this problem.

Again, to Which Values?

If we can separate out technique of choice from the necessary goal of change in values, the inevitable question arises as to which values. It is this critical question that prompts the last proposal:

Proposition 8. *Drawing upon the available models of the mature personality, it should be possible to develop testable hypotheses relative to the values to be supported in counselor-client interaction.*

The hazards in this are tremendous: Jahoda (1958) points out for instance that

> While it is easy to speculate about the relation of each criterion to a vast number of high values, we do not know whether such relations actually obtain. Does self-actualization really benefit the development of the species, as Fromm would claim? Is interpersonal competence a prerequisite for the happiness of the individual? Is happiness or productivity the value underlying an active orientation to problem-solving?

Yet what recourse have we other than the dictum that the individual will develop his own? More than that: the omniscient answers that these questions appear to require are not really necessary. We do not need to solve them for the next few millenia, the job is difficult enough if we get answers that are better than any others and that will work for the next 25 years or for that part of such a period until better answers emerge. In any case, the models provide the best answers that theory making and clinical experience have yet made available to us.

I do not want to be mistaken. The notion, for example, of a congress of psychologists determining by vote whatever values should be, scares the daylight out of me as well. This is not the way. Our faith must be put on the scientific derivation of desirable behavior, orientation to life, and their underlying values.

Should we embark on such an enterprise, after coming to terms with the values implicit in it, it would follow that the professed neutrality of the counselor relative to his client's values would have to be abandoned in favor of an affirmation of given values. The attendant possibility might arise of opening up the important process of values as referent points.

Least of all am I concerned with the shibboleth of democracy and authoritarianism in the counseling relationship. These ghosts were laid by Meehl and McClosky in 1947, and what is required is a courageous editor nowhere available to reprint that sterling article. An affirmative stand in values is contrary also to Patterson's summation (1959, p. 74). He says in part about the counselor that:

> He would not feel that the counseling relationship is the place to teach moral or ethical standards or a philosophy of life. He is confident, as apparently some are not, that the client in the therapeutic relationship will be aware of and influenced by social realities. He will leave to the family, the church and the school, as institutions representing the moral and ethical standards of society, the teaching of such standards.

These three sentences appear to represent the orthodox opinion in the field and yet I believe they must be subject to serious examination. They bypass the reality that values are in fact learned in the consulting room. But more important, they disregard the counseling situation as a learning experience of the greatest possible import, ethically bound as are very few others, constantly under the scrutiny of a highly self-conscious professional community. It is not an opportunity to be lightly dismissed. It is an opportunity for the learning of values to be affirmed, explored, and made the subject of our most serious concern.

The written word takes on a finality that goes beyond intention. Personal experience and consideration of these serious problems argues a greater tentativeness than these propositions offer. But the unequivocal certitude of a great deal of present thinking on values, counselor role, and client change, is too troublesome to leave alone. This much is certain: We must examine our present value commitments and carry them sharply in awareness. In the light of our growing knowledge of human behavior we must ourselves map the country and travel a road of our own choosing. We should be able to accept without quibbling the objective in counseling of modification of client behavior and therefore of attitudes and values. With the purpose unequivocally clear our task remains that of determining how it can best be accomplished whatever our present commitments.

REFERENCES

Ginsberg, E. & Associates. *Occupational choice, An approach to a general theory.* New York: Columbia Univer. Press. 1951.

Hobbs, N. Science and ethical behavior. *Amer. Psychol.*, 1959, *14*, 217-225.

Jahoda, Marie. *Current concepts of positive mental health.* Monograph Series No. 1, Joint Commission on Mental Health. New York: Basic Books, 1958.

Maslow, A. H. (Ed.) *New knowledge in human values.* New York: Harpers, 1959.

Meehl, P. E. Some technical and axiological problems in the therapeutic handling of religious and valuational material. Paper delivered at APA Convention, 1958.

Meehl, P. E., & McClosky, H. Ethical and political aspects of applied psychology. *J. abnorm. soc. Psychol.*, 1947, *42*, 91-98.

Montagu, M. F. *The direction of human development: Biological and social bases.* New York: Harpers, 1955.

Murphy, G. The cultural context of guidance. *Personal guid., J.*, 1955, *34*, 4-9.

Patterson, C. H. *Counseling and psychotherapy: Theory and practice.* New York: Harpers, 1959.

Samler, J. Basic approaches to mental health. An attempt at synthesis. *Personnel guid. J.*, 1959, *37*, 638-643.

Smith, J. E. *Value convictions and higher education.* New Haven: The Edward W. Hazen Foundation, 1958.

Wheelis, A. *The quest for identity.* New York: Norton, 1958.

Williamson, E. G. The meaning of communication in counseling. *Personnel guid. J.*, 1959, *38*, 6-14.

Behavioral Goals for Counseling

John D. Krumboltz[1]

The goals of counseling should be stated as those specific behavior changes (a) desired by each client, (b) compatible with his counselor's values and (c) externally observable. Such behavioral goals would be both more consistent with the guidance tenet of individual worth and more scientifically useful than the traditional goals of counseling such as "self-understanding" and "self-acceptance." The use of behavioral goals would result in (a) a clearer anticipation of what counseling could

Reprinted by permission of the author and *Journal of Counseling Psychology*, Vol. 13, No. 2 (Summer, 1966), 153-159.

John D. Krumboltz, Professor of Education and Psychology, Stanford University, Stanford, California.

[1]For helpful comments and suggestions on a preliminary draft of this manuscript, I am indebted to W. H. Cowley, Helen B. Krumboltz, Eleanore B. Luckey, H. B. McDaniel, David V. Tiedeman, C. Gilbert Wrenn and the graduate students in counseling at Stanford University. The views expressed are, of course, my own and do not necessarily reflect the views of those named here.

accomplish, (b) a better integration of counseling psychology with the mainstream of psychological theory and research, (c) a facilitation of the search for new and more effective techniques for helping clients and (d) the use of different criteria for assessing the outcomes of counseling with different clients.

I shall argue that stating the goals of counseling in terms of observable behavior will prove more useful than stating goals in terms of such inferred mental states as "self-understanding" and "self-acceptance." Self-understanding and self-acceptance are frequently listed among the goals of counseling although definitions of these terms lack precision. Let me make perfectly clear that I am not opposed to people having self-understanding and being self-accepting. Counselors who use these terms probably want the same kind of outcomes which I would want. But with terms as abstract as these, it is impossible to tell whether agreement exists and whether the goals are ever attained.

It is my contention that it would be far more useful to state the goals of counseling in terms of overt behavior changes. Utlimately counselors of all persuasions look to client behavior changes as justification for their procedures. Self-understanding and self-acceptance constitute intermediate mental states which some people assume make possible these ultimate modifications in behavior patterns. It is assumed that if clients can attain some degree of self-understanding and/or self-acceptance, they will be "freed" to change their overt behavior. Whether or not this assumption is justified is an empirical question, the evidence on which is discussed in Krumboltz (1966).

Disavowal of subjective states as goals of counseling is not new. Recently Brayfield (1962) argued that counseling psychologists had placed undue emphasis on egocentric self-regarding internal states and should instead use a performance criterion which would stress dependability, accountability, obligation and responsibility. Similarly, Samler (1962) cited three instances in which problems of prejudice, self-pity and poor workmanship were brought to the counselor. In each case, Samler argued, the important objective was that the client change his behavior in relevant ways whether or not his subjective feelings changed. Such logic finds a foundation in the concept of efficiency as advocated by Wishner (1955) and the concept of competence which was brilliantly developed by White (1959).

Why have objective statements of behavior change not already replaced subjective states as counseling objectives if they are superior? Subjective states are appealing because their very abstractness enables them to be interpreted to suit individual preferences. "Self-fulfillment" commands the same instant acceptance from some counselors as "patriotism" does from some politicians. It is only when attempts are made to specify concrete actions that dissension occurs. With abstract goals real differences between people may still exist but may not be discovered. The resulting harmony is reinforcing to many.

The fundamental obstacle to formulating behavioral objectives has been the assumption that we must write one list of objectives which applies to all counselees. It has been hoped that once we discover exactly what constitutes the "good life" we could analyze and list its elements as counseling objectives. Such attempts quickly bog down when it becomes apparent that what's good for GM is not good for MG. Hence, any list of behavioral objectives, if taken as desirable behavior for *all* clients, is justifiably vulnerable to criticism.

Criteria for Counseling Goals

Any set of goals for counseling should meet each of the following criteria:

1. *The goals of counseling should be capable of being stated differently for each individual client.* One set of statements cannot apply to all clients. The unique feature of counseling is the individualization it provides. If we take seriously the assertion that each client is entitled to our respect as an individual, then we should be willing to work toward different goals with each of our clients. The common goals that our society holds for all individuals are partially met by the regular instructional program in our schools and colleges. Helping different individuals attain their different goals provides a unique opportunity for counselors to be of service. If this is true, there may be a virtually unlimited number of goals toward which counselors might help their clients strive. The goals of one client might be in direct contradiction to the goals of another client. For example, one client might wish to learn how to become more assertive in his social responses, while another might wish to learn how to become less assertive. A counselor could legitimately work with both of these clients, helping each one to achieve the particular type of behavior he desired.

2. *The goals of counseling for each client should be compatible with, though not necessarily identical to, the values of his counselor.* To use an extreme example, a boy who wanted help in becoming a more effective bank robber would find few counselors willing to help him attain that particular goal. However, if the boy indicated a desire to consider the possible consequences of a bank robbing career in relation to other career possibilities, then probably many more counselors would be willing to help him think through the alternatives.

This second criterion implies that each counselor has some responsibility for evaluating the particular goals of his clients. This is not to say that he would necessarily attempt to change the goals of his clients, but he must make a judgment of whether or not he would be willing to help a client attain his particular goal. There might be goals acceptable to some counselors but not to others. For example, a client might ask a counselor for help in strengthening (or abandoning) his religious practices. It is quite conceivable that some counselors working in certain settings would be willing to help attain this goal while other counselors in different settings would not accept the assignment. The counselor's own interests, competencies and ethical standards should place limitations on what he is, and is not, willing to help his client accomplish (Krumboltz, 1965b).

3. *The degree to which the goals of counseling are attained by each client should be observable.* Some means must be available so that competent judges, regardless of their theoretical preferences, can agree that a particular goal has or has not been attained. This means that some overt indication of the client's behavior provides the basis for the judgment. Behavior, of course, is interpreted broadly to include any verbal or written statement, any responses that can be seen or heard, and any other responses that can be assessed reliably through some type of instrumentation.

Three Types of Behavioral Goals

There are three types of goals which meet the criteria listed above and which clearly fall within the scope of counselors' responsibilities. The three categories are not intended to be mutually exclusive or even all inclusive but may provide a convenient framework for organizing the tasks a counselor may accomplish.

Under each category illustrative examples of goals are listed. Clearly all possible goals of counseling can never be listed if we use the above criteria. Any type of behavior change desired by a client and agreed to by his counselor could be listed as an illustrative counseling goal.

1. *Altering Maladaptive Behavior.* Many clients are unhappy because they are engaging in a pattern of behavior which does not lead to the satisfactions they desire. Of course, many are not able to identify the maladaptive behavior pattern to the counselor, especially at first, but instead report their subjective feelings which result from the inappropriate behavior. For example, a client may report "I am lonely" while his typical behavior pattern is to spend all his spare time alone in his own room. Or if he spends time with other people, he may not have learned how to interact with them in a meaningful way.

In any event it is the counselor's job to help the client translate his problem into a behavioral goal that the client wants to attain and that the counselor believes will contribute to the welfare of his client. Considerable skill on the part of the counselor is required to make this translation. Listed below are some illustrative behavioral goals concerned with altering maladaptive behavior.

- Increasing socially assertive responses
- Decreasing socially assertive responses
- Increasing social skills necessary in meeting new people
- Decreasing fear responses to examinations
- Increasing ability to concentrate for longer periods of time on school work
- Decreasing the frequency of stealing
- Increasing participation in school activities
- Learning how to initiate social contacts with members of the opposite sex

- Learning to assume responsibility for a task and carry it through to completion
- Decreasing aggressive responses to smaller children
- Increasing aggressive responses to abusive peers
- Learning to respond calmly to hostile remarks
- Decreasing quarreling behavior with other members of the family
- Increasing ability to complete work on time
- Decreasing the frequency of reckless and fast driving
- Increasing the sharing of possessions with friends
- Decreasing excessive sharing with friends and acquaintances
- Increasing ability to say "no" to salesmen
- Increasing ability to return unsatisfactory articles to stores
- Decreasing threatening or violent behavior
- Learning to discriminate between insults and friendly teasing
- Decreasing weeping behavior in social situations
- Increasing ability to communicate with friends and acquaintances

2. *Learning the Decision Making Process.* Another major category of problems concerns decision making. Again the client may not present his problem as a behavioral goal in decision making but instead may simply indicate that a decision must be made, e.g., "What shall I do next year?" "Give me some tests that tell me what I'm good at." "I can't make up my mind between law and engineering." "I don't have the slightest idea of what I want to be." "Shall I get married now or wait until after graduation?"

Counselors seem universally agreed that they cannot provide ready-made solutions for such problems. Instead the counselor must help launch the client on a course of action that will increase the probability that the client will ultimately be satisfied with his own decision. His decision will probably be more satisfactory if he engages in some or all of the illustrative counseling goals listed below.

- Generating a list of all possible courses of action
- Gathering relevant information about each feasible alternative course of action
- Estimating the probability of success in each alternative on the basis of the experience of others and projections of current trends
- Considering the personal values which may be enhanced or diminished under each course of action
- Deliberating and weighing the facts, probable outcomes and values for each alternative
- Eliminating from consideration the least favorable courses of action
- Formulating a tentative plan of action subject to new developments and opportunities
- Generalizing the decision making process to future problems

3. *Preventing Problems.* The highest priority in the counseling profession should involve the prevention of problems. The development of a polio vaccine was far more beneficial than the treatment of persons who had already become victims of the disease. Similarly, developing educational programs that will prevent certain kinds of maladaptive behavior and inadequate decision making should deserve high priority. It is far easier to prevent a problem than to remedy it after it has occurred. Many of the problems that come to counselors need never have arisen if teachers had

been more skillful, if parents had been wiser, and if administrators had established more effective programs. It is not necessary, desirable or helpful, however, to blame others for the problems that come to counselors. Instead counselors need to ask what they can do to prevent such problems from arising in the future.

The most valuable and ethical behavior of professional persons consists of eliminating the need for their own services. At the present time we do not know just what programs and systems would prove effective in reducing the incidence of misery, discouragement and waste. Research designed to explore new possibilities should be encouraged. A few general examples may indicate the direction these efforts might take.

- Developing a school marking system so that even the poorest student in each class can be encouraged by seeing the extent of his own progress
- Implementing a system of helping young men and women select compatible marriage partners
- Planning an educational program in child rearing techniques for parents
- Helping to construct a curriculum more useful and effective for the students in it
- Evaluating the effectiveness of preventive and remedial programs

Consequences of Behavioral Statements of Counseling Goals

Why should stating goals behaviorally in this manner be more useful than stating internal mental states as goals? The consequences of shifting to a more behavioral orientation would be the following in my judgment.

1. *Counselors, clients and citizens could more clearly anticipate what the counseling process could, and could not, accomplish.* Counselors and clients would formulate tentative statements of desired behavior changes early in the counseling process. The very process of stating the goals in unambiguous language might have therapeutic effects. The clarification of goals would result in better public relations and public support. In the long run I can see no benefits from having a mystified clientele.

2. *Counseling psychology would become more integrated with the mainstream of psychological theory and research.* By conceiving of their professional problems as problems in behavior, counseling psychologists would be in a position to generate testable hypotheses from the research and theory in learning, perception, developmental and social psychology. The testing of such extrapolations in counseling settings would have important implications for all of psychology.

3. *The search for new and more effective techniques of helping clients would be facilitated.* With a variety of possible counseling goals, it seems safe to assume that no one counseling procedure would be universally applicable. Work is just beginning on alternative approaches. I have discussed elsewhere some of the philosophic objections to certain experimental guidance procedures (Krumboltz, 1964). It would seem to me that the

professional responsibility of each counselor is to seek whatever ethical methods most effectively and efficiently bring about the desired behavior changes. When we are clear on the behavioral goals we are trying to attain, when we have developed adequate procedures for assessing each goal, when our ingenuity has generated a number of alternative procedures which seem likely to attain each goal, then we can test and evaluate the effectiveness of each procedure and determine experimentally what methods produce which results best with what type of clients (Krumboltz, 1965a).

4. *Different criteria would have to be applied to different clients in assessing the success of counseling.* Outcomes would be evaluated in terms of the extent to which each individual had changed his own behavior in the desired direction. Investigators of counseling outcomes would not be able to state one single criterion (e.g., grade point average) which every client would be expected to increase. The reason that some evaluations of counseling have not produced more significant results may be that the criteria chosen were not equally appropriate for all members of the sample. For example, half the counseled students might have wished to increase their assertive responses while the other half wished to become less assertive. Even if counseling were successful in every single case, the average "assertiveness score" of the experimental group would still be equal to the average "assertiveness score" of the control group. Unless some provision is made for taking into account the different goals of different clients, evaluations of counseling are likely to continue to produce negative results.

A precedent for considering the individual goals of clients has been provided by Pascal and Zax (1956). Although their study may be questioned on certain methodological grounds, it nevertheless makes an important contribution by showing how each subject's own goals and prior behavior can be the baseline for evaluating whether or not changes in the desired direction occur. Bijou (in press) has shown how this can be done by counting the frequency of responses in certain categories. Brayfield (1963) also stressed this point when, in anticipating the present article, he stated, ". . . it remains now for someone to suggest that the counselee set the goals and that evaluation be undertaken in that context" (p. 341).

Discussion

In discussing these ideas informally with groups of counselors, psychologists and counselor educators, a number of questions have arisen. I shall attempt to restate some of the most frequent questions and try to answer them.

I do not regard the views I have expressed here as any final commitment. Questions and comments from my colleagues have been most helpful to me in clarifying my own views, and I hope that continued questioning and discussing will lead us all to a progressive refinement of our notions as to what counselors should accomplish.

Question: Are you saying that counselors have been wrong all these years in stating goals of counseling like self-actualization, self-fulfillment, self-understanding and self-acceptance?

Answer: Not at all. These would be fine goals if each were accompanied by a list of illustrative behaviors to define what it might mean for different clients. These abstract goals are not wrong; they are just not as useful as more specific statements would be.

Question: Don't people have feelings and isn't it important for counselors to be sensitive to these feelings?

Answer: Without doubt, people have feelings, and many have learned an extensive vocabulary for describing such feelings. I am not against people feeling they understand and accept themselves; I favor such feelings just as I favor people loving justice, truth and beauty. My point is that, stated as goals of counseling, such subjective feelings will not prove as useful as more objective statements of behavior. Being sensitive to the feelings of a client is certainly a necessary attribute for any counselor. That it is sufficient is questionable (Krumboltz, in press).

Question: But don't people act the way they do because of their feelings, insights and self-perceptions?

Answer: It seems more plausible that positive feelings are the by-product, not the cause, of competent behavior and the rewards it brings. As Hobbs (1962, p. 742) puts it,

> It seems to me that the traditional formulation of the relationship between self-understanding and effective behavior may be backwards. I suggest that insight is not a cause of change but a possible result of change. It is not a source of therapeutic gain but one among a number of possible consequences of gain.

Hence, if we succeed in helping people to act more competently, they will receive more positive feedback from their friends, relatives and employers; then their feelings about themselves will improve as a matter of course.

Question: What would be done about the large number of clients who come to the counselor reporting feelings of dissatisfaction and unhappiness but having no idea about what behavior they could change?

Answer: The possible causes of unhappiness are infinite. An understanding listener is all some people require. Others need help in formulating and implementing plans. The counselor's job is to help the client formulate more concrete goals and take appropriate action.

Question: Aren't behavioral goals pretty superficial? Don't they imply habitual action without comprehension? Wouldn't we be overlooking permanent personality changes? Aren't there some things we can't observe or measure that are nevertheless very important? Don't "self-understanding" and "self-acceptance" really imply much more than can be expressed in words?

Answer: These questions deserve more of an answer than space permits. Undoubtedly, many complicated behavior patterns have not yet been categorized and described, but an affirmative reply to these questions would imply that we should give up without trying.

To those who say there is "something more" than behavior (defined broadly) I would ask these questions: (a) Can you point to any individual who exhibits the "something more " trait? (b) Can you point to any individual who fails to exhibit this trait? (c) What does the first individual do or say differently than the second individual under what circumstances that leads you to conclude that he possesses the "something more" trait? (d) Why don't we list what he does or says under which circumstances as another possible behavioral goal?

The task of stating behavioral goals is hard work and the job has scarcely begun. But only when our goals are clearly stated and communicated will we be able to engage in the service and experimentation which will ultimately benefit clients, counselors and citizens alike.

REFERENCES

Bijou, S. W. Implications of behavioral science for counseling and guidance. In J. D. Krumboltz (Ed), *Revolution in counseling: implications of behavioral science.* Boston: Houghton Mifflin, in press.

Brayfield, A. H. Counseling psychology. In P. R. Farnsworth, Olga McNemar, & Q. McNemar (Eds.), *Annual review of psychology.* Vol. 14. Palo Alto, Calif.: Annual Reviews, 1963. Pp. 319-350.

Brayfield, A. H. Performance is the thing. *J. counsel. Psychol.,* 1962, 9, 3.

Hobbs, N. Sources of gain in psychotherapy. *Amer. Psychologist,* 1962, *17,* 741-747.

Krumboltz, J. D. The agenda for counseling. *J. counsel. Psychol.,* 1965, *12,* 226. (a)

Krumboltz, J. D. Behavioral counseling: rationale and research. *Personnel guid. J.,* 1965, *44,* 383-387. (b)

Krumboltz, J. D. Parable of the good counselor. *Personnel guid. J.,* 1964, *43,* 118-124.

Krumboltz, J. D. Promoting adaptive behavior: new answers to familiar questions. In J. D. Krumboltz (Ed.), *Revolution in counseling: implications of behavioral science.* Boston: Houghton Mifflin, in press.

Krumboltz, J. D. *Stating the goals of counseling.* Monograph published by the California Counseling and Guidance Association, 1966.

Pascal, G. R., & Zax, M. Psychotherapeutics: success or failure. *J. consult. Psychol.,* 1956, *20,* 325-331.

Samler, J. An examination of client strength and counselor responsibility. *J. counsel. Psychol.,* 1962, 9, 5-11.

White, R. W. Motivation reconsidered: the concept of competence. *Psychol. Rev.*, 1959, *66*, 297-333.

Wishner, J. A concept of efficiency in psychological health and in psychopathology. *Psychol. Rev.*, 1955, *62*, 69-80.

Some Proposed New Developments in Vocational Aspects of Counselor Education

John W. Loughary

Introduction

We agree, I think, that vocational guidance is not limited to providing occupational information to counselees, and therefore the related aspects of counselor education are not limited to such things as memorizing DOT codes and noting sources of free and inexpensive occupational information. Nor, on the other hand, does it help very much to reason that because all behavior is in a sense vocational behavior, all guidance is vocational.

For purposes of this paper vocational guidance is concerned with what counselors and others do to facilitate the process which eventually leads the individual to one or a series of relatively stable occupations. Therefore,

Reprinted by permission of the author. Presented at a conference, Vocational Aspects of Counselor Education, at George Washington University, 1965.

John W. Loughary, Professor of Education, University of Oregon, Eugene.

planning for counselor education necessitates an identification of desired counselor behavior, and more basic than that, specification of desired counselee behavior.

We need, then, a model for conceptualizing the kinds of behavior with which we are concerned. In order for such a model to guide research and development in vocational aspects of counselor education, it must provide at least tentative answers to the following questions:

1. What do we mean by vocation?
2. What are the general components of the process of vocational development?
3. Which aspects of the process can be influenced significantly by counseling functions?

The first question is important, in general, because of the changing meaning and function of work in our culture. It has specific importance here because of a distinction I will make between vocation and job—both of which occupy one's time, but for possibly quite different reasons. The second question is important for the purpose of relating independent research and program development efforts. It should provide a basis for identifying several manageable areas of research and development, and in such a way that results will be useful to total program development. The third question is aimed at deriving priorities for program development efforts suggested by the model.

The model suggested, therefore, is not one of counselor education, or of vocational guidance. Instead, it attempts to conceptualize the vocational development process. The process of vocational development is viewed as one of making decisions, and involves the individual's constant attempts to acquire, evaluate, and personalize information. The model was developed with the aid of two colleagues, Martin Acker and Oscar Christenson. It is offered as tentative: an early version of what we hope to evolve eventually.

The Process of Vocational Development
From an Information Point of View

Assumptions

As do most models, this one includes underlying assumptions. Those of which we are aware and believe important are listed below.

1. The belief that one's job (occupation) can provide a financial income as well as a major means of satisfying and utilizing one's aptitudes, competencies, and interests is unrealistic for an increasing proportion of the population.
2. Job is defined as the activity(s) by which one earns his living, and vocation, as that activity(s) which serve(s) as the major source of self-fulfillment—that is, from which one derives major psycho-social direction and identification. It is, of course, possible for one activity

to serve both functions. (I have elaborated on this notion elsewhere [Loughary, 1965] and will not repeat that presentation except to point out that the proposed definition allows the individual to deal with (a) preparing for and finding a satisfactory vocation(s) and (b) obtaining a job as separate problems.)

3. The job (as defined above) placement process will make use of computer technology and will become an increasingly precise function.

4. The counselor's function regarding the provision of vocational information is that of maintaining and controlling a system by which he can identify and retrieve specific information relative to the decisions being made by counselees. Ultimately, this implies that in-school or in-agency collections of information will be eliminated in a large part. Instead, needed information will be identified, retrieved, used, and returned to a storage system for updating. The system would be very comprehensive and serve a great number of agencies. It also means that a resource would be available for research regarding effective ways of organizing, presenting, and preparing information.

5. The vocational aspects of counselor education, while in significant part a component of resident education, must continue throughout the professional career of counselors.

6. Vocational exploration at a level of abstraction lower than a verbal level is required by most individuals in order to achieve a useful (in regard to decision making) understanding of the total implications of a job and/or vocation for which they may decide to prepare.

I would like to make it clear at this point that I am not substituting the job-vocation distinction for the traditional vocation-avocation concept. I mean the difference to be more than a semantic one. Webster defines avocation as "something one does in addition to his regular work, and usually for fun," and vocation as "any trade, profession, or occupation." Historically most people have derived their personal sense of importance, well-being, or purpose in large part from that thing they did to earn a living—namely their vocation. Most people also carried on some kind of avocational or recreational behavior. My contention is that an increasing number of jobs will not serve this dual function (income and purpose), and therefore an increasing number of people will need to:

(1) Hold a job for purposes of earning a living,
(2) Engage in recreational or vocational activity in order to relax and have fun, and
(3) Carry on serious work behavior of a more complex nature than their job in order to achieve a sense of purpose and self worth.

While for many, one kind of activity might well satisfy all three types of requirements, vocational planning should recognize the three kinds of needs implied.

I do not wish to continue the job-vocation terminology if it is confusing, but neither am I willing to settle for the vocation-avocation distinction because it misses the point—which I currently believe to be a valid and important one.

Further, in regard to work, I am not suggesting that work is losing its value in our culture but rather that its value is *changing*. We have already reached a point where work, defined as job, is not a way of life for everyone. Those who doubt this should spend some time talking with an educated truck driver, stamp press operator, mail carrier, or card punch operator, for example. These jobs are not a way of life for many who hold them. They may be acceptable ways of making a living, but little else from the point of view of the individual.

The failure to make this distinction, in my opinion, is an important reason why counselors fail to provide effective vocational guidance for so many. They persist in assuming that each counselee can find a job which will also provide a way of life, satisfying all the needs which that implies, and this is simply not consistent with the real world in which we live.

Information and Process

The diagram in Figure 1 [p. 458] attempts to portray in general terms the process of vocational development from an information processing perspective. The process, as indicated above, is essentially one of the individual obtaining various kinds of information and making decisions which move him toward satisfactory job and vocational status.

As shown, vocational development and job preparation-acquisition involve acquiring information about *work* and *self*. Three work information constructs are included and can be thought of as the individual's need for three kinds of information. First, there is the need to understand the functions of work in society (e.g., economical and social control). Second, and more specific, is the need for information regarding classes and characteristics of different work environments. Such an understanding is important for making decisions about what one wants to do. For example, while all secretaries perform many similar tasks and possess common competencies, differing work environments result in different jobs from the worker's point of view. In this sense the occupation of a secretary is different in a government agency than in large private corporations, and both are different from the secretary in a professional office. Finally, there is the need for information regarding specific work behavior; i.e., competencies or skills involved in occupations.

With regard to information about self there are also three constructs representing kinds of information needs. First, and most general, is an awareness of personal significance of the environment in which one lives. For example, what is the significance of one's geographic location, family background, social status, community, religion, school, etc.

The second kind of information about self is more specific. It is illustrat-

FIGURE 1

THE PROCESS OF VOCATIONAL DEVELOPMENT
FROM AN INFORMATION PROCESSING PERSPECTIVE

WORK INFORMATION   SELF INFORMATION

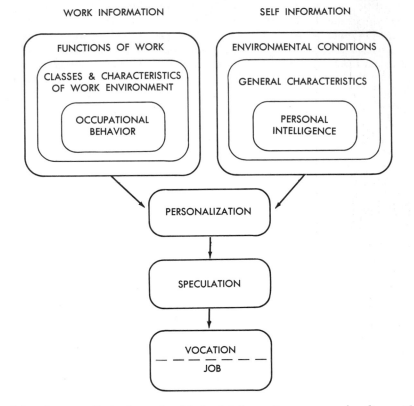

ed by, but not limited to, the kind of information we are familiar with
regarding aptitudes, achievement, personality, interests, etc. While I have
some concern over the traditional manner of organizing and presenting such
data (normative) and would like to see more done with the notion of
absolute measures, the kind of information is similar.

The third level of self information is much more nebulous. Perhaps it is
simply an idiographic understanding of the other two kinds of information,
but at this point it seems something in addition to that. Each of us would
seem to have very private, very intimate information about ourselves, something beyond that obtained through "objective" measurement, which, if
organized and sorted appropriately, can be extremely useful in planning and
deciding about vocations. For example, even prior to adolescence we have
experience working under pressure, following schedules, and pursuing assigned tasks under supervisory conditions which we find objectionable. From

such experiences the individual builds up a store of highly personal information about himself which can be useful for making decisions and plans for future activities.

Both information about work and information about self are changing continually, and this should be kept in mind while considering the diagram. More about this below after commenting briefly on the remaining components of the diagram.

We have suggested that both information about work and self are continually available (or potentially so) to the individual, and the first task is to acquire that which is pertinent. The second component of the process is what we have labeled personalization and involves merging, sorting, organizing, and abstracting the two classes of information so as to maximize their usefulness to the individual.

The next component, speculation, involves behaviors aimed at testing and experimenting with potential vocations and jobs. These behaviors are based on and generate from the results of the personalization component, and include the kinds of things usually involved in preparing for an occupation. Speculation has traditionally been done primarily at the verbal level (reading about a job, college, or a career, and attempting to imagine what they would be like) or consisted of exploratory behavior in real situations. This component offers tremendous potential for increasing the contribution of counselors, and thus has exciting possibilities for new developments in the vocational aspects of counselor education. I will elaborate and illustrate later.

The last component refers to the individual entering a job and vocation in the real world. It should be noted that the components of the system are not discrete. They overlap and can occur simultaneously. However, for purposes of guiding research and development efforts in counselor education, they can be considered useful as an aid to determining valid and manageable areas of concentration.

The ever changing status of information is further illustrated in Figure 2 [p. 460]. Here it is suggested that for any given individual the relationship between (1) functions of work, (2) characteristics of work environment and occupational behavior, and (3) self, changes continually. The forces of change are of two kinds from the perspective of the individual: (1) those controllable and influenced by the individual, (2) those not under control or influence of the individual. Obviously, the greater the control or influence maintained by the individual, the less he will be influenced by chance and the control of others.

Research and Development Problems

The last (next) section of the paper contains brief descriptions of several specific prepared new developments in the vocational aspects of counselor education. The limitations of time and space restrict the number

FIGURE 2

THE DYNAMICS OF
VOCATIONAL DEVELOPMENT

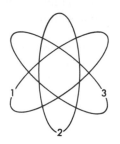

1. THE FUNCTIONS OF WORK
2. CHARACTERISTICS OF WORK ENVIRONMENTS
   AND SPECIFIC OCCUPATIONAL BEHAVIOR
3. SELF

of illustrations which can be provided. The present section of the paper attempts to compensate by outlining a more representative list of research and development questions derived from the model. Several problems are listed for each component of the model.

Work and Self Information

1. The work information constructs denote different levels of information specificity. What are the relationships between levels? For example, what effect does a particular attitude regarding the function of work have on one's perception and evaluation of various work environments, and upon specific job tasks?
2. What are the important variables which need to be considered in designing work information presentation procedures and materials? (e.g., age intelligence, past experiences, and interest)
3. How much and what kinds of information are needed in order to make satisfactory decisions about vocations and jobs?
4. Do media differ in regard to effectiveness of communication? If so, which media are most appropriate for various kinds of information?
5. How much and what kinds of self information are necessary to achieve adequate self-understanding for vocational development?
6. What are the maximum limitations regarding the amount of information which counselors and counselees can use effectively at any given time? What are the most effective ways of summarizing personal information?
7. How can counselees learn to identify useful personal intelligence?

Personalization of Information

1. When objective information is personalized, what changes in meaning take place? What are the major kinds of distortions which occur? and how can counselors anticipate and compensate for these?
2. What individual and group procedures are most effective for helping individuals personalize information? Can packaged systems be developed which will both aid the individual and reduce the counseling burden?
3. How can counselees learn to gain maximum use of personal intelligence?
4. Is it important to record personalized versions of information? How can such information be obtained? What formats are suitable? How should it be fed back to counselees?

Speculation

1. What levels of exploration and testing are most useful for various kinds of occupations?
2. How much speculation is needed in order to provide a reasonable basis for prediction and decisions?
3. How can the range of speculation resources be increased? Can packages be developed for general use? What resources are needed by counselors to contrive local and spontaneous speculation opportunities?
4. How can speculation innovations be evaluated?

General Process

1. Will the changing dimensions of vocational development require revisions in the parameters of vocational guidance? What changes might be needed regarding guidance for adults and working conditions for counselors?
2. What changes in counselor education programs will be needed to extend the competencies of practicing counselors?
3. How can information about developments be disseminated and exchanged rapidly and effectively within the profession?

There is the question whether these are counseling functions or not. For what reasons should they be assigned to the counseling domain rather than instruction? Let us for the present simply grant that counselors and counseling have by nature of traditional concern and professional competency a prior interest in the areas which are involved. The possibility that research and development will suggest that some are more appropriately assigned areas other than counseling should not concern us at this point.

Illustrations

Illustrations of proposed new developments in vocational aspects of counselor education are presented below. As indicated in each case, some of the projects are operational and others are in the conceptual stage.

Computer-Based Information Systems

Computers and their underlying technology offer great potential for advancing counseling. Two examples of what can be done with existing technology are given below. The first is primarily service oriented, and the initial value of the second is research.

The importance of educational and vocational information in the school guidance program is well established. Realistic and appropriate student decisions regarding educational and vocational plans depend upon accurate and adequate information. A tremendous amount and variety of information materials are available from several types of sources, including commercial publishers, special interest groups, and government agencies. As the supply of material has grown, the counseling profession has given serious attention to criteria for material construction, uses, and classification. Consequently, there exists not only a great amount of vocational and educational information for guidance but also a body of research and theoretical knowledge which can assist counselors help students make intelligent use of it.

The amount of information available to a given student or class, however, is essentially limited to what is available in the local school, supplemented by any additional informational materials that counselors or librarians might know of and obtain. Even the extensive educational and vocational information collections maintained by many schools are extremely limited in relation to what is actually available. However, were it possible for counselors to maintain nearly complete collections of educational and vocational information, such a practice would be highly unrealistic and inappropriate. The realistic objective for a counselor should not be to maintain a complete selection but rather to: (1) maintain a selected collection of materials appropriate to the particular needs of his counselees, and (2) have a system for selective acquisition of additional materials as needs change.

One means by which counselors could maintain educational and vocational information collections meeting these criteria would be through a center for current analytical data about available educational and vocational guidance materials. Such a center would have two basic requirements. First, it should be developed as a national program. Second, it would involve a computer-based data processing, storage, and retrieval system.

The system would expand the educational and vocational exploration areas for students. Thus, the study of vocations would not be limited to the information available in a given school. In addition, the system would permit counselors to make selective use of information in terms of a variety of criteria. Not only would counselors have information about a vastly increased amount of materials, but the information would also be coded with several criteria, thus making it possible to meet relatively specific student needs.

The system could have a variety of input, output modes, including manual, punch card, document readers, typewriter, teletypes, and cathode ray tube. A counselor would be able to input requests for information, including such specifications as cost limits and reading level, and receive either lists of available information, or in some cases actual occupational information.

Data from the system would be valuable for research purposes. It would be possible to identify specific areas in which more materials and information were needed to be developed, and the record of counselor inquiries would provide valuable data regarding the work, attitudes, and competencies of school counselors. It would be possible to identify specific areas in which more materials and information were needed to be developed and the record of counselor inquiries would provide valuable data regarding the work, attitudes, and competencies of school counselors.

A second development concerns the use of computers to help establish the relationship between counselor behavior and ensuing counselee behavior. The problem involves designing a data bank for storing information about:

1. Counselee characteristics.
2. Counselor behavior.
3. Ensuing counselee behavior.

Given such a system, it would be possible to determine which counseling procedures are most likely to produce the desired terminal behavior in question. Eventually counselor educators should be in a position to teach specific kinds of techniques and practices with greater assurance that they will produce desired results than would other procedures.

The problems involved in describing and specifying both counselor and counseling behavior are difficult, to say the least, but this should not deter efforts to develop the data bank described. If such a resource could be developed cooperatively by several counselor education programs, research could be more productive and less expensive than if pursued on a provincial basis.

Presentation Modes

It has been apparent for some time that written presentations of occupational information frequently fail to serve their purpose. Many individuals either won't read or don't understand the information. In part this is due to dull content and unimaginative writing style. In addition, a large number of counselees with which we are becoming increasingly concerned lack reading skills and are uncomfortable with written materials.

There is then reason to experiment with other media for conveying occupational information. I have recently been working on a system which would consist of about three hundred multi-voiced tape-film occupational information packages stored on a random access "juke box" like machine. The basic format of each package involves a theme or story line similar to that employed in the western and adventure serials heard on radio. The objective is to use media with which the counselee is comfortable and present occupational information in such a way that it makes affective as well as cognative sense to him. Photographs particularly should be an effective means of communicating certain aspects of vocational environments.

The organization of the materials and the number of packages is yet to be determined. Perhaps a number of systems will need to be devised in order to accommodate different populations. In all probability traditional classification systems will be defied, and existing standards for occupational information materials, challenged. If in the process ways of making information more meaningful and useful to counselees are discovered, then such will be justified.

Regional Closed-Circuit T.V. Clinics

Each of the components identified in the model involves functions for which counseling procedures need to be developed. As new procedures and techniques emerge, there is an equally critical need to update practicing counselors throughout the nation. Summer workshop and conferences help but are relatively cumbersome. Another way of extending counselor education to practicing counselors would be via regional closed-circuit television demonstrations, lectures, and clinics. The procedure has been useful in related fields, such as medicine. In addition to its value to individual counselors, this kind of communication could reduce provincialism and advance the art in an accelerated and comprehensive manner.

Another method for disseminating research and development findings to practicing counselors would be via pre-recorded video sonic tapes. Relatively inexpensive portable equipment is now available and undoubtedly will be acquired by counselor education programs.

Whatever method is used, technology exists which can help revitalize and extend counselor education.

Other Resources

There are a number of other areas of counselor education where innovations are needed. For example, counselors, whether in schools or other agencies, have an increasing number of professional contacts outside of their employing organization. Using the school counselor as an example, counselors need to work with representatives of Job Corps Centers, Upward Bound Projects, Head Start Projects, community college representatives, and who knows what else is to come. While most counselor education programs treat referral procedures and agencies to some degree, it seems likely that counselors must be prepared to work ever more cooperatively and extensively with people outside their organization. Left to their own devices, counselors will acquire knowledge about agencies as counselee needs dictate. This is a chancy arrangement at best and results in counselors failing to provide maximum resources for pupils. I would propose that more systematic attention be given to orienting counseling students in residence to the general services and policies of new agencies and programs. I would think it not impossible for each counselor education program to have an advisory committee made up of individuals from other agencies to help plan and implement work in this area.

A related but different kind of resource for counseling is federal funding legislation. Vocational guidance can now benefit from federal aid on the local as well as state level. Counselors can be key people in marshaling this kind of resource, and counseling students-in-residence should be made aware of the various federal aid programs and of the procedures for securing funds. More than orientation should be involved. It is not too much to expect that they know how to prepare a project proposal and applications. Similar objectives for practicing counselors could be achieved through orientation conferences and workshops sponsored by counselor education programs.

Conclusion

Each of the proposed new developments described above focuses on research and development in counseling. As these and other projects produce results, counselor education programs will need to be revised, expanded, and extended to post-residence study. This should provide for better counselor education and more effective counseling per se.

In addition, it needs to be recognized that counselors will need an increasing amount of systems support supplied by others. Particularly important are computer-based information and data processing systems and guidance packages employing new media. This kind of outside support, I believe, is necessary if counselors are to take advantage of current and future technology. It is both impossible and unwise for most school districts and agencies to pioneer every addition to their program. The concept of extensive outside support to counselors is an emerging one but is growing at an enormous rate. For example, as recently as 1960 computer manufacturers were not particularly interested in the education market or the needs of education. Now, five years later, nearly every major computer manufacturer has a division concerned entirely with educational research and development (and sales). Other manufacturing areas have taken similar steps.

To the extent that support systems affect counseling, counselor education programs must assume a responsibility for instruction and, equally important, for monitoring and guiding the development of support systems. I would not go so far as to propose something analagous to the Good Housekeeping Seal of Approval, but each manufacturer of guidance materials should have the benefit of advice from the profession. While the practicing counselor must be consulted in terms of the immediate and pressing needs of operational situations, the view from the larger perspective of counselor education should be included. Support systems must be based on future implications as well as current problems. They are frequently expensive to develop and, thus, resistant to change.

The concentration on research and development in counseling, which characterizes this paper, reflects the writers belief that the critical issue in counselor education today is not how we teach but what. The problem of program development has received much attention during the last several years, and as a result one can be less anxious about inadequate programs. We now need to give our attention to research and development with the aim of increasing the amount and specificity about what counselors can do for people.

As a final comment, it must be noted that the one most significant determining factor regarding new developments in vocational aspects of counselor education is the counselor educator. The extent, pace, and significance of innovations in counseling will depend in great degree to his willingness to acquire for himself the knowledge and competencies which have evolved since completing his formal education.

REFERENCE

Loughary, John W., Ed., and Stripling, Robert, and Fitzgerald, Paul, Assoc. Eds., COUNSELING, A GROWING PROFESSION, Chpt. 4, Washington, D.C., the American Personnel and Guidance Association, 1965.

Some Missing Links in Counseling Theory and Research

Milton Schwebel

The question as to what areas are most fruitful for research can be partially answered by discovering the big gaps in professional knowledge. Usually these are the unsolved issues that make the daily work of the counselor difficult, simply because he must grope his way. The question can be answered further by identifying fields or processes in counseling in which relatively little new knowledge has been accumulated. The recent semicentennial of Frank Parsons' death suggested a comparison of his ideas and those of 1960 as a point of departure to an appraisal of professional progress and plateaus, and of major vacuums in knowledge.

Not Quite So Old Hat

Rereading his little classic, *Choosing a Vocation [8]*, one is struck by a remarkable similarity between his outline of the counselor's tasks and the

---

Reprinted by permission of the author and *Personnel and Guidance Journal*, XLI, No. 4 (December, 1962), 325-331.
Milton Schwebel, Professor of Education, New York University, New York.

descriptions in current textbooks. If our contemporaries have a greater sophistication and a more technical vocabulary, his work conveys a freshness and confidence frequently lacking today. If it seems that we have broken the bounds of vocational counseling, hasty perusal of Parsons' work will reveal that the title of the book was not sufficiently comprehensive, for in his work with youth he was deeply interested in their well-rounded development: social, civic, physical as well as vocational.

Advances have been especially noticeable in the field of measurement and diagnosis. Writing almost a decade before Terman introduced the Binet-Simon test in this country, Parsons used original, individual and, of course, unstandardized procedures that seem now like an old Model-T Ford, but still have merit.

> Sometimes the counselor may wish to test the nerve and delicacy of touch. One way to do this is to have a series of very small circles a sixteenth or a thirty-second of an inch in diameter, and giving the applicant a fine-pointed pencil, ask him to put a dot precisely in the center of each little circle and one exactly in the middle between each two circles, and make a certain mark at a given point on each of the circles in the group [9, p. 22].

A few of his ideas such as characterological inferences based on physiognomy have been rejected since his day, as a result of scientific evaluation. Aside from these, Parsons, the "clinical diagnostician," would be very much at home today in a profession in which the arch-actuarialist, Paul Meehl, asks and answers several questions:

> How should we meanwhile be making our decisions? Shall we use our heads, or shall we follow the formula? Mostly we will use our heads, because there just isn't any formula... [7]

Parsons' counseling methodology was a forerunner of the processes used by today's clinical counselor. It would probably be appropriate to say that the contemporary counselor is not far removed from his earliest professional ancestor. Most of the difference relates first to the changes in diagnostic procedures already referred to, and, second, to those effects on clinical counseling that resulted from the influence of dynamic psychology, psychoanalytic thinking, and especially of the most direct representative of these in our profession—nondirective counseling and therapy. The impact of Rogers on counseling and guidance has made for the widest gap between Parsons and the counselor of our day. This is not to suggest that the gap is very wide, but only that it is there. Parsons was quite sensitive to the resistance and defensiveness of the client and took pains to instruct beginning counselors on the ways of coping with these. However, the versatile Bostonian apparently had not been influenced by his Viennese contemporary, and while he shared with Freud a belief in the necessity for a direct, analytical, and interpretive role on the part of the professional worker, he did not take into account and perhaps was unaware of the influence of repression and unconscious motivation in the behavior and choice process of the client.

Parsons was no novice in the field that approximates our study of occupations and the labor market. A social scientist of the muckraking era *[9]*, he admonished the vocational counselor to be "a careful student of industrial history and industrial geography. He should know how not merely to get the statistics, but how to use them" *[8, p. 71]*. He made great demands, for his counselor looked at the whole man and at the whole life of his whole man, and he was not afraid to assert certain values and to help the client adopt and implement them.

In summary, during the half century since his death, counseling has developed instruments that are helpful but not crucial to diagnostic work and has seen the rise of a counseling orientation that has influenced all counseling but is only a competing approach to clients and not an indispensable one. In addition, counseling has been immeasurably enriched by concepts from psychology and sociology that are important in understanding behavior.

Such a condensed evaluation of progress does not do justice to accumulated knowledge about interests, choice process, differential aptitudes, occupations, etc. One can recognize important strides and still strive for acceleration in the process of unlocking those mysteries of human development and its vicissitudes that challenge the counselor.

This viewpoint is shared with others. For example, a published thumbnail sketch of Victor Raimy contains the following: "He has been deep in clinical psychology ever since World War II, is a Diplomate in Clinical Psychology, and is fast losing faith in the interview as the sole means of changing behavior" *[14]*. In his review of Brower and Abt's *Progress in Clinical Psychology*, Raimy says

> diagnosis in the clinical field is little different in 1958 than in 1950, and no one seems willing to bet money that he knows how to improve the adjustment of persons with behavior disorders. For the impatient, and for those of faint heart, the present status of clinical psychology may well appear to be discouraging. If one broadens his perspective beyond the borders of a particular five-year or ten-year period, one may also be reminded that other areas of science have, each in their time, marched slowly across frequent plateaus *[14]*.

An experienced clinician like Raimy might well have added that we can cope with such plateaus in science as we do in counseling and psychotherapy, by re-examining the data, by re-evaluating our mode of perceiving them, and reconsidering with painful objectivity the theory that informs both our research and our practice.

In the epilogue of proceedings of a 1958 conference on research in psychotherapy, Rubinstein and Parloff *[15]* write that while much research has been done during the previous decade there was little support for any of the hypotheses.

> Basic problems in this field of research have remained essentially unchanged and unresolved. This may be due in large part to the fact that both the investigator and the therapist have managed to preserve

their favorite concepts, assumptions, values and hypotheses by hermetically sealing them in layers of ambiguity [*15, p. 292*].

Many of us can recall all too painfully the period in our professional lives when we adhered to particular doctrines which seemed sufficiently versatile to explain all the empirical data. In retrospect we see how plastic were the data, how easily they could be forced into a theoretical mold with which we needed to identify. We pay dearly for this in our professional development. The loss can be equally great by the easy acceptance of eclecticism which is, in its own way, a closed system when its assumptions are not well grounded. The only alternative is a paranoid-like suspicion of all our cherished theories and practices, of all our favored research problems, an approach that accords with the traditions of science.

The Almost-Axiomatic

Much research effort is devoted to testing that which may be beyond question. The problems of people can be the result either of faulty inheritance, of prenatal birth or postnatal injury, of adequate or inappropriate nurturance and education, of social injustice and family crises. Many of the problems that send our clients for help seem to arise in their interrelationships with people. When we commit ourselves to our profession we simply declare that we believe that their problems, created in a human relationship, however defined, are remediable in an interpersonal relationship, this time with a person who will provide adequate nurturance and instruction. Our profession would not have arisen were there not a social need for it, nor would we have entered it nor our clients sought our aid, did they and we not believe that we could help. The evidence over the years is quite consistent and convincing, Eysenck [*3*] notwithstanding, that we do help. The evidence is equally clear that some are helped little or not at all, no matter how we define the criteria of helping. Continued attempts to test whether counseling "works" thus seem wasteful. The important questions seem to be: What kinds of problems are we now able to alleviate? What kinds seem unaffected by our intervention? What is the nature of these problems? What are their causes? What new methods can we develop in light of these reformulations? And, of equal importance, which problems are irremediable by any known or conceivable methods, perhaps because their roots lie deeply in conditions that only a society itself can change, or in biological processes as yet beyond man's grasp?

Designing research in terms of these questions would be more likely to avoid plateaus in professional learning than continued study of the effectiveness of counseling-in-general. It is hoped that this would insure against a trend, especially noticeable in one branch of psychology, toward a proliferation of studies on various instruments and procedures that smack of the intellectual gymnastics of medieval scholastics who applied high intellect and boundless energy to the brilliant study of issues whose usefulness had long since been exhausted.

New Directions

Such a new orientation would turn attention away from treatment or remedial work, away from the improvement of diagnostic instruments, and turn it to the nature—not the description, but the nature of the problems that are treated. It would turn away from studies that *describe* the symptoms or even the dynamics of a client-category and turn to those that seek to understand the causes. It would build upon the scientific foundation exemplified by Williamson's 1939 book, *How to Counsel Students [17]*, a title that inadequately labels this handbook on the manifold problems of students, with special emphasis on their correlates if not their causes, and exemplified by Bordin's *[1]* and Pepinsky's *[12]* work in the 1940's on diagnostic categories.

If the counseling problems could be defined with greater precision, their causes could be identified, and we could turn our attention with greater reward to the development of treatment measures. There are, of course, other outcomes already alluded to: the unhappy recognition that some of these problems are beyond solution, or, more happily, beyond solution by currently employed methods, or only by methods conceivably employable within the counseling profession.

The Search for Causes

We can be easily deluded by the appearance of certain data when we begin to look for causes. The continued experience of failure in school and elsewhere does, as we would expect, have a deleterious effect upon the self-concept of the individual. It would be erroneous to conclude that the *cause* of his circumstances is a poorly valued self. Even when counseling that focuses on self-theory achieves change in self-valuation and brings about behavioral changes, the self-theory may have nothing whatsoever to do with success. It may even be a burden and an obstacle. Perhaps we are burning houses to roast our pigs, despite Charles Lamb's dissertation!

Few would deny that an evaluative process goes on in all of our counseling interviews, regardless whether the lead is taken by counselor or client. In one way or another this involves a form of diagnosis and, to a lesser degree, a search for causes. No matter what methods we use, our evaluation is delimited by our understanding of the human with whom we are working and the category of problems that has brought him to us. What we listen for, hear, and respond to, and how we respond depends in part on us as persons and in part on our orientation *[4, 13]*, that is, on a theory which has made particular assumptions about the causes of the problems and the methods of treatment. Our orientation delimits the repertoire of cause-effect response sets available to us in our attempt to understand a client.

Helpful as all of them have been, none of the dominant theories will suffice as a guide in understanding the problems of clients. It seems valid to assume that the causes will be found to belong to one or more of the following categories—biological, psychological, sociological, educational. Self-theory takes litte cognizance of the first and last of these factors; learning theory has similar shortcomings; psychoanlytically oriented counseling, which has come to the fore in our field at the very time that some of the analysts [16] are bewailing their limitations, is equally restrictive; finally, the trait-and-factor theory (if this empirical approach can be called a theory) is manifestly uninterested in causes, concerning itself primarily with the correlates of behavior as reflected in studies of groups of persons.

It seems doubtful that loyalty to any one theory will result in a material increase in knowledge of the etiology of client problems. The shortest route to that goal seems to be the direct one of studying the problems themselves and searching for their causes. A helping profession cannot escape the task of organizing its knowledge in such a way that its treatment procedures are clearly related to its diagnostic categories which in turn must be based on cause. In 1953 Tyler stated that "no evidence has been presented that different types of treatment corresponding to these (diagnostic) catagories can be distinguished" [17, p. 106]. Further investigation unrestricted by present theory might lead to more profound understanding of causation which might in turn suggest different treatment methodologies. Of equal significance, a knowledge of causes permits an institution or a community to take preventive measures, and it is for a profession of specialists to discover and publicize them.

The search for causes must be pressed to their ultimate source whether they be physiological, psychological, social, or educational. It hardly suffices to describe a behavior as an outgrowth of adolescence, or to attribute malfunctioning to parental discord, or to explain ambivalences in the choice process to characteristic indecision. Why do these conflicts occur?

Pseudo-psychologizing must not be allowed to mask the real causes by mistaking description of dynamics for cause and, hence, erroneously assigning responsibility to a mystical psyche. Firm links to the real problems of life can supply one with ample reason to question the exaggerated role that has been assigned to the psyche, and its relative isolation from physical social reality. Of course, this is an argument for drawing from scientific psychology (and sociology, etc.) and not from speculative psychology which should have become outdated at the time of Wundt.

The possible consequences of such an approach to research in our field can be understood by referring to a statement of Kohler's [5]. Psychologists face a problem unique to them in that the material that they study is so familiar. People, he said, do not tend to ask questions about facts with which they are thoroughly acquainted, only about unusual events. This may well be true for guidance and counseling. One can grow accustomed to the face of things and take for granted such facts of everyday life as, for example, intelligence tests.

One can find it tiring in classes on the use and interpretation of tests in guidance to reiterate that they mean "such and such" except for the many Puerto Rican children who have language and cultural handicaps, the other children in the New York area from foreign-language speaking homes, the many Negro children who come from economically and culturally deprived homes, the many working-class white children with similar conditions, the many middle-class children suffering the effects of disruptive forces at home, the emotionally disturbed children, the brain-damaged children. "Who's left?" the students ask. And then they inquire, if the tests measure "functioning intelligence," at what age, if any, should we give up remedial measures with all the handicapped and deprived people? When should we cease our efforts—if we ever begin—to give them a chance to show their potential?

The work of one prolific scientist, Pasamanick, bears on this problem. He has reported his research in almost 50 publications since 1946 and his impact on counseling and guidance is long overdue. His first significant study [10] revealed racial equality on the Gesell developmental techniques, the first time such equality had been found. Further examination of the data showed that unlike other racial comparative studies this was the first one in which Negroes were equal to white children not only in the early expressions of mental functioning but also in height and weight. He hypothesized that the mothers had received an apparently adequate prenatal diet because of wartime rationing and the improved economic status of wartime employment, and that the changed social conditions affected the physiological conditions for intra-uteral development, which in turn helped determine psychological functioning.

Pasamanick and his associates conducted a series of retrospective studies involving more than 8,000 children and concerning such disorders of interest to us as the following: reading disabilities, speech disorders, mental deficiency, and behavior disorders. Here is a statement of propositions basic to this major investigation:

> Inasmuch as prematurity and complications of pregnancy are associated with fetal and neonatal death, usually on the basis of injury to the brain, there must remain a fraction so injured who do not die; depending upon the degree and location of trauma they go on to develop a series of disorders extending from cerebral palsy, epilepsy, and mental deficiency through all types of behavioral and learning disabilities which are a result of lesser degrees of damage sufficient to disorganize behavioral development and lower thresholds to stress; and, further, that these abnormalities of pregnancy are associated with certain life experiences, usually socio-economically determined, with the consequence that they themselves and their resulting neuropsychiatric disorders find greater aggregation in the lower strata of our society [11, p. 2-3].

Some of his statements are startling, and they should, therefore, be presented with the reassurance that his work is in the scientific tradition. Pasamanick and Knobloch [11] state that the studies raise the question whether or not the distribution of intelligence really follows the bell-shaped curve. While this "normal distribution" has been found to apply to a few biological characteristics such as height and weight, the distribution "of most biological functions, particularly vital metabolic indices, indicates that these are far from being normally distributed." In their view, the range of intellectual potential is far narrower than has been thought. Stressing that the evidence is far from complete they state their belief, "that it is now possible to entertain a new *tabula rasa* theory which hypothecates that at conception individuals are quite alike in intellectual endowment except for the few quite rare hereditary neurologic defects. It appears to be life experience and socio-cultural mileu influencing biological and physiological function which, in the absence of organic brain damage, makes human beings significantly different behaviorally from each other" *[11, p. 16]*.

If Pasamanick's hypotheses continue to be supported, and if they lead ultimately to the corroboration of his impressions about human intelligence, he will shatter some strongly and widely held beliefs. Furthermore, the counselor's conceptualization of problems would be modified and, consequently, his repertoire of responses.

At the moment, indirect and inferential support for this optimistic view of human capabilities comes from a distant source. Reporting on his observations of education in the Soviet Union, Chauncey *[2]* of the Educational Testing Service referred to the Soviet assumption that all individuals except the organically defective are capable of mastering the academic program This assumption, he believes, is at least partially responsible for the fact that Soviet schools are graduating a significantly higher percentage of their students from the *academic* secondary school than we are.

Indirect support comes also from a closer source. The longitudinal studies at Fels Research Institute on mental growth and personality development clearly suggest that acceleration of mental development in an above-average-intelligence group of children is associated with specific personality characteristics. Sontag, Baker, and Nelson *[16]* report that significant IQ gains between the ages of four and six occur in association with "independence." Those children whose parents have trained them to be independent have developed a mode of behavior which is conducive to "learning to learn." Between the ages of six to ten, acceleration is associated with a constellation of characteristics that deserves comparison with McClelland's *[6]* "achievement motive."

This rich series of studies suggests that to attribute scholastic failure to low intelligence and to inadequate "potential" may well be superficial or inappropriate diagnosis.

These studies and especially Pasamanick's have been introduced to indicate the possibilities inherent in a fresh approach. In the spirit of science, all the old theories in counseling, as in psychology, sociology, economics, etc., are suspect, and the new ones, including his, even more so. As a profession sometimes called human engineering, counseling should draw upon all the sciences that relate to man, the biological no less than the others, and the goal can be nothing less than the discovery of the causes of the multifarious problems of clients.

It is these, the causes of problems, that appear to be the important missing links. When the etiology of educational, vocational, and social problems is clear and the origins understood, diagnostic treatment as well as preventive measures ought to be considerably more effective. When the counselor knows all of the possible causes of school failure, and need not resort to shaky and unproved "theories" about the unconscious or about native dullness, he can be expected to reshape his formulations and his professional behavior. The study of causes is a potentially rich field for research, offering immediate applications to concrete problems.

REFERENCES

1. Bordin, E. S. Diagnosis in counseling and psychotherapy. *Educ., psychol. Measmt.*, 1946, *6*, 169-184.
2. Chauncey, H. Some notes on education and psychology in the Soviet Union. *American Psychol.*, 1959, *14*, 307-312.
3. Eysenck, H. J. The effects of psychotherapy: an evaluation. *J. consult. Psychol.*, 1952, *16*, 319-324.
4. Fiedler, F. A comparison of therapeutic relationships in psychoanalytic, nondirective, and Adlerian therapy. *J. consult. Psychol.*, 1950, *14*, 426-445.
5. Kohler, W. *Dynamics in psychology.* New York: Liveright, 1940.
6. McClelland, D.C. *The achievement motive.* New York: Appleton-Century-Crofts, 1953.
7. Mechl, P. When shall we use our heads instead of the formula? *J. counsel. Psychol.*, 1957, *4*, 268-273.
8. Parsons, F. *Choosing a vocation.* Cambridge, Mass.: The Riverside Press, 1909.
9. Parsons, R. *The city for the people.* Philadelphia: C. F. Taylor, 1900.
10. Pasamanick, B. A comparative study of the behavioral development of Negro infants. *J. genet. Psychol.*, 1946, *59*, 3-44.
11. Pasamanick, B., & Knobloch, H. Epidemiologic studies on the complications of pregnancy and the birth process which have implications for the primary prevention of mental disorders in childhood. Paper presented at Meeting of International Preparatory Commission of the International Association for Child Psychiatry and Allied Professions. Cambridge, Mass., February 1960.
12. Pepinsky, H. B. The selection and use of diagnostic categories in clinical counseling. *Appl. Psychol. Monogr.*, 1948, *15*.
13. Porter, E. J., Jr. *Therapeutic counseling.* New York: Houghton Mifflin, 1950.
14. Raimy, V. Clinicists march on—a little. *Contemp. Psychol.*, 1960, *5*, 53.
15. Rubinstein, E. A., & Parloff, M. B. *Research in psychotherapy.* Washington, D.C. Amer. Psychol. Assoc., 1959.
16. Sontag, L. W., Baker, C. T., & Nelson, V. L. *Mental growth and personality development: a longitudinal study.* Monograph, Society for Research in Child Development, XXIII, 1958, *68*, (2).

17. Tyler, L. *Work of the counselor.* New York: Appleton-Century-Crofts, 1953.
18. Wheelis, A. *The quest for identity.* New York: Norton, 1958.
19. Williamson, E. G. *How to counsel students.* New York: McGraw-Hill, 1939.

Research in Vocational Development: Implications for the Vocational Aspects of Counselor Education

Henry Borow

Introduction

Brayfield (1, 2) aptly observed recently that vocational guidance cannot lay claim to the status of an independent scholarly or research discipline. Like many fields of professional practice it must draw its principles from a number of outside fields of study. Unfortunately, the strong flavor of pragmatism which marked vocational guidance from its inception in America as a formal movement early in the century led its pioneers to champion notions of method and to ignore sound conceptual models of vocational behavior to which such method might be applied.

Background paper prepared for Airlie House, Warrenton, Virginia Conference on Vocational Aspects of Counselor Education, December 12-15, 1965. Sponsored by The George Washington University under contract with the U. S. Office of Education.

Henry Borow, Professor of Psychological Studies, University of Minnesota, Minneapolis.

Actually, vocational guidance for the first half-century of its existence did have a theory of sorts. Any attempt to deal with behavior and to make predictions about what happens to behavior when one or another course of treatment is used upon it requires a "theory" in the sense of a prior set of notions about how behavior works. But like a number of other loosely formulated theories of behavior, that adopted by vocational guidance was largely impressionistic and lacked a sophisticated network of postulates and laws tied to controlled observation.

We are familiar by now with the premises about behavior which are built into the trait-measurement model of vocational choice and vocational guidance. The individual is assumed to possess a large number of personal attributes, largely fixed or static, which combine in various ways to dispose him toward success or failure in given curricula or occupational fields. His choice of an occupation under guidance is a cognitive process deliberately carried out by the method of "pure reasoning," as Frank Parsons termed it. It is obvious to us today that this uncomplicated conception of occupational choice behavior slighted or distorted (a) the dynamic, needs-based character of vocational striving and preference, (b) the unconscious processes which attend the making of value choices and decisions, (c) the potential modifiability of career behavior, and (d) the psychological meanings of the human work experience. Vocational guidance in practice was, and largely remains, a technique-centered, perhaps one should say, a technique-obsessed field of service emphasizing in one setting or another the compilation, classification, and dissemination of occupational information, the selection, administration and interpretation of vocational tests, and the analysis of interview method. Attention appeared to be devoted to everything about guidance except the integral nature of the adjusting organism itself.

Beginning in the 1950's, growing dissatisfaction with the classical, trait-measurement model in which vocational guidance was anchored led to the emergence of imaginative reconceptualizations of occupational behavior. The principal benchmarks of the newer models of vocational development are now well known. Prominent among them are the following:

1. *Concept of Psychological Life Stages* (3): Psychological growth can be described in terms of a series of stages in cognitive, emotional and social development. The life-stage notion provides a useful framework for the study of vocationally relevant behavior, particularly when longitudinal research designs are employed.

2. *Concept of the Career Pattern* (4, 5): Occupational choice behavior is not confined to a single, fixed decision but is best viewed as a time-extended process involving a series of socially and personally imposed choice points. This is a lawful or orderly, hence potentially predictable, movement from position to position within the career pattern that is related to the attributes and interwoven with the life experience of the individual. The particular decision made at any choice point will depend also upon economic and social contingencies which

are sometimes fortuitous, a circumstance which makes long-range occupational prediction hazardous.

3. *Vocational Developmental Tasks* (6): Acquiring vocational maturity involves confronting at each life stage a set of typical and necessary problem-solving experiences, the mastery of which furnishes the basis for achievement and successful coping behavior at the next successive stage.

4. *Implementation of the Self-Concept* (7): As part of the process of establishing a stable identity, the adolescent makes choices, both conscious and inadvertent, consistent with and fortifying to his emerging image of self. By no means all of these decisions are directly vocational in nature, but they are all part of an orderly and developing career pattern, broadly conceived.

5. *Occupational Role Models* (8): In acquiring and practicing adult behavior, the child or adolescent imitates the behavior of the significant adults in his experience who thus serve as his behavior role models. From the taking and testing of roles in this socially imitative manner, the subject internalizes values and broad habits of behavior such that they become relatively enduring facets of his psychological makeup. If he is fortunate in having exposure to effective adult role models, he may develop the capacity for delayed gratification of needs, take on useful habits of industry, and establish in his behavior the achievement orientation requisite to satisfactory vocational development, including rational decision-making and productive, satisfying work.

Concepts such as the foregoing have provided the means for building integrated models of occupational behavior set in a developmental, ongoing frame of reference. The value of such conceptualizations, of course, is that they allow for the generation and testing of a much wider and richer assortment of hypotheses about vocational life than is permitted by the classical and static actuarial model. It is the presenter's opinion that the model building and empirical investigations of the past fifteen years, with all of their shortcomings, have advanced our knowledge of the structure and meaning of occupationally relevant behavior far beyond the thousands of conceptually sterile prediction and validation studies of the entire first-half of the century.

A Selected Resume of Relevant Research

What have we learned thus far from the yield of the new research genre which may bear upon the issues of aim and content in counselor education? There follows below an enumeration, with brief descriptions, of some representative classes of research findings which the presenter believes must ultimately be reflected in the competence of practicing counselors and, hence, must in some significant way be incorporated into the design of professional training programs.

1. A number of motivational traits and response styles are acquired in the early formative years of personality development which, while not yet converging upon occupation, would appear to shape the course and effectiveness of the broad career pattern. Among them may be mentioned coping and mastery behavior (9), habits of industry, personal autonomy, and achievement orientation (10). Sometimes the relationship they hold to career may be more distinctly seen. For example, Rosen (11), who has analyzed achievement motivation, specified educational-occupational aspiration as one of the three major components of achievement-oriented behavior.

2. Children appear to acquire powerful prestige sterotypes of occupations from the general culture without having to learn them formally or deliberately. Gunn (12) has shown, for instance, that children cannot handle the concept of ranking occupations in a stable and meaningful way before fourth grade, are able to rank occupations meaningfully as fourth and fifth graders but invoke a service or social usefulness criterion in doing so and tend to see all jobs in a favorable light, begin to rank jobs by their status-conferring potency by the time they are seventh graders and arrange occupations in their minds very much the way adults do by the time they reach the tenth grade. Confirming evidence comes from Richard Nelson's (13) study and others. Children thus assimilate negative views of many occupations as they move through middle and late childhood and, correspondingly, restrict in a premature and ill-considered way the range of occupations they will later contemplate as possible careers. It is obvious that children do not wait till the schools begin to teach about occupational life before forming concepts and values about work which subtly but powerfully affect career-related decisions.

3. Younger children do not appear to distinguish between occupational aspiration and occupation expectation. For a second or third grader, to want a certain vocation is tantamount to having it. Ginzberg (14), Slocum (15), and others have shown that the limiting factors of personal attributes and economic reality enter career choice deliberation more prominently with advancing age, although not all studies agree with Ginzberg's conclusions about the age of onset of this period of tentative choice. Indirect corroboration of the position that reality-oriented behavior increases with age is provided by O'Hara and Tiedeman's (16) research report in the Harvard Studies in Career Development series. They found that self-estimated and objectively determined scores on interest, aptitudes, and values, in that order, converge on one another between the ninth and twelfth grades, and they infer that a process of progressive clarification of the self-concept occurs during these secondary school years which provides a firmer base for realistic planning and choice.

4. Stability of occupational preference also tends to increase with age. Tested vocational interest becomes more stable in mid-adolescence

and relatively durable in the early twenties. Many studies agree with Schmidt and Rothney's (17) finding that vocational choices fluctuate fairly commonly during the high school years. There is also a disparity between preferred and expected choices, academically less successful students and those of low socioeconomic class membership scaling down their expectations considerably more than is typical of academically successful students and of subjects from higher-level socioeconomic backgrounds.

5. Perhaps because vocational motives are not yet strongly developed, occupational information is quite limited, and preference yet quite unstable, devoting the counseling of junior high school students to an evaluation of the wisdom of stated vocational choices or to the working out of specific vocational choices seems unjustified. Super and Overstreet's (18) widely cited conclusion on this issue is that the vocational development of ninth grade boys is best viewed in terms of a criterion of planfulness, an orientation and disposition toward planning for the future rather than the making of specific occupational decisions per se.

6. In light of the shifting concern in the occupational study of pre-adolescents and young adolescents from earliness and specificity of choice toward more useful developmental criteria, a number of investigators have been at work on the development of new measures of vocational behavior. Promising among these are Crites' Vocational Development Inventory (19, 20), a questionnaire form, and Gribbons and Lohnes' Readiness for Vocational Planning Scales (21, 22), based on a semi-structure interview technique. A few years ago, Harris and Clark constructed a Sense of Responsibility Scale which appears to merit use in vocational development studies. While none of these instruments has yet produced unusually impressive findings, this presenter believes that they open to researchers the most promising avenues of attack we have had on the description and norming of career development behavior across age, sex, ability, and socioeconomic subsamples.

7. In agreement with the common belief, the quantity and quality of occupational information generated by children at both elementary and secondary school levels are distressingly poor. At least two studies (Super and Overstreet, Nelson) have indicated that children of high intelligence and upper social-class membership are somewhat better informed about their preferred occupations than are other samples of students. (23, 24) A common charge about lack of realism in the vocational planning of high school subjects centers on the findings that students frequently voice occupational preferences that are too ambitious for their announced educational plans. A survey involving a national sample of boys aged fourteen to sixteen years report that only 18 per cent of the subjects possessed a clear picture of the steps which would have to be taken to qualify for their choosen field. (25)

8. As previously noted, the broad, social sterotypes carried by occu-

pations are associated with the attractiveness or lack of appeal they have as potential career choices for youth. (26) In fact, it is very questionable whether objective and factual occupational information per se is as potent a determinant of occupational preference and aspiration as the broadly framed images of jobs as social ways of life. The precise manner in which these style-of-living occupational images are so universally and persuasively acquired is not yet fully understood.

9. In general, the rate of vocational development is associated with social class status. Culturally disadvantaged and delinquent youth evince slower and more sporadic development. (27) Tentative evidence suggests that the eroding effects of cultural impoverishment apply not alone to general social discomfort and unsatisfactory scholastic motivation and achievement, but to occupational planning as well. That some studies show that disadvantaged adolescents make earlier vocational choices is not an index of precocity in vocational development so much as a matter of their having come to the end of the line in educational opportunity and being forced to seek entry into the labor market as a way of avoiding utter purposelessness.

10. Respondents in both American and British surveys cite outside work experience as highly influential in the making of definite overt vocational decisions, especially so when the outside jobs have been in a field related to the preferred occupation. (28, 29) The significance of this finding for work-study programs and for vocational education programs in general seems immediately apparent, particularly in view of the general effect of heightened formal schooling requirements in delaying entrance of a substantial segment of youth into full-time work.

11. Evidence not conducive to the building of high morale and feelings of self-importance among counselors comes from studies on who influences the vocational choices of students. In Slocum and Empey's (30) studies in the State of Washington, students were more likely to point to outside work experience than to persons as the single most important factor in choice. Among human agents, parents were named most commonly by women students. Frequent mention was made also of the influence upon vocational choice of teachers, relatives, and friends. Wilson's (31) study among English secondary school subjects yielded similar results. Counselors are rarely named. It would be of considerable interest and importance to the counseling profession to know why. One reason would appear to lie in the fact that many student counselors, owing perhaps to lack of interest, lack of self-confidence, unfavorable student-counselor ratios, conflicts in duties, or some combination of these conditions simply do not perform vocational counseling as such. Pertinent here, too, is Dr. Kenneth Hoyt's observation that the counselor's influence on the total life of any student is probably small and the counselor must learn to live with this reality. Yet it seems likely that the counselor has potential for influence that is greater than is generally achieved. Krumboltz and Varenhorst's (32) recently published study,

for example, demonstrated that ninth-grade students lent greater credence to statements that were fictitiously attributed to counselors than when ascribed to peers or parents.

12. In an age in which the centrality of work in human life is being questioned by some authorities, work clearly occupies an increasingly prominent place in the lives of women. (33, 34) Indeed, the fact that the percentage of persons of labor force age who are currently employed in the United States is substantially unchanged from 1910 (despite drastic declines in the percentage of workers at both ends of the age scale) is traceable to the growing importance of woman's role as worker. Approximately one of three American workers today is female. About two out of five women of working age are currently in the labor force. The image of the typical female worker as a young woman who withdraws permanently from the labor force when she starts her family or when her husband becomes moe financially secure is palpably false. About 35 per cent of married women are now gainfully employed. Nine and one-half million women with children under eighteen years of age are employed. A modest estimate from the Bureau of Labor Statistics holds that the average working life expectancy for today's high school girls, irrespective of marriage and family contingencies, is 25 years. More frequently than men who face military service, the careers of women are interrupted by the obligations of marriage and family. Yet curriculum revision and school counseling have largely ignored these insistent realities. (35)

13. Personality structure converges upon the career history. Most will recall that Roe (36) hypothesized a determinable relationship between early child-rearing climate and latter vocational choice. While Roe (37) now concedes that the relation of early life experience and personality to occupation may be more complex than she once believed, there seems little cause to doubt the impact of personality on vocational development. Holland's (38, 39) work strongly suggests that preference for occupational labels may be related to general personality style, a view shared by certain other research workers. Getzels and Jackson's (40) highly creative subjects differed from the highly intelligent (but not highly creative) subjects in the quantity and range of their expressed vocational interests. It is to be hoped that future research will chart the connections between the personality variables and career pattern behavior in fuller detail.

14. It may be useful to identify some gaps in the topical domain of empirical research. No general concordance is found among research workers about the rate of vocational development. For example, not all investigators produce findings which agree with Ginzberg's proposed age ranges for the fantasy, tentative, and reality periods of vocational development. Secondly, while industrial psychologists and sociologists have learned much about the relation of actual working conditions to worker morale and performance, we must repeat the earlier observation

that little is yet known about how children acquire their occupational valuing system and vocational motives. Finally, while work is proceeding on new approaches to the clustering of occupations on the basis of their common loadings of human attributes, no definitive system for the functional sorting out of fields of work is yet at hand. The newly published *Third Edition of the Dictionary of Occupational Titles*, while admittedly an important research and counseling tool, represents only a very modest step in this particular direction. We can only say with some confidence that the fluid nature of the changing social and technological order will require more frequent job changes in the future. We must therefore discover the work rubrics possessing the highest degree of communality, and hence transferability, from job to job as the basis for devising a radically new occupational classification system for use in training and guidance.

The Future Face of Counselor Education: A Vocational Profile

No simple, clearly discernible relationship may be claimed to exist between research discovery in the field of vocational development, as herein reported, and the need for curriculum revision and new training methods in counselor education. The results of research do not have singleness of meaning for all who are concerned with the preparation of counselors. There is, moreover, the question of the underlying social values and aims in counselor education, and research findings have only a tangential rather than focal relation to this fundamental issue. Nonetheless, one can hardly dispute the claim that our expanding views of occupational behavior call for a searching reappraisal of counselor education programs with a view toward effecting substantial modification both in content and method.

Admittedly, the implications of research findings in vocational development for counselor education, as enumerated below, are idiosyncratic. They represent one observer's provisional judgment about some of the new directions we must travel in the preparation of qualified counselors in view of what we now know. Others will study the same research findings and emerge perhaps with a somewhat different set of implications and recommendations for training policy and practice. As a matter of fact, others have already done so in their own way. The presenter is aware of the recommendations for training, some consistent with and others incompatible with his own, that grew out of the report of the commission on Guidance in American Schools, (Wrenn Report), out of the 1964 Greyston Conference, and more recently, out of the June 1965 Invitational Conference on Government-University Relations in the Professional Preparation and Employment of Counselors (McGowan Report). The presenter's recommendations should be interpreted against the backdrop of the crucial importance he attaches to the sphere or work within the total psychological life process and his conviction that school counseling is now generally bedeviled with archaic assumptions and practices which violate both the realities of today's occupational universe and the newly emerging facts about the vocational development of youth.

It will be obvious that the adoption of even a few of the recommendations that follow below would require a marked lengthening of the counselor education curriculum. In the presenter's view, the 30 hours of graduate semester credit or 45 hours of graduate quarter-term credit which have been required in many programs are grossly inadequate to equip counselors-in-training for the formidable task which will confront them. Such programs are unrealistic, too, when judged against the expectations and demands which society now sets for counselors. It seems unarguable that counselor education programs will have to grow in length, quality, and disciplined rigor.

1. The study of the development of vocationally relevent motives must extend into early childhood. The secondary school counselor's ability to understand and help the student with vocational problems does not rest entirely with a cross-sectional analysis of present behavior. If it is to assist with the process of vocational development, counseling must become as sensitive to pertinent concepts and findings of child psychology as it has been in the past to those of the psychology of individual differences and of adolescent psychology.

2. Counselors-in-training must learn to view the student's emerging vocational motives through a developmental prism. If he were to acquire an appreciation of the fact that the criteria of vocational maturity differ with the particular developmental tasks and capacities that typify and differentiate successive life stages, the counselor would more effectively resist preoccupation with problems of choice and the temptation to restrict the aim of counseling to choice-making alone.

3. Personality variables associated with the capacity to achieve at a successful level in academic work and, ultimately, with the capacity to perform useful and satisfying work must be better understood by counselors. Thus, the study of how general personality theory and vocational development theory converge on each other should be part of the counselor's formal preparation. For the counselor, to learn that parental encouragement of independence and parental rewarding of acts of constructive independence nourishes achievement motivation in the child and influences both his aspirations and the effectiveness of his coping behavior is to deepen the counselor's insight into psychological growth processes.

4. Much greater attention in the curriculum of counselor education should be devoted to the dynamics of social class phenomena. The typical school counselor's generalized image of the student, what motivates him and what his values are, is often highly inaccurate. Even when he recognizes that the student is not academically oriented and rejects certain aspects of "proper," middle-class culture, the counselor may feel perplexed and threatened. The study of cultural disparity and

the analysis of the forces of social disorganization should be part of the training experience of all counselors who will meet a heterogeneous range of students in their professional work. Ideally, counselor education should function to eliminate the counseling bias which has in the past favored the high achieving, socially compliant, upwardly mobile youth. The training of counselors must be concerned with the cultivation of sensitivity about the social motives and perceptions of counselees of widely differing socio-economic class origins, particularly of culturally disadvantaged and socially alienated counselees and those who are caught up in culture conflict. The societal values, school-oriented emphases, and verbal techniques with which conventional counseling has been imbued have not generally been found to be applicable to such counselees, at least not in the earlier stages of the counseling relationship. Increasingly, counselors will need to equip themselves with or at least understand, the conceptual tools of the social worker and cultural anthropologist if they are to come to terms with such individuals and offer them effective help.

5. Vocational aspirations and plans, and the general course of vocational development itself, are not immutable. They are the products of a complex of antecedent sociocultural conditions and are, within limits, subject to change. As we have seen, traditional vocational guidance preoccupied itself with prediction rather than with the modification of vocationally relevant behavior. Contemporary vocational guidance can do better. Vocational development is not a static, predetermined process. It can and should be systematically influenced. Through continuing research, counseling must identify experience variables which facilitate the development and effective expression of educational-vocational motives and must learn how to apply knowledge of these variables to the shaping of vocational development. If this ambitious aim is to be attained, the insights of modern learning theory and practice must be brought to bear upon the preparation of professional counselors. As a beginning, counselors should familiarize themselves with the current vigorous movement in behavior modification theory and reinforcement counseling. While this movement has thus far centered chiefly on therapeutic counseling, it has clear and direct import for the work of educational and vocational counselors as well. It seems safe to predict that the literaure of counseling and guidance will signal a quickening of interest in behavior modification techniques. Not the smallest part of this interest will attach itself to the problems of facilitating vocational development processes and of maximizing the prospects of vocational maturity.

The revamped curriculum of counselor education will need to stress learning theory and practice with reference to the behavior modification functions of the counselor. Current concerns about the ethicality of behavior modification aims seems to the presenter to be no greater than the moral concern we have ever felt when we have entered into the lives of people and tried to influence them. Is not all education a planned attempt at behavioral change? Does the fact that we now have the prospect of a better technology at our disposal make what we do any less ethical?

6. Some years ago, the argument raged as to whether the schools needed a specialist to discharge guidance functions or whether these activities should be left in the hands of the classroom teacher and homeroom teacher. More recently, the school counselor has established his distinct professional identity but he has been somewhat self-conscious and protective about his new image. It is time now that the counselor-in-training be thoroughly and systematically exposed to the social psychology of the school, his place in it and in the network of sometimes harmonious, sometimes dissonant assumptions, values, objectives, and practices. When we consider the ambitious expectations that are held for today's counselor, it becomes clear that the counselor cannot effectively work as a wholly autonomous agent of the school. That part of the complex socialization process by which the student acquires attitudes, motives, and skills relative to the worker role is dependent upon many agents and agencies of behavioral change other than counselors alone. The traditional one-to-one relationship in counseling which we have cherished and perhaps overvalued will, of course, continue. But it is quite likely that the conception of the counselor as a room-bound agent of behavior change must be critically reappraised. The counselor of the future will likely serve as a social catalyst, interacting in a two-person relationship with the counselee part of the time, but also serving as a facilitator of the environmental and human conditions which are known to promote the counselee's total psychological development, including vocational development.

The 1965 Cubberley Conference at Stanford University, titled "Revolution in Counseling," stressed the potential role of the counselor as an effective arranger of the total school environment in promoting the improved psychological growth of students. Inevitably and increasingly, it would seem, counselor education must find ways of training the counselor to function broadly as a significant agent of social change in an interlocking system of many specialists within the formal institution that we call the school.

7. Vocational counseling, which was originally the province of social workers in this country, has once again become a prominent activity in out-of-school governmental and voluntary social agencies. School counselors have sometimes hermetically sealed themselves off against those outside agencies and have too often betrayed an attitude of indifference or contempt toward their services. The recent spate of federal enactments involving vocational help for the disabled, the technologically displaced, and out-of-school youth should have made it clear to school counselors that they hold no monopoly an the helping relationship. In fact, where vocational aspects of counseling are concerned, the more

significant work appears to be going on in non-school agencies, in quantity, at least, if not always in quality.

The psychological needs of youth including those needs anchored in vocational development, are continuous and are not restricted to one specific life stage of institutional setting. Counselor education programs, with their traditional concern about in-school problems and adjustments, have in the past largely ignored this reality. Training which makes the counselor-to-be more keenly aware of the extramural problems of youth and of the agencies established to serve youth can lead to closer cooperation between counselors at different educational levels (elementary, secondary, college) and between school counselors and those in other settings (public employment service, social work agencies, rehabilitation centers, youth opportunity centers, and the like). Counseling services, when articulated in this way across institutions and age periods, constitute a good example of what the idea of developmental counseling can become in practice. A recent significant attempt in this direction was the June 1965 Invitational Conference on Government-University Relations in the Preparation and Employment of Counselors. Counselor educators would do well to study the report of this conference recently released under the editorship of John McGowan.

8. One might hope that somewhere in the expanding curriculum of counselor education a place may be found for the study of curricular problems. The long-standing habits of thought which require complete separation of problems of curriculum from those of counseling are unfortunate. The counselor's goals for students can often be mediated through the formal curriculum if the latter can be manipulated.

A new approach to curriculum-making is called for. Traditionally, the establishment and revision of school curricula have been based on impressionistic and *a priori* conceptions of student capabilities and social needs. As a resource specialist who possesses useful knowledge of student motives and of developmental and learning processes, the counselor can contribute importantly to the analysis of problems of curriculum revision, particularly where culturally disadvantaged and nonacademic youth are concerned. Recent pilot programs with such youth in some school systems have lent tentative support to this recommendation. The need for the counselor's involvement with curriculum is particularly urgent in programs of vocational education. A heartening current trend is that which involves long overdue cooperation between vocational education researchers and counseling specialists in experimental projects under the Vocational Education Act (e.g., the National Interdisciplinary Seminar on Occupational Guidance in Vocational Education, to be held at The Ohio State University in January, 1966).

9. Two other suggestions for improving the formal program of counselor education should be mentioned briefly. First, it is well known that school counselors tend to confound curricular counseling with vocational counseling. Their limited knowledge of the outside occupa-

tional world, its requirements and problems, leads them to prefer curricular counseling or program advising to vocational counseling. Some institutions which encourage short industrial internships for their counselors-in-training report increased counselor sensitivity to problems of employment, the hiring requirements of industry, and the school work transition problems of the recent graduate. If industrial internships were to become more nearly standard in the training of counselors, we should probably witness an upsurge of appreciation of the phenomena of vocational development and an upturn of genuine vocational counseling in the school.

Finally, while most school counselors cannot realistically be expected to make major contributions to research in the field of vocational development, the future advancement of vocational guidance as a viable profession may depend in part on the research performed by actual practitioners. Brayfield (41) has argued persuasively that the practicing counselor is an important participant in occupational research and he cites three important contributions that the practitioner can make to the research enterprise. The best counselor education programs of the future, it is hoped, will balance the teaching of principles and practice with the cultivation of appreciation for the research enterprise and the transmission of functional research skills.

A final comment about the future development of counselor education in light of the recent work on vocational development and the increased demand on counselors for high competence. In a word, I would not be so concerned with what to eliminate from the counselor education curriculum as with what I should add. And what I should most assuredly add, as many of my previous recommendations may imply, is a strong and pervasive accent on the behavioral and social sciences.

REFERENCES

1. Brayfield, A. H. Research on vocational guidance: status and prospect. Part I. In H. Borow (Ed.) *Man in a world at work.* Boston: Houghton Mifflin, 1964. Pp. 310-323.
2. Brayfield, A. H. Vocational counseling today. In E. G. Williamson (Ed.), *Vocational counseling: a reappraisal in honor of Donald G. Paterson.* Minnesota Studies in Student Personnel Work, No. 11. Minneapolis: University of Minnesota Press, 1961. Pp. 22-58.
3. Super, D. E. *The psychology of careers.* New York: Harper & Brothers, 1957, Chap. 5.
4. Form, W. H. & Miller, D. C. Occupational career pattern as a sociological instrument. In S. Nosow & W. H. Form (Eds.), *Man, work, and society.* New York: Basic Books, 1962. Pp. 287-297.
5. Super, *The psychology of careers,* Chap. 5.
6. Super, D. E., *et al., Vocational development: a framework for research.*

New York: Bureau of Publications, Teachers College, Columbia University, 1957.

7. Super, *The psychology of careers,* Chaps. 8 and 9.
8. Slocum, W. L. Occupational and educational plans of high school seniors from farm and non-farm homes. *Bulletin* 564, Washington Agricultural Experiment Stations, State College of Washington, February 1956.
9. Murphy, Lois B. *The widening world of childhood: paths toward mastery.* New York: Basic Books, 1962.
10. McClelland, D. C. *et al., The achievement motive.* New York: Appleton-Century-Crofts, 1953.
11. Rosen, B. C. The achievement syndrome: a psychological dimension of social stratification. *Amer. Sociol. Rev.,* 1956, *21,* 203-211.
12. Gunn, B. Children's conceptions of occupational prestige. *Personn. Guid. J.,* 1964, *42,* 558-563.
13. Nelson, R. C. Knowledge and interests concerning sixteen occupations among elementary and secondary school students. *Educ. Psychol. Measmt.,* 1963, *23,* 741-754.
14. Ginzberg, E. *et al., Occupational choice.* New York: Columbia University Press, 1951.
15. Slocum,Occupational and educational plans of high school seniors from farm and non-farm homes.
16. O'Hara, R. P. & Tiedeman, D. V. The vocational self-concept in adolescence. *J. counsel. Psychol.,* 1959, *6,* 292-301.
17. Schmidt, J. L. & Rothney, J. W. Variability of vocational choices of high school students. *Personn. Guid., J.,* 1955, *34,* 142-146.
18. Super, D. E. & Overstreet, P. L. *The vocational maturity of ninth-grade boys.* New York: Bureau of Publications, Teachers College, Columbia University, 1960.
19. Crites, J. O. A model for the measurement of vocational maturity. *J. counsel. Psychol.,* 1961, *8,* 255-259.
20. Crites, J. O. Research on vocational guidance: status and prospect. Part II. In H. Borow (Ed.), *Man in a world at work.* Boston: Houghton Mifflin, 1964. Pp. 324-340.
21. Gribbons, W. D. & Lohnes, P. R. Predicting five years of development in adolescents from readiness for vocational planning scales. *J. educ. Psychol.,* 1965, *56,* 244-253.
22. Gribbons, W. D. & Lohnes, P. R. Shifts in adolescents' vocational values. *Personn. Guid. J.,* 1965, *44,* 248-252.
23. Super & Overstreet, *op. cit.*
24. Nelson, *op. cit.*
25. Survey Research Center Staff, Institute for Social Research, University of Michigan. *A study of adolescent boys.* New Brunswick, New Jersey: Boy Scouts of America, 1955.
26. O'Dowd, D. D. & Beardslee, D. C. College student images of a selected group of professions and occupations. *Cooperative Research*

Project No. 562 (8142), United States Office of Education, Department of Health, Education, and Welfare, April 1960.

27. Small, L. Personality determinants of vocational choice. *Psychol. Monogr.*, 1953, 67(1), 21.

28. Slocum, *op. cit.*

29. Wilson, M. D. The vocational preferences of secondary modern school children: Part VI. The development of a realistic attitude to vocations. *Brit. J. educ. Psychol.*, 1953, *23*, 163-179.

30. Slocum, W. L. & Empey, LaMar. Occupational planning by young women. *Bulletin* 568, Washington Argicultural Experiment Stations, State College of Washington, 1956.

31. Wilson, *op. cit.*

32. Krumboltz, J. D. & Varenhorst, B. Molders of pupil attitudes, *Personn. Guid. J.*, 1965, *43*, 443-446.

33. U. S. Department of Labor. *Manpower: challenge of the 1960's*. Washington, D. C.: U. S. Government Printing Office, 1960.

34. President's Commission on the Status of Women. *American Women*. Washington, D. C.: U. S. Government Printing Office, 1963.

35. Midwest Regional Pilot Conference. "New Approaches to Counseling Girls in the 1960's." Report of the conference held at University of Chicago, February 26-27, 1965.

36. Roe, A. Early determinants of vocational choice. *J. counsel. Psychol.*, 1957, *4*, 212-217.

37. Roe A. Personality structure and occupational behavior. In H. Borow (Ed.) *Man in a world at work*. Boston: Houghton Mifflin, 1964, Pp. 196-214.

38. Holland, J. L. Some explorations of a theory of vocational choice: I. One-and-two year longitudinal studies. *Psychol. Monogr.*, 1962, *76*, No. 26.

39. Holland, J. L. Explorations of a theory of vocational choice and achievement: II. A four-year prediction study. *Psychol. Rep.*, 1963, *12*, 547-594.

40. Getzels, J. W. & Jackson, P. W. Occupational choice and cognitive functioning: career aspirations of highly intelligent and highly creative adolescents. *J. abnorm. soc. Psychol.*, 1960, *61*, 119-123.

41. Brayfield, Research on vocational guidance: status and prospect. Part I.

Research in Guidance: Horizons for the Future

Buford Stefflre

The present relationship between research and practice in guidance is much like the relationship between research and practice in other areas of education. If we did, in the name of guidance, only those things which research has proven to be worth doing, we would have a good deal of free time on our hands. We act largely in the name of the three great educational motivators—instinct, inertia, and imitation! And yet—on the horizon we see the promise of better things.

Present knowledge in guidance can be divided into three categories. There is a very small category of knowledge which we know to be true as a result of sound research evidence. There is an extremely large category of

Reprinted by permission of the author and *Theory Into Practice,* II, No. 1 (February, 1963), 44-50.

Buford Stefflre, Professor of Education, Michigan State University, East Lansing.

"knowledge" which we "know" from common sense or scholastic revelation; such knowledge may be said to be part of the "conventional wisdom." Finally, there is a category of knowledge, which is growing rapidly, that indicates what we do not know! Well-designed research in guidance typically results in transferring "knowledge" from the second category to the third one. The most common conclusion reached as a consequence of carefully designed research in guidance is the verdict—"not proven."

Present State of Guidance Research

To be more specific with regard to our present situation, let us take a look at the research which deals with the value of counseling. In reviewing this research, the most defensible conclusion is that there is no solid evidence that counseling helps its recipients. An optimistic reaction to this same evidence is contained in the article "Counseling Theory" in the *Encyclopedia of Educational Research,* in which Leary and Harvey are quoted as follows: "The steady growth in prestige of . . . [psychotherapy] in the teeth of these two obstacles—its unscientific status and its inherent threats to the conscious ego—is a remarkable testimony to its basic effectiveness or to the capacity of otherwise intelligent professional workers to deceive themselves."[1] Regardless of our interpretation of the lack of proof regarding the value of counseling, the fact remains that such proof is not now existent. The difficulty of gathering evidence in this field is tremendous, inasmuch as the goals which we might evaluate are not the same for all classifications of individuals. In short, we are not always certain of what we are trying to accomplish in school counseling, but it seems clear that we are trying to achieve different ends with different students. In some cases we are trying to make a child more free in the expression of his impulses; in others we are trying to make him more controlled and more subject to the dictates of society. In some cases we are trying to get him to raise his level of aspiration; in others we are trying to get him to be more "realistic." Thus, counseling programs are now found in schools, not because of sound research evidence of their value, but rather because it is the considered opinion of specialists, teachers, students, administrators, and community members that counseling is a worthwhile educational activity.

Essentially the same conclusion is inevitable when we consider the value of systematic high-school guidance programs. The best research in this area is reported by Rothney and Roens in *Guidance of American Youth: An Experimental Study*[2] and Rothney in *Guidance Practices and Results.*[3] These studies both come to the conclusion that some value (though much less

---

[1]Third Edition. New York: Macmillan Company, 1960, p. 347.

[2]Rothney, John Watson Murray, and Roens, Bert A. *Guidance of American Youth: An Experimental Study.* Cambridge, Massachusetts: Harvard University Press, 1950.

[3]Rothney, John Watson Murray. *Guidance Practices and Results.* New York: Harper and Brothers, 1958.

than anticipated) probably accrues to the high-school student who receives counseling. While these are the most definitive attempts to illustrate and prove the value of high-school guidance programs, their findings cannot be interpreted in any clear-cut fashion. The first study separated students into experimental and control groups on the basis of matching rather than randomization. The second study does not spell out exactly what the treatment effect was that the experimental group received; that is, the reader does not know what "counseling" meant in this context. The most defensible conclusion to be drawn from these two studies is that doing *something* is generally better than doing nothing. The results of both research studies, while not at all clear-cut in favoring the counseled group, can best be explained by the so-called "Hawthorne effect," which was discovered long ago in industry and is instinctively understood by the physician who supplies his patient with a placebo in the expectation that attention will succeed where more verifiable science falters.

To illustrate further the present state of guidance research, we can point to the fact that our nomenclature is so ambiguous that we are not even certain how many counselors we have working in the United States, how many schools have guidance programs, exactly what a counselor does, or how many counselors we still need. (One study of visiting teachers found that fifty different titles were used to designate this specialist!)

There is no clear and agreed-upon job description for school counselors; they are, in fact, engaged in a variety of tasks. Some function almost as psychologists, some as quasi-administrators, some as disciplinarians, some as liaison men trafficking in college admissions, some even as heavy-handed advice-givers and soothsayers—and this list is not exhaustive. Because of this lack of agreement with regard to the counselor's role, his education neither fits his present function nor reflects precisely what the universities training him think he should do. Research has not helped us to describe the function we are talking about, the specialist who is performing the function, or the purpose for which he was hired.

Furthermore, there is a large hiatus between guidance practice and the research that has been done. Practice seems to move by instinct and inertia, while researchers talk only to each other, and sparingly at that. An example of the lag between research and practice is the present expansion of elementary-school guidance programs. All over the country, administrators are seeking and hiring elementary-school counselors. There is as yet, however, no research evidence indicating that these people will be helpful. Certainly there are those who believe fervently that if guidance is good it is good at all levels. There are also those who think that if it is difficult to cure "maladjustment" it is better to prevent it, and the way to prevent it is to work with students at the youngest possible age. Such reasoning may or may not be logical, but it is certainly not based on research. Again, then, we find the field moving on the basis of faith, hope, "expert judgment," but not on the basis of research evidence.

Some Observations on Research Needs

In view of the present state of affairs, how can research be used to aid guidance practice and, in turn, the total educational activity of the schools? First, we need, as a profession, to come to some agreement in regard to what we mean by such terms as *counselor, pupil-personnel services, guidance,* and *discipline.* Until we have done this job of thinking through and defining, it seems unlikely that we will make any significant progress in research in this field. What guidance most needs at this time is a Linnaeus!

Second, we need much research that is local and descriptive. That is, we need much study of the process of guidance rather than of its ultimate product. Such studies are best done by local school counselors and do not involve any ultimate "proof" of the value of their work, but rather describe for us what they are doing. Such local research obviously should not be done without a careful consideration of its effects on the local setting, because it may intrude on the personal values of the professional staff or the community, it may offend certain groups or alter relationships within the school, it may use time which we can ill afford for such purposes. Before beginning such research, counselors should carefully consider who should be consulted and whether the results will be worth the effort. Once such consequences are considered however, there still might be much room for research studies which tell us how a counselor spends his day, what the perception of the community is with regard to the guidance program, what teachers see as their responsibilities for guidance, and other practical "bread and butter" questions.

Third, we need to recognize that knowledge of human behavior is not confined to the quantitative sciences. Certainly there is much more to be learned about the nature of adolescence from reading Salinger's *The Catcher in the Rye* than from reading the most recent issue of the *Journal of Consulting Psychology.* Guidance persons, like many workers in education, have blinded themselves to the humanities as a way of understanding behavior. We have leaned too long and too heavily on numbers. Do we learn about old age only by reading journal articles on gerontology, or can we not also learn by studying the self-portraits of Rembrandt? Before guidance can make significant contributions to education, it must turn again to the sources which traditionally have both satisfied and aroused our curiosity about the human condition. These sources are the literary and visual arts, and while they do not replace the need for more systematic statements, they certainly should supplement our exercises in the quantitative and the minute.

Fourth, we must recognize that along with a human need to "know" we have an equally human need "not to know." Some of our very supersophisticated research designs grow out of the latter need. The insistence on complete randomization when we know that it is impossible to achieve, the use of very involved statistical manipulations for data which do not merit such careful treatment, the obsession with assumptions underlying statistics when their violation sometimes does not really alter the conclusions—all are evidences of our need not to know. Such a need, perhaps stemming from the guilt of some unresolved academic voyeurism, needs to be brought out into the open and clarified if we are going to make progress in research in guidance. Absolute, ultimate answers—free from the pedant's attack—will not soon be found in guidance research.

Fifth, we must be more concerned about illuminating ends and less concerned about examining means. Certainly the kind of clarification offered by Barry and Wolf in *Modern Issues in Guidance-Personnel Work*,[4] which helps us sort out the purposes of guidance programs, is much needed. We cannot expect any dramatic breakthrough in guidance, or for that matter in education, until we have clearly thought through what it is we are trying to do. We could make a plea, then, for less correlation and more conceptualization.

Sixth, in some cases we ought to delay research and substitute demonstration projects. In elementary-school guidance, for example, it seems that there is no general agreement as to what the program should involve. Since we know very little about the field, perhaps our "research" should deal with the evolving of theory rather than its testing. Demonstration or pilot projects would permit us to try out various approaches to this new field. One school, for example, might hire an elementary-school counselor who behaves and is trained much like a secondary-school counselor. Another could have a psychologist who might serve as a resource person on child growth and development. A third might hire a social worker to carry on therapy with children. There are many other possibilities within this field. Trying out several methods in schools is one way to begin to decide what is the best use of the elementary-school counselor and to determine what problems evolve from various approaches. Such research, which would be essentially theory-building, is much needed in guidance.

Horizons for the Future

Now let us look at some promising research which offers a brighter horizon for the future. Major longitudinal studies, such as Flanagan's Project Talent and Super's Career Pattern Study give us much hope. These studies promise no immediate answers to our questions, but they will provide us with a base of data which will permit sounder research and study. They may well do for our understanding of guidance what the Terman studies did for our understanding of the gifted student.

A second kind of study which has much promise is exemplified by Coleman's *The Adolescent Society*,[5] which examines the values and atti-

---

[4]Barry, Ruth, and Wolf, Beverly. *Modern Issues in Guidance-Personnel Work.* New York: Bureau of Publications, Teachers College, Columbia University, 1957.
[5]Coleman, James S. *The Adolescent Society: The Social Life of the Teenager and Its Impact on Education.* Glencoe, Illinois: Free Press, 1961.

tudes of schools and their impact on the learning and behavior of youth. Coleman has pointed to the importance of considering not only the individual but also the context within which the individual learns. Such studies may constitute a major breakthrough in understanding the behavior of adolescents and the levers instrumental in changing it.

A third kind of research is exemplified by Jahoda's *Current Concepts of Positive Mental Health,*[6] in which she does a splendid job of classifying the definitions of mental health and helping us see that before we can work for mental health we need to agree on what it is. This kind of taxonomic conceptualization is badly needed in the whole field of guidance.

Still another kind of research which leads to optimism is that done by Bandura and Walters, in which they investigate the backgrounds of aggressive adolescents—*Adolescent Aggression: A Study of the Influence of Child-Training Practices and Family Interrelationships.*[7] Few studies have exploded so many stereotypes so completely. This is an excellent example of research which transfers knowledge from our original second category—things that we know we know simply because they are part of the conventional wisdom—to our third category—things that we know we do not know. This kind of iconoclastic, stereotype-breaking research is badly needed.

Finally, the studies of H. H. Anderson of Michigan State University, in which he compares the values of children in such countries as Russia, Germany, Mexico, and the United States, provide a valuable perspective to workers in guidance as well as to others in education. Anderson's research is the kind that will pull us out of our provincialism and permit us to see that the world is larger than one school system or one country.

Conclusion

These five kinds of research seem to me to be the sort that will lead guidance out of its present state into a more promising future. They have in common a strong belief that counting is not a substitute for thinking! Too much guidance research has been concerned with the manipulation of figures; too little of it, with the manipulation of ideas. The horizons for the future depend on the clarification of concepts more than they depend on the calculation of figures.

In summary, then, the present state of guidance research is not reassuring. We are not able to demonstrate the value of what we are doing, nor are we even able to agree on who is doing it nor what should be done. As a result, we make radical moves, for example, in increasing the number of elementary-school counselors, before we have any clear understanding of why we are doing what we are doing. We need clarification of concepts, we

[6]Jahoda, Marie. *Current Concepts of Positive Mental Health.* New York: Basic Books, Inc., 1958.

[7]Bandura, Albert, and Walters, Richard H. *Adolescent Aggression: A Study of Child-Training Practices and Family Interrelationships.* New York: Ronald Press, 1959.

need a return to the importance of the humanities, we need local descriptive studies, we need to understand *why* we act, as well as *how* we act, and most of all, we need to know when we do not know. We must unmask easy answers and reveal that they are often but fraudulent substitutes for hard questions.

Ethical Standards: American Personnel and Guidance Association

Preamble

The American Personnel and Guidance Association is an educational, scientific, and professional organization dedicated to service to society. This service is committed to profound faith in the worth, dignity, and great potentiality of the individual human being.

The marks of a profession, and therefore of a professional organization, can be stated as follows:

1. Possession of a body of specialized knowledge, skills, and attitudes known and practiced by its members.

Reprinted by permission of *Personnel and Guidance Journal*. Published by the American Personnel and Guidance Association, 1605 New Hampshire Avenue, N.W. Washington, D. C.

2. This body of specialized knowledge, skills, and attitudes is derived through scientific inquiry and scholarly learning.

3. This body of specialized knowledge, skills, and attitudes is acquired through professional preparation, preferably on the graduate level, in a college or university as well as through continuous in-service training and personal growth after completion of formal education.

4. This body of specialized knowledge, skills, and attitudes, is constantly tested and extended through research and scholarly inquiry.

5. A profession has a literature of its own, even though it may, and indeed must, draw portions of its content from other areas of knowledge.

6. A profession exalts service to the individual and society above personal gain. It possesses a philosophy and a code of ethics.

7. A profession through the voluntary association of its members constantly examines and improves the quality of its professional preparation and services to the individual and society.

8. Membership in the professional organization and the practice of the profession must be limited to persons meeting stated standards of preparation and competencies.

9. The profession affords a life career and permanent membership as long as services meet professional standards.

10. The public recognizes, has confidence in, and is willing to compensate the members of the profession for their services.

The Association recognizes that the vocational roles and settings of its members are identified with a wide variety of academic disciplines and levels of academic preparation. This diversity reflects the pervasiveness of the Association's interest and influence. It also poses challenging complexities in efforts to conceptualize:

a. the characteristics of members;
b. desired or requisite preparation or practice; and
c. supporting social, legal and/or ethical controls.

The specification of ethical standards enables the Association to clarify to members, future members, and to those served by members the nature of ethical responsibilties held in common by its members.

The introduction of such standards will inevitably stimulate greater concern by members for practice and preparation for practice. It will also stimulate a general growth and identification with and appreciation for both the common and diverse characteristics of the definable roles within the world of work of Association members.

There are six major areas of professional activity which encompass the work of members of APGA. For each of these areas certain general principles are listed below to serve as guide lines for ethical practice. These are preceded by a general section which includes certain principles germane to the six areas and common to the entire work of the Association members.

Section A

General

1. The member exerts what influence he can to foster the development and improvement of the profession and continues his professional growth throughout his career.

2. The member has a responsibility to the institution within which he serves. His acceptance of employment by the institution implies that he is in substantial agreement with the general policies and principles of the institution. Therefore, his professional activities are also in accord with the objectives of the institution. Within the member's own work setting, if, despite his efforts, he cannot reach agreement as to acceptable ethical standards of conduct with his superiors, he should end his affiliation with them.

3. The member must expect ethical behavior among his professional associates in APGA at all times. He is obligated, in situations where he possesses information raising serious doubt as to the ethical behavior of other members, to attempt to rectify such conditions.

4. The member is obliged to concern himself with the degree to which the personnel functions of non-members with whose work he is acquainted represent competent and ethical performance. Where his information raises serious doubt as to the ethical behavior of such persons, it is his responsibility to attempt to rectify such conditions.

5. The member must not seek self-enhancement through expressing evaluations or comparisons damaging to other ethical professional workers.

6. The member should not claim or imply professional qualifications exceeding those possessed and is responsible for correcting any misrepresentations of his qualifications by others.

7. The member providing services for personal remuneration shall, in establishing fees for such services, take careful account of the charges made for comparable services by other professional persons.

8. The member who provides information to the public or to his subordinates, peers, or superiors has a clear responsibility to see that both the content and the manner of presentation are accurate and appropriate to the situation.

9. The member has an obligation to ensure that evaluative information about such persons as clients, students, and applicants shall be shared only with those persons who will use such information for professional purposes.

10. The member shall offer professional services only through the context of a professional relationship. Thus testing, counseling, and other services are not to be provided through the mail by means of newspaper or magazine articles, radio or television programs, or public performances.

Section B

Counseling

This section refers to practices involving a counseling relationship with a counselee or client and is not intended to be applicable to practices involving administrative relationships with the persons being helped. A counseling relationship denotes that the person seeking help retain full freedom of choice and decision and that the helping person has no authority or responsibility to approve or disapprove of the choices or decisions of the counselee or client. "Counselee" or "client" is used here to indicate the person (or persons) for whom the member has assumed a professional responsibility. Typically the counselee or client is the individual with whom the member has direct and primary contact. However, at times, "client" may include another person(s) when the other person(s) exercise significant control and direction over the individual being helped in connection with the decisions and plans being considered in counseling.

1. The member's *primary* obligation is to respect the integrity and promote the welfare of the counselee or client with whom he is working.

2. The counseling relationship and information resulting therefrom must be kept confidential consistent with the obligations of the member as a professional person.

3. Records of the counseling relationship including interview notes, test data, correspondence, tape recordings, and other documents are to be considered professional information for use in counseling, research, and teaching of counselors but always with full protection of the identity of the client and with precaution so that no harm will come to him.

4. The counselee or client should be informed of the conditions under which he may receive counseling assistance at or before the time he enters the counseling relationship. This is particularly true in the event that there exist conditions of which the counselee or client would not likely be aware.

5. The member reserves the right to consult with any other professionally competent person about his counselee client. In choosing his professional consultant the member must avoid placing the consultant in a conflict of interest situation, *i.e.,* the consultant must be free of any other obligatory relation to the member's client that would preclude the consultant being a proper party to the member's efforts to help the counselee or client.

6. The member shall decline to initiate or shall terminate a counseling relationship when he cannot be of professional assistance to the counselee or client either because of lack of competence or personal limitation. In such instances the member shall refer his counselee or client to an appropriate specialist. In the event the counselee or client declines the suggested referral, the member is not obligated to continue the counseling relationship.

7. When the member learns from counseling relationships of conditions which are likely to harm others over whom his institution or agency has responsibility, he is expected to report *the condition* to the appropriate responsible authority, but in such a manner as not to reveal the identity of his counselee or client.

8. In the event that the counselee or client's condition is such as to require others to assume responsibility for him, or when there is clear and imminent danger to the counselee or client or to others, the member is expected to report this fact to an appropriate responsible authority, and/or take such other emergency measures as the situation demands.

9. Should the member be engaged in a work setting which calls for any variation from the above statements, the member is obliged to ascertain that such variations are justifiable under the conditions and that such variations are clearly specified and made known to all concerned with such counseling services.

Section C

Testing

1. The primary purpose of psychological testing is to provide objective and comparative measures for use in self-evaluation or evaluation by others of general or specific attributes.

2. Generally, test results constitute only one of a variety of pertinent data for personnel and guidance decisions. It is the member's responsibility to provide adequate orientation or information to the examinee(s) so that the results of testing may be placed in proper perspective with other relevant factors.

3. When making any statements to the public about tests and testing care must be taken to give accurate information and to avoid any false claims or misconceptions.

4. Different tests demand different levels of competence for administration, scoring, and interpretation. It is therefore the responsibility of the member to recognize the limits of his competence and to perform only those functions which fall within his preparation and competence.

5. In selecting tests for use in a given situation or with a particular client the member must consider not only general but also specific validity, reliability, and appropriateness of the test(s).

6. Tests should be administered under the same conditions which were established in their standardization. Except for research purposes explicitly stated, any departures from these conditions, as well as unusual behavior or irregularities during the testing session which may affect the interpretation of the test results, must be fully noted and reported. In this connection, unsupervised test-taking or the use of tests through the mails are of questionable value.

7. The value of psychological tests depends in part on the novelty to persons taking them. Any prior information, coaching, or reproduction of test materials tends to invalidate test results. Therefore, test security is one of the professional obligations of the member.

8. The member has the responsibility to inform the examinee(s) as to the purpose of testing. The criteria of examinee's welfare and/or explicit prior understanding with him should determine who the recipients of the test results may be.

9. The member should guard against the appropriation, reproduction, or modifications of published tests or parts thereof without express permission and adequate recognition of the original author or publisher.

Regarding the preparation, publication, and distribution of tests reference should be made to:

"Tests and Diagnostic Techniques,"—Report of the Joint Committee of the American Psychological Association, American Educational Research Association, and National Council of Measurements used in Education. Supplement to *Psychological Bulletin*, 1954, 2, 1-38.

Section D

Research and Publication

1. In the performance of any research on human subjects, the member must avoid causing any injurious effects or after-effects of the experiment upon his subjects.

2. The member may withhold information or provide misinformation to subjects only when it is essential to the investigation and where he assumes responsibility for corrective action following the investigation.

3. In reporting research results, explicit mention must be made of all variables and conditions known to the investigator which might affect interpretation of the data.

4. The member is responsible for conducting and reporting his investigations so as to minimize the possibility that his findings will be misleading.

5. The member has an obligation to make available original research data to qualified others who may wish to replicate or verify the study.

6. In reporting research results or in making original data available, due care must be taken to disguise the identity of the subjects, in the absence of specific permission from such subjects to do otherwise.

7. In conducting and reporting research, the member should be familiar with, and give recognition to, previous work on the topic.

8. The members has the obligation to give due credit to those who have contributed significantly to his research, in accordance with their contributions.

9. The member has the obligation to honor commitments made to subjects of research in return for their cooperation.

10. The member is expected to communicate to other members the results of any research he judges to be of professional or scientific value.

Section E

Consulting and Private Practice

Consulting refers to a voluntary relationship between a professional helper and help-needing social unit (industry, business, school, college, etc.) in which the consultant is attempting to give help to the client in the solving of some current or potential problem.*

1. The member acting as a consultant must have a high degree of self-awareness of his own values and needs in entering a helping relationship which involves change in a social unit.

2. There should be understanding and agreement between consultant and client as to directions or goals of the attempted change.

3. The consultant must be reasonably certain that he or his organization have the necessary skills and resources for giving the kind of help which is needed now or that may develop later.

4. The consulting relationship must be one in which client adaptability and growth toward self-direction are encouraged and cultivated. The consultant must consistently maintain his role as a consultant and not become a decision maker for the client.

5. The consultant in announcing his availability for service as a consultant follows professional rather than commercial standards in describing his services with accuracy, dignity, and caution.

6. For private practice in testing, counseling, or consulting the ethical principles stated in all previous sections of this document are pertinent. In addition, any individual, agency, or institution offering educational and vocational counseling to the public should meet the standards of the American Board on Professional Standards in Vocational Counseling, Inc.

Section F

Personnel Administration

1. The member is responsible for establishing working agreements with supervisors and with subordinates especially regarding counseling or clinical relationships, confidentiality, distinction between public and private material, and a mutual respect for the positions of parties involved in such issues.

2. Such working agreements may vary from one institutional setting to another. What should be the case in each instance, however, is that agreements have been specified, made known to those concerned, and when-

---

*This definition is adapted from "Dimensions of the Consultant's Job" by Ronald Lippitt, *The Journal of Social Issues,* Vol. XV, No. 2, 1959.

ever possible the agreements reflect institutional policy rather than personal judgment.

3. The member's reponsibility to his superiors requires that he keep them aware of conditions affecting the institution, particularly those which may be potentially disrupting or damaging to the institution.

4. The member has a responsibility to select competent persons for assigned responsibilities and to see that his personnel are used maximally for the skills and experience they possess.

5. The member has responsibility for constantly stimulating his staff for their and his own continued growth and improvement. He must see that staff members are adequately supervised as to the quality of their functioning and for purposes of professional development.

6. The member is responsible for seeing that his staff is informed of policies, goals, and programs toward which the department's operations are oriented.

Section G

Preparation for Personnel Work

1. The member in charge of training sets up a strong program of academic study and supervised practice in order to prepare the trainees for their future responsibilities.

2. The training program should aim to develop in the trainee not only skills and knowledge, but also self-understanding.

3. The member should be aware of any manifestations of personal limitations in a student trainee which may influence the latter's provision of competent services and has an obligation to offer assistance to the trainee in securing professional remedial help.

4. The training program should include preparation in research and stimulation for the future personnel worker to do research and add to the knowledge in his field.

5. The training program should make the trainee aware of the ethical responsibilities and standards of the profession he is entering.

6. The program of preparation should aim at inculcating among the trainees, who will later become the practitioners of our profession, the ideal of service to individual and society above personal gain.

Confidence and Confidentiality

John L. Phillips, Jr.

Adam Margoshes

In a recent article, Clark (1965) raises an important question of ethics not covered by the formal professional statements of psychology, counseling and education: how should a school counselor act when confronted with a conflict of interests between the administrative policy of the school and the confidentiality of information given by his client? The experts cited by Clark from the Ethical Standards of the American Personnel and Guidance Association (1961) are pertinent to the issue at hand, but his conclusions appear not to flow inexorably from them.

The following excerpts are taken directly from the *Ethical Standards of the American Personnel and Guidance Association* (APGA, 1961). Italics

Reprinted by permission of Professor Phillips and *The School Counselor*, Vol. 13, No. 4 (May, 1966), 235-238.

John L. Phillips, Jr. is Professor of Psychology, Boise College, Boise, Idaho and the late Adam Margoshes was Assistant Professor of Psychology, Shippensburg State College, Shippensburg, Pennsylvania.

have been left as in the original, because we believe that the meaning of the writers of the *Standards* comes through more clearly when this is done than it does when italics are changed to fit a particular argument. The following paragraphs from Section B—Counseling—seem to bear on the question:[1]

1. The member's *primary* obligation is to respect the integrity and promote the welfare of the counselee or client with whom he is working.
2. The counseling relationship and information resulting therefrom must be kept confidential consistent with the obligations of the member as a professional person.
3. Records of the counseling relationship including interview notes, test data, correspondence, tape recordings, and other documents are to be considered professional information for use in counseling, research, and teaching of counselors, but always with full protection of the identity of the client and with precaution so that no harm will come to him.
4. The counselee or client should be informed of the conditions under which he may receive counseling assistance at or before the time he enters the counseling relationship. This is particularly true in the event that there exists conditions of which the counselee or client would not likely be aware.
5. The member reserves the right to consult with any other professionally competent person about his counselee client. In choosing his professional consultant the member must avoid placing the consultant in a conflict of interest situation, *i.e.*, the consultant must be free of any other obligatory relation to the member's client that would preclude the consultant being a proper party to the member's efforts to help the counselee or client.
7. When the member learns from counseling relationships of conditions which are likely to harm others over whom his institution or agency has responsibility, he is expected to report *the condition* to the appropriate responsible authority, but in such a manner as not to reveal the identity of his counselee or client.
8. In the event that the counselee or client's condition is such as to require others to assume responsibility for him, or when there is clear and imminent danger to the counselee or client or to others, the member is expected to report this fact to an appropriate responsible authority, and/or take such other emergency measures as the situation demands.

---

[1]Like Clark, we have concentrated on the APGA *Standards* because it seems to be the code most relevant to the concerns of school counselors; but the *Ethical Standards of Psychologists* (American Psychological Association, 1962) and the *Code of Ethics of the Education Profession* (National Education Association, 1963) are consonant, on essential points, with this one.

The reader will note that, with the single exception of the number eight, all of these paragraphs are essentially elaborations and specifications of the first one: *the counselor's primary responsibility is to the client.* Paragraph eight merely recognizes the obvious fact that there may be emergencies which the counselor is not equipped to handle. It does not seem to us at all mandatory to infer from these quotations, as Clark does, that "when a pupil is a minor with the attendant legal, moral, and other responsibilities of the parent and school, such information must be shared with them in some form or manner, and therefore has only limited confidentiality" (Clark, 1965)[2]. Such information *may* be shared with them, certainly; but only if, in the judgment of the counselor, such a sharing will promote the welfare of the client.

Clark offers as an alternative to "predetermined solutions based on rules of ethics" (Clark, 1965), a formula whereby the counselor's professional authority is determined by the school. The amount of confidentiality is in turn determined by the degree of authority thus granted. This policy leads to the conclusion that "if a rare instance should occur when the interests of the school and the pupils are in an irreconcilable conflict and the counselor must choose between them, the interests of the school should usually be given precedence" (Clark, 1965).

Emphatically not! It is precisely at this point of conflict that the APGA *Standards'* provisions for client welfare become important. If the client's interest is to be protected only until some other interest conflicts with it, he would certainly be wise not to rely upon that protection, and if he cannot rely upon it, the effectiveness of any counseling process can be expected to deteriorate accordingly. True, Clark emphasizes that "the counselor is responsible for communicating these conditions or limits on the confidentiality of information to pupils before the establishment of a counseling relationship." But this procedure, while perhaps adequate to the safeguarding of confidentiality in counseling relationships with mature adults, is not enough when dealing with adolescents and younger children. Because they cannot be relied upon to defend their own interests, that defense devolves upon the counselor: the minor requires not less, but *more* protection than the adult— in counseling confidentiality as in other areas.

We are dealing here with a variant of the venerable "individual vs. the state" dilemma, and it is within our democratic tradition to resolve it by

---

[2]Actually, far the strongest argument in favor of Clark's contention that the institution should set ethical standards is not even mentioned in his article. Paragraph nine of the section on counseling states that "should the member be engaged in a work setting which calls for any variation from the above statements, the member is obligated to ascertain that such variations are justifiable under the conditions and that such variations are clearly specified and made known to all concerned with such counseling services." Our contention is that "variations" that may be expected to result in harm to a client are justifiable only in situations described in Paragraph eight, cited above.

charging one person with the responsibility of promoting the individual's welfare; there are plenty of others responsible for protecting society. Counseling in the past 20 years has placed more and more emphasis on a mutual examination of the client's basic motivational system (Wrenn, 1952). Such an examination requires a high level of trust on the part of the client, and it seems fairly obvious that this trust will not be placed in a counselor who has the reputation of relaying confidential information to anyone who wants it badly enough to apply pressure to get it. *Confidence,* if we may coin an aphorism, *depends on confidentiality.*

After presenting his "delegated authority" alternative to full professional responsibility, Clark goes on to say that arrangements relative to this authority "should be arrived at by mutual consent of the administrator and the counselor before the counselor is involved in counseling interviews" (Clark, 1965). We agree. But the discussion with the administrator should be held *before the counselor accepts employment, a*nd his status as a professional person should be a condition of that employment.

The counselor who neglects to establish this condition faces the prospect of having "the nature and confidentiality of the counselor's communications with pupils in counseling interviews, the form in which pertinent information from such interviews is to be transmitted, the method of transmission, and appropriate receivers of such information" defined clearly and explicitly by the delegating authority. This definition has an advantageous effect, according to Clark, for it "places the responsibility for decisions in an individual case upon the professional judgment of the counselor and not upon predetermined solutions based on rules of ethics" (Clark, 1965). Surely Clark is not suggesting that rules of ethics be abandoned as guides to conduct. What he seems to be saying is that instructions from the delegating authority make the process of decision-making clearer for the counselor, who now merely consults his store of professional knowledge to find the most efficacious method of implementing the authority's policy. The counselor is thus relieved of the burden of questioning this policy where it might possibly conflict with his client's interests. But by narrowing his concern from the ethical to the purely technical (which Clark apparently perceives as the most important aspect of professionalism) the counselor is *abdicating* responsibility rather than assuming it.

Our position is that full professional status, even though it requires adherence to an established code of ethics, demands the highest order of competence and full responsibility for making decisions in the counseling process. It is the counselor, and no one else, who must decide what course of action will best promote the welfare of the client. This position seems to express the consensus of the profession, since, according to Clark's data, over 90 per cent of the counselors he polled disagreed "with the position that a counselor should furnish any information obtained in a counseling position to parents or the principal upon legitimate request" (Clark, 1965).

The giving or withholding of such information is certainly a heavy responsibility, and we believe it should be entrusted only to a truly *professional* person.

REFERENCES

American Personnel and Guidance Association, Commiteee on Ethics. Code of Ethics. Personnel Guid., J., 1961, *40,* 206-209.

American Psychological Association. Ethical standards of psychologists. *American Psychol.* 1963, *18,* 56-60.

Clark, Charles M. Confidentiality and the school counselor. *Personnel Guid. J.,* 1965, *43,* 482-484.

National Education Association. *Code of ethics of the education profession.*

The Two-Year Graduate Program in Counselor Education: A Re-examination

F. C. Noble

While the formal adoption of the *Standards for Counselor Education in the Preparation of Secondary School Counselors by* ACES at the 1964 Convention may rightly be viewed as an important step in the upgrading and professionalization of the school counselor, one aspect of the Standards continues to be troublesome. The demand for a second graduate year of training is laudable—within the present context of recruitment and certification—but it can be viewed as a somewhat makeshift expediency, when what is needed is a significant breaking away from traditional patterns. The second graduate year is needed only because state certification laws make it necessary for a prospective counselor to first prepare for another profession—teaching—before he can enter into preparation for his chosen field.

Reprinted by permission of the author and *Counselor Education and Supervision*, IV, No. 3 (Spring, 1965), 160-162.

Frank C. Noble, Associate Professor of Psychology, George Peabody College for Teachers, Nashville, Tennessee.

An examination of the suggested program of studies in the new Standards makes it obvious that *the bulk of the material to be covered is already a part of most well-established master's degree programs in counselor education. The significant additions are in more emphasis on the "foundations and dynamics of human behavior and the individual in his culture"— the social and behavioral sciences—and in an extension of the supervised practice and internship experiences. It seems apparent that a major portion of the additional graduate year is to be used in an attempt to provide the prospective counselor with a grounding in psychology, sociology, and other disciplines which he presumably either failed to get as an undergraduate or has forgotten.* For the typical counselor candidate the former is most often the case; since he has been forced to prepare to teach, and since psychology and sociology are infrequently taught in secondary schools, he has had very little opportunity to study in these two areas which are most basic to counseling as a profession.

In any case, the new look in counselor education would emphasize the social and behavioral sciences during the two years of graduate study. *Unfortunately, if the student has not had undergraduate preparation in these areas, he cannot be expected to enter them at the graduate level. Consequently, credit-counting being what it is (often absurd), he will need special permission to count undergraduate courses toward a graduate degree or (and this is more likely) special "graduate courses" for counselors will be offered.* Too often these will be given by counselor educators who are themselves not thoroughly versed in the disciplines under consideration. Will the result be in accord with the high hopes of the new Standards?

This is, of course, all supposition—and more than a little cynical, but what is the alternative? If what is sought is a firm foundation in these disciplines which undergird the counseling profession, it would seem more logical to provide this training during the undergraduate years. The proposal is simple: why not make the "two-year program" into a three-year program beginning in the junior undergraduate year?

If the iron hand of teacher certification could be loosened, it would be possible to admit students to counselor education programs just as they are currently admitted to advanced standing in the various teacher-education curricula. Based on two previous years of contact and an opportunity for relatively extensive testing and observation, it should be possible to base admission here on factors other than purely academic aptitude.

Students admitted to the counselor education program at this point should be committed to continuing through three additional years, and the faculty evaluation should be done with this in mind. That is to say, requirements for admission to the counselor education program should probably be somewhat higher than those for admission to teacher-education curricula since the counseling program requires committment to graduate work.

Students who successfully pass the screening would be assigned a counselor educator as an adviser and take a combined major in the social and behavioral sciences. In addition, some of the course work in counseling, ordinarily reserved for the graduate year, would be completed. Each school would develop its own program, but statistics, appraisal of the individual, principles of guidance, and the information service might well be taken as undergraduate courses. In the senior year the student-counselor would engage in an extended clerkship experience in a public school working under the supervision of an experienced counselor. The clerkship would include observation of counseling and classroom teaching and some actual practice in guidance activities. The student should probably have experience in giving and scoring group tests and compiling the data for guidance and administrative purposes. He should also be given special assistance in understanding the school as a social institution becoming involved, at least as an observer, in board meetings, PTA meetings and faculty committees. The scope of the clerkship experience would depend on the amount of time allotted and the particular pattern of course work that has been undertaken, but should be viewed as a pre-professional orientation. Students at this level would not be allowed to enter into formal counseling relationships.

With this background, both in theoretical foundations in the social and behavioral sciences and the practical school experience, the student would be prepared to enter into actual counseling practicum relatively early in the graduate year. A closely supervised practicum might be offered during the first semester with a field work experience in a public school as a part of the second half of the year. The particular pattern would, of course, be a matter left to the discretion of the institution, but with three years of full-time study, there should be sufficient time to plan a truly meaningful program.

It is not argued here that this would produce a "finished" counselor, since no program can accomplish this, but it would provide, in the author's estimation, a more adequate beginning than the two years of graduate study proposed by the Standards. If we can shake loose from the rigidity of present counselor certification requirements, perhaps both approaches could be employed. Which approach is better would then become an empirical question awaiting only the establishment of adequate criteria for the evaluation of effectiveness.

Counselors Need Teaching Experience

George R. Hudson

Were it not for the existing shortage of qualified teachers and counselors, there would be little need to discuss the desirability of teaching experience for one who wants to become a guidance counselor. Anyone who entered the field of teaching prior to World War II well recalls the premium put upon experience. In order to get a desirable job, the beginner frequently had to serve an "apprenticeship" in a position that offered very little in terms of location or salary. Contrast that picture with the current situation when a city system will send a representative three thousand miles across the country to tell a university placement officer that he will hire every senior who has majored in education.

Reprinted by permission of the author and *Counselor Education and Supervision*, Vol. 00 (Spring, 1961), 24-27.

George R. Hudson, Associate Professor of Education, The Pennsylvania State University, University Park.

In the face of such a shortage of teachers and counselors perhaps it is understandable why, in some instances, persons with no teaching experience have been employed as counselors; but it may be well to review some of the reasons for making teaching experience a prerequisite for counselors and to consider how this prerequisite can be achieved without reducing the supply of badly-needed counselors.

To become professionally competent as a school guidance counselor at least one full year of graduate work is necessary, even though the certification requirements in some states do not come up to this standard. It is extremely doubtful whether graduate work in any phase of education should be undertaken without prior teaching experience.

A teacher's first year or two, or in some cases more, may well be considered a period of exploration, a time of assessing and being assessed by the world of education. Some teachers know after a year in the classroom that for them there must be an easier way to earn a living. Better to discover this before spending an extra year in preparation! A few sometimes discover that they would rather teach a different age group and may plan to go, for example, from high school to college positions. Other teachers learn through experience what aspects of teaching and related duties appeal to them most. It may be the actual presentation of subject matter to children with a resulting desire to learn more about the subject itself. It may be that working with exceptional children offers the real challenge. It may be administration; and it may be guidance. Regardless of the teacher's choice, it will be a better one (and the graduate work more meaningful) if it is based upon actual association with children and with co-workers in a school situation and not upon what one *thinks* he will prefer before he has ever taught.

It is not uncommon to hear teachers say that they learned more during their first year of teaching than they did in all four years of undergraduate work, at least figuratively speaking. Indeed few would question the statement that two years' experience is twice as valuable as one year. During his first year the teacher may well be so busy trying to learn and play the many roles of teacher that he is unable to look objectively at himself in those roles. It is a little bit like learning to play bridge. The beginner is so involved in remembering the rules that he does not have time to enjoy the game. Once the "rules" of teaching have been learned, a teacher will then feel more free to try his wings. He will find it easier to look beyond subject matter and to see the students. At that point in his career he will start to become a teacher in the broadest, truest sense of the word. This, of course, is the very basis for principals' preferring to hire experienced teachers. Certain skills and techniques must be developed and improved in the classroom; they cannot be mastered from text books alone, nor even from practice teaching.

If teaching experience makes one a better teacher, so does it make one a better counselor; for the counselor and the teacher are both educators. They are both involved in helping students learn. Since most of his duties involve working directly with students and with teachers, the counselor who has been a successful teacher will have a greater understanding of students and a greater appreciation of the classroom teacher's point of view than the counselor who has not taught.

As a teacher he will have an opportunity to note in a group setting the many ways in which individuals differ—physical size, intelligence, abilities, interests, ambitions, morals, social and economic background, parental aspiration—the list could go on indefinitely. He will become aware of their common needs as well, needs that may be physical, personal, social or intellectual in nature. He will discover how students learn (and why they sometimes do not), how they work and play together, how they feel about each other, what their problems are, individually and collectively, and how they adjust to those problems.

Since a counselor must work closely with classroom teachers, it is essential he be accepted by them. A counselor without teaching experience is likely to be looked upon with suspicion, as a person who does not know what teaching entails and who thus cannot appreciate the complexities of a teacher's job. In some measure these suspicions are justifiable.

The counselor who has been a teacher knows what it is to be responsible for a homeroom and to keep a register, to write lesson plans and grade papers by the hundred, to serve as club sponsor, to handle a crowded study hall, to keep an eye on "traffic" in the halls between classes—and also to teach one or more subjects for five, six or seven periods a day. Such a counselor will know the practical difficulty of applying in a large classroom a principle everyone accepts in theory, the principle of instruction based upon the needs of each individual class member. He will appreciate the difference between dealing, let us say, with a behavior problem in the privacy of the counselor's office as opposed to dealing with it in the classroom in the presence of thirty or more fascinated student spectators. He will know how frustrating it can be as a teacher to have a student called out of class unexpectedly on the day of an especially important lesson (and he can resolve to avoid making that mistake when he becomes a counselor). He will learn to deal with parents who demand too much of their children or who do not demand anything, including school attendance. (As a counselor he will get even more experience of this kind!) In short, by becoming intimately aware of the teacher's job he will be in a much better position to know how counselors and teachers can complement each other in their work with students.

Teaching experience will help one decide whether or not to become a counselor and will serve as the foundation upon which formal counselor preparation is based. Courses in principles and practices of guidance, measurement, testing, occupational information, counseling; courses in the psychology of adolescence, of adjustment, of learning—these courses will enable one to envision their future application in the light of his own past experience. As guidance theories and techniques are learned they can be evaluated, rejected, modified or accepted on the basis of what has been discovered in dealings with students, parents and co-workers. These courses, apparently theoretical to the inexperienced person, become most practical to the experienced teacher.

There is supporting evidence for these statements. In the spring of 1955 in a series of meetings sponsored by The Pennsylvania State University and the Pennsylvania Cooperative Program in Educational Administration, over two hundred principals, counselors, teachers, parents and students agreed that teaching experience was essential for counselors. In the spring of 1956, sixty-six counselors throughout Pennsylvania were asked what experiences, other than course work, helped them in their professional training. Teaching experience led the list with ninety-seven per cent of the counselors attesting to its value for them personally.

In order to make teaching experience a prerequisite for counseling without further reducing the supply of counselors, three things must be done. Prospective counselors must be made aware that there are definite advantages, in terms of long range professional growth and development, in getting teaching experience prior to becoming counselors. In addition counselor educators must accept responsibility for seeing that their students do not complete their professional preparation (certification) before getting teaching experience, preferably a minimum of two years. This does not mean that students should not begin their graduate work for two years; indeed, they should be encouraged to work toward their degrees summers while they are accumulating experience. And, finally, principals should refuse to hire counselors with no teaching experience. By looking ahead a few years, school administrators can estimate with a high degree of accuracy what their counselor needs will be in the future. The wise principal is the one who looks over his staff, decides which teachers might make good counselors, and then encourages those people to begin graduate work in guidance, either in a sabbatical year or in a series of summer sessions. (The National Education Defense Act of 1958 provides for financial assistance for persons training to be counselors.) Such action on the part of the principal will assure his school of an adequate supply of counselors who have demonstrated their ability to work successfully with parents, fellow teachers, and with that community's greatest single resource—its youth.

REFERENCES

Follow-up of Graduates of the Counselor Education Program. Unpublished report, Department of Education, The Pennsylvania State University, 1956.

Guidance. Summary of conferences sponsored by the Department of Education, The Pennsylvania State University, 1955 (Mimeo).

Kremen, Benjamin K., *A National Study of Counselor Certification.* Division of Higher Education, Fresno State College, Fresno, California. (Undated) (Mimeo)

Stewart, Lawrence (Chairman). Professional Training, Licensing and Certification, *Personnel and Guidance Journal,* 1958, 37, 162-166.

U. S. Office of Education (Brewster) *Guidance Workers Certification Requirements,* 1960.

A Rationale Against Teaching Experience for School Counselors

Frank A. Nugent

The Problem

A question which has generated a great deal of heat during national surveys by counselors and counselor educators on school counselor role and function is the need for mandatory teaching experience for prospective counselors. The author's feeling is that some of the controversy surrounding this point would be cleared up if the importance of preserving a counseling relationship were considered foremost in the delineation of counselor function, role and education. In this paper, a rationale will be presented against legislating teaching experience for counselors predicated upon the nature of the counseling relationship.

Reprinted by permission of the author and *The School Counselor*, XIII, No. 4 (May, 1966), 213-215.

Frank A. Nugent, Professor of Psychology, Director, Counseling Center, Western Washington State College, Bellingham, Washington.

Experts' Agreement on Counseling Relationship

The counseling relationship could be a clarifying factor in this question of teaching before counseling because irrespective of setting, counseling experts concur that the counseling relationship has some essential components to it. Learning and neobehaviorist theorists as well as cognitive and psychoanalytic groups perceive an optimal counseling relationship as being basically non-punitive, non-authoritative and non-threatening *[2, 4, 5,].*

Evaluation of Arguments for Compulsory Teaching

Most proponents of prescribed teaching experience start with the assumption that what makes a good teaching relationship automatically makes for an effective counseling relationship. Yet, it is common knowledge that the good teacher must be an effective disciplinarian, a fair evaluator and a skilled leader in teaching large groups of very diversified students his subject matter. This description is the antithesis of the non-authoritative, non-evaluative role of the counselor whose strength lies in developing either a working relationship with individuals or relationships with small groups with similar problems. Thus, teaching experience, in some cases, might hamper the development of counseling skills rather than promote them. The writer has noted that some students in interview courses and counseling practice who have taught for a number of years find it difficult to switch from an authoritative to a non-authoritative role even when they are aware of need for change of attitudes and techniques. This difficulty appears to increase proportionately with the length of teaching experience. Campbell *[1]* has demonstrated that people going into counseling with a teaching background tend to use sub-roles in counseling similar to their teaching experiences. These individuals make significantly more use of tutoring, advising, and information-giving than do counselors with no teaching background. Olsen *[6]* expressed similar reactions in his discussion of new counselors.

If teaching and counseling relationships have different components, one further disadvantage accrues in requiring teaching experience for counselors. It is possible that some potentially excellent counselors might not be successful teachers, with the result that they might lose the opportunity of contributing their skills in an area where good candidates are at a premium.

But the proponents of compulsory teaching argue that the relationship of teachers and counselors is enhanced when the counselor has been in the classroom and has experienced problems teachers face. In the experiences of the writer in teaching, counseling, supervising or consulting in the public schools, these productive relationships between counselors and teachers often do not exist. Frictions may arise with teachers feeling that their former colleague has been promoted to a "soft" job in the front office where he more than likely will ally himself with administrators and students against the teaching staff. In addition, some teachers may have underlying apprehensions that they are demonstrating weakness when they refer students to counselors, and these apprehensions become more acute if counselors are recognized as previously superior teachers. Counselors may contribute to these frictions and apprehensions, when, as former successful teachers, they begin to evaluate teaching or disciplinary methods of faculty members when a student is referred. If selection of counselors were centered upon the ability to develop counseling relationships rather than on successful teaching experience, counselors and teachers would be more likely to set up more constructive communication. In this atmosphere, teachers could feel more relaxed about referral to counselors because the principles of non-evaluative, non-authoritative relationships apply to them as well as to pupils.

Environmental Experience an Important Supplement

Hoyt [3] justifiably contends that exposure to a school setting improves the chances for integrated action of counselors with teachers and administrators. The rationale presented here does not negate the importance of environmental experience. Rather, it is suggested that concerted action is more likely if selection of counselors is based first on the potential to develop counseling relationships, with school experience being a critical supplement rather than the reverse procedure prevalent today. This change in emphasis still permits the teaching ranks to be the major reservoir for prospective counselors. This is as it should be, for many effective teachers are potentially good counselor candidates. But it also permits internships, supervised experience, and group guidance activities to be used as effective school environmental experiences. This approach leaves the door open for individuals who have not taught but who show interest, ability, and personality traits needed for school counseling.

Summary

In summary, the following guidelines are suggested toward resolving the controversy about the need of teaching experience for counselors.

1. Teaching relationships and counseling relationships are inherently different. Thus, teaching experience does not automatically work in favor of good counseling—and at times may be a hindrance.

2. A compulsory teaching requirement might eliminate potentially good counseling candidates who are otherwise highly qualified.

3. Some experience in a public school setting is needed by counselors to make them more productive in understanding problems unique to the public school environment.

4. For these reasons, it is recommended:
   a. The major consideration in selection of school counselors should be the ability to develop and preserve a counseling relationship.
   b. Within this framework of the counseling relationships, public school experiences must be included in the background of counselors. This experience most often will be teaching, but it might also

be internships, laboratory experiences, or group guidance activities.

c. Counselor educators and supervisors need to be alert to the need to re-educate former school teachers who are in counselor preparation to transfer from a teaching to a counseling relationship, since inherently there are significant differences.

REFERENCES

1. Campbell, R. E. Counselor personality and background and his interview sub-role behavior. *J. counsel. Psychol.*, 1962, *9*, 329-334.
2. Hadley, J. M. *Clinical and counseling psychology.* New York: Alfred E. Knopf, 1958.
3. Hoyt, K. B. Guidance & constellation of service. *Personnel Guid. J.*, 1962, *40*, 690-697.
4. Nugent, F. A. Implementing an appropriate counselor image on the schools; an educative process, *Counselor educ. supv.*, 1962, *2*, 49-51.
5. Nugent, F. A. High school counselors and discipline: a theoretical clarification. *Counselor educ. supv.*, 1963, *3*, 44-49.
6. Olsen, L. C. Success for new counselors. *J. counsel. Psychol.*, 1963, *10*, 350-355.

The NDEA and Counselor Education

C. H. Patterson

The preparation and education of school counselors under the National Defense Education Act of 1958 has upgraded many practicing counselors, many of whom had little if any training, and has added many additional counselors, even if only partially trained, to the field. The conditions under which such counselors have been prepared, however, warrant some attention. While perhaps necessary for quickly improving the educational preparation of counselors in our schools and useful to help trained counselors keep up with new developments, the Institute approach is hardly one which is desirable for long term preparation of counselors, or for the strengthening of counselor education programs in our colleges and universities.

Reprinted by permission of the author and *Counselor Education and Supervision*, III, No. 1 (Fall, 1963), 4-7.
C. H. Patterson, Professor of Education, University of Illinois, Urbana.

The programs of counselor preparation, designated as Institutes, have certain characteristics which are inimical to the development and improvement of continuing programs of counselor education. These characteristics have been to some extent necessary to upgrade partially trained individuals already employed as counselors. They also, however, appear to represent a policy of the U. S. Office of Education. This policy, while committed to the goal of improving counselor education, in actual practice does not seem to be achieving this goal, Rather, it appears to be having effects which are detrimental rather than beneficial to counselor education programs in our colleges and universities.

The major policy which is questioned is the requirement that students supported by NDEA must be taught in segregated groups. This requirement has been supported on the bases that this would allow for the acceleration of training, that it would allow for experimentation with new approaches to counselor education, and that the continuous participation of the same group together provides a desirable teaching and learning experience.

I would suggest that there is no evidence that any of these goals have been or are being achieved by the NDEA program. Further, however, even if they should be assumed to be desirable without evidence of their effectiveness, there are sufficient undesirable results of this practice to warrant abandoning it. These results are related to the students, the staff, and the counselor education programs of the institutions involved.

The students in these Institutes constitute a segregated and isolated group. They have all, or nearly all, of their classes together. They do not mix with other students. They do not feel or consider themselves a part of the college or university as do other students. They have, essentially, their own and separate staff of instructors. They are not usually exposed to any great extent to the regular, permanent counselor education staff, and thus are deprived of exposure to varying points of view. They become isolated in their total lives, essentially being limited in social contacts to each other. The total picture is one of undesirable isolation, restriction and narrowness in their total lives, an inbreeding which is undesirable personally and professionally. Observation indicates that they are not happy about this.

The effects upon counselor education staff members are not desirable, either. The Institute instructors, like the students, tend to be isolated from the rest of the staff, even though they may participate to a limited extent in the regular counselor education program. But to a large extent, Institute staff members are not members of the regular staff, but are employed specifically for Institute instruction. Without reflection on their competence, they are nevertheless younger and less experienced than the regular staff. Students who select an institution for their education because of the reputation of the regular staff find that in the Institute they have no contact with the staff members with whom they hoped to study, although they may read their books and articles.

This condition will continue as long as NDEA students are segregated. Moreover, it will become worse. Institute staff members have no tenure, do not accumulate credit toward retirement or sabbatical leaves, are not in the regular lines for promotion in rank or pay. This being the case, the better ones will seek and accept regular positions, leaving Institutes to be staffed by the less competent and by new, inexperienced instructors. While this provides some good experience for new instructors, it is not the best situation for the development of new staff members.

The influence on the regular programs of the institutions involved is not beneficial. While a few institutions have expanded their staff and programs in conjunction with NDEA Institutes, this cannot be attributed to the influence of NDEA, but would have occurred anyway. In fact, the continuation of NDEA Institutes is detrimental to the development of permanent counselor education programs. As long as Institutes continue, there is little if any need to increase the regular, permanent staff. The staffing of Institutes with temporary appointments actually decreases the number of permanent staff openings which would be available. Finally, there is no evidence that the Institutes have developed any new or desirable methods or approaches to counselor education which have been incorporated into regular counselor education programs.

The result of the isolation of NDEA Institutes from the regular counselor education programs has been detrimental to students, staff, and the institutions, and thus to counselor education in general. In effect, each institution with an Institute operates two counselor education programs. Although students may receive the same degree after the same period of time, the content may be quite different. Transcripts and degrees which may be identical do not represent the same thing.

It would appear desirable for the future of counselor education that the policy of segregation and isolation be dropped. Federal support for counselor education should take the form which it has taken in other areas. Stipends or fellowships may be provided to individual students. Such students would enroll in regular counselor education programs. In a survey of Institute directors, Klopf and Cohen (1) found that 57.1 per cent preferred a fellowship program to the Institute program, and an additional 15.8 per cent desired both. Support for the expansion and improvement of counselor education programs should come from long term teaching grants to the institutions. This would allow them to expand staff and offerings by selecting staff members who would be assured some permanence and who could participate in the regular benefits of faculty positions.

It would appear that the time has come to recognize the implications of continuing under the present system of NDEA support of counselor education. This amounts to federal control of education, in a direction which is not conducive to the future of counselor education.

In summary, we may say that as a method of upgrading practicing counselors, the Institute approach has made a significant contribution. The need for such an approach is now past, however. There is evidence that the bottom of the barrel is being scraped in recruitment for such Institutes. There may still be a place for short term institutes for refresher purposes and to bring to practicing counselors new developments in counseling and related fields.

The current need is for developing and improving programs for the adequate preparation of individuals who have had no previous training or experience in counseling, by providing support for students and institutions for full time continuing study. Our goal, then, should be to communicate to legislators these needs, and encourage and support legislation to meet these needs. The President's [John F. Kennedy] education bill (HR 3000, the National Education Improvement Act of 1963) included a provision which would make possible the kind of support to counselor education which is needed. In my opinion, we should forget about the NDEA, and declare ourselves for the kind of support which will strengthen and improve our existing counselor education programs. The Institute pattern has served its purpose, and its perpetuation will be detrimental rather than helpful. It would appear that it might be better that NDEA be allowed to lapse than that it continue in its present form, leading to the development of two programs of counselor education in our colleges and universities.

BIBLIOGRAPHY

1. Klopf, G., & Cohen, Nancy K. The impact of NDEA counseling and guidance institutes on the professional education of school counselors. *Counselor Educ. Superv.*, 1962, *1*, 151-161.

Index of Names

Adman, A., 296, 320
Adams, J. F., 72, 107, 129, 197, 226, 318
Adams, G. S., 171, 172, 199
Allport, G. W., 380
Anastasi, A., 173, 197, 427
Anderson, H., 341
Andrew, D., 72, 226, 253, 280
Apostal, R. A., 107
Arbuckle, D. S., 16, 72, 95, 197, 202, 226, 253, 340
Arnold, D. L., 62, 64, 72, 113, 129

Baer, M. F., 253, 265, 280
Bakken, C. J., 123, 129
Baron, D., 171, 172, 199
Barr, J. A., 16, 72, 95, 226, 280
Barry, R., 5, 6, 16, 47, 72, 226, 280, 318, 322, 327, 340
Beers, C., 26, 27
Bennett, M. E., 16, 95, 226, 253, 318
Berdie, R. F., 16, 197, 226, 253, 275, 280, 318
Bernard, H., 220, 227
Binet, A., 28
Bingham, W. V., 209, 226
Blanchard, H. L., 72, 95, 197, 226, 253, 280
Blocher, D., 401
Blocher, O. H., 222, 226
Bordin, E. S., 212, 216, 227
Borow, H., 477
Bower, E. M., 137, 146
Bowman, F. Q., 130
Boy, A. V., 72, 197, 207, 227, 280, 318
Brammer, L. M., 209, 216, 217, 227, 229
Brewer, J. M., 25, 44, 47
Buchheimer, A., 107
Buros, O. K., 28, 173, 197
Burrows, A. H., 147
Busacher, W. E., 130
Byrne, R. H., 16, 107, 129, 197, 219, 220, 223, 227, 319

Callis, R., 280
Camp, D., 8, 16, 139, 146, 319
Carle, R. F., 96, 342
Carter, T. M., 122, 129, 340
Chase, F. S., 341
Chenault, J., 340
Cohen, N., 336, 337, 340
Conant, J. B., 41, 47, 98, 107, 325, 340
Cortale, M. J., 220, 227
Costar, J. W., 108, 130, 198, 228, 254, 281
Cottingham, H. F., 16, 72, 97, 107, 129, 197, 227, 253, 280, 319
Cottle, M. O., 122, 129

Cox, R., 296, 319
Crane, M., 275, 281
Crawford, C. C., 406
Cremin, L. A., 46, 47, 327, 340, 354
Crissey, O. L., 294, 319
Crites, J. O., 42, 49
Cronbach, L. J., 173, 177, 197
Crow, A., 5, 16, 17, 72, 73, 95, 107, 129, 146, 197, 198, 227, 253, 280, 281, 319, 340, 342
Crow, L., 5, 16, 17, 72, 73, 95, 107, 129, 146, 197, 198, 227, 253, 280, 281, 319, 340, 342
Cunningham, M., 146
Cuony, E. R., 240, 253
Cutts, N. E., 146

Darley, J. G., 177, 198, 209, 227, 269, 282
Davis, A., 180, 198
Davis, J. B., 26
Delacato, C. H., 107
Demos, G. D., 108, 130
Denney, R., 18, 329, 342
Detjen, E. W., 107
Detjen, M. F., 107
Dietz, J. W., 5, 17
Drasgow, J., 179, 198
Dressel, P. L., 130, 188, 190, 198, 228, 254, 281
Dugan, W. E., 210, 220, 227
Dunn, M., 96

Eckerson, L. O., 98, 100, 101, 102, 103, 104, 108, 110, 391
Edelfelt, R. A., 109, 147
Erickson, C. E., 74, 219, 227, 240, 255, 264, 265, 271, 275, 282
Evans, D. L., 100, 103, 110

Farwell, G. F., 18, 47, 73, 96, 108, 130, 188, 198, 199, 227, 253, 254, 281, 319
Faust, V., 108
Feldman, M. J., 327, 341
Ferree, G., 341
Fick, R. L., 178, 197
Field, F. L., 76, 96, 286, 317, 320
Flaum, L. S., 72, 95, 197, 226, 253, 280
Foley, J. O., 202, 230
Foster, C. M., 102, 108
Fox, W. H., 239, 254
Franklin, B., 20, 21
Fredericks, J. R., 113, 130
Freeman, F. S., 163, 173, 198
French, J. W., 32, 39, 49
Fritzemeier, L. H., 220, 227
Froehlich, C. P., 6, 8, 17, 57, 73, 95, 198, 203, 209, 223, 227, 271, 281

Fullmer D. W., 220, 227
Fusco, G. C., 146

Gage, N. L., 173, 199
Gardner, E. F., 198
Garry, R., 108
Getzels, J., 330, 341
Gilbert, N. S., 115, 130, 221, 227
Gilmore, J. L., 109
Ginsberg, E., 253
Glanz, E. C., 17, 47, 73, 95, 198, 228, 254, 319
Glazer, N., 18, 329, 342
Glueck, E., 99, 108
Glueck, S., 99, 108
Goldstein, H. A., 62, 64, 73, 113, 130
Goodwin, F. P., 26
Gordon, I. J., 17, 95
Gorman, W., 313, 320
Gottsegen, G. B., 146
Gottsegen, M. G., 146
Gowan, J. C., 108, 130
Grant, C. W., 202, 229, 286, 320
Green, D. A., 294, 319
Green, M., 341

Hadley, J. M., 228
Hagenah, T., 16, 177, 197, 198, 226, 253, 280, 318
Hahn, M. E., 213, 217, 228, 272, 281
Hamrin, S. A., 20, 47, 55, 57, 73
Hancher, V. M., 325, 341
Harris, M. W., 147
Harrison, E. L., 108
Hart, R. N., 100, 108
Hatch, R. N., 8, 17, 62, 73, 95, 108, 130,188,190,198, 228, 254,281, 319
Hayden, V. D., 147
Healy, W., 27
Heisey, M., 104, 108,396
Hess, R., 180, 198
Hill, G. E., 97, 101, 103, 108, 109, 113, 130, 294, 319, 327, 341
Hilton, O., 122, 130
Hodges, W. L., 146
Hollinshead, B. S., 33, 47
Hollis, J. W., 17, 73, 95, 198, 228, 254, 281
Hollis, L. V., 17, 73, 95, 198, 228, 254, 281
Holmes, J., 341
Hopke, W., 16, 72, 197, 253
Hoppock, R., 240, 253, 254
Hoyt, K. B., 151, 198, 327, 336, 341, 344
Hudson, G., 336, 341, 515
Hughes, E. C., 254
Hulslander, S. C., 9, 17, 228
Hummel, R. C., 42, 49

Humphreys, J. A., 17, 47, 73, 78, 95, 198, 228, 247, 248, 254, 270, 281, 319
Hutson, P. W., 17, 47, 73, 198, 228

Iffert, R. E., 32, 39, 47
Isaacson, L., 254

Jager, H. A., 31
Johnson, A., 146
Johnson, M., 130
Johnson, M. C., 32, 39, 49
Johnson, W. F., 17, 96, 109, 147, 199, 228, 254, 286, 319
Jones, A. J., 17, 47, 73, 130, 199, 228, 281, 319

Kaczkowski, H. R., 191, 192, 199
Katz, M., 228
Kaupp, L. E., 239, 254
Kehas, C. D., 96, 342
Kelley, J. A., 96
Keppers, G. L., 296, 319
Kinker, H. R., 239, 254
Kitson, H. D., 4, 5, 17, 275, 281
Kluckhohn, C., 324, 341
Knapp, R. H., 109
Koeppe, R. P., 100, 105, 109
Kowitz, G. T., 109
Kowitz, N. C., 109
Kroel, A. M., 147, 255, 341
Krumboltz, J. D., 444

Lallas, J. E., 109
Landy, E., 47, 147, 255, 340, 341
Lane, D., 99, 103, 110
Layton, W. L., 16, 197, 226, 253, 280, 318
Lee, J. M., 109
Little, J. K., 36, 48
Litwack, L., 341
Lloyd-Jones, E., 109, 213, 228
Loeb, M. X., 147
Loughary, J. W., 73, 228, 281, 454
Louisell, D. W., 124, 130
Lundberg, H. W., 147
Lundy, C. T., 100, 102, 110
Lynes, R., 329, 341

MacLean, M. S., 272, 281
MacMinn, P., 296, 319
Magary, J. F., 147
Margoshes, A., 507
Martinson, R. A., 17, 48, 96, 109, 281
Martyn, K. A., 62, 64, 73, 113, 130
Mathewson, R. H., 13, 17, 48, 73, 199, 220, 228, 319, 322, 329, 341
McCary, J. L., 120, 121, 130
McCully, C. H., 338, 341
McDaniel, H. B., 17, 48, 57, 73, 96, 109, 228, 254, 281, 319, 341

McDaniels, C., 341
McDougall, W. P., 100, 109
McGowan, J. F., 17, 73, 199, 228, 319,
    342
McKinney, F., 202, 228
McQuarry, J. P., 11, 18
McQueen, M., 78, 96
Meeks, A. R., 109
Merrill, G., 25
Miller, C. H., 18, 48, 73, 147, 199, 228,
    254, 281
Miller, F. W., 85, 96, 120, 130, 228,
    274, 278, 281, 296, 319
Millett, J. D., 14, 18
Mollenkopf, W. G., 31, 32, 39, 49
Moore, B. B., 209, 226
Moore, G., 342
Moser, H. P., 42, 49
Mosher, R. L., 96, 342
Munsterberg, D., 27
Murphy, G., 11, 18, 23, 48, 320, 330,
    334, 342
Myers, G., 5, 18

Newman, W. H., 100, 109
Nitzschke, D. F., 101, 108, 109
Noble, F. C., 342, 512
Norris, W., 110, 254
North, R. D., 17, 47, 73, 78, 95, 198,
    228, 247, 248, 254, 255, 281, 319
Nugent F. A., 219, 228, 342, 520
Nunnally, J. C., 177, 199

O'Donnell, R. J., 220, 229
O'Hara, R. P., 42, 49
O'Hern, J., 341
Ohlsen, M. M., 18, 73, 96, 199, 229,
    245, 254, 282
Oldridge, B., 110
Opstad, P. E., 220, 229
Orgel, R. G., 110
Otis, A. S., 28, 173
Otto, M., 14, 18
Overstreet, P. L., 42, 49

Parsons, E., 25, 48
Patouillet, R., 102, 110
Patterson, C. H., 18, 48, 74, 96, 147,
    199, 212, 213, 217, 229, 254, 282,
    320 338, 524
Payne, A. F., 4, 18
Pearman, J. R., 147
Pearson, P., 69, 74, 90, 96
Pepinsky, H. B., 203, 212, 213, 229
Pepinsky, P. N., 203, 212, 213, 229
Perlmutter, B. J., 343
Perrone, P. A., 100, 103, 110
Perry, C., 320
Perry, P. A., 47, 340
Peters, H. J., 18, 47, 73, 96, 108, 110,
    130, 147, 188, 198, 199, 227, 253,

Peters, H. J. (continued)
    254, 262, 272, 281, 282, 319, 363,
    418
Phillips, J. L., 507
Pierson, G. A., 48, 202, 229, 286, 320,
    338, 342
Pierson, W. D., 122, 130
Pine, G. J., 72, 197, 207, 227, 280, 318
Poirier, B. B., 296, 320
Polmantier, P., 342

Quaranta, J. J., 110
Quattlebaum, V., 147

Ratigan, W., 327, 331, 342
Reed, A., 25, 26, 28, 48
Reitan, H. H., 100, 109
Remmers, H. H., 173, 199
Riccio, A. C., 110, 199, 200, 230, 255,
    282, 320
Richards, M., 296, 320
Rickover, H., 323, 342
Riesman, D., 18, 329, 342
Rimel, E. G., 239, 254
Roe, A., 42, 48
Roeber, E. C., 74, 240, 253, 255, 264,
    265, 271, 275, 280, 282
Roens, B. A., 167, 199
Rogers, C. R., 203, 204, 205, 206, 207,
    208, 213, 229
Rosencrance, F. C., 147
Ross, R. G., 296, 319
Rothney, J. W., 167, 199
Routh, T. A., 214, 229
Rummell, J. F., 173, 199
Ryden, A., 250

Samler, J., 433
Sanford, N., 42, 48
Santavicca, G. G., 296, 320
Saum, J. A., 109
Schmidt, L. D., 17, 73, 115, 124, 130,
    131, 199, 228, 319, 342, 343
Scholl, C. E., 228
Schwebel, M., 320, 467
Shaw, M. C., 371
Shertzer, B., 40, 48, 100, 102, 110, 147,
    410
Shoben, E. J., 327, 342
Shostrom, E. L., 209, 216, 217, 227,
    229
Simpson, R. J., 120, 130
Skill, T. E., 313, 320
Smallenberg, H., 17, 48, 96, 109, 281
Smith, G. E., 6, 18, 74, 219, 229, 240,
    255, 264, 265, 266, 267, 271, 275,
    282
Smith, H. M., 98, 100, 101, 102, 103,
    108, 110
Smith, M. R., 213, 228
Soldahl, T. A., 115, 131

Sorenson, A. G., 219, 229
Spindler, G., 330, 342
Stalnaker, J., 39, 48
Stefflre, B., 8, 17, 62, 73, 95, 109, 110, 147, 198, 218, 220, 223, 229, 270, 276, 281, 282, 319, 342, 492
Stewart, C. C., 64, 74
Stewart, L., 18, 49, 101, 110, 199, 229, 255, 282, 320, 336, 337, 342
Stice, G., 31, 32, 39, 49
Stoops, E., 18, 74, 199, 229, 255, 282
Stone, S. C., 410
Strang, R., 157, 199, 207, 230
Stripling, R. O., 99, 103, 110
Strong, M. W., 96
Super, D. E., 10, 18, 42, 49, 320, 342
Swanson, E. O., 16, 197, 226, 253, 280, 318
Symonds, P. M., 166, 199

Teague, L. L., 193
Tennyson, W. W., 113, 131
Terman, L. M., 28
Thompson, A. S., 320
Thompson, G. G., 198
Thompson, J. M., 110
Thorne, F. C., 206, 211, 213, 230
Thorpe, L. P., 171, 172, 199
Tiedeman, D. V., 42, 49, 76, 96, 255, 286, 317, 320
Tolbert, E. L., 199, 230, 255, 282
Torgeson, W. S., 31, 39, 49
Traube, M. R., 216, 230
Travers, R. M. W., 271, 282
Traxler, A. E., 13, 17, 18, 47, 49, 73, 74, 78, 95, 96, 191, 198, 199, 216, 228, 230, 247, 248, 254, 255, 269, 270, 281, 282, 319
Trow, W. C., 101, 110
Tuel, J. K., 371
Tyler, L. E., 18, 35, 49, 200, 214, 216, 217, 230, 282, 338, 343

Van Hoose, W. H., 110

Wahlquist, G. L., 18, 74, 199, 229, 255, 282
Ware, M. L., 131
Warnath, C., 18, 42, 49, 199, 229, 255, 282, 320, 336, 337, 342
Warner, R., 37, 49, 230
Warters, J., 18, 49, 74, 163, 188, 191, 200, 282, 320
Weaver, E. W., 26
Weiss, L. A., 163, 200
Weitz, H., 18, 200, 343
Wesman, A. G., 200
White, M. A., 147
Whitson, M. E., 171, 172, 199
Whyte, W., 329, 343
Wigmore, D., 122
Wilkins, W. D., 343
Willey, R. D., 72, 96, 111, 226, 253, 280
Williamson, E. G., 202, 209, 210, 211, 213, 230, 343
Winslow, J. T., 274, 282
Wolberg, L. R., 216, 230
Wolf, B., 5, 6, 16, 47, 72, 226, 280, 318, 322, 327, 340
Wolfbein, S. L., 99, 111
Wolfle, D., 39, 49
Wrenn, C. G., 18, 42, 49, 74, 123, 131, 202, 230, 269, 282, 287, 299, 320, 343
Wriston, H. M., 324, 326, 343

Yates, J. W., 343
Young, E. F., 28, 29

Zeran, F. R., 200, 220, 230, 254, 255, 282, 320

Subject Index

Abilities and aptitudes, 153 (see Tests)
Academic aptitude tests, 153 (see Tests)
Achievement tests (see Tests)
Allport-Vernon-Lindzey Study of Values, 177-178
American Academy of Pediatrics, 145
American Association of School Administrators, 145
American College Personnel Association, 288-289
American College Testing (ACT), 251
American Medical Association, 145
American Nurses Association, 145
American Personnel and Guidance Association, 38, 42, 126, 129, 145, 287-288, 293-294, 298-301, 307-310, 338, 344, 499-506
American Psychiatric Association, 145
American Psychological Association, 137, 139, 145, 213, 226, 293, 298-299
American Rehabilitation Counseling Association, 290
American School Counselor Association, 100, 101, 102, 105, 107, 115, 129, 290, 298, 300-301
American School Health Association, 145
American Speech and Hearing Association, 145
Anecdotal records, 158-163
Appraisal services (see Student appraisal)
Army Alpha Examination, 28
Association for Counselor Education and Supervision, 100-102, 105, 107, 129, 289, 297-298, 301-307
Association for Measurement and Evaluation in Guidance, 290
Association for Supervision and Curriculum Development, 95, 145
Attendance services, 135-136
Autobiography, 167-170
Audio-visual materials, 261 (see also Films)

Bell Adjustment Inventory, 177
Business-Industry-Education Day, 241

California State Dept. of Education, 103, 139, 146
California Test of Personality, 177
Carnegie Foundation, 39-40
Career Days, 240-241
Career Development Theory, 42
Career Planning Courses, 239-240
Case Conferences, 186-187

Certification, 311-315
  for school psychologists, 139
  for school social workers, 143
Civilian Conservation Corps, 23
Classroom Distance Scale, 170
Client-centered counseling, 203, 204-209
Clinical counseling, 203-204, 209-211
College Days, 241-244
College Entrance Examination Board, 251
Commission on Financing Higher Education, 33
Commission on Guidance in American Schools, 42, 299
Commission on Human Resources and Advanced Training, 39
Confidentiality in counseling, 222
Council for Exceptional Children, 145
Council of Chief State School Officers, 133, 146
Counseling, 58-59, 201-225
  and confidentiality, 222, 507-511
  and discipline, 61, 219-222
  and psychotherapy, 217-219
  and teaching, 79, 202
  as a learning process, 213-216
  as assistance in choice-making, 216
  as personality development, 216-217
  as role clarification, 217
  client-centered, 203-209
  clinical, 203-204, 209-211
  current approaches, 212-217
  definitions of, 202-203, 212-217
  eclectic, 203-204, 211-212
  goals of, 219
  historical perspective of, 202-212
  in elementary school, 97-111, 391-395
  in secondary school, 116
  issues in, 222-223
  services in schools, 223-224
  summary card, 193-194
  theories and research, 467-475
Counselor
  and civil liability, 125-126
  and criminal liability, 124
  and self-evaluation, 275-276
  and values (see Values and counseling)
  as change agent, 401-405, 444-452
  as learner, 214-215
  background and qualifications, 333-337, 515-523
  certification of, 311-315
  personality of, 204, 208, 334-335
  preparation of, 298-311, 337-339, 454-466, 477-489, 512-514, 524-527

Counselor (continued)
   responsibility to society, 210, 223
   selection of, 294-298
Culture-bias of tests, 180, 427-432
Cumulative records (*see* Personnel records)

Dean of Girls, 28-29
Dept. of Elementary School Principals, 145
Dictionary of Occupational Titles, 21, 24
Differential Aptitude Tests, 153, 175
Directive counseling (*see* Clinical counseling)
Discipline and counseling, 84, 219-222
Dual deviation technique, 171

Eclectic counseling, 203-204, 211-212
Economic Opportunity Act of 1964, 42
Education and occupational planning, 117
Educational information, 236-246, 256-258
Educational placement, 249-252
Educational Testing Service, 31
Elementary and Secondary Education Act of 1965, 43
Elementary school
   need for guidance services, 97-100
   role of counselor, 97-111, 391-400
Ethical standards, 293-294, 499-506
Evaluation, 56-60, 262-279 (*see also* Research)
   school surveys, 263-264
   follow-up studies, 265-269, 274
   of guidance services, 269-279

Field trips, 241
Films, 234, 236, 261
Financial aid, 256-257
Follow-up studies, 265-269, 274
Friendship Target Test, 170

George-Barden Act, 30-31
George-Dean Act, 30
"Guess Who" test, 170
Guidance
   and intellectual development, 323-324
   and manpower utilization, 324-327
   and personal adjustment, 327-328
   and values, 328-331
   as a profession, 285-320, 344-353
   child, 27
   coordination of, 332-333
   courses in, 240
   definitions and functions, 4-9, 322-331
   elementary, 396-400
   evaluation of, 269-279
   history of, 25-31, 354-362

Guidance (continued)
   issues in, 321-343, 507-527
   materials, 237-238
   need for, 19-25, 97-100
   principles and concepts, 9-15, 44-45
   scope of, 331-332
   services, 57-60
   vocational, 25-26, 454-466, 477-489
Guidance Program
   and community, 68-71
   organizational patterns, 60-64
   planning and developing, 65-68, 116
   role of administrator in, 410-417
   role of counselor in, 64-65
   role of teacher in, 75-94

"Halo effect," 165-166
Health services, 136, 153
Historical approaches to counseling, 202-212
Higher Education Act of 1965, 43
Homeroom, 63, 245-246

Illinois Institute of Juvenile Research, 27
Information services, 59, 231-261
In-Service education, 85-94
Intelligence tests (*see* Tests)
Interest inventories, 154, 176-177
International Association of Pupil Personnel Workers, 145
Interprofessional Research Commission on Pupil Personnel Services, 144
Interview, 183
Issues in counseling, 222-223
Iverson case, 125-126

Job placement, 247-249

Kuder Preference Record-Personal, 178
Kuder Preference Record-Vocational, 154

Mental Health Analysis, 177
Mental hygiene movement, 26-27
Metropolitan Achievement Tests, 175
Military services, sources of information on, 260
Mooney Problem Check List, 178
Multiple Aptitude Tests, 153
Multiple counseling, 203

National Association of Guidance Supervisors and Counselor Trainers, 109
National Association of Pupil Personnel Administrators, 145, 292
National Association of Secondary School Principals, 145
National Association of Social Workers, 145, 147, 291-292
National Association of Women Deans and Counselors, 292

National Defense Education Act, 33-37, 338-339, 524-527
National Defense Fellowships, 34
National Education Association, 40, 48, 145, 293
National Employment Counselors Association, 290-291
National Institute of Mental Health, 40
National Merit Scholarship Program, 39, 251
National Occupational Conference, 29
National Science Foundation, 31-32, 36, 39
National Teacher Corps, 44
National Vocational Guidance Association, 29, 289, 293, 298
National Youth Administration, 23
New York State Assoc. of Deans and Guidance Personnel, 242, 254
North Central Assoc. of Colleges and Secondary Schools, 35, 40
Northwestern University, 35
Nurse, school, 136

Observation, 156-158
Occupational information, 236-246, 258-259
Occupational Information and Guidance Service, 30
Occupational index, 29-30
Occupational Outlook Service, 30
Ohio Social Acceptance Scale, 170
Ohio State Dept. of Education, 113-130
Ohio State University, 113-130
Orientation, 232-236

Parents, conferences, 118-119, 183-186
Personal data blanks, 166-167
Personal-social information, 236-246, 260-261
Personality inventories, 177-178
Personality theory, 213, 216-217
Personality vs. skill issue, 204, 208
Personnel records, 187-193
Personnel work in industry, 27-28
Physician, school, 136
Placement services, 118
President's Advisory Committee on Education, 30
Privileged communication of counselors, 121-124
Problem Check Lists, 167, 178
Project Talent, 40
Projective tests, 178
Psychological examiner, 139
Psychological services, 136-139
Psychologist, school, 136-139
Psychotherapy and counseling, relationship of, 217-219
Public Law 85-864, 33
Public relations, 120
Pupil appraisal (*see* Student appraisal)

Pupil personnel services, 132-145, 418-426
Progressive education, 354-362

Rating scales, 163-166
Referral services, 80, 117
Research, 59-60, 119, 262-279, 492-498
    and counseling theory, 467-475
    competencies of counselors in, 262-263
    evaluation of guidance services, 269-279
    follow-up studies, 265-269, 274
    in vocational development, 477-489
    publications, 315-317
    school surveys, 263-265
Rockefeller Bros. Fund, 41-42
Rorschach test, 178

S.R.A. Youth Inventory, 178
Science Information Service, 34
Secondary school
    role of counselor, 112-127
    staff consulting, 119
Self-report forms, 166-167
Single-group experiment, 273
Smith-Hughes Act, 21, 30
Social worker, school, 139-143
Sociogram, 171-172
Sociometric devices, 170-172
Standardized tests (*see* Tests)
Strong Vocational Interest Blank, 154
Student Appraisal, 57-58, 116-117, 151-193
    areas of the individual requiring study, 152-155
    principles for programs of, 151-152
    tools and techniques of, 156-193
        anecdotal records, 158-163
        autobiography, 167-170
        case conferences, 186-187
        interview, 183
        observation, 156-158
        personal records, 187-193
        psychological tests, 173-182
        rating scales, 163-166
        role of teacher, 79
        self-report forms, 166-167
        sociometric devices, 170-172
        teacher-parent conferences, 183-186
Student handbook, 233-235
Student Personnel Association for Teacher Education, 289
Student Personnel Folder, 192
Superior and Talented Student Project, 35
Syracuse Scales of Social Relations, 170

Teacher
    and the guidance program, 75-94
    and information services, 244-245
    and job placement, 247

Teacher (continued)
  and student appraisal, 151-193
  as counselor, 79, 83-85, 202
Tests, 173-182
  achievement, aptitude and intelligence, relationships of, 174-176
  classifications of, 173-176
  culture-bias of, 180, 427-432
  definitions of, 166
  differential aptitude batteries, 175-176
  errors in interpreting, 182
  factors influencing performance, 182
  history of, 28
  interest inventories, 176-177
  limitations of, 179-182
  personality inventories, 177-178
  values of, 178-179
Testing Calendar, 251-252
Thayer Conference, 138
Thematic Apperception Test, 178
Theories of counseling, 202-217 (see also Counseling)
  and behaviorism, 444-452

Theories of Counseling (continued)
  and learning, 213-216
  and personality, 213, 216-217
Thurstone Temperament Schedule, 178
Toledo Council of Social Agencies, 142
Two-group experiment, 272-273

U.S. Employment Service, 23
U.S. Office of Education, 32, 36, 39-40
  Counseling and Guidance Branch, 37
  Commissioner of Education, 34, 36

Values and counseling, 23, 209-210, 223, 328-331, 380-390, 406-409, 433-443
Visiting teacher, 139
Vocation Bureau of Boston, 25

Wechsler Intelligence Scales, 175
White House Conference on Children and Youth, 38
Who's Who in My Room Test, 170
Wisconsin Supreme Court Case, 126